W9-CDD-200

SPORTS MARKETING

THIRD EDITION

SPORTS MARKETING

A STRATEGIC PERSPECTIVE

Matthew D. Shank

Professor of Marketing and Chair
Department of Management and Marketing
Northern Kentucky University

PEARSON
Prentice
Hall

UPPER SADDLE RIVER, NEW JERSEY 07458

Library of Congress Cataloging-in-Publication Data

Shank, Matthew D.
　Sports marketing : a strategic perspective / Matthew D. Shank—3rd ed.
　　p. cm.
　Includes bibliographical references and index.
　ISBN 0-13-144077-2
　1. Sports—United States—Marketing.　2. Sports—Economic aspects—
United States.　I. Title.

GV716.S42 2004
796′.06′98—dc22　　　　　　　　　　　　　　　　2004044696

Acquisitions Editor: Katie Stevens
Editorial Director: Jeff Shelstad
Assistant Editor: Melissa Pellerano
Editorial Assistant: Rebecca Lembo
Media Project Manager: Peter Snell
Executive Marketing Manager: Michelle O'Brien
Managing Editor: John Roberts
Production Editor: Kelly Warsak
Permissions Supervisor: Kathy Weisbrod
Manufacturing Buyer: Indira Gutierrez
Cover Design: Bruce Kenselaar
Cover Photo: Getty Images Inc.
Director, Image Resource Center: Melinda Reo
Manager, Rights and Permissions: Zina Arabia
Manager, Visual Research: Beth Brenzel
Manager, Cover Visual Research and Permissions: Karen Sanatar
Image Permission Coordinator: Joanne Dippel
Photo Researcher: Elaine Soares
Composition: Integra
Full-Service Project Management: Heather Meledin/Progressive Publishing Alternatives
Printer/Binder: Hamilton Printing Company
Cover Printer: Coral Graphics

Credits and acknowledgments borrowed from other sources and reproduced, with permission, in this textbook appear on appropriate page within text.

Microsoft® and Windows® are registered trademarks of the Microsoft Corporation in the U.S.A. and other countries. Screen shots and icons reprinted with permission from the Microsoft Corporation. This book is not sponsored or endorsed by or affiliated with the Microsoft Corporation.

10 9 8 7 6 5 4 3 2
ISBN 0-13-144077-2

To Lynne, My Favorite Sports Fan and Participant

BRIEF CONTENTS

CONTENTS

PREFACE

OVERVIEW

One of the greatest challenges for sports marketers is trying to keep pace with the ever changing, fast-paced environment of the sports world. Since the first edition of this text was published six years ago, amazing changes have taken place and challenges to sports marketers emerge daily. First, costs have been rising quickly. Athlete salaries continue to escalate. Alex Rodriguez was recently traded to the New York Yankees, who now pay salaries totaling over $107 million to their starting lineup. To pay for this, new stadiums and arenas have been built at a rapid pace. Industry experts estimate that more than $7 billion will be spent on new facilities for professional teams before 2006.

Each ticketholder will also pay more to attend the games in these plush new facilities. Ticket prices continue to increase and drive the common fan out of the sport arena. For instance, the average seat at a NBA game doubled from $22.52 in 1991 to $44.68 in 2003. But this may not be the largest problem in sports, as TV ratings continue sinking. NBC's coverage of the 2000 Summer Games drew the lowest ratings for a Summer or Winter Olympics since 1968. The NBA finals ratings in 2003 fell 38% to a new 32 year low. That same year, the NCAA men's college basketball title game drew its lowest rating since CBS started airing the event in 1982. Major League Baseball's All-Star game in 2003 tied for the worst-ratings ever and Fox Sports' telecast of the World Series that year produced the lowest-rated World Series in history. New leagues such as the National Pro Fastpitch continue to emerge, and recently formed leagues like the WUSA, WPBA, and the XFL have played their last game.

The one constant in this sea of change is the incredible appetite of consumers for sports. We get sports information on the Web, watch sports on network and cable tv, read about sports in the newspaper and sports magazines, talk to friends about sports, purchase sports merchandise, participate in sports, and attend sporting events in record numbers. The sports industry has experienced tremendous growth over the last fifteen year and is currently estimated to be a $350 billion industry in the United States. Moreover, the sports industry is flourishing around the globe. The expansion of the sports industry has triggered a number of important outcomes: More sports related jobs are being created and more students are interested in careers in the sports industry. As student interest grows, demand for programs in sports administration and classes in sports marketing have also heightened.

In this book, we will discover the complex and diverse nature of sports marketing. Moreover, a framework will be presented to help explain and organize the strategic sports marketing process. Even if you are not a sports enthusiast, you should become excited about the unique application of marketing principles and processes to the sports industry.

WHY THIS BOOK?

Programs and courses in sports marketing are emerging at universities across the country. Surprisingly, few sports marketing textbooks exist and none is written from a strategic marketing perspective. In the first edition of this book, I sought to fill this void. The second edition represented an effort to improve the first edition and capitalize on its strengths. The third edition attempts to continuously improve the content and focus on the current relevant issues in sport marketing. My goals for the third edition are to provide:

- *A framework or conceptual model of the strategic marketing process that can be applied to the sports industry.* The contingency framework is presented as a tool for organizing the many elements that influence the strategic sports marketing process and recognizes the unpredictable nature of the sports industry. In addition, the contingency framework allows us to explore complex relationships between the elements of sports marketing.

- *An appreciation for the growing emphasis on the globalization of sport.* As such, international sport topics are integrated throughout the text, and are also highlighted in chapters with a "Spotlight on International Sports Marketing."

- *An examination of current research in the area of sports marketing.* The study of sports marketing is still in its relative infancy and academic research of interest to sports marketers (e.g., sports sponsorships, using athletes as endorsers, and segmenting the sports market) has grown exponentially since the first edition of this text. It is important that students learn how academic research is applied to the "real world" of sports marketing.

- *An understanding of the ethical issues emerging in sports and their impact on sports marketing decision.* In today's scandal laden environment, it's important for students of sports marketing to be able to identify and respond to ethical issues of the day. As such, "Spotlight on Sports Marketing Ethics" are sprinkled throughout the text. Hopefully, these ethical spotlights will stimulate lively class discussion.

- *A balanced treatment of all aspects of sports marketing at all levels.* This book attempts to capture the diverse and rich nature of sporting marketing by covering the marketing of athletes, teams, leagues, and special events. Although it is tempting to discuss only "major league" sports because of their intense media coverage, the book explores different sports (e.g., cricket and women's football) and different levels of competition (e.g., collegiate and recreational). Moreover, the book discusses the activities involved in marketing to participants of sports—another area of interest to sports marketers.

- *An introduction of the concepts and theories unique to sports marketing and review the basic principles of marketing in the context of sports.* Even though many of the terms and core concepts are repetitive, they often take on different meanings in the context of sports marketing. Consider the term sports involvement. Although you probably recognize the term product involvement from your Principles of Marketing and/or Consumer Behavior class, what is sports involvement? Is involvement with sports based on participation or watching sports? Is involvement with sports deeper and more enduring than it is for other products that we consume? How can sports marketers apply sports involvement to develop a strategic marketing plan? As you can see, the core marketing concept of involvement in the context of sports presents a whole new set of interesting questions and a more comprehensive understanding of sports marketing.

- *Comprehensive coverage of the functions of sports marketing.* While some texts focus on specialized activities in sports marketing, such as sports media, this book seeks to cover all of the relevant issues in designing an integrated marketing strategy. Extensive treatment is given to understanding consumers as spectators and participants. In addition to planning the sports marketing mix (product, price, promotion, and place), we will examine the execution and evaluation of the planning process.

GROUND RULES

This text is organized into four distinct but interrelated parts. Each part represents an important component in the strategic sports marketing process.

PART I: CONTINGENCY FRAMEWORK FOR STRATEGIC SPORTS MARKETING

In Chapter 1, we introduce sports marketing and illustrate the breadth of the field. In addition, we will take a look at the unique nature of sports products and the sports marketing mix. Chapter 2 presents the contingency framework for strategic sports marketing. This chapter also highlights the planning, implementation and control phases of the strategic sports marketing process. In Chapter 3, the impact of the internal and external contingencies on the strategic sports marketing process is examined. Internal contingencies such as the sports organization's mission and organizational culture are considered, as are external contingencies like competition, the economy and technology.

PART II: PLANNING FOR MARKET SELECTION DECISIONS

Chapter 4 presents an overview of the tools used to understand sports consumers—both participants and spectators. Each step in the marketing research process is discussed, illustrating how information can be gathered to aid in strategic decision-making. In Chapters 5 and 6, respectively, participants and consumers of sport are studied. Chapter 5 examines the psychological and sociological factors that influence our participation in sport, while Chapter 6 looks at spectator issues such as fan motivation. In addition, we will discuss the relationship between the participant and spectator markets. Chapter 7 explores the market selection decisions of segmentation, targeting, and positioning in the context of sport.

PART III: PLANNING THE SPORTS MARKETING MIX

Chapters 8 to 15 explain the sports marketing mix, the core of the strategic marketing process. Chapters 8 and 9 cover sports product issues such as brand loyalty, licensing, and the new product development process. Chapter 10 introduces the basic promotion concepts, and Chapter 11 gives a detailed description of the promotion mix elements of advertising, public relations, personal selling, and sales promotions. Chapter 12, the final chapter on promotion, is devoted to designing a sports sponsorship program. In Chapter 13, the sports distribution function is introduced. Then the discussion turns to sports retailing, the stadium as place, and sports media as a type of distribution channel. The final chapters of Part III tackle the basic concepts of pricing (Chapter 14) and pricing strategies (Chapter 15).

PART IV: IMPLEMENTATION AND CONTROLLING THE STRATEGIC SPORTS MARKETING PROCESS

While the previous sections have focused on the planning efforts of the strategic marketing process, Part IV focuses on the implementation and control phases of the strategic marketing process. Chapter 16 begins with a discussion of how sports organizations implement their marketing plans. In this chapter, we see how factors such as communication, motivation, and budgeting all play a role in executing the strategic plan. We also examine how sports marketers monitor and evaluate the strategic plans after they have been implemented. Specifically, three forms of control (process, planning assumption, and contingency) are considered.

PEDAGOGICAL ADVANTAGES OF SPORTS MARKETING

To help students learn about sports marketing and make this book more enjoyable to read, the following features have been retained from previous editions of Sports Marketing: A Strategic Perspective.

- Text organized and written around the contingency framework for strategic sports marketing
- Each chapter incorporates global issues in sport and how they affect sports marketing
- Sport marketing hall of fame featuring pioneers in the field integrated throughout the text
- Text incorporates up-to-date research in the field of sport marketing
- Internet exercises at the end of each chapter
- Experiential exercises at the end of each chapter that ask you to apply the basic sports marketing concepts and perform mini-research projects
- Vignettes throughout the text to illustrate core concepts and make the material come to life
- Detailed glossary of sports marketing terms
- Use of ads, Internet screen captures and photos to illustrate core concepts of sports marketing
- Appendix describing careers in sports marketing
- Appendix presenting Internet addresses of interest to sports marketers
- Video(s) featuring the WNBA and NASCAR

ENHANCEMENTS TO THE THIRD EDITION

While I have attempted to retain the strengths of the previous editions of Sports Marketing: A Strategic Perspective, I also hoped to improve the third edition based on the comments of reviewers, faculty who adopted the text and most importantly, students who have used the book. New additions include the following features:

- Up-to-date examples illustrating the core sports marketing concepts in the text. As mentioned previously, the sports industry is rapidly changing and nearly 80 percent of the examples introduced in the second edition are now obsolete. It was my goal to find new, relevant examples to illustrate key points in every chapter of the text. These new examples are meant to keep the book fresh and the student engaged.
- New advertisements and illustrations have been incorporated into each chapter to highlight key sports marketing concepts and make the material more relevant for students. These ads, and photos are examples of sports marketing principles that have been put into practice and bring the material in the text "to life."
- The spotlights on international sports marketing have also been revised and updated for the third edition to highlight this key area of growth in the sports industry.

- New screen captures of relevant Web sites to illustrate key concepts. Because the Internet is now playing such a large role in sports marketing, screen captures from various Web sites have been incorporated throughout the text to bring the material to life for the students. In addition, Internet exercises appear at the end of each chapter, and discussions of the Internet as an emerging tool for sports marketers appear throughout.
- New spotlights on ethical issues in sport to address this growing concern in the context of sport. Hopefully, these articles will allow students to recognize ethical issues that they may face as sports marketers and stimulate classroom discussion surrounding ethics in sport.
- Since the writing of the second edition, the number of Web sites devoted to sports business has grown substantially. The third edition includes the latest Web sites of interest in sports marketers and the sites that have withstood the test of "Web" time.
- Three new cases have been added at the end of Parts I–III. These cases will provide students with an opportunity to analyze and solve "real world" sports marketing challenges

INSTRUCTIONAL SUPPORT

Various teaching supplements are available to accompany this textbook. They consist of an Instructor's Manual, Test Item File, and PowerPoint presentation. These items may be found online only at www.prenhall.com, the homepage for Prentice Hall's online Instructor's Resource Center (IRC). In order to access these materials, please follow the instructions below:

- Go to www.prenhall.com.
- Use the "Search our Catalog" field across the top to search for this textbook.
- Once you locate the book's catalog page, locate the "Instructor" link on the left menu bar and click on it.
- Scroll down the Instructor Resources page and you will see supplement download links. (Look for the small disk icons.)
- Click on any download link; you will be taken to a login page. Follow the instructions to register if you have not already done so. Once your status as an instructor has been validated (allow 24-48 hours), you will receive an e-mail message confirming your username and password. You only need to register once to access any Prentice Hall instructor resource.

ACKNOWLEDGMENTS

Each time I begin the process of researching and writing a new edition, I tell myself that "this has to be easier than the last edition." To the contrary, the challenges of improving and refining Sports Marketing: A Strategic Perspective continues to grow (as does the field). Even though this is a sole authored textbook, the project could never have been completed without the expertise and encouragement of many others. Although there are countless people to thank, I was greatly assisted by the thoughtful reviews that undoubtedly improved the third edition of the text. These reviewers include:

Ronald Borrieci, *University of Central Florida*
James Cannon, *University of South Alabama*

Renee Florsheim, *Loyola Marymount University*
Patricia Kennedy, *University of Nebraska, Lincoln*
Stephen McKelvey, J.D., *University of Massachusetts, Amherst*
Michael Smucker, *Texas Tech University*

I also wish to thank the reviewers who reviewed and helped shape the first and second editions. These colleagues include:

Ketra Armstrong, *The Ohio State University*
Chris Cakebread, *Boston University*
Joseph Cronin, *Florida State University*
Pat Gavin, *New Mexico State University*
Lynn Kahle, *University of Oregon*
Jerry Lee Goen, *Oklahoma Baptist University*
Deborah Lester, *Kennesaw State University*
Ann Mayo, *Seton Hall University*
David Moore, *University of Michigan*
Gregory Pickett, *Clemson University*
Joseph Terrian, *Marquette University*
Lou Turley, *Western Kentucky University*
Kathleen Davis, *Florida Atlantic University*
Robert E. Baker, *Ashland University*
Susan Logan Nelson, *University of North Dakota*
Mark McDonald, *University of Massachusetts, Amherst*
Eddie Easley, *Wake Forest University*

In addition to these formal reviews, I am especially grateful to the informal comments that I received from many of you who adopted the first two editions and provided me with feedback. I have tried to incorporate all of your suggestions and comments.

I am very grateful to many of my colleagues at Northern Kentucky University (NKU) who have supported me throughout this process. In addition to my colleagues at NKU, thanks go to all of my students at NKU who have helped fuel my interest in sports marketing. When the second edition went to press, I was in the process of developing a sports business major at NKU. The program is now in its second year with well over 100 majors. I'd like to thank all of those sports business students who have used the book at NKU and pointed out their likes and dislikes.

A number of organizations have been very helpful in providing permission to use ads and articles throughout the text. Thanks goes out to all the individuals within these organizations who have made this book more meaningful and readable for students.

One of the goals of this text was to provide real-world examples and applications that would make the material come to life. This effort was certainly enhanced through the assistance of Rod Taylor and Tom Wessling. Special thanks goes to Rod Taylor who spent countless hours editing the first edition of the text and making it much more user-friendly and interesting. In addition to real world examples, three case studies have been added to the third edition. I am extremely grateful to my friend and colleague Bill Shelburn from the University of South Carolina, Aiken who outlined these cases.

Finally, I am indebted to the Prentice Hall team for their encouragement and making the third edition a reality. Special thanks go to Katie Stevens, Melissa Pellerano, and Kelly Warsak for their support, professionalism, and suggestions throughout the project.

PART I

CONTINGENCY FRAMEWORK FOR STRATEGIC SPORTS MARKETING

CHAPTER 1

EMERGENCE OF SPORTS MARKETING

After completing this chapter, you should be able to:

- Define sports marketing and discuss how the sports industry is related to the entertainment industry.
- Describe a marketing orientation and how the sports industry can use a marketing orientation.
- Examine the growth of the sports industry.
- Discuss the simplified model of the consumer–supplier relationship in the sports industry.
- Explain the different types of sports consumers.
- Define sports products and discuss the various types of sports products.
- Understand the different producers and intermediaries in the simplified model of the consumer–supplier relationship in the sports industry.
- Discuss the elements in the sports marketing mix.
- Explain the exchange process and why it is important to sports marketers.
- Outline the elements of the strategic sports marketing process.

Mary is a typical "soccer mom." At the moment, she is trying to determine how to persuade the local dry cleaner to provide uniforms for her daughter's Catholic Youth Organization soccer team.

George is the president of the local Chamber of Commerce. The 10-year plan for the metropolitan area calls for developing four new sporting events that will draw local support while providing national visibility for this growing metropolitan area.

Sam is an events coordinator for the local 10K road race, which is an annual fund raiser for fighting lung disease. He is faced with the difficult task of trying to determine how much to charge for the event to maximize participation and proceeds for charity.

Ramiz is the Athletic Director for State U. In recent years, the men's basketball team has done well in postseason play, therefore, ESPN has offered to broadcast several games this season. Unfortunately, three of the games will have to be played at 10 P.M. local time to accommodate the broadcaster's schedule. Ramiz is concerned about the effect this will have on season ticket holders because two of the games are on weeknights. He knows that the last athletic director was fired because the local fans and boosters believed that he was not sensitive to their concerns.

WHAT IS SPORTS MARKETING?

Many people mistakenly think of sports marketing as promotions or sports agents saying, "Show me the money." As the previous examples show, sports marketing is more complex and dynamic. **Sports marketing** is "the specific application of marketing principles and processes to sport products and to the marketing of nonsports products through association with sport."

Mary, the soccer mom, is trying to secure a sponsorship; that is, she needs to convince the local dry cleaner that they will enjoy a benefit by associating their service (dry cleaning) with a kid's soccer team.

As president of the Chamber of Commerce, George needs to determine which sports products will best satisfy his local customers' needs for sports entertainment while marketing the city to a larger and remote audience.

In marketing terms, Sam is trying to decide on the best pricing strategy for his sporting event.

Finally, Ramiz is faced with the challenge of balancing the needs of two market segments for his team's products. As you can see, each marketing challenge is complex and requires careful planning.

To succeed in sports marketing one needs to understand both the sports industry and the specific application of marketing principles and processes to sports contexts. In the next section, we introduce you to the sports industry. Throughout this book, we continue to elaborate on ways in which the unique characteristics of this industry complicate strategic marketing decisions. After discussing the sports industry, we review basic marketing principles and processes with an emphasis on how these principles and processes must be adapted to the sports context.

Coca Cola's stadium signage is just one example of sports marketing.

Source: Used by permission of The Coca Cola Company.

UNDERSTANDING THE SPORTS INDUSTRY

SPORT AS ENTERTAINMENT

Webster's defines **sport** as "a source of diversion or a physical activity engaged in for pleasure." Sport takes us away from our daily routine and gives us pleasure. Interestingly, "entertainment" is also defined as something diverting or engaging. Regardless of whether we are watching a new movie, listening to a concert, or attending an equally stirring performance by Shaquille O'Neal, we are being entertained.

Most consumers view movies, plays, theatre, opera, or concerts as closely related forms of entertainment. Yet, for many of us, sport is different. One important way in which sport differs from other common entertainment forms is that sport is spontaneous. A play has a script and a concert has a program, but the action that entertains us in sport is spontaneous and uncontrolled by those who participate in the event. When we go to a comedic movie, we expect to laugh, and when we go to a horror movie, we expect to be scared even before we pay our money. But the emotions we may feel when watching a sporting event are hard to determine. If it is a close contest and our team wins, we may feel excitement and joy. But if it is a boring event and our team loses, the entertainment *benefit* we receive is quite different. Because of its spontaneous nature, sport producers face a host of challenges that are different than those faced by most entertainment providers.

Nonetheless, successful sport organizations realize the threat of competition from other forms of entertainment. They have broadened the scope of their businesses, seeing themselves as providing "entertainment." The emphasis on promotional events and stadium attractions that surround athletic events is evidence of this emerging entertainment orientation. Consider the NBA All-Star Game. What used to be a simple competition between the best players of the Western Conference and the best players of the Eastern Conference has turned into an entertainment extravaganza. The event (not just a game anymore) lasts four days and includes slam-dunk contests, a rookie game, concerts, 3-point shooting competition and plenty of other events designed to promote the NBA.[1] In 1982, the league created a separate division, NBA Entertainment, to focus on NBA-centered TV and movie programming. NBA TV has created orginal programming featuring shows like NBA Player Nation, Real Playoffs, Insiders, Virtual GM, and Hardwood Classics. As Alan Brew, a corporate identity specialist at Addison, a branding and communication firm states, "The line between sport and entertainment has become nearly nonexistent."[2]

Underscoring the notion of sport as entertainment is Richard Alder, president of the Atlanta Knights of the International Hockey League (IHL), who states that "This is a league for the masses and not the classes. [Minor league hockey] is entertainment with the ice as the stage. The NHL is the coat and tie league. We're not. They're the Mercedes, the best hockey league in the world. We're the Chevrolet. Of course, more people drive Chevys." Coincidentally, Alder worked for 16 years as a vice president of marketing for the Ringling Brother and Barnum & Bailey Circus.[3] Additional examples of the relationship between sports and entertainment abound.

After originally trying to compete head to head against ESPN, the Fox Sports Network wants to position its product as a more entertainment-based alternative. With its hit show, The Best Damn Sports Show leading the way, Fox has six more sports entertainment shows under development. Similarly, comedians have become a mainstay on NFL pregame shows. For example, Jimmy Kimmell (of the Man Show fame) does segments on Fox NFL Sunday and George Lopez appears on HBO's Inside the NFL. ESPN has also started to create original programming with movies and a dramatic series.

Of course, one the most highly visible examples of "sporttainment" is the WWE or World Wrestling Entertainment. For the past two decades, the WWE has managed to build a billion dollar empire that maintains the highest rated cable show and has also produced No. 1 box office films, No. 1 NY Times bestselling books, and CDs as high as No. 2 on the Billboard charts. Vince McMahon, the founder and chairmen has been called the P. T. Barnum of our time.

Organizations that have not recognized how sport and entertainment relate are said to suffer from marketing myopia. Coined by Theodore Levitt, **marketing myopia** is described as the practice of defining a business in terms of goods and services rather than in terms of the benefits sought by customers. Sports organizations can eliminate marketing myopia by focusing on meeting the needs of consumers rather than on producing and selling sports products.

A MARKETING ORIENTATION

The emphasis on satisfying consumers' wants and needs is everywhere in today's marketplace. Most successful organizations concentrate on understanding the consumer and providing a sports product that meets consumers' needs while achieving the organization's objectives. This way of doing business is called a **marketing orientation.**

Marketing-oriented organizations practice the marketing concept that organizational goals and objectives will be reached if customer needs are satisfied. Organizations employing a marketing orientation focus on understanding customer preferences and meeting these preferences through the coordinated use of marketing. An organization is marketing oriented when it engages in the following activities.[4]

- **intelligence generation**—analyzing and anticipating consumer demand, monitoring the external environment, and coordinating the data collected
- **intelligence dissemination**—sharing the information gathered in the intelligence stage
- **responsiveness**—acting on the information gathered to make market decisions such as designing new products and services and developing promotions that appeal to consumers

Using the previous criteria (intelligence gathering, intelligence dissemination, and (responsiveness), one study examined the marketing orientation of minor league baseball franchises.[5] Results of the study indicate that minor league baseball franchises do not have a marketing orientation and that they need to become more consumer focused. Although the study suggests that minor league baseball franchises have not moved toward a marketing orientation, some sports organizations realize that profitability is based on adopting this business philosophy. One organization that has attempted to apply a marketing orientation is the LPGA (Ladies Professional Golf Association).

The LPGA's effort to make the fans a priority is being led by Commission Ty Votaw. Recently, Votow laid out a five year business plan designed to increase the tour's visibility and grow the tour. In order to do so, Votaw created a "fan first" initiative that has a relatively simple, but important, premise: if fans are able to find a connection with the players then they will begin or continue to support the tour. To create that connection, Votaw is asking players to adopt the five points of celebrity—performance, relevance, joy and passion, appearance, and approachability.

Nancy Lopez, a longtime tour veteran, stated that "there are so many sports vying for the attention of fans . . . we need to to do what we can to make them go see the LPGA. Whether the LPGA's marketing orientation is successful in the long term remains to be seen, but in the short run it seems to be working. Attendance has increased by 10 percent in 2003, TV viewership is up 22 percent on cable and 29 percent on broadcast, the average purse has more than doubled and total prize money has grown some 87 percent in the same time span. All these factors are positive indicators that the marketing orientation is paying dividends.[6]

GROWTH OF THE SPORTS INDUSTRY

Sport has become one of the most important and universal institutions in our society. It is estimated that the sports industry generates approximately $200 billion dollars a year. As shown in Figure 1.1, this total is based on a number of diverse areas within the industry including gambling, advertising, sponsorships, etc. As ESPN founder Bill Rasmussen points out, "The games are better, and well the athletes are just amazing and it all happens 24 hours a day. America's sports fans are insatiable."[7] For better or worse, sports are everywhere. The size of sport and sports industry can be measured in different ways. Let us look at the industry in terms of attendance, media coverage, employment, and the global market.

ATTENDANCE

Not only does sport spawn legions of "soccer moms and dads" who faithfully attend youth sport events, but also for the past several years, fans have been flocking to major league sports in record numbers. The NFL experienced a record-setting year in paid attendance with 17.6 million fans watching in 2002 for an average attendance of 66,100. In addition, 90 percent of NFL games sold out last year in time to lift TV blackouts, which was the highest percentage ever. The 2002 to 2003 season produced a small attendance decrease (0.6 percent) at NBA games with an average of 16,887 fans enjoying the action. However, the league is poised to rebound on the shoulders on rookie LeBron James. After a poor showing in 2002 because of the labor strife, attendance for Major League Baseball finished down 0.4 percent in 2003. The commissioner's office attribues part of the slide to the poor economy, the war in Iraq, and other uncontrollable factors like the SARS scare in Toronto.[8] Even with a soft economy, NHL attendance nearly matched that of the NBA in 2002–2003 and was substantially higher than a decade ago. Similar to the other leagues, paid attendance fell about 1 percent league-wide, but overall attendance was still close to an all-time high.

MEDIA COVERAGE

Although millions of Americans attend sporting events each year, even more of us watch sports on network and cable television or listen to sports on the radio. For example, while 67,603 fans were in attendance at Super Bowl XXXVII in San Diego, an estimated 41 percent of the country was watching on TV.[9] Likewise, some 171 million people watched NBC coverage of the Summer Olympic Games from Sydney, Australia;[10] however, this number is minimal compared with the estimated 7 billion people who watched worldwide. ESPN, the original sports-only network launched in 1979, reaches 87 million homes with 4,900 hours of live, original sports programming, and ESPN2 reaches 85 million viewers.[11]

Traditional networks are trying to keep pace with the demand for sports programming. The four major networks devote in excess of 2,000 hours to sports programming annually and a family with cable has access to 86,000 hours of sports TV. NBC spent a record $2.3 billion to secure the broadcast and cable rights for the Olympic Games in 2004, 2006, and 2008. In addition, NBC paid $1.27 billion to televise the Olympics in 2000 and 2002. Recently, NBC extended its stronghold on the Olympics by winning the broadcast rights to the 2010 and 2012 Games for $2.2 billion. Add to this the four-year deal worth $2.64 billion paid by NBC and Turner Sports to televise NBA contests or the $18 billion paid by the networks to the NFL, and you can see the value of sports to the league and the networks.[12] These numbers show no signs of slowing down in the future. In 1999, CBS agreed to pay $11 billion for a six-year contract with the NCAA.

The huge demand for sports broadcasting has led to the introduction of more sport-specific channels. New sports networks such as the College Sports Television (www.cstv.com), Blackbelt TV, the Tennis Channel, and the Women's Sports Network

FIGURE 1.1 Sports Industry Total Revenues

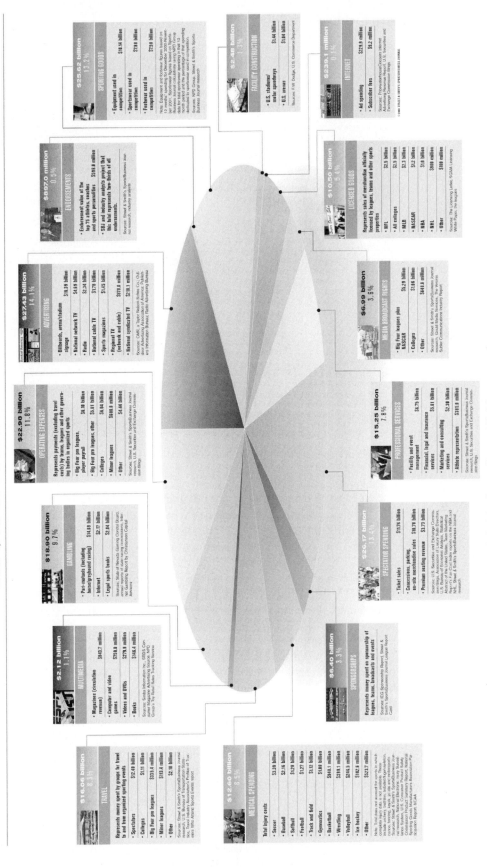

SPECIAL REPORT: DOLLARS IN SPORTS

HOW $194.64 BILLION IS SPENT IN SPORTS

Source: Sports Business Journal. Copyright © 1998–2004. Street & Smith's Sports Group. All rights reserved.

The growth of sports information on the Web.
Source: Reprinted courtesy of ESPN.com.

are emerging because of consumer demand. This practice of "narrowcasting," reaching very specific audiences, seems to be the future of sports media.

In addition to traditional sports media, new media such as the Internet and pay-per-view cable television are growing in popularity. Satellite stations, such as DIRECTV, allow spectators to subscribe to a series of sporting events and play a more active role in customizing the programming they want to see. For example, DIRECTV offers the NHL Center Ice package where subscribers can choose from 40 out-of-market (i.e., not local) regular season NHL games per week for just $139.

EMPLOYMENT

Another way to explore the size of the sports industry is to look at the number of people the industry employs. *The Sports Market Place Registry,* an industry directory, has more than 24,000 listings for sports people and organizations.[13] A *USA Today* report estimates that there are upward of 4.5 million sports-related jobs in marketing, entrepreneurship, administration, representation, and media.[14] Some estimates range as high as 6 million jobs. In addition to the United States, the United Kingdom employs some 400,000 people in their $6 billion a year sports industry.[15] Consider all the jobs that are created because of sports-related activities such as building and staffing a new stadium. The Sports Business Directory lists 13 career areas in sport. These include event suppliers, event management and marketing, sports media, sports sponsorship, athlete services, sports commissions, sports lawyers, manufacturers and distribution, facilities and facility suppliers, teams, leagues, college athletics, and finance.

The number of people working directly and indirectly in sports will continue to grow as sports marketing grows. Sports marketing creates a diverse workforce from the

SPOTLIGHT ON INTERNATIONAL SPORTS MARKETING

Can Man U Score in America?

On match day, the devout begin to congregate on Chester Road in Manchester, about a 15-minute walk from their cathedral. The road takes them past many shrines: There is Bishop's Blaize, a local pub where supporters chant from the Manchester United hymnal 30 minutes before game time. At the corner of Chester and Sir Matt Busby Way (so named for an inspirational coach of the past), the faithful take a left and pass a giant mural featuring the faces of legendary team members such as George Best and Eric Cantona. Finally, the processional winds over some railroad tracks to one of the most hallowed grounds in soccer: Old Trafford, home to the 125-year-old Manchester United Red Devils football club.

The veneration of Manchester United is hardly restricted to a gritty British city, however. Man U is the true prophet of football, or soccer, to a devoted worldwide following of 53 million fans, according to polls done for the club by researcher MORI. In fact, it is the most popular team in the world—making the New York Yankees, Dallas Cowboys, and Los Angeles Lakers seem bush league by comparison. And it has leveraged its hold on its fans into a global business that spreads far beyond soccer.

Maggie English, a 43-year-old customer-services manager in London, is one of them. "I have traveled all over Europe to support them," she says. "I went eight years without missing a game. I went to Turkey three times for the day and Russia once for the day to see them play." Adds Graham May, 39, a building-contracts manager in North Manchester: "I would be a millionaire if I hadn't spent so much on football."

Such true believers help explain how Man U turns such a handsome profit: In fiscal 2002, the publicly traded club kicked out $50.3 million in profits on $230 million in revenues, and it expects to generate revenues this year of $260 million, club officials say.

To spin that much cash, Man U goes far beyond its primary sources—ticket sales and a lucrative TV deal with Rupert Murdoch's British Sky Broadcasting Group PLC. It sells everything from Man U coffee mugs to bedsheets and scarves. It runs its own subscription-TV service, Manu.TV, that beams game highlights and player interviews to 75,000 subscribers over four channels airing six hours a day, seven days a week. It sells its own credit cards, home mortgages, consumer loans, and insurance policies. It runs an online auction business similar to eBay Inc. and is opening a string

of Red Cafe restaurants from Singapore to Manchester. Says Marketing Director Peter Draper: "We are trying to package loyalty and affinity."

In July, Man U will take another big step to expand its global following when it takes its star-studded show to the United States for four largely sold-out exhibition matches in Seattle, Los Angeles, Philadelphia, and New York. The club's aim is twofold: to penetrate America's $15 billion annual professional sports market and to persuade Wall Street to invest in a growing global brand. "This is about the long-term development of the marketplace," says Peter F. Kenyon, CEO of Manchester United PLC.

That may be easier said than done. First, Man U may have to make the trip without its biggest star, golden-haired midfielder and tabloid idol David Beckham, who has led the team to 8 English Premier League championships in the past 11 years. Rumors have swirled for months that Beckham will move to another European club, which would bring Man U a transfer fee in the $50 million range. Indeed, on June 10, the club announced that it had reached agreement with Barcelona—a deal Beckham promptly vetoed. But some such deal may soon take place, with Real Madrid and A.C. Milan thought to be among the contenders.

Even if Beckham makes the U.S. tour, it's hardly clear that Americans are ready to embrace pro soccer. True, 28 million Americans play the game. The U.S. Men's National Team reached the quarterfinals of the 2002 World Cup, the U.S. Women's National Team continues to dominate competitions and attract crowds, and the United States will play host to the Women's World Cup this fall. Americans are even flocking to see *Bend It Like Beckham,* a film about a young Englishwoman of Indian descent who wants to play professionally.

But beyond those successes, soccer struggles to gain a foothold in the crowded American sports market. Even though Major League Soccer, the top professional league here, has been making steady attendance gains, the 10-team league still loses money and has not yet attracted a broad fan base. Skeptics abound. "I think soccer in the United States is a participation sport and not a spectator sport," says Craig Tartasky, president of Vertical Sports Marketing, a Bethesda (MD) consultancy.

While in the United States, Man U officials will be trying to capitalize on the curiosity factor. Finance director Nick Humby will head to Wall Street to try to interest investors in the club's business model—one that combines

(Continued)

(Continued)

a winning tradition with shrewd stewardship of the Man U brand. With its U.S. sponsors, Man U will be running soccer clinics in cities where it plays exhibition matches—and trying to squeeze as much publicity out of the U.S. media as possible.

Wall Street may well listen, because Man U's business acumen is on par with Beckham's uncanny ability to curve a free kick around an opposing wall of players into a corner of the goal. The debt-free club used its own cash to build a 67,700-seat stadium that sells out every match. "We always invest at a level we can afford," says Humby. Management also insists on rigorous financial discipline that limits players' salaries to 50 percent of revenues, compared with the 70 percent or even 100 percent at some other English teams. Man U's willingness to let Beckham go, while it may alienate some fans, reflects the team's iron rule that no player must loom larger than the team as a whole. Coach Sir Alex Ferguson, apparently irritated by Beckham's glamour-boy lifestyle—his wife, Victoria, is a former Spice Girl—benched him in several games this spring. And the huge transfer fee would buy Man U other stars; experts say the team has its eye on Brazilian striker Ronaldinho.

Man U also prospers because its popularity has attracted big multinational consumer companies. Nike Inc. last year agreed to pay $450 million over 13 years to design and supply new clothing and equipment and take over Man U's entire merchandising business, giving it more global punch. "The scale that we brought was unattainable for them," says Nike co-President Charlie Denson. Man U is also teaming up with other iconic brands, such as Pepsi and Budweiser.

But will the club's popularity rub off in the United States? It counts about 4 million hard-core U.S. fans, according to MORI, but it will need millions more to make that backing financially meaningful. The stakes are high, since Man U is already approaching saturation in Europe and Asia. "No soccer team has penetrated the U.S. market, and Man U needs to do so," says Jeffrey Bliss, president of Javelin Group, a sports-marketing consultant in Alexandria, Va.

Certainly a big U.S. splash could lay the groundwork for more growth. But it may be a long time before Man U generates U.S. adherents like Chris Mann, a 57-year-old English factory worker who plans to catch a pair of the U.S. games. "Man U is my life," he says. "We call it the religion. We call Old Trafford the cathedral. You have to go worship the team." Now, the question is whether the prophet of football can spread the word to those soccer heathens in America.

Man U's Money Machine

Total Revenue 2002: $230 million

Ticket sales: 39%
Primarily home games at 67,700-seat stadium at Old Trafford, the biggest in England. Every game sells out.

Media: 36%
Sale of live TV rights for English Premier League games and European and English cup matches. Two-thirds comes from EPL and English cup TV rights, the rest from European cup.

Commercial: 18%
Income from key sponsorships such as Nike and Vodafone and Man U's emerging financial-services business.

Merchandising: 7%
Royalties from merchandise sales, with Beckham paraphernalia especially hot.

Source: Stanley Holmes, Heidi Dawley, and Gerry Khermouch. *Business Week,* June 2003, No. 38, p. 108. http://www.businessweek.com/index.html.

players who create the competition, to the photographers who shoot the competition (see Appendix A for a discussion of careers in sports marketing).

GLOBAL MARKETS

Not only is the sports industry growing in the United States, but it is also growing globally. As the previous spotlight on international sports marketing discusses,

Manchester United is a premier example of a powerful global sports organization that continues to grow.

THE STRUCTURE OF THE SPORTS INDUSTRY

There are many ways to discuss the structure of the sports industry. We can look at the industry from an organizational perspective. In other words, we can understand some things about the sports industry by studying the different types of organizations that populate the sports industry such as local recreation commissions, national youth sports leagues, intercollegiate athletic programs, professional teams, and sanctioning bodies. These organizations use sports marketing to help them achieve their various organizational goals. For example, agencies such as the United States Olympic Committee (USOC) use marketing to secure the funding necessary to train and enter American athletes into the Olympic Games and Pan American games.

The traditional organizational perspective, however, is not as helpful to potential sports marketers as a consumer perspective. When we examine the structure of the sports industry from a consumer perspective, the complexity of this industry and challenge to sports marketers becomes obvious. Figure 1.2 shows a **simplified model of the consumer–supplier relationship.** The sports industry consists of three major elements: consumers of sport, the sports products that they consume, and the suppliers of the sport product. In the next sections, we explore each of these elements in greater detail.

FIGURE 1.2   Simplified Model of the Consumer—Supplier Relationship in the Sports Industry

Consumers	Products	Producers and Intermediaries
Spectators	Events	Ownership
Participants	Sporting goods	Sanctioning bodies
Corporate or Business	Personal training for sport	Sponsors
	Sports information	Media
		Agents
		Equipment manufacturers

Sports marketing fills the stands.

THE CONSUMERS OF SPORT

The sports industry exists to satisfy the needs of three distinct types of consumers: spectators, participants, and sponsors.

THE SPECTATOR AS CONSUMER

If the sporting event is the heart of the sports industry, then the spectator is the blood that keeps it pumping. **Spectators** are consumers who derive their benefit from the observation of the event. The sports industry, as we know it, would not exist without spectators. Spectators observe the sporting event in two broad ways: they attend the event, or they experience the event via one of several sports broadcast media.

Spectator consumers are also of two types. Some are individuals, whereas others are corporations. As shown in Figure 1.3, there are two broad types of consumers: individual consumers and corporate consumers. Similarly, there are two broad ways in which consumers can become spectators: in person or via the media. This creates four distinct consumer groups. Individuals can attend events in person by purchasing single event tickets or series (season) tickets. Not only do individuals attend sporting events, but so too do corporations. Today, stadium luxury boxes and conference rooms are designed specifically with the corporate consumer in mind. Many corporate consumers can purchase special blocks of tickets to sporting events. At times, there may be a tension between corporate consumers' and individual consumers' needs. Many believe that corporate consumers, able to pay large sums of money for their tickets, are pushing out the individual consumer and raising ticket prices.

Both individual spectators and corporations can also watch the event via a media source. The corporate consumer in this case is not purchasing the event for its own viewing, but, rather, acting as an intermediary to bring the spectacle to the end user groups or audience. For example, CBS (the corporate consumer) purchases the right to televise the Masters Golf Tournament. CBS then controls how and when the event is experienced by millions of individual spectators who comprise the television audience.

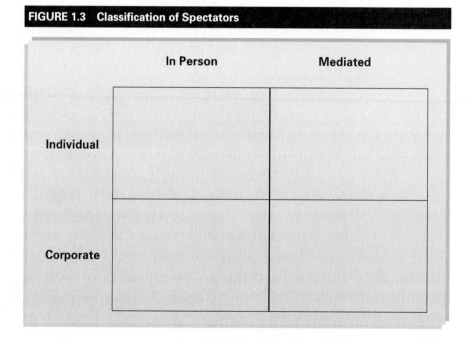

FIGURE 1.3 Classification of Spectators

Historically, the focus of the sports industry and sports marketers was on the spectator attending the event. The needs of the consumer at the event were catered to first, with little emphasis on the viewing or listening audience. Due to the power of the corporate consumer, the focus has changed to pleasing the media broadcasting the sporting event to spectators in remote locations. Many season ticket holders are dismayed each year when they discover that the starting time for events has been altered to fit the ESPN schedule. Because high ratings for broadcasted sporting events translates into breathtaking deals for the rights to collegiate and professional sports, those who present sporting events are increasingly willing to accommodate the needs of the media at the expense of the on-site fan. The money associated with satisfying the needs of the media is breathtaking. For example, in 1997, the NFL signed a contract with a major television network for nearly $18 billion dollars.[16] Less than a month later, the players also reaped the benefits of this contract by having the salary cap raised to slightly over $75 million in 2003. Identifying and understanding the different types of spectator consumption is a key consideration for sports marketers when designing a marketing strategy.

THE PARTICIPANT AS CONSUMER

In addition to watching sports, more people are becoming active **participants** in a variety of sports at a variety of competitive levels.[17] Table 1.1 shows "frequent" participation in sports fitness and outdoor activities. As the number of participants grows, the need for sports marketing expertise in these areas also increases.

As you can see, there are two broad classifications of sports participants: those that participate in unorganized sports and those that participate in organized sports.

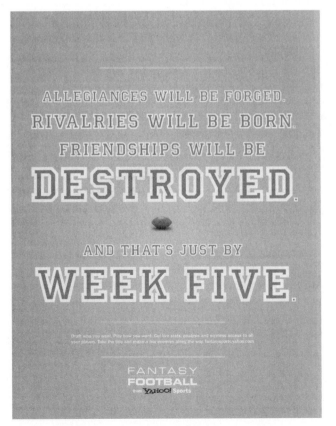

Fantasy sports blurring the line between spectator and participant.

Source: Reproduced with permission of YAHOO! Inc.

TABLE 1.1 Frequent Participants (in millions of people)

	Number of Participants
Fitness (exercise with equipment)	
Free Weights (100+ days/year)	15,826,000
Treadmill (100+ days/year)	11,266,000
Weight/Resistance Machines (100+ days/year)	9,354,000
Fitness (nonequipment)	
Fitness Walking (100+ days/year)	17,160,000
Stretching (100+ days/year)	16,749,000
Running/Jogging (100+ days/year)	10,485,000
Team sports	
Basketball (25+ days/year)	16,982,000
Soccer (25+ days/year)	7,783,000
Softball (25+ days/year)	5,438,000
Racquet sports	
Tennis (25+ days/year)	3,954,000
Table Tennis (25+ days/year)	2,355,000
Racquetball (25+ days/year)	1,054,000
Outdoor activities	
Fishing (15+ days/year)	15,561,000
Camping (15+ days/year)	10,220,000
Hiking (15+ days/year)	8,181,000
Winter sports	
Downhill Skiing (15+ days/year)	1,385,000
Snowboarding (15+ days/year)	985,000
Snowmobiling (15+ days/year)	704,000
Water sports	
Jet Skiing (15+ days/year)	1,589,000
Water Skiing (15+ days/year)	1,240,000
Sailing (15+ days/year)	927,000
Extreme sports	
Inline Skating (25+ days/year)	6,854,000
Skateboarding (52+ days/year)	3,442,000
Mountain Biking (25+ days/year)	1,732,000
Noncompetitive sports	
Recreational Walking (52+ days/year)	40,085,000
Recreational Swimming (52+ days/year)	15,427,000
Recreational Biking (52+ days/year)	14,785,000
Recreational sports	
Billiards/Pool (25+ days/year)	9,582,000
Golf (25+ days/year)	8,301,000
Bowling (25+ days/year)	8,246,000

Source: SGMA/American Sports Data, Inc. Used by permission of SGMA International. www.sgma.com.

Unorganized Sport Participants/Organized Sport Participants

Amateur
    Youth recreational instructional
    Youth recreational elite
    Schools
    Intercollegiate
Professional
    Minor/Secondary
    Major

Unorganized sports are the sporting activities people engage in that are not sanctioned or controlled by some external authority. Kids playing a pick-up game of basketball, teenagers skateboarding, or people playing street roller hockey, as well as fitness runners, joggers, and walkers are only a few of the types of sporting activities that millions of people participate in each day. The number of people who participate in unorganized sports is difficult to estimate. We can see how large this market is by looking at the unorganized sport of home fitness. In 2002, Americans spent nearly $4 billion on exercise equipment.[18] We can see that the size of the market for unorganized sports is huge, and there are many opportunities for sports marketers to serve the needs of these consumers.

Organized sporting events refer to sporting competitions that are sanctioned and controlled by an authority such as a league, association, or sanctioning body. There are two types of participants in organized events: amateur and professional.

Amateur sporting events refer to sporting competitions for athletes who do not receive compensation for playing the sport. Amateur competitions include recreational youth sports at the instructional and elite (also known as "select") levels, high school sports controlled at the state level through leagues, intercollegiate sports (NCAA Division 1-3, NAIA, and NJCAA), and adult community-based recreational sports. Professional sports are also commonly classified by minor league or major league status.

Sponsors as Consumer

Other equally important consumers in sports marketing are the many business organizations that choose to sponsor sports. In **sports sponsorship,** the consumer (in most cases, a business) is exchanging money or product for the right to associate its name or product with a sporting event. The decision to sponsor a sport is complex. The sponsor must not only decide on what sport(s) to sponsor, but must also consider what level of competition (recreational through professional) to sponsor. They must choose whether to sponsor events, teams, leagues, or individual athletes.

Unorganized sports participation also interests sports marketers.

Congratulations
Kevin Harvick on your
brilliant Brickyard win.

The Brickyard is the most fabled track in American automobile racing. A win there puts you in the company of the true greats of the sport. Way to go, Kevin! You demonstrated once again that you are one of the hottest drivers on the Winston Cup circuit. Winning takes a great team as well as great driving, and Richard Childress Racing, with its six NASCAR Winston Cup championships, knows everything there is to know about teamwork. As an associate sponsor of the #29 GM Goodwrench Monte Carlo, and the Official Lighting Supplier of Richard Childress Racing, SYLVANIA is proud to be part of the team.

SEE THE WORLD IN A NEW LIGHT SYLVANIA

Be sure to catch all the excitement of the first SYLVANIA 300 on September 14 at the New Hampshire International Speedway.

Sylvania leverages their sponsorship of NASCAR driver Kevin Harvick.

Source: Used by permission of OSRAM SYLVANIA. All rights reserved.

Although sponsorship decisions are difficult, sponsorship is growing in popularity for a variety of reasons. As Pope discusses in his excellent review of current sponsorship thought and practices,[19] sponsorship can help achieve corporate objectives (e.g., public awareness, corporate image building, and community involvement), marketing objectives (e.g., reaching target markets, brand positioning, and increasing sales), media objectives (e.g., generate awareness, enhance ad campaign, and generate publicity), and personal objectives (management interest). Although $5.6 billion were spent by corporations on sports sponsorships in 1999, according to the IEG sponsorship report, that number more than doubled to $9.57 billion in 2003. Sponsorship revenue for the 2002 Winter Olympic Games in Salt Lake City reached a record $840 million, surpassing the $633 million spent at the 1996 games in Atlanta.

THE SPORTS PRODUCT

Perhaps the most difficult conceptual issue for sports marketers is trying to understand the nature of the sports product. Just what is the sports product that participants, spectators, and sponsors consume? A **sports product** is a good, a service, or any combination of the two that is designed to provide benefits to a sports spectator, participant, or sponsor.

GOODS AND SERVICES

Goods are defined as tangible, physical products that offer benefits to consumers. Sporting goods include equipment, apparel, and shoes. We expect sporting good retailers to sell tangible products such as tennis balls, racquets, hockey equipment, exercise equipment, and so on. By contrast, **services** are defined as intangible, nonphysical products. A competitive sporting event (i.e., the game itself) and an ice-skating lesson are examples of sport services.

Sports marketers sell their products based on the **benefits** the products offer to consumers. In fact, products can be described as "bundles of benefits." Whether as participants, spectators, or sponsors, sports products are purchased based on the benefits consumers derive. Ski Industry America, a trade association interested in marketing the sport of snowshoeing, understands the benefit idea and suggests that the benefits offered to sports participants by this sports product include great exercise, little athletic skill, and low cost (compared with skiing). It is no wonder snowshoeing has recently emerged as one of the nation's fastest growing winter sports.[20]

Spectators are also purchasing benefits when they attend or watch sporting events. For example, while 2 million attended, some 2.1 billion TV viewers watched some portion of the 2002 Winter Olympic Games in Salt Lake City. The Olympic Games provide consumers with benefits such as entertainment, ability to socialize, and feelings of identification with their countries' teams and athletes. Moreover, organizations such as Federal Express, which paid $205 million over 27 years for the naming rights to the Washington Redskins sports complex that opened in 1999, believe the association with sports will be worth far more than the investment.[21] The benefits that organizations receive from associating with the sports product include enhanced image, increased awareness, and increased sales of their products.

DIFFERENT TYPES OF SPORTS PRODUCTS

Sports products can be classified into four categories. These include sporting events, sporting goods, sports training, and sports information. Let us take a more in-depth look at each of these sports products.

Sporting Events   The primary product of the sports industry is the **sporting event.** By primary product we are referring to the competition, which is needed to produce all the related products in the sports industry. Without the game there would be no licensed merchandise, collectibles, stadium concessions, and so on. You may have thought of sports marketing as being important for only professional sporting events, but the marketing of collegiate sporting events and even high school sporting events is becoming more common. For example, *High School Hoops* is a new mainstream glossy preview magazine jointly produced by the Sporting News and School Sports. The first-of-its-kind magazine is devoted solely to the coverage of nationwide prep basketball.

Historically, a large distinction was made between amateur and professional sporting events. Today, that line is becoming more blurred. For example, the Olympic Games, once considered the bastion of amateur sports, is now allowing professional athletes to participate for their countries. Most notably, the rosters of the Dream Teams of USA Basketball fame and the USA Hockey team are almost exclusively professional athletes. This has been met with some criticism. Critics say that they would rather give the true amateur athletes their chance to "go for the gold."

Athletes   Athletes are participants who engage in organized training to develop skills in particular sports. Athletes who perform in competition or exhibitions can also be thought of as sports products. David Beckham, Chamique Holdsclaw, and Lance Armstrong are thought of as "bundles of benefits" that can satisfy consumers of sport both on and off the court. The latest athlete to achieve this "superproduct" status is the multimillion dollar phenomenon named Eldrick "Tiger" Woods. Tiger seems to have it all. He is handsome, charming, young, multiethnic, and most important—talented. Tiger's sponsors certainly think he is worth the money. Nike, Buick, NetJets, and American Express have all purchased a piece of Tiger for millions in sponsorship fees. The Nike contract alone is worth an estimated $100 million.[22] But, the "bundle of benefits" that accompany an athlete varies from person to person. The benefits associated with Allen Iverson are different from those associated with Kevin Garnett or gold medal winner Sarah Hughes. Regardless of the nature of the benefits, today's athletes are not thinking of themselves as athletes but as entertainers. "Being like Mike [Jordan] means being a polished celebrity who can slam, spike and strut for the highlight reel; give good sound bite without embarrassing himself, his sport and his sponsors; and be able to find that Disneyland film crew amid the pandemonium of winning a world championship."[23]

Arena   A final sports product that is associated with the sporting event is the site of the event—typically an arena or stadium. Today, the stadium is much more than a place to go watch the game. It is an entertainment complex that may include restaurants, bars, picnic areas, and luxury boxes. Most stadium seating is designed for entertainment purposes. For example, ChoiceSeat was introduced at Super Bowl XXXII and promises to be the stadium seat of the future. The ChoiceSeat is a Pentium-powered touch screen that allows individuals to access real-time camera views from a variety of camera angles, replays, player and game statistics, and merchandising information. With this new technology, the seat within the stadium becomes an attractive product to market.[24] Similarly, the Purdue Boilermakers are experimenting with a prototype known as e-Stadium that will provide player and coach biographies, up-to-the-minute statistics and other "infotainment" using PDA technology.[25]

SPORTING GOODS

Sporting goods represent tangible products that are manufactured, distributed, and marketed within the sports industry. The sporting goods and recreation industry, consisting of four segments, was nearly a $70 billion dollar industry in 2002.[26] The four segments and their relative contribution to the industry sales figure include sports equipment ($17.5 billion), sports transportation products such as recreational vehicles and water scooters ($17.9 billion), sports apparel ($22.3 billion), and athletic footwear ($9.3 billion). Although sporting goods are usually thought of as sports equipment, apparel, and shoes, there are a number of other goods that exist for consumers of sport. Sporting goods include equipment, licensed merchandise, collectibles, and memorabilia.

Equipment   Sports equipment sales were relatively flat in 2002 with a very slight increase from the previous year experienced. The largest product category, in terms of sales, was exercise equipment ($3.8 billion) followed by golf equipment ($2.4 billion), firearms and hunting ($1.9 billion), camping ($1.7 billion), team sports ($1.6 billion), and fishing ($1 billion).[27]

Licensed Merchandise   Another type of sporting good that is growing in sales is licensed merchandise. **Licensing** is a practice whereby a sports marketer contracts with other companies to use a brand name, logo, symbol, or characters. In this case, the brand name may be a professional sports franchise, college sports franchise, or a sporting event. Licensed sports products usually are some form of apparel such as team hats, jackets, or jerseys. Licensed sports apparel accounts for 60 percent of all sales. Other licensed sports products such as novelties, sports memorabilia, trading cards, and even home goods are also popular.

The Licensing Letter reports that sales of all licensed sports products reached $12.1 billion in 2003, a 7% increase over the previous year's retail sales. This growth is expected to continue based on research from the National Sporting Goods Manufacturers Association. U.S. retail sales of licensed products for the four major professional sports leagues (NBA, NFL, MLB, and NHL) and colleges and universities have more than doubled in the 1990s, from $5.35 billion in 1990 to $10.95 billion in 2003.[28]

Through this period, the various major professional sports leagues developed a sprawling network of licensing arrangements with more than 600 companies. Another 2,000 companies have arrangements with the various college and university licensing groups. As far as the retail distribution of product, a network of "fan shops" grew to over 450 in number and licensed products found their way into sporting goods stores, department stores, and eventually, the mass merchants. To compete, most of the major sporting goods chains and many department stores developed separate areas devoted exclusively to licensed goods.[29] Sales of licensed sports products will continue to grow as other "big league" sports gain popularity. For example, NASCAR has seen the sale of licensed goods increase from $60 million in 1990 to $500 million in 1994 and to $1.2 billion in 2003.

Collectibles and Memorabilia   One of the earliest examples of sports marketing can be traced to the 1880s when baseball cards were introduced. Consider life before the automobile and the television. For most baseball fans, the player's picture on the card may have been the only chance to see that player. Interestingly, the cards were featured as a promotion in cigarette packages rather than bubble gum. Can you imagine the ethical backlash that this practice would have produced today?

Although the sports trading card industry reached $1.2 billion in 1991, industry wide yearly sales plummeted to $700 million in 1995 and are now stable at between $400 and $500 million.[30] What caused this collapse? One answer is too much competition. David Leibowitz, an industry analyst, commented that "With the channel of distribution backed up and with too much inventory, it was hard to sustain prices, let alone have them continue to rise. From the beginning of the 1970s there were 3 major card companies (Topps, Dondruss and Fleer) and now there are over 80 companies. In addition to a flooded market, the cartoon fad cards like Pokeman and Yu-Gi-Oh have hurt the sports trading card industry. Other problems include labor problems in sports, escalating card prices and kids with competing interests.

There is, however, some evidence that the industry will rebound. Perhaps the biggest boost will be selling and trading cards on the Internet.[31] The first major company in this market was the industry leader, Topps. Each week on etopps.com the company promotes 6 new limited edition cards or IPOs (Initial Player Offerings). The buyer can then purchase the card and takes physical possession, sell the card in an auction, or hold the card until it appreciates in value. The new product has been a huge success for Topps and could be the future of the card industry.

PERSONAL TRAINING FOR SPORTS

Another growing category of sports is referred to as **personal training.** These products are produced to benefit participants in sports at all levels and include fitness centers, health services, sports camps, and instruction.

Fitness Centers and Health Services   When the New York Athletic Club was opened in 1886, it became the first facility opened specifically for athletic training. From its humble beginning in New York, the fitness industry has seen an incredible boom. "Pumping iron" was a common phrase in the 1970s and early 1980s. Moreover, the 1970s aerobics craze started by Dr. Ken Cooper added to the growth of health clubs across the United States.

It is no secret that a physically fit body is becoming more important to society. The growth of the fitness industry follows a national trend for people to care more about their health. In 1993, there were 11,655 clubs in the United States billed as "health and fitness" centers. In 2002, this number had grown to a record high of 17,807 clubs. Moreover, health club membership climbed to a record high 36.3 million people and is expected to double by 2010. Why are people joining health clubs in record numbers?

The sports collector's dream—the Baseball Hall of Fame.

According to a 2002 study conducted by the International Health, Racquet, and Sportsclub Association, the factors that will continue to support the growth of health club membership in the United States include the following:

1. The growing number of health clubs that make it more convenient for consumers.
2. The continued and increased promotion of the benefits of exercise by organizations like the U.S. Surgeon General.
3. More Americans are concerned about the adverse effects of poor exercise and eating habits.[32]

Sports Camps and Instruction Sports camps are organized training sessions designed to provide instruction in a specific sport (e.g., basketball or soccer). Camps are usually associated with instructing children; however, the "fantasy sports camp" for aging athletes has received considerable attention in the past few years. Fantasy sports camps typically feature current or ex-professional athletes, and the focus is more on having fun than actual instruction. Nearly every major league baseball team now offers some type of fantasy camp for adults. For example, Chicago Fantasy Baseball Camp allows you (if you're over 30 years old) to be a major leaguer for a week. The experience consists of social activities, games, and instruction with former major league players, but this does not come cheap. The price for participating is roughly $3,000 per person.

Along with camps, another lucrative sports service is providing personal or group instruction in sports. The difference between instruction and camps is the ongoing nature of the instruction versus the finite period and intense experience of the camp. For example, taking golf or tennis lessons from a professional typically involves a series of half-hour lessons over the course of months or sometimes years. Contrast this with the camp that provides intense instruction over a week-long period.

SPORTS INFORMATION

The final type of sports product that we discuss is sports information. **Sports information** products provide consumers with news, statistics, schedules, and stories about sports. In addition, sports information can provide participants with instructional materials. Sports specific newspapers (e.g., *The Sporting News*), magazines (e.g., *Sports Illustrated*), Internet sites (e.g., cnnsi.com), television (e.g., The Golf Channel), and radio (e.g., WFAN) can all be considered sports information products. All these forms of media are experiencing growth both in terms of products and audience. Consider the following examples of new sports information media. ESPN launched its new magazine in March

The Bassmaster official Web site provides information for fishing enthusiasts.
Source: Reprinted courtesy of ESPN.com.

1998 to compete with *Sports Illustrated,* which leads all sports magazines with a circulation of over 3.2 million. The current circulation for ESPN The Magazine is 1.7 million, but all indications are that there is room at the top for two sports magazine powerhouses.[33] In addition, the ESPN2 audience has increased to more than 85 million homes.[34]

The fastest growing source of sports information is on the World Wide Web. The ESPN Chilton Sports Poll estimates that 34 percent of all computer owners and people with access to computers get sports information online and use the computer for that purpose an average of 2.4 times per week.[35] Due to the tremendous amount of information that sports fans desire (e.g., team stats, player stats, and league stats) and the ability of Web sites to supply such information, Web sites and sports marketing make a perfect fit. One example of the success of providing sports information via the World Wide Web is www.ESPN.com (ESPN's Web site).

ESPN has not only introduced a successful magazine, but it has also become a leader in providing sports information on its Web site with a combined home and work reach of 15 million unique users. ESPN's site has been so successful because it targets the right customers, has a great product, leverages the ESPN name, and has one of the highest advertising rates on the Web.[36]

THE MULTIDIMENSIONAL NATURE OF THE SPORTS PRODUCT

As you can see from our previous discussion, there are a wide variety of sports products. Our earlier definition of the sports product incorporated the distinction between goods and services. Although this is a traditional approach to categorizing consumer products, the complexity of the sports product makes the goods–services classification inadequate. Consider the rich diversity of the sports products that we have just considered. Everything from a hockey puck to the NCAA championship game of the Final Four in basketball is included in our definition. Because of this diversity and complexity, we have added an additional dimension to the sports product known as the body–mind continuum. The body–mind continuum is based on the notion that some sports products benefit consumers' minds, while other products act on consumers' bodies. Figure 1.4

FIGURE 1.4   The Sports Product Map

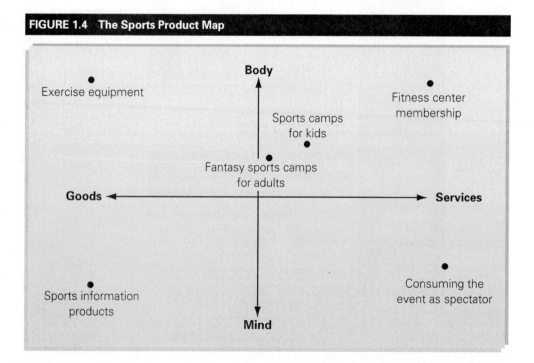

illustrates the multidimensional nature of sports products using two dimensions: goods–services and body–mind. These dimensions make up the **sports product map.**

As you can see, we have positioned some sports products on this map. Exercise equipment is shown as a good that works on the body of the consumer. At the other end of the map, attending or watching a sporting event is considered a service that acts on the mind of consumers. Perhaps we can best describe the differences based on the mind–body and goods–services dimension by exploring sports camps. Sports camps for children are primarily instructional in nature. The primary product being sold is the opportunity for kids to practice their physical skills. However, the fantasy camp targeting adults is a product that acts more on the mind than body. The adults are purchasing the "fantasy" to interact with professional athletes rather than the physical training.

Understanding where sports products fall on this map is critical for sports marketers. Marketers must understand how they want their sports product to be perceived by consumers so they can understand what benefits to stress. For example, the marketers of a sporting event may want to sell the intangible excitement or the tangible features of the arena. This strategic decision is based on a number of factors that will be considered in detail throughout this text.

PRODUCERS AND INTERMEDIARIES

Producers and intermediaries represent the manufacturers of sports products or the organizations that perform some function in the marketing of sports products. Organizations or individuals that perform the function of producer or intermediary include team owners, sanctioning bodies, agents, corporate sponsors, media, and sporting goods manufacturers. In the following paragraphs, we take a look at each of these producers and intermediaries as they relate to the various sports products.

Sports Labor   Owners of professional sports franchises, partnerships that own sporting events, and universities that "own" their athletic teams all represent producers of sporting events. One of the unique aspects of the sports industry is that often times businesspeople purchase a team because they always dreamed of becoming involved in sports. Typically, sports owners are entrepreneurs who have made their riches in other businesses before deciding to get involved in the business of sports. All too often these owners may be realizing a dream, but fail to realize a profit. Just think of the risks in owning your own team. Pro sports teams have seasonal revenue streams, few chances to expand, and frequent labor problems, and are dependent on the health of just a select few employees.

Many sports-related financial ownership deals—be it racehorses, minor league baseball teams, or indoor soccer franchises—score high on appeal and low on profits. J. W. Stealey, former owner of the Baltimore Spirit (now Blast) professional indoor soccer team, exemplifies the typical sports owner. He says, "Sports has always been my life. Owning a team is, to be honest, an ego kind of a deal, with all the attention from the media and involvement with the players." However, there is just one catch. "Although I keep expecting us to turn a profit, we never have."[37]

Although ownership of professional franchises is still a dream for many individuals, corporations are quickly becoming the dominant force in ownership. In recent years the dominant trend was for media giants to purchasing teams to own their sports programming. Irwin Stelzer, a Washington economist, says "Buying a team is just a surer way of buying the rights [to programming]." In fact, media companies own about 10 percent of North American sports franchsies. However, media groups are now rethinking their sports business strategies. The Anaheim Angels owned by Walt Disney, the LA Dodgers owned by News Corp., and AOL Time Warner are all examples of media companies looking to unload their sports franchises.[38] Interestingly, the NFL forbids corporate ownership of franchises.

Sanctioning Bodies Sanctioning bodies are organizations that not only market sports products, but also, more important, delineate and enforce rules and regulations, determine the time and place of sporting events, and provide athletes with the structure necessary to compete. Examples of sanctioning bodies include the NCAA, NFL, NHL, IOC (International Olympic Committee), and NASCAR. Sanctioning bodies can be powerful forces in the sports industry by regulating the rules and organizing the structure of the leagues and sporting events.

The PGA (Professional Golf Association) of America is one of the largest sanctioning bodies in the world. It is comprised of more than 22,000 members that promote the game of golf to "everyone, everywhere." In addition to marketing the game of golf, the PGA organizes tournaments for amateurs and professional golfers, holds instructional clinics, and hosts trade shows.[39] Although the PGA has a long history of advancing golf, this sanctioning body most recent controversy surrounds women in golf. More specifically, Martha Burk, the head of the National Organization of Women's Organizations protested the 67th Masters played at Augusta National because the club does not admit women. The PGA Tour Commissioner, Tim Finchem, contends that Augusta's membership policy is a private matter and the PGA will not get involved. Burk believed that since the PGA is recognizing the event as official and taking its prize money, the sanctioning body is condoning Augusta's stance on female membership. Burk is also threatening to target PGA Tour corporate partners for a boycott of the event.[40] Yet even more controversy surrounding gender emerged for the PGA in 2003 as Annika Sorenstam received an invitation to play in the Colonial, becoming the first woman to play on the men's tour in 58 years.

NCAA: One of the most powerful sanctioning bodies.
Source: Copyright © 2003. The National Collegiate Athletic Association. All rights reserved worldwide.

Sponsors Sponsors represent a sport intermediary. As we discussed, corporations can serve as a consumer of sport. However, corporations also supply sporting events with products or money in exchange for association with the event. The relationship between the event, the audience, and the sponsor is referred to as the event triangle.[41] The basis of the event triangle is that the event, the audience, and the sponsor are all interdependent or depend on each other to be successful. All three groups work in concert to maximize the sport's exposure. The events showcase talented athletes and attract the audience who watch the event in-person or through some medium. The audience, in turn, attracts the sponsor who pays the event to provide them with access to the audience. In addition, the sponsor promotes the event to the audience, which helps the event reach its attendance goals. It is safe to say that sponsors represent an important intermediary or link between the event and the final consumers of sports— the audience.

Media Earlier in this chapter, we commented on the growth of media in bringing sporting events to consumers. In fact, the media, which is considered an intermediary, may be the most powerful force in sports today and is getting stronger. Televised sports pulled in roughly $5 billion in sales in 2000 with the major networks (ABC, NBC, CBS, and FOX) accounting for over 70 percent of the market.[42] The primary revenue generator for these networks is selling prime advertising time. As the price of advertising time rises, so does the cost of securing broadcast rights; however, the networks are willing to pay.

Sports organizations cannot survive without the mass exposure of the media, and the media needs sports to satisfy the growing consumer demand for this type of entertainment. As the demand for sports programming increases, innovations in media will emerge. For example, in the new millennium interactive media will allow fans to control what game they are watching and what appears on the screen. The television audiences will be able to view player and game statistics at their convenience.

Agents Another important intermediary in bringing the athlete to the consumer is the sports **agent.** From a sports marketing perspective, sports agents are intermediaries whose primary responsibility is leveraging athletes' worth or determining their bargaining power. The first "super-agent" in sports was Mark McCormack (see Sports Marketing Hall of Fame). Prior to his emergence, agents had never received the exposure and recognition that they enjoy today. Interestingly, it is not the agents themselves that have provoked their current rise to prominence, but rather the increased bargaining power of their clients.

The bargaining power of the athletes can be traced to two factors. First, the formation of new leagues in the 1970s, such as the American Basketball Association (ABA) and the World Hockey Association (WHA), resulted in increased competition to sign the best athletes. This competition drove the salaries to higher levels than ever before and made agents more critical. Second, free agency and arbitration have given players a chance to shop their talents on the open market and question the final offer of owners. In addition, owners are now able to pay players the higher salaries because of the multimillion dollar national television contracts and cable television revenues.

Although most people associate agents with contract negotiations, agents do much more. Here are some of the other responsibilities of the agent:[43]

- determines the value of the player's services
- convinces a club to pay the player the aforementioned value

SPORTS MARKETING HALL OF FAME

Mark McCormack

Many people trace the beginnings of modern sports marketing to one man—Mark McCormack. In 1960, Mark McCormack, a Cleveland lawyer, signed an agreement to represent Arnold Palmer. With this star client in hand, McCormack began the International Management Group, better known as IMG. Today, IMG is a multinational sports marketing organization that employs over 3,000 people, has sales of over $1 billion, and represents some of the finest professional athletes in the world.

In addition to his contribution to sports marketing in the United States, McCormack has globalized sports marketing. He opened an Asian office of IMG in Tokyo in 1969, led in the sponsorship of events in Europe, and continues to expand into the Middle Eastern markets. One example of McCormack's enormous reach into international markets is IMG's Trans World International. TWI is the largest independent producer of sports programming in the world. One of its shows, Trans World Sports, is viewed in more than 325 million homes in over 76 countries. Along with representing athletes and producing sports programming, IMG runs several sports academies that serve as training facilities for elite athletes. Additionally, IMG manages and creates sporting events such as the Skins Game, Superstars Competition, and CART races. Unfortunately for the sports world, Mr. McCormack died in May 2003 at the age of 72.

Source: Susan Vinella, "Sports Marketing Pioneer Dead at 72"; "IMG's McCormack Hailed as Visionary," *Plain Dealer,* May 17, 2003, a1; Eric Fisher, "IMG Founder McCormack Spiced Up the Sports World," *The Washington Times,* May 18, 2003, c3.

- develops the package of compensation to suit the player's needs
- protects the player's rights under contract (and within the guidelines set by the collective bargaining agreement)
- counsels the player about postcareer security, both financial and occupational
- finds a new club upon player free agency
- assists the player in earning extra income from endorsements, speeches, appearances, and commercials
- advises an athlete on the effect their personal conduct has on their career

Sports Equipment Manufacturers   **Sports equipment manufacturers** are responsible for producing and sometimes marketing sports equipment used by consumers who are participating in sports at all different levels of competition. Some sporting equipment manufacturers are still associated with a single product line whereas others carry a multitude of sports products. For example, Platypus Sporting Goods only manufactures cricket balls. However, Wilson manufactures football, volleyball, basketball, golf, tennis, baseball, softball, racquetball or squash, and youth sports equipment.

Although it is obvious that equipment manufacturers are necessary to supply the equipment needed to produce the competition, they also play an important role in sports sponsorship. Sports equipment manufacturers become sponsors because of the natural relationship they have with sports. For instance, Rawlings, one of the best known baseball glove manufacturers, sponsors the American and National League Golden Glove Award, which is given to the best defensive players in their position. Spalding sponsors the NCAA Volleyball Championship by supplying the official game balls. In addition, Spalding is the official game ball of the WNBA.

BASIC MARKETING PRINCIPLES AND PROCESSES APPLIED TO SPORT

THE SPORTS MARKETING MIX

Sports marketing is commonly associated with promotional activities such as advertising, sponsorships, public relations, and personal selling. Although this is true, sports marketers are also involved in product and service strategies, pricing decisions, and distribution issues. These activities are referred to as the **sports marketing mix,** which is defined as the coordinated set of elements that sports organizations use to meet their marketing objectives and satisfy consumers' needs.

The basic marketing mix elements are the sports product, price, promotion, and distribution. When coordinated and integrated, the combination of the basic marketing mix elements are known as the marketing program. The marketing mix or program elements are controllable factors because sports marketing managers have control over each element. In the following sections, we take a closer look at the four marketing mix elements as they apply to the sports industry.

PRODUCT STRATEGIES

One of the basic sports marketing activities is developing product and service strategies. In designing product strategies, decisions regarding licensing, merchandising, branding, and packaging are addressed. In addition, sports marketing managers are responsible for new product development, maintaining existing products, and eliminating weak products. The Toronto Blue Jays decision to change the team logo for the third time in eight seasons, Charlotte's new NBA expansion team deciding on "Bobcats" for its nickname, and Callaway introducing a new driver are product issues of interest to sports marketers.

Because so much of sports marketing is based on services rather than goods, understanding the nature of services marketing is critical for the sports marketing manager. Services planning entails pricing of services, managing demand for services, and evaluating service quality. For instance, sports marketing managers want to know fans' perceptions of ticket ushers, concessions, parking, and stadium comfort. These service issues are especially important in today's sports marketing environment because fans equate value with high levels of customer service.

DISTRIBUTION STRATEGIES

Traditionally, the role of distribution is finding the most efficient and effective way to get the products into the hands of the consumers. Issues such as inventory management, transportation, warehousing, wholesaling, and retailing are all under the control of distribution managers. The advent of sporting goods superstores such as Dick's Sporting Goods or the Sports Authority, offering sports memorabilia on the Home Shopping Network, and marketing sports products on the Internet are examples of the traditional distribution function at work. Sports marketing managers are also concerned with how to deliver sports to spectators in the most effective and efficient way. Questions such as where to build a new stadium, where to locate a recreational softball complex, or how to distribute tickets most effectively are potential distribution issues facing sports marketers.

PRICING STRATEGIES

One of the most critical and sensitive issues facing sports marketing managers today is pricing. Pricing strategies include setting pricing objectives, choosing a pricing technique, and making adjustments to prices over time.

The price of tickets for sporting events; fees for personal seat licenses, pay-per-view and television sports programming; and the rising costs of participating in recreational sports such as golf, are all examples of how the pricing function affects sports marketing.

PROMOTION STRATEGIES

Just ask someone what comes to mind when they think of sports marketing, and the likely response is advertising. They may think of athletes such as Anna Kournikova or Brett Favre endorsing a product or service. Although advertising is an element of promotion, it is by no means the only one. In addition to advertising, promotional elements include communicating with the various sports publics through sponsorships, public relations, personal selling, or sales promotions. Together these promotional elements are called the promotion mix. When designing promotional strategies, sports marketers must consider integrating their promotions and using all aspects of the promotion mix.

THE EXCHANGE PROCESS

Understanding the exchange process is central to any successful marketing strategy. As generally defined, an **exchange** is a marketing transaction in which the buyer gives something of value to the seller in return for goods and services. For an exchange to occur, several conditions must be satisfied:

- There must be at least two parties.
- Each party must have something of value to offer the other.
- There must be a means for communication between the two or more parties.
- Each party must be free to accept or decline the offer.
- Each party must believe it is desirable to deal with the other(s).

Traditionally, a marketing exchange consists of a consumer giving money to receive a product or service that meets their needs. Other exchanges, not involving money, are also possible. For example, trading a Pedro Martinez rookie baseball card for a Randy Johnson card represents a marketing exchange between two collectors.

Examples of elements that make up other exchanges appear in Figure 1.5. The two parties in the exchange process are called exchange players. These two participants are

FIGURE 1.5   Model of the Sports Marketing Exchange Process

Something of Value
Money
Time
Personal energy

Exchange Players
Sports spectators
Sports participants
Organizations

Exchange Players
Sporting events
Sporting good manufacturers
Teams

Something of Value
Entertainment
Better quality of life
Enhanced image

consumers of sport (e.g., spectators, participants, or sponsors) or producers and intermediaries of sport. Sports spectators exchange their time, money, and personal energy with sports teams in exchange for the entertainment and enjoyment of watching the contest. Sports participants exchange their time, energy, and money for the joy of sport and the better quality of life that participating in sports brings. In sponsorships, organizations exchange money or products for the right to associate with a sporting event, player, team, or other sports entity.

Although these are rather elementary examples of the exchange process, one of the things that makes sports marketing so unique is the complex nature of the exchange process. Within one sporting event, multiple exchanges will occur. Consider a Winston Cup NASCAR event. There are exchanges between spectators and the track ownership (i.e., money for entertainment); spectators and product vendors who are licensed by NASCAR (i.e., money for goods associated with racing); track owner and NASCAR sanctioning body (i.e., money for organizing the event and providing other event services); media and NASCAR (i.e., event broadcast coverage for money); product sponsors and driving team owner (i.e., promotional benefits for money); and track owner and driving team owner (i.e., producer of the competition for money). As you may imagine, trying to sort out all these exchanges, much less determine the various marketing strategy involved in each exchange, is a complicated puzzle that can only be solved by having a full understanding of the industry within each sport. Although the nature of each sporting event and industry is slightly different, designing a marketing strategy incorporates some fundamental processes that span the sports industry.

THE STRATEGIC SPORTS MARKETING PROCESS

Sports marketers manage the complex and unique exchange processes in the sports industry by using the strategic sports marketing process. The **strategic sports marketing process** is the process of planning, implementing, and controlling marketing efforts to meet organizational goals and satisfy consumers' needs.

To meet these organizational goals and marketing objectives, sports marketers must first anticipate consumer demand. Sports marketers want to know what motivates consumers to purchase, how they perceive sports products or services, how they learn about a sports product, and how they choose certain products over others.

One way sports marketers anticipate demand is by conducting marketing research to gather information about the sports consumer. Another way that sports marketers anticipate demand is by monitoring the external environment. For instance, marketing research was used to determine the feasibility of locating a new NASCAR speedway in Northern Kentucky. According to developer, Jerry Carroll, "The report was two volumes and it not only said a major racetrack would work in this area, but it would be a grand slam." In addition, Carroll anticipated demand by examining the external environment. He found out that there are about 51 million people within a 300-mile radius of the proposed track and that "NASCAR fans and other racing fans, don't think anything of driving 300 miles for a race."[44] Thus far, the research has proven to be true as the Kentucky Speedway has been a huge success since opening its door for the 2000 season.

Next, sports marketers examine different groups of consumers, choose the group of consumers in which to direct the organization's marketing efforts, and then determine how to position the product or service to that group of consumers. These market selection decisions are referred to as segmentation, targeting, and position. The final aspect of the planning phase is to offer products that are promoted, priced, and distributed in ways that appeal to the targeted consumers.

Canadiens Targeting Younger Fans with a New Club

The Montreal Canadiens have never been lacking for fans.

Consistently among the league's attendance leaders (they led the NHL last season with 20,673 a game), and with 23 Stanley Cup banners, the club probably could rest on tradition and still sell the overwhelming majority of seats at the Bell Centre.

But with no championships in the last decade, the Canadiens' brass feels it needs to reach out to younger fans and has unleashed an extensive fan development project akin to the ones found in expansion markets.

For the coming season, the club has launched an official fan club—the first in its 85-year history—and also aligned with Hockey Quebec for a joint grassroots program that will reach 150,000 youth hockey players.

"We're targeting the younger generation that hasn't been treated to the Stanley Cup," said Ray Lalonde, the team's vice president of sales and marketing.

"Guys my age have seen the Canadiens win six or seven Cups," said Lalonde, who is 41. "Young kids haven't seen much they can remember. They haven't had the privilege of seeing Guy Lafleur or the great teams of the '70s. Yet they are the ones who are buying consumer products, watching on television, going to our Web site."

The fan club is targeted at kids ages 5 to 15. For a C$19.95 ($14.63 U.S.) membership fee, they'll get a ticket to a game, in addition to promotional items that Lalonde valued at C$90 ($65.99 U.S.). Backup goaltender Mathieu Garon is the official spokesman for the club, and each member will get a Garon puck and poster.

The Hockey Quebec program is titled "Learn, Respect and Fun," or the somewhat more graceful "Respect Apprentissage et Plaisir" in French, and aims to stress morals, values and sportsmanship along with hockey instruction. Participants sign a "contract" with the Canadiens and their general manager, Bob Gainey, agreeing to uphold good values on and off the ice. They then will receive patches bearing the Canadiens logo that they can sew onto their hockey jerseys.

Both the fan club and sportsmanship programs are simultaneously administered in French and English. Underwriting the costs are several sponsors, with the doughnut chain Tim Horton's sponsoring the Hockey Quebec program and packaged goods brand Saputo backing the fan club.

Source: Andy Bernstein *Sports Business Journal.* Copyright © 1998–2004 Street & Smith's Sports Group. All rights reserved.

Following the planning phase of the strategic sports marketing process, the next step is implementation. Implementation refers to executing or carrying out the plans. For implementation to be successful, the sports organization must consider a number of organizational design elements, including communication, staffing, skills, coordination, rewards, information, creativity, and budgeting.

Once the plans have been implemented, the final step of the strategic sports marketing process is referred to as the control phase. During the control phase, plans are evaluated to determine whether organizational objectives have been met. If objectives are not being reached, adjustments are made to planning and the process continues.

To gain a better understanding of the strategic marketing process, we look at the following article about the Montreal Canadiens attempt to use sports marketing principles to reach out to younger fans.

Summary

The sports industry is experiencing tremendous growth, and sports marketing is playing an important role in this emerging industry. Chapter 1 provided a basic understanding of sports marketing and the sports industry. Sports marketing is "the specific application of marketing principles and processes to sport products and to the marketing of nonsports products through association with sport." The study and practice of sports marketing is complex and interesting because of the unique nature of the sports industry.

Today sports organizations define their businesses as entertainment providers. In addition, sports organizations know that to be successful in the competitive environment of sports, they must practice a marketing orientation. An organization with a marketing orientation concentrates on understanding consumers and providing sports products that satisfy consumers' needs.

Sports marketing will continue to grow in importance as sports become more pervasive in the U.S. culture and around the globe. This phenomenal growth of the sports industry can be seen and measured in a number of ways. We can identify growth by looking at the increasing numbers of sport spectators, the growth of media coverage, the increase in sports participation, rising employment opportunities, and the growth in sports internationally. To better understand this growing and complex industry, a simplified model of the consumer–supplier relationship was presented.

The simplified model of the consumer–supplier relationship in the sports industry consists of three major elements: consumers of sport, sports products, and producers and intermediaries. Three distinct types of sports consumers are identified in the model. These consumers of sport include spectators who observe sporting events, participants who take part in sporting events, and sponsors who exchange money or product for the right to be associated with a sporting event. The spectators, participants, and sponsors use sports products.

A sports product is a good, service, or any combination of the two that is designed to provide benefits to a sports consumer. The primary sports product consumed by sponsors and spectators is the sporting event. Products related to the event are athletes such as Derek Jeter and arenas such as the Staples Center, which both provide their own unique benefits. Other categories of sports products common to the sports industry include sporting goods (e.g., equipment, apparel and shoes, licensed merchandise, collectibles, and memorabilia), personal training services for sports (e.g., fitness centers and sports camps), and sports information (e.g., news and magazines). Because there is a variety of sports products, it is useful to categorize these products using the sports product map.

Producers and intermediaries represent the third element of the simplified model of the consumer–supplier relationship in the sports industry. Producers include those organizations or individuals that help "manufacture" the sporting event, such as owners, sanctioning bodies, and sports equipment manufacturers. Intermediaries are also critical to the sports industry because they bring the sport to the end user of the sports product. Sponsors, the media, and agents are the three intermediaries presented in this chapter.

Although sports marketers must have a thorough understanding of the sports industry to be successful, the tool of their trade is the sports marketing mix. The sports marketing mix is defined as the coordinated set of elements that sports organizations use to meet their marketing mix objectives and satisfy consumers' needs. The elements of the marketing mix are sports products, distribution or place, pricing, and promotion.

In addition to the marketing mix, another central element of marketing is the exchange process. The exchange process is defined as a marketing transaction in which the buyer gives something of value to the seller in return for goods and services. One of the things that makes the sports industry so unique is the complex nature of the exchange process and the many exchanges that take place within a single sporting event.

To manage the complexities of the sports industry and achieve organizational objectives, sports marketers use the strategic sports marketing process. The strategic sports marketing process consists of three major parts: planning, implementation, and control. The planning process begins by understanding consumers' needs, selecting a group of consumers with similar needs, and positioning the sports product within this group of consumers. The final step of the planning phase is to develop a marketing mix that will appeal to the targeted group of consumers and carry out the desired positioning. The second major part of the strategic sports marketing process is putting the plans into action or implementation. Finally, the plans are evaluated to determine whether organizational objectives and marketing goals are being met. This third, and final, part of the strategic sports marketing process is called control.

Key Terms

- agent
- amateur sporting event
- benefits
- exchange
- goods
- licensing
- marketing myopia
- marketing orientation
- organized sporting events
- participants

- personal training
- producers and intermediaries
- services
- simplified model of the consumer–supplier relationship
- spectators
- sport
- sporting event
- sporting goods
- sports equipment manufacturers

- sports information
- sports marketing
- sports marketing mix
- sports product
- sports product map
- sports sponsorship
- strategic sports marketing process
- unorganized sports

Review Questions

1. Define sports marketing and discuss how sports are related to entertainment.
2. What is a marketing orientation, and how do sports organizations practice a marketing orientation?
3. Discuss some of the ways that the sports marketing industry is growing?
4. Outline the simplified model of the consumer–supplier relationship in the sports industry.
5. What are the three distinct types of sports consumers? What are the different types of spectators? How are sports participants categorized?
6. Define sports products. What are the different types of sports products discussed in the simplified model of the consumer–supplier relationship in the sports industry?
7. Describe the different producers and intermediaries in the simplified model of the consumer–supplier relationship in the sports industry.
8. What are the basic elements of the sports marketing mix?
9. What is the marketing exchange process, and why is the exchange process critical for sports marketers?
10. Define the strategic sports marketing process, and discuss the various elements in the strategic sports marketing process.

Exercises

1. Provide five recent examples of sports marketing that have been in the news and describe how each relates to our definition of sports marketing.
2. How does sport differ from other forms of entertainment?
3. Provide an example of a sports organization that suffers from marketing myopia and another sports organization that defines its business as entertainment. Justify your choices.
4. Attend a high school, college, and professional sporting event and comment on the marketing orientation of the event at each level of competition.
5. Provide three examples of how you would *measure growth* in the sports marketing industry. What evidence do you have that the number of people participating in sports is growing?
6. Discuss the disadvantages and advantages of attending sporting events versus consuming a sporting event through the media (e.g., television or radio).
7. Develop a list of all the sports products produced by your college or university. Which are goods and which are services? Identify ways in which the marketing of the goods differs from the services.
8. Choose any professional sports team and describe how it puts the basic sports marketing functions into practice.

Internet Exercises

1. Using Internet sites, support the growth of the sporting goods industry.
2. Compare and contrast the Internet sites of three professional sports teams. Which site has the strongest marketing orientation? Why?

Endnotes

1. John Mossman, "Denver to Host 2005 NBA All-Star Game," The Associated Press (June 16, 2003).
2. David Barboza, "Michael Jordan Movie Is Sports Marketing in New and Thinner Air," *The New York Times* (May 1, 2000), C16.
3. Michael Farber, "Putting on a Show," *Sports Illustrated* (October 17, 1994), 30–33.
4. A. K. Kohli and B. J. Jaworski, "Marketing Orientation: The Construct, Research Propositions, and Managerial Implications," *Journal of Marketing* 54 (2): 1–18.
5. Jeffery D. Derrick, "Marketing Orientation in Minor League Baseball." www.cjsm.com/Vol1/derrick.html
6. "The LPGA's Fan Friendly Attitude," www.ausport.gov.au/fulltext/1997/cjsm/u1n3/derrick.htm (September 17, 2002).
7. Michele Himmelberg, "The Sporting Life; Long Hours, Low Pay, Starting at the Bottom, What Fun!" *Orange County Register* (June 14, 1999), c1; Don Walker, "Money Game: Sports Becoming Big Business," *Journal Sentinel,* www.jsonline.com/news/gen/jan00/csports23012200.asp.

8. Eric Fisher, "Baseball Renaissance Still on Hold," *The Washington Times* (September 28, 2003), C03.

9. "Super Bowl Ratings Up 1 Percent," (January 27, 2003), sportsillustrated.cnn. com/football/playoffs/news/2003/01/27.

10. Jeff Houck, "Logo Land Examining Olympic Corporate Sponsorship Deals," www.foxsports.com/business/bites/z000914olym pic_money.sml.

11. "ESPN Customer Marketing and Sales," www.espnabcsportscms.com/adsales/portfolioespn.go. com/espninc/pressreleases/funfacts.html.

12. John Higgins, "MLB: Who's at Bat," *Broadcast and Cable* (July 3, 2000), 8.

13. Stedman Graham, Joe Jeff Goldblatt, and Lisa Delphy, *The Ultimate Guide to Sport Event Management and Marketing* (Chicago: Irwin, 1995), 6.

14. Michele Himmelberg, "The Sporting Life; Long Hours, Low Pay, Starting at the Bottom, What Fun!" *Orange County Register* (June 14, 1999), c1.

15. Nick Pandya, "Sporting a New Career," *The Guardian* (February 27, 1999), 2.

16. Vito Stellino, "Big NFL Figures Disguise Modest Corporate Reality; Financially, Few Teams Play Major-League Ball," *The Baltimore Sun* (July 27, 1999), 1C; Larry Weisman, "TV Cash Expands NFL Millionaires Club," *USA Today* (June 16, 1999), 1C.

17. www.sgma.com/press/2003.

18. "Sale of US Recreational Products on Positive Pace," www.sportinggoodsbusiness.com, July 23, 2003.

19. Nigel Pope, "Overview of Current Sponsorship Thought," www.cjsm.com/Vol2/pope21.htm.

20. Geoffrey Smith, "Sports: Walk, Don't Schuss," *Business Week*. www.businessweek.com/ 1997/49/b3556153.htm.

21. Skip Rozin, "Welcome to U.S. Widget Stadium," *Business Week* (September 11, 2000), 125–126.

22. "Tiger Woods; World's Greatest Golfer & Richest Black Athlete," *Jet* (December 4, 2000), 51. www.tigerwoods.com/sponsors.

23. Jeff Jensen, "All the Sports World's a Stage," *Advertising Age*, vol. 65 (October 24, 1994), 1, 3–4.

24. "Venue Media Teams with Williams to Provide Choice Seat Interactive Network at Super Bowl XXXII," *Yahoo!—The Williams Companies Inc. Company News*. www.biz.yahoo.com/bw/980123/ venue_medi_1. html.

25. "Purdue to (Palm) Pilot Wireless Football Fan Experience: Boilermaker Fans Try Out e-Stadium Prototype," *Ascribe Newswire* (September 5, 2003).

26. "Sale of U.S. Recreational Products on Positive Pace," www.sportinggoodsbusiness.com, July 23, 2003.

27. "Sale of U.S. Recreational Products on Positive Pace," www.sportinggoodsbusiness.com, July 23, 2003.

28. "Sports Licensed Products Still Sluggish," www.sportlink.com/press_room/ 2000_releases/m2000–010.html.

29. *1998 State of the Industry Report, Sporting Goods Manufacturers Association*, www.sportlink.com/ research/1998_research/industry/98soti.html.

30. Thomas Corwin, "Sports-Card Dealers Strike Out; Web Traders Hurting Bricks-and-Mortar Stores, Owners Say," *The Plain Dealer* (November 4, 2000), 1C.

31. Thomas Corwin, "Sports-Card Dealers Strike Out; Web Traders Hurting Bricks-and-Mortar Stores, Owners Say," *The Plain Dealer* (November 4, 2000), 1C.

32. "U.S. Health Club Industry Reaches a Record High," *Club Industry*, May 1, 2003.

33. Russell Adams, "Top Sports Titles Find There's Room for Two," www.sportsbusinessjournal.com/ article.cms?.

34. ESPN Customer Marketing and Sales, www.espnabcsportscms.com/adsales/ portfolioespn.go.com/espninc/pressreleases/ funfacts.html.

35. Don Walker, "Money Game: Sports Becoming Big Business, Journal Sentinel," www.jsonline.com/ news/gen/jan00/csports23012200.asp.

36. "ESPN.com Sets Record for Unique Users in October," www.espn.go.com/mediakit/ public_relation/12_09_02.html.

37. Jill Andresky Frasier, "Root, Root, Root for Your Own Team," *Inc.* (July 1997), 111.

38. "Media Companies Begin Ditching Ownership of Sports Teams, Mergers and Acquisitions," *The Dealmaker's Journal* (June 1, 2003), p.1; Christopher Grimes, "Media Owners Get Ready to Strike Out Baseball Franchises," *Financial Times* (April 12, 2003), p. 26.

39. "The Role of the PGA in America," www.pga.com/FAQ/pga_role.html.

40. Mick Elliot, "Would-Be Boycotter Determined to Pursue PGA at Vulnerable Time," *Tampa Tribune* (October 31, 2002), p. 8.

41. Phil Schaaf, *Sports Marketing: It's Not Just a Game Anymore* (Amherst, MA: Prometheus Books, 1995), 46–75.

42. Dan Caesar, "Stealing the Show," *St. Louis Post Dispatch* (June 11, 2000), D1, 4.

43. "Frequently Asked Questions," *Sim-Gratton, Inc.* www.home.istar.ca/~simagent/faq.html.

44. Andrea Tortora, "NASCAR Track City's Future?" *The Enquirer* (November 16, 1997).

CHAPTER 2

CONTINGENCY FRAMEWORK FOR STRATEGIC SPORTS MARKETING

After completing this chapter, you should be able to:

- Understand the contingency framework for strategic sports marketing.
- Describe and apply the strategic sports marketing process.
- Define the internal and external contingencies and relate them to the strategic sports marketing process.
- Explain the planning decisions fundamental to the strategic sports marketing process.
- Describe how and why sports marketers understand consumers' needs.
- Understand the concepts of segmentation, targeting, and positioning.
- Identify the elements of the sports marketing mix.
- Describe the implementation phase of the strategic sports marketing process.
- Discuss the control phase of the strategic marketing process.
- Identify different ways to assess the success of your planning.

As the next article illustrates, the foundation of any effective sports organization is a sound, yet flexible, strategic framework. The process should be systematic and well-organized, but must be readily adaptable to changes in the environment. Each strategic marketing process may have unique characteristics, but the fundamentals are all the same. To help make sense of the complex and rapidly changing sports industry, we use a contingency framework to guide the strategic sports marketing process. For the remainder of this chapter, let us look at an overview of this process.

Globetrotters Dribble Out a New Marketing Plan

Trying to put a new spin on an 80-year-old brand is no easy task. For decades, the Harlem Globetrotters thrilled fans of all ages around the world. Even though the NBA is basking in popularity, the Globetrotters nearly dropped the ball. The problem was that the Globetrotters organization did not change with the times. Its act grew stale while the NBA grew hip. The solution—unveil a new strategic marketing direction, keeping in mind the changing environment and internal strengths and weaknesses of the Globetrotters.

Mannie Jackson, team owner and former Globetrotter player, attempted to capitalize on the strengths of the Globetrotters. As Jackson pointed out, "There's a lot of equity in the brand, and so now we are trying to build it, protect it, and embellish it."

Jackson has already realized the long-standing appeal his team has with families and children. According to Jon Jameson, vice president of marketing at Denny's restaurants, the team "stands for quality, family entertainment, and outstanding role models for children." Although the Globetrotters' clean-cut image may be a curse for the older end of the youth market, they are one of the few entertainment properties that appeal to the 6 to 10 age group.

What has Jackson done to rejuvenate the Globetrotters marketing mix? During the first year of Jackson's tenure (1993), the team boasted updated music and comedy bits, added a team mascot, and recruited an additional touring team. Jackson also cut all but four of the team's players and beefed up scouting to make the team more competitive. Today, it's a combination of great basketball and entertainment that excite fans. Not unexpectedly, the Harlem Globetrotter USA audience is 70 percent Caucasian. In 2003, the African-American audience accounts for 13 percent, a demographic that is unequaled by other professional sports teams, especially one that performs in over 200 urban and rural areas across the USA. In some urban areas, the non-white attendees reach 40 percent while in many small towns the crowds are exclusively white. It is this crossover broad base appeal that makes this organization's 77-year legacy so interesting and rich. In the past 10 years, attendance of African-Americans has more than doubled.

In 2003, a new flavor was also evident in the player's game attire, which is designed by FUBU as a result of a licensing partnership between the Harlem Globetrotters and the clothing company. For Us By Us (FUBU), is an urban clothing fashion designer that targets "urban life style" youth around the world. FUBU has become the most popular crossover brand of this fast moving "hip-

Owner Mannie Jackson and the Harlem Globetrotters.

hop" era. In addition to outfitting the team, FUBU created a line of Harlem Globetrotters clothing, The Platinum FUBU Harlem Globetrotter line, that debuted in stores in the fall of 2002. FUBU experienced a surprising year of brisk sales with the line selling over $40 million in retail sales in the first year in 5,000 locations worldwide.

The 1999, 2000, and 2002 "Q" ratings show further evidence of the Globetrotters popularity, particularly in the African-American community. The "Q" rating administrator, Marketing Evaluations, Inc. surveyed over 1,800 people asking them to rate 1,700 performers in sports and entertainment by recognition and likeability, resulting in a statistical quotient of appeal, trust, and popularity. According to the 2002 "Q" Ratings, when compared to all 1,700 performers averages, African-Americans were nearly twice as likely to be familiar with The Harlem Globetrotters (73%), and three times as likely to choose the Globetrotters as one of their favorites (32%). Overall, the Globetrotters rank second to Michael Jordan and ahead of Tiger Woods in popularity and Q-scores, and in the top 2 percent of all 1,700 performers!!

Jackson says that as the team heads into its 77th season, he has never stopped appreciating the Globetrotters from the fans' perspective. In addition to reviving the team financially, Jackson has made a commitment for the

(Continued)

(Continued)

Globetrotters to live up to their nickname of "Ambassadors of Goodwill." Under Jackson's ownership, the Globetrotters have donated over $10 million to charities around the world. All of this shows—having a marketing orientation and practicing strategic marketing pays off in more ways than one.

Sources: Cyndee Miller "Mannie Jackson Celebrates 10th Season as Harlem Globetrotter Owner" *Jet*, May 26, 2003, p. 51. "Globetrotters Dribble Out a New Marketing Plan," *Sports Marketing* (September 23, 1996), 34. Courtesy of the *Marketing News;* Jeff Houck, "Harlem Renaissance: Better Business Practices Put Globetrotter Back on Top." (August 14, 2000). www.foxsportsbusiness.com/trends/z000811globetrotters1.sml.

CONTINGENCY FRAMEWORK FOR STRATEGIC SPORTS MARKETING

Sports marketing managers must be prepared to face a continually changing environment. As Burton and Howard pointed out, "marketers considering careers or already employed in sports marketing must be prepared for unexpected, often negative actions that jeopardize a sport's organization's brand equity."[1] Think about what can happen over the course of an event or a season. The team that was supposed to win the championship cannot seem to win a game. The star player gets injured halfway through the season. Attendance at the sporting event is affected by poor weather conditions. Leagues are shut down by lockouts. Team owners threaten to move the franchise, build new stadiums, and change personnel. All this affects the sports marketing process.

At the collegiate level, a different set of situations may alter the strategic marketing process. For example, players may be declared ineligible because of grades, star players may leave school early to join the professional ranks, programs may be suspended for violation of NCAA regulations, or conferences may be realigned.

One example of a crisis situation at the collegiate level occurred when an announcement was made that one of the NCAA football programs most competitive and visible universities would be leaving the conference. This school's decision to leave the conference would have a tremendous impact on all the schools in the conference. It was also speculated that the school's leaving the conference would have a direct impact on its local economy and the revenues from the football program.

A study was conducted to determine the perception of the local business community with respect to the economic impact of the football program.[2] Findings revealed that the university and conference had a high social impact on the community, but less of an economic one on the individual business owners. Businesses that held season tickets felt even stronger than nonseason ticket holders about the positive impact the football program had on the community. Based on these findings, recommendations were made to promote the fact that the athletic program had a positive economic impact on the community. Unfortunately, recommendations such as the one just described were suggested after the crisis occurred.

The authors of this study advised taking a more proactive approach in the future, which would either avoid or prepare for crisis situations. More specifically, the authors suggested two remedies for identifying or resolving crises. First, sports organizations should conduct frequent marketing audits to review performance and identify market opportunities and threats. Second, formal marketing plans should be constructed and continually monitored to avoid or adapt to crisis situations. Most important, the authors stated that "a marketing plan could have been developed that would have blueprinted the team's approach to avoiding the impending crisis (perhaps lobbying efforts, new team recruitment, etc.) and defined a **contingency strategy** for adoption if the crisis were to prove inevitable."

It is also possible for positive opportunities to occur within the marketing environment. For example, the football program at Northwestern University, a perennial cellar-dweller in the Big Ten Conference, suddenly emerged as a national power in the mid-1990s. The Miracle Mets of 1969 made an unexpected late season run and eventually captured the World Series. The 1980 U.S. Olympic hockey team is yet another example of a team that defied the odds. These are all positive "crises" that presented opportunities for sports marketers.

Sports marketers need to be prepared for either positive or negative changes in the environment. These factors are out of the sports marketer's control, but they must be acknowledged and managed. Sports marketers must be prepared to cope with these rapid changes. One model that provides a system for understanding and managing the complexities of the sports marketing environment is called the **contingency framework for strategic sports marketing.**

CONTINGENCY APPROACHES

Contingency models were originally developed for managers who wanted to be responsive to the complexities of their organization and the changing environments in which they operate.[3] Several elements of the contingency framework make it especially useful for sport marketers. First, sports marketers operate in unpredictable and rapidly changing environments. They can neither predict team or player success nor control scheduling or trades. A quote by former New York Mets Marketing Vice President, Michael Aronin, who spent 13 years with Clairol, captures the essence of this idea: "Before, I had control of the product, I could design it the way I wanted it to be. Here the product changes every day and you've got to adapt quickly to these changes."[4]

Second, the contingency approach suggests that no one marketing strategy is more effective than another. However, one particular strategy may be more appropriate than another for a specific sports organization in a particular environment. For example, sports marketers for the Boston Red Sox have years of tradition on their side that influence their strategic planning. This marketing strategy, however, will not necessarily meet the needs of the relatively new teams such as the Columbus Blue Jackets. Likewise, strategies for an NCAA Division I program are not always appropriate for a Division II program. The contingency framework can provide the means for developing an effective marketing strategy in all these situations.

Third, a contingency model uses a systems perspective, one that assumes an organization does not operate in isolation but interacts with other systems. In other words, although an organization is dependent on its environment to exist and be successful, it can also play a role in shaping events outside the firm. Think about the Chicago Black Hawks and all the resources required from the environment to produce the core product—entertainment. These resources include professional athletes; owners; management and support personnel; and minor league franchises to supply talent, facilities, other competitors, and fans. The different environments that the Chicago Black Hawks actively interact with and influence include the community, the NHL, sponsors, employees and their families, and the sport itself. Understanding the relationship between the organization and its many environments is fundamental to grasping the nature of the contingency approach. In fact, the complex relationship that sports organizations have with their many publics (e.g., fans, government, businesses, and other teams) is one of the things that makes sports marketing so unique.

One way of thinking about the environments that affect sports organizations is to separate them on the basis of internal versus external contingencies. The external contingencies are factors outside the organization's control; the internal are considered controllable from the organization's perspective. It is important to realize that both the internal and external factors are perceived to be beyond the control, though not the influence, of the sports marketer.

The essence of contingency approaches is trying to predict and strategically align the strategic marketing process with the internal and external contingencies. This alignment is typically referred to as strategic fit or just "fit." Let us look at the contingency approach shown in Figure 2.1 in greater detail.

The focus of the contingency framework for sports marketing, and the emphasis of this book, is the strategic sports marketing process. The three primary components of this process are planning, implementation, and control. The planning phase begins with understanding the consumers of sports. As previously discussed, these consumers may be participants, spectators, or perhaps both. Once information regarding the potential consumers is gathered and analyzed, market selection decisions can be made. These decisions are used to segment markets, choose the targeted consumers, and position the sports product against the competition. The final step of the planning phase is to develop the sports marketing mix that will most efficiently and effectively reach the target market.

Effective planning is merely the first step in a successful strategic sports marketing program. The best-laid plans are useless without a method for carrying them out and

FIGURE 2.1 Contingency Framework for Strategic Sports Marketing

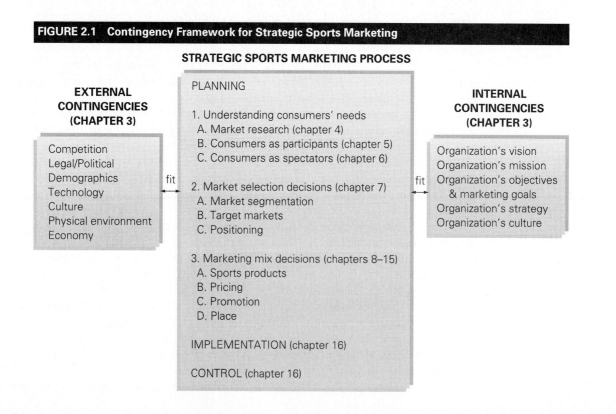

monitoring them. The process of executing the marketing program, or mix, is referred to as implementation. The evaluation of these plans is known as the control phase of the strategic marketing plan. These two phases, implementation and control, are the second and third steps of the strategic sports marketing process.

As you can see from the model, a contingency framework calls for alignment, or fit, between the strategic marketing process (e.g., planning, implementation, and control) and external and internal contingencies. Fit is based on determining the internal strengths and weaknesses of the sports organizations, as well as examining the external opportunities and threats that exist. **External contingencies** are defined as all influences outside the organization that can affect the organization's strategic marketing process. These external contingencies include factors such as competition, regulatory and political issues, demographic trends, technology, culture and values, and the physical environment. **Internal contingencies** are all the influences within the organization that can affect the strategic marketing process. These internal contingencies usually include the vision and mission of the organization, organizational goals and strategies for reaching those goals, and the organizational structure and systems.

STRATEGIC SPORTS MARKETING PROCESS: THE HEART OF THE CONTINGENCY FRAMEWORK

The **strategic sports marketing process** was defined in Chapter 1 as the process of planning, implementing, and controlling marketing efforts to meet organizational goals and satisfy consumers' needs (see also Figure 2.2). The **planning phase,** which is the most critical, begins with understanding the consumers of sport through marketing research

FIGURE 2.2   Strategic Sports Marketing Process

PLANNING PHASE

Step 1: Understanding Consumers' Needs
   A. Marketing research
   B. Consumers as participants
   C. Consumers as spectators

Step 2: Market Selection Decisions
   A. Marketing segmentation
   B. Target markets
   C. Positioning

Step 3: Marketing Mix Decisions
   A. Sports products
   B. Pricing
   C. Promotion
   D. Place

IMPLEMENTATION PHASE

CONTROL PHASE

and identifying consumer wants and needs. Next, market selection decisions are made, keeping the external and internal contingencies in mind. Finally, the marketing mix, also known as the four Ps, is developed to meet the identified consumer needs.

Once the planning phase is completed, plans are executed in the **implementation phase.** In this second phase of the strategic sports marketing process, decisions such as who will carry out the plans, when the plans will be executed, and how the plans will be executed are addressed. After implementing the plans, the third phase is to evaluate the response to the plans to determine their effectiveness. This is called the **control phase.** Let us examine the three phases of the strategic sports marketing process in greater detail.

PLANNING PHASE

UNDERSTANDING CONSUMERS' NEEDS

The first step in the planning phase is conducting marketing research to identify and examine sports consumers' needs. Marketing research is conducted using a variety of techniques. Surveys, the most widely used marketing research tools, are conducted at sporting events, over the telephone, or by mail to understand the attitudes and purchase behaviors (e.g., attendance) of sport consumers. Questions concerning who attends sporting events, the reasons that consumers attend sporting events, and consumers' attitudes toward various sports are all used by sports marketing managers to help formulate strategies to meet the needs of sports spectators and those who participate in sports.

An example of an area where sports marketers use marketing research to identify the needs of consumers can be found in the fitness industry. A survey was conducted by American Sports Data asking individuals why they most recently joined a health club. Young adults under the age of 35 thought it was important to join a health club to look better, increase strength, develop muscles, and meet new friends. The over-35 crowd joined to improve their health, deal with stress, or as medical or physical therapy.[5] Understanding the unique needs of these different groups of consumers is essential in designing appropriate marketing strategies that will meet these specific needs.

MARKET SELECTION DECISIONS

The process of selecting appropriate markets and positioning your sports entity effectively is the next stage in the planning phase of the strategic sports marketing process. **Market selection decisions** are sometimes referred to as STP, or segmentation, targeting, and positioning. These decisions should only be made after careful evaluation of the consumers' needs. It is important to bear in mind that the all the steps in the strategic marketing process follow a sequential order and are systematically organized. Only after choosing a target can the sports entity be positioned to that distinct market segment. Let us examine each of these steps.

SEGMENTATION

Grouping consumers based on common needs is referred to as **market segmentation.** Sports marketers frequently segment markets based on one or a combination of the following characteristics:

- demographics (e.g., age, sex, marital status, occupation, education, and ethnic background)
- geographic (where people live)
- geodemographic (the demography that defines a region where people live)

SPOTLIGHT ON INTERNATIONAL SPORTS MARKETING

Major League Baseball International: Segmenting the Market Based on Where People Live

As the World Series gets under way, the first word in its title has actually started to mean something.

These days, about 28 percent of all major-leaguers, including the Florida Marlins' Miguel Cabrera (Venezuela) and the New York Yankees' Hideki Matsui (Japan), come from parts of the planet outside the 50 states. The figure is an astounding 46 percent in the minors. And in the last few years, the people who run baseball have made renewed efforts to bolster the international fan base.

"Our efforts in that regard are absolutely critical," commissioner Bud Selig said. "The potential to grow the game is great here, but the potential elsewhere is tremendous."

Why do the people in Major League Baseball care so much about globalizing the game? They are not thinking about establishing franchises outside North America; logistics make that impractical, at least for now. Mostly, they are thinking about getting added revenue from three sources:

1. The sale of overseas broadcast rights.

2. Sponsorship arrangements, primarily with U.S. companies that do business in Asia and Latin America.

3. The marketing of team-logo merchandise, which, in some countries, has considerable sales appeal as Americana.

To grow that part of the business, Major League Baseball International is going to considerable lengths. During the World Series, it is producing its own video feed, separate from that of Fox Sports, to be broadcast to over 200 countries. Announcers Gary Thorne and Rick Sutcliffe are explaining the game to foreign viewers and highlighting foreign players. Earlier this year, Major League Baseball opened a new office in Tokyo to go along with existing outposts in London and in Sydney, Australia.

For the 2005 season, serious consideration is being given to playing a regular-season series somewhere in Europe, most likely in Italy, perhaps just before the All-Star Break. Last fall, about the time the New York Mets' Mike Piazza was posing outside the Colosseum in Rome, a baseball official was looking at Rome's Olympic Stadium as a possible venue.

Also in the talking stages is a baseball World Cup that might be held in this country during spring training. The competition would involve national teams made up largely of major-leaguers, teams representing Japan, South Korea, the Dominican Republic, Puerto Rico, Venezuela, Mexico, Cuba, and the United States, among other countries.

"The NBA's international business exploded after the Dream Team played in the 1992 Olympics," said Paul Archey, baseball's senior vice president for international business operations. "We think a World Cup could do the same for us. And we wouldn't have just one Dream Team. We'd have eight or nine, with no guarantee the U.S. would win."

While baseball won't reveal how much money it's making overseas, Archey says that the amount has grown substantially over the last few years and that 70 percent of the total comes from broadcast rights. In Japan, the most lucrative overseas market, the 2003 All-Star Game got better television ratings than it did in the United States. To try to spur interest in other countries—the kind of interest that results in higher rights fees, more sponsorship deals, and more sales of Yankees caps and Red Sox jerseys—baseball is moving on several fronts. The most noticeable is the staging of overseas events. There's the semiannual All-Star tour of Japan, with similar trips being contemplated for Australia, South Korea, and Taiwan.

And this season, as part of baseball's broader outreach, the Montreal Expos played 22 "home" games in San Juan, Puerto Rico.

But the prospective European excursion has particular appeal to baseball executives because of what Europe has going for it—a lot of money, a lot of new cable and satellite television stations in need of programming, and, to put the best face on it, a lot of room for growth.

"Europe has been a tough market for us because it's so soccer-crazy," said Russell Gabay, baseball's executive producer of television operations. "You've got to get people to see baseball and touch it." The philosophy under which Major League Baseball International operates is that it can't make money someplace long-term unless people there are playing the game. Only then, the theory goes, will they watch games on television or buy licensed products.

With that in mind, baseball has poured about $25 million into a number of development programs. One introduces the game to youngsters in grade-school gym classes. Another sends U.S. college coaches overseas. A third provides equipment to national baseball federations. A fourth offers a "road show" featuring a batting

(Continued)

(Continued)

cage and pitching tunnel. A fifth sends American stars abroad as ambassadors. Piazza, for instance, went to Berlin and Rome last November.

Baseball's goal is to help countries develop national teams and ultimately send a few players to the major leagues. "Establishing heroes in each country is critical to the development of our sport," said James Pearce, baseball's director of market development. "The nationalistic nature of sports is so powerful."

It's no accident that Major League Baseball's revenue in Japan soared with the arrival of Ichiro Suzuki in Seattle and Matsui in the Bronx. The interest level is high among Venezuelans and Dominicans, who have plenty of their own players to watch. More foreign stars means higher foreign broadcast fees and more merchandise sales. What Bud Selig wouldn't give for a superstar from Italy.

Source: www.sportsbusinessnews.com, October 21, 2003.

- benefits (what consumers desire in products and services)
- behavioral (e.g., consumption and usage patterns)
- psychographic (e.g., personality and lifestyle)

Demographics are perhaps the most popular way to segment sports consumers because of the ease of capturing demographic data. Table 2.1 provides a demographic comparison of motor sports fans. With this information, organizations could choose to sponsor the motor sport whose fans' demographic profiles most closely match its desired target market. Other considerations when choosing a target market(s) are discussed next.

TARGET MARKETS

After choosing the appropriate method or basis for categorizing groups of consumers, target market(s) must be chosen. **Target marketing** is described as choosing the segment(s) that will allow an organization most efficiently and effectively to

Consumers receive different benefits from fitness classes.

TABLE 2.1 Demographics: Who Goes to Races?

	CART	NASCAR	NHRA
Attendance			
Male	75%	62%	70%
Female	25%	38%	30%
Single	45%	22%	38%
Married	9%	64%	52%
Widowed or divorced	16%	14%	10%
Age			
Under 18	N/A	3%	2%
18–24	19%	15%	7%
25–34	35%	29%	28%
35–44	27%	25%	35%
45–54	13%	16%	21%
55+	6%	12%	7%
Education			
High school or less	N/A	12%	8%
High school graduate	24%	88%	42%
Some college or college graduate	60%	38%	49%
Post graduate	8%	N/A	3%
Income			
Under $19,999	9%	21%	10%
$20,000–$29,999	17%	17%	20%
$30,000–$39,999	17%	19%	20%
$40,000–$49,999	13%	14%	17%
Over $50,000	44%	29%	33%
Occupation			
Professional	21%	27%	36%
Manager or proprietor	25%	N/A	N/A
Technical or clerical sales	41%	21%	48%
Craft person	N/A	13%	N/A
Student	N/A	N/A	N/A
Other	13%	39%	8%

Source: Cart (SRi/Bruskin), NASCAR (Simmons Market Research Bureau, Inc. and Performance Research) and NHRA.

attain its marketing objectives. As discussed, these marketing objectives are formulated prior to the market selection decisions. Therefore, target markets represent the group of consumers around which the entire strategic sports marketing process is built.

To choose successful market segments, sports marketers must keep the following requirements in mind. Target markets must be[6]

- sizable (large enough in terms of the number of consumers)
- measurable (characteristics of the market are easily identifiable, such as gender or geographic region)
- reachable (must have a means of accessing the consumers)
- demonstrate behavioral variation (consumers within a market must share common needs, whereas consumers outside the target market behave differently)

Segmenting the runners market.

Source: Used by permission of Runner's World Magazine.

POSITIONING

The final market selection decision is positioning. **Positioning** is fixing the sports product in the minds of the target market. In other words, how does the target market perceive your product or service? For example, many minor league hockey franchises position their sport as fun-filled, family entertainment at a low price. For example, the International Hockey League (IHL), considered one of the most marketing-oriented sports leagues, has adopted a philosophy of providing major league sports at minor league prices. To implement this positioning, the IHL ran a print advertisement stating

Major League Entertainment. Minor League Price. Most professional sports leagues seem to have forgotten one key component when structuring their ticket prices. The fan. In fact, unless you're independently wealthy or you've just won the lottery, you probably can't afford to attend many games, much less bring your family. Not so in the IHL. We've

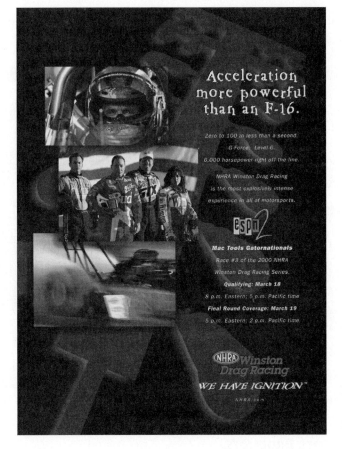

NHRA positioning drag racing as explosive excitement.

Source: Used by permission of National Hot Rod Association.

combined major league entertainment with an average ticket price of about $10 to become the number one fan value in professional sports today. So check out an IHL game in a major league market near you and see what you might be missing. We guarantee it won't be all your spending money.[7]

Arena football positions itself as a hard-hitting, action-packed game that can be watched in the comfort of an air-conditioned arena. Turner Sports Broadcasting positions its televised NBA games as live, unscripted, and completely unpredictable drama as just some of the unique characteristics of sport.

The key to proper positioning is understanding what the target market wants or needs from the product or service. Marketing research is necessary to understand consumers' perceptions of positioning. Major League Baseball introduced the "I Live For This" ad campaign to celebrate the passion and dedication its players have for the game. This campaign stems from marketing research in which fans said they would be more inclined to connect with baseball if they knew more about the players and what made them so successful.

MARKETING MIX DECISIONS

After the market selection decisions are made, the **marketing mix decisions** are fully developed. The objective of the marketing mix is to implement the positioning established by the chosen target market. This is done by coordinating the marketing mix variables, or the four Ps—product, price, place, and promotion.

Arena football positions itself as real fun, real close, real football.

Source: Copyright © 2001–2003. Arena Football League. All rights reserved.

SPORTS PRODUCTS

As discussed in Chapter 1, a sports product is a good, service, or any combination of the two that is designed to provide benefits to a sports spectator, participant, or sponsor. These benefits may be intangible or tangible. For example, the competition and entertainment generated by the San Diego State University Aztecs versus the University of Wyoming Cowboys football game is an intangible service that is consumed by thousands of fans at the game, watching on television, or listening to the radio. The football used in the game and manufactured by Wilson Sporting Goods, however, is a pure good with tangible attributes, including the size of the ball, the type of leather used, and the price.

PRICING

Price is simply something of value that is given in exchange for something else of value. For example, money paid in exchange for admission to a sporting event; annual salary paid to hockey star Jaromir Jagr ($11.5 million) in exchange for his talents; or the time volunteers donate to the ATP Tennis Tournament in exchange for the thrill of getting to meet the players and watch the event for free, are all forms of pricing. It is the job of sports marketers to set and control pricing. More important, the price must reflect the quality of the product as well as how the product is promoted and distributed to consumers.

PLACE

As discussed in Chapter 1, place or distribution takes on several meanings in the context of sports marketing. Traditionally, place is associated with getting goods to the customer in an efficient manner. A channel of distribution is the chain of marketing organizations that interact to bring the product from producer to end user. For example, Mizuno manufactures baseball gloves, which are sold and shipped to The Sports Authority retail outlets, and purchased by the consumer.

The other, equally important distribution issue for sports marketers is bringing the competition to the fans. New technologies, such as the Internet and satellite television, are making this easier than ever before. MLB and its media partners, such as ESPN, have also recognized the need to provide sports programming when viewers desire entertainment. For example, witness the advent of Sunday night baseball. Historically, baseball games were played only on Sunday afternoons, but now the growth of larger prime-time audiences hungry for sports have caused teams to change their traditional scheduling. Issues involving whether to build new sports facilities and where to locate them are equally critical sport distribution issues.

PROMOTION

All forms of promotion are based on communicating with consumers. Sports marketers communicate with target groups through advertisements, public relations efforts, sales promotions, personal selling, and sponsorships. Each one of these elements, or a combination of these elements, comprises a firm's promotional efforts. This is known as the promotional mix.

Promoting high school sports on the Web.

Source: Copyright © Elder High School 2001. All rights reserved.

IMPLEMENTATION PHASE

The best plan is only a plan—that is, good intentions—unless it degenerates into work. The distinction that makes a plan capable of producing results is the commitment of key people to work on specific tasks.[8]

At this stage of the strategic sports marketing process, we gathered information about potential consumers, made market selection decisions, and developed our marketing mix. Now that we completed our planning phase, the next step is to put our plan into action. This step of the strategic sports marketing process is called implementation. During this phase, promotional efforts, distribution plans, product issues, and pricing strategies are all carried out. The best plans are meaningless unless properly implemented.

One example of the ramifications of implementation gone bad is the Philadelphia KiXX, indoor professional soccer team. Fans interested in purchasing tickets were instructed to call the team via its toll-free number, which ends in KiXX. Mistakenly, many fans misdialed KICKS instead. Much to the fans surprise, the KICKS extension connects them to a fantasy sex line rather than the team's ticket office.[9] The Cincinnati Bengals represent another example of problems in implementation. Fans in Cincinnati were not very happy with the hapless Bengals performance on the field after the opening of the new Paul Brown stadium. In fact, the taxpayers of Hamilton County filed a lawsuit stating the Bengals convinced county officials that they needed generous lease terms to be competitive on the field but failed to take reasonable steps to improve their team after the lease was signed. Subsequently, a judge has dismissed the lawsuit, but an appeal has already been filed.[10]

What steps need to be taken during implementation and by whom? The successful implementation of a marketing plan requires that specific activities take place. The major activities that are necessary for implementing a plan, shown in Table 2.2, include

TABLE 2.2　Activities Associated with Implementation

Organizing
• Organizational structure
• Task assignments

Leadership and Interaction
• Communication
• Motivation

Resource Acquisition and Allocation
• Financial and human resources
• Technology

Coordinating and Timing of Activities
• Marketing resources
• Other functional area resources (e.g., production, finance)

Information Management
• Acquisition
• Utilization

organizing, leadership and interaction, resource acquisition and allocation, coordinating and timing of activities, and information management.[11]

ORGANIZING

Organizing is the first of the functional activities associated with implementation. In the marketing sense, organizing is the assigning of tasks, the grouping of tasks into organizational units, and allocating resources to organizational units. One of the key issues to consider in this aspect of implementation is how the sports organization should be structured to best carry out the strategic marketing process.

One example of a traditional organizational structure is the functional organization, where marketing activities are carried out by specialized departments, such as advertising, marketing research, new product development, and so on. Other sports organizations find it more effective to organize by product type, customer type, geographic region, or perhaps use a hybrid organization, which combines all these features.

As previously discussed, sports organizations operate in extremely turbulent environments, where frequent and unpredictable changes are characteristic. For example, it is common for professional sports organizations to experience high turnover in the front office as well as on the field. Organization structures that provide flexibility enhance organizational effectiveness.

LEADERSHIP AND INTERACTION

Two additional activities that are required to implement marketing plans successfully are having strong leaders and interacting well with others within the sports organization. Marketing leaders must emerge who can communicate the strategic sports marketing process within and outside the organization. For instance, the marketing department must communicate the importance of fan relation efforts to the players. These leaders must also have the ability to motivate their workforce so the plans are implemented effectively and efficiently.

Sports marketing managers must excel at communicating the importance of their plans to employees within the organization, also known as internal customers. For sports marketing plans to succeed, management must sometimes focus on internal marketing—marketing efforts aimed at a company's own employees who have contact with the ultimate consumer of the sport or sports product.

Leadership off the court.

RESOURCE ACQUISITION AND ALLOCATION

Another of the activities necessary for implementation is the ability to acquire and allocate human, financial, and technological resources. Sports organizations are downsizing just like the rest of corporate America, and managers are continually being asked to do more with less. This includes carrying out plans developed in the strategic sports marketing process.

One example of financial trouble resulting from inefficient human resource allocation is Pro Beach Volleyball where the players serve as management and labor at the same time. By doing so they are forced to choose between their own short-term gain and the leagues' long-term best interest.

COORDINATING AND TIMING OF ACTIVITIES

The coordination and timing of marketing activities is essential to a successful marketing effort. An advertisement designed to run during the holiday season could be destroyed if it is plagued by mistakes in timing and coordination.

Similarly, marketers must be quick to respond to sudden changes in team or player popularity. Fueled by the emergence of Michael Vick, the Atlanta Falcons increased their home attendance by 27 percent in 2002 and have dramatically altered their marketing strategy to meet the popularity of the star quarterback. Similarly, the arrival of LeBron James in Cleveland might not mean instant success on the court for the last place team, but he already has boosted attendance. After the NBA lottery, 25 operators tried to keep pace with calls for season tickets.

Slazenger coordinating its marketing efforts around the holidays.

Source: Used by permission of David Geoffrey & Associates d.b.a. Slazenger Golf.

INFORMATION MANAGEMENT

To make sound decisions regarding the implementation of the strategic marketing plan, information is critical. Having access to the necessary information and being able to interpret that information is the foundation of information management. Some of these types of information and how they are used to reformulate planning are discussed in the next section.

CONTROL PHASE

The process of measuring results, comparing the results with the marketing objectives, communicating the results to the entire organization, and modifying the plan to achieve the desired results is known as the control phase. Upon implementing the sports marketing plan, the organization must attempt to understand whether the plan is achieving the desired results. If the plan is meeting or exceeding the proposed marketing objectives, no modifications are necessary. For example, the Calgary Stampeders of the Canadian Football League and Molson Brewery extended their sponsorship agreement through 2006 Molson's long partnership with the Stampeders continues its tradition of investing in Alberta sports and the community. Dean Fiala, Sales Director for Molson said that "Molson is known for its association with sports and we're excited to build on that connection and our partnership with the Stampeders."[12] However, when objectives are not being met, companies make other types of adjustments. As the following article on the revolving door of sports sponsorships points out, "nothing is forever and few things are for very long."

MEASURING RESULTS

The results measured by the sports organization depend on the nature of the objectives set in the previous phase of the sports marketing plan. Assessment can be thought of in broad terms—to determine the overall success of the marketing plan. A marketing audit may then be conducted to explore the organization's marketing efforts. Alternately, assessment can be conducted to determine the success of very specific objectives. Let us briefly examine sales analysis, profitability analysis, customer satisfaction, and marketing audit.

SALES ANALYSIS

One common marketing objective that must be continuously monitored is sales data. The formal process of examining sales figures is called sales analysis. Sales analysis is a comparison of current sales with past sales, industry sales, sales by competitors, and forecasting sales as a method of evaluating a firm's performance.[13]

In the control phase of the strategic sports marketing process, sales analysis is usually based on examining sales relative to objectives set by forecasting sales. Through the use of simple analytical techniques, sales figures can be evaluated in a number of ways. For example, sales can be measured in unit volume, which is based on the number of units sold. Sales can also be assessed based on dollar volume, or on the monies received from sales. In addition, sales can be measured relative to competitors in the industry or by market share. Market share is the proportion of an organization's total sales in a particular market.

Revolving Sponsors a Big Part of Sports

In the high-stakes world of sports sponsorships, nothing is forever and few things are for very long.

There is, for example, golf's Nationwide Tour. Invented in 1990, it was sponsored by the Ben Hogan Company until 1992. Then Nike took over until 1999, followed by Buy.com in 2000 and now Nationwide Insurance.

That's three title sponsors in five years. Winless players like Jeff Freeman and Eric Meeks, trudging through Triple-A level tournament golf, have enough other problems without worrying about whose name is on the tour.

English soccer's League Cup changes sponsors with regularity. The competition is now called the Carling Cup, thanks to a three-year deal with Coors. This is the same event that was called the Worthington Cup for five years and the Coca-Cola Cup before that.

Revolving sponsorships are an old story in college football. The Capital One Bowl once flew the banner of the Florida Department of Citrus as well as Comp USA and OurHouse.com. At various times, the Independence Bowl's bills were paid by Poulan/Weedeater, Sanford, which manufactures writing instruments, and MainStay Management.

Bank One Bank has its name on the Arizona Diamondbacks ballpark and now is a presenting sponsor of the Chicago Bears, expanding its relationship with the NFL team that began when George Halas opened an account there in 1934. Nobody knows how much Papa Bear deposited.

Does this sponsorship stuff really work? The people paying for the privilege seem to think so.

"You may not buy a brand because of association with an event, but it serves to support image," said John Eckel, senior vice president for sports and automative marketing for Hill and Knowlton.

"It used to be you'd hang a banner for awareness and that was enough. It has become so much more sophisticated. You must get into the right sponsorship and leverage it properly. Just buying sponsorships is never enough.

"It's a $20-plus billion sponsorship market and 80 percent of that is in sports."

A lot of the message is subliminal.

It could be as simple as the sponsor's name across a coach's headset. "A viewer might say, 'If he's using that brand, it must be reliable.'" Eckel said.

Unless, of course, a play gets botched.

Few companies are more involved with sports than Anheuser-Busch. Tony Ponturo is the company's vice president for corporate media and sports marketing.

"At the end of the day, we are not in the sports purchasing business," Ponturo said. "We are in the growing beer sales and market share business."

Tradition often gets shattered by sponsorships.

The Chicago White Sox played in Comiskey Park for the better part of a century. Now the place is called U.S. Cellualr Field, named for the wireless phone company that paid $68 million over 20 years for the right to hang its name over the front door. The new sponsor did not, however, replace the dugout-to-bullpen land lines.

"Our strategy was based on how to get our brand name out there on a consistent basis," said Jay Ellison, vice president of operations of U.S. Cellular. "It's a tactical, daily opportunity. You see the traffic. You see the brand impression.

"We had a sponsorship and took it further to naming rights. It was a cost-effective way to keep our name out there."

And a necessary one in the competitive world of wireless communications.

Let U.S. Cellular buy a ballpark. Nextel went for the whole NASCAR stock racing series in a 10-year, $700 million deal after R. J. Reynolds, the series sponsor for 33 years, bowed out.

Was Nextel, sortie a reaction to U.S. Cellular's baseball buy?

"Meaning no disrespect, we don't react to U.S. Cellular in any area," said Mark Schweitzer, senior vice president for marketing at Nextel.

For Nextel's, already equipped with sponsorship relationships in hockey, football, and baseball, stock cars looked like a perfect fit.

"We had been interested in NASCAR for some time," Schweitzer said. "The rate of growth in the sport seemed to us a great value and the fact that it was exclusive was very much a factor. There's not other sport where you can own the league name."

One sponsor in, another out.

When Enron's bankroll turned into Monopoly money, workers hastily removed that company's name from the ballpark in Houston and replaced it with Minute Maid. The same thing happened in Foxboro, Mass., when CMGI's books started spilling red ink. All the signs came down at the new stadium, replaced by Gillette.

In St. Louis, the Rams play in Edward Jones Stadium. It used to be called the TWA Dome but then TWA went out of business, perhaps in part because it spent too much discretionary capital on naming rights for a ballpark.

Adelphia Coliseum, home of the Tennessee Titans, now is simply called The Coliseum after Adelphia's revenue stream dried up. The same thing happened with PSINet Stadium, home of the Baltimore Ravens.

Buying stadium names is a big thing for the high tech crowd. There's Qualcomm in San Diego, Alltel in Jacksonville, Network Associates in Oakland, Ericsson in Carolina, and 3Com in San Francisco.

Some years ago, when Pete Rozelle was still commissioner of the NFL, the final question at his annual Super Bowl press conference concerned sponsorships.

Noting the increasing corporate interest in sports, an inquiring mind wondered whether the NFL's showcase event might be vulnerable to a takeover.

"Could we one day have the Preparation H Super Bowl?" he asked a nonplussed Rozelle.

It hasn't happened.

Not yet.

Source: Hal Bock, *Associated Press.* July 6, 2003, D. 9. Reprinted with permission of LexisNexis, a division of Reed Elsevier Inc. All rights reserved.

Although each unit of measurement (i.e., unit volume, dollar volume, and market share) is useful, the most comprehensive and effective approach is to explore all these measures when conducting a sales analysis. Each method provides the organization with a slightly different perspective on their overall marketing efforts.

In addition to looking at the big picture, or total aggregate sales figure, sports marketers routinely examine more specific components of their overall sales. Often, the big picture is not the best picture. Smaller units of analysis—such as sales figures by geographic region, product categories, customer type, or even individual salespeople are generally more useful in guiding the strategic sports marketing process.

PROFITABILITY ANALYSIS

One of the primary methods for evaluating the success of any sports organization is profitability. Profitability refers to the amount of money an organization earns after expenses, or the difference between revenues generated by products and the cost incurred.

The most basic unit of measuring profitability is the profit margin. Expressed as the ratio of profits to revenues, profit margins are another "hard" measure of an organization's health. As with sales analysis, the organization's overall profit margin is important, but perhaps not as useful as examining the profitability of various product lines or services offered. Therefore, profitability analysis may best be conducted on smaller units to help guide the strategic sports marketing process.

CUSTOMER SATISFACTION

Although sales and profits represent traditional hard measures of success, customer satisfaction has become one of the most critical objectives as more sports organizations strive for a customer or marketing orientation. Customer satisfaction is difficult to quantify, so multiple measurement methods can be useful.

Informally, organizations can assess customer satisfaction levels by communicating and listening to their customers' wants and needs. More formally, customer hotlines, observation of customers, and comment or complaint cards are used to gauge customer satisfaction. In addition to these measures, the most common form of evaluating customer satisfaction is conducting marketing surveys.

MARKETING AUDIT

Very specific objectives can be measured by examining things such as sales, profits, and customer satisfaction. For a more holistic view of the sports marketing organization, a marketing audit is recommended. A marketing audit is a systematic and exhaustive appraisal of an organization's marketing activities.

What makes a marketing audit effective? First, an effective audit is systematic. That means the audit is organized and follows a logical process—its goal is a series of action items to guide strategic marketing planning. In addition, a systematic audit is unbiased. A marketing audit should be performed by an independent, outside source that can remain objective during the process. An effective audit should also be exhaustive. That is, the audit should seek to cover all the firm's marketing activities in as much detail as possible. Finally, marketing audits should be conducted on a regularly scheduled timetable.

To conduct an audit, sports marketing managers should meet with an independent outside source to agree on the timing, format, and objectives of the audit. Most important, the scope of the audit, or the number of activities to examine, would be agreed on. Sports marketing audits usually include a review of the following areas: marketing orientation, marketing objectives, strategic planning process, target markets, products and services, promotion, planning, pricing, and distribution issues. Some sample marketing audit questions are shown in Table 2.3.

TABLE 2.3 Sampling of Marketing Audit Questions

I. Market Orientation

1. Has the firm established a marketing orientation? That is, has the firm identified the benefits that particular customers seek and developed programs based on this input?

2. Is the firm's main goal to maximize customer satisfaction or to get as many customers as possible?

II. Marketing Planning

A. *External Environment*

1. Social: What major social and lifestyle trends will have an affect on the firm? What action has the firm been taking in response to these trends?

2. Competition: Which organizations are competing with us directly by offering a similar product? Which organizations are competing with us indirectly by securing our prime prospects' time, money, energy, or commitment?

3. Technological: What major technological changes are occurring that affect the firm?

B. *Needs Assessments*

1. Are needs assessments undertaken?

2. Have secondary data been used in the needs assessments? If so, is the information current? Classified in a useful manner? Impartial? Reliable? Valid?

3. What does the firm want to learn from the needs assessments?

C. *Objectives and Mission*

1. What is the mission of the firm? What business is it in? How well is its mission understood throughout the organization? Five years from now, what business does it want to be in?

2. What are the stated objectives of the organization? Are they formally documented? Do they logically lead to clearly stated marketing goals?

III. Target Market Strategies

1. Are the members of each product's target markets homogeneous or heterogeneous with respect to geographic, sociodemographic, and behavioral characteristics?

2. Is the size of each market segment sufficiently large or important to develop a unique marketing mix for it?

3. Are the market segments measurable and accessible? That is, are the market segments accessible to distribution and communication efforts?

4. What publics other than target markets (financial, media, government, citizen, local, general, and internal) represent opportunities or problems for the firm?

5. What steps has the firm taken to deal effectively with key publics?

IV. Distribution Decisions

1. Should the firm try to deliver its offerings directly to customers, or can we better deliver selected offerings by involving other organizations?

2. Are members of the target market willing and able to travel some distance to buy the product?

3. How good is access to facilities? Can it be improved? Which facilities need priority attention in these areas?

V. Product Strategies

1. What are the major products offered by the firm? Do they complement each other, or is there unnecessary duplication?

2. Where is the firm and each major product in its life cycle (calculated by using market share or sales)?

VI. Pricing Strategies

1. What are the firm's objectives in pricing each product?

2. What discounts are offered and with what rationale?

3. Has the firm considered psychological dimensions of price in its initial price decisions as well as in its price revision decisions?

VII. Promotion Strategies

1. Are there clear objectives for each element of the promotion mix? How are promotion activities related to these objectives?

2. How does a typical customer find out about the firm's products? Word of mouth? Personal selling? Advertising? Publicity?

3. How is public relations normally handled by the firm? By whom?

4. What is the specific purpose of each sales promotion activity? Why is it offered? What does it try to achieve?

5. What level of sponsorship opportunity do you have (i.e., local versus global)?

6. Are you actively selling your sponsors all the services that they may need (e.g., luxury boxes, program advertisements, signage, ticket mention, employee nights, promotional services, etc.)?

Source: Principles of Marketing, 2/e, by Lamb/Hair/McDaniel. Copyright © 1994. Reprinted by permission of South-Western College Publishing, a division of International Thomson Publishing, Inc., Cincinnati, Ohio 45227.

SPOTLIGHT ON SPORTS MARKETING ETHICS

Move Toward Athletic Reform Long Overdue

Think of Gordon Gee as Don Quixote with a bow tie. In confronting the culture of collegiate athletics, the Vanderbilt chancellor has picked a fight that promises frustration.

Reforming big-time college sports is a noble aim, but a fool's errand, like teaching trigonometry to a turtle. The problems are too profound to be easily solved. The goal is too grandiose to be quickly achieved. If Gordon Gee is determined to tilt at this particular windmill, he is advised to pack a lunch.

In eliminating Vanderbilt's athletic department, Gee threw down a gauntlet whose echo has carried from coast to coast. The move was largely symbolic—Vanderbilt's 14 varsity sports still operate under the authority of the Office of Student Athletics, Recreation and Wellness—but in his effort to bring college sports back under the wider university umbrella, Gee has made a first, tangible step toward sanity.

At the root of many of the recent college sports scandals are the dual demons of excessive autonomy and insufficient accountability. When the NCAA cites a "lack of institutional control," as it did with San Diego State's football probation, what it's saying is that the university administration has allowed athletics too loose a leash.

"We've created a culture of isolation," Gee told the New York Times. "Athletic departments are connected to the university only by a heating plant or a telephone line. We're going to have to have them integrated."

In case after case, at Baylor and St. Bonaventure, at Ohio State and Georgia, at Alabama and Michigan, oversight has been overlooked. University presidents driven to raise funds have been remiss about raising eyebrows. As a consequence, proud universities have been embarrassed and their degrees tarnished by the hiring of dubious characters, the admission of sham students, and their shared contempt for the core mission of college education.

"To me, it could have been foretold 25 years ago—when schools started building their own residence halls for athletes, and their own classrooms," said Bob Pastoor, the University of San Diego's vice president for student affairs. "Now we're seeing student-athletes totally separated from the rest of the university. It goes against the grain of the student-athlete (ideal).

"It doesn't strike me as strange that something's happened. As athletic directors report to presidents who spend 50 percent of their time off the campus, the less supervision the athletic directors receive."

On too many American campuses, the student-athlete is an oxymoron, a hired hand who majors in eligibility while awaiting the first opportunity to turn pro. His coach makes more money than the governor, and makes no pretense that he is paid to generate revenue rather than scholars. His athletic director is too busy soliciting donations to monitor corruption, or too strapped for cash to care.

For many college presidents, the secret to success lies not in the ability to inspire, but the willingness to indulge.

"I find that the three major administrative problems on a campus," former Cal Chancellor Clark Kerr once told Time magazine, "are sex for the students, athletics for the alumni and parking for the faculty."

The University of San Diego has it about right. Athletics remains a part of the university instead of apart from the university. There is still an athletic department and an ongoing search for a new athletic director, but there are few of the perspective problems that have beset so many higher-profile programs.

"It's an interesting thing that (Gee's initiative) has gotten as much press as it has," USD's Pastoor said. "The great majority of colleges in the country are operating the way he has just positioned Vanderbilt. That may not apply to many large universities and especially large football and basketball universities. But for us, athletics reports to me as the vice president for student affairs, which sends a message in itself.

"They're not separated from the rest of the university. They are not isolated. And that structure sends a message to the student-athletes."

That structure is no guarantee against academic fraud, illicit payoffs or recruiting shenanigans, but it does provide some additional safeguards. It's the same guiding principle that has placed civilians in charge of America's generals—the need for dispassionate supervision.

"I think the bottom line is hiring people with integrity, who understand the mission of the institution—that it is an academic institution," Pastoor said. "But we (as an industry) keep hiring people who get in trouble at other places. It perpetuates that good-ol'-boy network. To me, presidents have to take a responsibility there when people are doing searches."

When San Diego State President Stephen Weber redrew his organizational chart after the forced resignation of AD Rick Bay, he recognized a need for another layer of responsibility. The decision to place Vice President Sally

Roush atop the athletic department was a move toward what may ultimately be known as the Vanderbilt model.

It's a small step, to be sure, but it's a start. In theory, at least, more auditors mean fewer errors.

Source: Tim Sullivan, Copley News Service, September 23, 2003.

"I think there's going to be internal pressure to those of us who supervise athletics," Bob Pastoor said, "to make sure we don't end up in the headlines."

Summary

Chapter 2 provides an overview of the contingency framework for the strategic sports marketing process. Although there are many ways to think about constructing a sports marketing plan, it is best to lay a foundation that is prepared for the unexpected. The contingency framework is especially useful for sports marketers because of the complex and uncertain conditions in which the sports organization operates. The unexpected changes that occur over the course of a season or event may be positive or negative. The changes that occur may be either controllable or uncontrollable events that affect the sports organization. Uncontrollable occurrences are typically in the marketing environment and are referred to as external contingencies, whereas internal contingencies are within the control of the organization (sometimes beyond the scope of the marketing function).

The contingency framework includes three major components: the internal contingencies, the external contingencies, and the strategic sports marketing process. The external contingencies, or uncontrollable factors, that influence the strategic marketing process, include competition, regulatory and political issues, demographic trends, technology, sociocultural issues, and the physical environment. The internal contingencies, which also affect strategic marketing decisions, include vision and mission of the organization, marketing goals and organizational objectives, organizational culture, and organizational design issues. The external and internal contingencies are the focus of Chapter 3.

The heart of the contingency framework is the strategic sports marketing process, which is defined as the process of planning, implementing, and controlling marketing efforts to meet organizational goals and satisfy consumers' needs. The planning phase has three steps. It begins with marketing research to examine the needs of current and potential markets. These consumer markets may be differentiated on the basis of participants or spectators. Next, market selection decisions are formulated. These include market segmentation, or dividing consumers into homogeneous groups based on common characteristics. The similarities among consumers are based on demographics (e.g., age, sex, and income), psychographics (lifestyle), geographics (where the consumer lives), geodemographics (what consumers look like who live in a particular region), benefits (what the consumer wants in the sports product), and behavioral

(consumption and usage patterns). Once the market is segmented, sports marketers must select the target market. The target market is defined as the segment that will allow an organization to reach its marketing objectives most efficiently and effectively. The final market selection decision is positioning. Positioning refers to fixing the sports product in the minds of the target market. In other words, how do we want our target market to perceive our sports product? What benefits do we want to sell?

The final step in the planning stage is to develop the appropriate marketing mix to reach the selected target market and achieve the desired positioning. The sports marketing mix consists of product, pricing, promotion, and place decisions. It is critical that the elements of the marketing mix, or the four Ps, be coordinated. We want to assure that the pricing is aligned with the perceived quality of the product and that the place the sports product is delivered is consistent with the promotional message received by consumers. In sports marketing, the coordination of the marketing mix can be especially challenging because marketers have so little control over the core product or the competition itself. For example, it is not easy to lower ticket prices if the team is performing poorly.

The implementation phase of the strategic sports marketing process refers to carrying out or executing the plans just discussed. Obviously, the best plans are worthless unless they are properly acted on or implemented. The success of implementation is based on how the sports organization is set up, how leaders communicate and motivate the employees, the marketing and financial resources available, and information management.

The third and final phase of the strategic sports marketing process is the control phase. The control phase is the process of measuring results, comparing the results with the marketing objectives, and revising objectives based on the evaluation of the objectives. The results of the marketing efforts are based on analyzing sales figures, profits, and customer satisfaction. A more global assessment of the sports organizations' marketing efforts is gained by conducting a marketing audit. The audit explores all the critical marketing areas, such as the marketing orientation of the organization, market selection decisions, and the marketing mix variables.

Key Terms

- contingency framework for strategic sports marketing
- contingency strategy
- control phase
- external contingencies

- implementation phase
- internal contingencies
- market segmentation
- market selection decisions
- marketing mix decisions

- planning phase
- positioning
- strategic sports marketing process
- target marketing

Review Questions

1. Describe the contingency framework for strategic sports marketing. Why is the contingency approach especially useful to sports marketers?
2. Outline the strategic marketing process, and comment on how it is related to the external and internal contingencies.
3. How do sports marketers attempt to understand consumers' needs? Why is this such an important first step in the planning process?
4. What are the three broad market selection decisions? Why is the market selection decision portion of the strategic marketing process sometimes considered to be the most important?
5. Define and discuss segmentation, target markets, and positioning.
6. What is the marketing mix? Why is it important to have an integrated marketing mix?
7. What is meant by the implementation phase of the strategic marketing process? Describe the activities commonly associated with implementing the marketing plan.
8. What is meant by the control phase of the strategic marketing process? How are the results of the planning phase evaluated?
9. Describe a marketing audit. When should a marketing audit be conducted and by whom? What are some of the broad categories of a marketing audit?

Exercises

1. Interview the marketing manager of a sporting goods retailer or sports organization about their strategic sports marketing process. Ask how the external and internal contingencies affect planning.
2. Find two sports organizations that, in your opinion, have undergone or are about to undergo a crisis situation. How should these organizations handle the crisis from a marketing perspective?
3. Choose three teams in the same sport (e.g., Braves, Indians, or Yankees) or three sports products in the same product category (e.g., Titleist, Cobra, and Ping golf clubs), and discuss how each makes market selection decisions. Comment specifically on similarities and differences in segmentation, targeting, and positioning.
4. Companies choose various sponsorship opportunities to reach different segments and target markets. Give examples of three different sponsorship opportunities and their perspective market segments and target markets.
5. Describe the marketing mix for the following sports products and services:

   - Wilson Sporting Goods tennis equipment
   - University of Notre Dame football program
   - golf lessons at a local country club
   - local high school basketball program
   - Air Jordans from Nike

6. Develop a hypothetical professional sports franchise in the sport of your choice and discuss the marketing mix you would implement. How are your marketing mix decisions related to your market selection decisions?
7. Construct and then conduct a brief marketing audit of your university's athletic program.

Internet Exercises

1. Find the Web site of any minor league hockey franchise and based on their site, describe how they are segmenting their consumer or fan market.
2. Find three sponsorship opportunities via the Internet and describe the target market(s) the sponsorship is trying to reach.
3. Discuss the marketing mix for an on-line sporting goods store.

Endnotes

1. Rick Burton and Dennis Howard, "Recovery Strategies for Sports Marketers: The Marketing of Sports Involves Unscripted Moments Delivered by Unpredictable Individuals and Uncontrollable Events," *Marketing Management,* vol. 9, no. 1 (Spring 2000), 43.
2. E. Stephen Grant and R. Edward Bashaw, "A Collegiate Football Program Confronts a Sports Marketing Crisis: Results and Implications of a Descriptive Study," *Sports Marketing Quarterly,* vol. IV, no. 1 (1995), 35–40.
3. W. Richard Scott, *Organizations: Rational, Natural, and Open systems* (Upper Saddle River, NJ: Prentice Hall, 1987), 87–89.
4. Bernard J. Mullin, Stephan Hardy, and William Sutton, *Sport Marketing* (Champaign, IL: Human Kinetics Publishers, 1993), 16.
5. Martin G. Letscher, "Sports, Fads and Trends," *American Demographics,* vol. 19, no. 6 (June 1997), 53–56.
6. Joel Evans and Barry Berman, *Marketing,* 5th ed. (New York: Macmillan, 1992), 255–226.
7. Michael Farber, "Putting on a Show," *Sports Illustrated* (October 17, 1994), 30–33.
8. Peter Drucker, *Management: Tasks, Responsibility, Practices* (New York: Harper Row, 1974).
9. William Power, "Soccer Team Discovers There Are Lots of Ways to Get Your Kicks," *The Wall Street Journal* (December 5, 1997), B1.
10. "Judge Dismisses Bengal Lawsuit," *Cincinnati Business Courier* (September 5, 2003).
11. Adapted from William Zikmund and Michael D'Amico, *Marketing,* 4th ed. (St. Paul, MN: West Publishing, 1993).
12. "Molson Celebrates Extended Partnership with Calgary Stampeders," *Canada Newswire* (June 16, 2003).
13. Courtland Bovee and John Thill, *Marketing* (New York: McGraw-Hill, 1992), 190–192.

CHAPTER 3

EXTERNAL AND INTERNAL CONTINGENCIES

After completing this chapter, you should be able to:

- Describe external contingencies and explain how they affect the strategic sports marketing process.
- Discuss the importance of monitoring external contingencies and environmental scanning.
- Describe the major internal contingencies and explain how they affect the strategic sports marketing process.
- Explain and conduct a SWOT analysis.

As discussed in Chapter 2, the strategic marketing process must carefully consider the "fit" between external and internal contingencies. To review, external contingencies are those factors outside the control of the organization that can affect marketing decisions. For instance, the growing emphasis on technology or women as sports participants must be considered when developing new sports products. Internal contingencies are those factors controlled by the organization such as its vision and mission, organizational objectives, and organizational culture.

A complex relationship exists between internal contingencies and the strategic marketing process. Sports marketers must ensure the marketing strategies are aligned with the broader organizational purpose. This purpose is often based on changes that occur in the environment. It is at this point that external and internal contingencies must complement one another. Let's take a further look at the various factors that make up the external and internal contingencies.

EXTERNAL CONTINGENCIES

As defined in Chapter 2, environmental contingencies are all influences outside the organization that might affect the strategic sports marketing process. External contingencies include competition; technology; cultural and social trends; physical environment; political, legal, and regulatory environment; demographics; and the economy. Let us take a brief look at each of these factors and how they might affect marketing strategy.

COMPETITION

Assessing the competitive forces in the **marketing environment** is one of the most critical components in the strategic sports marketing process. **Competition** is the attempt all organizations make to serve similar customers.[1]

Sellers realize that, to successfully reach their objectives, they must know who the competition is—both today and tomorrow. In addition, sellers must understand the strengths and weaknesses of their competitors and how competitor strategies will affect their own planning. An example of many "sellers" attempting to fill the same customer need can be found in Indy Car racing.

Competition between "the old" and "the new" ensued when the 80th Indianapolis 500 took on the first U.S. 500. As Tony George, president of the Indianapolis Motor Speedway, suggested, "It's a crucial day for us." The world was watching to see whether Indy could withstand a boycott by Championship Auto Racing Teams, Inc. (CART), which had the world's most popular drivers on its side. There were 17 rookie drivers in the field of 33 at Indy, but it was the U.S. 500 drivers that provided the day's embarrassing moment when 12 cars piled up approaching the starting line.[2] It seems as though the INDY Racing League (IRL) may have had the last laugh as CART is facing extinction. Recently, after losing 43 million dollars through the first six months of the 2003 season, the Open Wheels Racing Series is considering buying CART.[3]

THE NATURE OF COMPETITION

Sports marketers most often categorize their competition as product related. There are three types of product-related competition. The first of these is termed **direct competition,** the competition between sellers producing similar products and services. High school football games on a Friday night in a large metropolitan area pose direct competition in that the "product" being offered is very similar. One interesting example of direct competition is found within the game schedule of the NBA Indiana Pacers. High school basketball is so popular in Indiana that the Pacers rarely play a home game on Friday or Saturday night because of the competition posed by high school games.

Another type of product competition is between marketers of substitute products and services, the competition between a product and a similar substitute product. For example, when several professional sports teams have scheduled an overlap, a consumer may have to choose to attend the Philadelphia 76ers (NBA), the Philadelphia Phillies (MLB), or the Philadelphia Eagles (NFL). Another example of substitute products is when spectators choose to watch a sporting event on television or listen to a radio or web broadcast rather than attend the event.

The third type of product-related competition, called **indirect competition,** is more general in nature and may be the most critical of all for sports marketers. Marketers of sporting events at any level realize their true competition is other forms of entertainment. Professional, collegiate, and high school sporting events compete with restaurants, concerts, plays, movies, and all other forms of entertainment for the consumer dollar. In fact, a recent study was conducted to examine how closely other forms of entertainment are related to sports.[4] Preliminary findings suggest that respondents most preferred entertainment activities are going out to dinner, attending parties, playing sports, watching movies, attending sporting events, attending live music or theatre, watching TV, shopping for pleasure, watching sports on TV, dancing, and gambling. In addition, video games seem to be competing in the same "entertainment space" as watching sports on TV. Obviously, the toy industry has capitalized on this notion by creating a multitude of sports-related video games. In fact, some people fear that today's interactive, virtual reality video games may replace watching "real games" on TV. Similarly, playing sports and gambling are perceived to be in the same perceptual space. Sport marketers may want to better understand the excitement and risks associated with gambling and add these attributes when marketing sports participation.

Indirect competition is present when even the popular USC and UCLA football games fail to sell out their respective home stadiums (the Rose Bowl and the L.A. Coliseum). There is simply too much entertainment competition in Southern California compared to Ann Arbor, Michigan (University of Michigan) or South Bend, Indiana (Notre Dame).

TECHNOLOGY

Technology represents the most rapidly changing environmental influence. New technologies affect the field of sports marketing daily. Advances in technology have a direct impact on how sports marketers perform their basic marketing functions, whereas others aid in the development of new sports products. For example, new technologies are emerging in advertising, stadium signage, and distributing the sports product. Internet sites are one of the fastest growing new technologies to affect sports marketing (see Appendix B for examples of Internet sites of interest to sports marketers). Internet sites have been developed to provide information on sports (e.g., www.nascar.com), sites of sporting events (e.g., www.daytona500.com), teams (e.g., www.penske.com), and individuals (e.g., www.rustywallace.com). Nascar.com

Providing sports information via the Internet.

Source: Used by permission of IBM Corporation. © 2004. All rights reserved.

is one of the fastest growing major sports sites. In 2003, the site made significant increases as it will exceed 1.5 billion page views by year's end and average 2.7 million unique users.[5]

Contrast this number with the 433,000 unduplicated visitors that logged on to NBColympics.com for the opening day at the 2000 Summer Games. The official Olympic Games Internet site attracted over 7.2 billion visitors, surpassing the original estimate of 6.5 billion. The explosion in hits made the Sydney Games the most popular event ever on the Internet and coincides with lower-than-expected television viewing figures in the United States.[6]

Of course, ESPN.com is still the king of sports information on the Internet and part of sports fans' daily routines. ESPN was launched in April 1995 and now reaches 15.4 million unique users, which is nearly greater than that of sportsline.com and AOL Sports combined. Among ESPN.com's users, 66 percent are ages 18 to 34, and 94 percent are men whose average household income is $72,100.[7]

In addition, the Internet has emerged as another popular way to broadcast live events to fans. Beginning in 1995 AudioNet, Inc. (www.Audionet.com) was one of the pioneers of live game broadcasts via the Internet. Today each of the major leagues offer their fans opportunities to follow games online. For example, MLB.com is providing a live worldwide webcast of every postseason game in 2003 for just $2.95 per game. The NFL is offering audio webcasts for nearly all its games, but care must be taken. The NFL wants fans to watch games on TV and complement this experience with new information gathered using new media such as the Internet.

The University of Nebraska game against San Jose State on September 2, 2000, was the first ever intercollegiate football game to be video webcast. The webcast resulted in more than 200,000 video streams around the world. Nebraska Athletic Director Bill Byrne summed it up nicely by stating that "we believe the Internet brings us one step closer to our fans, particularly those who are miles from home and have limited access to our normal radio and TV broadcasts."[8,9]

In addition to providing information and game coverage to consumers, the Internet has emerged as a popular alternative to purchasing tickets at a box office. Nearly 7.5 million tickets were sold online by Major League Baseball teams in 2002 and the estimate is that this number will jump to 15 million annually within five years. Rob Bowman, head of MLB Advanced Media, expects more teams will also provide online forums for fans to sell tickets they've decided not to use and he expects 15 teams will allow fans to print their own bar-coded tickets.[10]

Teams and leagues have already formed partnerships with high-tech companies. For example the NHL has signed a deal with Montreal-based Airborne Entertainment, a wireless content provider. Airborne will produce content such as real-time scores, the NHL Numbers Crunch Fantasy Game, NHL ring tones, and other features for wireless users. Of interest, NHL fans rank number one among the major sports leagues in personal computer ownership and access to the web via broadband connections.[11] The NBA has reached an agreement with Intel to develop and distribute interactive NBA content. League czar Davis Stern says, "With this new agreement with Intel, we believe that essentially we've created the recipe for new ways that sports and entertainment will be delivered in the future. Providing fans with unmatched access to a new level of interactive media such as daily customized highlights and classic footage available on demand from our vast archives enables us to offer personalization for the user's experience."[12] Interestingly, many owners are emerging from high-tech companies who are using their technology experience and strength to benefit their sports franchises. Examples of high-tech owners include Charles Wang of the New York Islanders and Chairman of Computer Associates International; Paul Allen of the

Seattle Seahawks, Portland Trailblazers, and cofounder of Microsoft; Ted Leonsis of the Washington Capitals, Washington Wizards, and America Online; Daniel Snyder of the Washington Redskins and Web marketer; Mark Cuban of the Dallas Mavericks and founder of broadcast.com; and Chris Peters of the Professional Bowlers Association and software designer.

OUT-OF-MARKET TECHNOLOGY

One of the latest technologies that will affect both consumers' ability to watch sports and marketers' ability to define their target audience more narrowly is "out-of-market sports packages." Out-of-market packages or **out-of-market technology** uses direct-to-home (DTH) technology to give subscribers a selection of sports telecasts not available on regular cable. Currently, there are two major companies offering these packages—DIRECTV and the Dish Network. Currently, DIRECTV, continues to grow with 11.8 million subscribers, which is about a 9 percnt increase over last year. The two satellite service providers appeal both to the die-hard sports fans and the displaced fan that can no longer watch their team locally. The total "out-of-market" market consists of roughly 21 million subscribers. However, industry experts say the packages will provide a steady revenue stream once the DTH companies build a sizable subscriber base.[13]

Major League Baseball, the NHL, the NFL, MLS, and the NBA have all negotiated deals to transmit games to viewers outside the home- and visiting-team markets. Fans pay from as much as $209 a season to subscribe to "NFL Sunday Ticket," an out-of-market package of 200 NFL regular season games, to as low as $49 to receive the MLS Shootout, featuring the games of one out-of-market team.

In addition to the Internet and DTH satellite, other new technologies are surfacing on a daily basis and changing the way sports are marketed. For instance, stadium signage has become dynamic rather than stationary. A Budweiser sign behind home plate may change into a promotion for McDonald's during the course of an inning or a pitch. The Fox network has invested in viewing improvements like the CatcherCam and a super slow motion camera that will shoot 100 frames per second. The innovative network also unveiled the Fly Cam for coverage of NASCAR. Fly Cam is an "elevated remote control camera positioned on cables that will run from the middle of pit row to the area where the car reenters the race-track."[14] The virtual, first down line has become a staple for all NFL and college football broadcasts. Additionally, HDTV (high definition) broadcasts are becoming more and more popular in sport.[15] Finally, more traditional technologies, such as ever-expanding cable networks and in-home shopping, are giving more choices to consumers of sport.

So far, our discussion of technology is based more on how technology influences spectators and the distribution of sport. How do technologically advanced products affect sports participants and their performance? Although most sporting goods have experienced major technological improvements since the early 1990s, two sports that live and die by technology are golf and tennis.

The tennis racquet revolution is not being dictated by larger sweet spots or new space-age materials, but simply by longer racquets. This new racquets range from one to two inches longer than the standard 27-inch racquet and are well within the 32-inch legal limit set by the International Tennis Federation. *Tennis* Technical Advisor Tracy Leonard says, "the extra-long is definitely the most significant racquet innovation since the wide-body. It is the third element of power, and equally significant to crushing the ball as were the large head and wide-beam breakthroughs."[16]

Howard Brody, a University of Pennsylvania physicist who specializes in racquet science, adds:

From my calculations, it gives the player definite advantages—it increases serving accuracy by 5 percent per extra inch, and you don't have to be a physicist to figure out the benefit of more reach, especially on shots that normally hit the top of the frame. If my opponent has one, I'd better get one too, especially if I'm a shorter player. A guy like (5-foot-8) Michael Chang will gain even a bigger advantage than taller tour pros.[17]

Technology has even made it easier for people to participate in sports. For instance, golfers are just beginning to take advantage of online tee times (e.g., teetimes.com and thegolfer.com).[18] Similarly, the Powerful Peach Triathlon has increased registration using Web technology.[19] Nearly half of the race participants have registered online.

In addition to changing the way sports are played, technology is altering the ways sports are consumed by fans at the event. Over time, technologies will allow fans to become more and more interactive. For example, Diamond Sports has equipped stadium seats with a handset that allows fans to vote on a figure skating champion. This same technology could be extended for other "made for marketing" events, such as the NBA's Slam-Dunk Contest.

Although some marketers have a hard time grasping the special language of technology, they still agree that a whole new culture of technology has emerged. Phoenix Suns owner Jerry Colanglo describes the new wave of emerging technology

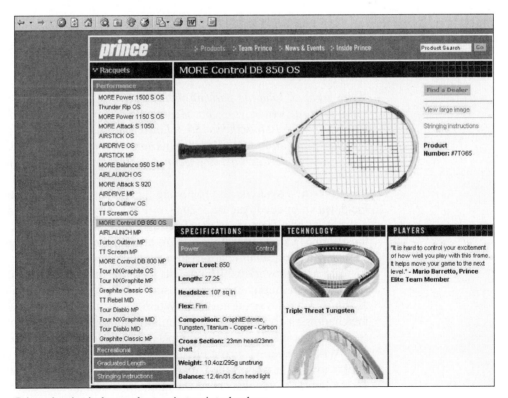

Prince showing its latest advances in tennis technology.
Source: Copyright © 2003 Prince Sports, Inc. All rights reserved.

Technology can take you only so far.

Though our business at Canon is to push technology to the limit, we are also aware of its limitations. To us, technology's applications are only as great as the capabilities of those it serves. Which is why Canon is as interested in the expansion of human potential as we are in the acceleration of technological innovation. To this end, Canon is deeply involved in projects that benefit people, especially the young. Canon's support of sports programs, such as Junior Golf, is a prime example. It is our belief that the lessons learned on the playing field—discipline, perseverance, determination and fair play, among them—are essential to the full development of human potential beyond athletics, maybe even beyond the bounds of technology as we know it. Now imagine how far that can take us all.

Canon

The finest technology still has not replaced hard work.

Source: Used by permission of Canon U.S.A.

and what this will mean for Bank One Ballpark, home of the Arizona Diamondbacks:

We're going to load the park up with interactive technologies and virtual reality game stations from which you can see the field. I want to build an interactive virtual Cooperstown West into the stadium. I also want to have a computerized dossier on every fan that comes into my park, so I can know what technological services and experiences each customer desires. This new technology means we can wire into every pocketbook.[20]

Other new stadiums are following this technological revolution. Lincoln Financial Field, which opened August 3, 2003, in Philadelphia was billed as the first in the next generation of ultramodern, fan-friendly entertainment venues. It is said to have the most sophisticated **technology** ever to be deployed in an open-air stadium, integrating a range of operational functions into a single computer network.

The new network, which consists of more than 1,000 devices, will connect everything from computers to merchandising stands, kiosks, and cash registers. It will serve as the stadium's central nervous system for ticketing, turnstiles, stadium operations, merchandising, food service, and communications. The network will also provide high-speed Internet access to the stadium's luxury suites and press areas.

"When it opens, Lincoln Financial Field will stand as a national showcase for outdoor stadiums, as well as the City of Philadelphia," said Tom Cretella, CEO of Harbor Technologies. "Every aspect of the stadium is designed to deliver the ultimate entertainment experience." Most importantly, Cretella said "the new technology will better allow the Eagles to serve their fans."[21]

A computer-driven video sport is another area of technological impact. Video sports games are called simulations due to their lifelike approximation of real sporting events. In fact, the danger for franchises lies in fans caring more about these games and simulations than they do for the "real" sports. Nearly 36 percent of video games sold are sports related. Stated differently, sports games account for $1 billion of the $5.5 billion spent last year on games for systems like PlayStation, Xbox, and GameCube.[22] The leading interactive sports software brand in the world is Electronic Arts (EA) Sports (www.easports.com), with games including FIFA Soccer, John Madden Football, NHL Hockey, Knockout Kings, NBA Live Basketball, Tiger Woods PGA Tour, Triple Play Baseball, and NASCAR Thunder. Its latest product set to hit the market is SSX3, which pits you and your snowboard "against the mountain." Paul Allen, cofounder of Microsoft and owner of the Portland Trail Blazers, believes "the only thing holding back sports simulation products is the level of reality that can be achieved." Microsoft's line of sports simulation products can be explored at www.microsoft.com/sports.

CULTURAL AND SOCIAL TRENDS

Culture is described as the shared values, beliefs, language, symbols, and tradition passed on from generation to generation by members of a society. Perhaps the most important aspects of any culture are the shared and learned values. **Cultural values** are widely held beliefs that affirm what is desirable by members of a society. Several of the core American values of interest to sports marketers include individualism, youthfulness, achievement and success, and family.

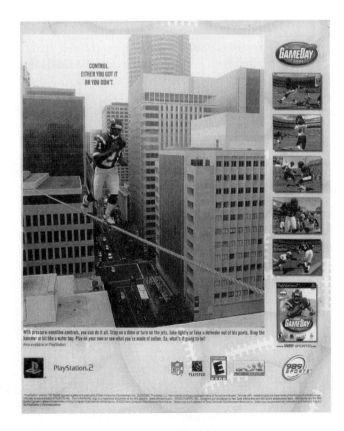

Playstation's Game Day: A leader in the sports video game industry.

Source: Used by permission of Playstation.

Sports are symbolic of many core American values. In fact, what could be more American than baseball, our national pastime? ESPN used this rich tradition in a series of television advertisements promoting its Major League Baseball coverage. These advertisements claim "It's baseball—you're American—watch it."

All these core values are directly or indirectly relevant to sports marketing. For instance, certain sports or sporting events stress individualism. Individualism is based on nonconformance or the need to be unique. Nothing could be more directly linked to individualism than the X-treme Games, featuring sports such as skateboarding and street luge.

The central or underlying values inherent in all sports are achievement and success. Virtually every sports marketing theme is either directly or indirectly linked to the achievement and success of an individual athlete or a team.

Youthfulness is another core American value that is continually stressed by sports marketers. People participate in sports and watch sports to feel young and have fun. Those in the mature market are making strides at staying in shape; they are also watching their own age cohorts still participating in sports at a professional level via any number of senior tours (men's and women's golf, tennis, and bowling). In addition, products like Just for Men are endorsed by sports legends Keith Herdandez, Walt "Clyde" Frazier, and Michael Waltrip who all use the product to "stay looking great."

Another core American value is family and the need to feel a sense of belonging. According to a recent study, team sports, which foster the sense of "group identity" continue to play an important role in the lives of American children. Nearly 75 percent of American children (ages 6 to 17) play a team sport in either an organized or recreational setting. Organized team sports are played by over half (54 percent) of kids from the ages of 6 to 17.[23]

PHYSICAL ENVIRONMENT

The **physical environment** is natural resources and other characteristics of the natural world that have a tremendous impact on sports marketing. For instance, the climate of a region dictates the types of sports that are watched and played in that area. In fact, various sports were developed because of the physical characteristics of a region. Skiing and hockey in the North and surfing on the Coasts are obvious examples.

The mature market—staying young and having fun in record numbers.

Sports marketers attempt to control the physical environment for both spectators and sports participants. For example, the 1997 Australian Open (tennis) was hit by a heat wave that affected both players and spectators. Tournament officials closed the roof on center court and artificially controlled the physical environment. Many players, however, wanted their matches rescheduled, and others argued that they had trained for the heat. This attempt to artificially control mother nature seems to have backfired, or at least come under scrutiny.[24] Another interesting example of control of the physical environment comes from the world of golf, where Dan Bjorkman is attempting to build the first 18 hole fully carpeted golf course. The course won't have to be watered and Bjorkman estimates that it will save him approximately $600,000 annually in maintenance costs.[25]

Artificial turf replaced natural grass surfaces in stadiums in the late 1960s. In the new millenium, all new stadiums being built have switched back to natural grass. Grass not only seems to be easier on the athletes in terms of potential injuries, but fans also seem to appreciate the "natural" look of grass. Likewise, domed stadiums seem to have run their (un)natural course. The newer stadiums are all open-air venues, which have greater appeal for spectators. The retro-look, built-of-brick, newer stadiums have created a nostalgic atmosphere of baseball as it was meant to be played.

In addition to the climate, the physical environment of sports marketing is concerned with conservation and preserving natural resources. This trend toward conservation is most often referred to as "green marketing." Marketing ecologically responsible products and being conscious about the effects of sports on the physical environment is one of the concerns of green marketing. For instance, many golf course management groups have come under attack from environmentalists concerned about the effect of phosphate-based chemicals used in keeping golf courses green.[26] Other groups have criticized the sport of fishing as cruel and unusual punishment for the fish.

POLITICAL, LEGAL, AND REGULATORY ENVIRONMENT

Sports marketers are continually faced with **political, legal,** and **regulatory environment** that affect their strategic decisions. Politics have always played a major role in sports and are becoming an increasingly important part of the sports landscape. In professional sports, politicians are involved in promoting or discouraging passage of stadium tax issues. Since 1953, most stadiums have been owned by city governments.[27] The question is "How far does one go in sacrificing taxpayers' wealth to promote civic pride?" Additional evidence of the relationship between government and sports marketing is the growing number of sports commissions. Since 1980, the number of sports commissions, designed to attract sporting events to cities, states, or regions, has increased from 10 to roughly 150.[28]

The legal environment of sports has certainly taken on a life of its own in the new millennium. Sports officials (i.e., league commissioners, judges, sports arbitrators, coaches, and athletic directors) are continually confronted with legal challenges that arise on and off the playing field. These officials must be adept at interpreting the language of collective bargaining, recruiting student-athletes, understanding Title IX, avoiding antitrust, licensing team logos, and handling other sports law issues.

One of the most famous pieces of legislation, passed in 1972 under President Richard Nixon, was Title IX. Simply, Title IX states that "no person in the United States shall, on the basis of sex, be excluded from participation in, be denied the benefits of, or be subjected to discrimination under any education program or activity receiving Federal financial assistance." Interestingly, the law that has had the most dramatic impact on the growth of women's sports participation does not even mention the word "sports." Perhaps the most famous Title IX decision was a 1997 ruling by the U.S. Supreme Court in the *Brown University v. Cohen* case. The courts ruled that Brown University did not meet any part of the three-step Title IX compliance.

This three-part test includes the following:

1. Are opportunities for female and male athletes proportionate to their enrollment?
2. Does the school have a history of expanding athletic opportunities for the underrepresented sex?
3. Has the school demonstrated success in meeting the needs of those students?

Unfortunately, Title IX implementation has led to reduction in men's sports programs. Rather than adding women's sports programs, universities have chosen to cut men's sports such as baseball and wrestling to address the problem of proportionality.[29]

As mentioned earlier, sports legal issues involve much more than Title IX and antitrust issues. Recent examples of sports legal issues in the news include cases of breach of contract, player-on-player/coach/fan violence, and trademark infringement. The latest disturbing trend, especially in light of heightened security is fans attacking players, coaches, and umpires on fields of play. One of the most recent, highly publicized events happened in September 2002 at Comiskey Park when Royals' first-base coach Tom Gamboa was assaulted by 34-year-old William Ligue Jr. and his 15-year-old son. Ligue's son spent one month in jail after pleading guilty to charges of aggravated battery and mob action. He was sentenced to five years probation and 30 hours of community service, while his father has pleaded not guilty to the same charge.

Due to the billions of dollars of sports-licensed merchandise sold each year, a more common form of legal issues in sport is a trademark violation. In one example, American Media, Inc. (parent company of the National Enquirer and Globe) was sued by the U.S. Olympic Committee (USOC) for using images of Olympic athletes without their consent and using the word "Olympics" in a publication entitled Olympics USA.[30] Similarly, the IOC has filed a lawsuit against 1,800 Internet sites abusing the Olympic name.[31] In yet another example, Callaway Golf recently stopped the sale of counterfeit clubs on eBay.com.

A regulatory body or agency is responsible for enacting laws or setting guidelines for sports and sports marketers. Regulatory agencies can either be controlled by government or nongovernment agencies. One example of a nongovernment regulatory body that has tremendous control over sports and sports marketing practices is The Federation Internationale de Football Association (FIFA). FIFA is the international federation for the world's most popular sport, soccer. The FIFA, which was formed in 1904, mandates to promote soccer through development programs for youth and to supervise international competition to ensure the rules and regulations of the game are being followed. In addition, FIFA is responsible for maintaining the unified set of rules for soccer called the *Laws of the Game*.

Although FIFA is concerned with regulating the game itself, it also controls many facets outside the game that have an impact on sports marketing. For example, FIFA is committed to improving stadiums for the fans and protecting them against the rising costs of attendance. Another example of FIFA's control over sports marketing is that virtual advertising—superimposing marketing messages on the field during televised broadcasts—is forbidden.

In addition, FIFA works with ISL Marketing to secure sponsors for major soccer events, such as the World Cup. As a regulatory agency, FIFA attempts to make sure that the sponsors do not intrude in any way on the integrity of the game. FIFA General Secretary, Joseph Blatter, describes the delicate but beneficial relationship between FIFA and its sponsors as follows: "It's important for the sponsors not to influence—or even try to influence—the game itself, any more than it is FIFA's role or intention to influence how these companies do their own business."[32]

DEMOGRAPHICS

Assessing the **demographic environment** entails observing and monitoring population trends. These trends are observable aspects of the population such as the total number of consumers and their composition (i.e., age or ethnic background) or the geographic dispersion of consumers. Let us look at several aspects of the demographic profile of the United States, including size of the population, age of the population, shifts in ethnic groups, and population shifts among geographic regions.

SIZE OF THE POPULATION

Currently, the U.S. population stands at approximately 292 million consumers and is growing at a rapid pace. It is estimated that by the year 2010, the U.S. population will increase by as much as another 24 million.[33] As with the U.S. population, the world population is also expanding at an alarming rate. The present world population is over 6 billion and is growing at a rate of roughly 76 million per year. This is of special interest to marketers of sports entities who are considering expansion into international markets.

AGE

Age is one of the most common variables used in segmenting and targeting groups of consumers. As such, sports marketers must continually monitor demographic shifts in the age of U.S. consumers. The "graying of America" has and will continue to exert a huge influence. The older adult population is expected to grow at a rate of 62 percent by the year 2010, whereas the U.S. population as a whole is projected to increase at a rate of 19 percent.[34] This trend is a function of the baby boom generation growing older.

Studies show that by the year 2015, mature adults will make up almost 25 percent of the entire population; this number will grow even larger to comprise one-third of the population by the year 2050.[35] This means that in about 50 years, one out of every three Americans will be 55 years of age or older.[36] Apparently, with new technological advances bringing about breakthroughs in medicine, a lower mortality rate, and preventive approaches to health, Americans are living longer.

Moreover, the 76-million-strong baby boom generation is already entering midlife and will soon age. Four out of every 10 adults in the United States are baby boomers; in the year 2000, they were between 35 to 50 years old. Also of significance is the baby bust generation (children of baby boomers) that follows in the wake of its parental tidal wave. In 2000, there were an estimated 19 million children under five years of age, compared with the 16 million in 1980.[37]

SHIFTS IN ETHNIC GROUPS

The United States has been called a melting pot because of its diversity and multiethnic population. The number of white Americans is diminishing, while roughly 31 percent of the U.S. population is represented by some minority group. By 2050, non- Hispanic whites will account for only 54 percent of the U.S. population. In terms of sheer size, nearly 81 million people represent either the African American, Asian, or Hispanic ethnic groups. All three of these ethnic groups have rising income levels, which translate into more purchasing power. Although all minority groups are growing, the fastest-growing segment between 1990 and 2000 was Asian Americans, with $254 billion in annual buying power. This group nearly doubled in size, although Asian Americans still represent only 4.2 percent of the U.S. population. The next fastest-growing minority was Hispanic Americans ($452 billion of annual buying power), who represent 12.5 percent of the U.S. population. African Americans still remain the largest minority group, with 12.9 percent of the population and $572 billion in annual buying power.[38]

Each of these ethnic groups are important subcultures that share a portion of the larger (white) American culture, but also have unique consumption characteristics. There are a number of benefits in developing a marketing mix that appeals to specific ethnic groups. In an early example, the Dodgers' attendance boomed in the early 1980s, when they featured pitcher Fernando Valenzuela, who appealed to the Hispanic market in Los Angeles.

POPULATION SHIFTS

Through 2020, the greatest population shift will be evident in the South and West. Based on 2000 census data the population in the western states grew by nearly 20 percent and 17 percent in the South, compared to lower rates of growth in the Midwest and Northeast (8 percent and 5.5 percent respectively). The states with the highest growth in absolute number of people are California, Texas, and Florida. In terms of percentage growth, Nevada led the way in the decade of the 1990s with an enormous 66% increase in population. The next fastest growing states include Arizona (40 percent), Colorado (31 percent), Utah (30 percent), and Idaho (29 percent).[39]

There is no definitive explanation for this shift, although some believe it is due to the previously discussed aging of America or the growth of employment opportunities in these areas. Keep in mind that, until 1957 when the Brooklyn Dodgers moved to Los Angeles, there were no Major League Baseball teams west of St. Louis.

Along with exploring population shifts by state, sports marketers must assess the dispersion of people within an area. Are people moving back to urban areas, or is the "flight to the suburbs" still occurring? The 2000 census showed the greatest growth to be in suburban areas. There are still fewer people living in or moving back to the central city. These measures of population dispersion are having an impact on where new professional teams are locating and where new stadiums are being built.

THE ECONOMY

The economic environment is another important but uncontrollable factor for sports marketers to consider. Economic factors that affect sports organizations can be described as either macroeconomic or microeconomic elements. A brief explanation of each follows.

MACROECONOMIC ELEMENTS

Economic activity is the flow of goods and services between producers and consumers. The size of this flow and the principle measure of all economic activity is called the gross national product (GNP). The business cycle, which closely follows the GNP, is one of the broadest macroeconomic elements. The four stages of the business cycle are as follows:

Prosperity—the phase in which the economy is operating at or near full employment, and both consumer spending and business output are high.

Recession—the downward phase, in which consumer spending, business output, and employment are decreasing.

Depression—the low phase of the business cycle, in which unemployment is highest, consumer spending is low, and business output has declined drastically.

Recovery—the upward phase when employment, consumer spending, and business output are rising.

Each cyclical phase influences economic variables, such as unemployment, inflation, and consumers' willingness to spend. Decisions about the strategic sports marketing process are affected by these fluctuations in the economy. Ticket sales may boom during times of economic growth. In addition, the growth period may have an even greater impact on corporate demand for luxury boxes and season tickets. If the country is in either a recession or a depression, consumers may be reluctant to purchase nonessential goods and services such as sporting goods or tickets to sporting events Mistakenly, the sports industry sometimes seems to operate under the "ignorance is bliss" philosophy when it comes to the economy. As Steve Wilstein points out "salaries for athletes kept rising, TV deals soared, and ticket prices spiraled ever upward as if the leagues were living in their own fantasyland, immune to economic cycles." Although Wilstein believes the sports that are hardest hit by the economy are those already on the periphery (e.g., the Women's Professional Bowling Tour), even the major sports are hit hard by a poor economy.[40]

Although the relationship between the purchase of sporting goods and tickets to sporting events is likely to be associated with good economic times, this may not always be the case. During a recession or depression, sports may serve as a rallying point for people. Consumers can still feel good about their teams, even in times of economic hardship. This is one of the important, but sometimes neglected, societal roles of sport.

MICROECONOMIC ELEMENTS

Whereas **macroeconomic elements** examine the big picture, or the national income, **microeconomic elements** are those smaller elements that make up the big picture. One of the microelements of concern to sports marketers is consumer income level. As economist Paul Samuelson points out, "Mere billions of dollars would be meaningless if they did not correspond to the thousand and one useful goods and services that people really need and want."[41] Likewise, having sports products would be meaningless if consumers could not afford to purchase them. A primary determinant of a consumer's ability to purchase is income level.

Consumer income levels are specified in terms of gross income, disposable income, or discretionary income. Of these types of income, discretionary is of greatest interest to sports marketers. This is the portion of income that the consumer retains after paying taxes and purchasing necessities. Sports purchases are considered a nonnecessity and, therefore, are related to a consumer or family's discretionary income. According to a new analysis by TGE Demographics, Inc., two-thirds of American households have some discretionary income they can spend on nonnecessities. In addition, the number of families with discretionary income is expected to rise.[42]

MONITORING THE EXTERNAL CONTINGENCIES

As discussed, external contingencies are dynamic, and sports marketers must keep abreast of these continually changing influences. A systematic analysis of these external factors is the first step approached by sports marketers using the contingency framework. In addition, as the sports industry becomes more competitive, one of the keys to success will be identifying new market opportunities and direction through assessing the external contingencies. The method used to monitor the external contingencies is known as environmental scanning.

ENVIRONMENTAL SCANNING

An outward-looking, environmental focus has long been viewed as a central component of strategic planning. In fact, it has been argued that the primary focus of strategic planning is "to look continuously outward" and to keep the organization in step with the anticipated changes in the external environment. This process of monitoring external contingencies is called environmental scanning. More formally, **environmental scanning** is a firm's attempt to continually acquire information on events occurring outside their organization to identify and interpret potential trends.[43]

A sports organization can do several things to enhance its environmental scanning efforts. First, the organization can identify who will be responsible for environmental scanning. The only way to move beyond the pressures of daily business activities is to include environmental scanning responsibilities in the job description of key members of the organization.

Second, the organization can provide individuals conducting the environmental scan with plenty of information on the three Cs: customers, competition, and company. Your scanners cannot correctly monitor the environment without having a solid base of information about the following: customer expectations and needs; the strengths, weaknesses, distinctive competencies, and relative market positioning of the competition; and the strengths, weaknesses, distinctive competencies, and relative market positioning of your own company—as well as the major developmental opportunities that await exploitation.

Third, the organization can assure integration of scanned information through structured interactions and communication. All too often, information needed to recognize new market opportunities is identified but never gets disseminated among the various functional areas. That is, marketing, finance, and operations may all have some information, or pieces to the puzzle, but unless these individuals share the information, it becomes meaningless. Organizations with the most effective environmental scanning systems schedule frequent interactions among their designated scanners.

Fourth, the organization can conduct a thorough analysis of ongoing efforts to improve the effectiveness of environmental scanning activities. This systematic study consists of evaluating the types of scanning data that are relevant and available to managers. This focus on previous environmental scanning efforts can often lead to the identification of new market opportunities.

Fifth, the organization can create a culture that values a "spirit of inquiry." When an organization develops such a spirit, it is understood that the environmental scanning process is necessary for success. In addition, it is understood that environmental scanning is an ongoing activity that is valued by the organization.

Environmental scanning is an essential task for recognizing the external contingencies and understanding how they might affect marketing efforts. However, there are two reasons why environmental scanning practices fail to identify market opportunities or threats. First, the primary difficulty in effectively scanning the environment lies in the nature of the task itself. As scanning implies, sports marketers must look into the future and predict what will likely take place. To make matters even more difficult, these predictions are based on the interaction of the complex variables previously mentioned, such as the economy, demographics, technology, and so on. Second, predictions about the environment are based on data. Sports marketers are exposed to enormous amounts of data and only with experience can individuals selectively choose and correctly interpret the "right data" from the overwhelming mass of information available to them.

INTERNAL CONTINGENCIES

Organizational leaders develop a strategic direction based on the external contingencies that were just discussed. These strategic choices for the organization are also shaped by the core values of the decision makers. In turn, these strategic decisions provide the direction of the strategic sports marketing process. Although the sports marketer should have an understanding of internal contingencies and how they influence the strategic marketing process, they are thought of as more managerial in nature. In other words, these organizational decisions are usually made by top management rather than sports marketing managers.

Internal contingencies are all influences within the organization that can affect the strategic sports marketing process. Let us describe some of the internal contingencies that sports marketers must consider within the contingency framework.

VISION AND MISSION

One of the first steps in developing a strategic direction for an organization is shaping a vision. The **vision** has been described as a long-term road map of where the organization is headed. It creates organizational purpose and identity. A well-written vision should be a prerequisite for effective strategic leadership in an organization. The vision should address the following:

- Where does the organization plan to go from here?
- What business do we want to be in?
- What customer needs do we want to satisfy?
- What capabilities are required for the future?

As you can see, the organizational questions addressed in the vision are all oriented toward the future. The mission, however, is a written statement about the organization's present situation. The purpose of a written mission statement is to inform various stakeholders (e.g., consumers, employees, general public, and suppliers) about the direction of the organization. It is particularly useful for motivating employees internally and for communicating with consumers outside the organization. Here are examples of mission statements constructed by New Balance athletic footwear company and the Green Bay Packers.

MISSION OF NEW BALANCE

To be recognized as the world's leading manufacturer of high-performance footwear. We support this mission by conducting our internal and external relationships according to these core values: Teamwork, Total Customer Satisfaction, and Integrity.[44]

MISSION OF THE GREEN BAY PACKERS

The Green Bay Packers' mission is to be a dominating force in professional football's competitive arena.

On the field, the Packers will continually strive to present their fans with the highest level of performance quality available.

In their operating activities and relations with the NFL, the Packers will also continually strive for excellence in the quality of work performed.

On-field and operating personnel will, at all times, maintain the highest ethical and moral standards in their actions, recognizing that they are all representatives of the Packers' franchise and traditions.

Overall, the Packers will commit themselves to doing their part in representing the State of Wisconsin with competitiveness, respect, and dignity.[45]

These mission statements address several key questions:

- What business are we currently in?
- Who are our current customers?
- What is the scope of our market?
- How do we currently meet the needs of our customers?

In addition to addressing these four key questions, the mission statements for New Balance and the Green Bay Packers also contain statements about the core values of the organization. In fact, these core values are fundamental to carrying out the vision and mission of the organization.

How do mission and vision influence the strategic sports marketing process? Both vision and mission define the consumers of sport in broad terms. For example, New Balance sees its customers from a global perspective, whereas the Packers use the term "fans" to represent its consumers. Also, vision and mission define the products and services that are being marketed to consumers. New Balance, in stating its core product is high-performance footwear, takes a somewhat limited view in defining its products and services. In addition, the vision and mission help to identify the needs of consumers and ultimately guide the marketing process in meeting these needs.

Nike provides an excellent illustration of the dependent relationship among vision, mission, and the strategic marketing process.[46] Originally, the product was aimed toward the serious track athlete who wanted a low-priced, high-quality performance shoe for competition. By 1969, Nike had begun to build a strong brand reputation as the shoe for competitive athletes. Over time, however, Nike redefined and broadened its vision and mission. In 1978, footwear represented 97 percent of Nike's total sales. Today, this percentage has decreased to roughly 67 percent as Nike produces footwear and apparel to meet the needs of almost every consumer in global markets. Nike's strategic decision to sell more than just high-performance footwear aimed to only the serious athlete has changed the entire marketing mix. Now, more Nike products are being sold at more places than ever before. In fact, Nike's mission is "to bring inspiration and innovation to every athlete in the world. If you have a body, you are an athlete."[47]

ORGANIZATIONAL OBJECTIVES AND MARKETING GOALS

ORGANIZATIONAL OBJECTIVES

The **objectives** of the organization stem from vision and mission. They convert the vision and mission into performance targets to be achieved within a specified timeframe. Objectives can be thought of as signposts along the road that help an organization focus on its purpose as stated in the mission statement. More specifically, an objective is a long-range purpose that is not quantified or limited to a time period.[48]

Organizational objectives are needed to define both financial and strategic direction. Organizational leaders typically develop two types of objectives: financial objectives and strategic objectives. Financial objectives specify the performance that an organization wants to achieve in terms of revenues and profits. Achieving these financial performance objectives is critical to the long term survival of the organization. Some examples of financial objectives include the following:

- growth in revenues,
- increase in profit margins, and
- improved return on investment (ROI).

Strategic objectives are related to the performance and direction of the organization. Achieving strategic objectives is critical to the long term market position and competitiveness of an organization. Whereas strategic objectives may not have a direct link to the bottom line of an organization, they ultimately have an impact on its financial performance. Here are a few examples of general strategic objectives:

- increased market share,
- enhanced community relations efforts, and
- superior customer service.

MARKETING GOALS

Marketing goals guide the strategic marketing process and are based on organizational objectives. A **goal** is a short-term purpose that is measurable and challenging, yet attainable and time specific.[49]

Here is a sampling of common marketing goals:

- increase ticket sales by 5 percent over the next year,
- introduce a new product or service each year,
- generate 500 new season ticketholders prior to the next season, and
- over the next six months, increase awareness levels from 10 to 25 percent for women between the ages of 18 and 34 regarding a new sports product.

Although multiple goals are acceptable, goals in some areas (e.g., marketing and finance) may conflict, and care must be taken to reduce any potential conflict. After developing marketing goals, the organization may want to examine them based on the following criteria:[50]

- *Suitability*—the marketing goals must follow the direction of the organization and support the organization's business vision and mission.
- *Measurability*—the marketing goals must be evaluated over a specific timeframe (such as the examples just discussed).
- *Feasibility*—the marketing goals should be within the scope of what the organization can accomplish, given its resources.
- *Acceptability*—the marketing goals must be agreed upon by all levels within the organization. Top management must feel that the goals are moving the organization in the desired direction; middle managers and first line supervisors must feel the goals are achievable within the specified timeframe.
- *Flexibility*—the marketing goals must not be too rigid, given uncontrollable or temporary situational factors. This is especially true when adopting the contingency framework.
- *Motivating*—the marketing goals must be reachable but challenging. If the goals are too easy or too hard, then they will not direct behavior toward their fulfillment.
- *Understandability*—the marketing goals should be stated in terms that are clear and simple. If any ambiguities arise, people may inadvertently work against the goals.
- *Commitment*—employees within the sports marketing organization should feel that it is their responsibility to ensure goals are achieved. As such, managers must empower employees so everyone in the organization is committed and will act to achieve goals.
- *People Participation*—as with commitment, all employees in the organization should be allowed to participate in the development of marketing goals. Greater

employee involvement in setting goals will foster greater commitment to goal attainment.

- *Linkage*—as discussed earlier, marketing goals must be developed with an eye toward achieving the broader organizational objectives. Marketing goals incongruent with organizational direction are ineffective.

ORGANIZATIONAL STRATEGIES

Organizational strategies are the means by which the organization achieves its organizational objectives and marketing goals. Whereas the organizational vision, mission, objectives, and goals are the "what," the organizational strategy is the "how." It is, in essence, the game plan for the sports organization. Just as football teams adopt different game plans for different competitors, sports organizations must be able to readily adapt to changing environmental conditions. Remember, flexibility and responsiveness are the cornerstones of the contingency framework.

In general, there are four levels of strategy development within organizations: corporate strategy, business strategy, functional strategy, and operational strategy.[51] The relationship among these strategy levels is pictured in Figure 3.1. Notice that there must be a good fit among the levels, vertically and horizontally for the firm to succeed.

Corporate-level strategies represent the overall game plan for organizations that compete in more than one industry. Business-level strategies define how a business unit gains advantage over competitors within the relevant industry. Functional-level strategies are those developed by each functional area within a business unit. For example, the strategic sports marketing process is the functional-level strategy developed by sports marketing managers, just as financial strategy is the purview of their finance manager counterparts. The operational level strategies are more narrow in scope. Their primary goal is to support the functional-level strategies. Let us take a look at the relationship among the four levels of strategy at the Walt Disney Company to see how a good fit among strategies can lead to overall organizational effectiveness.[52]

The Walt Disney Company is a diversified company with interests in a number of related entertainment industries. The entertainment industries of interest to Disney include: parks and resorts (Walt Disney World, Disney Cruise Lines, Anaheim Mighty Ducks); the internet group (abcnews.com, Disney.com); studio entertainment

FIGURE 3.1   Relationship Between Levels of Strategy

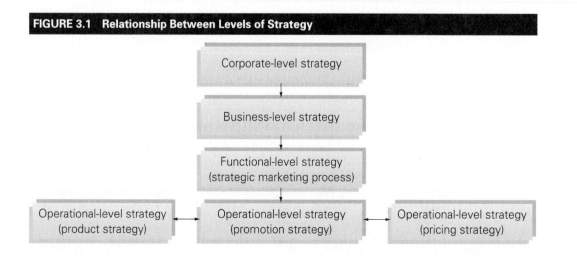

(Miramax, Touchstone, Walt Disney Pictures); media networks (ABC, ESPN, SOAPnet); consumer products (Disney licensing, Disney publishing); and Walt Disney International. Interestingly, the professional sports franchise is described as part of the parks and resorts segment. Also of interest is that the ownership of the sports team supports the entertainment mission of Disney.

The corporate strategy for Disney is based on competing globally in all of these entertainment industries. The corporate strategy should allow Disney to obtain the broader organizational goals and pursue its vision and mission.

At the business level, Disney management specifies strategies for each business unit within each of the industry segments. For example, the Mighty Ducks and Walt Disney World would each have a unique business-level strategy, even though they are in the same group—parks and resorts. These strategies are aimed at gaining competitive advantage within each relevant industry. However, each business-level strategy must support the corporate-level strategy, goals, vision, and mission.

At Disney, there are numerous functional areas within the organization. For example, the Mighty Ducks functional areas may include finance and administration, general management and operations, business affairs, civic affairs, sales, and marketing. Leadership within each of these functional areas would be responsible for designing their own strategies to meet their respective business-level strategies.

Finally, within the functional areas such as sales and marketing, operational-level strategies are developed. Promotion, ticket sales, product, and pricing strategies must all be designed and coordinated to attain the sales and marketing objectives set forth in the functional-level strategy. As you can see, sports marketing managers responsible for each operational unit must be concerned with satisfying not only their own goals, but also the objectives of the broader organization.

CORPORATE LEVEL

Most professional sports franchises are owned by individuals or corporations that have many business interests. Sometimes these businesses are related, and sometimes the professional sports franchise is nothing more than a hobby of a wealthy owner. Today, the latter is becoming far less common as corporations include sports franchises in their portfolio. Even more rare is the sports franchise owned and operated as the primary, if not sole, source of owner income (e.g., Mike Brown family and the Cincinnati Bengals).

There are typically two types of diversified companies—those that pursue related diversification and those that pursue unrelated diversification. In related diversification, the corporation will choose to pursue markets in which they can achieve synergy in marketing, operations, or management. In other words, the corporation looks for markets that are similar to their existing products and markets. The underlying principle in related diversification is that a company that is successful in existing markets is more likely to achieve success in similar markets. Unrelated diversification, however, refers to competing in markets that are dissimilar to existing markets. The primary criteria for choosing markets are based on spreading financial risk over different markets.

Professional sports franchises can be owned privately by one or more individuals, publicly owned corporations, or some combination of both. Today, roughly 52 public companies own at least some of the 130 or so major league franchises.[53] Roughly 10 percent of these sports franchises are owned by media companies that view sport as a very related and natural diversification.[54] Time Warner Media owns baseball, basketball, and hockey teams. The Tribune Company, which owns super station WGN, also owns the Chicago Cubs. GE, which owns NBC, also owns the New York Knicks and Rangers. The list goes on and on. Along with the media giants, the leagues are recognizing the advantages of team ownership by corporations that are involved in related markets.

Developing Corporate-Level Strategy Corporate-level strategies must make three types of decisions. First, top managers must determine in which markets they want to compete. Sports organizations have a core product and service, plus they also compete in ancillary markets. The core product has been defined as the game itself and the entertainment provided to consumers, whereas secondary markets include sale of licensed merchandise, fantasy sports camps, sports magazines, sports art, and so on. The leaders of a sports organization must also attempt to identify ways of capitalizing on the similarities in markets. For instance, fans for the core product often represent a natural target market for additional products and services. Examples such as Disney and the media moguls owning sports franchises illustrate the synergy in markets.

The second type of decision deals with enhancing the performance within each of the chosen markets. Top managers constantly need to monitor the mix of markets in which the organization competes. This evaluation might lead to decisions that involve pursuing growth in some markets or leaving others. These decisions are based on the performance of the market and the ability of the organization to compete successfully within each market.

The third type of decision involves establishing investment priorities and placing organizational resources into the most attractive markets. For a sports organization, this could involve decisions regarding stadium renovation, player contracts, or investing more heavily in merchandising. Corporate decisions within a sports organization must constantly recognize that the core product, the competition itself, is necessary to compete in related markets.

BUSINESS-LEVEL STRATEGY

The next level of strategic decision-making is referred to as business-level, or competitive, strategies. Business-level strategies are based on managing one business interest within the larger corporation. The ultimate goal of business-level strategy decisions is to gain advantage over competitors. In the sports industry, these competitors may be other sports organizations in the area or simply entertainment in general.

One strategic model for competing at the business level contains four approaches to gaining the competitive advantage. These approaches include low-cost leadership, differentiation, market niche based on lower cost, and market niche based on differentiation. Choices of which of the four strategies to pursue are based on two issues: strategic market target and strategic advantage.

Strategic market targets can include a broader market segment or a narrow, more specialized market niche. Strategic advantage can be gained through becoming a low-cost provider or creating a real or perceived differential advantage.

The focus of low-cost leadership is to serve a broad customer base at the lowest cost to any provider in the industry. Although there may be a number of competitors pursuing this strategy, there will be only one low-cost leader. Many minor league teams compete as low-cost leaders due to the lower operating costs relative to their major league counterparts. Differentiation strategies attempt to compete on the basis of their ability to offer a unique position to a variety of consumers. Typically, companies differentiate themselves through products, services, or promotions. With differentiation strategies, companies can charge a premium for the perceived value of the sports product. Professional sports franchises attempt to differentiate themselves from competitors by providing a high-quality product on and off the field. This is done through

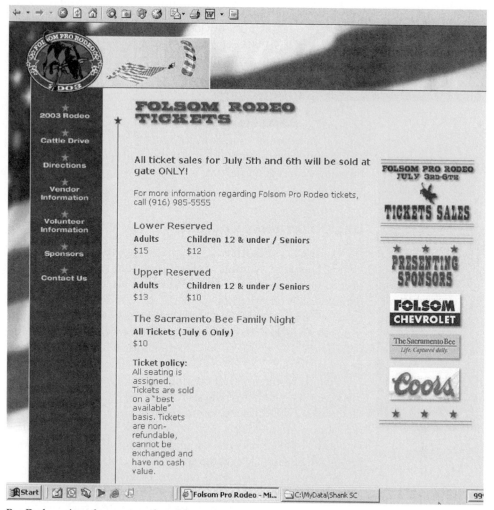

Pro Rodeo using a low-cost market niche strategy.
Source: Used by permission of Folsom Rodeo.com. All rights reserved.

a unique blend of sports promotion, community relations, stadium atmosphere, and a winning team.

Although low-cost leadership and differentiation strategies have mass-market appeal, the market niche strategies are concerned with capturing a smaller market segment. These market segments may be based on consumer demographics, geographic location, lifestyle, or a number of other consumer characteristics. Within the market niche chosen, sports organizations can gain strategic advantage through a focus on low cost or differentiation. Two examples of low-cost market niche strategy include Association of Volleyball Professionals (AVP) where tournament ticket prices are free for general admission and the Pro Rodeo Cowboys Association (PRCA) whose events are priced between $10 and $15.

FUNCTIONAL-LEVEL STRATEGY

Each functional area of the organization (e.g., marketing, personnel, and operations) must also develop a game plan that supports the business-level and corporate-level initiatives. Again, the contingency framework calls for "fit" between each level of strategy within the organization. It is also important to coordinate among each functional area. For example, the marketing strategies should dovetail with personnel and operations strategies. The strategic marketing process discussed in Chapter 2 provides the functional-level strategy for the organization's marketing efforts.

OPERATIONAL-LEVEL STRATEGY

Within the strategic sports marketing process, several narrower strategies must be considered. For example, plans must be designed, implemented, and evaluated in areas such as promotion, new product and service development, pricing, sponsorship, and ticket distribution. Each strategy at the operational level must also fit the broader strategic marketing process, as well as be integrated across the marketing function.

ORGANIZATIONAL CULTURE

As we discussed earlier in the chapter, culture is described as the shared values, beliefs, language, symbols, and tradition that is passed on from generation to generation by members of a society. Culture can affect the importance placed on sports by a region or nation, whether we participate in sports, and even the types of sports we enjoy playing or watching. A similar concept applied to organizations is called organizational culture. **Organizational culture** is the shared values and assumptions of organizational members that shape an identity and establish preferred behaviors in an organization.[55]

As one of the internal contingencies, organizational culture influences the sports marketer in a number of ways. First, the organizational culture of a sports organization dictates the value placed on marketing. For instance, the Cincinnati Reds have only one person guiding their marketing efforts. Contrast this with the Toronto Blue Jays, who have eight employees just in marketing, and you begin to see the relative value an organization can place on the sports marketing function.

Second, organizational culture is important because it is linked with organizational effectiveness. In a study of campus recreation programs, organizational culture was found to be positively associated with organizational effectiveness.[56] That is, a positive culture is associated with an effective organization. A positive culture rewards employees for their performance, has open communication, has strong leadership, encourages risk taking, and is adaptive. The ability to adapt to change is one of the most important dimensions from the contingency framework perspective.

Third, the organizational culture of professional sports organizations and college athletic programs not only has an impact on the effectiveness of the organization, but also can influence consumers' perceptions of the organization. For example, the Oakland Raiders, under owner Al Davis, have an organizational culture that values risk taking and doing anything necessary to get the job done. This organizational culture translated to the team's successful and ruthless performance on the field. Subsequently, the fans began to adopt this outlaw image. Ultimately, the black and silver bad boys of football have attracted a fan following that has come to expect this rebel image.

University athletic departments and their programs are also defined by the organizational culture. Athletic programs are known to either value education or attempt to win at all costs. In Cincinnati, two Division I basketball programs have organizational cultures that, on the surface, could not be more different. Xavier University is known for its emphasis on academics (high student-athlete graduation rates) and athletics, whereas the University of Cincinnati program is sometimes jokingly referred to as

"Hugs Thugs" (named after head coach Bob Huggins). In this case, the athletic programs have influenced consumers' perceptions and may also influence the broader university culture.

ASSESSING THE INTERNAL AND EXTERNAL CONTINGENCIES: SWOT ANALYSIS

To this point, we have looked at both the external and internal contingencies. To guide the strategic sports marketing process, an organization conducts a SWOT analysis. SWOT is an acronym for strengths, weaknesses, opportunities, and threats. The strengths and weaknesses are controllable factors within the organization. In other words, a firm must evaluate its strengths and weaknesses based on the internal contingencies. The opportunities and threats are assessed as a result of the external contingencies found in the marketing environment. These elements may be beyond the control of the sports organization.

The strategic sports marketing process must first examine its own internal contingencies. These internal strengths and weaknesses include human resources, financial resources, and whether organizational objectives and marketing goals are being met with the current marketing mix. Products and services, promotional efforts, pricing structure, and methods of distribution are also characterized as either strengths or weaknesses.

After assessing the organizational strengths and weaknesses, the firm identifies external opportunities and threats found in the marketing environment. As discussed earlier in

Many sports marketers realize new opportunities based on the growth in women's sports.

Source: Used by permission of Nike Advertising.

the chapter, sports marketing managers must monitor the competition; demographic shifts; the economy; political, legal, and regulatory issues; and technological advances. Each of these external factors may affect the direction of the strategic marketing process.

The intent of conducting a SWOT analysis is to help sports marketers recognize or develop areas of strength capable of exploiting environmental opportunities. When sports marketers observe opportunities that match a particular strength, a strategic window is opened. More formally, **strategic windows** are limited periods of time during which the characteristics of a market and the distinctive competencies of a firm fit together well and reduce the risks of seizing a particular market opportunity.[57] For example, IMG, a leading sports and entertainment marketing company has created "IMG X Sports" to capitalize on the growing popularity in extreme and lifestyle sports. In addition to capitalizing on strengths, sports marketers develop strategies that eliminate or minimize organizational weaknesses.

At this stage, you should have a broad understanding of how each of the external contingencies may affect your marketing plan. Table 3.1 provides a common list of questions to consider when developing the opportunities and threats (OT) portion of your SWOT analysis.

TABLE 3.1 Assessing External Contingencies

1. **Social**—What major social and lifestyle trends will have an impact on the sports participants or spectators? What action has the firm been taking in response to these trends?

2. **Demographics**—What impact will forecast trends in size, age, profile, and distribution of population have on the firm? How will the changing nature of the family, the increase in the proportion of women in the workforce, and changes in ethnic composition of the population affect the firm? What action has the firm taken in response to these developments and trends? Has the firm reevaluated its traditional sports products and expanded the range of specialized offerings to respond to these changes?

3. **Economic**—What major trends in taxation and in income sources will have an impact on the firm? What action has the firm taken in response to these trends?

4. **Political, Legal, and Regulatory**—What laws are now being proposed at federal, state, and local levels that could affect the strategic marketing process? What recent changes in regulations and court decisions have affected the sports industry? What action has the firm taken in response to these legal and political changes?

5. **Competition**—Which organizations are competing with us directly by offering a similar product? Which organizations are competing with us indirectly by securing our customers' time, money, energy, or commitment? What new competitive trends seem likely to emerge? How effective is the competition? What benefits do our competitors offer that we do not?

6. **Technological**—What major technological changes are occurring that affect the sports organization and sports industry?

SPOTLIGHT ON SPORTS MARKETING ETHICS

Sports Offers a Human Timeout from the Inhumanity

Do not feel guilty Thursday for channel hopping between March Madness images of absurd extremes, for spending an hour with Wolf Blitzer before taking a 20-second T.O. with Dickie V. It's okay to put down the duct tape and plastic long enough for a quick survey of the upsets sabotaging your chances in the office pool, because being human means needing a refuge from the inhuman horrors that shape Saddam Hussein's reality TV.

Live from Baghdad, college basketball fans will watch Hussein's regularly scheduled programming with tight throats and heavy hearts, then switch to whichever network ends up broadcasting the straight-faced announcers talking about young athletes coping with "adversity." Yes, the games must go on. Myles Brand, NCAA chief and former Indiana president, has decreed, "We're not going to let a tyrant determine how we lead our lives."

The world was a much better place when Brand's biggest worry was Bobby Knight.

All of America wishes the bully of the moment merely threw chairs and berated refs. So with the Iraqi dictator threatening to unleash chemical and biological agents on a military force that includes kids in Carmelo Anthony's age group, some have challenged Thursday's first-round tournament tipoff on moral and common-sense grounds.

Why add packed sports arenas to the dizzying maze of possible terrorist targets? How in God's name can we spend time tracking bracket-busting three-pointers, and discussing Jim Livengood's selection-committee foulups involving the school he works for (Arizona) and the school he graduated from (Brigham Young), when men and women are risking their lives for our freedoms?

Tough questions, easy answers. On the domestic security front, go with Tom Ridge's playbook: games shouldn't be postponed or canceled unless credible intelligence suggests a subregional site has landed on some madman's hit list.

As for the moral dilemma of breaking down zone defenses while man-to-man blood spills, remember that the vast majority of soldiers in harm's way want our planes, trains, and automobiles to operate, and our theaters, restaurants, and stadiums to remain open.

The truest words I've heard spoken within this context come from Jay Robertson, a New York Giants assistant under Jim Fassel, who saw too many friends die while serving as a Marine company commander in Vietnam.

"We called (America) 'the world' because we felt like we were on a different planet," Robertson told me. "When you got sports news . . . it meant so much, because we were starving for anything representing home. I begged my parents to send me the sports pages, and every week or two they'd come in a big envelope.

"Our battalion commander had the film of that great Notre Dame–Michigan State 10 to 10 game two weeks after it was played. We had soldiers in the mess tent watching it who weren't sports fans, but who just needed to watch."

Soldiers needed to watch and hear about the Fighting Irish and Spartans then just like they needed to watch and hear about the Giants and Bills in the Gulf War Super Bowl, and just like they need to watch and hear about the Orangemen and Longhorns now. Americans thousands of miles removed from the battlefield have always needed a similar escape from the anxiety and fear, a fact inspiring President Franklin D. Roosevelt to send his "Green Light" letter to baseball commissioner Kenesaw Mountain Landis five weeks after the Pearl Harbor attack, a letter he began, My dear Judge . . . "I honestly feel that it would be best for the country to keep baseball going."

They played through World War II, the Korean War, Vietnam, and the Gulf War, good choices all. They didn't play in the immediate wake of the 9/11 attacks, and Bud Selig and Paul Tagliabue made the right calls there, too.

The rules are different when the killing fields are next door. The mass murder of civilians in New York, Washington, D.C., and Pennsylvania was so traumatic and so close; America couldn't possibly find a reprieve in the race for the NL East crown. Same goes for the murder of a President. The NFL played on before the country could recover from the Kennedy assassination, and Pete Rozelle later conceded he would take that regret to his grave.

There's no manual to consult in cases of coast-to-coast crises, but other than Rozelle's decision and Avery Brundage's dreadful choice to rush the 1972 Munich Games back into business after the murder of 11 Israeli athletes, most sports leaders and leagues have acted appropriately during such times. The NCAA might've waited a night to play its Indiana-North Carolina championship game in 1981, waited until it had more reason to believe President Reagan would survive a would-be assassin's bullet.

But Selig did right by the Mariners and As in canceling their season-opening series in Japan. No matter how friendly the hosts or how secure the facilities, this just isn't the time to be sending goodwill ambassadors around the globe.

It is the time to stay home and keep everyday American life going. The Oscars should be awarded, Broadway should lift its curtains, and spring training should keep dealing in the blissful baseball currency of hope sweet hope.

And when they're not whispering prayers, lighting candles, or buying duct tape Thursday, sports fans should feel free to take a break from the Middle East and check in on the Midwest Region.

You don't need a letter from Franklin D. Roosevelt to understand: It's only human to need a 20-second time-out from the inhumanity of war.

Source: Ian O'Connor, *USA Today,* March 20, 2003.

Summary

The contingency for strategic sports marketing consists of three components: the strategic sports marketing process, external contingencies, and internal contingencies. The purpose of Chapter 3 was to gain a better understanding of the external and internal contingencies that affect the strategic sports marketing process. External contingencies are those elements outside the control of the sports organization. Alternatively, internal contingencies are managed by the sports organization.

Because the marketing environment is so complex and dynamic, sports marketers use a method for monitoring external contingencies called environmental scanning. Environmental scanning is the sports organization's attempt to acquire information continually on events occurring outside the organization and to identify and interpret potential trends. Sports marketers must continually monitor the environment to look for opportunities and threats that may affect the organization.

The external contingencies that affect the strategic sports marketing process include competition; technology; cultural and social trends; physical environment; political, legal, and regulatory environment; demographic trends and the economy. As with any industry, understanding competitive threats that exist is critical to the success of all sports organizations. Competition for sporting events and sports organizations comes in many forms. Typically, we think of competition as being any other sporting event. However, other forms of entertainment are also considered competitive threats for sports organizations. Technological forces represent another external contingency. Advances in technology are changing the way that consumers watch sports, play sports, and receive their sports information. Cultural and social trends must also be carefully monitored. Core values, such as individualism, youthfulness, and the need for belonging, can have an impact on the target markets chosen and how sports products are positioned to spectators and participants. The physical environment, such as the climate and weather conditions, is another external contingency that can have a tremendous influence on the success or failure of sporting events. Another of the uncontrollable factors is the political, legal, and regulatory environment. Proposed legislation, such as the banning of all tobacco advertising and sponsorship at sporting events, could have a tremendous impact on the motorsports industry. Demographic trends are another critical external contingency that must be monitored by sports marketers. For instance, the graying of America will bring about changes in the levels of participation in sports and the types of sports in which the "mature market" will participate. Finally, economic conditions should be considered by sports marketers. Sports marketers must monitor the macroeconomic elements, such as the national economy, as well as microeconomic issues, such as the discretionary income of consumers in the target market.

In addition to external contingencies, internal contingencies also play a significant role in shaping the strategic sports marketing process. Internal contingencies, thought of as managerial, controllable issues, include vision and mission of the sports organization, organizational objectives and marketing goals, organizational strategies, and organizational culture. The vision and mission of the sports organization guide the strategic sports marketing process by addressing questions such as: What business are we in? Who are our current customers? What is the scope of our market? How do we currently meet the needs of our customers? The organizational objectives and marketing goals stem from the vision and mission of the sports organization. The objectives of the organization are long term and sometimes unquantifiable. Alternatively, marketing goals are short term, measurable, and time specific. It is extremely important to remember that the marketing goals are directly linked to decisions made in the strategic sports marketing process. Another internal contingency that influences the strategic sports marketing process is organizational strategy. The organizational strategy is how the sports organization plans on carrying out its vision, mission, objectives, and goals. There are four different levels of strategy development within the organization. These include corporate-level strategies, business-level strategies, functional-level strategies, and operational-level strategies. Marketing is described as a functional-level strategy. The operational-level strategies such as pricing and promotion must fit the broader strategic sports marketing process. A final internal contingency is the organizational culture or the shared values and assumptions of organizational members that shape an identity and establish preferred behaviors in an organization.

External and internal contingencies are systematically considered prior to the development of the strategic marketing process. The process that many organizations use to analyze internal and external contingencies is called a SWOT analysis. SWOT is an acronym for strengths, weaknesses, opportunities, and threats. The strengths and weakness are internal, controllable factors within the organization that may influence the direction of the strategic sports marketing process. For example, human resources within the organization may represent strengths or weaknesses within any organization. However, the opportunities and threats are uncontrollable aspects of the marketing environment (e.g., competition and economy). The purpose of conducting a SWOT analysis is to help sports marketers recognize how the strengths of their organization can be paired with opportunities that exist in the marketing environment. Conversely, the organization may conduct a SWOT analysis to identify weaknesses in relation to competitors.

Key Terms

- competition
- cultural values
- culture
- demographic environment
- direct competition
- economic activity
- environmental scanning
- goal

- indirect competition
- internal contingencies
- macroeconomic elements
- marketing environment
- microeconomic elements
- objectives
- organizational culture
- organizational strategies

- out-of-market technology
- physical environment
- political, legal, and regulatory environment
- strategic windows
- technology
- vision

Review Questions

1. Define the marketing environment. Are all elements of the marketing environment considered uncontrollable? Why or why not?
2. What is environmental scanning? Why is environmental scanning so important? Who conducts the environmental scan, and how is one conducted?
3. Define competition. What are the different types of competition?
4. How has technology influenced the sports marketing industry? Discuss how "out-of-market" technology benefits sports spectators.
5. Identify several cultural and social trends in our society and describe their impact on sport and sports marketing.
6. What are the core American values, and why are they important to sports marketers?
7. How does the physical environment play a role in sports marketing? How can sports marketers manipulate or change the physical environment?
8. Define the political and regulatory environment. Cite several examples of how this can influence or dictate sports marketing practices.
9. Describe the different demographic trends of interest to sports marketers. How will these demographic trends influence the strategic marketing process?
10. Differentiate between macro- and microeconomic elements. Which (macro- or microelements) do you feel plays an important role in sports marketing? Why?
11. How can sports marketers assess the external environment? What are some sources of secondary data that may assist in understanding the current and future external environment?

Exercises

1. Describe all the ways the changing marketing environment will have an impact on NASCAR racing. How should NASCAR prepare for the future?
2. Your university's athletic program has a number of competitors. List all potential competitors and categorize what type of competition each represents.
3. Find examples of how technology has influenced the sporting goods industry, a professional sports franchise, and the way spectators watch a sporting event. For each example indicates the technology that was used prior to the new technology.
4. Develop advertisements for athletic shoes that reflect each of the core American values discussed in this chapter.
5. Interview five international students and discuss the core values used by sports marketers in their culture. Do these values differ from the core American values? For example, do the British value individualism more or less than Americans? What evidence do they have to support their claims?
6. How does the physical environment of your geographic area or location play a role in sports marketing?
7. Describe how changing demographic trends have led to the development of new sports leagues, the shifting of professional sports franchises, and new sports products. Provide three specific examples of each.

Internet Exercises

1. Experience a portion of any sporting event via Internet broadcast. What did you enjoy the most about this experience, and what could be done to improve this technology?
2. Find three sports products on the Internet that stress technological developments. Do the companies communicate their technological advantages differently?
3. Search the Internet for articles or sites that discuss the pros and cons of the banning of tobacco advertisements at sporting events.

Endnotes

1. Bill Bearden, Thomas Ingram, and Buddy LaForge, *Marketing*, 2nd ed. (New York: Irwin/McGraw Hill, 1998).
2. Ed Hinton, "Sunday Drivers," *Sports Illustrated* (June 3, 1996), 20–24.
3. "CART Just Might Have to Take What It Can Get," www.sportsbusinessnews.com.
4. M. D. Shank and K. Verderber, "Understanding the Nature of Sports Competition," *International Conference on Sport and Society* (June 1999), Marquette, MI.
5. Welcome to NASCAR.com, http://www.nascar.com/guides/about/.
6. Scott McDonald, "Olympic Web Site Attracts Record 7.2 Billion Hits." www.foxsports.com/business/bites/z000926oly_hits.sml.
7. "ESPN.com Sets Record for Unique Users in October." (December 9, 2002), espn.go.com/mediakit.
8. "Foxsports.com and University of Nebraska's Live College Football Webcast Serves More Than 200,000 Video Streams," *Business Wire* (September 6, 2000).
9. K. Kerschbaumer, "Cornhusker Fans Surf for Tackles," *Broadcasting and Cable*, (August 28, 2000).
10. Michael Hiestand, "Online Sales Allow Leagues to Gain Money, Ticket Holder Information," *USA Today* (May 1, 2003), 2C.
11. Wayne Karl, "Tech-savvy Fans Fuel Growth in Digital Revenue." www.sportbusinessjournal.com.
12. Adapted from "NBA, Intel Reach Agreement." www.nba.com/news/intel_000913.html.
13. Matt Richtel, "Satellite vs. Cable: Entertainment Battle Is Revving Up," *The New York Times* (April 16, 2003), 12.
14. John Jackson, "Latest Fox Toy Will Put Racing Fans in the Pits," *Chicago Sun Times* (February 14, 2003), p. 181.
15. Andy Bernstein, "More Evolution Than Revolution in TV Tech," www.sportsbusinessjournal.com.
16. Bill Gray, "Long Time Coming," *Tennis* (September 1995), 32–35.
17. Ibid.
18. Chris Jenkins, "Tee Times Online Catching On," *USA Today* (April 13, 2000), 15c.
19. Michael Alpert, "Powerful Peach Triathlon Gets Boost from Online Registration," *The Atlanta Journal and Constitution* (July 6, 2000), 10jj.
20. Donald Katz, "Welcome to the Electronic Arena— The Digital Age Is Upon Us, and the Sporting World Will Never Be the Same," *Sports Illustrated* (July 3, 1995), 60–77.
21. Philadelphia Eagles Team with Harbor Technologies; Harbor Technologies Selected to Develop Advanced Computer Network for New Lincoln Financial Field, *Business Wire* (June 25, 2003).
22. Victor Godinez, "Sports Games Lap the Field in Video Market," *The Dallas Morning News* (July 26, 2003).
23. "U.S. Trends in Team Sports 2003," www.sgma.com.
24. "New Balls, Cool Rules for Australian Open," (October 8, 1997). www.pointcast.com.
25. Michael, Hiestand, "Play Real Golf on Fake Grass," *USA Today* (June 12, 2003), 2C.
26. Ron Chepesiuk, "The Greening of America," *Wildlife Conservation*, vol. 96, no. 4 (July 1993), 54–59. Rob Shapard, "Environment at the Fore Front: Keys for Greener Municipal Golf Courses," *American City and Country*, vol. 112, no. 4 (April 1997), 52–59.
27. D. V. Baim, *The Sports Stadium as a Municipal Investment* (Westport, CT: Greenwood, 1994).
28. "States and Sports: Hawaii Eyes Tourism Dollars," www.sportserver.com.
29. Michael Jones, *Sports Law* (Upper Saddle River, NJ: Prentice Hall, 1999).
30. P. Solomon Banda, "American Media Inc. Sued Over Olympic Trademark," (September 12, 2000). www.foxsportsbusiness/bites/z000912 oly_trademark.sml.
31. "Out, Out Damn Site; IOC Attempts to Evict Cybersquatters," (July 13, 2000). www.foxsports business/bites/z000713olympic_websites1.sml.
32. "For the Good of the Game," (1996). www.fifa.com/fifa/handbook/fgg/fgg.intro.html.
33. U.S. Census Bureau. *National Population Projections*. www.census.gov/population/www/projections/natproj.html.
34. W. Lazer and E. Shaw, "How Older Americans Spend Their Money," *American Demographics* (September 1987), 36–41.
35. H. Spotts and C. Schewe, "Communicating with the Elderly Consumer: The Growing Health Care Challenge," *Journal of Health Care Marketing* (September 1989), 36–44.

36. Judith Waltrip, "Secrets of the Age Pyramids," *American Demographics* (August 1992), 46.

37. U.S. Census Bureau, *Current Population Reports: Population Projections of the United States by Age, Sex, Race and Hispanic Origin: 1995 to 2050.* www.census.gov/prod/1/pop/p25–1130.

38. Kay Anderson, "Diversity: America's New Face, Home Accents Today," June, 2002, 68–69; U.S. Census Bureau, "Census Briefs and Special Reports." www.census. gov/population/www/cen2000/briefs.html.

39. U.S. Census Bureau, "Census Briefs and Special Reports." www.census.gov/population/www/ cen2000/briefs.html.

40. Steve Wilstein, "Think the NBA Can't Go Belly Up? Think Again" Associated Press (September 26, 2003), http://news.mysanantonio.com.

41. Paul A. Samuelson, *Economics,* 10th ed. (New York: McGraw Hill, 1976).

42. Berna Mider, "Fun Money," *American Demographics,* vol. 19, no. 3 (March 1977), 33.

43. Matthew D. Shank and Robert A. Snyder, "Temporary Solutions: Uncovering New Market Opportunities in the Temporary Employment Industry," *Journal of Professional Services Marketing,* vol. 12, no. 1 (1995), 5–17.

44. Fact Sheet (NB). www.newbalance.com/bean/ misson.html.

45. "Green Bay Packers: Community—Mission Statement," (1997 to 1998). www.packers.com/ community/mission.html.

46. Kenneth Labich, "Vice vs. Reebok: A Battle for Hearts, Minds & Feet," *Fortune* (September 18, 1995), 90–106. Bik Saporito, "Can Nike Get Unstuck?" *Time* (March 30, 1998), 48–53.

47. "Nike Mission," *www.nike.com/nikebiz*.

48. Subhash C. Jain, *Marketing Planning and Strategy,* 3rd ed. (Cincinnati: South-Western Publishing, 1990).

49. Ibid.

50. George Steiner, *Strategic Planning* (New York: Free Press, 1979).

51. Aurthur Thompson and A. J. Strickland, *Strategic Management: Concepts and Cases,* 10th ed. (New York: Irwin/McGraw Hill, 1998).

52. "Walt Disney Annual Report," Disney.go.com/ corporate/investors/financials/annual/2002.

53. *Team Marketing Report,* "Inside the Ownership of Professional Team Sports" (1997), 29–30.

54. "Media companies begin ditching ownership of sports teams," *Mergers and Acquisitions,* June 1, 2003, 1; Ronald Grover, Amy Barrett, and Richard Melcher, "Playing for Keeps," *Business Week* (September 22, 1997), 32–33.

55. E. H. Schein, *Organizational Culture and Leadership* (San Francisco: Josey-Bass, 1988).

56. W. James Weese, "Do Leadership and Organizational Culture Really Matter?" *Journal of Sport Management* (1996), 197–205.

57. George S. Day, *Strategic Market Planning* (St. Paul: West, 1984).

CASE: PART I

The Georgia Alley Cats

Tim Mosser stood up from his desk and walked to the window in his office. For a moment he stared at the parking lot outside, which served as the main parking area for the civic center where the Alley Cats, the professional hockey team he worked for, played their games. It was 6:30 on a Thursday evening, only a hour before a home match for the Alley Cats. He wondered whether there would be any more cars in the lot tonight then there had been for the team's last home game. Tim was the director of sales and promotions for the Alley Cats, a franchise in the East Coast Hockey League. The Alley Cats had been in the league for four years and Tim had been with the team from its inception. The team was located in a central Georgia city with a population of 50,000 residents and the surrounding metropolitan area had a population of 170,000 residents. A minor league baseball team was the only other professional sports franchise in the city at the time the Alley Cats started operation.

Two major investors, Ron Sharpson and Steve Bouton, owned the franchise. Sharpson owned two successful auto dealerships and had always wanted to own a professional sports franchise. Football was his favorite sport, but he enjoyed the contact in hockey. Although he had not played the sport, he liked to watch it and to entertain his friends and business clients at the games. Steve Bouton, his coowner, grew up in Michigan with hockey is in his blood. He played hockey in youth leagues and high school. After college he moved south and enjoyed great success in the construction business. He never lost his love of the sport and had convinced Sharpson to join his efforts to bring professional hockey to his new home town.

Major league franchises in baseball, basketball, football, and hockey all enjoyed large increases in attendance during the sports boom of the 1990s. Minor league hockey was no exception to this success. It included the East Coast Hockey League, of which the Alley Cats were a member. Minor league baseball had grown the fastest of all these sports with new leagues in medium sized and even small cities once considered too small to support a professional team. The success of these leagues encouraged other investors to attempt the same strategy with hockey. Minor league hockey already existed in the colder regions of the country but the Southeast was an untapped market.

There had been little interest in the cold weather sport among sports fans in the Southeast. Football was the favorite sport of this region, particularly college football. The state of Georgia had two highly successful Division I college teams and a Division I AA team, which had won several national championships. The new hockey league had to educate fans about the nuances of the game and promote it as more than simply a sport. Professional hockey had to be sold as a form of entertainment. In New England and the upper Midwest the winters were cold enough for hockey to be played outdoors. Boys grew up playing hockey and it was a popular sport in the colleges. The Southeast did not have that tradition, and the Alley Cats could not draw from that fan base. Promotions and the concept of offering an evening of entertainment for the family and not just for avid hockey fans were keys to the success of the franchise, despite being far removed from its Canadian origins.

These factors made Tim's position more important to the financial success of the team than they would have in a Northern city of similar size. This fact appealed to Tim when he took the position. He viewed it as a challenge. He felt that if he were successful in a small city in the Southeast then he would certainly be able to move to a larger minor league franchise in the Northern portion of the country and eventually to his ultimate goal of a general manager's position with a National Hockey League team. At first he was reluctant when he was approached about the position by a representative of the owners, but he eventually recognized the opportunity. Also, the challenge of working at a brand new franchise appealed to him.

Tim met the challenge of providing entertainment for the casual hockey fans. He created a special promotion for every home game and was voted the best promotions manager in the league by his peers for the first two years he was with the Alley Cats. Attendance, however, started to fall after the second year and Tim felt there were several reasons.

Civic Center

A critical factor in the franchise's success was the lease arrangement the Alley Cats had with the city's civic center. The first year of the team's existence saw them play their home games in the Berk Auditorium. This building was over 25 years old and better suited to concerts and plays than to hosting hockey matches. It was not built with hockey in mind and had a poor ice-making system. It also had a capacity of only 5,000 which was considered too small by the East Coast Hockey League officials. City officials had promised Sharpson and Bouton that they could move their team into the new downtown civic center, which was then being built. It was designed to accommodate hockey and had a seating capacity of over 8,300. In their second year of existence the Alley Cats moved into their new home. Initially they were quite happy with the facility. They paid only a nominal rental fee, had total control of all food and beverage concessions at games, and received half of all parking fees. The city council, however, which supervised the facility, quickly realized it had vastly underestimated the cost of maintaining it. In their eagerness to attract a professional hockey franchise to the city they made a far too generous arrangement with Alley Cats management.

The lease arrangement was tied to game attendance. The Alley Cats were required to pay the city only a nominal fee for rent. Any ticket revenue above an attendance figure of 2,500 patrons per game was to be divided equally between the Alley Cats and the civic center management. For the first two years of the team's existence, attendance averaged over 4,200 patrons per game. In the past two years, however, attendance at games rarely exceeded 3,000 fans. This figure was enough to barely cover the city's cost of maintaining the facility. The decline in attendance for the past two years had placed a financial strain on the city. Also, to worsen matters, the situation had become a public relations nightmare for city officials.

The local newspaper gave the financial problems extensive coverage. There had been a bitter fight to win approval for the construction of the civic center. Many people, including a portion of the city council, had not been in favor of the construction of the facility. They felt that the bond issue required to finance it placed the city under too heavy a debt load. Several members felt the city had been too eager to get the team as a tenant at the facility. When the financial problems surfaced one of the members contacted the local newspaper, which was more than willing to provide detailed coverage of the problems to its readers. Several council members were quite sensitive to the criticism they received from citizens over the matter.

The major argument against the center voiced among these members was that it was a huge financial obligation to incur for a city with a declining population. The latest census confirmed this fact. It showed that the population within the city limits had fallen by over 7,000 residents since the time of the previous census. Council members pointed to a decline in the services provided by the city as the primary factor for this decrease in residents. Residents, who had the income to do so, had fled to the suburbs. It was the opinion of these council members that the city had more pressing problems than constructing a sports and entertainment facility to further the economic and political interests of a few individuals. More pressing problems such as adequate housing for the poor, funding for schools, and improvements in the highway system needed to be addressed first. They contended that the mayor had pushed through the bond issue because it would be good for his political career. These council members claimed he had aspirations to, at some point, run for the governor's office and it would be beneficial for him to state that during his administration the city built a civic center and brought professional hockey to it.

The city council had gone back to Alley Cat ownership and asked to renegotiate the terms of the lease. Sharpson and Bouton stated that they had entered into the agreement in good faith and they were not interested in discussing any changes until the end of the agreement, which would not occur for another four years. Tensions increased between the two owners and the city council. The newspaper coverage of this strife added to these tensions.

Competition

The first two years of the franchise's existence had been successful. With no other professional sports competition during the fall and winter months, the Alley Cats had the city to themselves. In any city there is a core of individuals who are willing to pay to see professional or college sports. Since there was no Division I college team in the city or even within a 50 mile radius, the Alley Cats' only competition was the class A minor league baseball team. That team was affiliated with an American League team, and since most of the fans in the area were National League fans, the local team enjoyed only a moderate following.

The Alley Cats were able to appeal to the businesses in the city who were interested in using the team's matches as a means of entertaining business clients. Also, they appealed to the sports-minded segment of the population who wanted to view a professional sporting event in the fall and winter months. These two market segments were large enough to sustain the Cats for their first two years of operation. In the third year of their existence a major change occurred.

An indoor professional football team established operations in the city and also played their games in the civic center. This football league was attempting to cash in on the same fan euphoria and economic prosperity that fueled the expansion of professional sports in the 1990s. Very quickly it became clear that the city could not adequately support another professional franchise. Though the Stallions, the new football franchise, played their games in the spring, they proved to be a major competitor for the sports entertainment dollar in the city. Almost overnight Tim saw season ticket sales for the Alley Cats start to decline. This was particularly true among businesses that had supported the team previously. Though this was indoor football, with its shortened field and unique rules, it was still football. The game that most of the city's sports fans grew up with and was their first love.

Economic analysts of sports are aware that there is a finite amount of sports dollars in a city. Only a fraction of the total population is willing to spend discretionary income to attend sporting events. Tim had done a good job of appealing to that segment of the population by actively promoting the Alley Cats and attempting to educate sports-minded consumers about hockey. When the

Stallions arrived, many of these fans shifted their loyalty to the new team. They wanted to support professional sports; but when they faced a choice between the new sport of hockey and the sport they had grown up with, football, they chose the familiar one.

Another factor that contributed to the decline in attendance was, for many, the novelty of the Alley Cats had worn off. It had been a new product when it first came to the city with exciting game promotions. After a point, however, it was difficult to come up with new promotions and fans looked elsewhere to spend their sports dollars. Additionally, there was a decline in the teams' on-ice performance. The team was reasonably successful their first two years, making the playoffs each year. The last two years, however, the team posted a poor winning percentage and failed to make the playoffs.

Demographics

One other factor that Tim had to deal with was the demographic makeup of the area's population. The city in which the Alley Cats played had a large African American population. Within the city, this ethnic group represented almost 70 percent of the total population. In the surrounding metropolitan area that percentage declined to less than 40 percent. Hockey was not a popular sport among African Americans. Very few actually played the game and only a few African Americans had ever played in the National Hockey League. Only a handful of this minority group attended any of the Cats' games. When population figures were evaluated in terms of the size of a metropolitan area needed to support a professional hockey team, total population for the city and metropolitan area had been used. In reality, these figures should have been reduced drastically. Instead of a metropolitan area of 220,000 potential customers, the franchise was really located in a market of under 120,000 individuals, a small population base from which to draw.

Local Economy

One other factor that presented problems for the Alley Cats was the local economy. The unemployment rate had been below four percent when the franchise had started operation in the late 1990s. By 2001 that figure had ballooned to over seven percent. Several large textile firms had closed their doors or severely reduced their workforces. The local economy felt a ripple effect. A large military base, one of the linchpins of the local economy, had reduced its military personnel by more than 30 percent with a subsequent loss of civilian jobs. As a result, the Alley Cats were faced with less discretionary income among their customer base.

With these problems in mind, Tim Mosser needed to develop a marketing strategy to bring fans back to the civic center to support the Cats. He knew he could not have any influence on the local economy and he could not just hope that the Stallions football team would go away. He also knew a mistake had been made by the owners in determining the size of the fan base, but he could not change these conditions. His bosses, Ron Sharpson and Steve Bouton, expected an increase in attendance very soon. Tim knew that his position with the team was in jeopardy if he could not produce this increase and few alternatives were available to him given the present environment.

DISCUSSION QUESTIONS

1. Discuss the alternatives available to Tim Mosser to reverse the trend of declining attendance?
2. What influence does the level of discretionary income among consumers in a community have on the success of a professional sports franchise?
3. What external factors contributed to the success of professional sports franchises during the second half of the 1990s?
4. What changes could be negotiated with the city council to make the lease arrangement of the civic center a more agreeable one for both parties?

PART II

PLANNING FOR MARKET SELECTION DECISIONS

CHAPTER 4

RESEARCH TOOLS FOR UNDERSTANDING SPORTS CONSUMERS

After completing this chapter, you should be able to:

- Discuss the importance of marketing research to sports marketers.
- Explain the fundamental process for conducting sports marketing research.
- Identify the various research design types.
- Describe the process for questionnaire development.
- Understand how to prepare an effective research report.

As the River Rat example illustrates, marketing research is a fundamental tool for understanding and ultimately satisfying customers' needs. As described in Chapter 1, one way of demonstrating a marketing orientation is to gather information used for decision making. Another way of establishing a marketing orientation is to disseminate information and share the marketing information with those responsible for making decisions. Marketing research is viewed as an essential element in marketing-oriented organizations.

The information gathered through marketing research can be as basic as where consumers live, how much money they make, and how old they are. Research also provides information for decision makers in identifying marketing opportunities and threats, segmenting markets, choosing and understanding the characteristics of target markets, evaluating the current market positioning, and making marketing mix decisions.

More specifically, marketing research may provide answers to questions such as the following:

- What new products or services would be of interest to consumers of sport?
- What do present and potential consumers think about our new ad campaign?
- How does the advertising and promotion mix affect purchase decisions?
- What are the latest changes or trends in the marketplace?
- How are consumers receiving sports information and programming?
- What are sports fans spending, and what are they buying?

Marketing Research in Action: The Albany River Rats

The Albany River Rats of the American Hockey League conducted a detailed study to gather information that would guide the planning phase of their strategic marketing process. The research objectives were to examine media usage, consumption behavior, and intentions (e.g., number of games attended and likelihood of attending again), and to explore the demographic characteristics of River Rat fans (e.g., age and gender). In addition, the study was designed to look at how survey responses differed according to fan demographics. For instance, are males more or less likely than females to attend a River Rat's game in the future?

To meet these research objectives, fans were asked to complete a survey at River Rat home games. A total of 1,421 surveys were returned and used for data analysis. Survey questions included:

- How many River Rat games have you attended?
- Would you come to a game again?

- What are the best two nights of the week to attend a River Rats game?
- To what radio stations do you listen?
- On what radio stations have you heard River Rat commercials?
- What newspapers do you read?
- What are your favorite television stations?
- Do you find the intermissions fun?
- Demographic information (age, gender, occupation, and hometown)

Analysis of the overall fan base helped to guide the strategic marketing process for the River Rats. More specifically, the survey helped to target their advertising efforts more efficiently.

Source: Adapted from Mark Hinkle, "River Rats Fan Survey Results and Analysis" (March 2, 1995), Unpublished technical report.

- Who are the biggest sponsors of professional sports leagues or college sports?
- How interested are fans in my team, my players, and in the sport itself?
- How do consumers perceive my team, league, or event relative to competitors?
- What is the best way to promote my sports product or service?
- Who participates in sports, and in what sports are they are participating? Also, where are they participating, and how often?
- Are current consumers satisfied with my sports products and services? What are the major determinants of customer satisfaction?
- What price are consumers willing to pay for my sports product or service?
- What image does the team, player, or event hold with current consumers and potential consumers?

These are just a few of the questions that may be addressed through marketing research. **Marketing research** or **sports marketing research** is the systematic process of collecting, analyzing, and reporting information to enhance decision making throughout the strategic sports marketing process.

Three key issues emerge from this definition. First, marketing research must be systematic in its approach. Systematic research is both well organized and unbiased. The well-organized nature of good research is dependent on adherence to the marketing research process, which is discussed later in this chapter. Researchers must also be careful not to make up their minds about the results of a study prior to conducting it; therefore, researchers must conduct the study in an unbiased manner.

Second, the marketing research process involves much more than collecting data and then reporting it back to decision makers. The challenge of research lies in taking the data collected, analyzing it, and then making sense of the data. Marketing researchers who can collect data, dump it in the computer, and spit out reports are a dime a dozen. The most valuable marketing researcher is the person who has the ability to examine the data and then make recommendations about how the information should be used (or not used) in the strategic marketing process.

Third, the importance of marketing research is found in its ability to allow managers to make informed decisions. Without the information gathered in research, management decision making would be based on guesses and luck. As Woody Hayes, Ohio State's great football coach, once said about the forward pass, "Three things can happen and two of them are bad!"

Finally, the definition states that marketing research is useful throughout the entire strategic sports marketing process. Traditionally, the focus of marketing research has been on how the information can be used in better understanding consumers during the planning phase of the strategic sports marketing process. It is also important to realize that marketing research is relevant at the implementation and control phases of the strategic marketing process. For example, research is used in the control phase to determine whether marketing goals are being met. The following article illustrates how research spending has grown in importance to professional sports.

Research Budgets Increase as Leagues Seek Growth

See that guy chowing on a hot dog, guzzling his beer, and shouting a steady stream of cheers and jeers at the players on the field? What is he thinking? Someone, somewhere is finding out.

Market research about sports fans is suddenly big business. Leagues and teams are relying on syndicated and more costly custom research surveys to study their fans' awareness, avidity, propensity for purchasing specific products, brand loyalty, and just about everything else you can imagine.

The major sports leagues have established in-house research departments, hiring someone specifically to oversee sports research. The NFL and MLB made the move within the past year, and the MLB now spends 25 percent of its marketing and advertising budget on research.

Scarborough Research said that since it formed its sports division five years ago, interest has been so great that it has increased its markets surveyed by one-third.

Tracy Schoenadel, vice president of TNS Intersearch/ESPN Sports Poll, said leagues and teams are doing more focus groups, more telephone surveys and more on-site polls. "They are even getting much better about doing research in the off-season to get ready," she said.

Bill Doyle, vice president of Performance Research, said, "In the past 10 years, market research within sports has gone from almost being nonexistent to being their primary sales tool, with a big jump especially in the last year or two."

Ed Horne, president of NHL Enterprises, added: "We have always done research on TV ratings, but we are paying much greater attention and spending more resources for other types of quantitative and qualitative research."

The leagues are becoming more active to keep fans happy and to make their pitch to sponsors.

New MLB research director, Dan Derian, said that in a universe with so many entertainment options—sports compete not just with each other but with movies and TV series—executives need to understand how to entice and keep their fans while reaching out to untapped markets. Derian regularly tracks which clubs and markets. Derian regularly tracks which clubs and markets are hot, how issues like scheduling and interleague play affect ratings, and the game's popularity.

Jacqueline Parkes, senior vice president of advertising and marketing with MLB, said, "We are always planning forward and need to know we are making the right decisions for the game."

"The leagues need numbers to sell themselves not just to fans but also to business partners. The old way of selling to sponsors and advertisers by emphasizing relationships—both personal ones as a salesman and the image connection between the client and the sport—no longer cuts it," said Howard Goldberg, senior vice president of sports marketing at Scarborough Research. "Every team or league has to justify their value today. It's about accountability."

Roger VanDerSnick, NASCAR's managing director of brand and consumer marketing, said the results of custom research helped close the major sponsorship deal with Nextel.

The research showed that NASCAR fans are more likely than nonfans to use wireless products, and use them more often, use the Internet more often, and are more likely to buy into computer and other tech accessories.

VanDerSnick said NASCAR spends as much as 10 times more on research than just a few years ago. He said custom research costs vary widely—you can have a few questions answered for $5,000 or do a comprehensive study for $120,000.

Doyle said NASCAR's use of research to land Nextel is the "deal of the future. That is the direction leagues are going to need to go."

He said a precursor to the NASCAR deal was custom research the Indy Racing League conducted about five years ago. He said the IRL didn't know what it was looking for but just kept digging into its fans, finding they were twice as likely as nonfans to be Internet savvy. That led the IRL to get Northern Light as the primary sponsor.

The information gathering has gotten more sophisticated to keep up with new marketing strategies. Schoenadel said her company now measures the effect of logos on field signs so teams, networks, and sponsors can evaluate whether a particular client would be better off as a sponsor or just as an advertiser buying television spots.

As for the leagues, while much of the info is still syndicated research gathered in large-scale telephone surveys covering a wide array of topics, the leagues and teams now can easily access and dissect the information provided by surveys, using desktop computer technology to pull together information for presentations, Goldberg says.

For instance, Schoenadel said, the NFL can go online before a meeting and pull out information that shows how many NFL fans use Hertz, or even how many avid NFL fans do. Baseball breaks down the information to create its own Media Tracker and Fan Tracker that MLB sends to 1,000 executives involved in the game. Parkes said these summaries are growing even more detailed—MLB recently provided minute-by-minute All-Star Game ratings as well as comparisons to the NBA Finals and other summer programming.

Goldberg said syndicated research has gotten more in-depth, too: Scarborough's 32-page questionnaire booklet sent to follow-up phone surveys asks detailed questions about avidity levels covering not only major sports but also other potential competitors, including the

WUSA, the IRL, competitive fishing, and professional rodeo. Scarborough is even expanding questions about ticket sales to help the industry understand fan perceptions about season tickets and mini-plans, promotional giveaways, and pricing issues.

"We talk regularly with the researchers to define what we need, including different categories to develop new business partners," Horne said. "When custom research revealed NHL fans to be tech savvy, the league sought more usage data in technology-related categories," Horne said.

The desktop access enables the leagues to break syndicated research out by market to provide teams local information. For instance, the NFL recently performed a premium-seat-holder ticket price survey to help teams understand the level of satisfaction and interest in renewal. The varying needs from market to market are one factor driving leagues to pursue custom research.

"The clubs usually have very specific, targeted questions," said Cary Meyers, the NFL's new director of consumer intelligence. One club requested a survey studying how to extend its reach into a geographic area it was not tapping into fully.

But even on a national level, custom research is becoming crucial. "The syndicated research does tracking over time, which is so important, but it can't get deeper," said Schoenadel. "It can be the basis to form other objectives studied in custom research."

Meyers agreed: "We try to exhaust our resources at the syndicated level first, but we need a unique point of view so we are adding more and more custom research to the mix."

A good example is last fall's national Hispanic study, which Marjorie Rodgers, NFL senior director of brand marketing, said the league is using to pitch sponsors and to plan how to market to Hispanic fans. The study examined the favorite sports among Hispanics, how much NFL merchandise they own, how much they watch the NFL on TV, and product usage on such major categories as cars, beer, and soda. It also provided local data to markets with substantial Hispanic populations. Meyers said the league will use the study to identify areas to do more specific research.

Next up, Meyers said, is a custom study aimed at understanding the league's most avid fans and how they developed their interest and passion for the game. The goal is then to translate the data into a response—figuring out how to nurture that passion in future generations of potential fans.

Similarly, MLB used research after last year's All-Star Game ended inconclusively to help determine ways to improve the game. Fans were livid after MLB allowed the game to end in a tie. Based in part on research, the league

(Continued)

(Continued)

decided that the league that won this year's All-Star Game would have home-field advantage for the World Series.

Parkes said MLB polled fans in the weeks leading up to this year's All-Star Game to determine awareness. Fans were also polled in the immediate aftermath to determine attitudes.

Horne said a recent study that revealed high levels of fan avidity and a sense of connection with teams and players inspired the NHL's recent Seventh Man contest, designed to highlight the league's biggest fans.

Len Perna, president/CEO of Turnkey Sports, said the Florida Panthers recently tested the effectiveness of ticket promotions and discounts in deepening relations with casual fans and learned that most of these cheaper tickets

weren't drawing newcomers but merely devoted fans who were "shopping the offers."

"They were cannibalizing their own full-price ticket sales," said Mark Shugoll, CEO of Shugoll Research, which partners with Turnkey on sports research projects.

MLB's Parkes and the NFL's Rodgers said that most teams won't hire a researcher but that more sales and marketing executives now have research backgrounds and, therefore, will devote more resources and energy to research.

"There is now a hunger for information at the local level," said Meyers. Rodgers added, "They use the league office as a central resource."

Source: Stuart Miller, Street & Smith's Sports Group Publication. Sportsbusinessjournel.com.
Copyright © 1998–2004. Street & Smith's Sports Group. All rights reserved.

THE MARKETING RESEARCH PROCESS

As previously mentioned, marketing research is conducted using a systematic process, or the series of interrelated steps shown in Figure 4.1. Before discussing each step in the research process in greater detail, two points should be kept in mind. First, the basic framework or process for conducting marketing research does not change, although every marketing research problem will. For example, the Detroit Red Wings may engage in research to understand fan satisfaction or the effectiveness of a between-period promotion. Each of these research questions are different. However, the basic marketing research process used to address each question is the same.

Second, you should understand that the steps of the research process are interdependent. In other words, defining the problem in a certain way will affect the choice of research design. Likewise, selecting a certain type of research design will influence the selection of data collection tools. Let us now examine each of the steps in the research process.

DEFINING THE PROBLEM OR OPPORTUNITY

The first and most important step of the marketing research process for sports marketers is to define the problem or opportunity. **Problem definition** requires the researcher to specify what information is needed to assist in either solving problems or identifying opportunities by developing a **research problem statement.** If the research addresses the correct problem or opportunity and seeks to properly define the problem or opportunity, then the project could be successful. However, the data collected may be useless if it is not the information needed by the sports marketing manager.

How does the researcher identify problems or opportunities that confront the sports organization? Initially, information is gathered at a meeting between the researcher and his or her client. In this meeting, the researcher should attempt to collect as much information as possible to better understand the need for research. Table 4.1 shows a list of the typical questions or issues addressed at the first information gathering meeting.

Defining the problem or opportunity

Choosing the research design type

Identifying data collection methods

Designing data collection forms

Designing the sample

Collecting, analyzing, and interpreting

Preparing the research report

FIGURE 4.1   Marketing Research Process

TABLE 4.1   Issues Addressed at Initial Research Meeting

- A brief background or history of the organization or individual(s) requesting the research
- A brief background of the types of research the organization has done in the past, if any
- What information the organization wants and why (i.e., what they plan to do with the information once it is obtained)?
- Who is the targeted population of interest for this research?
- What are the expectations in terms of the timeframe for the research and costs of conducting the study?

RESEARCH OBJECTIVES

Based on this initial meeting, the researcher should have collected the proper information to develop a set of research objectives. **Research objectives** describe the various types of information needed to address the problem or opportunity. Each specific objective will provide direction or focus for the rest of the study.

Here is an example of the research objectives developed for the Sport Sponsorship Survey conducted by Sports & Media Challenge.[1] The broad purpose of the study was to provide information that would assist corporate sports sponsors in better aligning themselves with sports personalities and organizations. More specifically, the research objectives were as follows:

- Rank the most desired characteristics and attributes preferred by sponsors.
- Determine the best process to select personalities and teams for sponsorship purposes.
- Determine the current level of satisfaction and any problems associated with sponsorship purposes.
- Determine the level of sponsorship activity and future trends.
- Determine the types of sports and endorsers needed for sponsorship purposes.
- Profile the types of companies using sports sponsorship as a marketing tool.

Understanding the Value of Sponsorship

Sponsors are increasingly concerned about what results they are getting for their sponsorship dollars. In the 1980s when sponsorship was the "hot" marketing tool, corporate involvement boomed. Properties "came-a-callin" and companies were willing to answer that call. Accountability seemed less an issue than the chance for corporate chieftains to exercise their egos. The chance to sidle up to big name stars or to have one's company associated with a major cause or event, irrespective of the value of that alignment to the company, was often overpowering. As the 1990s draw to a close, the scenario has changed. Big money still chases sponsorships, but with a twist. The value of sponsorships is being called into question much more often than in the past. Every aspect of the marketing mix, from advertising to direct marketing to sales promotion to couponing is under intense scrutiny and sponsorship is no exception.

The cry now heard in more and more corporations is: "Just what are we getting out of these sponsorships, anyway?" Marketing directors and even CEOs are being challenged to justify their forays into event marketing and to quantify the value of their sponsorships. So, how does one go about determining what a sponsorship is doing for a company? How does one determine whether or not a sponsorship is returning anything to the bottom line?

It seems to us that one difficulty that event marketers have in trying to figure out just what their sponsorships are doing is that they are either unable or unwilling to find out the answer! In some instances, the feeling is that there is no real accurate gauge for determining success, especially if the sponsorship is pursued as a means of "improving relationships" or "boosting employee morale." These seemingly "soft" criteria are considered by some in the field to be impossible to measure.

Yet another reason for avoiding measures of effectiveness is fear! Some event marketers try to avoid solid measurement because they worry that the answer will not be to their liking (a phobia we in the advertising business also suffer from on occasion). They know in their "guts" that the sponsorship was beneficial, but avoid trying to quantify these feelings for fear of being proven wrong.

Ironically, the slower we pursue measuring the value of sponsorship, the quicker we may hasten sponsorship's demise. If we do not provide fair and objective estimates of the effects of sponsorship, there may be less money available for sponsorship activities as marketing dollars are allocated elsewhere—perhaps to those areas of marketing that can demonstrate effectiveness.

Evaluating a sponsorship is not usually straightforward.

- There may be imperfect or even conflicting evidence as to what happened.

- There may be a problem deciding what is the relationship between cause and effect.

- Because other elements of the marketing mix may be active at the time of the sponsorship, isolating the effects of the sponsorship may be problematic.

- Because one sponsorship may work differently from another there may be no all-purpose solution for measuring impact.

Despite these problems, we should not give up. In fact, we should pursue solutions as vigorously as possible. Sponsorship is not a "bolt-on" extra to the marketing mix. It is an integral—and, one hopes, a continuing—part of it. So, not only will measuring the effectiveness of sponsorship keep it a viable marketing force, good measurement can, in turn, make the next sponsorship even more effective. If we hope to improve the effectiveness of sponsorship, and thus our entire marketing program, we must make the effort to find out what worked, what didn't work, and why.

THE SPONSORSHIP EFFECTIVENESS GUIDELINES

Any program designed to evaluate a sponsorship must address these issues. While these issues may seem painfully rudimentary, it is surprising how infrequently they are considered.

1. What did we expect to happen?
2. What did happen?
3. Can we isolate the effect of the sponsorship from other marketing activities?
4. What were the reasons for the results, either good or bad?
5. What have we learned from the experience and what will we do better next time?

Let's take a closer look at each of these.

1. What did we expect to happen?
If we are going to look for the results of a sponsorship, it's essential that we start with the end in mind. What kind of results were we hoping for? This sounds obvious, but it is very often ignored. The answer is likely to be found in the original marketing strategy for the brand. Remember sponsorship is not an isolated event. It is an integral part of the brand's overall marketing program—or should be if it isn't.

While a well-integrated marketing program can have many components, there are three basic elements:

- The business objective
- The target audience
- The desired action

BUSINESS OBJECTIVE

The overall business objective to which the sponsorship is expected to contribute is normally expressed in terms of sales, volumes, shares, or prices. Of course, other success criteria may also be in place.

Whichever one we look at, the important thing is to relate our measurements and expectations to the objective—and be realistic about what the sponsorship can actually contribute. If the overall marketing objective is maintenance of a brand share or a small volume increase, it would be wrong to look for huge leaps in these measures on the basis of the sponsorship alone. For example, if our annual business objective is to increase share by two percentage points, how much of that increase can we realistically expect to be accounted for by a sponsorship, no matter how large the commitment.

Not all sponsorships need to show big sales increases to be successful. In fact, our experience suggests that most sponsorships do not generate huge sales increases. Nevertheless, a dramatic sales increase is often taken, without much thinking, as the sole measure of success.

The reason for this, we believe, is that too often a sponsorship is looked at as a "megapromotion" designed to generate a large, immediate bump in sales. However, a sponsorship is more apt to be a brand building tool, one more element of the marketing mix that contributes, over time, to the overall impressions people have of a brand. In the same way that long-term advertising campaigns can help build a brand, so too, can a sponsorship program help build the brand over the long term. A sponsorship is not something that necessarily produces an immediate, short term sales impact. Of course, if the sponsorship is specifically designed to generate immediate sales, then measuring an immediate sales gain probably is the right thing to do. Yet, most sponsorships aren't designed to generate sales in the short term but are often expected to nonetheless!

TARGET AUDIENCE

In attempting to answer the question "What am I getting out of my sponsorship?" we have to consider all the different audiences that a sponsorship can address. Sponsorships are often used to influence or build relationships with various constituencies: consumers, key accounts, vendors, financial institutions, investors, community and civic organizations, and employees.

Here again, what we measure—or, more precisely, whom we measure—often depends on what the brand is supposed to accomplish in the marketplace. If the brand is aimed at young women, any research designed to measure the effectiveness of the sponsorship must be based on a sample of young women. (Of course, it will help if the sponsored property, cause, or event is something that appeals to young women!) Even the biggest brands, and likewise the biggest sponsored properties, don't fulfill a need for everyone.

However, if the sponsorship is designed to energize employees—a worthy objective that may be outside a broader marketplace goal—then a structure has to be in place that will measure just how well the sponsorship accomplished this goal. For example, a company can use its sponsorship as a sales incentive. If its sales people meet or exceed specific sales goals, the company will send the employee and his or her family to the sponsored event. In this case, the company has an excellent measurement device, the meeting or exceeding of set sales quotas, for evaluating its sponsorship.

DESIRED ACTION

A sponsorship should always be in sync with what the overall marketing program is trying to get target customers to do or think. If the marketing program sets out to encourage trial of a new brand, then so should the sponsorship. Consequently, the success of the sponsorship should be determined by how well it encourages trial. If a brand's communications program is designed to increase in-home consumption of a product normally consumed away from home, then the sponsorship should be evaluated on the degree to which it encouraged in-home consumption.

In both of these examples, though, how much trial and how much in-home consumption accounted for by the sponsorship must be predetermined so as to best evaluate sponsorship's impact. Setting specific levels and, more importantly, tracing the results to the sponsorship versus other marketing activity can be problematic. We'll examine some ways to go about tightly tying marketplace results to the sponsorship a little later.

The advice to make sure that the desired action of the sponsorship is consistent with that of the overall marketing program may seem obvious; yet it is not uncommon that a sponsorship is independent from what the brand is trying to get customers to do. Sometimes, no consideration is given at all to what specific action the brand is trying to get customers to take when the value of the sponsorship is being assessed.

2. What did happen?

If we have laid out criteria for what we want to have happen as a result of our sponsorship, it's a heck of a lot easier to evaluate the success or failure of the sponsorship.

Simply put, we want to know if our target audience responded to the sponsorship in the desired way. For example, did it change their perceptions or beliefs about the brand or company? Have they bought more of the product? Have more calls been made to a free phone number to order the product?

(Continued)

(Continued)

3. Isolating the Effects of the Sponsorship

Once we have seen what's happened in the marketplace after our sponsorship has run its course, the next step is to examine critically whether the results are really due to the sponsorship and not some other marketing efforts. Perhaps one of the nastiest problems sponsors face is determining just how much the sponsorship contributed to the marketing goal. Separating the effects of the sponsorship from the effects of other elements of the marketing mix is no small feat. Difficult though it may be, we should still do our best to design measures that reflect the ways we think the sponsorship will work.

For example, DDB has created a tracking study for clients and prospects who are Olympic sponsors. This study allows us easily to determine whether or not consumer awareness of a brand's Olympic sponsorship affects their perception of the superiority of that brand.

For other clients, we have taken their historical sales data as well as information they have on various elements of the marketing mix, such as spending on advertising, sales promotion, price discounting, sponsorships, and so on, and have built "influence models" that can isolate the effects of each element on sales.

4. Reasons for success or failure

In our rush to measure the impact of sponsorship, it is often easy to lose sight of the real reason we need to measure its effect—so we can continue investing in a successful sponsorship or discontinue (or greatly modify the tactics associated with) an ineffective one. We need to know what went right so we can build on that success and not make needless changes, or diagnose what went wrong so the next sponsorship will work better.

Diagnosing success or failure is a matter of detective work, and will involve pulling together and comparing all the information we have about elements of the sponsorship, as well as overall marketplace activity. In particular, we need to examine both the strategic foundation upon which the sponsorship was built and the execution of what took place. In other words, was this truly the best sponsorship for achieving our marketplace objectives, and did we properly market the sponsorship and implement the right tactics both on-premise and to the larger "off-premise" audience?

5. What have we learned from the process and what can we do better the next time?

It is impossible to summarize the range of learning that might come out of the process of measuring sponsorship's impact and how what we learn will affect what we do the next time. Perhaps a few first-hand examples, though, may illustrate why the process is so important.

- In work with an Olympic sponsor, customer awareness of the brand's sponsorship was extremely high. However, perceptions of the brand being "the best in the category" changed only minimally. Thorough examination of all the commercials used in the Olympics' campaign made it clear that the brand used the Olympics as a promotional device for specific items in the line, but did little to exploit the "quality rub-off" that an Olympic alignment can offer. Our recommendation was to cut back (though not eliminate) the number of Olympic-themed promotional commercials, and to increase the number of "brand building" messages that use the brand's Olympic sponsorship as a "proof point" of the brand's quality. As we gear up for the 2000 Olympics, we are about to develop this type of advertising campaign.

- A manufacturer of industrial products with whom we work used its sponsorship of U.S. NASCAR motor-racing to create a special catalog of co-branded "NASCAR-Manufacturer" merchandise available only to its employees. The merchandise was free to employees, the tab being picked up by the company. (Employees could not order more than one unit of each item). The program was a big hit, generating more than $60,000 worth of orders in a few weeks. We looked at which items were particularly popular among employees and recommended to the client that they merchandise these items at retail outlets where their industrial products are purchased. A program is now under way to do exactly that.

A FINAL THOUGHT

The best time to start planning how you will evaluate the effectiveness of a sponsorship is before you even decide which property or properties to sponsor. Or, if you are already committed to a property, then determine what your objectives are and what measures should be put into place for determining whether or not those objectives were met.

Following the Sponsorship Effectiveness Guidelines is not easy and requires a lot of up-front preparation. However, the time you spend at the beginning of the process can pay huge dividends later when the day of reckoning comes, that day when you're asked: "So, what exactly are we getting out of our sponsorships?"

Source: Adapted from Martin Horn and Karen Baker, Measuring the Impact of Sponsorship, *International Journal of Sports Marketing & Sponsorship*, vol 1. no. 2 (Sept–Oct 1999) 296(6).

TABLE 4.2 Marketing Research Proposal Outline

Background and History
Defining the Problem or Opportunity
Research Objectives
Research Methodology
    a. Sample
    b. Procedures
    c. Topical areas
Time Estimate
    a. Design of instrument
    b. Data collection
    c. Data entry
    d. Data analysis
    e. Final report preparation
Cost Estimate

WRITING A MARKETING RESEARCH PROPOSAL

To ensure agreement on the direction of the research between the researcher and the client, a research proposal is developed. A **research proposal** is a written blueprint that describes all the information necessary to conduct and control the study. The elements of the research proposal include background for the study, research objectives based on the need for the research, research methodology, timeframe, and cost estimates. An outline for developing a research proposal is shown in Table 4.2.

CHOOSING THE RESEARCH DESIGN TYPE

Once the researcher is certain that the problem is correctly defined, the research design type is considered. The **research design** is the framework for a study that collects and analyzes data. Although every study is unique and requires a slightly different plan to reach the desired goals and objectives, three research design types have emerged. These design types are called exploratory, descriptive, and causal designs. Whatever research design or designs are ultimately chosen, it is important to remember the crucial principle in research is that the design of the research should stem from the problem.[2]

EXPLORATORY DESIGNS

Exploratory designs are useful when research problems are not well defined. For instance, the general manager for the River Rats may say that ticket sales are down, but he is unsure why. In this case, an exploratory research design would be appropriate because there is no clear-cut direction for the research. The research is conducted to generate insight into the problem or to gain a better understanding of the problem at hand. For example, the researcher may recommend examining AHL attendance trends or conducting one-on-one interviews with team management to determine their ideas about the lack of attendance. Because exploratory research design types address vague problems, a number of data collection techniques are possible. These data collection techniques will be addressed during the next phase of the research process.

DESCRIPTIVE DESIGNS

If the research problem is more clearly defined, then a descriptive design is used. A descriptive design type describes the characteristics of a targeted group by answering questions such as who, what, where, when, and how often. The targeted group or population of interest to the decision maker might be current season ticket holders, people in the geographic region who have not attended any games, or a random group of people in the United States.

The River Rats study used a descriptive research design. The targeted group in this case was fans attending River Rat home games. Characteristics of the group of interest in the study included where the fans were coming from (geographic area), how often they attended games, when they were most likely to attend games (weekends, weekdays, day, or evening), and demographics (age and gender).

In addition to describing the characteristics of a targeted group, descriptive designs show the extent to which two variables differ or correlate. For example, a researcher may want to examine the relationship between game attendance and merchandising sales. Using the River Rat's example, researchers wanted to understand the relationship between age of the fans and likelihood of attending games in the future. A descriptive research design type would allow us to examine the relationship or correlation between these two variables (age and future attendance).

If a positive relationship were found between age and likelihood of attending games in the future, then the older you get, the more likely you would be to attend future River Rat games. That is, as the age of the fan increases, the likelihood of going to future games also increases (see Figure 4.2a). However, a negative relationship means that as age increases, the likelihood of going to games decreases (see Figure 4.2b). Knowing the shape of this relationship will help the River Rat's marketers make decisions on who to target and how to develop the appropriate marketing mix for this group. What do you think the relationship between age and attendance would look like?

CAUSAL DESIGNS

Using a descriptive design, we can explore the relationship between two variables, such as age and likelihood of attending games in the future. However, what this does not tell us is that age causes the likelihood of attending to either increase or decrease. This can only be determined through a causal design.

Causal designs are useful when problems are very clearly defined. More specifically, causal designs examine whether changing the level of one variable causes the level of another variable to change. This is more commonly called a cause-and-effect relationship.

In an example of a causal design, the River Rats could conduct a study to determine whether varying the level of advertising on a local radio station has any effect on attendance. In this case, level of advertising is the independent variable and attendance

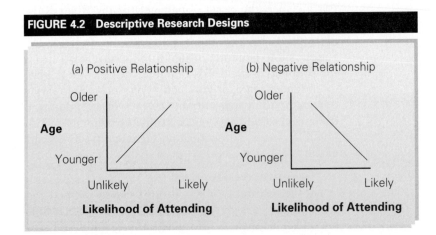

FIGURE 4.2 Descriptive Research Designs

is the dependent variable. The **dependent variable** is the variable to be explained, predicted, or measured (i.e., attendance). The **independent variable** is the variable that can be manipulated or altered in some way (i.e., level of advertising or perhaps whether to advertise at all).

To show cause-and-effect relationships, three criteria must be satisfied. The first criterion for causality is that the occurrence of the causal event must precede or be simultaneous to the effect it is producing. Using our example, advertising must precede or occur at the same time as the increase in attendance to demonstrate a cause-and-effect relationship.

The second criterion for causality involves the extent to which the cause and the effect vary together. This is called **concomitant variation.** If advertising expenditures are increased, then season ticket sales should also increase at the same rate. Likewise, when advertising spending is decreased, season ticket sales should also decline. Keep in mind, however, that concomitant variation does not prove a cause-and-effect relationship, but it is a necessary condition for it.

A third criterion used to show causal relationships requires the elimination of other causal factors. This means that another variable or variables may produce changes in the independent variable. This possibility is called a spurious association or spurious correlation. In the dynamic sports marketing environment, it could be difficult to isolate and eliminate all possible causal factors. For instance, an increase in attendance may be due to the success of the team, ticket prices, and addition of other promotions (e.g., puck night) rather than increased advertising. A researcher must attempt to either eliminate these other potential factors, hold them constant, or adjust the results to remove the effects of any other factors.

IDENTIFYING DATA COLLECTION TECHNIQUES

As with the previous steps in the research process, decisions regarding data collection techniques are very much a function of problem definition and research design type. If the research problem is loosely defined and requires an exploratory research design, then there are more alternatives for collecting that information. However, for well-specified problems using a causal design, the choice of data collection techniques decreases dramatically.

Data collection techniques can be broadly categorized as secondary or primary. **Secondary data** refer to data that were collected earlier but are still related to the research question. This data may come from within the sports organization or from outside the organization. For example, useful internal secondary data might include a history of team merchandise sales figures, event attendance figures, or fan satisfaction studies that were conducted previously. External secondary data, or data from outside the organization, may come from any number of the sources presented later in this chapter.

Although a researcher should always try to use existing data before conducting his or her own inquiries, it is sometimes impossible to find data relevant to the problem at hand. In that case, research must turn to the other data collection alternative, primary data. **Primary data** is information gathered for the specific research question at hand.

Before turning our discussion to the various types of primary and secondary data, it is important to note that both types of data are useful in understanding consumers. For example, sports marketers from the Phoenix Cardinals may want to look at trends in merchandising sales for each NFL team before undertaking a study to determine why their sales have decreased. In this case, secondary data is a useful supplement to the primary data they would also need to collect.

SECONDARY DATA

As just mentioned, secondary data may be found within the sports marketing organization (internal secondary data) or from outside sources (external secondary data). External secondary data can be further divided into the following categories:[3]

- government reports and documents;
- standardized sports marketing information studies;
- trade and industry associations; and
- books, journals, and periodicals.

GOVERNMENT REPORTS AND DOCUMENTS

As we discussed in Chapter 3, environmental scanning is an essential task for monitoring the external contingencies. Government reports and documents are excellent sources of data for sports marketers exploring the marketing environment. Government sources of data can provide demographic, economic, social, and political information at the national, state, and local levels. This information is generally abundant and can be obtained at no cost. There are thousands of government sources that are useful for environmental scanning. In fact, many are now published on the Internet. Let us look at a few of the most useful sources of government data.

Bureau of the Census of the U.S. Department of Commerce (www.census.gov) The Bureau of the Census is one of the most comprehensive sources of secondary data that is readily available via the Internet. Here are some of the census documents that may be of interest: Census of Population, Census of Retail Trade, Census of Service Industries, and Census of Manufacturing Industries.

The Statistical Abstract of the United States (www.census.gov/stat_abstract) The *Statistical Abstract of the United States*, which is published each year by the Bureau of the Census, is an excellent place to begin a search for secondary data. In addition to more general statistical information on the population and economy, the *Statistical Abstract* has a section entitled, "Parks, Recreation and Travel." Within this section, statistics can be found on both participants and spectators.

Chambers of Commerce Usually, Chambers of Commerce have multiple sources of demographic information about a specific geographic area, including education, income, and businesses (size and sales volume). This type of information can be helpful to sports marketers conducting research on teams or events within a metropolitan area.

Small Business Administration (SBA) SBA-sponsored studies can be a valuable source for the environmental scan. The sources include statistics, maps, national market analyses, national directories, library references, and site selection.

STANDARDIZED SPORTS MARKETING INFORMATION STUDIES

Although government sources of secondary data are plentiful, they are generally more useful for looking at national or global trends in the marketing environment. Standardized sports marketing information studies, such as the ESPN Sports Poll or the Sports Business Research Network, focus more specifically on sports consumers and markets. In fact, these sources of secondary data can provide extremely specialized information on consumers of a specific sport (e.g., golf) at a specific level of competition or interest (avid golfers). Table 4.3 shows the table of contents for a standardized study available for better understanding the golf market in North America.

These studies are called standardized because the procedures used to collect the information and the type of data collected are uniform. Once the information is collected, it is then sold to organizations that may find the data useful. Although the data

TABLE 4.3 **North American Golf Report Table of Contents**

Executive Summary
Golf Supply
  Golf Supply by Country
  Population per 18 Holes
  Courses by State
Golf Development
  Golf Development by Country
  Golf Course Openings (1850–1999)
  Recent Golf Course Openings (1985–1999)
  New Openings by State (1990–1999)
Golfer Participation
  Golfer Participation by Country
  Golfer Participation by State
  Number of Golfers by State
Regional Breakdown of Supply, Growth and Participation
Trade in Golf-Related Goods
  Imports and Exports by Country

Source: http://www.golf-research-group.com/reports/report/22/content.html.
Used by permission of the Golf Research Group. All rights reserved.

TABLE 4.4 **Standardized Sports Marketing Information Studies**

Team Marketing Report's Sports Sponsor Factbook
Team Marketing Report's Stadium Signage Report
Team Marketing Report's Inside the Ownership of Professional Sports Team
IEG's Sponsorship Report
IEG's Intelligence Reports
Sports & Media Challenges Sports Sponsorship Survey
National Sporting Good Manufactuers' Sports Media Index
National Sporting Good Manufactuers' Country Market Research Studies
American Sports Data's American Sport Analysis Reports
National Golf Foundation's Golf Business Publications
Gallup Poll's Sports Participation Trends
Simmons Market Research Bureau's Study of Media & Market, Sports & Leisure
ESPN Chilton Sports Poll
Yankolovich Monitor Sports Enthusiast Profile

collected are more specific than other sources of secondary data, the data may still not directly address the research question. Table 4.4 shows a sampling of the standardized sources of secondary data that may be useful to sports marketers.

TRADE AND INDUSTRY ASSOCIATIONS

There are hundreds of associations that can be helpful in the quest for information. Sports associations range from the very broad in focus (e.g., NCAA) to the more specific (e.g., The Association of Black Sporting Goods Professionals). For example, the Women's Sport Foundation (www.womenssportsfoundation.org), established in 1974 by Billie Jean King, works to improve public understanding of the benefits of sports and fitness for females of all ages. To support this educational objective, the foundation has a number of publications and research reports that serve as excellent sources of secondary data. In fact, the Women's Sport Foundation now has a cyberlibrary that

The growing number of women's sports participants are being monitored through secondary marketing research.

contains 25 years of information gathered on topics and issues such as business, coaching, ethics, gender equity, history, homophobia, leadership and employment, media, medical, participation, sexual harassment, special needs, and training and fitness. Here is just a small sampling of trade and sport associations:

North American Society for Sport Management
European Association for Sport Management
Institute of Sport and Recreation Management
National Association of Sports Commissions
Sport Management Association of Australia and New Zealand
Sporting Goods Manufacturers Association
National Collegiate Athletic Association

BOOKS, JOURNALS, AND PERIODICALS

In addition to the books and journals listed here, a comprehensive list of referenced articles published in sports marketing is available, at no cost, from the University of Connecticut's Laboratory for Leisure, Tourism, and Sport. The reference list can also be found on the Internet (http://playlab.uconn.edu/frl.htm). In addition, a comprehensive list of periodicals related to sport can be found on the Sport Information Resource Center's Web site (www.sportquest.com).

BOOKS

IEG's Complete Guide to Sponsorship
Sport Marketing (Mullins, Hardy, & Sutton)
Sports Marketing: Competitive Business Strategies for Sport (Brooks)
Sport Marketing (Pitts and Stotlar)
Team Marketing Report's Newsletter
Cases in Sport Marketing (McDonald and Milne)
Case Studies in Sport Marketing (Pitts)
Successful Sports Marketing and Sponsorship Plans (Potlar)
Sports Marketing: Global Marketing Perspectives (Schlossberg)
Sports Marketing: It's Not Just a Game Anymore (Schaaf)
Sports Marketing: Famous People Sell Famous Products (Pemberton)
Sports Marketing: The Money Side of Sports (Pemberton)
Sports Marketing/Team Concept (Leonardi)
The Sports Marketing Guide (Wascovich)
Keeping Score: An Inside Look at Sports Marketing (Carter)

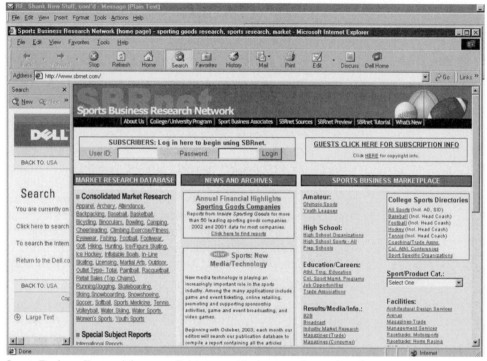

Sports Business Research is an excellent source of primary and secondary data.
Source: www.sbrnet.com. Sports Business Research Network.

Ultimate Guide to Sport and Event Marketing (Graham, Goldblatt, and Delpy)
Sports Marketing: Managing the Exchange Process (Milne and McDonald)

ACADEMIC JOURNALS OF INTEREST TO SPORTS MARKETERS

Sports Marketing Quarterly
Journal of Sport Behavior
Journal of Sport and Social Issues
Journal of Sport Management
Journal of Services Marketing
International Journal of Sports Marketing and Sponsorship
Sport Management Review

PRIMARY DATA

Data collected specifically to answer your research questions are called **primary data.**
There are a wide variety of primary data collection techniques. Again, remember that
your method of collecting primary data is dependent on the earlier choice of research
design. Let us look briefly at some of the primary data collection methods and their
pros and cons.

DEPTH INTERVIEWS

Depth interviews are a popular data collection technique for exploratory research.
Sometimes called "one-on-ones," depth interviews are usually conducted as highly
unstructured conversations that last about an hour. *Unstructured* means that the
researcher has a list of topics that need to be addressed during the interview, but the
conversation can take its natural course. As the respondent begins to respond, new
questions may then emerge and require further discussion.

The primary advantage of depth interviews is that detailed information is gathered on the research question. Researchers may also prefer depth interviews to other primary methods when it is difficult to coordinate any interface with the target population. Just think of the difficulty in trying to organize research using professional athletes as the target population. For instance, a sports marketing researcher may want to determine what characteristics a successful athlete-endorser requires. To address this research question, depth interviews may be conducted with professional athletes who have been successful endorsers, athletes who have never endorsed a product, brand managers of products being endorsed, or any other individuals who may provide insight into the research question. The responses given in these interviews then would be used to determine the characteristics of a successful endorser.

Depth interviews may also be appropriate when studying complex decision making. For example, researchers may want to find out how others influence your decision to attend a sporting event. The information gathered in the depth interviews at the initial phase of this research may then be used in the development of a survey or some other type of primary research. In yet another example, depth interviews were used in a study to understand the decision-making process used by corporate sponsors.[4]

FOCUS GROUPS

Another popular exploratory research tool is the use of focus groups. A **focus group** is a moderately structured discussion session held with eight to 10 people. The discussion focuses on a series of predetermined topics and is led by an objective, unbiased moderator. Much like depth interviews, focus groups are a qualitative research tool used to gain a better understanding of the research problem at hand. For instance, focus groups may be useful in establishing a team name or logo design, what food to offer for sale in the concession areas, how best to reposition an existing sporting goods retailer, or what kinds of things would attract children to a collegiate sporting event. Let us look at two examples of sports organizations that have used focus groups.

Louisiana State University's athletic department used focus group, among a number of other research techniques, to better understand reactions to possibly raising season ticket prices for the 2004 season.[5] The results and discussion from these groups provided the direction for the strategic sports marketing process at LSU. In another example, the Ottawa Lynx, the Triple A affiliate of the Baltimore Orioles, used focus group information to help understand how to draw more fans. Through these focus groups, the Lynx assessed what people think of the team and why the community is not supporting the team. Findings included putting more emphasis on marketing to kids and getting the team more involved in the local community, so fans would identify with the players.[6]

Focus group and observers.

TABLE 4.5 Planning and Implementing Focus Groups

Q. How many people should be in a focus group?
A. Traditionally, focus groups are composed of 8 to 10 people. However there is a current trend toward minigroups of 5 to 6 people. Minigroups are easier to recruit and allow for better and more interaction among focus group participants.

Q. How many people should I recruit, if I want eight people in my group?
A. The general rule of thumb is to recruit 25 percent more people than the number needed. For example, if you are planning on holding minigroups with 6 people, you should recruit eight. Unfortunately, some respondents will not show up for the group, even if there is an incentive for participation.

Q. What is a good incentive for participants?
A. Naturally, a good incentive depends largely on the type of individual you want to attract for your group. For example, if your group wants to target runners who might be participating in a local 10K race, $35 to $50 may be the norm, including dinner or light snacks. However, if your group requires lawyers to discuss the impact of Title IX on the NCAA, an incentive of $75 to $100 may be more appropriate. In addition to or instead of cash, noncash incentives could also serve as an incentive for participation. For example, free tickets or merchandise may work better than cash for some groups.

Q. Where should the focus groups be conducted?
A. The best place to conduct focus groups is at a marketing research company that has up-to-date focus group facilities. The facility is usually equipped with a one-way mirror, videotape, microphones connected to an audio system, and an observation room for clients. In addition, more modern facilities have viewing rooms that allow the client to interact with the moderator via transmitter while the group is being conducted.

Q. How should I choose a moderator?
A. There is no rule of thumb, but research has identified a set of characteristics that seem to be consistent among good moderators. These characteristics include the following: quick learner, friendly leader, knowledgeable but not all-knowing, excellent memory, good listener, a facilitator—not a performer, flexible, empathic, a "big-picture" thinker, and a good writer. In addition, a good moderator should have a high degree of sports industry knowledge or product knowledge.[7]

Q. How many groups should be conducted?
A. The number of groups interviewed is dependent on the number of different characteristics that are being examined in the research. For example, Notre Dame may want to determine whether regional preferences exist for different types of merchandise. If so, two groups may be conducted in the North, two groups in the South, and so on. Using the previous example, if lawyers were the participants in a focus group, two or three total groups may suffice. Any more than this and the information would become redundant and the groups would become inefficient.

Q. What about the composition of the groups?
A. A general rule of thumb is that focus group participants should be homogenous. In other words, people within the group should be as similar as possible. We would not want satisfied, loyal fans in the same group as dissatisfied fans. Similarly, we would not want a group to be composed of both upper-level managers and the employees that report to them. In the latter case, lower-level employees may be reluctant to voice their true feelings.

Conducting focus groups, like those in the LSU and Ottawa examples, requires careful planning. Table 4.5 provides questions and answers that must be considered when planning and implementing focus groups.

PROJECTIVE TECHNIQUES

Another source of data collection is through the use of projective techniques. **Projective techniques** refer to any of a variety of methods that allow respondents to project their feelings, beliefs, or motivations onto a relatively neutral stimulus. Projective techniques were developed by psychologists to uncover motivations or to understand personality. The most famous projective technique is the Rorschach test, which asks respondents to assign meaning to a neutral inkblot. Although the Rorschach may not have value for sports marketing researchers, other projective techniques are useful. For instance,

1. People who wear Fila footwear are _____ .

2. When I think of Fila, I _____ .

3. I would be most likely to buy Fila shoes for _____ .

FIGURE 4.3 Sentence Completion Test

sentence completion, word association, picture association, and cartoon tests could be employed as data collection techniques. Figure 4.3 demonstrates the use of sentence completion to gain insight into consumer attitudes toward Fila. The responses to these sentences could be analyzed to determine consumer perceptions of the target market for Fila (question 1), the brand image of Fila (question 2), and product usage (question 3).

SURVEYS

Data collection techniques are more narrowly defined for descriptive research design types. As stated earlier, a descriptive study describes who, where, how much, how often, and why people are engaging in certain consumption behaviors. To capture this information, the researcher would choose to conduct a survey. Surveys allow sports marketing researchers to collect primary data such as awareness, attitudes, behaviors, demographics, lifestyle, and other variables of interest. For example, the Cleveland Indians handed out roughly 30,000 surveys over 14 games to understand fans' perceptions of the team's on-the-field winning prospects, the quality of the team's management and commitment to winning, and pricing issues. Glenn Goodstein, director of J. D. Power's newly formed sports division, points out that "10 years ago, if the teams won, that was all that mattered—who cared what fans thought. But that is changing. Soon, about 75 percent of more than 100 professional sports teams in the country will be doing (this kind of research)."[8]

Surveys that are considered "snapshots" and describe the characteristics of a sample at one point in time are called **cross-sectional studies.** For example, if a high school athletic program wanted to measure fan satisfaction with its half-time promotions at a basketball game, cross-sectional design would be used. However, if a researcher wanted to investigate an issue and examine responses over a longer period of time, a **longitudinal study** would be used. In this case, fan satisfaction would be measured, improvements would be made to the half-time promotions based on survey responses, and then fan satisfaction would be measured again at a later time. Although longitudinal studies are generally considered more effective, they are not widely used due to time and cost constraints.

EXPERIMENTS

For well-defined problems, causal research is appropriate. As stated earlier, cause-and-effect relationships are difficult to confirm. **Experimentation** is research in which one or more variables are manipulated while others are held constant; the results are then measured. The variables being manipulated are called independent variables, whereas those being measured are called dependent variables.

An experiment is designed to assess causality and can be conducted in either a laboratory or a field setting. A laboratory, or artificial setting, offers the researcher greater degrees of control in the study. For example, Major League Baseball may want to test the design of a new logo for licensing purposes. Targeted groups could be asked to evaluate the overall appeal of the logo while viewing it on a computer. The researchers could then easily manipulate the color and size of the logo (independent variables) while measuring the appeal to fans (dependent variable). All other variation in the design would be eliminated, which offers a high degree of control.

Unfortunately, a trade-off must be made between experimental control and the researchers' ability to apply the results to the "real purchase situation." In other words, what we find in the lab might not be what we find in the store. Field studies, therefore, are conducted to maximize the generalizability of the findings to real shopping experiences. For example, MLB could test the different colors and sizes of logos by offering them in three different cities of similar demographic composition. Then, MLB could evaluate the consumer response to variations in the product by measuring sales. This common approach to experimentation used by sports marketers is called test marketing.

Test marketing is traditionally defined as introducing a new product or service in one or more limited geographic areas. Through test marketing, sports marketers can collect many valuable pieces of information related to sales, competitive reaction, and market share. Information regarding the characteristics of those purchasing the new products or services could also be obtained. First Union Bank ran a two-week test market to determine consumer preference for two debit cards. One of the debit cards featured NASCAR driver Wally Dallenbach and the other was an Atlanta Braves card. The test showed that consumers preferred the NASCAR card—1,800 people chose the Dallenbach version compared with only 300 that chose the Braves' card.[9] Another test market recently occurred in Columbus, Ohio, for Major League Lacrosse. Columbus, known as a good test market city because of its demographic composition, featured a star-studded demonstration match. If the game drew more than 5,000 spectators, the league was likely to consider Columbus as a strong possibility for a new franchise.[10]

Although test marketer information is invaluable to a sports marketer wanting to roll out a new product, it is not without its disadvantages. One of the primary disadvantages of test marketing is cost and time. Products must be produced, promotions or ads developed, and distribution channels secured—all of which cost money. In addition, the results of the test market must be monitored and evaluated at an additional cost. Another problem related to test marketing is associated with competitive activity. Often, competitors will offer consumers unusually high discounts on their products or services to skew the results of a test market. In addition, competitors may be able to quickly produce a "me-too" imitation product or service by the time the test market is ready for a national rollout.

The problems of cost, time, and competitive reaction may be alleviated by means of a more nontraditional test market approach called a **simulated test market.** Typically, respondents in a simulated test market participate in a series of activities, such as (1) receiving exposure to a new product or service concept, (2) having the opportunity to purchase the product or service in a laboratory environment, (3) assessing attitudes toward the new product or service after trial, and (4) assessing repeat purchase behavior.

DESIGNING DATA COLLECTION INSTRUMENTS

Once the data collection method is chosen, the next step in the marketing research process is designing the data collection instrument. Data collection instruments are required for nearly all types of data collection methods. Guides are necessary for depth interviews and focus groups. Data collection forms are needed for projective techniques. Even experiments require data collection instruments.

One of the most widely used data collection instruments in sports marketing is the questionnaire or survey. All forms of survey research require the construction of a questionnaire. The process of designing a questionnaire is shown in Figure 4.4.

SPECIFY INFORMATION REQUIREMENTS

As the first step of **questionnaire design,** the information requirements must be specified. In other words, the researcher asks what information needs to be gathered via the questionnaire. This should be addressed in the initial step of the research process if

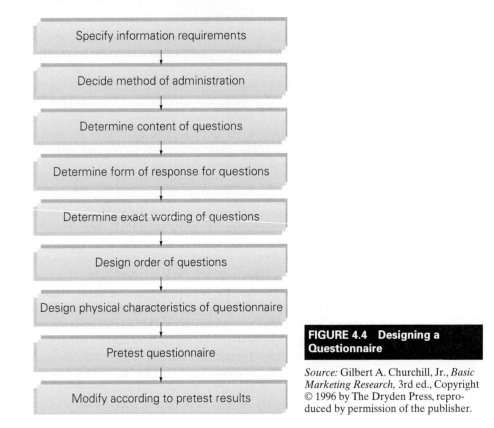

FIGURE 4.4 Designing a Questionnaire

Source: Gilbert A. Churchill, Jr., *Basic Marketing Research,* 3rd ed., Copyright © 1996 by The Dryden Press, reproduced by permission of the publisher.

the problem is carefully defined. Remember, in the first step of the marketing research process, research objectives are developed based on the specified information requirements. The research objectives are a useful starting point in questionnaire design because they indicate what broad topic will be addressed in the study.

DECIDE METHOD OF ADMINISTRATION

The method of administration is the next consideration in questionnaire design. The most common methods of administration are via mail, phone, e-mail, Web sites, or personal interview. Each method has its own unique advantages and disadvantages that must be considered (see Table 4.6). For example, if a short questionnaire is designed to measure fan attitudes toward the new promotion, then a phone survey may be appropriate. However, if the research is being conducted to determine preference for a new logo, then mail or personal interviews would be necessary.

DETERMINE CONTENT OF QUESTIONS

The content of individual questions is largely governed by the method of administration. However, several other factors must be kept in mind. First, does the question address at least one research objective? Second, are several questions necessary to answer an objective? Contrary to popular belief, more is not always better. Third, does the respondent have the information necessary to answer the question? For example, a respondent may not be able to answer questions regarding personal seat licenses if they do not have a full understanding or description of what is meant by a PSL. Finally, will the respondent answer the question?

Web surveys are continuing to grow in popularity.

Source: Used by permission of the Washington Baseball Club LLC.

TABLE 4.6   Comparison of Methods of Administration

	Methods of Administration			
Issues	*Mail*	*Telephone*	*Stadium and Event Interviews*	*Internet*
Costs	Inexpensive	Moderately expensive	Most expensive because of time	Inexpensive
Ability to use complex survey	Little, because self-administered	Same	Greatest because interviewer is present	Little, because self-administered
Opportunity for interviewer bias	None	Same	Greatest because interviewer is present	None
Response rate	Lowest	Moderate	Greatest	Low
Speed of data collection	Slowest	High	Medium to high	High

Sometimes respondents possess the necessary information, but they elect not to respond. For instance, questionnaires may sometimes ask sensitive questions (e.g., income levels) that respondents will not answer.

DETERMINE FORM OF RESPONSE

After deciding on the content of the questions, the form of response should be considered. The form of the response is dependent on the degree of structure in the question. Unstructured questionnaires use a high number of open-ended questions. These types of questions allow respondents to provide their own responses rather than having to choose from a set of response categories provided by the researcher. The following are examples of open-ended questions:

- How do you feel about personal seat licenses?
- How many years have you been a season ticket-holder?
- How will the personal seat license affect your attitude toward the team?

DETERMINE EXACT WORDING OF QUESTIONS

One of the most rigorous aspects of questionnaire design is deciding on the exact wording of questions. When constructing questions, the following pitfalls should be avoided:

- **Questions Should Not Be Too Lengthy**—Lengthy, run-on questions are difficult to interpret and have a higher likelihood of being skipped by the respondent.
- **Questions Should Not Be Ambiguous**—Clarity is the key to good survey design. For instance, "Do you like sports?" may be interpreted in two very different ways. One respondent may answer based on participation, whereas another may answer from a spectator's viewpoint. In addition, there may be ambiguity in how the respondent defines sport. Some respondents would call billiards a sport, whereas others may define it as a game.
- **Questions Should Not Be Double Barreled or Contain Two Questions in One**— For example, "Do you enjoy collecting and selling baseball cards?" represents a double-barreled question. This should be divided into two separate questions. "Do you enjoy collecting baseball cards?" and "Do you enjoy selling baseball cards?"
- **Questions Should Not Lack Specificity**—In other words, clearly define the questions. "Do you watch sports on a regular basis?" is a poorly written question in that the respondent does not know the researcher's definition of regular. Does the researcher mean once per week or once per day?
- **Questions Should Not Be Technical in Nature**—Avoid asking respondents a question that will be difficult for them to answer. For instance, "What type of swing weight do you prefer in your driver?" may be too technical for the average golfer to answer in a meaningful fashion.

DETERMINE QUESTION SEQUENCE

Now that the question wording has been determined, the researcher must determine the proper sequence of the questions. First, a good questionnaire starts with broad, interesting questions that hook the respondents and capture their attention. Similarly, questions more narrow in focus, such as demographic information, should appear at the end of the questionnaire. Second, questions that focus on similar topical areas should be grouped together. For example, a fan satisfaction questionnaire may include sections on satisfaction with concessions, stadium personnel, or game promotions.

Finally, proper question sequencing must consider branching questions and skip patterns. Branching questions direct respondents to questions based on answers to previous questions. For example, the first question on a questionnaire may be, "Have you ever been to a River Rats game?" If the respondent answers "yes," the respondent might continue with a series of questions concerning customer satisfaction. If the respondents answer "no," then they might be asked to skip forward to a series of questions regarding media preferences. Because branching questions and skip patterns are sometimes confusing to respondents, they should be avoided if at all possible.

DESIGN PHYSICAL CHARACTERISTICS OF QUESTIONNAIRE

One of the final steps in the questionnaire development process is to consider carefully the physical appearance of the questionnaire. If the questionnaire is cluttered and looks unprofessional, respondents will be less likely to cooperate and complete the instrument. Other questionnaire design issues include the following:

- Questionnaire should look simple and easy to fill out.
- Questionnaire should have subheadings for the various sections.
- Questionnaire should provide simple and easy-to-understand instructions.
- Questionnaire should leave sufficient room to answer open-ended questions.

PRETEST

After the questionnaire has been finalized and approved by the client, the next step in the questionnaire design process is to pretest the instrument. A **pretest** can be thought of as a "trial run" for the questionnaire to determine if there are any problems in interpreting the questions. In addition to detecting problems in interpreting questions, the pretest may uncover problems with the way the questions are sequenced.

An initial pretest should be conducted with both the researcher and respondent present. By conducting the pretest through personal interview, the researcher can discuss any design flaws or points of confusion with the respondent. Next, the pretest should be conducted using the planned method of administration. In other words, if the survey is being conducted over the phone, the pretest should be conducted over the phone.

The number and nature of the respondents should also be considered when conducting a pretest. The sample for the pretest should mirror the target population for the study, although it may be useful to have other experienced researchers examine the questionnaire before full-scale data collection takes place. The number of people to pretest depends on time and cost considerations. Although pretests slow down the research process, they are invaluable in discovering problems that would otherwise make the data collected meaningless.

DESIGNING THE SAMPLE

After the data collection instrument has been designed, the research process turns to selecting an appropriate sample. A **sample** is a subset of the population of interest from which data is gathered that will estimate some characteristic of the population. Securing a quality sample for sports marketing research is critical. Researchers rarely have the time or money to communicate with everyone in the population of interest. As such, developing a sample that is representative of this larger group of consumers is required.

To design an effective and efficient sample, a variety of sampling techniques are available. Sampling techniques are commonly divided into two categories: **nonprobability sampling** and **probability sampling.** The primary characteristic of nonprobability sampling techniques is that the sample units are chosen subjectively by the researcher. As such, there is no way of ensuring whether the sample is representative of the population of interest. Probability sampling techniques are objective procedures in which sample units have a known and nonzero chance of being selected for the study. Generally, probability sampling techniques are considered stronger because the accuracy of the sample results can be estimated with respect to the population.

NONPROBABILITY SAMPLING

The three nonprobability sampling techniques commonly used are convenience, judgment, and quota sampling. **Convenience sampling techniques** are also called accidental sampling because the sample units are chosen based on the "convenience" of the researcher. For example, a research project could be conducted to assess fans' attitudes toward high school soccer in a large metropolitan area. Questionnaires could be handed out to fans attending Friday night games at three different high schools. These individuals are easy to reach but may not be representative of the population of interest (i.e., high school fans in the area).

Other researchers may approach the same problem with a different data collection method. For example, three focus groups might be conducted to gain a better understanding of the fans' attitudes toward high school soccer. Using this scenario, long-time, loyal soccer fans might be chosen as participants in the three focus groups. These participants represent a **judgment sample** because they are chosen subjectively and, based on the judgment of the researcher, they best serve the purpose of the study.

A quota sampling technique may also be used to address the research problem. In **quota sampling,** units are chosen on the basis of some control characteristic or characteristics of interest to the researcher. For instance, control characteristics such as gender and year in school may be appropriate for the soccer study. In this case, the researcher may believe there may be important distinctions between male and female fans and between freshmen and seniors. The sample would then be chosen to capture the desired number of consumers based on these characteristics. Often, the numbers are chosen so that the percentage of each sample subgroup (e.g., females and juniors) reflect the population percentages.

PROBABILITY SAMPLING

As stated earlier, the stronger sampling techniques are known as probability sampling. In probability sampling, the sample is chosen from a list of elements called a sampling frame. For example, if students at a high school define the population of interest, the sampling frame might be the student directory. The sample would then be chosen objectively from this list of elements.

Although there are many types, a simple random sample is the most widely used probability sampling technique. Using this technique, every unit in the sampling frame has a known and equal chance of being chosen for the sample. For example, Harris Interactive (http://www.harrisinteractive.com/) e-mails a random and representative sample of the U.S. population drawn from a database of more than 6.5 million respondents who have agreed to cooperate. Respondents who agree to participate are directed to the appropriate URL for each survey. The Internet-based methodology allows Harris to randomly sample a minimum of 10,000 people each month on various topics of interest to decision makers in the sports and entertainment industry. A probability sampling technique, such as simple random sampling, allows the researcher to calculate the degree of sampling error, so the researcher knows how precisely the sample reflects the true population.

SAMPLE SIZE

Another question that must be addressed when choosing a sample is the number of units to include in it, or the sample size. Practically speaking, sample sizes are determined largely on the basis of time and money. The more precise and confident the researchers want to be in their findings, the greater the necessary sample size.

Another important determinant in sample size is the homogeneity of the population of interest. In other words, how different or similar are the respondents. To illustrate the effect of homogeneity on sample size, suppose the River Rats are interested in determining the average income of their season ticket holders. If the population of interest includes all the season ticket holders and each person has an income of $50,000, then how many people would we need to have a representative sample? The answer, because of this totally homogeneous population, is one. Any one person that would be in our sample would give us the true income of River Rat season ticket holders.

As you can see from this brief discussion, sample size determination is a complex process based on confidence, precision, the nature of the population of interest, time, and money. Larger samples tend to be more accurate than smaller ones, but researchers must treat every research project as a unique case that has an optimal sample size based on the purpose of the study.

SPOTLIGHT ON INTERNATIONAL SPORTS MARKETING

Measuring the Impact of Cricket Sponsorship

With Cornhill Insurance bringing an end to their 23-year-old relationship with cricket, and Natwest switching their sponsorship from county to international cricket, an independent* study by Performance Research shows cricket fans** recall and value sponsors, but asks whether sponsors are doing enough?

So can fans remember the names of the companies involved with cricket sponsorship? The answer appears to be yes, during spontaneous awareness questioning over 60 different companies were mentioned, and just 2 percent of fans were unable to mention any sponsors. The most frequently mentioned sponsor was Cornhill Insurance, which was mentioned by roughly three-fourths (71 percent) of fans, followed by Natwest (50 percent), and Benson & Hedges (30 percent). The England team sponsor, Vodafone, was mentioned by 22 percent of fans.

What does this all mean? How important is spontaneous awareness for sponsors? Some observers believe spontaneous awareness is an unnecessary objective, a luxury, which may only benefit commodity products such as soft drinks or confectionary. The ability to spontaneously recall sponsors at the point-of-purchase can drive sales, but what can sponsors like Cornhill Insurance and Natwest take from this?

Quite simply the affiliation with a property in terms of credibility and image enhancements can only be effective if the target market is aware of the sponsorship. Although, in this instance aided sponsor awareness may be sufficient to provoke further investigation into the relative merits of each company and the services they offer.

So how did these companies fare when the fans were asked to identify cricket sponsors from a list? Almost all of the fans identified Natwest (98 percent) and Cornhill Insurance (94 percent), while Foster's (94 percent), who sponsor the Oval; and Vodafone (87 percent), a relative newcomer to cricket sponsorship also did well.

After establishing that cricket fans can remember sponsors, the study then asked fans to describe how they felt about the companies as a result of their association with cricket. Roughly one-half of the fans chose the statement *"Sponsorship makes a valuable contribution to cricket and makes me feel better about sponsors."* So for a sponsor associated with test match cricket, positive inferences concerning the credibility of the company are certainly possible.

How can cricket sponsorship be developed further? With awareness levels reaching almost saturation point, sponsors may look beyond awareness and look to leverage their sponsorships. The next step is to build on the positive impressions reported toward sponsors and develop meaningful relationships with fans, enabling them to see how a sponsorship can benefit them, both as cricket fans, and as consumers using that brand.

Finally, when questioned about loyalty to sponsors' products, roughly one-fourth (25 percent) of the cricket fans reported they would *"Almost always"* or *"Frequently"* preferentially choose a sponsors' product because of their involvement with cricket. Good news, but still comparatively low when compared to the loyalty levels reported toward sponsors of other sports in the United Kingdom.

*Staff from Performance Research collected the names and phone numbers of cricket fans attending the 5th Test between England and the West Indies at the Foster's Oval. In the following two weeks 201 cricket fans were recontacted by telephone and asked to complete a short questionnaire. The margin of error for this sample is no more than ±7 percent.

**The respondents were read four statements and were asked to choose one which best described how they support cricket. Roughly one-half (46 percent) of the respondents described themselves as "Avid cricket fans" by choosing the statement; "I make a point to frequently watch and attend cricket matches."

Source: http://www.performanceresearch.com/framesets/f_sponsor_links.htm. Copyright © 2004. Performance research, Newport, Rhode Island. All rights reserved.

DATA ANALYSIS

After the data is collected from the population of interest, data analysis takes place. Before any analytical work occurs, the data must be carefully scrutinized to ensure its quality. Researchers call this the editing process. During this process, the data is examined for impossible responses, missing responses, or any other abnormalities that would render the data useless.

Once the quality of the data is ensured, coding begins. Coding refers to assigning numerical values or codes to represent a specific response to a specific question. Consider the following question:

How likely are you to attend River Rats' games in the future?

1. Extremely unlikely
2. Unlikely
3. Neither unlikely nor likely
4. Likely
5. Extremely likely

The response of *extremely likely* is assigned a code of 1, *unlikely* a code of 2, and so on. Each question in the survey must be coded to facilitate data analysis.

After editing and coding are completed, you are ready to begin analyzing the data. Although there are many sophisticated statistical techniques (and software programs) to choose from to analyze the data, researchers usually like to start by "looking at the big picture." In other words, researchers want to describe and summarize the data before they begin to look for more complex relationships between questions.

Often, the first step in data analysis is to examine two of the most basic informational components of the data—central tendency and dispersion. Measures of central tendency (also known as the mean, median, and mode) tell us about the typical response, whereas measures of dispersion (range, variance, and standard deviation) refer to the similarity of responses to any given question.

To give us a good feel for the typical responses and variation in responses, frequency distributions are often constructed. A frequency distribution, such as the one shown in Table 4.7, provides the distribution of data pertaining to categories of a single variable. In other words, frequency distributions or one-way tables show us the number (or frequency) of cases from the entire sample that fall into each response category. Normally, these frequencies or counts are also converted into percentages.

After one-way tables or frequency distributions are constructed, the next step in data analysis involves examining relationships between two variables. A cross-tabulation allows us to look at the responses to one question in relation to the responses to another question. Two-way tables provide a preliminary look at the association between two

TABLE 4.7 Frequency Distribution or One-Way Table

How likely are you to attend River Rats' games in the future?

	Respondents	
	Number	*Percent*
1. Extremely unlikely	20	13.3
2. Unlikely	30	20.0
3. Neither unlikely or likely	25	16.7
4. Likely	45	30.0
5. Extremely likely	30	20.0
Total	150	100%

TABLE 4.8 Two Way Table or Cross-Tabulation

How likely are you to attend River Rats' games in the future?

		Gender	
		Male	*Female*
1. Extremely unlikely		5	15
2. Unlikely		5	25
3. Neither unlikely or likely		10	15
4. Likely		30	15
5. Extremely likely		25	5
	Total	75	75

questions. For example, the two-way table shown in Table 4.8 explores the relationship between the likelihood of going to River Rats' games and gender. Upon examination, the two-way table clearly shows that females are less likely to attend River Rats' games in the future than males. Implications of this finding may include the need to conduct future research to better understand why females are less likely to attend River Rats' games than males and the design of a marketing mix that appeals to females.

PREPARING A FINAL REPORT

The last step in the marketing research process is preparing a final report. Typically, the report is intended for top management of the sports organization, who can either put the research findings into action or shelve the project. Unfortunately, the greatest research project in the world will be viewed as a failure if the results are not clearly communicated to the target audience.

How can you prepare a final report that will assist in making decisions throughout the strategic marketing process? Here are some simple guidelines for preparing an actionable report:

- **Know Your Audience**—Before preparing the oral or written report, determine your audience. Typically, the users of research will be upper management, who do not possess a great deal of statistical knowledge or marketing research expertise. Therefore, it is important to construct the report so it is easily understood by the audience who will use the report, not by other researchers. One of the greatest challenges in preparing a research report is presenting technical information in a way that is easily understood by all users.
- **Be Thorough, Not Overwhelming**—By the time they are completed, some written research reports resemble volumes of the *Encyclopedia Britannica.* Likewise, oral presentations can drag on for so long that any meaningful information is lost. Researchers should be sensitive to the amount of information they convey in an oral research report. Oral presentations should show only the most critical findings, rather than every small detail. Generally, written reports should include a brief description of the background and objectives of the study, how the study was conducted **(methodology),** key findings, and marketing recommendations. Voluminous tables should be located in an appendix.
- **Carefully Interpret the Findings**—The results of the study and how it was conducted are important, but nothing is as critical as drawing conclusions from the data. Managers who use the research findings often have limited time and no inclination to carefully analyze and interpret the findings. In addition, managers

are not only interested in the findings alone, but they also want to know what marketing actions can be taken based on the findings. Be sure you do not neglect the implications of the research when preparing both oral and written reports.

Summary

Chapter 4 focuses on the tools used to gather information to make intelligent decisions throughout the strategic sports marketing process. More specifically, the chapter describes the marketing research process in detail. Marketing research is defined as the systematic process of collecting, analyzing, and reporting information to enhance decision making throughout the strategic sports marketing process.

The marketing research process consists of seven interrelated steps. These steps include defining the problem; choosing the research design type; identifying data collection methods; designing data collection forms; designing the sample; collecting, analyzing, and interpreting data; and preparing the research report. The first step is defining the problem and determining what information will be needed to make strategic marketing decisions. The tangible outcome of problem definition is to develop a set of research objectives that will serve as a guide for the rest of the research process.

The next step in the marketing research process is to determine the appropriate research design type(s). The research design is the plan that directs data collection and analysis. The three common research design types are exploratory, descriptive, and causal. The choice of one (or more) of these design types for any study is based on the clarity of the problem. Exploratory designs are more appropriate for ill-defined problems, whereas causal designs are employed for well-defined research problems.

After the research design type is chosen, the data collection method(s) is selected. Once again, decisions regarding data collection are contingent upon the choice of research design. Data collection consists of two types—secondary and primary. Secondary data refers to data that was collected earlier, either within or outside the sports organization, but still provides useful information to the researcher. Typically, sources of secondary data include government reports and documents; trade and industry associations; standardized sports marketing information studies; and books, journals, and periodicals. Primary data is information that is collected specifically for the research question at hand. Common types of primary data collection techniques include, but

are not limited to, in-depth interviews, focus groups, surveys, and experiments.

The fourth step in the research process is to design the data collection instrument. Regardless of whether you are collecting data by in-depth interviews, focus groups, or surveys, data collection instruments are necessary. The most widely used data collection technique in sports marketing research is the questionnaire. As such, it is important that sports marketing researchers understand how to construct a questionnaire properly. The steps for questionnaire design include specifying information requirements, deciding the method of administration (i.e., mail, phone, and stadium interview), determining the content of questions, determining the form of response for questions, deciding on the exact wording of the questions, designing the order of the questions, designing the physical characteristics of the questionnaire, pretesting the questionnaire, and modifying it according to pretest results.

Once the data collection forms are constructed, the next step in the research process is choosing a sampling strategy. Rarely, if ever, can we take a census where we communicate with or observe everyone of interest to us in a research study. As such, a subset of those individuals is chosen to represent the larger group of interest. Sampling strategy identifies how we will choose these individuals and how many people we will choose to participate in our study.

Data analysis is the next step in the marketing research process. Before the data can be analyzed, however, it must be edited and coded. The editing process ensures the data being used for analysis is of high quality. In other words, it makes sure that there are no problems, such as large amounts of missing data or errors in data entry. Next, coding takes place. Coding refers to assigning numerical values to represent specific responses to specific questions. Once the data are edited and coded, data analysis is conducted. The method of data analysis depends on a variety of factors, such as how to address the research objectives. The last step in the marketing research process is to prepare a final report. Oral and written reports typically discuss the objectives of the study, how the study was conducted, and the findings and recommendation for decision makers.

Key Terms

- concomitant variation
- convenience sampling techniques
- cross-sectional studies
- data collection techniques
- dependent variable

- experimentation
- focus group
- independent variable
- judgment sample
- longitudinal study

- marketing research
- methodology
- nonprobability sampling
- pretest
- primary data

- probability sampling
- problem definition
- projective techniques
- questionnaire design
- quota sampling

- research design
- research objectives
- research problem statement
- research proposal
- sample

- secondary data
- simulated test market
- sports marketing research
- test marketing

Review Questions

1. Define sports marketing research. Describe the relationship between sports marketing research and the strategic marketing process.
2. What are the various steps in the marketing research process?
3. Define problem and opportunity definition and explain why this step of the research process is considered to be the most critical.
4. What are some of the basic issues that should be addressed at a research request meeting?
5. Outline the steps in developing a research proposal.
6. Define a research design. What are the three types of research designs that can be used in research? How does the choice of research design stem from the problem definition? Can a researcher choose multiple designs within a single study?
7. Describe some of the common data collection techniques used in sports marketing research. How does the choice of data collection technique stem from the research design type?
8. What are some of the central issues that must be considered when conducting focus groups?
9. What are the pros and cons of laboratory studies versus field studies?
10. Outline the nine steps in questionnaire design. What are some of the most common errors in the wording of questions?
11. Define nonprobability sampling and probability sampling techniques. What are three types of nonprobability sampling?
12. What is a sampling frame? How do researchers decide on the appropriate sample size for a study?
13. What are some of the guidelines for preparing oral and written research reports?

Exercises

You are interested in purchasing a new minor league baseball franchise. The franchise will be located in your area. To reduce the risk in your decision making, you have requested that a sports marketing firm submit a detailed research proposal. The following questions pertain to this issue:

1. What is the broad problem/opportunity facing you in this decision? Write the research objectives based on the problem formulation.
2. What type of research design type do you recommend?
3. The sports marketing firm has submitted the following preliminary questionnaire. Please provide a detailed critique of their work.

   Age: _____   Gender: _____

   Are you likely to go to a baseball game at the new stadium?

   Yes ____   No ____

   How many minor league games did you go to last year?

   0–3 ____   4–6 ____   6–9 ____   10+ ____

   What types of promos would you like to see?

   Beer Night _____   Straight-A Night _____   Polka Night _____

4. Now that you have looked at their survey, create a questionnaire of your own. Would any other data collection techniques be appropriate, given the research problem?
5. What sampling technique(s) do you recommend? How is the correct sample size determined, given your choice of sampling technique?

Internet Exercises

1. Using secondary data sources on the Internet, find the following and indicate the appropriate URL (Internet address):
   a. Number of women who participated in high-school basketball last year
   b. Attendance at NFL games last year
   c. Sponsors for the New York City Marathon
   d. Universities that offer graduate programs in sports marketing
2. Using the Internet, find at least five articles that relate to the marketing of NASCAR.
3. Using the Internet, locate three companies that conduct sports marketing research. What types of products and services do the companies offer?

Endnotes

1. "1997 Sports Sponsorship Survey." www.media challenge.com/survey/CSsurvey.html.
2. Gilbert Churchill, *Basic Marketing Research,* 3rd ed. (Ft. Worth: Dryden Press, 1996).
3. Ibid.
4. Kristie McCook, Douglas Turco, and Roger Riley, "A Look at the Corporate Sponsorship Decision Making Process." *Cyber Journal of Sport Marketing,* vol. 1, no. 2 (1997). www.cad.gu.edu.au/market/cy . . . rnal_of_sport_marketing/mcook.html.
5. "Mike Triplett, "Tigers' Bertman is ready to make pitch," *Times-Picayune* (August 21, 2003), 1.
6. "Dave Gross, "Lynx Reach Out and Ask Fans for Imput," *The Ottawa Sun* (December 12, 2002), 81.
7. Gilbert Churchill, *Basic Marketing Research,* 3rd ed. (Fort Worth: Dryden Press, 1996).
8. "Cleveland Indians Look to Long-Term Viability Through Market Research," *Akron Beakon Journal* (April 16, 1999).
9. "IEG Network: Assertions." www.sponsorship.com/forum/assertions.html.
10. Craig Mertz, "Pro Lacrosse League to Test Local Support," *The Columbus Dispatch* (July 7, 2000), 5D.

CHAPTER 5

UNDERSTANDING PARTICIPANTS AS CONSUMERS

After completing this chapter, you should be able to:

- Define participant consumption behavior.

- Explain the simplified model of participant consumption behavior.

- Describe the psychological factors that affect participant decision making.

- Identify the various external factors influencing participant decision making.

- Describe the participant decision-making process.

- Understand the different types of consumer decision making.

- Discuss the situational factors that influence participant decision making.

As the article on Pilates illustrates, new participant sports are growing in popularity all the time. Think about the sports and recreational activities in which you participated during the past month. Maybe you played golf or tennis, lifted weights, or even went hiking. According to data from the National Sporting Goods Association (NSGA) provided in Table 5.1, millions of Americans participate in a variety of physical activities each year.

At this point you may be asking yourself, "Why are sports marketers concerned with consumers who participate in sports?" Recall from our discussion of sports marketing in Chapter 1 that one of the basic sports marketing activities was encouraging participation in sports. Sports marketers are responsible for organizing events such as the Boston Marathon, the Iron Man Triathlon, or the Gus Macker 3-on–3 Basketball Tournament where thousands of consumers participate in sports. Moreover, sports marketers are involved in marketing the equipment and apparel necessary for participation in sports. As you might imagine, sports participants constitute a large and growing market both in the United States and internationally.

To successfully compete in the expanding sports participant market, sports organizations must develop a thorough understanding of participant consumption behavior and what affects it. **Participant consumption behavior** is defined as actions performed when searching for, participating in, and evaluating the sports activities that consumers believe will satisfy their needs. You may have noticed this definition relates to the previous discussion of the marketing concept and consumer satisfaction.

Pilates Craze: It's the Hottest Exercise Trend

The fastest growing fitness trend is a far stretch from the grueling no-pain, no-gain pounding of the 1990s.

Pilates training is stretching to new heights and gaining countless followers with its kinder, gentler style that stretches and strengthens not only the body, but the mind and spirit as well.

Participation in Pilates is up nearly 100 percent in 2002, reports the latest Sports Participation Trends Report put out by the Sporting Goods Manufacturers Association. Yoga and fitness bicycling have made small climbs in the past year, while high-impact aerobics has hit the skids big time.

According to the experts, many aerobic junkies of the past have traded in the jarring gym workout for a more mindful approach to staying fit and healthy.

Pilates is not only a contemporary approach to fitness, but it's also being widely used in rehabilitation to overcome an injury or address chronic pain, says Pilates expert, Laura Helsel. Once a well-kept secret among dancers and celebrities, gym goers—the fit, unfit, and injured—are taking to the mats in droves around the Greater Toronto Area (GTA).

"It's an insane increase," says Helsel, owner of Riverdale Pilates studio in Toronto. "People are really interested in its holistic approach. You come away stronger, standing straighter, with an overall sense of less tension."

Fitness expert Gloria Atkinson agrees: "People are looking to stay fit and healthy in noninjurious ways and they're looking for a change and something different. And Pilates is really different, especially for cardio junkies who in the past equated harder with better."

Pilates has been dubbed the intelligent exercise: "Today people are working out smarter, not harder," says Atkinson, a Pilates instructor and group exercise director at the Ontario Racquet Club (ORC) in Mississauga. "It's definitely the way of the future."

The fact that Pilates provides an effective and efficient workout, adaptable to various body types and fitness levels, even those injured, makes it a popular offering at clubs. The relaxing, yet challenging, low-to-no weight-bearing exercise method focuses on breathing and results in total body strengthening, postural stability, and spinal alignment, says Atkinson.

"It builds core stability, so participants come away being able to apply its techniques to everyday activities, like lifting and turning, to avoid injuries," says Atkinson.

Pilates is not about weight loss, says Atkinson. It increases fitness and overall wellness through improved posture and developing longer, leaner muscles (which, by the way, do keep metabolisms revved up).

The aim is to rebalance the muscles around the joints through a series of exercises usually done on mats, using plastic bands and balls and, in some studios, utilizing resistance apparatus called reformers.

Helsel agrees that today people are willing to go slower to make greater gains. By focusing on gently straightening and strengthening without straining, Pilates offers a wonderful workout and a great way to stay in shape safely.

Source: Joanne Richard, *Sun Media*. (June 20, 2003) Copyright © 2003 Lexis Nexis, a division of Reed Elsevier Inc. All rights reserved.

Sports marketers must understand why consumers choose to participate in certain sports and what the benefits of participation are for consumers. For instance, do we play indoor soccer for exercise, for social contact, to feel like part of a team, or to enhance our image? Also, the study of participant consumer behavior attempts to understand when, where, and how often consumers participate in sports. By understanding consumers of sport, marketers will be in a better position to satisfy their needs.

The definition of participant consumption behavior also incorporates the elements of the participant decision-making process. The **decision-making process** is the foundation of our model of participant consumption. It is a five-step process that consumers use when deciding to participate in a specific sport or activity. Before turning to our model of participant consumption behavior, it must be stressed that the primary reason for understanding the participant decision-making process is to guide the rest of the strategic sports marketing process. Without a better understanding of sports participants, marketers would simply be guessing about how to satisfy their needs.

TABLE 5.1   Top 30 Participation Activities in the United States

Activities and Sports	Number of Participants (in millions)
1. Bowling	53.2
2. Treadmill exercise	43.4
3. Freshwater fishing (not fly)	42.6
4. Tent camping	40.3
5. Billiards/Pool	39.5
6. Stretching	38.4
7. Fitness walking	38.0
8. Day hiking	36.8
9. Basketball	36.6
10. Running/Jogging	35.9
11. Stationary cycling (recumbent, spinning, upright)	29.1
12. Dumbbells	28.9
13. Hand weights	28.5
14. Weight/Resistance machines	27.8
15. Golf	27.8
16. Calisthenics	26.9
17. Barbells	24.8
18. In-line skating	21.6
19. Darts	19.7
20. RV camping	18.7
21. Target shooting (pistol, rifle)	17.6
22. Soccer	17.6
23. Abdominal machine/device	17.4
24. Hunting (shotgun/rifle)	16.5
25. Tennis	16.4
26. Touch football	14.9
27. Saltwater fishing	14.9
28. Horseback riding	14.6
29. Fitness swimming	14.5
30. Ice skating	14.5

Source: SGMA International. Used by permission of SGMA International. www.sgma.com.
This information is based on participation numbers ages six and up in 2002.

MODEL OF PARTICIPANT CONSUMPTION BEHAVIOR

To help organize all this complex information about sports participants, we have developed a model of participant consumption behavior that will serve as a framework for the rest of our discussion (see Figure 5.1). At the center of our model is the participant decision-making process, which is influenced by three components: (1) internal or psychological processes such as motivation, perception, learning and memory, and attitudes; (2) external or sociocultural factors, such as culture, reference groups, and family; and (3) situational factors that act on the participant decision-making process.

PARTICIPANT DECISION-MAKING PROCESS

Every time you lace up your running shoes, grab your tennis racquet, or dive into a pool, you have made a decision about participating in sports. Sometimes these decisions are nearly automatic because, for example, we might jog nearly every day. Other decisions, such as playing in a golf league, require more careful consideration because

Three lifelong sports participants in training.

 SPOTLIGHT ON INTERNATIONAL SPORTS MARKETING

Howzat? Soccer Kicks Cricket Out as Top Game

Soccer has overtaken cricket as the sport most played by Australians, according to a new poll.

A Morgan Poll found soccer's national participation rates in March this year had risen above cricket for the first time.

An estimated 1,218,000 Australians aged 14 or more played soccer, while 1,057,000 played cricket, the poll found.

Soccer was the sport most played by males but netball retained its rating as the preferred participation sport for females, with soccer second.

Overall, basketball (892,000 people) ranked as the third most played sport by Australians, netball (762,000) fourth, and Australian Rules football (585,000) fifth.

Volleyball (sixth) was more popular than contact sports including rugby league (seventh) and rugby union (eighth).

The pollsters interviewed about 100,000 people between April last year and March this year.

In Queensland polling, soccer and handball were the most popular sports played at schools and soccer was the most popular after-school and weekend sport.

Queensland Sport Minister Terry Mackenroth said the Queensland survey, carried out earlier this year, included more than 16,000 students.

The survey was carried out as part of a government program to encourage greater sporting activities among students.

GOOD SPORTS

Results from a Morgan Poll, which found soccer had overtaken cricket as the sport most played by Australians.*

- Soccer: 1,218,000 people
- Cricket: 1,057,000
- Basketball: 892,000
- Netball: 762,000
- Aussie Rules: 585,000
- Volleyball: 501,000
- Rugby league: 405,000
- Rugby union: 240,000

*Note: Figures are participation rates in March 2003. Source: Roy Morgan Poll of about 100,000 Australians aged 14 and over, April 2002–March 2003.
Source: Keith Jackson. *Illawara Mercury.* Illawarra Newspapers Holdings Pty, Ltd. Australia. Reprinted with permission of The Associated Press.

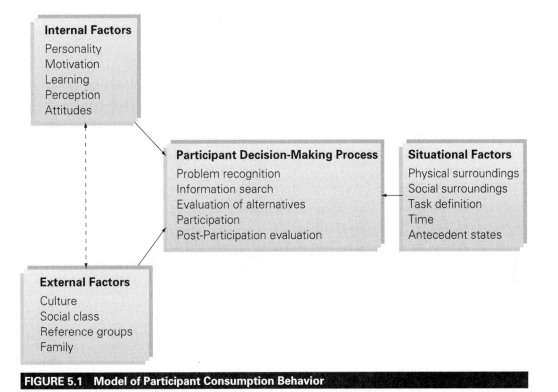

Internal Factors
Personality
Motivation
Learning
Perception
Attitudes

Participant Decision-Making Process
Problem recognition
Information search
Evaluation of alternatives
Participation
Post-Participation evaluation

Situational Factors
Physical surroundings
Social surroundings
Task definition
Time
Antecedent states

External Factors
Culture
Social class
Reference groups
Family

FIGURE 5.1   Model of Participant Consumption Behavior

of the time and cost involved. The foundation of our model of participant consumption behavior is trying to understand how consumers arrive at their decisions.

Participant decision making is a complex, cognitive process that brings together memory, thinking, information processing, and making evaluative judgments. The five steps that make up the process used to explain participant decision making are shown in Figure 5.1. It is important to remember that every individual consumer arrives at decisions in a slightly different manner because of their own psychological make-up and environment. However, the five-step participant decision-making process moving from problem recognition through postparticipation evaluation, is relatively consistent among consumers and must be understood by sports marketers to develop strategies that fit with consumers' needs.

As we progress through the participant decision-making process, let us consider the case of Jack, a 33-year-old male who just moved from Los Angeles to Cincinnati. Jack has always being active in sports and would like to participate in an organized sports league. Because of work and family commitments, Jack only has the time to participate in one league. He is unsure about what sport to participate in, although he does have a few requirements. Because he is a newcomer to the city, Jack would like to participate in a team sport to meet new people. Also, he wants the league to be moderately competitive so as to keep his competitive juices flowing. Finally, he would like to remain injury free, so the sport needs to be non- or limited-contact. Let us see how Jack arrives at this important decision by using the participant decision-making process.

PROBLEM RECOGNITION

The first step in the participant decision-making process is problem recognition. During problem recognition, consumers realize they have a need that is not presently being met. **Problem recognition** is the result of a discrepancy between a desired state and an actual state large enough and important enough to activate the entire decision-making process.[1] Stated simply, the desired state reflects the "ideal" of the participant.

Many consumers see a discrepancy between the "ideal" and "actual" body.

In other words, what is the absolute best sport for Jack to participate in, given his unique needs? If there is a difference between ideal and actual levels of participation, then the decision-making process begins.

The desire to resolve a problem and to reach goals, once recognized by consumers, is dependent on two factors: (1) the magnitude or size of the discrepancy and (2) the relative importance of the problem. Let us look at how these two factors would affect problem recognition. Jack currently jogs on a daily basis and wants to participate in a competitive, organized, and aggressive team sport. Is the discrepancy between actual state (individual, recreational, and nonaggressive) and desired state (team play, competitive, and aggressive) large enough to activate the decision-making process? Let's assume that it is and consider the second condition of problem recognition, the importance of the problem.

The second condition that must be met for problem recognition to occur is that the goal must be important enough to Jack. Some consumers may recognize the difference between participating in recreational sports versus an organized league. Would the benefits of participating in the new organized league (hopefully making some friends and being more competitive) outweigh the time, expense, and energy required to play? If the problem is important enough to Jack, then he moves on to the next stage of the decision-making process—information search.

What strategic implication does problem recognition hold for sports marketers? Generally, we would first identify the actual and desired states of sports participants or potential participants. Once these states have been determined, sports marketers can offer activities and events that will fill these needs and eliminate "problems." In addition, sports marketers can attempt to alter the perceived ideal state of consumers. For example, it is common for health clubs to show the "ideal" body that can be achieved by purchasing a membership and working out.

INFORMATION SEARCH

After problem recognition occurs, the next step in the participant decision-making process is information search. **Information search** occurs when a participant seeks relevant information that will help resolve the problem. The sources of information sought by consumers can be broken down into two types: internal and external sources.

Internal sources of information are recalled from our own memories and are based on previous exposure to sports and activities. The internal information activated from memory can provide us with a wealth of data that may affect the decision-making process. Jack has spent most of his life participating in sports and recreational activities so information based on past experience is readily available. For instance, because Jack has played in an organized league in the past, he would use internal information to recall his experiences. Did he enjoy the competition of organized sport? Why did he stop participating in the sport?

External sources of information are environmentally based and can occur in three different ways. First, Jack might ask **personal sources,** such as friends or family, to provide him with information about possible organized team sports in which to participate. Friends and family are important information sources that can have a great deal of influence on our participation choices. Second, **marketing sources,** such as advertisements, sales personnel, brochures, and Web sites on the Internet are all important information sources. In fact, sports marketers have direct control over this source of information, so it is perhaps the most critical from the perspective of the sports organization. The third type of external information source is called an **experiential source.** Jack may watch games in several different sports leagues to gather information. His decision is influenced by watching the level of competition.

Some participants may require a great deal of information before making a decision, whereas others require little to no information. The amount of information and

On-line information source.

Source: Copyright © 2000–2004. Kayak Online. All rights reserved. http://www.kayakonline.com/

the number of sources used is a function of several factors, such as the amount of time available, the importance of the decision, the amount of past experience, and the demographics and psychographics of the participants.

The extent of the information search also depends on the **perceived risk** of the decision. Perceived risk stems from the uncertainty associated with decision making and is concerned with the potential threats inherent in making the wrong decision. For individual sports participants, perceived risk surfaces in many different forms. Perceived risk may be the embarrassment of not having the skill necessary to participate in a competitive league (social risks) or being concerned about the money needed to participate (economic risks). Also, an important perceived risk for many other adult participants is health and safety (safety risks).

At this stage of the participant decision-making process, sports marketers must understand as much as they can about the information sources used by consumers. For instance, marketers for the Cincinnati Recreational Commission want to know the information sources for teams, what is the most effective way to provide teams with information, how much information is desired, and to whom they should provide this information. Moreover, sports marketers want to understand the perceived risks for potential participants such as Jack. This information is essential for developing an effective promotional strategy that targets both teams and individual participants.

EVALUATION OF ALTERNATIVES

Now that the information search has yielded all the available participation alternatives that have some of the basic characteristics that appeal to Jack, he must begin to evaluate the alternatives. Jack thinks about all the organized, team sports in which he might participate and chooses a subset to which he will give further consideration. The few sports given the greatest consideration are called the **evoked set** of alternatives. Jack's evoked set might consist of four sports: softball, basketball, bowling, and indoor soccer.

After consumers develop their evoked set, comprised of acceptable alternatives, they must evaluate each sport based on the important features and characteristics. These features and characteristics that potential consumers are looking for in a sport are called **evaluative criteria.** The evaluative criteria used by Jack include team sport, organized or league play, moderate level of competition, and moderately aggressive sport. It is important to realize that each of the four evaluative criteria carries a different weight in Jack's overall decision-making process. To continue with our example, let us say that Jack attaches the greatest importance to participating in a team sport. Next, Jack is concerned with participating in a league or organized sport. The level of aggression is the next most important criterion to Jack. Finally, the least important factor in choosing from among the four sports is the level of competition.

In complex decision making, Jack would evaluate each of the sports against each of the evaluative criteria. He would base his final decision regarding participation on which sport measures best against the various factors he deems important. The two most important criteria—team sport and league play—are satisfied for each of the four sports in the evoked set. In other words, all the sports that Jack is evaluating are team sports, and all have league play. Therefore, Jack moves on to his next criteria, level of aggression. Ideally, Jack wants to remain injury free so he eliminates indoor soccer and basketball from further consideration. Bowling seems to be a clear winner in satisfying these criteria, and Jack is aware of several competitive bowling leagues in the area. As such, Jack decides to participate in a bowling league.

The **evaluation of alternatives** has two important implications for sports marketers. First, sports marketers must ensure their sports are included in the evoked set of potential consumers. To accomplish this objective, consumers must first become aware of the alternative. Second, sports marketers must understand what evaluative criteria are used by potential consumers and then develop strategies to meet consumers' needs based on these criteria. For example, marketers of bowling have determined that there are two different participant bowling markets: league or organized and recreational bowlers.

Recreational bowlers are growing in numbers and care most about the facilities at which they bowl and the related services provided. The evaluative criteria used by recreational bowlers might include the type of food served, other entertainment offered (e.g., arcade games and billiards), and the atmosphere of the bowling alley. League bowlers, however, constitute a diminishing market. This segment of bowlers cares most about the location of the bowling center and the condition of the lanes.[2]

PARTICIPATION

The evaluation of alternatives has led us to what marketers consider the most important outcome of the decision-making process—the participation decision. The participation stage of the decision-making process might seem to be the most straight-forward, but many things need to be considered other than actually deciding what sport to play. For instance, the consumer's needs may shift to the equipment and apparel needed to participate. Jack may decide that he needs a new bowling ball, shoes, and equipment bag to look the part of bowler for his new team. Thus, marketers working for equipment manufacturers are interested in Jack's participant consumption behavior. In addition, Jack may have to decide which bowling alley offers the best alternative for his needs. He may choose a location close to home, one that offers the best price, or the alley that has the best atmosphere. Again, these criteria must be carefully considered by sports marketers, because participants make choices regarding not only what sports they want to participate in, but also where they want to participate.

Other things might occur that alter the intended decision to participate in a given sport. At the last minute, Jack's coworkers may talk him out of playing in a competitive men's league, in lieu of a co-rec, work league. There might be a problem finding an opening on a roster, which would also change Jack's decision-making process at the last moment. Perhaps the bowling team that Jack wanted to join is scheduled to play during a trip that he had planned. All these "unexpected pleasures" may occur at the partici-pation stage of the decision-making process.

POSTPARTICIPATION EVALUATION

You might think that the decision-making process comes to an abrupt halt after the participation decision, but there is one more very important step—**postparticipation evaluation.** The first activity that may occur after consumers have made an important participation decision is **cognitive dissonance.** This dissonance occurs because con-sumers experience doubts or anxiety about the wisdom of their decision. In other words, people question their own judgment. Let us suppose Jack begins participating in a com-petitive bowling league, and the first time he bowls, he is embarrassed. His poor level of play is far worse than everyone else on the team. Immediately, he begins to question his decision to participate.

Whether dissonance occurs is a function of the importance of the decision, the difficulty of the choice, the degree of commitment to the decision, and the individual's tendency to experience anxiety.[3] Jack does not know his teammates well and only paid $50 to join the league, so he may decide to quit the team. However, he does not want to let his team down and ruin his chance of making new friends, so high levels of dissonance may cause him to continue with the team. In either case, the level of dissonance that Jack feels is largely based on his own personality and tendency to experience anxiety.

Another important activity that occurs after participation begins is evaluation. First, the participant develops expectations about what it will be like to play in this competitive bowling league. Jack's expectations may range from thinking about how much physical pain the sport will cause to thinking about how many new friends he will make as a result of participating. Next, Jack evaluates his actual experience after several games. If expectations are met or exceeded, then satisfaction occurs. However, if the experience or performance is poorer than expected, then dissatisfaction results. The level of satisfaction Jack experiences will obviously have a tremendous impact on future participation and word-of-mouth communication about the sport.

TYPES OF CONSUMER DECISIONS

We have just completed our discussion of Jack's decision-making process and have failed to mention one very important thing. Not all decisions are alike. Some are extremely important and, therefore, take a great deal of time and thought. Because we are creatures of habit, some decisions require little or no effort. We simply do what we have always done in the past. The variety of decisions that we make about participation in sport can be categorized into three different types of participation decision processes. The decision processes, also known as levels of problem solving, are habitual problem solving, limited problem solving, and extensive problem solving.

HABITUAL PROBLEM SOLVING

One type of decision process that is used is called **habitual problem solving (or routinized problem solving).** In habitual problem solving, problem recognition occurs, followed by limited internal information search. As we just learned, internal search comes from experiences with sports stored in memory. Therefore, when Jack is looking for information on sports next year, he simply remembers his previous experience and satisfaction with bowling. The evaluation of alternatives is eliminated for habitual decisions because no alternatives are considered. Jack participates in bowling again, but this time there is no dissonance and limited evaluation occurs. In a sense, Jack's decision to participate in bowling becomes a habit or routine each year.

LIMITED PROBLEM SOLVING

The next type of consumer decision process is called **limited problem solving.** Limited problem solving begins with problem recognition and includes internal search and sometimes limited external search. A small number of alternatives are evaluated using a few evaluative criteria. In fact, in limited problem solving, the alternatives being evaluated are often other forms of entertainment (e.g., movies or concerts). After purchase, dissonance is rare and a limited evaluation of the product occurs. Participation in special sporting events, such as a neighborhood 10K run or charity golf outing, are examples of sporting events that lend themselves to limited problem solving.

EXTENSIVE PROBLEM SOLVING

The last type of decision process is called **extensive problem solving (or extended problem solving)** because of the exhaustive nature of the decision. As with any type of decision, problem recognition must occur for the decision-making process to be initiated. Heavy information search (both internal and external) is followed by the evaluation of many alternatives on many attributes. Postpurchase dissonance and postpurchase evaluation are at their highest levels with extensive decisions. Jack's initial decision to participate in the bowling league was an extensive decision due to his high levels of information search, the many sports alternatives he considered, and the comprehensive nature of his evaluation of bowling.

For many people who are highly involved in sports, participation decisions are more extensive in nature, especially in the initial stages of participating in and evaluating various sports. Over time, what was once an extensive decision becomes routine. Participants choose sports that meet their needs, and the decision to participate becomes automatic. It is important for marketers to understand the type of problem solving used by participants so the most effective marketing strategy can be formulated and implemented.

PSYCHOLOGICAL OR INTERNAL FACTORS

Now that we have looked at the participant decision-making process, let us turn our focus to the internal, or psychological, factors. Personality, motivation, learning, and perception are some of the basic **psychological or internal factors** that will be unique to each individual and guide sports participation decisions.

PERSONALITY

One of the psychological factors that may have a tremendous impact on whether we participate in sports, the sports in which we participate, and the amount of participation, is personality. Psychologists have defined **personality** as a set of consistent responses an individual makes to the environment.

Although there are different ways to describe personality, one common method used by marketers is based on specific, identifiable personality traits. For example, individuals can be thought of as aggressive, orderly, dominant, or nurturing.[4] Consider the potential association between an individual's personality profile and the likelihood of participating in a particular sport. The self-assured, outgoing, assertive individual may be more likely than the apprehensive, reserved, and humble person to participate in any sport. Moreover, the self-sufficient individual may participate in more individual sports (e.g., figure skating, golf, or tennis) than the group-dependent individual.

In one study, Generation X-ers were found to be more interested in fast-paced, high-risk activities, such as rock climbing and mountain biking.[5] As such, action sports may be a good choice for the happy-go-lucky, venturesome personality type of the Generation X-ers. Action or Extreme sports are defined as the pantheon of aggressive, nonteam sports, including snowboarding, in-line skating, super modified shovel racing, wakeboarding, ice and rock climbing, mountain biking, and snow mountain biking.[6] Another example of the relationship between sports participation and personality traits can be seen in Table 5.2. As illustrated, golfers most often described themselves as responsible,

A growing number of consumers participate in high-risk sports.

TABLE 5.2 Golfer's Self-Reported Traits and Personality Characteristics

Best Descriptors	%	Poorest Descriptors	%
Responsible	80%	Bitter	3%
Family-oriented	75	Sick a lot	3
Self-confident	70	Extravagant	6
Intelligent	66	Risk-averse	6
Fun-loving	64	Virgin	6
Team player	63	Fun-loving	8
Sensitive	62	Lonely	8
Ambitious	61	Outside the mainstream	14
Competent	61	Sexy	15
Practical	60	Born again	16

Source: Yankolovich Partners. "How Golfers are Likely to Describe Themselves."
Yankolovich Monitor Sports Enthusiast Profile.

family-oriented, self-confident, and intelligent. The poorest descriptors for golfers were *bitter, sick a lot, extravagant,* and *risk-averse.* Interestingly, golfers described themselves as team players, although they participate in this highly individual sport.

Although personality and participation may be linked, care must be taken not to assume a causal relationship between personality and sports participation. Some researchers believe sports participation might shape various personality traits (i.e., sports is a character builder). Other researchers believe we participate in sports because of our particular personality type. To date, little research supports the causal direction of the relationship between personality and participation in sport.

Not only does personality dictate whether someone participates in sports, but it may also be linked with participation in particular types of sports. The violent, aggressive personality type may be drawn to sports such as football, boxing, or hockey. However, the shy, introverted personality type may be more likely to participate in individual sports, such as tennis and running. Knowing the relationship between participation and personality profiles can help sports marketers set up the strategic sports marketing process so it will appeal to the appropriate personality segment. In addition, sports marketers of large participant sporting events use personality profiles to attract potential corporate sponsors who may want to appeal to the same personality segment.

MOTIVATION

Why do people participate in sports? What benefits are people looking for from participating in sport, and what needs do participating in sport satisfy? Results from a recent study suggest there are three basic reasons for participation (see Table 5.3).

The study of human motivation helps to better understand the underlying need to participate in sports. **Motivation** is an internal force that directs behavior toward the fulfillment of needs. In our earlier discussion of the participant decision-making process, problem recognition resulted from having needs that are not currently being met. As the definition indicates, motivation is discussed in terms of fulfilling unmet needs. Although there is no argument that all humans have needs, there is disagreement about the number of needs and the nature of them.

One popular theory of human motivation based on classification of needs is called **Maslow's hierarchy of needs** (see Figure 5.2). Maslow's hierarchy of needs consists of five levels. According to Maslow, the most basic, primitive needs must be fulfilled before the individual can progress to the next level of need. Once this higher level of

TABLE 5.3 Why People Participate in Sports

Personal Improvement

Release of tension or relaxation, sense of accomplishment, skill mastery, improved health and fitness, other people's respect for one's athletic skill, release of aggression, enjoyment of risk taking, personal growth, development of positive values, and sense of personal pride

Sport Appreciation

Enjoyment of the game, sport competition, and thrill of victory

Social Facilitation

Time spent with close friends or family and sense of being part of a group

Source: George Milne, William Sutton, and Mark McDonald, "Niche Analysis: A Strategic Measurement Tool for Managers," *Sport Marketing Quarterly,* vol. 5, no. 3 (1996), 17–21.

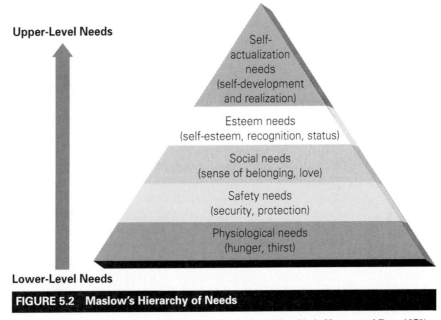

FIGURE 5.2 Maslow's Hierarchy of Needs

Source: A. H. Maslow, *Motivation and Personality,* 2nd ed. (New York: Harper and Row, 1970).

need is satisfied, the individual is then motivated to fulfill the next higher level of need. Let us look at the hierarchy of needs as it relates to participation in sports.

The first and most basic level of needs in Maslow's hierarchy are called **physiological needs.** These are the biological needs that people have—to eat, drink, and meet other physiological needs. For some individuals, there may be a physiological need to exercise and have some level of activity. Once this lower order need is met, safety needs are addressed.

Safety needs are concerned with physical safety, as well as the need to remain healthy. Sports equipment manufacturers address the need participants have for physical safety. With respect to the need for health, many participants cite that the primary reason for joining health clubs is to maintain or improve their health.

The next need level is based on **love and belonging.** Many people choose to participate in sport because of the social aspects involved. One of the early need theories of motivation includes "play" as a primary social need.[7] For some individuals, sports participation is their only outlet for being part of a group and interacting with others. The need to be part of a team and be respected by teammates has been demonstrated in a number of studies.

As these social needs are satisfied, **esteem** needs of recognition and status must be addressed. Certainly, sport plays a major role in enhancing self-esteem. For example, bungee jumping provides an excellent illustration of how sport influences esteem. The president of the U.S. Bungee Association (USBA), Casey Dale, describes the motives of people who use risky activities as a self-image booster. "People are less satisfied than they used to be with being pigeonholed by what they do, so they want to change their self-image. A quick fix is to become this extreme, risk-taking individual. All of a sudden, Bill the accountant goes bungee jumping off a 20-story bridge, and all of his coworkers see him in a new light."[8]

Finally, the highest order need, **self-actualization,** should be met. This refers to the individual's need to "be all that you can be" and is usually fulfilled through participation in mountain climbing, triathlons, or any sport that pushes an individual to the utmost of his or her physical and mental capacities. For example, ultramarathons in which runners compete in 100K road races certainly test the will of all participants. Another example of self-actualization can be found in the amateur athlete who trains his or her whole life for the Olympic Games.

As a sports marketer, strategies for increasing participation may be enhanced if you identify and understand the needs of consumers. In some instances, participation might fill more than one need level. Consumers may satisfy physiological needs, safety needs, social needs, esteem needs, or possibly self-actualization needs. For instance, marketing a health-club membership might appeal to consumers wanting to fulfill any of the need levels in the hierarchy. The members' physiological needs are being met through exercise. Safety needs might be met by explaining that the club has state-of-the-art exercise equipment that is designed to be safe for all ages and fitness levels. Social needs are addressed by describing the club as a "home away from home" for many members. The need for esteem for health-club members might be easily satisfied by depicting how good they will look and feel after working out. Finally, self-actualization needs may be fulfilled by working out to achieve the ideal body.

The needs that have just been presented can be described in two ways: motive direction and motive strength. Motive direction is the way that a consumer attempts to reduce tension by either moving toward a positive goal or moving away from a negative outcome. In the case of sports participation, an individual wants to get in good

Sports participants fulfilling the need for self-actualization.

physical condition and may move toward this goal by running, biking, lifting weights, and so on. Likewise, this same individual may want to move away from eating fatty foods and drinking alcohol.

Of particular interest to sports marketers is the strength of the sports participation motive. Motivational strength is the degree to which an individual chooses to actively pursue one goal over another. In sports marketing, the strength of a motive is characterized in terms of **sports involvement.** Sports involvement is the perceived interest in and personal importance of sports to an individual participating in a sport.[9]

Triathletes are an excellent example of an extreme level of sports involvement because of the importance placed on training for events. In their study, Hill and Robinson demonstrated that extreme involvement in a sport affects many aspects of the athletes' lives.[10] Participation could have positive effects, such as increased self-esteem, improved moods, and a better sense of overall wellness. Conversely, high involvement in a sport (e.g., triathlon) may produce neglected responsibilities of work, home, or family, and feelings of guilt, stress, and anxiety. Said simply, extremely involved individuals frequently have a difficult time balancing their lives.

Sports marketers are interested in involvement because it has been shown to be a relatively good predictor of sports-related behaviors. For example, a study found that level of involvement was positively related to the number of hours people participate in sports, the likelihood of planning their day around a sporting event, and the use of sports-related media (e.g., television, newspaper, or magazines).[11] Knowledge of sports involvement can help sports marketers develop strategies for both low- and high-involvement groups of potential participants.

Obsession never sleeps: the high involvement golfer.

Source: Copyright © Destination Hotels & Resorts, LLC. All rights reserved.

PERCEPTION

Think for a moment about the image you have of the following sports: soccer, hockey, and tennis. You might think of soccer as a sport that requires a great deal of stamina and skill, hockey as a violent and aggressive sport, and tennis as a sport for people who belong to country clubs. Ask two friends about their images of these same sports, and you are likely to get two different responses. That is because each of us has our own views of the world based on past experience, needs, wants, and expectations.

Your image of sport results from being exposed to a lifetime of information. You talk to friends and family about sports, you watch sports on television, and listen to sports on the radio. In addition, you may have participated in a variety of sports over the course of your life. We selectively filter sports information based on our own view of the world. Consumers process this information and use it in making decisions about participation.

The process by which consumers gather information and then interpret that information based on their own past experience is described as perception. **Perception** is defined as the complex process of selecting, organizing, and interpreting stimuli such as sports.[12] Ultimately, our perception of the world around us influences participant consumer behavior. The images that we hold of various sports and of ourselves dictate, to some extent, what sports we participate in. One of the primary goals of sports marketing is to shape your image of sports and sports products.

Before sports marketers can influence your perceptions, they must get your attention. **Selective attention** describes a consumer's focus on a specific marketing stimulus based on personal needs and attitudes. For example, you are much more likely to pay attention to advertisements for new golf clubs if you are thinking about purchasing a set.

Sports marketers fight with other sports and nonsports marketing stimuli for the limited capacity that consumers have for processing information. One job of the sports marketer is to capture the attention of the potential participant. But how is this done? Typically, sports marketers capture our attention through the use of novel promotions, using large and colorful promotional materials, and developing unique ways of communicating with consumers.

While sports marketers attempt to influence our perceptions, each participant brings a unique set of experiences, attitudes, and needs that affect the perceptual process. Generally speaking, consumers perceive things in ways that are consistent with their existing attitudes and values. This process is known as **selective interpretation.** For example, someone who has played hockey all their life may not see it as a dangerous and violent sport, whereas others hold a different interpretation.

Finally, **selective retention,** or the tendency to remember only certain information, is another of the influences on the perceptual process. Selective retention is remembering just the things we want to remember. The hockey player does not remember the injuries, the training, or the fights—only the victories.

Although sports marketers cannot control consumers' perceptions, they can and do influence our perceptions of sports through their marketing efforts. For example, a sports marketer trying to increase volleyball participation in boys ages 8 to 12 must first attempt to understand their perception of volleyball. Then the sports marketer tries to find ways of capturing the attention of this group of consumers, who have many competing sports and entertainment alternatives. Once they have the attention of this group of potential participants, a marketing mix is designed to either reinforce their perception of volleyball or change the existing image.

In addition to understanding consumers' images of volleyball, sports marketers are also interested in other aspects of perception. For instance, how do potential participants

Influencing the perception of running among the youth market.
Source: Used by permission of waycoolrunning.com. All rights reserved.

perceive advertisements and promotional materials about the sport? What are the parents' perceptions of volleyball? Do the parents perceive volleyball to be costly? The answer to all these questions depends on our own unique view of the world, which sports marketers attempt to understand and shape.

LEARNING

Another psychological factor that affects our participation decisions is learning. **Learning** is a relatively permanent change in response tendency due to the effects of experience. These response tendencies can be either changes in behavior (participation) or in how we perceive a particular sport. Consumers learn about and gather information regarding participation in various sports in any number of ways. **Behavioral learning** is concerned with how various stimuli (information about sports) elicit certain responses (feelings or behaviors) within an individual. **Cognitive learning,** however, is based on our ability to solve problems and use observation as a form of learning. Finally, **social learning** is based on watching others and learning from their actions. Let us look briefly at these three theories of learning as they apply to sports participation.

FIGURE 5.3 **Model of Operant Conditioning**

Specific behavior → Behavior is rewarded or punished → Likelihood of that behavior recurring increases or decreases

BEHAVIORAL LEARNING

One behavioral learning theory of importance to sports marketers is operant conditioning. Conditioning teaches people to associate certain behaviors with certain consequences of those behaviors. A simplified model of operant conditioning is illustrated in Figure 5.3.

Let us illustrate the model of operant conditioning using participation in snow skiing. We may decide to try snow skiing (specific behavior) as a new sport. Next and unfortunately, our behavior is punished as we continually fall down, suffer social embarrassment, and are uncomfortably cold. Finally, the likelihood of engaging in this behavior in the future is decreased because of the negative consequences of the earlier attempts at skiing. However, if the skiing participant is rewarded through the enjoyment of the sport and being with others, then he or she will continue to ski more and more.

The theory of operant conditioning lies at the heart of loyalty to a sport. In other words, if the sports we participate in meet our needs and reinforce them, then we will continue to participate in those sports. The objective of the sports marketer is to try to heighten the rewards associated with participating in any given sport and diminish any negative consequences.

America's greatest car designer, Harley Earl. The world's greatest golfer, Tiger Woods.

The one car company where they both hang their hats.

BUICK
THE SPIRIT OF AMERICAN STYLE

The innovative 2003 Rendezvous at buick.com. ©2003 GM Corp. All rights reserved.

The Nike golf hat elicits a learned response of a famous golfer.
Source: © 2004 GM Corporation. All rights reserved.

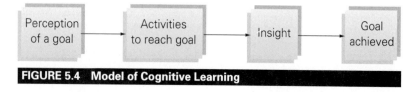

FIGURE 5.4   Model of Cognitive Learning

COGNITIVE LEARNING

Although much of what we learn is based on our past experience, learning also takes place through reasoning and thought processes. This approach to learning is known as cognitive learning. Cognitive learning is best known as learning through problem solving or insight, as shown in Figure 5.4.

Consider a goal that concerns some of us—weight loss. Once this goal is established, consumers search for activities that allow them to achieve the goal. The activities necessary to achieve weight loss might include dieting, participating in aerobics, weight training, playing basketball, or jogging. When consumers finally realize what specific activities they feel are necessary to achieve the desired goal, insight occurs. Finally, and hopefully, the goal of weight loss is achieved.

By using the concept of cognitive learning, the first focus of sports marketers is to understand the goals of potential consumers or participants. In addition, marketers must make potential participants aware of how the sport or sports product will help participants achieve their goals.

SOCIAL LEARNING

Much of our learning takes place by watching how others are rewarded or punished for their actions. This way of learning is called social learning. As children, we watched our friends, family members, and our heroes participate in various sports. To a large extent, this early observation and learning dictates the sports in which we choose to participate later in life. In social learning, we not only see someone benefiting from sport, but we also learn how to participate in the sport ourselves.

Those individuals we choose to observe and the process of observation are called models and modeling, respectively. The job of the sports marketer is to present positive models and present sports in a positive light, so others will perceive the benefits of sports participation. For example, Venus and Serena Williams may be seen as role models for young African American athletes thinking about participating in tennis, or Peyton Manning may be a model for young men interested in football.

ATTITUDES

Because of the learning and perceptual processes, consumers develop attitudes toward participating in sports. **Attitudes** are learned thoughts, feelings, and behaviors toward some given object. What is your attitude toward participation in bowling? One positive aspect of bowling is the chance to interact socially with other participants. However, bowling does not burn a lot of calories and may be seen as expensive. Your overall attitude toward bowling is made up of these positive and negative aspects of the sport.

Attitudes represent one of the most important components of the overall model of sports participation because they ultimately guide the decision-making process. Our attitudes are formed on the basis of an interaction between past experience and the environment in which we live. A simple model of attitude formation or how attitudes are developed is shown in Figure 5.5.

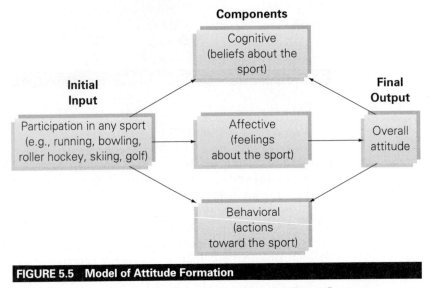

FIGURE 5.5 Model of Attitude Formation

Source: Adapted from Del Hawkins, Roger Best, and Kenneth Coney, *Consumer Behavior: Building Marketing Strategy,* 7th ed. (New York: McGraw-Hill, 1998). Reproduced with permission of the McGraw-Hill Companies.

As the model of attitude formation suggests, an attitude is based on our thinking, feeling, and actions toward a sport. These three components interact to form an overall attitude. Let us look briefly at its three components: cognitive, affective, and behavior.

The **cognitive component** of attitude holds the beliefs that people have toward the object. Beliefs can be either a statement of knowledge regarding bowling or thoughts someone has toward bowling. They are neither right nor wrong and vary from individual to individual. For example, here are some beliefs about participation in bowling that consumers might hold:

- Bowling is expensive.
- Bowling is time consuming.
- Very few women bowl.
- Bowling is for old people. (*Note:* The largest participant group for bowling is 18- to 34-year-olds.)

The **affective component** of attitude is based on feelings or emotional reactions to the initial stimulus. Most beliefs, such as the ones shown for cognitive attitude, have a related affective evaluation. More recently, affects, or feelings, have taken a more central role in explaining attitudes than beliefs or behaviors. In other words, some people equate attitudes with feelings that are held toward an object.[13]

Here are some potential affective statements:

- I hate bowling.
- Bowling is a boring sport.

The final component is called the **behavioral component** and is based on participants' actions. In other words, does the individual participate in bowling? How often does the individual bowl? What are the individuals' behavioral intentions, or how likely will they be to bowl in the future?

Generally, sports marketers must understand consumer attitudes to maintain or increase participation in any given sport. Only after attitudes are assessed can sports marketing strategies be formulated to improve upon or change existing attitudes. In our previous example, bowling equipment manufacturers and bowling alley management companies would need to change their beliefs that potential participants have about bowling. Additional strategies may attempt to change potential participants' feelings about bowling by repositioning the sport's current image. Finally, marketers may get potential participants to try bowling, which could lead to possible changes in their beliefs and feelings about the sport.

SOCIOLOGICAL OR EXTERNAL FACTORS

Now that we have looked at the major internal or psychological factors that influence participation decisions, let us turn our attention to the sociological factors. The **sociological or external factors** are those influences outside the individual participant that affect the decision-making process. The external factors are also referred to as sociological because they include all aspects of society and interacting with others. The external factors discussed in this chapter include culture, social class, reference groups, and family.

CULTURE

Participating in sports and games is one of the most long-standing traditions of civilization. Since the time of the ancient Greeks, participation in sports was expected and highly valued.[14] In the United States, sports are criticized for playing too important a role in our society. Many detractors frown at public monies being spent to finance private stadiums for professional athletics or institutions of higher education spending more on a new coach than on a new president for the university.

Culture is the set of learned values, beliefs, language, traditions, and symbols shared by a people and passed down from generation to generation. One of the most important aspects of this definition of culture includes the learning component. **Socialization** occurs when we learn about the skills, knowledge, and attitudes necessary for participating in sports. Sports marketers are interested in better understanding how the socialization process takes place and how they might influence this process.

A model of sports socialization is presented in Figure 5.6, which provides a framework for understanding how children learn about sports. Although the sports socialization process begins at increasingly younger ages, it extends throughout the life of the individual. Sports marketers are interested in learning how the socialization process

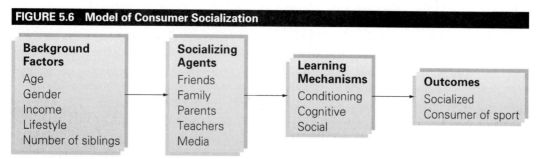

FIGURE 5.6   Model of Consumer Socialization

Source: John Mowen, *Consumer Behavior,* 3rd ed. (New York: Macmillan, 1993).

differs on the basis of gender, income, family lifestyle, and the number of children in the family.

Socializing agents also have a tremendous impact on the process. These factors represent the direct and indirect influences on the children. Sports marketers are also interested in understanding the relative impact of each socializing agent on a child's interest in participating in sports. For instance, is watching parents or professional athletes a better predictor of sports participation among children? One study has shown that children look to parents first, but if they are unacceptable or unwilling role models, children turn to other people.[15]

The learning mechanisms of observation and reinforcement are just two ways that the socialization process is facilitated. As discussed earlier, observation refers to looking to others as models for sports participation. For example, older siblings may serve as models for sports participation at earlier ages, whereas friends may become a more important learning mechanism as children age. Reinforcement may occur as children receive praise for participation in sport from parents, coaches, and friends.

The final element in the socialization model is the emergence of a socialized sports participant. Here, the child becomes actively engaged in sports participation. From the sports marketer's perspective, when children participate in sports at an early age, they may have better potential to become lifelong participants. Certainly, sporting goods manufacturers are interested in having children associate their brands with the enjoyment of sport at the earliest possible age. Aside from the learning that takes place during the socialization process, values represent another important aspect of any culture. **Values** are widely held beliefs that affirm what is desirable in a culture. Several of the core values that reflect U.S. culture are shown in Table 5.4.

Some of the core American values listed in Table 5.4 have intimate ties to sports participation in the United States. Obviously, the last value mentioned, fitness and health, relates directly to our preoccupation with participating in sports. The activity value has a direct impact on the way Americans spend their leisure time, including sports participation. Likewise, achievement and success are a theme that is continually underscored as consumers participate in sports.

Although they are not directly related, other core U.S. values may tangentially affect sports participation. For example, the value of individualism and being oneself

TABLE 5.4 Core American Values

Core American Value	Descriptor
Achievement and success	Sense of accomplishment
Activity	Being active or involved
Efficiency and practicality	Saves time and effort; solves problems
Progress	Continuous improvement
Material comfort	Money; status
Individualism	Being themselves
Freedom	Democratic beliefs
External conformity	Adaptation to society
Humanitarianism	Overcoming adversity; supporting
Charity	Giving to others
Youthfulness	Looking and acting young
Fitness and health	Exercise and diet

Source: Leon Shiffman and Leslie Kanuk, *Consumer Behavior*, 5th ed. (Upper Saddle River, NJ: Prentice Hall, 1994).

may manifest itself in the types of sports or activities in which we choose to participate. Many sports, such as surfing, hang-gliding, climbing, and hiking, allow a consumer to express his or her own personality. Youthfulness is also expressed through participation in sport as consumers keep "young at heart" by staying active. Consumers may also participate in sporting events to help raise money for charities.

SOCIAL CLASS

Throughout history, people within various cultural systems have been grouped together based on social class. Whether it is the "haves" versus the "have nots" or the "upper class" versus the "lower class," social class distinctions have always been present. **Social class** is defined as the homogeneous division of people in a society sharing similar values, lifestyles, and behaviors that can be hierarchically categorized.

Important to this definition is the idea that individuals are divided into homogeneous classes, or strata. Typically, social strata are described in terms of a hierarchy ranging from lower to upper class. Consumers are grouped into the various social classes based on the interaction of a number of factors. Occupation, income, and education are usually considered the three primary determinants of social class. In addition, possessions (e.g., home and car) and affiliations (e.g., club membership, professional organizations, and community organizations) are also believed to be important factors.

Although researchers agree that there are distinct social strata, there is little agreement on how many categories there are in the hierarchy. For instance, some researchers believe a seven-tiered structure (as illustrated in Figure 5.7) explains social

---

FIGURE 5.7 The Structure of Social Class

INCOME →

Upper Americans

Upper-Upper (0.3%): The "capital S society" world of inherited wealth
Lower-Upper (1.2%): The newer social elite, drawn from current professionals
Upper-Middle (12.5%): The rest of college graduate managers and professionals; lifestyle centers on private clubs, causes, and the arts

Middle Americans

Middle Class (32%): Average pay white-collar workers and their blue-collar friends; live on "the better side of town," try to "do the proper things"
Working Class (38%): Average pay blue-collar workers; lead "working-class lifestyle" whatever the income, school, background, and job

Lower Americans

A Lower Group of People, but Not the Lowest (9%): Working, not on welfare; living standard is just above poverty; behavior judged "crude," "trashy"
Real Lower-Lower (7%): On welfare, visibly poverty stricken, usually out of work (or have "the dirtiest jobs"); "bums," "common criminals"

Source: Richard P. Coleman, "The Continuing Significance of Social Class to Marketing," *Journal of Consumer Research*, vol. 10 (December 1983), 265–280.

TABLE 5.5 Household Income for Select Sports and Activities

Activity	Household Income (in thousands)	Activity	Household Income (in thousands)
Basketball	$58	Roller Hockey	$73
Bowling	$60	Running/Jogging	$63
BMX Bicycling	$49	Sailing	$82
Day Hiking	$66	Saltwater Fishing	$64
Downhill Skiing	$83	Snorkeling	$83
Fitness Bicycling	$71	Snowboarding	$63
Fitness Swimming	$69	Soccer	$59
Fitness Walking	$66	Surfing	$74
Football (Tackle)	$54	Tennis	$68
Golf	$80	Tent Camping	$58
Horseback Riding	$65	Yoga/Tai Chi	$68

Source: Sporting Goods Manufacturers Association, http.//www.sportsbusinessdaily.com.

class in the United States. Others, however, believe in a simple two-tiered system (i.e., upper and lower).

Regardless of the class structure, sports marketers are interested in social class as a predictor of whether a consumer will participate in sports and, if they do participate, the types of sports in which a consumer might participate. Table 5.5 shows the relationship between average household income and participation in 22 selected sports activities.

Other research has shown that more than one in four Americans would like to have more time for leisure activities such as bowling and softball. A disproportionate number of those people who want more leisure time are lower income, blue-collar workers.[16] In addition, the U.S. Fish and Wildlife Service found that anglers are above average in income and are moderately well educated.[17]

REFERENCE GROUPS

"Be Like Mike" and "I Am Tiger Woods" illustrate the power of reference group influence. More formally, **reference groups** are individuals who influence the information, attitudes, and behaviors of other group members. Sports participation is heavily influenced through the various reference groups to which an individual may belong.

Witness the Tiger Woods phenomenon and the hordes of children who have now begun to participate in golf as a result of his influence. This type of reference group, which has an impact on our participation in sports as well as on our purchase of sports products, is called an aspirational group. Although many famous athletes recognize the influence they can have on children, others refuse to accept the responsibility that reference group influence demands (e.g., the now-retired Charles Barkley of the NBA stating, "I am not a role model").

Celebrity athletes are not the only individuals who have an impact on sports participation. Friends and coworkers are also considered a **primary reference group** because of the frequent contact we have with these individuals and the power they have to influence our decisions. Many of us participate in sports because friends and coworkers urged us to join their team, play a set of tennis, or hit the links. Primary reference groups may exert a powerful influence among high-school athletes as participation continues to grow at this level.

SPORTS MARKETING HALL OF FAME

The Babe: Babe Didrikson Zaharias

Mildred "Babe" Didrikson Zaharias was known by sports fans all over as the "best at everything." Her early success as an all-around athlete began as she played on basketball, softball, and track and field teams, named the Golden Cyclones, sponsored by the Employers Casualty Insurance Company. Babe represented the Golden Cyclones by herself in the 1932 Olympic track and field qualifying trials and entered eight of the 10 events. She ended up winning six of the events, and her legend was born.

As an amateur, Babe won two gold medals and one silver in track and field events at the 1932 Olympics. She began a professional career that included stints in basketball, baseball, boxing, football, and hockey. Didrikson's most impressive sport of all, however, was golf. Returning to amateur status in golf, Babe ran up an unprecedented 17 straight wins, including a victory in the 1947 British Women's Amateur—never before won by an American. In 1949, she was one of the founding members of the LPGA.

In addition to her impressive athletic achievements, Babe was the consummate sports promoter and marketer. For example, she participated in publicity stunts such as harness racing and pitched against New York Yankee Joe Dimaggio. She published a book of golfing tips, had her own line of golf clubs through Spalding Sporting Goods, and appeared in movies such as the classic *Pat and Mike*. Through her example and performance, Babe Didrikson Zaharias legitimized women's sports. Her excellence in so many sports made her a marketer's dream. Just imagine her today.

Source: Elizabeth Lynn, *Babe Didrikson Zaharias: Champion Athlete* (New York: Chelsea House, 1989).

FAMILY

Another primary reference group that has one of the greatest influences on sports participation is the family. As you might guess, family plays a considerable role because sports marketers target families as spectators. But how does **family influence** affect participation in sport? Consider families of friends or your own family. It is common for family members to exert a great deal of influence on each other with respect to decisions about sports participation and activities. For example, children may either directly or indirectly get parents involved in a sport (e.g., in-line skating, soccer, or biking) so the entire family can participate together. Conversely, parents may urge their kids to get off the couch and get involved in sports.

Traditionally, fathers have had the greatest impact on their children's (mostly their sons) sports participation. Dad might have encouraged junior to play organized football because he did or go fishing because his father took him fishing. Of course, these scenarios are vanishing, as is the traditional family structure.

Long gone are the days of the mom, dad, two kids, and a dog. Long gone is the *Leave It to Beaver* mentality where fathers are breadwinners and mothers are homemakers. Today's modern family structure typically includes dual-income families with no kids (DINKS), divorced parents, single parents, or parents who are dually employed with kids (DEWKS).

Each of these modern family structures may influence participation in sports for both adults and children. For instance, dual-income families with no kids may have the time and the money to participate in a variety of "country club" sports. However, single or divorced parents may face time and financial constraints. Sports products such as the "10-minute workout" and 30-minute aerobic classes are targeted to working moms on the move. In addition, the tremendous increase in sales of home exercise equipment may be traced back to the constraints of the modern family structure.

High School Sports Participation Climbs

More high school students are playing sports in the United States than ever before, and girls are closing the participation gap in a hurry.

Boys still outnumber girls in sports by more than a million, according to the latest survey by the National Federation of State High School Associations (NFHS). But the bulk of the difference comes from football, and there is no girls sport with comparable numbers.

"The girls' figures have pretty much been on a rise ever since the survey was started, because they got off to a slower start," NFHS spokesman Bruce Howard said Wednesday

NFHS has been surveying its member associations from the 50 states and the District of Columbia since 1971, and the number of girls competing in one or more sports rose by more than 49,000 last year to a record 2,856,358.

The number of boys in sports increased just over 28,000 to 3,988,738, not a record but the most in 25 years.

"The mid to late 1970s was kind of the height of the baby boom era, and there was an increase in enrollment and participation," Howard said. "It trickled back down again, but really, since the mid- to late–1980s we've had a gradual climb upward in both enrollment and participation."

The total of about 6.9 million boys and girls last year marked the fourteenth straight year with an increase in participation and the fifth straight year with a record number of participants.

Also, the rate of participation as a percentage of the total student enrollment continued to rise.

Basketball remained the most popular sport for girls, with 457,165 participants. Next were outdoor track and field (415,602), volleyball (396,682), softball (357,912), soccer (301,450), cross country (163,360), tennis (162,810), and swimming and diving (141,468).

For boys, the greatest participation was in football, with 1,023,142. Basketball was next with 540,874 participants, followed by outdoor track and field (498,027), baseball (453,792), soccer (345,156), wrestling (239,845), cross country (191,833), golf (162,805), tennis (144,844), and swimming and diving (94,612).

Texas remained the state with the most participants with 771,633, followed by California (652,333), New York (333,987), Illinois (319,727), Michigan (304,971), Ohio (301,885), Pennsylvania (249,985), Minnesota (220,219), Florida (212,408), and New Jersey (209,452).

Source: Steve Herman. Associated Press, *Associated Press Online* (September 3, 2003). Reprinted with permission of The Associated Press.

Children's ability to participate in organized sport may also be hampered by the single-parent family, although women are increasingly taking on the traditional male sex role of coach, sports participant, and sports enthusiast. Also, fathers are increasingly encouraging daughters to participate in sport, another sign of changing sex roles.

SITUATIONAL FACTORS

Now that we have looked at how the psychological and sociological factors influence the participant decision-making process, let us turn to the situational factors. Unlike the psychological and sociological factors that are relatively permanent in nature, the situational factors are temporary aspects that affect participation. For instance, the culture in which we make our participation decision is considered a long term environmental factor. Likewise, personality is a set of consistent responses that we make to our environment. However, **situational factors** are those temporary factors within a particular time or place that influence the participation decision-making process.[18]

Consider the following examples of situational influences on **participant behavior.** Your best friend is in town and, although you do not normally enjoy golfing, you do so anyway to spend time with your friend. You typically run five miles per day, but an unexpected ice storm put a halt to your daily exercise routine. You have to study for final exams, so you settle for a 30-minute workout versus your normal 75 minutes. Each of these examples represents a different type of situational influence on participant decision making.

Girls' sport participation is eroding traditional gender roles.

Consumer researchers have identified five situational influences that affect decision making. The five primary types of situational influences include physical surroundings; social surroundings; time; reason for participation, or task definition; and antecedent states. Let us briefly look at each in the context of participant decision making.

PHYSICAL SURROUNDINGS

The location, weather, and physical aspects of the participation environment comprise the **physical surroundings.** In sports participation, the physical surroundings play an extremely important role in decision making. When the weather outside is good, people who might not participate in sports normally do so. Likewise, the weather can have a situational influence on where we choose to participate. The runner described in the earlier example may decide to jog indoors rather than skip the workout. In addition to the weather, location might influence our decision to participate. For example, nonskiers may be tempted to try skiing if they are attending a sales conference in Vail or Aspen. Other aspects of the physical environment, such as a perfectly groomed championship golf course or scenic biking trail can also influence our participation decisions in a positive manner. From the perspective of the sports marketer, any attempt to increase participation must carefully consider the physical surroundings. Even the worst athletes in the world enjoy playing in nice facilities.

SOCIAL SURROUNDINGS

The effect of other people on a participant during participation in a sport is another situational influence, called **social surroundings.** In other words, who we are with may have a positive or negative impact on participation decisions. The earlier golf example presented a case where the presence of a friend caused the person to participate. Likewise, golfing in the presence of unfamiliar coworkers at a corporate outing can be an unpleasant and intimidating experience. In this case, participation might be avoided altogether.

Crowds represent another social situation that is usually avoided. For example, if the tennis courts or golf courses are full, you might decide to participate in another sport that day. Biking and hiking represent two other activities where crowds are usually perceived to have a negative impact on participation. In other words, people generally do not like to bike or hike in large crowds. However, some people may take pleasure when participating among large crowds. Consider, for example, runners who feel motivated when participating in events with thousands of other runners.

TIME

The effect of the presence or absence of **time** is the third type of situational influence. In today's society, there are increasing time pressures on all of us. Changes in family structure, giving rise to dual-income families and single parents, have made time for participation in sports even scarcer. Slightly more than half of all U.S. residents under the age of 50 complain of a lack of leisure time and this percentage is even higher for dual-income families. How many times have you heard someone say, "I don't have the time to work out today?"

Because of time constraints, sports marketers are concentrating on ways to make our participation activities more enjoyable and more time effective. For example, few of us can afford to take five hours out of our day to enjoy 18 holes of golf. As such,

Social surroundings may have a negative or positive influence on participation.

golfing associations are always communicating ways to speed up play. Similarly, few of us feel like we have the time to drive to the gym each day. The marketers' response to this was the development of the 30-minute workout and the enormous home health equipment industry.

REASON FOR PARTICIPATION OR TASK DEFINITION

Another situational influence, **task definition,** refers to the reasons that occasion the need for consumers to participate in a sport. In other words, the reason the consumer participates affects the decision-making process. Some participants may use jet skis or scuba dive once a year while they are on vacation. Other consumers may participate in a fantasy baseball camp, once in a lifetime.

These examples represent special occasions or situational reasons for participating. Moreover, the participation occasion may dictate the sports apparel and equipment we choose. For example, a consumer participating in a competitive softball league might wear cleats, long softball pants, and batting gloves. However, the recreational participant playing softball at the company picnic would only bring a glove.

ANTECEDENT STATES

Temporary physiological and mood states that a consumer brings to the participant situation are **antecedent states.** In certain situations, people may feel worn out and lack energy. This physiological state may motivate some people to workout and become reenergized at the end of a long day of work. However, feeling tired can elicit another response in others, such as "I'm too tired to do anything today."

Certainly, other situational mood states, such as being "stressed out," can activate the need to participate in sports or exercise. Yet, feeling tired or hungry can cause us to decide against participation. At the very least, our mood can influence our decision to ride or walk 18 holes of golf.

It is important to remember that antecedent means "prior to" or "before." Therefore, the mood or physiological condition influences our decision making. For example, people who are experiencing bad moods may turn to sports to lift their spirits. Contrast this with someone who feels great because they have just participated in a sporting event.

Summary

The focus of Chapter 5 is understanding the sports participant as a consumer of sports. Sports marketers are not only concerned with consumers who watch sporting events, but also with the millions of consumers who participate in a variety of sports. To successfully market to sports participants, sports marketers must understand everything they can about these consumers and their consumption behaviors. Participant consumption behavior is defined as the actions performed when searching for, participating in, and evaluating the sports activities that consumers believe will satisfy their needs.

To simplify the complex nature of participant consumption behavior, a model was developed. The model of participant consumption behavior consists of four major components: the participant decision-making process, internal or psychological factors, external or sociological factors, and situational variables. The participant deci-

sion-making process is the central focus of the model of participant consumption behavior. It explains how consumers make decisions about whether to participate in sports and in which sports to participate. The decision-making process is slightly different for each of us and is influenced by a host of factors. However, the basis of the decision-making process is a five-step procedure that consumers progress through as they make decisions. These five steps include problem recognition, information search, evaluation of alternatives, participation, and postparticipation evaluation. The complexity of this process is highly dependent on how important the decision is to participants and how much experience consumers have had making similar decisions.

The internal or psychological factors are those things that influence our decision-making process. These psychological factors include personality, motivation, perception, learning, and attitudes. Personality is a set of consistent responses we make to our environment. Our personality can play a role in which sports we choose to participate in or whether we participate in any sports. For example, an aggressive personality type may be most likely to participate in boxing or hockey. Motivation is the reason we participate in sports. Some of the more common reasons we participate in sports are for personal improvement, appreciation of sport, or social facilitation. The strength of our motives to participate in sports is referred to as sport involvement. Another important psychological factor that influences our participation decisions is perception. Perception influences our image of the various sports and their participants as well as shaping our attitudes toward sports participation. Learning also affects our participant behavior. We learn whether to participate in sports because we are rewarded or punished by our participation (behavioral theories), because we perceive sports as a way to achieve our goals (cognitive theories), and because we watch others participating (social theories). A final internal or psychological factor that directly influences our sports participation decisions is attitudes. Attitudes are defined as learned thoughts, feelings, and behaviors toward some given object (in this case, sports participation). Our feelings (affective component of attitude) and beliefs (cognitive component) about sports participation certainly play a major role in determining our participation (behavioral component).

The external or sociological factors also influence the participant decision-making process. These factors include culture, social class, reference groups, and fam-

ily. Culture is defined as the learned values, beliefs, language, traditions, and symbols shared by people and passed down from generation to generation. The values held by people within a society are a most important determinant of culture. Some of the core American values that influence participation in sports include achievement and success, activity, individualism, youthfulness, and fitness and health. Social class is another important determinant of participant decision making. Most people erroneously associate social class only with income. Our social class is also determined by occupation, education, and affiliations. Another important sociological factor is the influence of reference groups. Reference groups are individuals who influence the information, attitudes, and behaviors of other group members. For example, our friends may affect our decision to participate in a variety of recreational sports and activities. One reference group that has a great deal of influence over our attitudes and participation behavior is our family.

The final component of the model of participant behavior is situational factors. Every decision that we make to participate in a given activity has a situational component. In other words, we are always making a decision in the context of some unique situation. Five major situational influences that affect participant decision making include physical surroundings (physical environment), social surroundings (interaction with others), time (presence or absence of time), task definition (reason or occasion for participation), and antecedent states (physiological condition or mood prior to participation).

Key Terms

- affective component
- antecedent states
- attitudes
- behavioral component
- behavioral learning
- cognitive component
- cognitive dissonance
- cognitive learning
- consumer socialization
- culture
- decision-making process
- esteem
- evaluation of alternatives
- evaluative criteria
- evoked set
- experiential source
- extensive problem solving (or extended problem solving)
- external sources
- family influence

- habitual problem solving (or routinized problem solving)
- information search
- internal sources
- learning
- limited problem solving
- love and belonging
- marketing sources
- Maslow's hierarchy of needs
- model of participant behavior
- motivation
- participant consumption behavior
- perceived risk
- perception
- personality
- personal sources
- physical surroundings
- physiological needs
- postparticipation evaluation

- primary reference group
- problem recognition
- psychological or internal factors
- reference groups
- safety needs
- selective attention
- selective interpretation
- selective retention
- self-actualization
- situational factors
- social class
- socialization
- social learning
- socializing agents
- social surroundings
- sociological or external factors
- sports involvement
- task definition
- time
- values

Review Questions

1. Define participant consumption behavior. What questions does this address with respect to consumers of sport? From a marketing strategy perspective, why is it critical to understand consumer behavior?
2. Outline the components of the simplified model of participant consumer behavior?
3. Outline the steps in the decision-making process for sports participation. What are the three types/levels of consumer decision making? How do the steps in the decision-making process differ for routine decisions versus extensive decisions?
4. Define personality. Why is it considered one of the internal factors of consumption behavior? Do you think personality is related to the decision to participate in sports? Do you think personality is linked to the specific sports we choose to play?
5. Describe Maslow's hierarchy of needs. How is Maslow's theory linked to sports marketing?
6. What is meant by the term *sports involvement* from the perspective of sports participants? How is sports involvement measured and used in the development of the strategic marketing process?
7. Define perception and provide three examples of how the perceptual processes apply to sports marketing.
8. Describe the three major learning theories. Which learning theory do you believe best explains the sports in which we choose to participate? Why is learning theory important to sports marketers?
9. Describe the three components of attitude. How do these components work together? Why must attitudes be measured to increase sports participation?
10. Define culture and explain the process of sports socialization. Describe the core American values.
11. Define social class and explain the characteristics of individuals at each level of the seven-tiered structure.
12. Explain how reference groups play a role in sports participation.
13. Discuss the traditional family structure and then the nontraditional family structures. How do today's nontraditional families influence sports participation? Is this for the better or the worse?
14. Explain each of the five situational factors that influence the participant decision-making process.

Exercises

1. Trace the simplified model of participant behavior for a consumer thinking about joining a health club. Briefly comment on each element of the model.
2. Ask three males and three females about the benefits they seek when participating in sports. What conclusions can you draw regarding motivation? Are there large gender differences in the benefits sought?
3. Interview five adult sports participants and ask them to describe the sports socialization process as it relates to their personal experience. Attempt to interview people with different sports interests to determine whether the socialization process differs according to the specific sports.
4. Watch three advertisements for any sporting goods on television. Briefly describe the advertisement and then suggest which core American value(s) are reflected in the theme of the advertisement.
5. Develop a survey instrument to measure attitudes toward jogging. Have 10 people complete the survey and then report your findings. How could these findings be used by your local running club to increase membership (suggest specific strategies)? Are attitudes and behaviors related?
6. Interview five children (between the ages of eight and 12) to determine what role the family and other reference group influences have had on their decision to participate in sports. Suggest promotions for children based on your findings.
7. Prepare a report that describes how time pressures are influencing sports participation in the United States. How are sports marketers responding to increasing time pressures?

Internet Exercises

1. Using the World Wide Web, prepare a report that examines sport participation in Australia. What are the similarities and differences in the sports culture of Australia versus that of the United States?
2. Find and describe two sports Web sites that specifically appeal to children. How does this information relate to the process of consumer socialization?
3. Find and describe a Web site for a health club. How does the information relate to the consumer decision-making process to join the club?

Endnotes

1. Del Hawkins, Roger Best, and Kenneth Coney, *Consumer Behavior: Building Marketing Strategy,* 7th ed. (New York: McGraw-Hill, 1998).
2. Ian P. Murphy, "Bowling Industry Rolls Out Unified Marketing Plan," *Marketing News* (January 20, 1997), 2.
3. Del Hawkins, Roger Best, and Kenneth Coney, *Consumer Behavior: Building Marketing Strategy,* 7th ed. (New York: McGraw-Hill, 1998).
4. R. B. Cattell, H. W. Eber, and M. M. Tasuoka, *Handbook for the Sixteen Personality Factors Questionnaire* (Champaign, IL: Institute for Personality and Ability Testing, 1970).
5. Douglas M. Turco, "The X Factor: Marketing Sport to Generation X," *Sport Marketing Quarterly*, vol. 5, no. 1: 21–23.
6. Terry Lefton and Bernhard Warner, "Alt Sportspeak: A Flatliner's Guide," *Brandweek* (January 27, 1997), 25–27.
7. H. Murray, *Exploration in Personality: A Clinical and Experimental Study of Fifty Men of College Age* (New York: Oxford University Press, 1938).
8. "You Can Buy a Thrill: Chasing the Ultimate Rush" www.demographics.com/publications/ad/9 7_ad/9706_ad/ad970631.htm.
9. Fred M. Beasley and Matthew D. Shank, "Fan or Fanatic: Refining a Measure of Sports Involvement," *Journal of Sport Behavior*, vol. 21, no. 4 (1998), 435–443.
10. Ronald Paul Hill and Harold Robinson, "Fanatic Consumer Behavior: Athletics as a Consumption

Experience," *Psychology & Marketing*, vol. 8, no. 2 (1991), 79–99.
11. Fred M. Beasley and Matthew D. Shank, "Fan or Fanatic: Refining a Measure of Sports Involvement," *Journal of Sport Behavior*, vol. 21, no. 4 (1998), 435–443.
12. Robert Sekular and Randolph Blake, *Perception*, 2nd ed. (New York: McGraw-Hill, 1990).
13. John Kim, Jeen-Su Lim, and Mukesh Bhargava, "The Role of Affect in Attitude Formation: A Classical Conditioning Approach," *Journal of the Academy of Marketing Science*, vol. 26, no. 2 (1998), 143–152.
14. Harry Edwards, *The Sociology of Sport* (Homewood, IL: Dorsey Press, 1973).
15. Elizabeth Moore-Shay and Britts Berchmans, "The Role of the Family Environment in the Development of Shared Consumption Values: An Intergenerational Study," *Advances in Consumer Research*, vol. 2. Kim Corfman and John G. Lunch, Jr., eds. (Provo, UT: Association for Consumer Research, 1996), 484–490.
16. "Something to Wish for: Time to Relax," *US News and World Report* (November 11, 1996), 17.
17. Diane Crispell. "Targeting Hunters" *American Demographics*. www.demographics.com/publications/ad /94_ad/9401_ad/ad508.htm.
18. Russel Belk, "Situational Variables and Consumer Behavior," *Journal of Consumer Research* (December 1975): 157–163.

CHAPTER 6

UNDERSTANDING SPECTATORS AS CONSUMERS

After completing this chapter, you should be able to:

- Understand the similarities and differences between spectator and participant markets.
- Describe the eight basic fan motivation factors.
- Explain how game attractiveness, economic factors, and competitive factors relate to game attendance.
- Describe the demographic profile of spectators and explain the changing role of women as spectators.
- Understand the relationship between stadium factors and game attendance.
- Discuss the components of the sportscape model.
- Describe the multiple values of sport to the community.
- Explain sport involvement from a spectator's perspective.
- Discuss the model of fan identification.

In Chapter 5, we examined participants as consumers. This chapter examines another group of consumers of great importance to sports marketers—spectators. Before we turn to our discussion of spectator consumption, two key points need to be addressed. First, the model of participant consumption behavior discussed in Chapter 5 can also be applied to spectator consumption. Think for a moment about your decision to attend sporting events. Certainly, there are sociological factors that influence your decision. For instance, reference groups such as friends and family may play a major role in influencing your decision to attend sporting events. Psychological factors, such as personality, perception, and attitudes, also affect your decision to attend sporting events. For example, the more ambitious and aspiring you are, the more likely you may be to attend sporting events. In addition, situational factors can affect your decision to attend sporting events. Maybe you were given tickets to the game as a birthday gift (e.g., task definition).

As you can see, the factors that influence participant decision making are also applicable to spectator decisions. However, the focus of this chapter is to understand

Some of the most enthusiastic spectators in the world are soccer fans.

why people attend sporting events and to examine what additional factors relate to game attendance. Rather than using the framework for participant consumption behavior, however, we concentrate on the wants and needs of spectators. Understanding the consumer's needs and wants, in turn, is important when developing an effective marketing mix for spectators.

The second key point addresses the basis for considering spectators and participants as two separate markets. Many people who watch and attend sporting events also participate in sports and vice versa. For example, you may watch March Madness and also play basketball on a recreational basis. Research has shown, however, that two different consumer segments exist.[1] In fact, marketing to "either participants or spectators would miss a large proportion of the other group." Let us look at Figure 6.1 to illustrate the differences between spectators and participants.

Each diagram in Figure 6.1 depicts the potential relationship between spectator and consumer markets for golf, basketball, NASCAR, and running. Golf (see Fig. 6.1a) represents a sport where there is large crossover between participants and spectators. A study conducted by Milne, Sutton, and MacDonald supports this notion, finding that 84 percent of the golf participant market overlaps the golf spectator market.[2] In another study, it was found that 87.3 percent of the spectators in attendance at an LPGA event also participated in golf.[3]

A similar pattern is shown for basketball (see Fig. 6.1b). The results of the study indicated an 81 percent overlap between basketball participation and watching pro basketball. Surprisingly, this same relationship did not exist for college basketball spectators. In that case, the overlap in the participation market and the college basketball spectator market was only 43 percent. The study also found that there was only a 36 percent overlap between spectators of professional basketball and spectators of college basketball—evidence that there are not only differences in spectators and participants, but also among spectators at different levels of the same sport.[4]

The other two sports shown in Figure 6.1, NASCAR racing and running, demonstrate more extreme differences in the spectator and participant markets. There is virtually no overlap between the spectators and participants of NASCAR (see Fig. 6.1c). Obviously, the NASCAR participant market is virtually nonexistent. However, new "fantasy camps" are springing up across the United States for spectators who want to try racing. For example, participants can enroll in classes with Richard Petty Driving Experience. The "Rookie Experience" is designed for the "layperson who has a strong

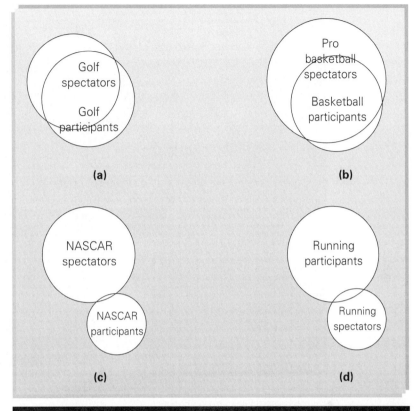

FIGURE 6.1   Relationship Between Spectator and Participant Markets

There is no overlap in the spectator and participant market for bull fighting.

desire to experience the thrill of driving a Winston Cup race car." For prices starting at $349, racing enthusiasts can begin to experience driving around the track at speeds up to 145 mph. Top speeds vary according to driver ability, track location, and program. Race fans can also experience a heart-pounding ride around one of the tracks with a professional instructor. Prices for the ride start at $99.00 and speeds will reach up to

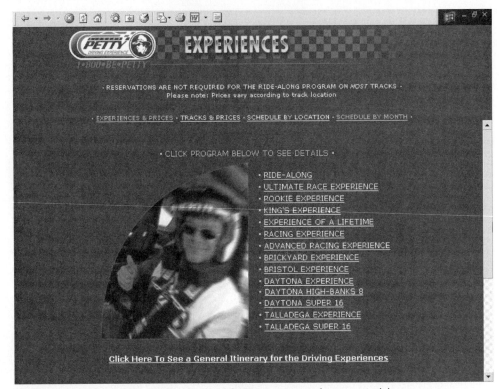

Richard Petty Driving School: Allowing NASCAR spectators to become participants.
Source: Richard Petty Driving Experience™ Copyright © 2004 RPDE. All rights reserved.

165 mph. There are very few requirements, and participants soon will feel like their favorite racecar driver.[5]

Figure 6.1d depicts the potential participant and spectator markets for running. As opposed to the previous examples, the participant running market is much larger than the spectator running market. In addition to the size of the markets, there are also differences in motivations for spectators and participants. Participants, for instance, may be motivated to run for reasons of personal improvement. However, spectators are likely to watch to provide support to a family member or friend.

In addition to looking at the overlap (or lack thereof) between participants and spectators on a sport-by-sport basis, other research has explored the differences between these two groups for sports in general. Table 6.1 summarizes the findings of a study conducted by Burnett, Menon, and Smart, which examined spectator and participant socioeconomic characteristics and media habits. Based on the results of this and other studies, sports participants and sports spectators seem to represent two distinct markets that should be examined separately by sports marketers.

Before we explore spectators in greater detail, it is important to note that this market can be differentiated into two groups on the basis of consumer behavior. The first group consists of spectators who attend the sporting event. The second group of spectators consumes the sporting event through some medium (e.g., television, radio, or Internet). This chapter is primarily concerned with understanding why consumers attend sporting events and what factors influence attendance. Let us begin by looking at some of the major factors that influence the decision to attend sporting events rather than watch them from the comfort of home.

TABLE 6.1 Differences Between Spectators and Participants

- Spectator and participant markets differ from each other with respect to socioeconomic characteristics and media habits.
- Consumers categorized as heavy participants were more likely to be male, better-educated, white-collar workers, minorities, and young, compared with the heavy spectator group.
- Consumers categorized as heavy participants also differ from heavy spectators with respect to media usage. Heavy participants are more likely to use business news-reporting media. In addition, heavy participants are more likely to watch intellectually appealing programming.
- Compared with male participants, male spectators exhibit an interest in a wider variety of media, especially television.
- Heavy participants and heavy spectators are different with respect to how they can be reached by advertising and how they perceive advertising.

Source: Adapted from John Burnett, Anil Menon, and Denise T. Smart, "Sports Marketing: A New Ball Game with New Rules," *Journal of Advertising Research* (September–October 1993), 21–33.

FACTORS INFLUENCING ATTENDANCE

It is opening day in Cleveland and the hometown Indians are set to take on the New York Yankees. Fred has gone to the traditional opening day parade and then attended the ball game for the past five years. The game promises to be a great one as the Indians are returning from last year's winning season and playing the rival Yankees. Fred will be joined at the game by his eight-year-old son and a potential business client.

As this hypothetical scenario illustrates, there are a variety of factors influencing Fred's decision to attend the season opener. He wants to experience the new stadium and watch the team that he has identified with since his childhood. As a businessman, Fred views the game as an opportunity to build a relationship with a potential client. As a father, Fred views the game as a way to bond with his son. In addition to these factors, Fred is prone to gambling and has placed a $50 bet on the home team. Finally, Fred thinks of opening day as an entertaining event that brings the whole community together and, as a lifelong resident, he wants to feel that sense of belonging.

Certainly, the interaction of the factors mentioned affected Fred's decision to attend the game. Sports marketers must attempt to understand all the influences on game attendance to market effectively to Fred and other fans like him. A variety of studies has examined some of the major issues related to game attendance, including fan motivation factors, game attractiveness, economic factors, competitive factors, demographic factors, stadium factors, value of sport to the community, sports involvement, and fan identification. Let us explore each factor in greater detail.

FAN MOTIVATION FACTORS

The foundation of any strategic sports marketing process is understanding why spectators attend sporting events or **fan motivation factors.** The basic motives for watching sports are categorized as self-esteem enhancement, diversion from everyday life, entertainment value, eustress, economic value, aesthetic value, need for affiliation, and family ties. It is important to note that these fundamental motives represent the most basic needs of fans. Because of this, the eight motives are often related to other factors, such as sports involvement and fan identification that are discussed later in the chapter. Let us now examine the eight underlying motives of fans identified in a study conducted by Wann.[6]

- **Self-Esteem Enhancement**—Fans are rewarded with feelings of accomplishment when their favorite players or teams are winning. These fans, more commonly are called "fair weather fans;" their association with the team is likely to increase when the team is winning and decrease when the team is doing poorly.

The phenomenon of enhancing or maintaining self-esteem through associating with winning teams has been called BIRGing, or basking in reflected glory.[7] When BIRGing, spectators are motivated by a desire to associate with a winner and, thus, present themselves in a positive light and enhance their self-esteem. Madrigal developed a model to explain why BIRGing might occur. He found that the three antecedent conditions that are related to BIRGing are expectancy disconfirmation, team identification, and quality of the opponent. In other words, BIRGing increases when the team does much better than expected, when the fan has high levels of association with the team, and when the team upsets stronger opponents.[8]

Spectators who dissociate themselves from losing teams because they negatively affect self-esteem accomplish this through CORFing, or cutting off reflected failure. The BIRGing and CORFing behaviors even have a high-tech influence on fans. A recent study found that fans are more likely to visit their team's Web site after a victory and less likely to visit the site after a defeat.[9]

- **Diversion from Everyday Life**—Watching sports is seen as a means of getting away from it all. Most people think of sports as a novel diversion from the normal routines of everyday life. In a recent article, the University of Nebraska Cornhusker fans were cited as having intense emotional ties to the team and it was stated that football served as a diversion from everyday life in Nebraska. "For several hours on a Saturday afternoon the struggling farmers of rural Nebraska—the inspiration for the school's nickname—can put aside their own problems and focus on someone else's."[10]

  In a recent example, there was great debate about whether and when Major League Baseball and other sports would resume their schedules after the events of September 11. Ultimately, it was decided that play should go on to serve as diversion and to ensure that the American way of life was not disrupted.

- **Entertainment Value**—Entertainment is closely related to the previous motive for attendance, sports serve as a form of entertainment to millions of people. As discussed in previous chapters, sports marketers are keenly aware of the heightened entertainment value of sports. In fact, one of the unique aspects of attending a sporting event is the uncertainty associated with the outcome. The drama associated with this uncertainty adds to the entertainment value of sports. Among spectators, the entertainment value of sports is believed to be the most highly motivating of all factors. In fact, Harris Interactive Company states that "contrary to popular belief, lowering ticket prices is not the best way—or even the most profitable way—to get people into seats. Creating an entertainment experience with flexible season tickets, VIP perks, etc., is a far better alternative. In short, people want to have fun, and for an increasing number of sports attendees this may have very little to do with the actual competition."[11]

  A number of professional sports are attempting to find interesting and innovative ways to increase their entertainment value for the fans on the field of play. John Madden, current Fox analyst and former Oakland Raiders head coach, suggested that the NFL adopt his "fair-play game plan," which features the following: more protection for the quarterback, a quicker instant-replay system, full-time and younger officials, more seasons before free agency, and more "event" promotion of games.[12] Baseball's commissioner, Bud Selig, continues to try and address the speed of play and has shaved an average of six minutes off

SPORTS MARKETING HALL OF FAME

David Stern

David Stern, the Commissioner of the NBA since 1984, has earned his place in sports marketing history. Stern is currently called the best commissioner in sport, the best in NBA history, and perhaps the best of any sport, ever. Prior to Stern, the NBA had a shaky network reputation, plummeting attendance figures, and no television contract.

During his tenure as commissioner, Stern took a floundering NBA and turned it "into an entity that is the envy of professional sports—an innovative, multifaceted, billion-dollar global marketing and entertainment company whose future literally knows no bounds." Stern has redefined the NBA and focused his marketing efforts on licensing, special events, and home entertainment. The league has gone from the arena business to radio, television, concessions, licensing, real estate, and home video—all under Stern's leadership. When the NBA was experiencing a public relations nightmare because of the number of players believed to be on drugs, it was again Stern who cleaned up the mess.

The All-Star Weekend, the made-for-television NBA lottery, making basketball the most popular sport in America with kids, and marketing the NBA across the world are all part of the sports marketing legacy that is David Stern.

Source: Adapted from E. M. Swift, "Corned Beef to Cavier," *Sports Illustrated* (June 3, 1991), 74–87.

each game.[13] However, some more innovative changes have been proposed by others to spice up the game, including: use of instant replay; allowing hitters to step out of the box only once per at-bat or an automatic strike would be called; only five visits per game to the mound; limiting pick-off throws to three per runner per base; waiving the waiver system; enforcing the batter's box; and inventing the "team" error.[14] Tennis, also suffering at the gate, has not seen any rule changes or major innovations since the addition of the break in the early 1970s. David Higedon, a tennis writer, has suggested that the entertainment value of tennis would be greatly improved by implementing some of the following ideas: allowing only three second serves per game, stopping the quieting of the crowds, eliminating five-set matches, and shortening the season.[15] Even track and field marketers have considered shortening meets and changing the way the events are run (e.g., limit the shot put to one throw instead of six).[16] Major League Soccer has sought to alter its product after successive seasons of slipping attendance. Most notably, the league will shorten its season from 32 to 28 games.[17] The NBA implemented new rules for the 2000 to 2001 season to quicken the pace of play, especially late in the games.[18] These new rules included reducing the number of timeouts per game per team from seven to six, reducing the number of fourth-period timeouts per team from four to three, reducing the maximum number of timeouts per team during the last two minutes of the fourth period from three to two, and reducing the length of timeouts in regulation play and overtime from 100 to 60 seconds.

- **Eustress**—Sports provide fans with positive levels of arousal. In other words, sports are enjoyable because they stimulate fans and are exciting to the senses. For example, imagine the excitement felt by Indy fans when the announcer says, "Gentlemen, start your engines" or the anticipation surrounding the opening kick-off for fans at the Super Bowl.
- **Economic Value**—A subset of sports fans are motivated by the potential economic gains associated with gambling on sporting events. Their enjoyment stems from having a vested interest in the games as they watch. Because this motive is only present for a small group of spectators, the economic factor is the

least motivating of all factors. However, the number of spectators who gamble on sports continues to rise, especially among college students. Keith Whyte, executive director for the National Council on Problem Gambling, says, "college campuses bring together a lot of Internet access, a propensity for sports wagering, and most students have credit cards. We are seeing signs that it is becoming a problem." In fact, four years ago there were 700 or so Web sites taking bets and now there are over 1,400 online gambling Web sites, about 72 percent of which offer sports betting. In addition, it was estimated that a total of 64 billion dollars was bet on sports over the Internet in 2003.[19] To curb this trend, a bill was introduced in February 2000 by Senator Sam Brownback to make betting on college and amateur sports illegal anywhere in the United States.[20] Thus far, no Internet gambling bill has ever reached the President's desk.

- **Aesthetic Value**—Sports are seen by many as a pure art form. Basketball games have been compared with ballets, and many fans derive great pleasure from the beauty of athletic performances (e.g., gymnastics and figure skating).
- **Need for Affiliation**—The need for belonging is satisfied by being a fan. Research has shown that reference groups, such as friends, family, and the community, influence game attendance. The more an individual's reference group favors going to a game, the more likely they are to attend games in the future. Additionally, individuals who become fans of a team later in life (adolescence and adulthood) are more likely to be influenced by friends in forming an attachment with a particular team.[21]

In addition to influencing game attendance, one study found that reference groups can also affect other game-related experiences, such as perceived quality of the stadium, perceived quality of the food service, overall satisfaction with the

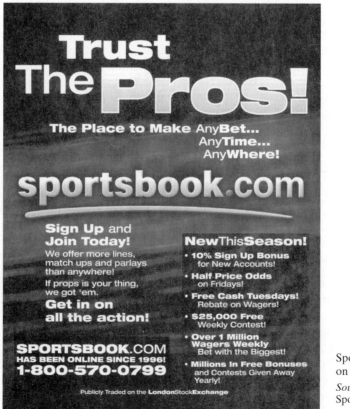

Sports gambling is growing on the Web.

Source: Copyright © 2000. Sportsbook.com. All rights reserved.

stadium, and perceived ticket value. For instance, individuals who perceive their reference group as opposing going to games will also have less satisfaction with the stadium environment.

- **Family Ties**—Some sports spectators believe attending sporting events is a means for fostering family togetherness. The entire family can spend time together and lines of communication may be opened through sports. Interestingly, women are more motivated than men to attend sporting events to promote family togetherness.[22] Research has also shown that "fathers" are the persons that have the greatest influence in becoming a fan of a specific team. This is especially true for individuals who became fans early in life (preteen years). This finding has important implications for sports marketers in creating opportunities for fathers to interact with children in team-related activities.[23]

What sports are people most likely to attend with their families and kids? According to a November 1999 poll by Harris Interactive,[24] 65 percent of respondents said they would take their families to watch men's tennis, followed by NFL games (56 percent) and PGA events (52 percent). Interestingly, the greatest percentage of respondents indicated they would take their kids (versus families) to watch professional wrestling (12 percent).

GAME ATTRACTIVENESS

Another factor related to game attendance is the perceived attractiveness of each game. **Game attractiveness** is a situational factor that varies from game to game and week to week. The perceived quality of a single game or event is based on the skill level of the individuals participating in the contest (i.e., the presence of any star athletes), team records, and league standings. In addition to these game-attraction variables, if the game is a special event (opening day, bowl game, or all-star game), game attractiveness is heightened. The more attractive the game, the more likely attendance will increase.

ECONOMIC FACTORS

Both the controllable and uncontrollable **economic factors** can affect game attendance. The controllable economic factors include aspects of the sports marketing environment that can be altered by sports marketers, such as the price of tickets and the perceived value of the sports product. The uncontrollable economic factors are things such as the average income of the population and the economic health of the country.

Generally, the greater the perceived value of the game and the greater the income of the population, the greater the game attendance. Surprisingly, one study found that attendance has no relationship to increased ticket prices.[25] In other words, raising ticket prices does not negatively affect game attendance. Other researchers, however, have found just the opposite.[26]

Sports teams pay a high price in fan loyalty every time a player leaves to join another team, according to research by economics professors Steve Shmanske and Leo Kahane.[27] Their analysis of baseball rosters and financial data for major league teams from 1990 to 1992 shows that owners who trade players frequently to get a winning team may end up hurting their revenues instead.

Winning teams do attract fans. Each additional percentage point in a major league team's winning percentage attracts about 32,000 fans that season and 25,000 fans the next season. But exorbitant player contracts and frequent trades may hurt attendance. A $1 increase in the average price of an MLB ticket decreases attendance by about 180,000. In addition, every time a regular player is traded to another team, attendance decreases. An average player's departure may cost 48,000 ticket sales. When a star leaves, as many as 84,000 tickets may not be sold. Given the average ticket price, the average player may be worth $420,000 to $540,000, and the star player may draw up to $730,000 in ticket sales. Trades are not necessarily bad for the baseball business, say the authors, but frequent trades are a sure way to alienate fans.

COMPETITIVE FACTORS

As discussed in Chapter 3, competition for sporting event attendance can be thought of as either direct (other sports) or indirect (other forms of entertainment). Ordinarily, the lesser the competition for spectators' time and money, the more likely they will be to attend your sporting event.

One form of direct competition of interest to sports marketers is the televised game. Sports marketers need to understand spectators' media habits and motivations to appeal to this growing segment. In addition, sports marketers want to learn whether to treat the viewing audience as a separate segment or whether it overlaps with spectators who attend games.

Some of these issues were addressed in a series of studies conducted to understand consumers' motivations for watching televised sports. Overall, the excitement, enthusiasm, and entertainment value associated with the telecasts are the primary motivating factors.[28] Interestingly, the need for watching televised sports differed by gender. Women indicated they were more motivated to watch sports for the social value and the fact that friends and family were already doing so. Men, however, were motivated to watch sports on television because they enjoy the telecasts and find them entertaining.

With respect to their viewing behavior, men are more interested in watching sports on television, want more sports coverage, watch more sports coverage, and follow it up by watching news reports of the action more frequently than do their female counterparts. In short, men appear more highly involved in televised sports.

How does consuming the game via some alternative media such as radio or television affect game attendance? One study examined the influence of television and radio broadcasting on the attendance at NBA games. The results indicated that television broadcasts of home games would have a negative impact on attendance, with over 60 percent of the fans indicating they would watch the game on television rather than attend. However, watching televised sports can also have a positive impact on home game attendance. For instance, the more one watches away games on television, the more one attends home games. In addition, the more one listens to the radio (for both home and away games), the greater the likelihood of attending home games.[29]

DEMOGRAPHIC FACTORS

Demographic factors or variables, such as population, age, gender, education, occupation, and ethnic background, are also found to be related to game attendance. Although the number of women attending sporting events is greater than ever before, males are still more likely to be in attendance. The sports that possess the highest retention of male fans include the NFL, NASCAR, and college football. The most avid female fans flock to figure skating, professional wrestling, and NASCAR.[30]

In addition, male sport fans tend to be younger, more educated, and have higher incomes than that of the general population. With the exception of baseball, the majority of ticket holders at sporting events now have annual income levels of $80,000 or more. According to the most recent census data, only 15 percent of American households reach this level of income, a relatively small market segment.[31] Interestingly, The National Hockey League, PGA Tour, and ATP (tennis) have the greatest percentage of fans with household incomes over $50,000.[32]

As you might imagine, it is very difficult to come up with *the* profile of the typical sports fan because of the varying nature of sport. However, it is important not to generalize and run the risk of neglecting a potentially huge market.[33]

STADIUM FACTORS

New stadiums are being built across the United States. Moreover, team owners who cannot justify or afford new stadiums are moving to cities that will build a new facility or attempt to renovate the existing stadium. Obviously, these stadium improvements are believed to affect the bottom line for team owners or for university presidents.

Stadium factors refer to variables such as the newness of the stadium, stadium access, aesthetics or beauty of the stadium, seat comfort, and cleanliness of the stadium. One study found that all these factors are positively related to game attendance. That is, the more favorable the fans attitude toward the stadium, the higher the attendance.[34]

Similar results were found in study a conducted for *Money* magazine by IRC Survey Research Group.[35] This study looked at what 1,000 sports fans value when attending professional sporting events. The major findings, in order of importance, are:

- Parking that costs less than $8 and tickets under $25 each
- Adequate parking or convenient public transportation
- A safe, comfortable seat that you can buy just a week before the game
- Reasonably priced snack foods, such as a hot dog for $2 or less
- Home team with a winning record
- A close score
- A hometown star who is generally regarded as being among the sport's 10 best players

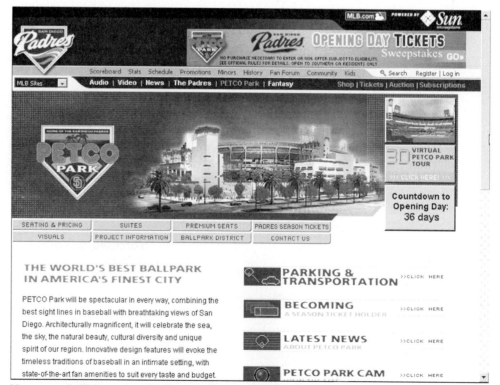

New sports facilities, such as the Petco Park in San Diego, influence attendance.
Source: Used by permission of MLB. All rights reserved.

- Reasonably priced souvenirs
- A game that ends in less than three hours
- A wide variety of snack foods

Interestingly, the four most important things identified in the study were unrelated to the game itself. If you make people pay too much or work too hard, they would rather stay home. Apparently, only after you are seated in your comfortable chair with your inexpensive food do you begin to worry about rooting for the home team.

In addition, spectators were concerned about having a clean, comfortable stadium with a good atmosphere. Part of the positive atmosphere is having strict controls placed on rowdy fans and having the option of sitting in a nonalcohol section of the stadium. An emerging area of some importance to new stadium design, as well as to stadium rehabilitation, is the need to provide more and larger restrooms. Because stadium atmosphere seems to be so important to fans, let us examine it in greater detail.

SPORTSCAPE

As you might have noticed, stadium atmosphere appears to be a critical issue in game attendance. Recently, studies have been conducted in the area of stadium environment or "sportscape."[36] **Sportscape** refers to the physical surroundings of the stadium that affect the spectator's desire to stay at the stadium and ultimately return to the stadium. Figure 6.2 shows the relationship between these sportscape factors and spectator behavior.

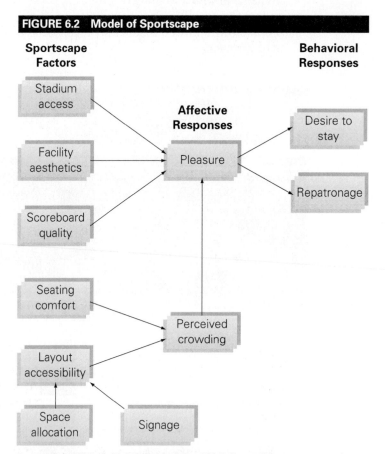

FIGURE 6.2 Model of Sportscape

Source: K. L. Wakefield, J. G. Bridgett, and H. J. Sloan, "Measurement and Management of the Sportscape," *Journal of Sport Management*, vol. 10, no. 6 (1996), 16. Reprinted by permission.

As shown in Figure 6.2, sportscape factors include stadium access, facility aesthetics, scoreboard quality, seating comfort, and layout accessibility. Each sportscape factor serves as input to the spectator's affective response or judgment of pleasure or displeasure with the stadium. The affective response, as we learned in Chapter 5, is the "feeling" component of attitudes. Similarly, the affective response with the sportscape is the feeling of perceived pleasure or displeasure the spectator has with the stadium. The perceptions of the stadium sportscape are linked to behavioral responses or actions of the spectator. In this case, the two behavioral responses are the desire to stay in the stadium and repatronage, or returning to the stadium for future events. Let us further examine the sportscape factors and their impact on spectators' pleasure.

Stadium Accessibility Many of us have left sporting events early to avoid traffic hassles or walked long distances to get to a game because of limited parking. For example, I recently attended a game at Wrigley Field in Chicago and, because of limited parking spaces, had to walk over three miles to get to the game. By the time I reached my seat, it was the third inning! This experience certainly resulted in displeasure with the entire game experience.

Stadium access includes issues such as availability of parking, the ease of entering and exiting the parking areas, and the location of the parking relative to the stadium. From the spectator's perspective, anything that can make it easier to get in and out of the stadium quicker will positively affect a return for future games.

Facility Aesthetics **Facility aesthetics** refers to the interior and exterior appearance of the stadium. The exterior appearance includes stadium architecture and age of the stadium. New stadiums, with historic architectural designs, are springing up across the United States. Research has shown that newer stadia do increase game attendance.

The interior of the stadium includes factors such as color of the stadium walls, facades and seats, the presence of sponsors' signage, and the presence of symbols from the team's past. For example, The Metrodome, the domed home of University of Minnesota football has been rated the poorest stadium in the Big Ten Conference because of its sterile game day atmosphere. It's so bad, that the university is proposing the construction of a new stadium on campus.[37] Compare this with Fenway Park in Boston, one of the oldest and most unique stadiums in the United States. As former pitcher Bill Lee stated, "Fenway Park is a religious shrine. People go there to worship."

Obviously, professional sports franchises are not the only ones who care about facility aesthetics. University marketers and athletic departments are equally concerned with their venues. In a recent article, the top 10 college football venues were ranked based on atmosphere and aesthetics, tradition, and how well the team plays at home. The number one stadium in college sport was Ben Hill Griffin Stadium, also known as the "Swamp," at the University of Florida. The rest of the best in college facilities include the following: (2) Notre Dame Stadium—University of Notre Dame, (3) Husky Stadium—University of Washington, (4) Neyland Stadium—University of Tennessee, (5) Kyle Stadium—Texas A&M University, (6) Ohio Stadium—Ohio State University, (7) Tiger Stadium—Louisiana State University, (8) Memorial Stadium—University of Nebraska, (9) Michigan Stadium—University of Michigan, and (10) LaVell Edwards Stadium—Brigham Young University.[38]

Scoreboard Quality One of the specific interior design considerations that represents a separate dimension of sportscape is **scoreboard quality.** In fact, the scoreboard in some stadiums is seen as the focal point of the interior. Throughout the game, fans continually monitor the stadium scoreboard for updates on scoring, player statistics, and other forms of entertainment, such as trivia contests, cartoon animation, and music videos. Examples of scoreboard quality range from the traditional scoreboard at

Fenway Park, which is manually operated, to the NFL's biggest scoreboard at Heinz Field in Pittsburgh.

The scoreboard at Heinz measures 27 feet tall by 96 feet wide and is designed to create pure entertainment.[39] Most of the entertainment will be produced like a TV show and feature in-stand giveaways, trivia contests, features on players, and facts and figures about the field. Rick Fairbend, the executive producer/broadcast manager for the Steelers said that "[the fans] will be amazed at the whole entertainment package from now on."

Not to be outdone, the Philadelphia Eagles new Lincoln Financial Field has two state-of-the-art, large screen video displays, each measuring 26 feet by 97 feet. The Philadelphia Phillies have decided that the signature element of their new stadium will be the main scoreboard. Even smaller colleges like Coastal Carolina University are enjoying the benefits of custom scoreboards. Underscoring the importance of the scoreboard is Warren Koegel, Athletic Director at Coastal Carolina University, who believes that fans are used to high definition TV and large screen displays, so they made the decision to invest in top-of-the-line equipment.[40]

Perceived Crowding   As shown in Figure 6.2, seating comfort and layout accessibility are the two factors that were found to be determinants of spectators' perceptions of crowding. Perceived crowding, in turn, is believed to have a negative influence on the spectator's pleasure. In other words, spectator pleasure decreases as perceived crowding increases.

Perceived crowding not only has an impact on pleasure but also on spectator safety. For example, English football grounds are moving away from terraces (standing areas renown for hooliganism and violence) and toward a requirement of all-seater facilities. There has been a great deal of debate about reintroducing terracing. However, based on a report that identified all-seating as the factor that contributes the most to spectator safety, the British government has no plans to bring back terraces at English football grounds.[41]

Seating Comfort   **Seating comfort** refers to the perceived comfort of the seating and the spacing of seats relative to each other. Anyone who has been forced to sit among the more than 100,000 fans at a University of Michigan football game can understand the influence of seating on the game experience. Likewise, those who have been fortunate enough to view a game from a luxury box also know the impact of seating on enjoyment of the game. The latest seating innovation in new stadia is the "club seat." These seats typically offer the padded seat luxuries of a private box without the privacy. Club level seats commonly include climate-controlled lounges, multiple TV sets, buffets, parking benefits, concierge service, and more space between rows of seats.

Layout Accessibility   **Layout accessibility** refers to whether spectators can move freely about the stadium. More specifically, does the layout of the stadium make it easy for spectators to get in and out of their seats and reach the concession areas, restrooms, and so on. To facilitate access to these destinations, there must be proper **signage** to direct spectators and there must be adequate **space allocation.** Inadequate space and signage cause spectators to feel confused and crowded, therefore, leading to negative feelings about the game experience.

As stated previously, all the sportscape factors affect spectators' feelings about the game experience. These positive or negative feelings experienced by spectators ultimately affect their desire to stay in the stadium and return for other games. Although all the sportscape factors are important, research has shown that perceived crowding is the most significant predictor of spectators having a pleasurable game experience. In addition, the aesthetic quality of the stadium was found to have a major impact on spectators' pleasure with the game.[42]

The findings of the sportscape research present several implications for sports marketers and stadium or facilities managers. First, stadium management should consider reallocating or redesigning space to improve perceived crowding. This might include enlarging the seating areas, walkways, and the space in and around concession waiting areas. Second, before spending the money to do major renovations or even building a new stadium to improve aesthetic quality, focus on more inexpensive alternatives. For instance, painting and cleaning alone might significantly improve the aesthetic value of an aging stadium.

The Bank One arena in Cincinnati (formerly the Riverfront Coliseum, and then the Firstar Center) is an excellent example of how making renovations to an older facility can be an effective way to improve the sportscape. The $14 million spent on renovating the Bank One arena included redesigning the building's entrance to improve traffic flow and increase the number of ticket windows. In addition, the entrance was repainted and retiled. On the interior, the walls were moved both to expand the size of the main concourse and concession areas and to double the number of restrooms. Moreover, all 15,000 seats were replaced. These changes have provided downtown Cincinnati with a first-class facility that spectators feel good about, at a cost much lower than new construction.[43]

Based on the studies conducted by Wakefield and his colleagues, there seems to be no doubt that the stadium atmosphere, or sportscape, plays a pivotal role in spectator satisfaction and attendance. Moreover, the pleasure derived from the sportscape causes people to stay in the stadium for longer periods of time. Certainly, having spectators stay in the stadium is a plus for the team, who will profit from increased concession and merchandise sales. In describing the importance of the sportscape, Wakefield states, "Effective facility management may enable team owners to effectively compete for consumers' entertainment dollars even when they may be unable to compete on the field."[44]

VALUE OF SPORT TO THE COMMUNITY

Values, as you will recall, are widely held beliefs that affirm what is desirable. In this case, values refer to the beliefs about the impact of sport on the community. Based on the results of a recent study, spectators' perceptions of the impact of professional sport on a community can be grouped into eight value dimensions (see Table 6.2 for a brief description of values).

As you might expect, each value is related to spectators' game attendance and intentions to attend future games. For instance, spectators who believe sports enhance community solidarity are more likely to attend sporting events. Sport marketers should carefully consider these values and promote positive values when developing marketing strategy.

SPORTS INVOLVEMENT

In Chapter 5, involvement was examined in the context of sports participation. Measures of sports involvement have also been used to understand spectator behavior. From the spectator's perspective, **sport involvement** is the perceived interest in and personal importance of sports to an individual attending sporting events or consuming sport through some other medium. What sports are people most interested in? The results of the 2003 Harris Interactive poll indicate that more than twice as many people name professional football over baseball as their favorite sport. Fan interest and involvement in the remaining sports can be seen in Table 6.3.[45]

Detailed studies have looked at the involvement levels of golf spectators, baseball spectators, Division I women's basketball spectators, and sports spectators in general.[46] In addition, a study has examined the cross-cultural differences in sport

Revamped Stadium to Put Fans Close to Action

SQUEEZING SEATING BOWL WITHIN COLONNADES COMPELS CLOSENESS TO FIELD

Intimacy in professional athletic stadiums? You bet.

Look at baseball's beloved Wrigley Field and Fenway Park. There's the retro-look Oriole Park at Camden Yards in Baltimore, where intimacy was part of the 1980s construction plan.

Since then, putting fans close to the action has been part of every new stadium design, from baseball's PacBell Park in San Francisco to the National Basketball Association's Conseco Fieldhouse in Indianapolis.

And now look at the new Soldier Field. "Intimate" Soldier Field.

It's likely that no National Football League stadium will match the level of close-to-the-sidelines intimacy promised by the designers and builders of the palace for the Chicago Bears.

A SHRINE TO INTIMACY

Actually, they had no choice but to make Soldier Field a shrine to intimacy, said Alice Hoffman, president of Chicago's Hoffman Management Partners LLC, the developer's representative for the Chicago Bears.

Because the bowl's new seating was to fit within the existing colonnades, all the suites and clubs had to be placed on the east side of the stadium, Hoffman added. By contrast, most NFL stadiums have suites around the entire circumference of the field.

"The colonnades force intimacy because they're so close together, on the east and west sides," she said. "In fact, our bowl is an average, of 60 ft. closer to the field than any other [NFL] stadium. Putting all the suites and clubs on one side allowed us to have a very narrow sideline on that side, the east side."

In addition, the south end zone seats have been moved 60 feet closer than they were in the old Soldier Field. "That's good for soccer too," Hoffman said. "Soccer draws crowds of about 20,000 to 25,000, and that's what our lower bowl accommodates. So the soccer fans will be right up close to the action. We got our sidelines so close for football, we actually have to have removable seating on the northwest and southwest corners of the lower bowl to accommodate a 70-yard-wide international soccer field.

"On the whole bowl, all the seats are as close as they can be by NFL guidelines without violating safety guidelines. We were definitely trying to get people as close to the action as possible, yet make sure disabled patrons have clear sightlines, even when people stand up in front of them."

Because an entire stadium has been built inside an existing stadium, being close to the action will be central to the experience, agreed Barnaby Dinges of the Dinges Gang Ltd., an Evanston, Ill.-based communications consultancy hired by the Chicago Bears and the Chicago Park District to manage communications on the Lakefront Redevelopment Project.

"There will not be a bad seat," Dinges said.

SUPERSIZED SCOREBOARDS

Adding to the feeling of closeness will be two new video scoreboards, one beyond each end zone, north and south. They're 23 feet high and 82 feet wide, or about twice the size of the video board in Soldier Field for its last season in 2001. Along with the scoreboards, the highly vertical wall of suites will help retain fan noise inside the stadium and should be a "wall of sound" intimidating to opposing teams, Dinges said.

Rising above three levels of club seating on the east side, the suites will be stacked four stories high in the center and will taper down to three stories as the wall moves north and south, said Joseph Caprile, principal in Chicago-based LW+Z Joint Venture. (The project is a joint venture of two architecture firms: Chicago-based Lohan Caprile Goettsch Associates, with primary responsibility for the master plan, and North Burnham Park project, and Boston-based Wood & Zapata, with primary responsibility for the architectural design of the Soldier Field stadium.)

The stacking results in "a very defined glass wall," Caprile added. "And the glass used in the suites is a special, transparent glass, to the extent that the glass in the lower half of the suite virtually disappears. Because the suites are stacked, the front glass wall is sloped facing down on the field. Right above that transparent glass, are windows that will open. That's because a lot of these suites fans love hearing the fan noise, the cheers, and the occasional boos."

FAN AMENITIES

Concessions and bathroom facilities have also been upgraded. Fans will have far more options in concession areas, types of food and beverages, and washrooms. And unlike in the old Soldier Field, eating and drinking won't take fans out of the sightlines of the game.

"You can get a beverage and still keep in touch with the game on the field," Caprile added.

The new facility will also offer club lounges, a new amenity for Bears' fans. Located on the east side behind each of the three levels of club seating, the club lounges will be places for fans to congregate, relax, and order food and beverages that will be brought to them by servers. Fans will be able to use the club lounge on their own level, as well as the other two.

"Another thing that's interesting about the club lounges is that they are all tied together by a three-story atrium," Caprile said. "So you don't feel isolated from the other lounges. In the club lounges, you're primarily watching the game on TV, although on the lower club lounge, there's a bar at the 50-yard line where you can sit and have a drink and see the field."

Caprile's guess is that the intimacy designed into the new Soldier Field will help make it one of the liveliest venues in the NFL.

"I walk under that stadium and it truly reminds me of a performing arts center or an opera house, where the seating is brought very close to the event," he said.

Source: Jeffrey Steele. Revamped Stadium to Put Fans Close to the Action. *Midwest Construction*, vol 6. no. 6, p. 18, McGraw-Hill Co., Inc. (June 2003).

TABLE 6.2   Eight Value Dimensions of Sport to the Community

- **Community Solidarity**—Sport enhances the image of the community enhances community harmony, generates a sense of belonging, and helps people to feel proud
- **Public Behavior**—Sport encourages sportsmanship, reinforces positive citizenship, encourages obedience to authority, and nurtures positive morality
- **Pastime Ecstasy**—Sport provides entertainment and brings excitement
- **Excellence Pursuit**—Sport encourages achievement and success, hardwork, and risk taking
- **Social Equity**—Sport increases racial and class equality and promotes gender equity
- **Health Awareness**—Sport eliminates drug abuse, encourages exercise, and promotes an active lifestyle
- **Individual Quality**—Sport promotes character building and encourages competitive traits
- **Business Opportunity**—Sport increases community commercial activities, attracts tourists, and helps community economic development

Source: James J. Zhang, Dale G. Pease, and Sai C. Hui, "Value Dimensions of Professional Sport as Viewed by Spectators," *Sports and Social Isssues* (February 21, 1996), 78–94. Reprinted by permission of Sage Publications, Inc.

involvement (see Spotlight). Generally, these studies have shown that higher levels of spectator involvement are related to the number of games attended, the likelihood of attending games in the future, and the likelihood of consuming sport through media, such as newspapers, television, and magazines. Also of importance, high-involvement spectators were more likely to correctly identify the sponsors of sporting events.

FAN IDENTIFICATION

Sports involvement was previously defined as the level of interest in and importance of sport to consumers. A concept that extends this idea to a sports organization is fan identification. Two contrasting examples of fan identification were seen with the movement of NFL franchises. When the Cleveland Browns moved to Baltimore, Browns fans became irate, holding protests, and filing lawsuits trying to stop the team's move.[47] However, when the Houston Oilers moved to Nashville relatively little fan resistance was observed, indicating low levels of fan identification.

Sports marketers are interested in building and maintaining high levels of fan identification for organizations and their players. If high levels of identification are developed, a number of benefits can be realized by the sports organization. Before examining the benefits of fan identification, let us take a closer look at what it is. **Fan identification** is defined as the personal commitment and emotional involvement customers have with a sports organization.[48] A conceptual framework was developed

TABLE 6.3 Favorite Sports—Which of These Is Your Favorite?

	1985	1989	1992	1993	1994	1997	1998	2002	2003	Change 1985–2003
	%	%	%	%	%	%	%	%	%	%
Pro football	24	26	28	24	24	28	26	27	29	+ 5
Baseball	23	19	21	18	17	17	18	14	13	−10
Men's pro basketball	6	7	8	12	11	13	13	11	10	+ 4
Auto racing	5	4	5	6	5	5	7	10	9	+ 4
College football	10	6	7	8	7	10	9	9	9	−1
Men's college basketball	6	10	8	8	8	6	4	4	6	—
Men's golf	3	4	4	6	5	6	4	4	5	+ 2
Hockey	2	3	3	3	5	4	3	3	3	+ 1
Soccer	3	2	2	1	3	3	4	3	3	—
Track & field	2	2	1	1	2	2	3	1	3	+ 1
Women's tennis	NA	NA	NA	NA	NA	NA	NA	3	2	NA
Men's tennis	5	4	4	4	3	3	4	1	2	−3
Horse racing	4	3	3	2	2	2	2	1	2	−2
Women's pro basketball	NA	NA	NA	NA	NA	NA	*	1	1	NA
Bowling	3	5	2	2	1	1	2	2	1	−2
Women's golf	NA	NA	NA	NA	NA	NA	NA	NA	1	NA
Women's college basketball	NA	NA	NA	NA	NA	NA	1	1	*	NA
Not sure	*	1	4	1	2	2	1	3	1	—
Pro football's lead over baseball	1%	7%	7%	6%	7%	11%	8%	13%	16%	+ 15%

Note: Base: All adults who follow a sport. NA = Not asked. Previously did not distinguish between men and women's sports when asking this question.
Source: From Football Widens Lead as Nation's Favorite Sport, Baseball Slips, Says U.S. Poll. PRNewswire, (September 24, 2003). Reprinted by permission.

by Sutton, McDonald, Milne, and Cimperman for understanding the antecedents and outcomes of fan identification.[49] The model is shown in Figure 6.3.

Managerial correlates are those things such as team characteristics, organizational characteristics, affiliation characteristics, and activity characteristics that directly contribute to the level of fan involvement. Team characteristics include, most notably, the success of the team. Typically, the more successful the team, the higher the level of fan identification—because people want to associate themselves with a winner (BIRGing). However, some fans see loyalty to the team to be more important than team success. For instance, the Boston Red Sox and the Chicago Cubs continue to have high levels of fan identification even though they have not won the World Series since the turn of the twentieth century.

Organizational characteristics also lead to varying levels of fan identification. In contrast with team characteristics, which pertain to athletic performance, organizational characteristics relate to "off-the-field" successes and failures. Is the team trying to build a winning franchise or just reduce the payroll? Is the team involved in the community and community relations? Is the team owner threatening to move to another city if a new stadium is not built with taxpayers' monies? An example of the impact of team and organizational characteristics on fan identification was provided by the Florida Marlins. As soon as the team won the 1997 World Series (team characteristic that should foster high fan identification), the owner talked about selling the team, and the organization traded several of its star players (organizational characteristic that will diminish fan identification).

SPOTLIGHT ON INTERNATIONAL SPORTS MARKETING

A Comparative Analysis of Spectator Involvement: United States vs. United Kingdom

As the field of sports marketing expands into international markets, the success of U.S. sports entities will be dependent on understanding the core consumer abroad—the international sports fan. Recently, a study was conducted to better understand the domestic and U.K. sports fan by measuring sports involvement and by exploring the relationship between sports involvement and sports-related behaviors.

The findings indicated that there are two dimensions of sports involvement that are consistent across the U.S. and U.K. sample. The cognitive dimension refers to the way that consumers think about sports, and the affective dimension is the way that consumers feel about sports. Both the cognitive and affective factors were positively related to viewing sports on television, reading about sports in magazines and newspapers, attending sporting events, and participating in sports. That is, higher levels of involvement are related to more viewing, reading about, and attending sporting events.

There were some differences in the responses of people from the United States and the United Kingdom. People from the United Kingdom spent less time each week watching sports on television; however, they were more likely to read the sports section of the newspaper on a daily basis. Compared with the U.S. sample, people from the United Kingdom were less interested in local sports teams as opposed to national teams. Finally, the British respondents were more likely than their American counterparts to perceive sports as necessary, relevant, and important.

There were no significant differences in the responses of people from the two countries concerning (1) the likelihood of planning your day around watching a sporting event, (2) hours spent reading sports-related magazines, and (3) participation in sports-related activities.

Source: Adapted from Matthew Shank and Fred Beasley, "A Comparative Analysis of Sports Involvement: U.S. vs. U.K.," Advertising and Consumer Psychology Conference, Portland, OR, May 1998.

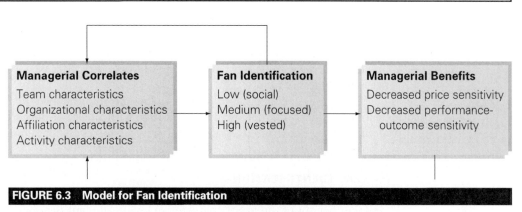

FIGURE 6.3   Model for Fan Identification

Source: William A. Sutton. *Sports Marketing Quarterly*. Reproduced with permission of Fitness Information Technology, Inc., in the format Textbook via Copyright Clearance Center.

Affiliation characteristics refer to the sense of community that a fan builds as a result of a team. According to Sutton et al., "The community affiliation component is . . . defined as kinship, bond, or connection the fan has to a team. Community affiliation is derived from common symbols, shared goals, history, and a fan's need to belong."[50] As discussed in the study on the impact of sports on the community, the sports team provides fans with a way to feel connected to the community and fulfill the **need for affiliation.** In addition, the more a fan's reference group (friends and family) favors going to games, the more the individual identifies with the team.[51]

Activity characteristics represent another antecedent to fan identification. In this case, activity refers to attending sporting events or being exposed to events via the

A Web page for high identification fans.
Source: Used by permission of Kristen Cornette, webmaster. All rights reserved.

media. As technology continues to advance, sports fans are afforded more opportunities to watch their favorite team via cable or pay-per-view, listen to games via radio, or link to broadcasts from anywhere via the Internet. With increased exposure, fan identification should be enhanced.

The interaction of the four preceding factors will influence the level of fan identification. An individual's level of identification with a team or player can range from no identification to extremely high identification. However, for simplicity, Sutton et al. describe three distinct categories of fan identification.[52]

LOW IDENTIFICATION

Fans who attend sporting events primarily for social interaction or for the entertainment benefit of the event characterize low-level identification. These "social fans" are attracted by the atmosphere of the game, promotions or events occurring during the competition, and the feelings of camaraderie that the game creates. Although this is the lowest level of fan identification, if fans are reinforced by the entertainment benefits of the game, then they may become more involved.

MEDIUM IDENTIFICATION

The next higher classification of fan involvement is called medium identification, or focused fans. The major distinguishing characteristic of these fans is that they identify with the team or player, but only for the short term. In other words, they may associate with the team, or player, if it is having an especially good year. However, when the team starts to slump or the player is traded, "focused" identification will fade. As with low-level identification, a fan that experiences medium levels of identification may move to higher levels.

HIGH IDENTIFICATION

The highest classification of fan involvement is based on a long term commitment to the sport, team, or player. These vested fans often recruit other fans, follow the team loyally, and view the team as a vital part of the community. Fans classified as high involvement exhibit a number of concrete behavioral characteristics. Most important, high-identification fans are the most likely to return to sporting events. Moreover, high-involvement fans are more likely to attend home and away games, have been fans for a greater number of years, and invest more financially in being a fan.

MANAGERIAL BENEFITS

The final portion of the fan identification model put forth by Sutton et al., describes the outcomes of creating and fostering vested fans. One outcome is that high-identification fans have decreased price sensitivity. Price sensitivity refers to the notion that small increases in ticket prices may produce great fluctuations in demand for tickets. Fans that stick with the team for the long run are more likely to be season ticketholders or purchase personal seat licenses to get the right to purchase permanent seats. Fans that exhibit low levels of identification may decide not to purchase tickets, even for small increases in ticket prices.

Another outcome of high levels of fan identification is decreased performance-outcome sensitivity. Stated simply, fans that are vested will be more tolerant of poor seasons or in-season slumps. Fans will be more likely to stick with the team and not give up prime ticket locations that may have taken generations to acquire.

Summary

In this chapter, we explored the spectator as a consumer of sport. Although there are many people who both participate in and observe sports, research suggests that there are two distinct segments of consumers. For instance, participants tend to be male, better educated, and younger than spectators.

There are a variety of factors that influence our decision to attend sporting events. These factors include fan motivation, game attractiveness, economic factors, competitive factors, demographic factors, stadium factors, value of sport to the community, sports involvement, and fan identification. Fan motivation factors are those underlying reasons or needs that are met by attending a sporting event. Researchers believe that some of the primary reasons fans attend sporting events are enhancement of self-esteem, diversion from everyday life, entertainment value, eustress (feelings of excitement), economic value (gambling on events), aesthetic value, need for affiliation, and time with family members.

Another factor that influences our decision to attend sporting events is game attractiveness. Game attractiveness refers to the perceived value and importance of the individual game based on what teams or athletes are playing (e.g., Is it the crosstown rival or is Ken Griffey Jr. in town?), the significance of the event to the league standings, whether the event is postseason versus regular season competition, or whether the event is perceived to be of championship caliber (e.g., the four majors in golf or the NCAA Final Four). In general, the greater the perceived attractiveness of the game, the more likely we will want to attend.

Economic factors also play a role in our decision to attend sporting events. As we discussed in Chapter 3, the economic factors that may affect game attendance can be at the microeconomic level (e.g., personal income) or macroeconomic level (e.g., state of the nation's economy). Although these are uncontrollable factors, the sports organization can attempt to control the rising cost of ticket prices to make it easier for fans to attend sporting events.

Competition is another important factor that influences our decision to attend sporting events or observe them through another medium. Today, sports marketers must define the competition in broad terms—as other entertainment choices, such as movies, plays, and theater compete with sporting events. Interestingly, sports organizations sometimes compete with themselves for fans. For example, one study found that televising home basketball games had a negative impact on game attendance.

Demographic factors such as age, ethnic background, and income are also related to spectator behavior. There is no such thing as a profile of the typical spectator. However, spectators are more likely to be male, young, more educated, and have higher incomes than that of the general population.

Perhaps the most important factor that influences attendance is the consumer's perception of the stadium. Stadium atmosphere appears to be a critical issue in attracting fans. The stadium atmosphere, or environment, has been referred to as the sportscape. The sportscape is the physical surroundings of the stadium that affect spectators' desire to stay at the stadium and ultimately return to the stadium. The multiple dimensions of sportscape include stadium access, facility aesthetics, scoreboard quality, seating comfort, and layout accessibility.

Another factor influencing game attendance and the likelihood of attending sporting events in the future is the perceived value of sport to the community. A study found that the more value attributed to sport, the more likely people were to attend. The value dimensions of sport to the community include community solidarity (bringing the community together), public behavior, pastime ecstasy (entertainment), pursuit of excellence, social equity, health awareness, individual quality (builds character), and business opportunities.

As discussed in Chapter 5, sports involvement referred to the consumer's perceived interest in and importance of participating in sport. Sports involvement has a related definition for those observing sporting events. High-involvement spectators are more likely to attend sporting events, read sports magazines, and plan their entire day around attending a sporting event.

A final factor related to spectator behavior is fan identification. Fan identification is the personal commitment and emotional involvement customers have with the sports organization. The characteristics of the team, the characteristics of the organization, the affiliation characteristics (sense of community), and the activity characteristics (exposures to the team) all interact to influence the level of fan identification. The higher the level of fan identification, the more likely fans are to attend events.

Key Terms

- aesthetic value
- demographic factors
- diversion from everyday life
- economic factors
- economic value
- entertainment value
- eustress
- facility aesthetics

- family ties
- fan identification
- fan motivation factors
- game attractiveness
- layout accessibility
- need for affiliation
- scoreboard quality
- seating comfort

- self-esteem enhancement
- signage
- space allocation
- sport involvement
- sportscape
- stadium access
- stadium factors

Review Questions

1. Describe the differences and similarities between spectators and participants of sport.
2. Discuss the spectators' eight basic motives for attending sporting events. Which of these are similar to the motives for participating in sports?
3. Provide two examples of how game attractiveness influences attendance.
4. What are the economic factors that influence game attendance? Differentiate between the controllable and uncontrollable economic factors.
5. Describe the typical profile of spectators of women's sporting events. How would a sports marketer use this information in the strategic sports marketing process?
6. Discuss, in detail, the sportscape model and how the sportscape factors affect game attendance.
7. What are the value dimensions of professional sport to the community? How would sports marketers use these values in planning the strategic sports marketing process?
8. Define sports involvement from the spectator perspective. Why is it important to understand the levels of involvement among spectators?
9. Discuss, in detail, the model of fan identification and its implications for sports marketers.
10. Explain the relationship among the eight basic fan motivation factors and the other factors that influence game attendance (i.e., game attractiveness, economic factors, competitive factors, demographic factors, stadium factors, value to the community, sports involvement, and fan identification).

Exercises

1. Go to a high school sporting event, college sporting event, and professional sporting event. At each event, interview five spectators and ask them why they are attending the events and what benefits they are looking for from the event. Compare the different levels of competition. Do the motives for attending differ by level (i.e., high school, college, and professional)? Are there gender differences or age differences among respondents?
2. Go to a sports bar and interview five people watching a televised sporting event. Determine their primary motivation for watching the sporting event. Describe other situations in which motives for watching sporting events vary.
3. Attend a women's sporting event and record the demographic profile of the spectators. What are your observations? Use these observations and suggest how you might segment, target, and position (market selection decisions) if you were to market the sport.
4. Attend a collegiate or professional sporting event. Record and describe all the elements of sportscape. How do these affect your experience as a spectator?
5. Ask 10 consumers about the value they believe a professional sports team would (or does) bring to the community. Then ask the same people about the value of college athletics to the community. Comment on how these values differ by level of competition.
6. How will marketing play a role in revitalizing the following sports: baseball, tennis, and cricket? How has marketing played a role in the increased popularity in the following sports: golf, basketball, and soccer?

Internet Exercises

1. Find examples via the Internet of how sports marketers have attempted to make it easier for fans to attend sporting events.
2. Locate two Web sites for the same sport—one for women and one for men (e.g., women's basketball and men's basketball). Comment on differences, if any, in how these sites market to spectators of the sport.
3. Locate two Web sites for the same sport—one American and one international (e.g., Major League Soccer and British Premier League). Comment on differences, if any, in how these sites market to spectators of the sport.

Endnotes

1. John Burnett, Anil Menon, and Denise T. Smart, "Sports Marketing: A New Ball Game with New Rules," *Journal of Advertising Research* (September–October 1993), 21–33.
2. George R. Milne, William A. Sutton, and Mark A. McDonald, "Niche Analysis: A Strategic Measurement Tool for Managers," *Sport Marketing Quarterly*, vol. 5, no. 3 (1996), 17–22.
3. Ibid.
4. Ibid.
5. *Richard Petty Driving Experience.* www.1800bepetty.com
6. Daniel L. Wann, "Preliminary Validation of the Sport Fan Motivation Scale," *Journal of Sport & Social Issues* (November 1995), 337–396.
7. R. B. Cialdini, R. J. Borden, A. Thorne, M. R. Walker, S. Freeman, and L. R. Sloan, "Basking in Reflected Glory: Three (Football) Field Studies," *Journal of Personality and Social Psychology,* vol. 34 (1976), 366–375.

8. Robert Madrigal, "Cognitive and Affective Determinants of Fan Satisfaction with Sporting Events," *Journal of Leisure Research*, vol. 27 (Summer 1995), 205–228.
9. Flip Boen, N. Vanbeselaere, J. Feys, "Behavioral Consequences of Fluctuating Group Success: An Internet Study of Soccer-Team Fans," *The Journal of Social Psychology*, vol. 142 (2002), 769–782.
10. Malcolm Moran, "For Nebraska, Football Is Personal," *USA Today* (October 27, 2000).
11. "Get Them Out to the Ballpark—and Off of the Couch," Harris Interactive, *Sporttainment News*, vol. 1, Issue 3 (June 12, 2001).
12. Dave Anderson, "John Madden: Game Plan for a Better NFL," *Athlon Sports* (July 1998), 23–30.
13. Paul Falevi and Mark Mashe, "Baseball's Winning Streak for Fans," *The Washington Post National Weekly Edition* (August 1998), 18–19.
14. Jayson Stark, "Get Your Rule Changes," *ESPN Baseball.* http://espn.go.com/mlb (February 4, 2003).

15. David Higdon, "13 Ways to Wake Up Pro Tennis," *Tennis* (May 1994), 43–46.

16. Jonathan Tesser, "S.O.S.," *Sport Magazine* (August 1998), 88–89.

17. Peter Brewington, "MLS Abandons Shootout, Shortens Season," *USA Today* (November 18, 1999).

18. "NBA Announces Rule Changes." www.nba.com/news/rules_changes_000815.html.

19. Jennifer Toland, "Cyber Gambling; Sports Fans Logging on for Online Wagering," *Sunday Telegram* (January 26, 2003) A1; Gary West, "No Need for Las Vegas or Bookies When There Is the Internet," *The Dallas Morning News* (March 19, 2002).

20. Rick Alm, "Brownback Aims to Ban All Betting on Colleges," *The Kansas City Star* (February 2, 2000), A1.

21. Richard Kolbe and Jeffrey James, "An Identification and Examination of Influences that Shape the Creation of Professional Team Fan," *International Journal of Sports Marketing and Sponsorship*, vol. 2 (2000), 23–38.

22. Daniel L. Wann, "Preliminary Validation of the Sport Fan Motivation Scale," *Journal of Sport & Social Issues* (November 1995), 337–396.

23. Richard Kolbe and Jeffrey James, "An Identification and Examination of Influences that Shape the Creation of Professional Team Fan," *International Journal of Sports Marketing and Sponsorship*, vol. 2 (2000), 23–38.

24. www.louisharris.com/pop_up/sports_poll/event_whom.asp.

25. R. A. Baade and L. J. Tiechen, "An Analysis of Major League Baseball Attendance, 1969–1987," *Journal of Sport & Social Issues*, vol. 14 (1990), 14–32.

26. Brad Edmondson, "When Athletes Turn Traitor," *American Demographics* (September 1997). www.demographics.com/publications/ad/97_ad/9709_ad/ad970916.htm.

27. Ibid.

28. Walter Gantz, "An Exploration of Viewing Motives and Behaviors Associated with Televised Sports," *Journal of Broadcasting*, vol. 25 (1981), 263–275.

29. James Zhang and Dennis Smith, "Impact of Broadcasting on the Attendance of Professional Basketball Games," *Sport Marketing Quarterly*, vol. 6, no. 1 (1997), 23–32.

30. "2003 ESPN Sports Fan Poll Is Now Available," Sporting Goods Manufacturers Association, www.sgma.com/press/2003.

31. Noel Paul, "High Cost of Pro-Sports Fandom May Ease Attendance at Most Major Events Drop—and Ticket Prices Are Expected to Follow," *Christian Science Monitor* (November 19, 2001), p. 16.

32. "2003 ESPN Sports Fan Poll Is Now Available," Sporting Goods Manufacturers Association, www.sgma.com/press/2003.

33. Donna Lopiano, "Marketing Trends in Women's Sports and Fitness," *Women's Sports Foundation*. www.lifetimetv.com/sports/index.html.

34. Kirk L. Wakefield and Hugh J. Sloan, "The Effects of Team Loyalty and Selected Stadium Factors on Spectator Attendance," *Journal of Sport Management* (1995), 153–172.

35. Jillian Kasky, "The Best Ticket Buys for Sports Fans Today," *Money*, vol. 24, no. 10 (October 1995), 146.

36. Kirk L. Wakefield, Jeffrey G. Blodgett, and Hugh J. Sloan, "Measurement and Management of the Sportscape," *Journal of Sport Management* (1996), 15–31.

37. Terry Hutchins, "Wisconsin Stadium Rated Tops in Big Ten," www.usatoday.com/sports, September 26, 2002.

38. Kevin Acee, "States of Grace; College Football's Finest Venues Are Almost Shrines to the Game," *The San Diego Union Tribune* (October 20, 2001), D2.

39. Ray Fittipaldo, "Game Day Entertainment Built Around NFL's Biggest Scoreboard," *Pittsburgh Post-Gazetter* (August 1, 2001).

40. NFL, NCAA, and High School Facilities Count on New Daktronics Football Scoreboards, *Business Wire* (September 10, 2003).

41. "British Sports Minister says 'The Terraces are History.'" (October 1997). www.nando.net/newsroom/spor. . ./feat/archive/102297/soc45127.html.

42. Kirk L. Wakefield, Jeffrey G. Blodgett, and Hugh J. Sloan, "Measurement and Management of the Sportscape," *Journal of Sport Management* (1996), 15–31.

43. Andy Hemmer, "Gardens Gets Skyboxes in Makeover," *Cincinnati Business Courier Inc.*, vol. 11, no. 48 (April 10, 1995), 1.

44. Kirk L. Wakefield, Jeffrey G. Blodgett, and Hugh J. Sloan, "Measurement and Management of the Sportscape," *Journal of Sport Management* (1996), 15–31.

45. "Football Widens Lead as Nation's Favorite Sport, Baseball Slips, Says U.S. Poll," PRNewswire, September 24, 2003, www.prnewswire.com

46. Deborah L. Kerstetter and Georgia M. Kovich, "An Involvement Profile of Division I Women's Basketball Spectators," *Journal of Sport Management*, vol. 11 (1997), 234–249. Dana-Nicoleta Lascu, Thomas D. Giese, Cathy Toolan, Brian Guehring, and James Mercer, "Sport Involvement: A Relevant Individual Difference Factor in Spectator Sports," *Sport Marketing Quarterly*, vol. 4, no. 4 (1995), 41–46.

47. Geoff Hobson, "Just Another Sunday," *The Cincinnati Enquirer* (December 7, 1996).

48. William A. Sutton, Mark A. McDonald, George R. Milne, and John Cimperman, "Creating and Fostering Fan Identification in Professional Sports," *Sport Marketing Quarterly*, vol. 6, no. 1 (1997), 15–22.

49. Ibid.

50. Ibid.

51. Kirk L. Wakefield, "The Pervasive Effects of Social Influence on Sporting Event Attendance," *Journal of Sport & Social Issues*, vol. 19, no. 4 (November 1995), 335–351.

52. William A. Sutton, Mark A. McDonald, George R. Milne, and John Cimperman, "Creating and Fostering Fan Identification in Professional Sports," *Sports Marketing Quarterly*, vol. 6, no. 1 (1997).

CHAPTER 7

SEGMENTATION, TARGETING, AND POSITIONING

After completing this chapter, you should be able to:

- Discuss the importance of market selection decisions.
- Compare the various bases for marketing segmentation.
- Understand target marketing and the requirements of successful target marketing.
- Describe positioning and its importance in the market selection decisions.
- Construct a perceptual map to depict any sports entity's position in the marketplace.

Market selection decisions are the most critical elements of the strategic sports marketing process. In this portion of the planning phase, decisions are made that will dictate the direction of the marketing mix. These decisions include how to group consumers together based on common needs, who to direct your marketing efforts toward, and how you want your sports product to be perceived in the marketplace. These important market selection decisions are referred to as segmenting, targeting, and positioning (STP). In this chapter, we examine these concepts in the context of our strategic sports marketing process. Let us begin by exploring market segmentation, the first of the market selection decisions.

SEGMENTATION

Not all sports fans are alike. You would not market the Xtreme Games to members of the American Association of Retired People (AARP). Likewise, you would not market the PGA's Champions Tour to Generation Xers. The notion of mass marketing and treating all consumers the same has given way to understanding the unique needs of groups of consumers. This concept, which is the first market selection decision, is referred to as market segmentation. More specifically, **market segmentation** is defined as identifying groups of consumers based on their common needs.

Market segmentation is recognized as a more efficient and effective way to market than mass marketing, which treats all consumers the same. By carefully exploring and understanding different segments through marketing research, sports marketers determine which groups of consumers offer the greatest sales opportunities for the organization.

If the first market selection decision is segmentation, then how do sports marketers group consumers based on common needs? Traditionally, there are six common bases for market segmentation. These include demographics, socioeconomic group, psychographic profile, geographic region, behavioral style, and benefits. Let us take a closer look at how sports marketers use and choose from among these six bases for segmentation.

BASES FOR SEGMENTATION

The bases for segmentation refer to the ways that consumers with common needs can be grouped together. Six bases for segmenting consumer markets are shown in Table 7.1.

DEMOGRAPHIC SEGMENTATION

One of the most widely used techniques for segmenting consumer markets is **demographic segmentation.** Demographics include such variables as age, gender, ethnic background, and family life cycle. Segmenting markets based on demographics is widespread for three reasons. First, these characteristics are easy for sports marketers to identify and measure. Second, information about the demographic characteristics of a market is readily available from a variety of sources, such as the government census data described in Chapter 4. Third, demographic variables are closely related to attitudes and sport behaviors, such as attending games, buying sports merchandise, or watching sports on television.

Age   Age is one of the most simplistic, yet effective demographic variables used to segment markets. Not only is age easy to measure, but it also is usually related to consumer needs. In addition, age of the consumer is commonly associated with other demographic characteristics, such as income, education, and stage of the family life cycle. A number of broad age segments exist such as the children's market, the teen market, and the mature market. Care must be taken, however, not to stereotype consumers when using age segmentation. How many 10-year-olds do you know who think they are 20 and how many 75-year-olds think they are 45?

TABLE 7.1   Common Bases for Segmentation of Consumer Markets

Demographic
- Age
- Gender
- Ethnic background
- Family life cycle

Socioeconomic
- Income
- Education
- Occupation

Psychographic
- Lifestyle
- Personality
- Activities
- Interests
- Opinions

Geographic
- World region
- Country
- Country region
- City
- Physical climate

Behavioral
- Frequency of purchase
- Size of purchase(s)
- Loyalty of consumers

Benefits
- Consumer needs
- Product features desired

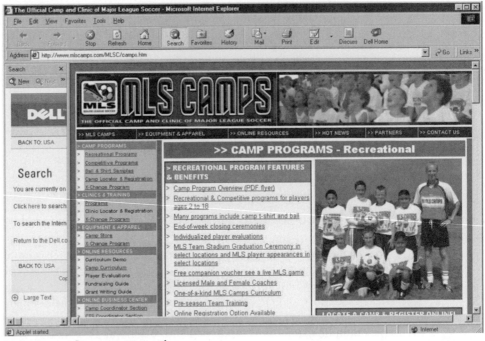

Major League Soccer targets youth.

Source: Used by permission of MLSC. All rights reserved.

Children. There has always been a natural association between children and sports. However, sports marketers are no longer taking the huge children's market for granted—and with good reason. Children have tremendous influence on purchase decisions within the family and are increasingly purchasing more and more on their own.[1]

Kids influence the sale of $200 billion of all products and services sold per year. In addition, children ages eight to 12 are believed to spend their own money at a rate of $19 billion annually.[2] Approximately 8 percent of all sports equipment is purchased by children, and 10 percent of all sports equipment purchases are influenced by children.[3] Children are participating in sports and are identifying with teams, players, and brands at younger ages each year.

Thus, sports marketers have recognized the power of the kids' market. They realize children will become the fans and the season ticketholders of the future. As such, they have segmented markets accordingly. An example of how the NBA is marketing to kids can be seen on page 186.

Major League Baseball is trying to increase its pipeline of players and future fans via its Urban Youth Initiative. MLB recently opened its first Youth Baseball Academy in Compton, California. The purpose of the academy is to grow the game of baseball by providing kids with coaching and instruction in both baseball and softball.[4] Wal-Mart is also getting into the kid's act by collaborating with FLW Outdoors, the leading marketer of competitive fishing and administers the $6 million Wal-Mart FLW Tour. The partners have developed a nationwide program called "Take a Kid Fishing," which promotes parents getting their kids "hooked on fishing."[5]

The children's segment is also growing in importance to those organizations marketing to kids via the Internet. For example, Toyrus.com recently introduced a new sporting goods site called sportrus.com with a "just for kids" area designed to help parents select sports equipment for kids ages five to 12. In another example, the

Professional sports are realizing the importance of the kid's market to their long-term success.

President's Council on Physical Fitness and Activity has launched a web site (www.presidentschallenge.org) to help motivate kids and families become more physically active.

Teens.   The teen market is currently estimated at $95 billion annually and growing.[6] The number of teens is also expected to rise exponentially, because the U.S. Census Bureau projects that by 2010 there will be 30.81 million teens in the United States.[7] A global study conducted by DMB&B of 25,000 teens in 41 countries found that basketball is the most popular game on the planet. Over 70 percent of teens are involved in basketball, and 76 percent of the teens surveyed are familiar with the NBA logo.[8] Numbers like these are causing sports marketers to take a hard look at the teen market in all sports, as the following article on NASCAR illustrates.

The Mature Market.   Another market that is expected to increase at a staggering pace is the age 55 and older, mature market. **Mature adults, age 55-plus** numbers some 59 million or roughly 21 percent of the U.S. population. Their staggering numbers equal the entire populations of New York and California, Washington State, and the District of Columbia, or New York, California, and Massachusetts combined. Additionally, people age 65-plus comprise 12.4 percent of the population and this number is expected to double to 70.3 million by 2030.[9] Stereotypically, the elderly are perceived to be inactive and thrifty. Nothing could be further from the truth. The mature market is living longer and becoming more physically active. In addition, income per capita of the mature market is 26 percent higher than the national average and this segment spends more than one trillion dollars on goods and services. As a result, sports marketers are capitalizing on this growing market in a variety of ways.

Traditionally, senior citizen discounts have been promoted in Major League Baseball. For example, the Milwaukee Brewers have created the 60+ fan club providing tickets, merchandise, and other special promotional offers to seniors. Promotions such as the "World's Oldest Tailgate Party" are designed to strengthen the relationship between the Brewers and the teams' senior fans.[10] Other examples of sports markets being segmented by age can be seen in the growing number of "senior" sporting tours and events. The Champions Tour of the PGA has nearly the following of the regular

NBA Scores with Book Publishing Program

The March release of a comic book featuring Dallas Mavericks players as superheroes is just the latest offering from the National Basketball Association's growing list of titles. Coordinated by the NBA's entertainment and players marketing division, the league has licensing agreements with six publishers and is looking to add more partners and titles, said the NBA's Charlie Rosenzweig.

The NBA works with publishers to reach different audiences with books in various formats, Rosenzweig explained. The Mavericks comic book, published by Ultimate Sports Entertainment, is the first of four comic books planned for this year that will feature specific teams and is the NBA's newest publishing venture. Another new deal is with Alpha Books, publisher of the Complete Idiot's line, which has resulted in the publication of *The Complete Idiot's Guide to the NBA*.

The NBA's longest-standing deals are with Scholastic, Doubleday, and *The Sporting News*. Four to six low-priced books are published annually with Scholastic, all aimed at the children's market. "They're a great partner," Rosenzweig said, noting that Scholastic is also a major contributor to the NBA's Read to Achieve literacy program, a project run by a separate NBA unit. Doubleday has published two books so far: the $50 *The Official NBA Encyclopedia* and *At the Buzzer*, a book/CD package. Talks are underway to do a third book with Doubleday. *The Sporting News* oversees the league's championship titles—Dynasty: *NBA 2002 Champion Los Angeles Lakers* is the most recent—as well as the league's annual guides and registers. *The Sporting News* aims to get the championship book out within 10 days after the final game and the title is then cross-promoted with the release of the DVD.

Cross-promotion with other NBA products is an important strategy for the league. Other products developed within the entertainment and players marketing division are DVDs, music CDs, and magazines. While each publisher sells its titles to its traditional accounts, the NBA's global merchandising group markets the titles to nontraditional outlets. Books are also available at the NBA's online store. And with the NBA drawing interest, and players, from around the world, the league is working to improve its global distribution capabilities. The international reach of Dorling Kindersley (DK) was one factor in the NBA inking a deal with that company to produce a number of photography books. The NBA has given DK access to its extensive photography collection. The first title, *Basketball's Best Shots*, came out last fall, and the next titles, due this fall, under the agreement are *Eyewitness Basketball* and *NBA's Greatest*.

Autumn, when the NBA season begins, is one of three prime times for promoting the league's books. The weeks surrounding the All-Star game are another window of opportunity, as is the spring, when the playoffs are underway. "We intend to grow this business and are looking at different opportunities," Rosenzweig said.

Source: Jim Milliot. *Publisher's Weekly* (April 28, 2003) p. 18. Copyright © 2003 Reed Business Information US, a division of Reed Elsevier Inc. All Rights Reserved.

tour events. Although not as successful as golf, other professional senior tours include tennis and bowling.

Seniors are also becoming more active as sports participants. The fastest-growing participation sports for seniors, classified as age 55 and older, include exercising to music and running or walking on the treadmill. Table 7.2 shows some of the most popular sports for the mature market.[11]

Gender More than 45 million women watch professional football on an average weekend, and a 2002 report by Scarborough Sports Marketing found that the number of women fans is booming with some 50 million women stating that they are avid fans of professional sports.[12] The sponsorship of women's sports has exceeded $1 billion dollars. The number of women playing hockey in Canada has quadrupled in the past five years. The WNBA has doubled in size over the past five years.[13] These examples, and many others, illustrate shifting gender roles in sport.

Historically, sports enthusiasts have been male. However, stereotypes are eroding quickly as women are becoming more involved in every facet of sport. More women are participating in sports, and more women are watching sports. Moreover, every

Teen Market Aim of New NASCAR

NASCAR hopes to attract younger fans with Nextel as the title sponsor for its top racing series.

NASCAR is no longer the same sport where Richard Petty won 200 races, North Wilkesboro was a regular stop, and the late Dale Earnhardt reigned.

Thursday's announcement that Nextel Communications will sponsor NASCAR's top stock-car series next year—NASCAR Nextel Cup—is another sign of a sport redefining its image. NASCAR no longer is the cigarette-toting fan from the South. Instead, the sport aspires to be the cellphone-carrying teen in Seattle.

"We've come a long way toward making NASCAR racing a national sport with fans spread across America," NASCAR chairman Bill France Jr., said in announcing that Nextel had signed a 10-year contract reported to be worth $700 million to replace Winston as series sponsor.

"We still have miles to go to achieve our goals, but we are confident we are well on our way."

NASCAR has taken an aggressive approach to exert more control of the U.S. market and spread its influence throughout the 115 countries that receive broadcasts or highlights of series races. Such a method was evident in how quickly Winston was replaced.

George Pyne, NASCAR's vice president, estimated that about 120 days elapsed between when Winston informed series officials to look for a new sponsor and Nextel was signed. That's despite a sluggish economy and a brief war that caused many companies to be cautious with their money. Normally deliberate in making decisions, NASCAR officials have made a series of recent announcements expanding the sport.

Consider what had happened this year before Nextel.

Toyota announced it would compete in the Craftsman Truck Series next season with expectations the company will field Cup cars by 2007.

California Speedway gets a second date next year, as North Carolina Speedway loses one of its two races as part of schedule realignment. More changes are expected next year, putting the South at risk of losing more races to another region.

NASCAR announced plans for more night races and later starting times, mainly to attract a larger West Coast TV audience. NASCAR completes a deal with Jerry Leigh, Inc. to make series-brand clothes for women.

More deals are to be struck, although none will be as big as signing Nextel, a wireless communications provider based in Reston, VA.

"I've got to believe that even though you're seeing a lot of things happening this year, I think a lot of this stuff has been in the works for a long time," said Jim Rocco, senior vice president of operations for Valvoline, which sponsors and co-owns the car of Johnny Benson.

It's not a coincidence that these decisions have been announced at about the same time.

"It's only a little over a year-and-a-half before negotiations on a new TV contract begin, so the timing is outstanding," said Humpy Wheeler, president and general manager of Lowe's Motor Speedway.

NASCAR, which ranks second to the NFL in TV ratings, received about $2.4 billion from Fox, NBC, and its partners to broadcast series races beginning in 2001. If the new initiatives attract additional fans, NASCAR would demand more money from the networks. The networks could recoup those extra costs with higher rates from sponsors.

"More eyeballs mean more advertising dollars," said Clay Campbell, president and general manager of Martinsville Speedway. "The bigger NASCAR can get . . . that's the name of the game as far as networks are concerned."

The biggest way NASCAR can grow is to reach a younger audience. Legislation against tobacco advertising prevented Winston from tapping the under-18 crowd. Nextel has no such problems. Many teens aren't aware of a world without cellphones.

Series officials were almost giddy Thursday when they talked about drawing younger fans—a generation unaware that Petty and Earnhardt are the only seven-time series champions or that North Wilkesboro hosted two Cup races a year from 1961–1996. A NASCAR study done in 2001 showed that 11 percent of people age 18 to 24 were series fans. The study did not look at fans any younger. That will change.

"The children of today are the consumers of tomorrow," NASCAR's Pyne said. Those consumers are valuable today.

Teenage Research Unlimited, an Illinois research firm focusing on the teen market, reported that the nation's teenagers spent $170 billion last year. The study found that teenagers spent an average of $101 a week either for themselves or on behalf of their parents.

That will purchase a lot of NASCAR merchandise. Today, tomorrow, and beyond. At least that's what series officials hope. All so a bunch of cars can race in circles most weekends.

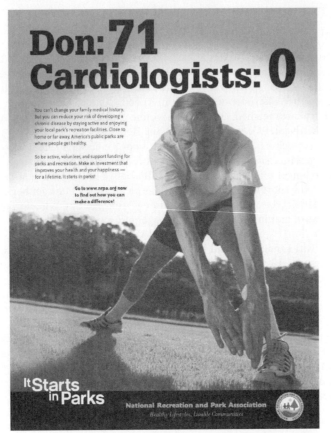

The National Recreation and Park Association is capitalizing on the growing mature market.

Source: Used by permission of the National Recreation and Park Association. All rights reserved.

TABLE 7.2 Most Popular Sports for Seniors Based on Frequent Participation (Age 55+ and older)	
Activity	*Year 2002*
1. Fitness Walking (100+ days/year)	6,515,000
2. Stretching (100+ days/year)	4,107,000
3. Treadmill Exercise (100+ days/year)	3,887,000
4. Golf (25+ days/year)	3,646,000
5. Freshwater Fishing (15+ days/year)	1,903,000
6. Recreational Vehicle Camping (15+ days/year)	1,736,000
7. Free Weights: Hand Weights (100+ days/year)	1,735,000
8. Bowling (25+ days/year)	1,725,000
9. Day Hiking (15+ days/year)	1,545,000
10. Weight/Resistance Machines (100+ days/year)	1,513,000
11. Stationary Cycling: Upright Bike (Regular) (100+ days/year)	1,298,000
12. Abdominal Machine/Device (100+ days/year)	1,185,000
13. Free Weights: Dumbbells (100+ days/year)	1,040,000
14. Running/Jogging (100+ days/year)	870,000
15. Calisthenics (100+ days/year)	827,000

SGMA International. Used by permission.

History of the NWFA

The National Women's Football Association (NWFA) was formed in August 2000 by well-known sports and entertainment entrepreneur, Catherine Masters. Masters, who has more than 25 years experience in the top levels of these industries, decided it was time for women to have the chance to play full contact football in a well-organized and professionally run league.

Starting with two teams, the Nashville Dream and the Alabama Renegades, the league held a preseason showcase of six games. This preseason ran from October 14, 2000 until December 2, 2000. The preseason was a rousing success with thousands of fans in the stands and incredible support from the media worldwide.

Between January and March of 2001, Masters added another eight teams bringing the total of teams for the 2001 season to 10. More than 5,000 fans packed the stands at the league's first championship game where the Philadelphia Liberty Belles beat the Pensacola Power. Then, between August 2001 and November 2001, Masters added another 11 teams bringing the total of teams gearing up for the 2002 season to 21.

In 2002 the NWFA broke all kinds of records in attendance, with 5600 fans attending the 2002 SupHer Bowl and created history with obtaining the first ever betting line on a women's football game. And, if that wasn't enough, the league negotiated and signed a five year TV rights broadcast deal with the exciting new football network. The league also brought in its first championship sponsor, The Essere Corporation. The Mass Mutiny and the expansion team, the Detroit Danger (name was changed to Demolition in 2003), played in the league's 2nd national championship game with Detroit winning the game. The NWFA produced and broadcast the 2002 Championship game to over 3 million homes.

In 2003, the NWFA added another eight teams bringing the total number of teams competing to 29. The two teams that won the right to play in the NWFA's 3rd National Championship Game were the Pensacola Power and the Detroit Demolition. Both teams had made previous appearances at the National Championship Game. Again, Detroit showed its talent and won the game in the 4th quarter 28-21. The game was played at Vanderbilt University stadium, the largest venue to ever host a women's football game. And, again, the league secured a betting line on the game. The league also scored some big points with bringing in a National and Championship sponsor, Dickens Energy Cider drink. This fuel replacement beverage will be seen at all team's games and the company will be the main sponsor of the league's National Championship games for three years. Again, the NWFA produced and broadcast the Championship game, this time to more than 5 million homes.

In 2004, the league will field 37 teams for the season. The league also has been the subject of many feature stories and articles in more than 250 major publications and TV networks including the CBS Evening News, The NBC Today Show, The New York Times, Nickelodeon, The Boston Globe, The Washington Post, and many local and regional networks and publications. The league's website had over 3.5 million hits in April of 2003.

Source: National Women's Football Association, www.womensfootballcentral.com/history.htm.

attempt is being made to make women's sports equitable with their male counterparts. For example, in the 2000 Olympics in Sydney, women competed in 24 of the 28 sporting events. In addition, the Sydney Olympics featured 21 extra women's events across nine sports, such as the triathlon and tae kwon do.

All this emphasis on women's sports translates into new opportunities for sports marketers. The women's segment is drawing much deserved attention as the above article that chronicles the history of the National Women's Football Association (NWFA) illustrates.

Ethnic Background   Segmenting markets by **ethnic background** is based on grouping consumers of a common race, religion, and nationality. Ethnic groups, such as African Americans (13 percent of the U.S. population), Hispanic Americans (12 percent of the U.S. population), and Asian Americans (4 percent of the U.S. population) are increasingly important to sports marketers as their numbers continue to grow. With segmenting based on ethnic background, marketers must be careful not to think of stereotypical profiles but to understand the unique consumption behaviors of each group through marketing research.

An example of how ethnic background can be an important consideration for sports marketers comes from the National Hockey League's diversity program called "Ice Hockey in Harlem." The goal of all the NHL's diversity efforts is to attract new players and new fans to the game. The reason for the increasing push in diversity is that more and more competition exists for sports fans and the NHL hopes to attract as many new fans as possible to the game. There are currently around 30 players of color in the NHL and the numbers are growing.[14]

Major League Soccer (MSL) has long espoused the philosophy of having an ethnic fan base. Commissioner Don Garber believes the MSL is, "perfectly suited to capitalize on what's going on in this country. We are a nation of increasing ethnic diversity. We are a nation that's finding itself in an increasingly growing global community. And that global community is linked by one language, a language that is shared by all, and that's the sport of soccer." Garber has also helped league officials and marketing folks understand that there are increasing numbers of immigrants—particularly in Hispanic communities—to whom soccer is a cultural necessity. Garber said, "capturing the ethnic fan" is essential in making that approach work. "It requires careful considerations. It means realizing that fans bang drums and stand throughout the game. It means courting Spanish-language media, Caribbean media, and other foreign-language interests."[15]

Another example of marketing to ethnic groups includes the introduction of "Deportes Hoy," the premier, Spanish-language sports daily. The sports information product will be circulated in Los Angeles, Orange, and San Diego Counties and will be targeted to reach everyone from the occasional to the most highly involved sports enthusiasts.[16] Similarly, SportsYA.com, which translates as "sports now," is the leading Internet brand among Hispanic users seeking sports information. Other examples of professional sports leagues attempting to build a diverse group of fans can be seen in the following article.

Family Life Cycle   The **family life cycle** was a concept developed in the 1960s to describe how individuals progress through various "life stages," or phases of their life. A traditional life cycle begins with an individual starting in the young, single "life stage." Next, an individual would progress through stages such as young, married with no children; young, married with children; to finally, older with no spouse. As you can see, the traditional stages of the family life cycle are based on demographic characteristics such as age, marital status, and the presence or absence of children.

Today, the traditional family life cycle is no longer relevant. In 2000, roughly half of all marriages end in divorce, and the number of single-parent households is on the rise. Changes in family structure such as these have led marketers to a more modern view of the family life cycle, shown in Figure 7.1.

Sports marketers segmenting on the basis of family life cycle have a number of options. Do they want to appeal to the young and single, the elderly couple with no kids living at home, or the family with young children? Sports that are growing in popularity, such as biking, segment markets based on a stage of the family life cycle. Just imagine the incompatible biking needs of a young, single person versus a young, married couple with children.

Professional sports has come under increased scrutiny in the past decade for its lack of family values. Rising ticket prices, drunken fans, and late games have all been cited as examples of professional sports becoming "family unfriendly." Realizing this, sports marketers have tried to renew family interest in sports and make going to the game "fun for the entire family." As discussed in Chapter 2, the Harlem Globetrotters have done this for years.

Along with the Globetrotters, there are many other examples of sports marketers trying to become more family friendly. For instance, the addition of Homer's Landing,

Leagues Work to Build Diverse Crowds

Four years ago, Major League Baseball (MLB) conducted a poll in which more than 80 percent of 3,000 adult women said they made the household purchasing decisions on behalf of the family, while 58 percent said they made the final call on how the family spends its weekends.

The league's study prompted the Anaheim Angels, who at that time were spending nothing on advertising to women, to reallocate 20 percent, or $300,000, of the club's $1.5 million marketing budget to attracting female heads of household, according to Robert Alvarado, the Angels' marketing director. Last year the Angels sold 15,000 tickets as part of their "family pack" offer, a fivefold increase over 2000, the first year of the Angels' newly segmented budget.

While the Angels' case illustrates how leaguewide initiatives can spur change at the local level, it's also a reminder of how much is often left up to the teams. But leagues with more aggressive and centralized fan diversity programs have proven in recent years that putting tools at teams' disposal does make a difference in attracting women, Hispanics, and African Americans to their sport.

MAJOR LEAGUE BASEBALL

Major League Baseball's fan demographic patterns since 1998 suggest the league may be relying too much on proactive teams like Anaheim. In 2002, MLB had the second-highest percentage (46.6) of female fans of all the leagues, but that was nearly stagnant after 1998, according to a study conducted by SportsBusiness Journal (SBJ) in conjunction with ESPN Sports Poll.

MLB also seems to be underachieving on the minority front, as the percentage of blacks following MLB is the same, 10.8 percent, as it was five years ago. And while the Hispanic fan base has grown more (18 percent) than every other league or organization except NASCAR, to have the largest and fastest-growing minority account for just 11.8 percent of fans in a sport loaded with Latin American players indicates that more could be done at the league level, some critics say.

"Everybody's talking about doing something because they've read the numbers," said Anthony Eros, president of Latino Sports Marketing, which has consulted the NBA, MLB, NFL, and MLS on marketing to Latinos. "From a PR perspective, [the leagues] do a good job, but from a hard marketing perspective, they don't. I've been hearing for years about how they need to reach the Latino marketplace. It seems as though we're still in the same place."

MLB did not return calls for comment.

For its part, since 1991 MLB has administered Reviving Baseball in the Inner Cities, an initiative that currently serves more than 120,000 boys and girls in 175 cities worldwide. But MLB still lacks a leaguewide fan outreach program that specifically targets Hispanics.

NASCAR

Based on rate of growth alone, no league or organization has done more in the last five years to diversify its fan base than NASCAR, which has seen double-digit increases in its Hispanic and African American fan base and has grown its female fan base more than any other league, according to the SportsBusiness Journal/ESPN poll.

NASCAR's Hispanic fan base over the last five years has risen 28 percent, from 8.3 percent in 1998 to 10.6 percent in 2002, according to the poll. Blacks, meanwhile, now account for 9.6 percent of NASCAR fans, a 17 percent increase over the 8.2 percent in 1998. And women have gone from 38.6 percent of the fan base in 1998 to 41.2 percent in 2002, a nearly 7 percent increase.

To be fair, NASCAR enjoyed the most room for growth over that period, and the 2002 percentages for Hispanics, African Americans, and women show that the series still lags behind every other major sport except the NHL.

Still, NASCAR's surge is no coincidence. In recent years the series has created a college tour of historically black and Hispanic-serving institutions, an Urban Youth Racing School, a technical institute for aspiring technicians, and a diversity council. Last year, NASCAR hired a senior manager of diversity affairs, Dora Taylor.

NFL

But judging a league's commitment and success based on growth alone can be misleading. The NFL ranks in the middle of the pack in terms of increases in the percentage of female, Hispanic, and African American fans during the last five years, with Hispanics' share of the fan base growing by 7 percent, blacks by less than 6 percent, and women remaining steady, according to the SBJ/ESPN poll.

That the NFL hasn't grown as rapidly in those categories as some of the other leagues, according to Marjorie Rodgers, the NFL's senior director of client and consumer marketing, is a function of the difficulty of building on already large numbers. According to the NFL, more than 375,000 women attend NFL games every weekend during the season. "To expect double-digit [growth] when you're already that high is unrealistic," Rodgers said.

The NFL has taken significant steps to reach female fans, in 1997, it became the first league to develop a full line of women's apparel. The NFL 101 program, which the league started to help teams teach the game to women,

(Continued)

(Continued)

has been adopted by 20 teams and some now offer 201 and 301 classes. The league has since built a similar template, called NFL en Español, to teach the game to Hispanic fans. Six teams offered the program in 2002.

NBA

The NBA has likely done more to expand internationally than any other league, having plucked players from around the globe and enhanced worldwide exposure through six different language Web sites. Players like Dallas' Eduardo Najera of Mexico and Houston's Yao Ming of China have helped bring greater interest among the populations in the United States that "associate with those countries," said Tim Andree, the NBA's vice president of communications.

Hispanics represent a higher percentage of the fan base in the NBA (14.5) than every league except Major League Soccer, while the NBA dwarfs the other leagues in terms of its African American fan base (18.3 percent). The NBA also has managed to cultivate those two segments, as the percentage of Hispanics has grown 13 percent since 1998 and African Americans 7 percent.

Only Major League Baseball and MLS have a higher percentage of female fans than the NBA (45.7 percent), although that represents a 3 percent decline since 1998. Andree said any decline is a function of the league's commitment to the female market, as the WNBA has likely drawn away some female fans.

NHL

Of the four major professional sports leagues, the NHL has seen the slowest growth in terms of minorities' share of the fan base. In 1998, Hispanics represented 10.3 percent of the NHL fan base, according to the SBJ/ESPN research, and five years later that number actually dropped to 10.2 percent. Blacks accounted for 8.7 percent of the NHL's fans in 1998, and in 2002 it dropped to 8.4 percent.

The percentage of female NHL fans, however, increased from 40.2 percent in 1998 to 41 percent in 2002, a minimal rate of growth but the best among its three counterparts.

The NHL has seen much slower growth because hockey is not a sport many American children grow up playing, and the league has consequently thrown its efforts at getting more boys and girls on the ice, according to Bernadette Mansur, the NHL's vice president of communications. Programs like NHL Diversity, founded in 1995 to support efforts to give low-income kids equipment and a chance to play, don't immediately put fans in seats, Mansur said. Instead, they help ensure a bigger American presence in the league in the future, which should lead to greater interest.

MLS

Major League Soccer (MLS), not surprisingly, has a higher percentage of Hispanic fans, at 19.2 percent, than any other league or organization. The Hispanic fan base has grown 10 percent in the last five years, but Mark Noonan, the MLS' vice president of marketing and fan development, said there's "certainly room for growth."

The league has monthly conference calls with every team, Noonan said, in which they address how best to reach a segment of the population that, based on the U.S. Census, nearly doubled from 1980 to 2000 to 35.3 million.

The key, Noonan said, is to "respect the culture" enough to go beyond just "adding Spanish flair" to U.S.-based initiatives. For example, Noonan said, Hispanic children don't respond well to initiatives that teach the game, because they already know more about soccer than anyone.

But for a relatively young league struggling to attract fans, where it finds those fans is secondary, Noonan said.

"As long as we continue to increase our attendance," he said, "whether they're Hispanic, kids, hard-core, or African American, I don't really care."

Source: Russell Adams. *Sports Business Journal*, Street & Smith's Sports Group. Copyright © 1998–2004. Street & Smith's Sports Group. All rights reserved.

an area where families can picnic before, during, and after the game, has become a "hit" for the St. Louis Cardinals. The Chicago Cubs and the other professional teams have initiated no-alcohol sections at their games to encourage a family environment. Moreover, many sports organizations have instituted family nights, which include tickets, parking, and food for a reduced price to encourage family attendance.

SOCIOECONOMIC SEGMENTATION

Thus far, we have discussed demographic variables such as age, gender, ethnic background, and family life cycle as potential ways to segment sports markets. Another way of segmenting markets that was found to be a good predictor of consumer behavior

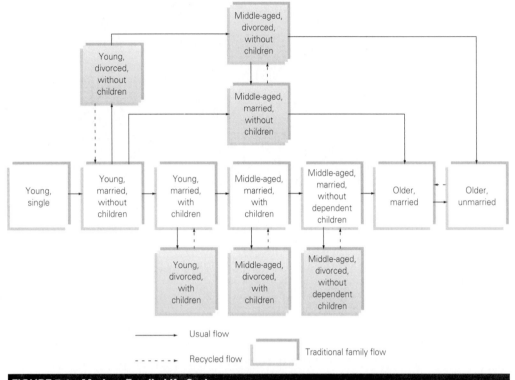

Usual flow

Recycled flow

Traditional family flow

FIGURE 7.1 Modern Family Life Cycle

Kawasaki is segmenting on the basis of the family life cycle.

Source: Used by permission of Kawasaki Motors Corp., U.S.A.

Polo is a sport that has typically appealed to the upper class.

is through **socioeconomic segmentation.** As previously defined a consumer's **social class** is a division of members of a society into a hierarchy of distinct status classes, so that members of each class have relatively the same status and members of all other classes have either more or less status.

Although most people immediately equate social class with income, income alone can be a poor predictor of social class. Other factors such as educational level and occupation also determine social standing. Usually, income, education, and occupation are highly interrelated. In other words, individuals with higher levels of education are typically in higher income and more prestigious occupations. Based on these factors (income, education, and occupation), members of a society are artificially said to belong to one of the social class categories. The traditional social class categories are upper-, middle-, and lower-class Americans. Participation in certain sports has been associated with the various social strata. For instance, golf and tennis are called "country club" sports. Polo is a sport of the "rich and famous." Bowling is usually thought of as the "blue-collar" sport of the working class.

As with sex roles, the relationship between social class and sport is now shifting. Golf is now being enjoyed by people of all income levels. Attending a professional basketball or football game, once affordable for the whole family, can now only be enjoyed by wealthy corporate season ticketholders. In addition, NASCAR fans are stereotypically "good ol' boys" with "blue-collar" values. However, NASCAR has turned into a multibillion-dollar-a-year industry and a marketing success story. During this tremendous growth, the sport is moving beyond its "good-ol'-boy" mentality and reaching a new market in yuppie America. Just consider the demographics of the NASCAR fan. More than a 42 percent of NASCAR fans have household incomes above $50,000 and more than a quarter hold professional or managerial jobs.[17,18]

PSYCHOGRAPHIC SEGMENTATION

Psychographic segmentation is described as grouping consumers on the basis of a common lifestyle preference and personality. Psychographic segments are believed to be more comprehensive than other types of segmentation, such as demographics, behavioral, or geodemographic. As consumer behavior researcher Michael Solomon points out, "Demographics allow us to describe *who* buys, but psychographics allows us to understand *why* they do."[19] For this reason, many sports marketers have chosen to segment their markets on the basis of psychographics. To gain a better understanding of consumers' lifestyles, marketers assess consumers' **AIO dimensions,** or statements describing activities, interests, and opinions (AIO). The three AIO dimensions are shown in Table 7.3.

TABLE 7.3   AIO Dimensions

Activities	Interests	Opinions
Work	Family	Themselves
Hobbies	Home	Social issues
Social events	Job	Politics
Vacation	Community	Business
Entertainment	Recreation	Economics
Club membership	Fashion	Education
Community	Food	Products
Shopping	Media	Future
Sports	Achievements	Culture

Source: William Wells and Douglas J. Tigert, "Activities, Interests, and Opinions," *Journal of Adevrtising Research,* vol. 11 (August 1971), 127–135. Courtesy of the *Journal of Advertising Research,* The Advertising Research Foundation.

Typically marketers quantify AIOs by asking consumers to agree or disagree with a series of statements reflecting their lifestyle. These statements can range from measures of general interest in sports to measures focusing on a specific sport. As seen in Table 7.3, many of these AIO dimensions relate indirectly or directly to sports. For example, sports, social events, recreation, and products may have a direct link to sports, whereas club memberships, fashion, community, and economics may be indirectly linked.

An example of psychographic segmentation in the golf market can be seen in Table 7.4. This table illustrates a golfer's lifestyle based on research from *SRDS: The Lifestyle Market Analyst/National Demographic and Lifestyle 2000.* This type of information examines activities and interests of golfers to determine what products and services might be successfully marketed to this group. For example, many professional golf tournaments are sponsored by large investment companies to capitalize on this popular activity of golfers.

TABLE 7-4   Golf Lifestyle Profiles Ranked by Index*

Top 10 Lifestyles		Bottom 10 Lifestyles	
Lifestyle	**Index**	**Lifestyle**	**Index**
Snow skiing frequently	186	Bible/devotional reading	81
Tennis frequently	178	Sewing	83
Stock/bond investments	154	Automotive work	88
Travel for business	152	Health/natural foods	88
Frequent flyer	153	Needlework/knitting	88
Wines	153	Science fiction	89
Real estate investing	147	Vegetable gardening	92
Watching sports on television	150	House plants	93
Own a vacation home	143	Own a cat	94
Boating/sailing	143	Entering sweepstakes	94

*(Index: U.S. Average = 100.)
Source: Reprinted from the 2000 edition of *The Lifestyle Market Analyst,* published by SRDS with data supplied by Polk.

GEOGRAPHIC SEGMENTATION

Geographics is a simple, but powerful, segmentation basis. Certainly, this is critical for sports marketers and as long-standing as "rooting for the home team." All sports teams use **geographic segmentation;** however, it is not always as straightforward as it may initially seem. For instance, the Dallas Cowboys, Chicago Bulls, Atlanta Braves, and the Fighting Irish are all known as "America's Teams."[20]

Geographic segmentation can be useful in making broad distinctions among local, regional, national, and international market segments. International or multinational marketing is a topic of growing interest for sports marketers. Witness, for example, Major League Baseball and the NBA both playing their first regular season games in Mexico, or the NFL discussing expansion into international markets. As the following spotlight on international marketing indicates, the leagues are also reaching their international fan base through the Internet.

The physical climate also plays a role in segmenting markets geographically. Classic examples include greater demand for snow skiing equipment in Colorado and surfboards in Florida. However, Colorado ski resorts have the greatest number of sports tourists who come from Florida, hardly thought of as a snow ski mecca.

SPOTLIGHT ON INTERNATIONAL SPORTS MARKETING

The Internationalization of the NBA Continues

With 73 players from foreign countries, including China's Yao Ming, France's Tony Parker, and Argentina's Emanuel Ginobili, on NBA rosters this season, the league has developed a large international presence on the court. But that pales in comparison to the interest on the Internet.

More than half the visits to NBA.com and its nine international Web sites during November came from outside the United States. Of the nearly 58 million visits (representing 6 million unique visitors) to NBA sites, 51 percent were from outside the United States.

The emergence of star players from overseas has drawn young, tech-savvy fans across the globe to the NBA's Web sites, said Brenda Spoonemore, NBA Entertainment senior vice president of interactive services. *"We have these incredible ambassadors,"* Spoonemore said. "Clearly basketball is one of the most participated-in sports worldwide. It's a great thing for us. It clearly tracks with the rest of our business." Spoonemore said internationally all aspects of the NBA's business have increased, including sponsorship sales and grass-roots events.

China, Canada, and Taiwan are the top three countries visiting the Web sites, including eight million visits from China alone.

The other sports leagues have not had the same draw overseas. In November, NHL.com had 3.75 million visitors, including 2.15 million outside the United States, mainly because of its popularity in Canada. Both the NFL and Major League Baseball say about 10 percent of their Internet visitors are from outside the United States.

The NBA has aggressively courted a worldwide audience. In 1999, NBA.com/japan debuted, with Canada, Espanol, United Kingdom, China, Germany, France, and Taiwan following. A Portuguese version for Brazil (NBA.com/brasil) launched in September.

According to NBA Latin America, 1.25 million visitors logged onto the Espanol site in November, up from 650,000 the previous November.

"As Latin players continue to succeed in the NBA, I think the interest will continue to grow," said Gabe Gabor, director of communications for NBA Latin America.

In addition to stories about their native stars, the sites feature local broadcast schedules and information about local basketball programs.

Source: The Internationalization of the NBA Continues, www.sportsbusinessnews.com, January 1, 2004.

Therefore, segments of sports consumers may exist in unlikely geographic markets. In this example, the psychographics of the sports consumer may be more important in predicting behavior than geographic location.

Although the climate plays an important role in sports, marketers have attempted to tame this uncontrollable factor. For instance, tons of sand was shipped to Atlanta, creating beach like conditions, for the first ever Olympic beach volleyball competition. Domed stadiums, since the opening (and now closing) of the Astrodome in Houston, have also allowed sports marketers to tout the perfect conditions in which fans can watch football in the middle of a blizzard in Minnesota.

BEHAVIORAL SEGMENTATION

For sports marketers engaged in the strategic sports marketing process, two common goals are attracting more fans and keeping them. Behavioral segmentation lies at the heart of these two objectives. **Behavioral segmentation** group consumers based on how much they purchase, how often they purchase, and how loyal they are to a product or service.

Interestingly, in today's professional sports environment, loyalty is an increasingly important topic. Many professional sports teams have held their fans and cities hostage, and cities are doing everything they can to keep their beloved teams. In 2003, nearly 67 percent of teams in the four major sports leagues in the United States will be playing in new stadia built since 1990.[21] This new construction and renovation was done largely to keep team owners satisfied and curb any threat of moving.

Franchises and players within each team move so rapidly that fan loyalty becomes a difficult phenomenon to capture. The day of the lifelong fan is over. Because of this, fans may identify more with individual players or even coaches (e.g., Derek Jeter and the Yankees, Shaquille O'Neal and the Lakers, or Joe Paterno and Penn State football) than they do with teams. According to some sports marketing experts, next to wins, fans like to see famous faces on the field.[22] This is true even in team-dominated sports, such as football. Prior to 1990, there was little movement of professional football teams. Since 1990, the Cardinals, Rams, Raiders, Browns, and Oilers have all moved.

Fans may be more concerned with the individual performance of Albert Pujols than they are with the St. Louis Cardinals. Certainly, sports marketers have to monitor this trend of diminishing loyalty to a team. However, some sports fans show extreme loyalty by purchasing personal seat licenses (PSLs). PSLs require fans to pay a leasing fee for their seats. This fee would guarantee the consumer his or her seat for several years. The PSL, of course, demonstrates the extreme devotion of a group of fans.

Sports marketers have recently taken a lesson in loyalty marketing from other industries and are creating loyalty marketing programs. A study by Pritchard and Negro[23] found that these programs are effective when they build on the genuine affinity fans have for their teams, rather than rewarding attendance alone. Increasing fan interaction with players, coaches, and the entire organization through direct access or personal communication was shown to be much more important to the success of loyalty programs than rewarding attendance.

Along with behavioral segmentation based on loyalty to a team or sports product, consumers are frequently grouped on the basis of other attendance or purchasing behaviors. For instance, lifelong season ticketholders represent one end of the usage continuum, whereas those who have never attended sporting events represent the other end. A unique marketing mix must be designed to appeal to each of these two groups of consumers.

BENEFITS SEGMENTATION

The focus of **benefits segmentation** is the appeal of a product or service to a group of consumers. Stated differently, benefits segments describe why consumers purchase a product or service or what problem the product solves for the consumer. In a sense, benefits segmentation is the underlying factor in all types of marketing segmentation in that every purchase is made to satisfy a need. Benefits segmentation is also consistent with the marketing concept (discussed in Chapter 1) that states that organizations strive to meet customers' needs.

Major shoe manufacturers, such as Nike, focus on "benefits sought" to segment markets. Some consumers desire a high-performance cross-training shoe, whereas others want a shoe that is more of a fashion statement. In fact, one study asked consumers what is important to them when purchasing athletic footwear. The highest percentage of consumers indicated that "comfort, fit, and feel" were very important (83 percent), followed by "suits active lifestyle" (63 percent), "has performance advantages" (56 percent), and "has fashion advantages" (54 percent). As this research finding illustrates, different consumers desire different benefits from their athletic footwear.[24]

Golf ball manufacturers also try to design products that will appeal to the specific benefits sought by different groups of golfers. The Titleist DT Spin offers a combination of long tee-to-green distance, wound-ball spin, improved feel, and guaranteed cut-proof durability. Whereas the Titleist DT Distance offers golfers longer and straighter two-piece distance with cut-proof durability. Sports marketers really hit a home run when they design products that satisfy multiple needs (i.e., distance, feel, accuracy, durability) of consumers.

CHOOSING MORE THAN ONE SEGMENT

Although each of the previously mentioned bases for segmentation identifies groups of consumers with similar needs, it is common practice to combine segmentation variables. An example of combining segmentation approaches is found in a study of the golf participant market.[25] A survey was conducted to determine playing ability, purchase behavior, and the demographic characteristics of public and private course golfers. The resulting profile produced five distinct market segments that combine some of the various bases for segmentation discussed earlier in the chapter. These five segments are shown in Table 7.5.

GEODEMOGRAPHIC SEGMENTATION

One of the most widely used multiple segment approaches in sports is **geodemographic segmentation.** Although geographic segmentation and demographic segmentation are useful tools for sports marketers, combining geographic and demographic characteristics seems to be even more effective in certain situations. For instance, many direct marketing campaigns apply the principles of geodemographic segmentation.

The basis for geodemographic segmentation is that people living in close proximity are also likely to share the same lifestyle and demographic composition. Because lifestyle of the consumer is included in this type of segmentation, it is also known as geolifestyle. Geodemographics allows marketers to describe the characteristics of broad segments such as standard metropolitan statistical areas (SMSA) all the way down to census blocks (consisting of roughly 340 houses). The most common unit of segmentation for

TABLE 7.5 Five Market Segments for Golf Participants

Competitors (18.6 percent)
- Have a handicap of less than 10
- Indicate love of game
- Play for competitive edge
- Practice most often
- Most likely to play in league
- Own most golf clothing
- Are early adopters (e.g., third wedge)
- Buy most golf balls

Players (25.7 percent)
- Have handicap between 10 and 14
- Use custom club makers
- Practice a lot
- Like competition
- Exercise and companionship are important
- Most likely to take out-of-state golf vacation

Sociables (17.8 percent)
- Have handicap between 15 and 18
- Often play with family
- Purchase from off-price retailers
- Play for sociability
- Most likely to take winter vacation to warm destination

Aspirers (18.4 percent)
- Have handicap between 19 and 25
- Love to play; hate to practice
- Most inclined to use golf for business purposes
- Golf shows are important as source of information
- Competition and sociability are unimportant reason to play

Casual (19.5 percent)
- Have handicap of 26 or more
- Do not practice
- More women in this segment
- Play less frequently than other segments
- Own the least golf clothing
- Purchase the fewest golf balls
- Recreation is most important factor for play
- Exercise and companionship are moderately important
- Least likely to take a golf vacation
- Most likely to shop in course pro shop

Source: Sam Fullerton and H. Robert Dodge, "An Application of Market Segmentation in a Sports Marketing Arena: We All Can't Be Greg Norman," *Sport Marketing Quarterly,* vol. 4, no. 3 (1995), 43–47. Reprinted with permission of Fitness Information Technology, Inc., Publishers.

geodemography is the zip code. Claritias, Inc., a marketing firm leading the charge in geo-demographics, established the PRIZM system in 1970s. PRIZM is used to identify potential markets for products. Each unit of geography is classified as one of the 62 PRIZM clusters, which have been given names that best characterize those populations. Some examples of the PRIZM cluster categories are shown in Table 7.6.

TABLE 7.6 Sample PRIZM Cluster Categories and Descriptions

Kids and Cul-de-Sacs—Ranked number 1 of all 62 clusters in married couples with children and large (4 plus) families. As this characteristic governs every aspect of their lives and activities, one rightly pictures these neighborhoods as a noisy medley of bikes, dogs, rock music, and sports.

God's Country—Populated by educated, upscale professionals, married executives who choose to raise their children in the far exurbs of major metropolitan areas. Their affluence is often supported by dual incomes. Lifestyles are family and outdoor centered.

Towns and Gowns—Describes most of our nation's college towns and university campus neighborhoods. With a typical mix of half locals (towns) and half students (gowns), it is totally unique. Thousands of penniless 18- to 24-year-old kids, plus highly educated professionals with a taste for prestige products beyond their means.

Winner's Circle—Second in American affluence and typified by new money, living in expensive new mansions in the suburbs of the nation's major metros. These are well-educated, mobile executives and professionals with teen-age families. Big producers, prolific spenders, and global travelers.

Source: How to Use PRIZM (Alexandria, VA: Claritas, 1996). Courtesy of Claritas, Inc., of Arlington, VA.

TARGET MARKETS

After segmenting the market based on one or a combination of the variables discussed in the previous section, target markets are chosen. **Target marketing** is choosing the segment(s) that will allow an organization to most efficiently and effectively attain its marketing goals.

Sports marketers must make a systematic decision when choosing groups of consumers they want to target. To make these decisions, each potential target market is evaluated on the basis of whether it is sizable, reachable, and measurable, and whether it exhibits behavioral variation. Let us look at how to judge the worth of potential target markets in greater detail.

EVALUATION OF TARGET MARKETS

SIZABLE

One of the first factors to consider when evaluating and choosing a potential target market is the size of the market. In addition to the current size of the market, sports marketers must also analyze the estimated growth of the market. The market growth would be predicted, in part, through environmental scanning, already discussed in Chapter 3.

Sports marketers must be careful to choose a target market that has neither too many nor too few consumers. If the target market becomes too large, then it essentially becomes a mass, or undifferentiated market. For example, we would not want to choose all basketball fans as a target market because of the huge variations in social class, lifestyles, and consumption behaviors.

However, sports marketers must guard against a target market that is too small and narrowly defined. We would not choose a target market that consisted of all left-handed female basketball fans between the ages of 30 and 33 who live in San Antonio and have income levels between $40,000 and $50,000. This market is too narrowly defined and would not prove to be a good return on our marketing investment.

One common trap that marketers fall into with respect to the size of the potential market is known as the majority fallacy. The **majority fallacy** assumes the largest group

TABLE 7.7 Market Segments vs. Market Niches

Segment	*Niche*
Small mass market	Very small market
Less specialized	Very specific needs
Top down (go from large market into smaller pieces)	Bottom up (cater to the smaller pieces of the market)

of consumers should always be selected as the target market. Although, in some instances, the biggest market may be the best choice, usually the competition is the most fierce for this group of consumers; therefore, smaller more differentiated targets should be chosen.

These smaller, distinct groups of core customers that an organization focuses on are sometimes referred to as a market niche. **Niche marketing** is the process of carving out a relatively tiny part of a market that has a very special need not currently being filled. By definition, a **market niche** is initially much smaller than a segment and consists of a very homogeneous group of consumers, as reflected by their unique need. The differences between market segments and niches are highlighted in Table 7.7. Milne and McDonald provide support for the use of niche markets in the sports industry by pointing out the proliferation of specialist magazines (e.g., *Triathlete, Cross Country Skier, Skydiving Magazine*), the TV coverage of new, niche sports on major broadcast network channels, and cable niche channels such as the Xtreme Sports Channel, and the continued interest of sponsors, such as Novell, Pepsi, and Van's Shoes, in affiliating with niche sports.[26]

One specific example of a niche market is individuals (as opposed to corporations) who have financially invested in the sports franchise through the purchase of season tickets for many seasons. In addition to their financial investment, these loyal fans have a high emotional investment in the team. To retain these valuable consumers, sports marketers must develop a specialized marketing mix to reinforce and reward the loyalty that these fans have shown to the organization.

REACHABLE

In addition to exploring the size of the potential target market, its ability to be reached should also be evaluated. Reach refers to the accessibility of the target market. Does the sports marketer have a means of communicating with the desired target market? If the answer to this question is no, then the potential target market should not be pursued.

Traditional means of reaching the sports fan include mass media, such as magazines, newspapers, and television. In today's marketing environment, it is possible to reach a very specific target market with technology such as the Internet. For instance, fans of women's soccer can interact on the "Women's Soccer World" at www.womensoccer.com. In addition to the Internet, satellite technology products, such as DIRECTV, are allowing sports fans across the United States access to their favorite teams. This, of course, opens new geographic segments for sports marketers to consider.

MEASURABLE

The ability to measure the size, accessibility, and purchasing power of the potential target market(s) is another factor that needs to be considered. One of the reasons demographic segmentation is so widespread is the ease with which characteristics such as age,

Reaching women's soccer fans on the web.

Source: Used by permission www.womensoccer.com.

gender, income level, and occupation can be assessed or measured. Psychographic segments are perhaps the most difficult to measure because of the complex nature of personality and lifestyle.

BEHAVIORAL VARIATION

Finally, if the target market is sizable, reachable, and measurable, sports marketers must examine behavioral variation. We want consumers within the target market to exhibit similar behaviors, attitudes, lifestyles, and so on. In addition, marketers want these characteristics to be unique within a target market. This component is the underlying factor in choosing any target market.

An example of behavioral variation among market segments is the corporate season ticketholder versus the individual season ticketholder. Although both corporate season ticketholders and individual season ticketholders may be fans at some level, their motivation for attending games and attitudes toward the team may be quite different. These variations would prompt different approaches to marketing to each segment.

HOW MANY TARGET MARKETS?

Now that we have evaluated potential target markets, do we have to choose just one? The answer depends largely on the organization's marketing objectives and its resources. If the firm has the financial and other resources to pursue more than one target market, it does so by prioritizing the potential target markets.

The market distinguished as the most critical to attaining the firm's objectives is deemed the primary target market. Other, less critical markets of interest are called secondary, tertiary, and so on. Again, a unique marketing mix may need to be developed for each target market, so the costs associated with choosing multiple targets are sometimes prohibitive.

POSITIONING

Segmentation has been considered and specific target markets have been chosen. Next, sport marketers must decide on the positioning of their sporting events, athletes, teams, and so on. **Positioning** is defined as fixing your sports entity in the minds of consumers in the target market.

Before discussing positioning, three important points should be stressed. First, positioning is dependent on the target market(s) identified in the previous phase of the market selection decisions. In fact, the *same* sport may be positioned differently to distinct target markets. As the box on NASCAR demonstrated earlier in the chapter, the positioning of the sport is changing with the opening of a new target market—the young.

Second, positioning is based solely on the perceptions of the target market and how its members think and feel about the sports entity. Sometimes positioning is mistakenly linked with where the product appears on the retailer's shelf or where the product is placed in an advertisement. Nothing could be further from the truth. Position is all about how the consumer perceives your sports product relative to competitive offerings.

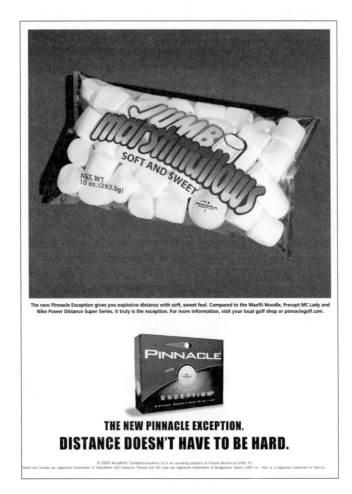

Pinnacle positioning itself versus the competition as long distance and soft feel.
Source: Courtesy of Acushnet Co.

Third, the definition of positioning reflects its importance to all sports products. It should also be noted that sports leagues (Arena Football versus NFL), sports teams (e.g., Dallas Cowboys as America's Team), and individual athletes (e.g., Tiger Woods as the youthful, hip golfer, or the NBA's bad boy, Allen Iverson) all must be positioned by sports marketers.

How does the sports marketer attempt to fix the sports entity in the minds of consumers? The first step rests in understanding the target market's perception of the relevant attributes of the sports entity. The relevant attributes are those features and characteristics desired in the sports entity by the target market. These attributes may be intangible, such as a fun atmosphere at the stadium, or tangible, such as having cushioned seating. Golf manufacturers such as Slazenger have positioned their equipment as the "standard of excellence" and having "impeccable quality."

In another example, consider the possible product attributes for in-line skates. Pricing, status of the name brand, durability, quality of the wheels, and weight of the skate may all be considered product attributes. If serious, competitive skaters are chosen as the primary target market, then the in-line skates may be positioned on the basis of quality of the wheels and weight of the skate. However, if first-time, recreational skaters are considered the primary target market, then relevant product attributes may be price and durability. Marketers attempt to understand all the potential attributes and then which ones are most important to their target markets through marketing research.

PERCEPTUAL MAPS

Through various advanced marketing research techniques, perceptual maps are created to examine positioning. **Perceptual maps** provide marketers with three types of information. First, perceptual maps indicate the dimensions or attributes that consumers use when thinking about a sports product or service. Second, perceptual maps tell sports marketers where different sports products or services are located on those dimensions. The third type of information provided by perceptual maps is how your product is perceived relative to the competition.

Perceptual maps can be constructed in any number of dimensions, based on the number of product attributes being considered. Figure 7.2 demonstrates a one-dimensional perceptual map, which explores the positioning of various spectator sports based on the level of perceived aggression or violence associated with the sports. This hypothetical example can be interpreted as follows: Boxing is seen as the most violent or aggressive sport, followed by football, hockey, and soccer. However, golf is the least aggressive sport. These results would vary, of course, based on who participated in the research, how aggression or violence is defined by the researchers, and what level of competition is being considered (i.e., professional, high school, or youth leagues).

FIGURE 7.2 One-Dimensional Perceptual Map of Sports

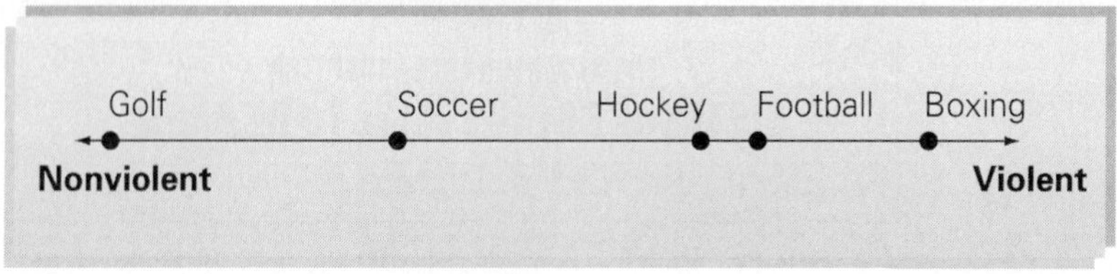

Dramatic differences in the positioning of hockey and figure skating.

Although it is easy to conceptualize one-dimensional perceptual maps, the number of dimensions is contingent upon the number of attributes relevant to consumers. For example, Converse positions its shoes for multiple uses like action sports, basketball, cheerleading, or cross-training. New Balance, however, positions its shoes solely on the basis of running.

TABLE 7.8 Six Dimensions or Attributes of Sports	
Dimension 1	Strength, speed, and endurance vs. methodical and precise movements
Dimension 2	Athletes only as participants vs. athletes plus recreational participants
Dimension 3	Skill emphasis on impact with object vs. skill emphasis on body movement
Dimension 4	Skill development and practice primarily alone vs. primarily with others
Dimension 5	A younger participant in the sport vs. participant ages from young to older
Dimension 6	Less masculine vs. more masculine

Source: James H. Martin, "Using a Perceptual Map of the Consumer's Sport Schema to Help Make Sponsorship Decisions," *Sport Marketing Quarterly,* vol. 3, no. 3 (1994), 27–33.

A study using perceptual mapping techniques found that consumers identify six dimensions of sport (shown in Table 7.8). Although it is possible to create a six-dimensional perceptual map, it is nearly impossible to interpret. Therefore, two-dimensional perceptual maps were constructed that compared 10 sports on the six dimensions identified by consumers.

Figure 7.3 shows a two-dimensional perceptual map using Dimension 4 (skill developed primarily with others versus skill developed alone) and Dimension 5 (younger athletes versus broad age ranges of participants). Interpreting this perceptual map, football is considered a sport where the participants are younger athletes and skill is developed primarily with others. Compared with football, golf is seen as a sport for a broader range of participants with skills developed more on your own. Using these results, sports marketers can better understand the image of their sport from the perspective of various target markets and decide whether this image needs to be changed or maintained.

FIGURE 7.3 Two-Dimensional Perceptual Map for Sports

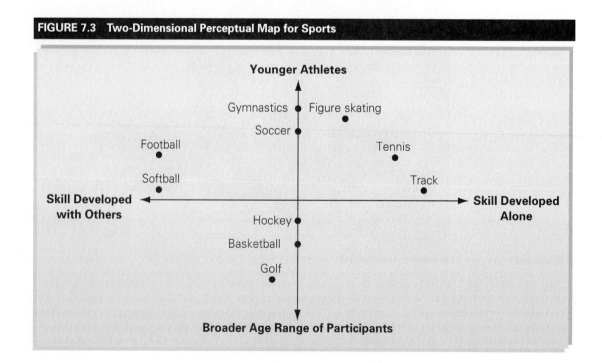

REPOSITIONING

As suggested, sport marketers may use the results of positioning studies to change the image of their sport. For instance, professional hockey is known for its aggressive play. Although this is appealing to some fans, it was not the image the NHL wanted to project. The NHL believed this aggressive play was overshadowing the essence of the game. Thus, the NHL sought to reposition hockey and eliminate some of the undue violence of the sport. **Repositioning** is changing the image or perception of the sports entity in the minds of consumers in the target market.

One way that the NHL has repositioned professional hockey is to provide stiffer penalties for fighting. Moreover, the NHL aired a series of lighthearted ads featuring celebrities such as Shania Twain, Jim Belushi, and Cuba Gooding Jr. The ads were trying to reach both hard-core and casual fans of hockey by having the celebrities explain terms such as "high-sticking" and "changing on the fly" in a humorous fashion.

Bowlers Look to Change Sport's Image

The waft of buffalo wings and chicken nuggets hung heavily in the air next to the podium at one of the odder venues of this year's Pan American Games.

Gaudy blues, oranges, pinks, and greens crisscrossed the carpet in designs depicting pins, bowling balls, and party streamers. They even turned luminous at night. Fans wolfed down fast food or drank the local Presidente beer as the first day of men's singles bowling, "boliche" in Spanish, began.

"It's true people have a certain perception of this sport," said Canadian manager Calvin Hugman. "They think of beer, cigars, and a generally unhealthy environment . . . of Homer Simpson or the Flintstones.

"But we're trying to change that and this sport is evolving," he added. "It's a game of physics, one of manipulating surfaces. It takes talent to throw a ball 60 feet and hit a dime.

"It's not just a blue-collar sport anymore."

Even the name of the sport in Spanish compounds the image problem. In some parts of South America the word also means a bar or nightclub. In the United States, of course, bowlers are referred to as "keglers."

But the sport's hemispheric popularity was clearly apparent as competitors from 19 countries—from Aruba to Panama to Uruguay—competed at the Plaza Bolera complex on Monday.

Aficionados have long been lobbying for bowling to become an Olympic sport, but were recently knocked back.

"For me, the image of booze and smoke is definitely what went against us," lamented Aruba's bowling delegate, David Groder. "It's seen as a diversion, a hobby. That's true, but most sports are hobbies.

"I maintain the hope that one day I will see this game at the Olympics."

Hugman said it came as a "big-time surprise" that the Olympics turned its back on the sport until at least 2012, attributing the failure to a "misunderstanding" of the sport at grass roots levels in North America.

"In Canada we're really going to work on that," he said.

For the time being, the president of the Brazilian federation, Cesar Maciel, said he would be content if the sport simply remains at the Pan Ams. The next Pan Am Games are in 2007, in Rio de Janeiro.

Bowling arenas might not seem a natural arena of choice in Brazil, and 17-year-old Luiza Rocha said there was a certain amount of "prejudice" there too.

"Not many people know what it is," said Rocha, who last year became South America's junior champion. "It's not something you'd automatically think of doing on the weekend in Brazil."

But the sport is growing there—and with American help. U.S. coach Fred Borden held clinics in Brazil this year to help promote the sport among youngsters.

And that age group appears to be the one most targeted.

Groder said one way of attracting youngsters was to make the sport stand out more. On Monday, some of the bowling balls simulated soccer or golf balls, others were transparent or had boxing glove designs.

"These new aggressive designs appeal to the young," he said. "That's down to the marketing guys."

Source: Ian Phillips. *Associated Press.* August 5, 2003. Reprinted with permission of The Associated Press. All Rights Reserved.

Hockey is not the only sports entity attempting to reposition itself. Following a series of scandals with coaches and athletes, the NCAA is also experiencing image problems. And let's not forget Laker star Kobe Bryant, who has some problems of his own. One sport constantly searching for a new image is bowling, as the previous box illustrates.

Summary

Chapter 7 focuses on the critical market selection decisions, also referred to as segmentation, targeting, and positioning. Segmentation, the first market selection decision, is identifying consumers with common needs. Typically, the bases for segmentation of consumer markets include demographics, socioeconomics, psychographics, behaviors, and benefits. Marketers using demographic segmentation choose groups of consumers based on common ages, gender, ethnic background, and stage of the family life cycle. Geographic segmentation groups people who live in similar areas such as cities, states, regions of the country, or even countries (e.g., the United States versus international markets). Socioeconomic segmentation groups consumers on the basis of similar income levels, educational levels, and occupations. Psychographic segments are especially useful to sports marketers, they are based on consumers' lifestyles, activities, interests, and opinions. Behavioral segments are groups of consumers that are similar on the basis of consumer actions, such as how often they purchase sports products or how loyal they are when purchasing a sports product. Finally, benefits segmentation are groups of consumers attempting to satisfy similar needs by consuming the sports product together. Sports marketers may choose to segment their markets using one of the previously mentioned segmentation variables (e.g., demographics) or combine several of the bases for segmentation (e.g., geodemographic).

Once market segments have been chosen, the next market selection decision is picking a target market. Target marketing is choosing the segment or segments that will allow the organization to most effectively and efficiently achieve its marketing goals. When evaluating potential target markets, care should be taken to ensure the markets are the right size (neither too large nor too small), reachable (accessible), measurable (i.e., size, purchasing power, and characteristics of the segments can be measured), and demonstrate behavioral variation (i.e., consumers share common characteristics within the target market).

The final market selection decision is positioning. After the target market has been chosen, sports marketers want to position their products or fix them in the minds of the target markets. Positioning is based on the perception or image that sports marketers want to develop or maintain for the sports product. For example, a minor league baseball team may want to position itself as an inexpensive, family entertainment alternative. To understand how a sports product is positioned relative to its competition, perceptual maps are developed through marketing research techniques. By looking at perceptual maps, sports marketers can identify whether they have achieved their desired image or whether they need to reposition their sports product in the minds of the target market.

Key Terms

- AIO dimensions
- behavioral segmentation
- benefits segmentation
- demographic segmentation
- ethnic background
- family life cycle
- geodemographic segmentation

- geographic segmentation
- market niche
- majority fallacy
- market segmentation
- market selection decisions
- mature adults, age 55-plus
- niche marketing

- perceptual maps
- positioning
- psychographic segmentation
- reposition
- social class
- socioeconomic segmentation
- target marketing

Review Questions

1. Describe the key components of market selection decisions and indicate how market selection decisions are incorporated into the larger strategic marketing process.
2. What is market segmentation? Provide some examples of how sports marketers segment the sports participant market (those who play) and the sports spectator market (those that watch).
3. Discuss the various ways to segment the sports market based on demographics. Which of the demographic bases are the most effective when segmenting the sports market and why?

4. Describe, in detail, the family life cycle and how it is used as a strategic tool when segmenting sports markets. What stage of the family life cycle are you currently in? How does this affect your sports participation and spectator behavior?
5. Provide examples of sports you believe would appeal to each of the six social class categories (upper-upper through lower-lower). What sports appeal to all social class segments?
6. What are AIOs? Why is psychographic segmentation so difficult to practice?
7. Provide several examples of the growth of international sports marketing.
8. What is behavioral segmentation? What are some of the common behaviors that sports marketers would use for segmentation purposes?
9. Define benefits segmentation and discuss why benefits segmentation is considered to be at the core of all segmentation. What benefits do you look for when attending a sporting event? Does your answer vary from event to event?
10. Define a target market. What are the requirements for successful target markets (i.e., how should each target be evaluated)? Provide examples of sports products or services that target two or more distinct markets.
11. How many target markets should a sports marketer consider for a single product?
12. Describe positioning and discuss how perceptual mapping techniques are used by sports marketers. What is repositioning?

Exercises

1. Find two advertisements for sports products that compete directly with one another. For example, you may want to compare Nike running shoes with Reebok running shoes or King Cobra golf clubs with Taylormade golf clubs. How is each product segmented, targeted, and positioned? Are there more differences or similarities in these market selection decisions?
2. How is the health and fitness industry segmented in general? Describe the segmentation, targets, and positioning of health and fitness clubs in your area.
3. You are hired as the director of sports marketing for a new minor league hockey franchise in Chicago, a city that already has an NHL team. Describe how you would segment, target, and position your new franchise.
4. Describe the primary target market for the following: NASCAR, the Kentucky Derby, "The Rhino" bowling ball, and the WNBA. Next, define a potential secondary target market for each of these sports products.
5. Interview five consumers who have recently attended a high school sporting event, five consumers who have recently attended a college sporting event, and five who have recently attended any professional sporting event. Ask them to identify why they attended this event and what benefits they were looking for? Were their needs met?
6. Develop a list of all the possible product attributes that may be considered when purchasing the following sports products: a tennis racquet, a basketball, and a mountain bike. After you have developed the list of attributes, ask five people which attributes they consider to be the most important for each product. Do all consumers agree? Are there some attributes that you may have omitted? Why are these attributes important in positioning?
7. How do you think the following races are positioned: Boston Marathon, "Run Like Hell" 5K Halloween Race, and the Bowling Green 10K Classic? Draw a two-dimensional perceptual map to illustrate the positioning of each race.
8. Provide examples of individual athletes, teams, and sports (leagues) that have had to develop repositioning strategies.

Internet Exercises

1. Using the Internet, find the demographic profile for fans attending LPGA (women's tour) versus PGA (men's tour). Are there differences? Use this information to comment on the market selection decisions for the LPGA.
2. Find two Internet sites that target children interested in sports and two Internet sites that target the mature market. Note any similarities and differences between the sites.

3. Find two Internet sites for soccer. One site should focus on U.S. soccer, whereas the other focus should be international. Comment on the relative positioning of soccer in the United States versus abroad based on information found on the Internet.

Endnotes

1. James U. McNeal, "Tapping the Three Kids' Markets," *American Demographics* (April 1998). "Kids in 2010," *American Demographics,* (September 1999).
2. Dawn Anfuso, "Study Shows Buying Power of Youth," www.imediaconnection.com (September 8, 2003).
3. "Young Consumers, Perils and Power," *The New York Times* (February 11, 1990).
4. Major League Baseball Targets Urban Youth, Marketing to Emerging Minorities, EPM Communications, vol. 15, no. 9 (September 5, 2003).
5. FLW Outdoors, Wal-Mart Partner to Get Kids Hooked on Fishing, *Financial News* (May 27, 2003).
6. Dawn Anfuso, "Study Shows Buying Power of Youth," www.imediaconnection.com (September 8, 2003).
7. Laura Zinn, "Teens: Here Comes the Biggest Wave Yet," *Business Week* (April 11, 1994) 76.
8. "New Consumer Product Offerings by NBA & WNBA." www.newspage.com/cgibin/ NA. . . . y?story= v0120209.6is&date=19980121.
9. http://www.suddenlysenior.com/maturemarket statsmore.html
10. "Brew Crew Creates Senior Club," *Sports Business News,* www.sportsbusinessnews.com (February 26, 2003).
11. "Age 55+—They Keep Ticking," www.sgma.com/press/2003. (June 10, 2003)
12. "NFL Targets Women," *Sports Business News*, www.sportsbusinessnews.com (February 3, 2002).
13. "The Dawn of a New Era for Women's Sports," *Sports Business News,* www.sportsbusinessnews.com (June 5, 2001).
14. James Walker, "Diversity on Ice," www.abcnews.com (January 16, 2002).
15. David Boyce, "Commissioner Plans for Growth," *The Kansas City Star* (July 29, 2000), D11.
16. "Group Seven Communications, Inc. Launches 'Deportes Hoy,' The Premier Spanish-Language Sports Daily,", www.guide-p.infoseek.com. (January 22, 1998)
17. "Meet the Amazing NASCAR Fan," http:// www.trackandtravel.com/demographics.html
18. Patrick Reusse, "It's Not Just Bubba Out There," *Star Tribune* (February 18, 2000), 1C.
19. Michael Solomon, *Consumer Behavior,* 3rd ed. (Upper Saddle River, NJ: Prentice Hall, 1996).
20. "America's Teams," *Sport* (November 1996), 33–37.
21. Dennis Howard and J. Crompton, *Financing Sport 2004*, 2nd ed. Morgantown, WV, Fitness Information Technologies.
22. Jon Morgan, "Oriole Makeover Likely to Put Sales in Foul Territory," *The Baltimore Sun* (August 2, 2000), 1A.
23. M. Pritchard and C. Negro, "Sport Loyalty Programs and Their Influence on Fan Relationships, *International Journal of Sports Marketing and Sponsorship*, vol. 3 (2001), 317–338.
24. "AFA National Consumer Survey." www.sportlink.com/footwear/. . . market97/ decisions_influences.html.
25. Sam Fullerton and H. Robert Dodge, "An Application of Market Segmentation in a Sports Marketing Arena: We All Can't Be Greg Norman," *Sport Marketing Quarterly,* vol. 4, no. 3 (1995), 42–47.
26. George Milne and Mark McDonald, *Sports Marketing: Managing the Exchange Process,* (Sudbury, MA: Jones and Bartlett Publishers, 1999).

CASE: PART II

The Eyes Over the Ball (EOB) Alignment Putting System

Bob Botsch was elated. After several attempts to develop his own putting aid he had succeeded. Bob taught political science at a small liberal arts college in South Carolina. He was also an avid golfer, who constantly tried to improve his golf scores. Bob was a very analytical person and he had become extremely frustrated at his lack of putting skill. He first started playing golf in college and through years of practice he had improved his skills in every aspect of the game except one, his putting. When he stood over any putt of 10 feet or less he lost all confidence in his abilities. He had tried many different cures for this problem in the past two years but none seemed to work.

Finally, after reading several books about putting, he developed the idea of placing a training device on his putter. From reading Dave Pelz's book about better putting he determined that he was not visualizing the proper line for his putts. He needed some device to provide him with a directional guide when he putted. He tried several different devices before he discovered that if he placed a plastic golf ball on top of his putter with a direction line painted on the top it permitted him to putt much more accurately. He determined that this simple device enabled him to focus his eyes over the golf ball. This improved his alignment and made it much easier for him to stroke the ball on the proper putting line.

The first device Bob tried had a red line drawn on top of the ball, that he glued to the top of a cavity-backed putter. After some modifications, he was able to glue the plastic ball, now cut in half, to a flat base that could slide into the slot on the top of the head of a cavity-backed putter. This allowed golfers to remove the device or add it whenever they desired. The only limitation was that the putter had to have a flat area on the top of the putter blade.

The success that Bob experienced with his device encouraged him to explore the possibility of selling this product. Although he had no previous experience in producing or selling any type of product, he did have one factor in his favor. Bob had a good friend who was an importer and toy manufacturer. His friend, Maury, had started a successful toy company, which imported its products from China. Bob and Maury had become good friends while they were both in graduate school. Bob had taken a year off from his graduate studies to help Maury build a warehouse for the storage of imported products. Maury became so involved with his business venture that he did not complete graduate school. He continued to expand his business and was quite successful.

Bob thought Maury would help him in his efforts to market the putting device. He made a trip to North Carolina to visit him and seek his advice. Maury was a bit hesitant at first when Bob described the device to him. He told Bob he would check with his supplier in China, see what type of information he could get about manufacturing and shipping costs, and then contact Bob. As Bob made the drive back to his home in South Carolina he wondered if he was willing to go through all the effort he now realized was required to make his device a commercial success.

A few weeks later Bob received a call from Maury, who told him that he had found a company in China that would manufacture the plastic device that Bob had shown him. Maury explained to him, however, that he was not interested in going any further in this endeavor until Bob had obtained a patent on his putting device. Without a patent, he explained, there was too much risk of someone else copying it. Maury had experienced this problem himself in his own business and he did not want Bob to have the same problem. Also, since he would be importing the product and storing it in his warehouse he did not want to take the risk of having several thousand of these devices in stock and no customers. If another company was able to produce a "knock off" it could steal a large portion of the potential sales.

Bob had been so focused on developing the device he had not given much thought about the need to patent it. He knew that it often took several years to obtain a patent and he wanted to get started on the manufacturing and sale of the product immediately. After his initial feelings of frustration, however, he realized that his friend was right.

Bob also realized he needed to determine if his putting aid would be considered a legal device by the United States Golf Association (USGA). This was the governing body for golf. If it deemed a golf club or ball to be illegal it would ban its use in its events. Without the approval of the USGA very few golfers would consider using Bob's putting aid. He knew that if he hoped to sell his product to serious golfers it had to be declared legal by that organization. He hoped at some point to possibly have a professional golfer endorse this product and he knew without the USGA's approval they would not consider it. Also it could not be used by golfers in any amateur competitions without USGA approval.

Before he went through the expense of obtaining a patent Bob decided to seek approval from the USGA. He wrote a letter of inquiry to USGA headquarters in New Jersey and shipped a copy of the putting device to them. He waited for two months and when he received no response he contacted them by telephone. They told him they had received the product but they had not made a decision. Two more months passed and he had still not received any word from the USGA. At this point Bob decided to contact another old friend.

Jack Marsh was another friend from college. He had graduated from the University of North Carolina School of Law and had specialized in patent law. Bob visited him the year before and had mentioned his device to him. Jack, who was also an avid golfer, had said he might be able to help Bob if he became serious about trying to obtain a patent for his product. Bob had laughed and said that as simple as the device was he didn't think a patent was necessary. Jack assured him that if he wanted to sell the product to anyone other than immediate friends he needed to have it patented.

Bob told his friend about his efforts to get a response from the USGA. Jack suggested that he would compose a letter and send it to the sanctioning organization. He explained that an organization like the USGA received thousands of inquiries about new products every year. It was Jack's opinion that they ignored most of these inquiries unless they were pursued vigorously. When the USGA received a letter from Jack they finally responded. Their ruling was that the putting device could be used as a training device and for casual play but that it would have to be removed from the putter during any round of golf that was USGA sanctioned. This meant it could not be used in any professional tournament or any amateur tournament that was an official USGA event.

This ruling at first disappointed Bob. He knew that sales to this group of golfers would be very limited. However, he had hoped that he might convince one of these professional golfers to use and then endorse the product. The vast majority of the approximately 26 million golfers in the United States were weekend and recreational golfers only. He was aware that many of these golfers took their cues in terms of equipment selection from tour professionals. An endorsement from just one of these professionals could be a powerful marketing tool.

After his initial disappointment Bob decided to concentrate his efforts to sell the device as a training tool. This did not exclude Professional Golf Association (PGA) or Ladies Professional Golf Association (LPGA) tour members from using it in practice situations and it still meant that he could sell it to the millions of nonprofessional golfers. Also, he decided to include a training booklet with the Eyes Over the Ball (EOB) device. He had read a great deal about putting in an attempt to improve his own putting. He had also done a great deal of experimentation and analysis. In addition, he was an educator who had authored a book and numerous academic papers. He felt he was qualified to write about this subject and the instructional booklet would be part of the product offering. Now that he had a ruling from the USGA, which clarified how his putting device could be used, he could proceed with the process of securing a patent.

The patent approval took much longer than Bob thought it would. Because of Bob's limited capital, Jack handled all the legal work and charged him only a portion of what the cost would have been if he had used another attorney. It took almost three years and $1,000 but Bob now had his patent and a name for his device. He called it the EOB (Eyes Over the Ball) Alignment and Putting System.

While Bob had been waiting for the approval of the patent he had tried to determine what distribution methods would be most effective for the EOB System. He had virtually no knowledge about marketing, but he was aware of the various methods used to sell golf equipment. Because he considered this a personal challenge, he did not want to approach a major equipment company such as Titleist or Calloway and simply sell the idea to them. Part of the appeal of developing this device was the idea that he could make this product a success on his own. Also, he did not have any experience with these companies and he felt they might take advantage of him. If his product did prove to be successful and he sold the rights to it to an equipment manufacturer at a low price, he would always regret it.

The first marketing outlet he decided to try was golf catalogs. Bob received several of these publications on a regular basis. He had ordered various products from them and he thought they were a perfect vehicle to sell his product. He contacted Golfsmith and Nevada Bob's, two of the biggest catalog houses. He sent both of them a sample of his device and waited for their response. To his surprise neither of these companies showed much interest. Golfsmith rejected the product. They informed him they did not think the device would sell well enough to justify the space it would require to list it in their catalog.

Nevada Bob's, which also has multiple retail sales locations across the country, was more encouraging. They stated they would buy 1,000 putting aids from him if he agreed to spend several thousand dollars on advertising. This offer presented a dilemma for Bob. He decided he could spend a total of $10,000 on his product. Half of this amount he had targeted for the cost of his inventory. That left him with $5,000 to spend on marketing and distribution. He wanted to try to succeed with his device but he was not going to quit his teaching position to pursue this fulltime. He viewed it as a sideline and, therefore, he could only devote limited resources of money and time to it. With this limited budget he did not think he could afford to spend the amount Nevada Bob's asked for advertising. Bob was now becoming aware of the costs associated with introducing a new product into the marketplace.

A second alternative he considered was the sale of the product at trade shows. Each year two major golf equipment shows took place. One occurred in Orlando, Florida, and the other in Las Vegas. At these two shows the major golf equipment manufacturers and many smaller ones present products they develop. Golf club professionals and retailers from all over the country attend these shows to evaluate new lines of golf clubs, apparel, and accessories. They purchased much of the merchandise they placed in their pro shops or stores for the upcoming golf season. In addition, there were numerous regional shows across the country at various times of the year. Once again Bob found that the capital he had available would not go very far. The cost of renting even a small display area at either the Orlando or Las Vegas show would be between $5,000 and $10,000. This would consume almost his entire budget. If he went to some of the smaller shows he would have to spend less but he could not reach as many potential customers. Also Bob did not see himself as a salesperson. He was not at ease standing in a booth all day long trying to convince people to buy his device.

A third alternative was to have independent sales representatives carry his product as part of their product line. Bob was aware that sales representatives called on pro shops and retail golf stores. These individuals already had established relationships with part of the target market Bob was trying to reach. If they would carry the product and take a commission on the putting devices they sold he would incur very little financial risk. Once again he had no luck. Several representatives looked at his product but none expressed any interest. They all reached the same conclusion. The product was a low priced item with the

potential of a one time sale. Unlike golf balls or gloves they could not continue to sell it to golfers time after time. They did not think the product had enough profit potential to warrant adding it to their merchandise lines.

Bob had reached a pivotal point with the development of his product. He believed in the product and its ability to improve a golfer's putting. He was convinced the EOB Alignment Putting System could be successful if he could just find the right way to get it into the hands of the consumer. He also realized that just having a good product was not enough. He did not have enough capital to market his device aggressively, but he wanted to retain control of his product rather than sell the rights to a golf equipment company or a catalog distributor. All his efforts to distribute the product had been met with failure. He was not sure what to do next.

DISCUSSION QUESTIONS

1. What market segment or segments of golfers are most likely to buy Bob's product?
2. Did the lack of an endorsement by a professional golfer seriously hinder the marketing of this product?
3. Can you identify any other means of distribution, other than those mentioned in the case, which could be used to get the product to consumers?
4. Did Bob make a serious mistake by deciding to market the product on his own rather than use a well-known golf equipment company?
5. What type of retail outlets are best suited for Bob's product and why?

PART III

PLANNING THE SPORTS MARKETING MIX

CHAPTER 8

SPORTS PRODUCT CONCEPTS

After completing this chapter, you should be able to:

■ Define sports products and differentiate between goods and services.

■ Explain how sports products and services are categorized.

■ Define branding and discuss the guidelines for choosing an effective brand name.

■ Discuss the branding process in detail.

■ Examine the advantages and disadvantages of licensing from the perspective of the licensee and licensor.

■ Identify the dimensions of service quality and goods quality.

■ Define product design and explain how product design is related to product quality.

Think about attending a Major League Baseball game at Wrigley Field in Chicago. Inside the stadium you find vendors selling game programs, scorecards, Major League Baseball-licensed merchandise, and plenty of food and drink. An usher escorts you to your seat to enjoy the entertainment. During the game, you are exposed to more product choices.

Every game experience presents us with a number of opportunities to purchase and consume sports products. Some of the products, such as the scorecards, represent a pure good, whereas others, such as the game itself, represents a pure service. Each sports product represents a business challenge with incredible upward and downward potential. In this chapter, we explore the multidimensional nature of sports products.

DEFINING SPORTS PRODUCTS

A **sports product** is a good, a service, or any combination of the two that is designed to provide benefits to a sports spectator, participant, or sponsor. Within this definition, the market concept discussed in Chapter 1 is reintroduced. As you recall, the marketing concept states that sports organizations are in the business of satisfying consumers' needs. To do this, products must be developed that anticipate and satisfy consumers' needs. Sports marketers sell products based on the benefits they offer

This baseball, glove, and bat represent pure goods.

This competition represents a pure service.

consumers. These benefits are so critical to marketers that sometimes products are defined as "bundles of benefits." For example, the sport of snowshoeing has recently emerged as one of the nation's fastest-growing winter sports. Ski Industry America, a trade association interested in marketing the sport of snowshoeing, suggests that the bundle of benefits this sports product offers include: great exercise, little athletic skill required to participate, and much less expense than skiing.[1]

In addition to sports and sporting goods, athletes can also be thought of as sports products that possess multiple benefits. For example, NBA teams are currently seeking players who can perform multiple roles on the court rather than those who have more specialized skills. The player who can rebound, is great defensively, dribbles well, and can play the post is invaluable to the franchise. The classic example of the "hybrid" player with multiple skills was Magic Johnson who played center and guard in the 1980 NBA Finals. Today's NBA stars, such as Kevin Garnett, Chris Webber, and Tim Duncan, exemplify the versatile player who offers many benefits to the team.

A number of athletes offer a unique bundle of benefits both on and off the court. Consider, for a moment, Miami Heat's star center, Shaquille O'Neal. The Shaq is clearly a top performer helping the Lakers earn a three-peat championship and being selected to his 11th All-Star game. In addition, Shaq has made several movies and raps, and owns his own sportswear company. The 7-foot-1-inch center has been aligned with numerous endorsement contracts, from Taco Bell to Payless shoes, and has helped a number of non-profit organizations. All of these activities contribute to the "product" we know as Shaq.[2]

GOODS AND SERVICES AS SPORTS PRODUCTS

Our definition of products includes goods and services. It is important to understand the differences in these two types of products to plan and implement the strategic sports marketing process. Because services such as watching a game are being produced (by the players) and consumed (by the spectators) simultaneously, there is no formal channel of distribution. However, when you purchase a pure good, such as a pair of hockey skates, they must be produced by a manufacturer (e.g., Bauer), sent to a retailer (e.g., Sports Authority), and then sold to you. This formal channel of distribution requires careful planning and managing. Let us explore some of the other differences between goods and services.

Goods are defined as tangible, physical products that offer benefits to consumers. Obviously, sporting goods stores sell tangible products such as tennis balls and racquets, hockey equipment, exercise equipment, and so on. By contrast, **services** are usually described as intangible, nonphysical products. For instance, the competitive aspect of any sporting event (i.e., the game itself) or receiving an ice-skating lesson, reflect pure services.

It is easy to see why soccer balls and exercise equipment are classified as pure goods and why the intangible nature of the game constitutes a pure service, but what about other sports products? For example, sporting events typically offer a variety of pure goods (such as food, beverages, and merchandise). However, even these goods have a customer service component. The responsiveness, courtesy, and friendliness of the service provider are intangible components of the service encounter.

Most sports products do not fall so neatly into two distinct categories, but possess characteristics of both goods and services. Figure 8.1 shows the goods–services continuum. On one end, we have sporting goods. At the other end of the continuum, we have almost exclusively, sports services. For example, a sports service that has received considerable attention in the past few years is the fantasy sports camp. Sports camps in a variety of team and individual sports have sprung up to appeal to the aging athlete.

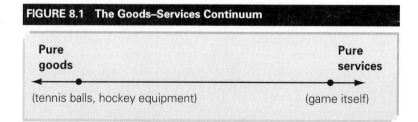

FIGURE 8.1 The Goods–Services Continuum

Pure goods ←————————————————————→ Pure services

(tennis balls, hockey equipment)   (game itself)

For instance, the L. A. Dodgers' Adult Baseball Camp offers life-long memories and mementos for $4,195. During the week, campers receive the following tangible goods: two L. A. Dodger uniforms (home and road) with name and number, L. A. Dodger cap, baseball autographed by an instructor, 50 baseball cards with the camper's picture and camp stats, videotaped highlights of the week at camp, L. A. Dodger T-shirt, team photo, camp certificate, and camp pin.

Thus far, the distinction between goods and services has been based on the tangible aspects of the sports product. In addition to the degree of tangibility, goods and services are differentiated on the basis of perishability, separability, and standardization. These distinctions are important because they form the foundation of product planning in the strategic sports marketing process. Because of their importance, let us take a look at each dimension.

TANGIBILITY

Tangibility refers to the ability to see, feel, and touch the product. Interestingly, the strategy for pure goods often involves stressing the intangible benefits of the product. For example, advertisements for Nike's F.I.T. performance apparel highlight not only the comfort of the product, but also the way the clothing will make you "ready to take on the challenges of wild and wicked workouts." Similarly, Formula 1 racing is paired with TAG Heuer watches in a sponsorship agreement and product line that leverages the benefits of both brands by asking "what are you made of." By pairing with Formula 1 racing, Tag Heuer hopes to capitalize on the intangible attributes of excitement, danger, excellence, and pushing yourself to be the best.

However, the strategy for intangible services is to "tangibilize them."[3] For example, a major league team may wish to highlight the tangible comforts of its new facility rather than promote the game itself. Sportscape dimensions, or the tangible aspects of the stadium such as the stadium design, seating, and aesthetics should be stressed, especially when the team is performing poorly.

STANDARDIZATION AND CONSISTENCY

Another characteristic that distinguishes goods from services is the degree of **standardization.** This refers to receiving the same level of quality over repeat purchases. Because sporting goods are tangible, the physical design of golf ball is manufactured with very little variability. This is even truer today, as many organizations focus on how to continuously improve their manufacturing processes and enhance their product quality.

Pure services, however, reflect the other end of the standardization and consistency continuum. For example, think about the consistency associated with different individual and team athletic performances. How many times have you heard an announcer state before a game, "Which team (or player) will show up today?" Meaning, will the team play well or poorly on that given day?

The Duke University men's basketball team, under the leadership of Mike Krzyzewski, has been one of the most consistent teams in college sports over the past 15 seasons. This, however, does not guarantee they will win the night you attend the game. Even the great Barry Bonds puts on a poor performance occasionally, as evidenced in the 2003 playoffs where he hit for a lowly .222 average in the series.

Consider another example of the lack of consistency within a sporting event. You may attend a doubleheader and see your favorite team lose the first game 14 to 5 and win the second game of the day by a score of 1 to 0. One of the risks associated with using individual athletes or teams to endorse products is the high degree of variability associated with their performance from day to day and year to year. Because sports marketers have no control over the consistency of the sports product, they must focus on those things that can be controlled, such as promotions, stadium atmosphere, and, to some extent, pricing.

PERISHABILITY

Perishability refers to the ability to store or inventory "pure goods," whereby services are lost if not consumed. Goods may be inventoried or stored if they are not purchased immediately, although there are many costs associated with handling this inventory. If a tennis professional is offering lessons, but no students enroll between the hours of 10:00 A.M. and noon, this time (and money) is lost. This "down time" in which the service provider is available but there is no demand is called **idle product capacity.** Idle product capacity results in decreased profitability. In the case of the tennis pro, there is a moderate inventory cost associated with the professional's salary.

Another example with much higher inventory costs is a professional basketball team that is not filling the stands. Consider the Cleveland Cavaliers, the NBA team with the poorest average attendance in the 2002 to 2003 season. The costs of producing one professional game include everything from the "astronomical" salaries of the players to the basic costs of lighting and heating the arena. If paying fans are not in the seats, the performance or service will perish, never to be recouped. As a general rule of thumb, the most perishable products in business are airline seats, hotel rooms, and athletic event tickets.

In an effort to reduce the problem of idle product capacity, sports marketers attempt to stimulate demand in off-peak periods by manipulating the other marketing mix variables. For example, if tennis lessons are not in demand from 10:00 A.M. to noon, the racquet club may offer reduced fees for enrolling during these times. Fortunately for the Cavs, the addition of LeBron James has created a new product offering to stimulate fan interest.

SEPARABILITY

Another factor that distinguishes goods from services is **separability.** If a consumer is purchasing a new pair of running shoes at a major shoe store chain, such as The Athlete's Foot, the quality of the good (the Reebok shoes) can be separated from the quality of the service (delivered by The Athlete's Foot sales associate). Although it is possible to separate the good from the person providing the service, these often overlap. What this suggests is that a manufacturer will selectively choose the retailers that will best represent their goods. In addition, manufacturers and retailers often provide detailed training to ensure salespeople are knowledgeable about the numerous brands that are inventoried.

As we move along the goods–services continuum from pure goods toward pure services, there is less separability. In other words, it becomes more difficult to separate the service received from the service provider. In the case of an athletic event, there is no separation between the athlete, the entertainment, and the fan. The competition is being produced and consumed simultaneously. As such, sport marketers can capitalize on a team or athlete when they are performing well. When things are going poorly, they may have to rely on other aspects of the game (food, fun, and promotions) to satisfy fans. The Dallas Cowboys have sold the history and tradition of the team to the fans. Despite several losing seasons the team has sold out 112 straight home games at Texas Stadium.

CLASSIFYING SPORTS PRODUCTS

In addition to categorizing products based on where they fall on the goods–services continuum, a number of other classification schemes exist. For sports organizations that have a variety of products, the concepts of product line and product mix become important strategic considerations. Let us look at these two concepts in the context of a goods-oriented sports organization and a services-oriented sports organization.

TABLE 8.1 Wilson Sporting Goods Product Mix

Baseball	Basketball	Football	Golf	Racquetball	Soccer
Gloves	Accessories	Footballs	Irons	Racquets	Soccer balls
Bats	Basketballs	Tees/Accessories	Woods	Gloves	Protective gear
Baseballs	Uniforms	Youth protective	Wedges	Eyewear	Bags
Protective Gear		Uniforms	Putters	Racquetballs	
Bags		NFL Accessories	Complete Sets	Footwear	
Accessories			Balls	Bags	
Uniforms			Bags	String	
			Gloves	Accessories	
			Accessories	Apparel	
			Retired Models		

Volleyball	Softball Fastpitch	Softball Slowpitch	Squash	Tennis	Badminton
Outdoor Balls	Gloves	Gloves	Racquets	Balls	Racquets
Indoor Balls	Bats	Bats	Bags	Footwear	Shuttlecocks
Uniforms	Balls	Balls	String	Legacy footwear	String
Ball Carts	Protective Gear	Accessories	Grips	Accessories	
Bags	Accessories			Platform Tennis	
				Court Equipment	
				Retired Models	
				Racquets	
				Bags	
				String	
				Grips	

Source: Wilson Sporting Goods, www.wilsonsports.com.

A **product line** is a group of products that are closely related because they satisfy a class of needs, are used together, are sold to the same customer groups, are distributed through the same type of outlets, or fall within a given price range. Wilson Sporting Goods sells many related product lines such as shoes, bats, gloves, softballs, golf clubs, and tennis racquets. The total assortment of product lines that a sports organization sells is the **product mix.** Table 8.1 illustrates the relationship between the product lines and product mix for Wilson Sporting Goods. The number of different product lines the organization offers is referred to as the breadth of the product mix. If these product lines are closely related in terms of the goods and services offered to consumers, then there is a high degree of product consistency.

Nike recently increased the breadth of its product mix by adding new brands and product lines. The company acquired Converse and its famous Chuck Taylor All-Star shoes, as well as Hurley International, a surf- and skateboard apparel brand. Other new acquisitions include Cole Haan dress shoes and Bauer hockey equipment. The strategic advantage of this related diversification is the use of Nike's established marketing muscle.[4] Synergy in distribution and promotion, as well as strong brand identification, should make Nike's launch into new markets a successful venture. Joycelyn Hayward, the manager of a sporting goods store that carries Nike summed it up best by saying, "Nike's ability to churn out innovative products and marketing plans has kept it ahead of rivals."[5]

Today, Nike is focusing on increasing their talent pool of athletes and expanding their growing product lines into new sports such as golf and hockey. For example, LeBron James joined the Knight stable for a $90 million, multiyear endorsement

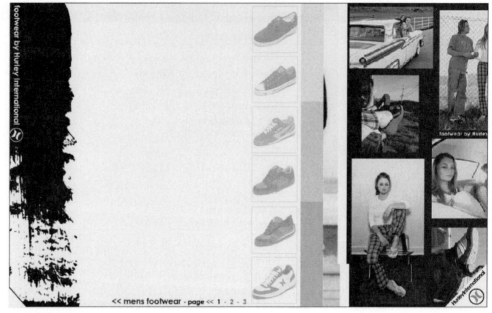

Nike extends product line with Hurley footwear and apparel.
Source: © Hurley International. www.hurley.com. All rights reserved.

contract prior to playing a college or professional game. Nike certainly hopes that James is the second coming of Jordan and that he will invigorate sales in the high-end market. In addition, Nike, under the leadership of Knight, is quickly moving into international markets. However their race with Reebok ends, Knight will always be remembered as the man who realized the true marketing power of sports celebrities.

The depth of the product lines describes the number of individual products that comprise that line. The greater the number of variations in the product line, the deeper the line. For example, the Wilson basketball product line currently features over 60 different basketballs, four of which are indoor and fifty-six of which are indoor/outdoor. Now, think about how the product concepts might relate to a more service-oriented sports organization, such as a professional sports franchise. All these organizations have gone beyond selling the core product, the game itself, and moved into other profitable areas, such as the sale of licensed merchandise, memorabilia, and fantasy camps. In essence, sports organizations have expanded their product lines or broadened their product mix.

Understanding the depth, breadth, and consistency of the product offerings is important from a strategic perspective. Sports organizations might consider adding product lines, and, therefore, widen the product mix. For example, Nike is using this strategy and capitalizing on its strong brand name. Alternatively, the sports organization can eliminate weak product lines and focus on its established strengths. In addition, the product lines it adds may be related to existing lines (product line consistency) or may be unrelated to existing lines (product line diversification).

Another strategic decision may be to maintain the number of product lines, but add new versions to make the line deeper. For instance, the MLS, which has 10 teams divided into Eastern and Western conferences, hopes to add two teams in 2005 and two more in 2006.[6] All of these product planning strategies require examining the overarching marketing goals and the organizational objectives, as well as carefully considering consumers' needs.

PRODUCT CHARACTERISTICS

Products are sometimes described as "bundles of benefits" designed to satisfy consumers' needs.[7] These "bundles" consist of numerous important attributes or characteristics that, when taken together, create the total product. These **product characteristics,** which include branding, quality, and design, are illustrated in Figure 8.2. It is important to note that each of the product characteristics interacts with the others to produce the total product. Branding is dependent on product quality, product quality is contingent on product design, and so on. Although these product features (i.e., branding, quality, and design) are interdependent, we examine each independently in the following sections.

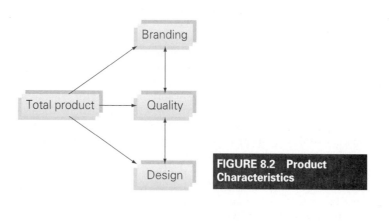

FIGURE 8.2 Product Characteristics

SPOTLIGHT ON INTERNATIONAL SPORTS MARKETING

Branded Like Beckham

Their relationship became strained when David Beckham met his wife Victoria, a British pop singer known as Posh Spice, and developed this "fashion thing," grumbled Sir Alex Ferguson, the curmudgeonly manager of Manchester United, when the soccer star he had reared since he was a teenager was sold to Real Madrid. This week, Mr. Beckham joined the Spanish club amid the blaze of publicity that follows him everywhere. Which is the whole point for the third-most-valuable sporting personality in the world, after America's basketball legend, Michael Jordan, and its top golfer, Tiger Woods.

Sports sponsorship is a huge business—even Mr. Beckham's contract-clinching medical was sponsored by a health-care firm. Roughly two-thirds of the almost $10 billion spent in sponsorship fees in North America last year was related to sports, estimate consultants with A. T. Kearney. The business is growing by some 9 percent a year. Globally, the market is probably twice as big, and growing faster. Add related advertising, marketing and so

forth, and other costs, and the value of a deal often triples. What makes Mr. Beckham such a hot property is that he is more than just a superb footballer.

Mr. Jordan is now a brand in his own right, with such things as Michael Jordan's Steak House and Cologne by Michael, "developed to reflect Michael's transition from super athlete to stylish executive." Mr. Woods, who at 27 is just younger than Mr. Beckham, is likely to become the first sporting billionaire—even before he reaches the middle-aged group to which his image mostly appeals (he promotes unflashy products such as Buick cars). For a fee, Mr. Beckham is willing to pitch such delights as Castrol motor oil in Vietnam. But his main plus is that he can reach the part of the market that advertisers struggle hardest to influence: trend-setters.

Last year, Mr. Woods replaced his Rolex (for a reported fee of $2 million a year) with a TAG Heuer, owned by LVMH. But Mr. Beckham can cause a sensation simply by getting a new hair style. Once, after he shaved his head, thousands of young men, from

(Continued)

(Continued)

Manchester to Tokyo, trooped to their hairdressers to be scalped.

As far as brand managers are concerned, Mr. Beckham's transfer might have been engineered in adland. He has a personal contract to promote Pepsi, an official sponsor of both Manchester United and Real Madrid. But although Nike sponsors United, Mr. Beckham wears Adidas boots, under a personal deal with the German firm. Its boss, Herbert Hainer, says Mr. Beckham's move is a "dream ticket" for Adidas because his firm also sponsors Real. United's main sponsor is Vodafone, which paid £30 million ($46 million) for a four-year deal ending next year. The world's biggest mobile-phone operator, which is midway though a separate two-year personal contract with Mr. Beckham, has no qualms about his move: it works with a Real sponsor, Siemens Mobile, a handset supplier.

When he was at United, Mr. Beckham collected a wage for playing football (said to be £70,000 a week) plus a fee (around £20,000 a week) for the club to use his image as part of its own merchandising. At Real it is said he will be earning less. But his personal sponsorship deals could become far more lucrative, though he will have to hand 50 percent to the Spanish club.

Real is likely to recoup Mr. Beckham's euro35 million ($41 million) transfer fee in just two or three years from the additional revenue that his joining is likely to generate, especially in Asia, where pictures of "golden balls" appear almost everywhere, and there are even gilded statues of him in Thai temples. More people watch Manchester United on TV in China than in England. Samantha McCollum of the London office of FutureBrand says that surveys of Asian fans show that around 30 percent follow the player rather than his team, which means that Real Madrid can expect an army of new supporters. Mr. Beckham's debut with the club next month will be against Beijing's Dragon team, the first in a series of pre-season games in Asia.

What do sponsors get for their money? Mainly a few days a year for photo-shoots, the filming of TV adverts, and appearances at corporate events. But gone are the pioneering days when a bored-looking celebrity endorsed a product on TV that nobody really believed he used. Today, both sponsor and player work hard to manage their respective brand risks.

Contracts can be arduous—insisting on, say, only a certain make of tennis racquet ever being held. Firms often impose tough "good behavior" clauses, to minimize "O. J. risk." The Hertz car-rental company quickly terminated its deal with O. J. Simpson when the American football star was accused of murdering his wife. For the most part, stars such as Mr. Beckham work hard at their image—not least because they hope to follow Mr. Jordan and maintain a brand value after their sporting days are over. Mr. Jordan has parlayed himself into a model businessman.

Mr. Beckham has been "good value," says Mike Caldwell, Vodafone's director of communications. He has rebranded as Vodafone the firm's Japanese subsidiary, J-Phone, and in Britain he helped to launch Vodafone live!, a new service with features such as picture-messaging. Although Finland's Nokia dominates handset sales in Europe, its phones have been outsold in the new service by a relatively unknown handset made by Japan's Sharp, which became known as "the Beckham phone."

Yet Vodafone does not always use Mr. Beckham. In Germany and Italy, its star is Michael Schumacher, the Formula One motor racing champion. Nor does Mr. Beckham appear in Vodafone ads in his football kit. In part this is not to offend fans of rival clubs, but mostly because the firm is using him as a "lifestyle icon."

That may be Mr. Beckham's most powerful role—and the way to extend his brand, a la Jordan, after he hangs up his soccer boots. Trend-spotters mark him out as a "metrosexual": a heterosexual urban man who enjoys fashion and grooming products, and even activities such as parenting, that are traditionally associated more with women. This may raise untrimmed eyebrows in Madrid. After he appeared in a series of pictures with his scantily clad wife, wearing painted nails and a studded wrist-band (Becks that is, not Posh), *El Mundo*, a Spanish newspaper, wondered how this strand of British "queerness" would play with Madrid's famously macho fans.

It will be interesting, to say the least. So, too, will be his efforts to make it in America, where Mr. Beckham is even less well-known than his briefly famous wife. During a recent attempt to promote themselves there, Mrs. Beckham told the New York Times: "We want to have our own brand. There are so many things that interest us—fashion, make-up, ..."

Alas for Mr. Beckham, his Spanish move means he will not now accompany Manchester United on a series of exhibition matches in America. Although no European soccer club could become as famous in America as the New York Yankees or Los Angeles Lakers, the tour would have raised Mr. Beckham's profile. Mr. Jordan and Mr. Woods seem safe, for now, atop the sports-sponsorship league.

Source: Copyright © 2003. The Economist Newspaper Ltd. All rights reserved. Reprinted by permission.

BRANDING

What first comes to mind when you hear University of Notre Dame, Green Bay, or adidas™? It is likely that the Fighting Irish name, along with the Lucky Leprechaun ready to battle, comes to mind for Notre Dame. The Packers are synonymous with Green Bay, Wisconsin, and the symbolic three stripes are synonymous with adidas. All these characteristics are important elements of branding.

Branding is a name, design, symbol, or any combination that a sports organization uses to help differentiate its products from the competition. Three important branding concepts are brand name, brand marks, and trademarks. A **brand name** refers to the element of the brand that can be vocalized, such as the Nike Air Jordan, the Minnesota Wild, and the Vanderbilt University Commodores. When selecting a brand name for sporting goods or a team name, considerable marketing effort is required to ensure the name symbolizes strength and confidence. Because choosing a name is such a critical decision, sports marketers sometimes use the following guidelines for selecting brand names:

- The name should be positive; distinctive; generate positive feelings and associations; be easy to remember and to pronounce. For team names, the positive associations include those linked with a city or geographic area.
- The name should be translatable into a dynamite attitude-oriented logo. As an example of a successful logo choice consider Binghamton University, who recently changed their name from the Colonials to the Bearcats. Athletic Director, Joel Thirer called the move a huge success based on the number of fans who now sport the Bearcat logo.[8]
- The name should imply the benefits the sports product delivers. For example, the name communicates the product attributes the target market desires.
- The name should be consistent with the image of the rest of the product lines, organization, and city. Again, this is especially important for cities naming their sports franchises. One example of this concept in action is MLS's Columbus Crew.[9] The Crew was chosen to represent the Columbus community in a positive manner. The name suggests the hard work, do-not-quit attitude that people in the Columbus community value.
- The name should be legally and ethically permissible. That is, the name cannot violate another organization's trademarks or be seen as offensive to any group of people. For example, a great many team names with reference to (and perceived negative connotations) Native Americans have been changed or are under scrutiny (e.g., Miami University of Ohio Redskins to RedHawks, Atlanta Braves, and Washington Redskins). There has even been an NCAA proposal to eliminate all references to American Indian mascots, nicknames, or logos. In the short term, the NCAA has decided to reject the proposal and let the schools conduct a self-analysis to determine whether the treatment is offensive.[10]

A **brand mark,** also known as the **logo** or **logotype,** is the element of a brand that cannot be spoken. One of the most recognizable logos in the world is the Nike Swoosh. Interestingly, Carolyn Davidson was paid just $35 in 1971 to create the logo that now adorns Nike products, as well as CEO Phil Knight's ankle in the form of a tattoo. It's important for sports marketers to realize that while the Nike logo was created for the paltry sum of $35 dollars, the cost of changing logos and nicknames can swell to $100,000. Some of the incidental costs of changing your brand include: surveys of constituent

SPOTLIGHT ON SPORTS MARKETING ETHICS

Debate Over Native American Team Names Still Heated

COLUMBUS—When Barry Landeros-Thomas' oldest daughter, Elysia, was 7, she came home crying after two boys at her Columbus school danced around her, slapping their mouths, making war whoops, and singing a song from a Disney movie.

They sang to her, "Savages, savages, barely even human."

The song came from "Pocahontas."

As innocent as young kids' antics may seem, Landeros-Thomas, 39, and his children, who are Native Americans, are hurt by such actions, which they say belittle them. Perceptions of Native Americans, learned through westerns or other movies and embodied in mascots and sports team names, perpetuate negative stereotypes and continue to subjugate Native Americans, Landeros-Thomas says.

The director of youth and education services at the Native American Indian Center of Central Ohio (NAICCO) in Columbus, Landeros-Thomas is trying to educate people about the racism inherent in Indian sports mascots and logos. He also worked on this issue in his previous post as coordinator of American Indian student services at Ohio State University's Multicultural Center in Columbus.

But it is his role as a father that pushes him to go year after year to the Cleveland Indians' home opening game to protest the team's Chief Wahoo mascot, he says. He will go to Jacobs Field on April 7.

In an e-mail sent by the American Indian Movement Support Group of Ohio and Northern Kentucky urging people to protest the Cleveland Indians in Cincinnati, the group writes: "Chief Wahoo promotes a negative stereotype of indigenous peoples. This red-faced, hook-nosed, grinning buffoon does not resemble any indigenous peoples. The name and logo do not 'honor' Native peoples, but perpetuate racist stereotypes only. Indians are not mascots."

Long road

It's been a slow, tough road for Landeros-Thomas and others to get people, mainly those who are not minorities, to understand and to acknowledge that Native American mascots don't honor Native Americans, but instead portray them in a negative light that is offensive to them.

Worst of all, places of learning won't budge.

"Most of this is perpetuated by our educational institutions," says Mark Welsh, program director at NAICCO. "We have been struggling to educate the educators. I'm learning our educators are slow learners."

On behalf of NAICCO, Welsh says he has sent letters to a few area school districts to ask them to change their Native American-related sports team names, receiving no reply. OSU's chapter of the National Coalition on Racism in Sports and the Media also has sent letters requesting a name change to 225 Ohio schools from the elementary to the college level that have Native American-related mascots, to professional sports teams, and to the National Collegiate Athletic Association, says Landeros-Thomas.

"From preschools to professional teams, we are dealing with the issue on multiple levels," he adds.

The only response he received was from a school acknowledging receipt of the letter, but responding that it wasn't going to change.

One victory for Native Americans has been Miami University of Ohio's 1996 decision to drop its Redskins name and become the RedHawks. In 1997, the minor league Canton-Akron Indians changed its name to the Akron Aeros.

Miami did so in deference to Native American sensitivities. The Akron team did so because of the team's relocation to Akron, according to a spokesman.

Outside Ohio, some schools have changed their Native American-related sports names in response to sensitivities about their derogatory meanings.

No professional baseball or football team has changed a nickname to a non-Indian one, according to Major League Baseball and the National Football League.

They're people too

Because of the difficulty in getting schools to truly understand their views, Landeros-Thomas, Welsh, and others have resorted to obviously offensive analogies to make their point.

"Suppose the Native American Indian Center of Central Ohio," says Welsh, "were to sponsor a football team and we called it the Columbus Caucasians, honoring our Caucasian ancestors. Our mascot is 'Popey.' We dress up 'Popey,' 'in honor,' in a black gown with a cross on his chest.

"At halftime," Welsh says, now pounding his fist on the table for emphasis, "he goes out with a bottle of wine and a loaf of bread, blessing someone and making the symbol of the cross.

"I bet 99.9 percent of the people would protest," says Welsh, who is generally calm and quiet. Being offensive is "precisely what they're doing with these (Native American) mascots."

The point is that Native Americans are people, who still exist today. Stereotypical images of them are just that—stereotypes that don't fit reality.

In a slide presentation showing more than 500 years of racist images used in America to represent Native Americans, blacks, Asians, Jews, and Hispanics, Landeros-Thomas points out that Native American mascots are offensive just like mascots representing other ethnic groups would be blatantly offensive.

Instead of the Cleveland Indians' Chief Wahoo, imagine the Cleveland Africans showing a mascot of a black man with an afro. Or the Cleveland Asians with an Asian man with glasses and slanted eyes. Or the Cleveland Hispanics with a man in a sombrero.

In whose honor?

If schools really wanted to honor Native Americans, Landeros-Thomas says, why not name a school after Chief Tecumseh? Tecumseh is the Shawnee leader revered for his efforts in uniting various tribes to fight for their homelands during the European settlement of the Ohio region.

Schools, for instance, named after George Washington or Theodore Roosevelt, honor the former U.S. presidents.

"But all these schools, you don't see a big guy dancing around like Teddy Roosevelt, dancing around with a big stick," says Landeros-Thomas. "That would be disrespectful."

According to research done by Landeros-Thomas and Welsh, the term "Redskin" comes from the practice of scalping, which was brought to America by Dutch settlers. As a way to take land from Native Americans, the federal and state governments would pay a bounty for their scalps.

To prove that they were native scalps, European settlers would stretch the scalped skin on a willow hoop. Once dried, the skin would turn red because of Native Americans' skin pigmentation.

Native Americans then learned scalping from the settlers.

Because of this history, Native Americans today are offended by the term Redskins in sports teams since it conjures up efforts to kill off their ancestors.

"It goes back to education," says Landeros-Thomas. "I've talked to innumerable school boards. You've got to go through lots of layers of defenses, of denials, of rationalizations to pull those scales from their eyes.

"Just because they don't see it as wrong doesn't mean it's right. People didn't see slavery as wrong."

Images of Native Americans in headdresses also don't represent them from the Ohio region, says Welsh. Native Americans who wore headdresses lived in the Great Plains.

Moreover, says M. C. Hapi, education specialist at the Ohio Historical Society's Newark Earthworks and Flint Ridge State Memorial sites, the feathers in a headdress are earned through honorable deeds. The feathers and dancing are considered sacred to Native Americans.

Having a sports mascot parade around in a headdress is like having a person dressed up like the Catholic Pope.

"It's undignified—the way you wouldn't want to see your Pope dancing around blessing the crowd," says Hapi, a descendant of the Cherokee and Choctaw Indians.

"If you want to honor me, why don't you ask us what we think represents honor," she wonders.

Source: Julie Shaw, Gannett News Service, March 30, 2003.

groups, designing the logo, retaining a marketing firm, developing a new ad campaign to create awareness, repainting of facilities, new stationary, replacing signage, new uniforms, and even a new mascot costume.[11]

A **trademark** identifies that a sports organization has legally registered its brand name or brand mark and thus prevents others from using it. Unfortunately, product counterfeiting or the production of low-cost copies of trademarked popular brands is reaching new heights. Product counterfeiting and trademark infringement are especially problematic at major sporting events, such as the Super Bowl or Olympic Games. For example, Collegiate Licensing Co, which represents about 150 colleges, found some 3,000 counterfeit items at football bowl games and the NCAA basketball tournament.

Sports logos gallery on the Web.
Source: Logo Server. Used by permission. All rights reserved.

THE BRANDING PROCESS

The broad purpose of branding a product is to allow an organization to distinguish and differentiate itself from all others in the marketplace. Building the brand will then ultimately affect consumer behaviors, such as increasing attendance, merchandising sales, or participation in sports. However, before these behaviors are realized, several things must happen in the **branding process** shown in Figure 8.3.

First, **brand awareness** must be established. Brand awareness refers to making consumers in the desired target market recognize and remember the brand name. Only after awareness levels reach their desired objectives can brand image be addressed. After all, consumers must be aware of the product before they can understand the image the sports marketer is trying to project.

After brand awareness is established, marketing efforts turn to developing and managing a **brand image.** Brand image is described as the consumers' set of beliefs about a brand, which, in turn, shape attitudes. Brand image can also be thought of as the "personality" of the brand. Organizations that sponsor sporting events are especially interested in strengthening or maintaining the image of their products through association with a sports entity (athlete, team, or league) that reflects the desired image. For instance, the marketers of Mercedes-Benz automobiles have established sponsorships with tennis events to reinforce a brand image of power, grace, and control.

FIGURE 8.3 The Branding Process

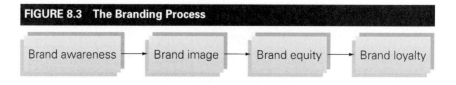

Sports marketers attempt to manage beliefs that we have about a particular brand through a number of "image drivers," or factors that influence the brand image. The image drivers controlled by sports marketing efforts include product features or characteristics, product performance or quality, price, brand name, customer service, packaging, advertising, promotion, and distribution channels. Each of these image drivers contributes to creating the overall brand image. After shaping a positive brand image, sports marketers can then ultimately hope to create high levels of brand equity.

Another link in the branding process is developing high levels of brand equity. **Brand equity** is the value that the brand contributes to a product in the marketplace. In economic terms, it is the difference in value between a branded product and its generic equivalent. Consumers who believe a sport product has a high level of brand equity are more likely to be satisfied with the brand. The satisfied consumers will, in turn, become brand loyal or repeat purchasers. Gladden, Milne, and Sutton have developed a unique model of assessing brand equity for the sports industry. The components of the model can be seen in Figure 8.4. The authors explain brand equity by extending the previous work of Aaker (1991), who believes there are four major components of brand equity. These are perceived quality, brand awareness, brand associations, and brand loyalty. Gladden, Milne, and Sutton describe the perceived quality of sport as the consumers' perceptions of a team's success. Obviously, this could be extended beyond the notion of a team to other sport products. Brand awareness is defined as the consumers' familiarity with a particular team or sport product. Brand associations refer to the intangible attributes of a brand or, in the case of sport, the experiential and symbolic attributes offered by an athletic team. The final component, brand loyalty, is defined as the ability to attract and retain consumers. As the authors point out, this is sometimes difficult because of the inconsistent and intangible nature of the sports product.[12]

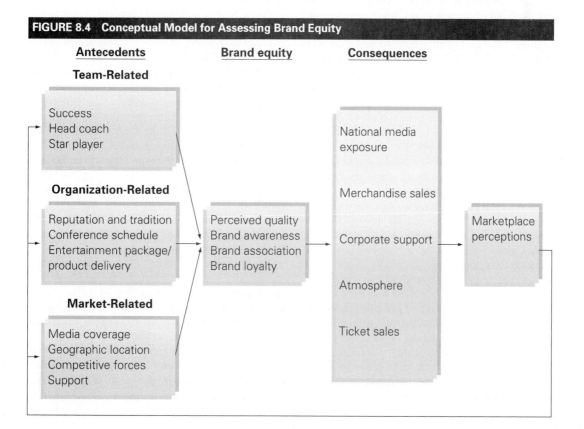

FIGURE 8.4 Conceptual Model for Assessing Brand Equity

When describing the full model of brand equity for sport, Gladden and his colleagues also discuss the antecedents and consequences of brand equity for a sports product. These antecedent conditions are particularly important for marketing managers to understand because they will have an impact on the level of brand equity. The three broad categories of antecedents include team-related factors, organization-related factors, and market-related factors.

Team-related factors are further broken down into the success of the team, head coach, and star player(s). Previous research has shown that winning or success is still a critical factor in establishing a strong brand and in achieving the desired outcomes such as merchandise sales, media exposure, etc. As the following article points out, "selling losing programs is never easy."

Although success is defined by wins and losses, it can also be thought of as the historical standard by which the team has been judged. Interestingly, the authors of the model also believe the head coach can be an important factor in establishing brand equity. The University of Louisville received a tremendous boost when they hired Rick Pitino and the Washington Redskins' brand was bolstered with the hiring of former

---

Selling Losing Programs Never Easy

Women football fans of the Ragin' Cajuns had a good reason to make sure they showed up early to Thursday's night matchup between their 0–7 University Lousisiana-Lafayette team and 1–6 New Mexico State Aggies.

There was a $3,800 diamond at stake.

In an effort to help boost attendance numbers to the battle for the cellar of the Sun Belt Conference matchup, the ULL athletics department partnered up with a local jewelry store. One of the first 500 women that went through the turnstiles would receive a diamond, with the 499 others receiving the imitation—cubic zirconias.

It's a promotion you'd likely never see at Penn State, Tennessee, Oklahoma, or USC. After all, gimmicks like these are for schools whose alumni base can't fill their stadiums, regardless of the team's record. And there's plenty of marketing creativity taking place among those schools that really have to work to fill the seats—especially for those that find themselves to be frequent members of ESPN.com's Bottom 10 list every week.

It's hard to sell just the football in Lafayette these days. Not only is the team's performance lacking luster, but the opponents that they play at home aren't too hot either. The Ragin' Cajuns are at the end of a three-game homestand in which their opponents—Louisiana-Monroe, New Mexico State, and Idaho—have combined to win just two games. The team knocked off New Mexico State on Thursday night in front of a crowd of just over 12,000 fans.

"Our biggest competition for the entertainment dollar here is festivals and hunting," says Daryl Cetnar, ULL's sports information director. "There are more than 100 festivals taking place, from frogs to rice to omelets, and everyone owns cabins out in the woods and knows when duck hunting season is."

So Cetnar and other school officials are hoping that promotions such as the find the diamond opportunity and free giveaways, like the fleece logo blanket given to each family that purchased tickets to a recent game, can keep the school's average attendance close to 15,000 this season.

The NCAA is expected to enforce a new rule that will require Division I-A teams to draw at least 15,000 fans per game—possibly as soon as next seaon—in order to remain in Division I-A.

That has to be a concern to schools like New York State University at Buffalo, which expanded their stadium to 31,000 seats in order to be eligible to play Division I-A in 1999. Since then, the Bulls have gone 6-47 and are in the midst of the longest losing streak in the nation at 18 games.

School officials estimate that attendance will be between 10,000 and 12,000 fans per game this season and they're working very hard to even make those numbers.

For the home opener against Division I-AA Colgate, 20,324 fans showed up to see the Red Raiders beat the Bulls, 38-15. Attendance numbers were boosted by some of the students, who were drawn to the game thanks to the school's attempt to break the Guinness World Record for number of people in a water balloon fight, which took place on the tennis courts close to the stadium. Others who came to the game to see reggae recording artist Shaggy, who performed at halftime.

"We've tried to incorporate halftime concerts one or two times a year," said John Lambert, Buffalo's associate athletic director for external relations. "Our marching band has been very good in understanding what we are trying to do and the students have really enjoyed them."

The school has also tried to draw fans by bringing in the country's top action sports stars, including renown skateboarder Tony Hawk and BMX specialist Dave Mirra, who performed his stunts inside the school's arena before the home opener.

Lambert says that the amount of tickets sold easily help defray the appearance fees of Hawk and Mirra.

Without many promotions, Buffalo's attendance has clearly suffered. The team's Sept. 27 game against fellow Mid-American Conference opponent Akron drew only 6,385 fans.

But trying to market events tied to the game doesn't always work.

Louisiana-Lafayette rents out spots on the grass field next to their stadium for $75 for the entire season. This season, they sold 160 spots to fans, who are supposed to use the area to tailgate before going inside to watch the game. But that doesn't always prove to be successful, especially when a school doesn't have a winning program.

"Our biggest problem that we've faced is that some of these people are not coming into the games and the 15,000-fan ticket count probably will be fans in the stands, not paid attendance. That's why it's a serious concern of ours that we have fans tailgating that are apparently not coming into the game."

For struggling schools in non-BCS conferences, home games against ranked opponents are a luxury they don't normally have. ULL has played teams like Minnesota and Oklahoma State on the road and Buffalo's only home game against a Top 25 team could come on Nov. 8, assuming Northern Illinois continues with its undefeated record.

East Carolina, who is now 1-6 after defeating Army on Saturday, had to play No. 2 Miami on the road, but the school is benefiting from being relatively formidable over the past five seasons.

That's one of the reasons why ECU hasn't had to work too hard to keep its attendance close to the 30,000 mark despite the team's record.

"We haven't had to do a whole lot in the past," said Craig Wells, assistant athletic director for media relations. "But once we were 0-4, we realized that we should start implementing some things."

In their first three games against Cincinnati, West Virginia and Miami, the Pirates were outscored 126-13.

So for a Tuesday night game against Houston, school officials—who wanted to make sure the crowd looked good in front of a national television audience—dreamed up every possible discount to increase attendance.

Any member of the military, any faculty or staff member and any public service worker could buy tickets for $5—an 80 percent discount from normal prices. Students had a chance to win free tuition for a semester, book vouchers, or a school parking permit.

"It's a pretty conservative area," Wells said. "We're in Bible Belt territory, so we have to make sure that we aren't going too far out of bounds in order to get people to our game."

With no other major college football program or professional sports team in close proximity to its Greenville, NC, campus, Easy Carolina doesn't have to worry about other major sporting events going up against them.

The same can't be said for SMU, which not only has to compete in the Dallas market, but also has to convince fans to come to their game. Since SMU was hit with the death penalty in 1987, the team has only had one winning season (in 1997, the Mustangs went 6-5).

"Dallas is very much a bandwagon sports town," said Shawn Heilbron, the school's associate athletic director for sales and marketing. "In the mid 90's, you could have your own section at Mavericks games. Now that they are winning, every game is sold out."

SMU certainly isn't doing much winning and in Texas there are plenty of good high school games to see on Friday night that could make a football fan a little less inclined to see the college variety on Saturday, even in the school's three-year old, $56.8 million Gerald J. Ford Stadium. But thanks in part to some fresh ideas, average attendance is around 20,000 fans per game this year, despite the school's 0-7 record.

SMU sold more than 1,000 tickets to cub and boy scouts for its game against UTEP on Oct. 4. The draw? After the game, the children watched movies on the scoreboard screen and slept on the field.

The effort of marketing to children is well worth it, says Heilbron, whose team at SMU built a play area for kids near the scoreboard, so that parents can watch while kids play. The play area helps bring in at least 500 tickets per game, Heilbron said. Buffalo has adopted a similar idea and has in the past brought in Nickelodeon characters like Jimmy Neutron to make the experience more meaningful.

On Nov. 15, for the school's game against Rice, all kids 13 and under will get in free with all other tickets costing $5. During the game, eight children will be selected from previously submitted online applications to perform game day jobs, including a stint as the stadium's PA announcer.

Despite the Mustangs' record, no child will get the chance to get into the game and run a play.

Source: Darren Rovell, ESPN, October 21, 2003. Reprinted courtesy of ESPN.com.

head coach Joe Gibbs. Similarly, a star player or players can boost brand equity, especially in the sports of baseball and basketball. For example, the LeBron phenomenon has given the Cleveland Cavaliers a new image and chance to reposition their franchise. Even the already powerful Yankees enhanced their brand by trading for Alex Rodriguez.[13]

The organization-related antecedents described in the model include reputation and tradition, conference and schedule, and entertainment package–product delivery. The reputation and tradition of the team off the field is believed to be a factor in building brand equity. An excellent example of problems in the front office influencing fan perceptions and brand equity is that of the hapless Arizona Cardinals. Owner Bill Bidwell has been scrutinized and criticized by the fans and media for years because of bad choices made on and off the field. The conference affiliation and schedule are also organizational factors influencing image. Gladden et al. believe college and professional teams who play in tougher conferences with long-standing rivals will create greater benefits for the team's equity in the long term. This must certainly hold some truth as college teams and conferences are constantly realigning. Most recently, Louisville, Cincinnati, Marquette, DePaul, and South Florida have all left Conference USA for the Big East. In turn, Conference USA has lined up SMU, Tulsa, Marshall, and Rice as replacement schools. Additionally, the ACC has added Miami, Virginia Tech, and Boston College to their membership.[14] Finally, the entertainment aspect of sport created and managed by the organization will affect brand equity. As mentioned previously, this is one of the controllable elements of the largely uncontrollable sports industry.

The market-related antecedents are those things such as media coverage, geographic location, competitive forces, and support. Media coverage refers to the exposure the sport product receives in the media via multiple outlets such as radio, TV, newspaper, and the Internet. Obviously, the images portrayed in the media and amount of coverage can have a huge bearing on all aspects of brand equity. Geographic location is also related to equity in that certain areas of the United States are linked with certain types of sport. As described in Milne and McDonald, "it may be easier to establish brand equity for a Division I men's basketball team in Indiana than it would be in Idaho." Competition must also be considered a market factor and the authors of the model describe it as the most influential in creating equity. In some instances, competition can enhance the value of a brand, but more typically competitive forces vying for similar consumers will weaken equity and its outcomes. Fan support is the final market force influencing equity. Quite simply, the greater the number of loyal fans or supporters, the greater the brand equity.

Although the preceding discussion has focused on the antecedents of brand equity to a sports product, the model also describes the related outcomes or consequences of establishing a strong brand. More specifically, the authors believe higher levels of brand equity will lead to more national media exposure, greater sales of team merchandise, more support from corporate sponsors, enhanced stadium atmospherics, and increased ticket sales.

How can marketers assess the equity of a brand such as the Yankees or Nike? One popular technique to measure brand equity evaluates a brand's performance across seven dimensions. Brand equity is then calculated by applying a multiple, determined by the brand's performance on the seven dimensions, to the net brand-related profits. These dimensions include leadership or the ability of the brand to influence its market, stability or the ability of the brand to survive, market or the trading environment of the brand internationality or the ability of the brand to cross geographic and cultural borders, trend or the ongoing direction of the brand's importance to the industry, support or the effectiveness of the brand's communication, and protection of the owner's legal title.[15]

Although there are a number of ways to measure brand equity in consumer goods, there have been very few attempts to look at the equity of sports teams. One exception was a study that measured the brand equity of MLB franchises.[16] To measure brand equity, the researchers first calculated team revenues for each franchise. These revenues are based on gate receipts; media; licensing and merchandise; and stadium-oriented issues; such as concession, advertising, and so on. The franchise value is then assigned a multiple based on growth projections for network television fees. Next, the total franchise value is subtracted from the value of a generic product to determine the brand equity. Because there is no such thing as a generic baseball team, the researchers used the $130 million fee paid by the two new expansion teams at the time of the study, Tampa Bay and Arizona. This $130 million fee represents the closest estimate to an unbranded team, since they had yet to begin play.

Interestingly, only seven of the 30 MLB teams show any brand equity. Based on the research, the following teams have positive brand equity (in rank order): New York Yankees, Toronto Blue Jays and New York Mets, Boston Red Sox, Los Angeles Dodgers, Chicago White Sox, and Texas Rangers. The teams with the lowest brand equity include the Montreal Expos, Pittsburgh Pirates, and Seattle Mariners. Given the fact that many of these "brands" have been around for decades, the brand equity for MLB franchises is surprisingly low.

Although the previous study used an economic basis for determining brand equity, other research has employed less precise, qualitative approaches. For example, a panel of sporting goods industry experts was asked to name the most powerful brands in sport. In this study of equity, sports brands were defined as those who directly manufacture sporting apparel, equipment, and shoes. Nike is in a league of its own when it comes to branding. Ever since the introduction of the Air Jordan basketball shoe, Nike has grown geometrically since the days when Phil Knight (CEO) sold shoes out of the trunk of his car.

Brand loyalty is one of the most important concepts to sports marketers, because it refers to a consistent preference or repeat purchase of one brand over all others in a product category. Marketers want their products to satisfy consumers, so decision making becomes a matter of habit rather than an extensive evaluation among competing brands. For example, Proctor & Gamble wants consumers to purchase Tide every time they need detergent, regardless of whether it is on sale or competitive products are being promoted.

SPORTS MARKETING HALL OF FAME

Phil Knight

A former University of Oregon track-and-field athlete and Stanford MBA, Knight is the founder and current CEO of Nike, Inc. By all accounts, Nike and Knight are still changing the face of sports marketing. Knight started his multibillion dollar empire by selling his specialized running shoes out of the trunk of his car.

The ultimate driving force of Nike's success has been Knight's ability to attract top sports stars and build marketing campaigns around them. Nike's first celebrity athlete was the University of Oregon's track star, Steve Prefontaine. When Nike was surpassed by Reebok in the late 1980s, they landed their biggest success story to date—MJ, Michael Jordan. Quickly, Nike regained its position as market leader and has not relinquished it since. Most recently, Knight has added high school phenom LeBron James to the stable of Nike endorsers. He's been named the Most Powerful Man in Sports and Knight considers his job is to "wake up consumers."

Sources: Michael McCarthy, "Wake Up Consumers? Nike's Brash CEO Dares to Do It All," *USA Today,* June 16, 2003, 1B. Keith Elliot Greenberg, Bill Bowerman and Phil Knight: *Building the Nike Empire* (Woodbridge, CT: Blackbird Press, 1994); David R. Collins, Philip H. Knight: *Running with Nike* (Ada, OK: Garrett Educational Corp., 1992).

To establish loyal consumers, Tide must address awareness and brand image. In 1987, brand managers of Tide decided that the awareness, image, and loyalty could be enhanced by establishing the Tide Racing NASCAR sponsorship. Today, Ricky Cravens drives the number 32 Tide car, and the NASCAR sponsorship has proven to be a tremendous success for P&G as loyal Cravens fans continue to be loyal to Tide products.

In sports marketing, teams represent perhaps one of the most interesting examples of loyalty. It is common to hear us speak of people as being "loyal fans" or "fair weather fans." The loyal fans endure all the team's successes and hardships. As the definition implies, they continue to prefer their team over others. Alternatively, the fairweather fan will jump to and from the teams that are successful at the time.

What are the determinants of fan loyalty to a team? Psychologist Robert Passikoff believes the interaction of four factors creates fan loyalty.[17] The first factor is the *entertainment value* of athletics. As we discussed in Chapter 6, entertainment value is one of the underlying factors of fan motivation. In addition, entertainment was discussed as one of the perceived values of sports to the community. The second component of fan loyalty is *authenticity*. Passikoff defines authenticity as the "acceptance of the game as real and meaningful." *Fan bonding* is the third component of fan loyalty. *Bonding* refers to the degree to which fans identify with players and the team. The bonding component is similar to the concept of fan identification discussed in Chapter 6. The fourth and final component of fan loyalty is the *history and tradition* of the team. For example, the Cincinnati Reds are baseball's oldest team and, although they may be lacking in other dimensions of loyalty, they certainly have a long history and tradition with the fans in the greater Cincinnati area.

To measure fan loyalty, self-identified fans are asked to rate their hometown teams on each of the four dimensions. Interestingly, the fan loyalty measure does not specifically include a team performance component. Contrary to popular belief, Passikoff believes winning and loyalty do not always go hand in hand. Table 8.2 provides the 2003 Fan Loyalty Index for best and worst franchises in Major League Baseball.

A study conducted by Passikoff in the summer of 2003 examined the fan loyalty of fans toward all major league sports. Interestingly, Major League Baseball scored the highest in fan loyalty followed by the NFL, NBA, and NHL. In fact, MLB has ranked first each year in the fan loyalty poll since 1999. According to Passikoff, all of the drivers of loyalty can be controlled by marketers with the exception of the entertainment value to the fans based, in part, on wins and losses.[18]

In our society, loyalty to sports teams, at the high school, college, and professional levels, is perhaps higher than it is for any other goods and services we consume. Unfortunately, team loyalty at the professional level is beginning to erode because of the constant threat of uprooting the franchise and moving it to a new town. This is perhaps one reason for the increased popularity of amateur athletics. Colleges will not threaten to move for a better stadium deal, and athletes do not change teams for better contracts (although they do leave their universities early for professional contracts).

TABLE 8.2 Fan Loyalty Index for Major League Baseball: The Best and Worst

The Best:	*The Worst:*
New York Yankees (1)	Anaheim Angels (26)
Houston Astros (2)	Montreal Expos (27)
San Francisco Giants (3)	Baltimore Orioles (28)
Boston Red Sox (4)	Tampa Bay Devil Rays (28)
Philadelphia Phillies (5)	Florida Marlins (30)

Source: Adapted from Brand Keys, Inc.

To increase fan loyalty, many teams are establishing fan loyalty programs, pairing new technology with existing marketing principles. Scott Loft, vice president of ticket sales for the NHL's Nashville Predators, says that his team is using customer relationship management technology to collect detailed information about fan demographics and psychographics. Interestingly, Loft believes this is a shift for sports organizations. Loft estimates that "90 percent of sports teams either don't care or don't bother to find out any information about their fan base."

The loyalty programs are driven by a card that it swiped at kiosks when fans enter a stadium or event. The fans benefit by earning points that can be redeemed for rewards such as free tickets, merchandise, and concessions. The teams benefit by collecting valuable information on their fan base that can later be used to direct strategic marketing decisions. Major League Baseball seems to have taken the lead in fan loyalty efforts, with teams such as the Cardinals, Padres, and A's, all successfully establishing programs.[19]

LICENSING

The importance of having a strong brand is demonstrated when an organization considers product licensing. **Licensing** is a contractual agreement whereby a company may use another company's trademark in exchange for a royalty or fee. A branding strategy through licensing allows the organization to authorize the use of brand, brand name, brand mark, trademark, or trade name in conjunction with a good, service, or promotion in return for royalties. According to Sleight, "Licensing is a booming area of the sports business with players, teams, event names, and logos appearing on a vastly expanding range of products."[20] For example, the NFL has approximately 350 licensees selling over 2,500 products such as apparel, sporting goods, basketball cards and collectibles, home furnishings, school supplies, home electronics, interactive games, home video, publishing, toys, games, gifts, and novelties.

Since the emergence of NFL Properties in 1963, licensing has become one of the most prevalent sports product strategies. From 1990 to 1994, the sale of licensed sports merchandise nearly doubled from $5.3 to $10.35 billion. Although the numbers have yet to reach the previous high water mark of nearly $14 billion in 1996, sales are on the upswing. In 2003, sales of licensed sports merchandise products increased 7 percent over the previous year to reach $12.1 billion.[21] In addition, there has been a 15 percent increase since 2001 based on sales growth in products from the four major professional leagues (NFL, MLB, NBA, and NHL), NASCAR and collegiate licensing. This positive trend is expected to continue over the next few years. The Sporting Goods Manufacturers Association, which monitors these trends, believes that the reasons behind the increased sales include:

- **New business models.** Many licensors have substantially restructured their licensee rosters, eliminating hundreds of former suppliers.
- **Favorable fashion trends.** Team sports looks have come back into style. Hip-hop artists have popularized authentic replica jerseys.
- **Global Sales.** Sales outside the United States represented less than 10 percent of total sales in 1998, but rose to 20 percent in 2003.
- **Television exposure.** In 2003, both the NBA and NFL launched 24-hour cable and satellite networks, which showcase their respective sports. NASCAR's TV coverage was the number one weekend sports property from February through September. Early in 2004, the NHL expanded its collection of retro apparel. And, on the collegiate front, "rivalry merchandise" gained attention in the media.
- **Video games.** Video games bring excitement and authenticity to major league sports. Each year young fans seem willing to purchase the current game to get the latest version with up-to-date team rosters.[22]

TABLE 8.3 2003 Retail Sales of Licensed Sports Products

	(in billions)
NFL	$2.5
College	2.5
MLB	2.3
NASCAR	1.2
NBA	1.0
NHL	.9
Other	.1

Source: Sporting Goods Manufacturers Association.

The 2003 retail sales of licensed sports products for the four major professional sports leagues and college and universities are shown in Table 8.3. This sales figure includes a variety of sports products such as sports memorabilia, novelty items, trading cards, and apparel. While clothing and apparel is estimated to account for nearly 60 percent of sales for all licensed sports products, all sorts of unusual new merchandise is being licensed such as leather pet clothing, Santa Claus figurines, prescription eyewear, and even contact lenses that bear the teams' logo and colors. International sports licensing has even started to sell condoms bearing the logo of the fans favorite soccer team.[23]

Indeed, licensing is everywhere, but just what are the benefits of merchandise licensing? First, let us look at the advantages and disadvantages for the licensee.

ADVANTAGES TO THE LICENSEE
- The licensee benefits from the positive association with the sports entity. In other words, the positive attributes of the player, team, league, or event are transferred to the licensed product or service.
- The licensee benefits from greater levels of brand awareness.
- The licensee benefits by saving the time and money normally required to build high levels of brand equity.
- The licensee may receive initial distribution with retailers and potentially receive expanded and improved shelf space for their products.
- The licensee may be able to charge higher prices for the licensed product or service.

DISADVANTAGES TO THE LICENSEE
- The athlete, team, league, or sport may fall into disfavor. For example, using an athlete such as Allen Iverson is risky given his past behavior, off-the-court as well as on-the-court.
- In addition to the licensee, the licensor also experiences benefits and risks due to the nature of the licensing agreement.

ADVANTAGES TO THE LICENSOR
- The licensor is able to expand into new markets and penetrate existing markets more than ever before.
- The licensor is able to generate heightened awareness of the sports entity and potentially increase its equity if it is paired with the appropriate products and services.

DISADVANTAGES TO THE LICENSOR

- The licensor may lose some control over the elements of the marketing mix. For instance, product quality may be inferior, or price reductions may be offered frequently. This may lessen the perceived image of the licensor.

Based on all these considerations, care must be taken in choosing merchandising–licensing partnerships. Certainly, "the manufacturer of the licensed product should demonstrate an ability to meet and maintain quality control standards, possess financial stability, and offer an aggressive and well-planned marketing and promotional strategy."[24]

In addition to carefully choosing a partner, licensors and licensees must also be on the lookout for counterfeit merchandise. One estimate has it that $1 billion worth of counterfeit sports products hit the streets each year. For instance, the NFL typically confiscates $1 million worth of fake goods during Super Bowl week. The Sydney Olympic games were home to an estimated $17 million in bad goods. In an attempt to stop or reduce counterfeit merchandise, Olympic officials used a new DNA technology. More specifically, an official Olympic product will have a special ink containing the DNA of an athlete. A handheld scanner will determine whether the tag matches the DNA and whether the merchandise is legitimate.[25]

This problem has become so pervasive that the leagues now have their own logo cops who travel from city to city and event to event searching for violations. In addition to this form of enforcement, the Coalition to Advance the Protection of Sports Logos (CAPS . . . see http://www.capsinfo.com/) was formed in 1992 to investigate and control counterfeit products. CAPS has picked up millions worth of counterfeit

Licensed mechandise on the Web.

Source: Copyright © 2004 FansEdge, Inc. All rights reserved.

products and production equipment since 1992. How can consumers guard against fakes? CAPS offers the following suggestions to consumers who are purchasing sports products.[26]

- **Look for Quality.** Poor lettering, colors that are slightly different from the true team colors, and background colors bleeding through the top color overlay are all signs of poor product quality.
- **Verification.** Counterfeiters may try to fake the official logo. Official items will typically have holograms on the product or stickers with moving figures, and embroidered logos should be tightly woven.
- **Check Garment Tags.** Poor-quality merchandise is often designated by split garment tags. Rarely, if ever, will official licensed products use factory rejects or seconds.

QUALITY

Thus far, we have looked at some of the branding issues related to sports products. Another important aspect of the product considered by sports marketers that will influence brand equity is quality. Let us look at two different types of quality: service quality and product quality.

QUALITY OF SERVICES

As sports organizations develop a marketing orientation, the need to deliver a high level of service quality to consumers is becoming increasingly important. For instance, at NFL Properties (NFLP), service quality is taken to the highest levels. NFLP is highly committed to understanding the individualized needs of each of its sponsors. Every sponsor of the NFL receives the name of a primary contact at NFLP who they can call at any time to discuss their marketing needs. They also recognize that each sponsor is in need of a unique sponsorship program, given their vastly different objectives and levels of financial commitment to the NFL.[27]

Although NFLP is an excellent example of an organization that values service quality, we have yet to define the concept. **Service quality** is a difficult concept to define, and as such, many definitions of service quality exist. Rather than define it, most researchers have resorted to explaining the dimensions or determinants of service quality. Unfortunately, there is also little agreement on what dimensions actually comprise service quality or how best to measure it.

Lehtinen and Lehtinen say service quality consists of physical, interactive, and corporate dimensions.[28] The physical quality component looks at the tangible aspect of the service. More specifically, physical quality refers to the appearance of the personnel or the physical facilities where the service is actually performed. For example, the physical appearance of the ushers at the game may affect the consumer's perceived level of service quality.

Interactive quality refers to the two-way flow of information that disseminates from both the service provider and the service recipient at the time of the service encounter. The importance of the two-way flow of information is why many researchers choose to examine service quality from a dyadic perspective. This suggests gathering the perceptions of service quality from stadium employees, as well as fans.

The image attributed to the service provider by its current and potential users is referred to as corporate quality. As just discussed, product performance and quality is one of the drivers of brand image. Moreover, Lehtinen and Lehtinen also cited customer service as one of the image drivers. This suggests a strong relationship between corporate quality, or image of the team, and consumers' perceptions of service quality.

Groonos describes service quality dimensions in a different manner.[29] He believes service quality has both a technical and functional component. Technical quality is described as "what is delivered." Functional quality refers to "how the service is delivered." For instance, "what is delivered" might include the final outcome of the game, the hot dogs that were consumed, or the merchandise that was purchased. "How the service is delivered" might represent the effort put forth by the team and its players, the friendliness of the hot dog vendor, or the quick service provided by the merchandise vendor. This is especially important in sports marketing, as "the total game experience" is evaluated using both the "what" and "how" components of quality.

The most widely adopted description of service quality is based on a series of studies by Parasuraman, Zeithaml, and Berry.[30] They isolated five distinct dimensions of service quality. These **dimensions of service quality** comprise some of its fundamental areas and consist of reliability, assurance, empathy, responsiveness, and tangibles. Because of their importance in service quality literature, a brief description of each follows.

Reliability refers to the ability to perform promised service dependably and accurately. **Assurance** is the knowledge and courtesy of employees and their ability to convey trust and confidence. **Empathy** is defined as the caring, individualized attention the firm provides its customers. **Responsiveness** refers to the willingness to help customers and provide prompt service. **Tangibles** are the physical facilities, equipment, and appearance of the service personnel.

To assess consumers' perceptions of service quality across each dimension, a 22-item survey instrument was developed by Parasuraman, Zeithaml, and Berry. The instrument, known as SERVQUAL, requires that the 22 items be administered twice. First, the respondents are asked to rate their expectations of service quality. Next, the respondents are asked to rate perceptions of service quality within the organization. For example, "Your dealings with XYZ are very pleasant" is a perception (performance) item, whereas the corresponding expectation item would be "Customers dealing with these firms should be very pleasant."

From a manager's perspective, measuring expectations and perceptions of performace allows action plans to be developed to improve service quality. Organizational resources should be allocated to improving those service quality areas where consumer expectations are high and perceptions of quality are low.

The original SERVQUAL instrument has been tested across a wide variety of industries, including banking, telecommunications, health care, consulting, education, and retailing. Most important, McDonald, Sutton, and Milne adapted SERVQUAL and used it to evaluate spectators' perceptions of service quality for an NBA team. The researchers fittingly called their adapted SERVQUAL instrument **TEAMQUAL.**[31]

In addition to finding that the NBA team exceeded service quality expectations on all five dimensions, the researchers looked at the relative importance of each dimension of service quality. More specifically, fans were asked to allocate 100 points among the five dimensions based on how important each factor is when evaluating the quality of service of a professional team sport franchise. As the results show in Table 8.4, tangibles and reliability are considered the most important dimensions of service quality. Tangibles, as you will recall from Chapter 6, form the foundation of the sportscape, or stadium environment. This study provides additional evidence that the tangible factors, such as the seating comfort, stadium aesthetics, and scoreboard quality, play an important role in satisfying fans. Understanding fans' perceptions of TEAMQUAL is critical for sports marketers in establishing long-term relationships with existing fans and trying to attract new fans. As McDonald, Sutton, and Milne point out, "Consumers who are dissatisfied and feel that they are not receiving quality service will not renew their relationship with the professional sport franchise."

TABLE 8.4 Importance Weights Allocated to the Five TEAMQUAL Dimensions

Dimensions	*Allocation*
Reliability—ability to perform promised services dependably and accurately	23%
Assurance—knowledge and courtesy of employees and their ability to convey trust and confidence	16
Empathy—the caring, individualized attention provided by the professional sports franchise for its customers	18
Responsiveness—willingness to help customers and provide prompt service	19
Tangibles—appearance of equipment, personnel, materials, and venue	24

Source: Mark A. McDonald, William A. Sutton, and George R. Milne, "TEAMQUAL: Measuring Service Quality in Professional Team Sports," *Sport Marketing Quarterly*, vol. 4, no. 2 (1995), 9–15. Reprinted with permission of Fitness Information Technology, Inc., Publishers.

QUALITY OF GOODS

The quality of sporting goods that are manufactured and marketed have two distinct dimensions. The first **quality dimension of goods** is based on how well the product conforms to specifications that were designed in the manufacturing process. From this standpoint, the quality of goods is driven by the organization and its management and employees. The other dimension of quality is measured subjectively from the perspective of consumers or end users of the goods. In other words, does the product perform its desired function? The degree to which the goods meet and exceed consumers' needs is a function of the organization's marketing orientation.

From the sports marketing perspective, the consumer's perception of **product quality** is of primary importance. Garvin found eight separate quality dimensions, which include performance, features, reliability, conformance, durability, serviceability, aesthetics, and perceived quality (see Table 8.5).

Whether it is enhancing goods or service quality, most sports organizations are attempting to increase the quality of their product offerings. In doing so, they can better compete with other entertainment choices, more easily increase the prices of their products, influence the consumer's loyalty, and reach new market segments willing to pay more for a higher quality product.

Some sports franchises have been criticized for attempting to increase the quality of their overall products, while driving up the price of tickets. Unfortunately, it is becoming more costly for the "average fan" to purchase tickets to any professional sporting event. In this way, sports marketers have targeted a new segment (corporations) and overlooked the traditional segments.

Other criticisms have been directed at the NCAA and professional sports for making it too easy for athletes to leave school and turn professional. For example, there were 40 college and high school players who declared for early entry into the 2003 NBA draft. This exodus of stars may have detrimental effects on "product quality" at the high school and college levels. It will be interesting to follow the case of Ohio State running back Maurice Clarett who recently won a court case allowing him to entry the NFL despite being less than two years out of high school.[32] It is yet to be seen, how many college, or even high school players, will follow Clarett's lead.

From a marketing standpoint, the fans are also suffering and may experience dissatisfaction. Teams no longer stay together long enough to get and capture the imagination of fans. Atlantic 10 commissioner Linda Bruno, stated, "It seems as soon as college basketball hooks on to a star, he's suddenly a part of the NBA. Athletes leaving early have definitely hurt the college game." Rick Pitino, whose opinion is widely respected,

TABLE 8.5 Quality Dimensions of Goods

Quality Dimensions of Goods	*Description*
Performance	How well does the good perform its core function? (Does the tennis racquet feel good when striking the ball?)
Features	Does the good offer additional benefits? (Are the golf clubheads constructed with titanium?)
Conformity to specifications	What is the incidence of defects? (Does the baseball have the proper number of stitches or is their some variation?)
Reliability	Does the product perform with consistency? (Do the gauges of the exercise bike work properly every time?)
Durability	What is the life of the product? (How long will the golf clubs last?)
Serviceability	Is the service system efficient, competent, and convenient? (If you experience problems with the grips or loft of the club, can the manufacturer quickly address your needs?)
Aesthetic design	Does the product's design look and feel like a high-quality product? (Does the look and feel of the running shoe inspire you to greater performance?)

Source: Adapted from D. A. Garvin, "Competing on the Eight Dimensions of Quality." *Harvard Business Review* (November–December 1987), 101–109. Copyright © 1987 by the President and Fellows of Harvard College; all rights reserved. Reprinted by permission of Harvard Business School Press.

adds, "Quite frankly, I think college basketball is in serious trouble." Interestingly, the early departures that are making the college game less appealing are doing nothing to strengthen the quality of the NBA. The NBA is saturated with players whose games never had a chance to grow or, as Stanford coach Mike Montgomery put it, "will have to be nurtured through [their] immaturity."[33]

A final product feature related to perceptions of product quality is product warranties. **Product warranties** are important to consumers when purchasing expensive sporting goods as they act to reduce the perceived risk and dissonance associated with cognitive dissonance. Traditional warranties are statements indicating the liability of the manufacturer for problems with the product. Interestingly, warranties are also being developed by sports organizations. The New Jersey Nets offered their season ticketholders a money-back guarantee if they were dissatisfied with the Net's performance. With the price of tickets skyrocketing for professional sporting events, perhaps these service guarantees will be the wave of the future.

PRODUCT DESIGN

Product design is one competitive advantage that is of special interest to sports marketers. It is heavily linked to product quality and the technological environment discussed in Chapter 3. In some cases, product design may even have an impact on the sporting event. For example, the latest technology in golf clubs does allow the average player to improve his or her performance on the course. The same could be said for the new generation of big sweet spot, extra long tennis racquet. In another example, the official baseball used in

Ping capturing the latest in product design and technology.

Source: Used by permission of Karsten Manufacturing Corporation.

the major league games was believed to be "juiced up." In other words, the ball was livelier because of the product design. As a result of this "juiced up" ball, home run production increased, much to the delight of the fans. From a sports marketing perspective, anything that adds excitement and conjecture to a game with public relation problems is welcomed. In the end, what matters is not whether the ball is livelier, but that the game is.

Baseballs are not the only products that are having an impact on the outcome of sporting events. But equipment changes aren't the only way to think about product design or redesign. The NHL has recently adopted rules changes to enhance the offensive output of games and ultimately make a more exciting product for the fans. The proposed rules changes, which will be implemented in the 2005 season include: (1) dropping the limit on goalie leg pads from 12 inches to 10 inches; (2) goalies will be prohibited from playing the puck behind their goal line; (3) tag-up offsides, which allows players to send the puck into the offensive zone while players are in the zone, as long as the players touch the blue line; (4) moving the goal line back from 13 feet to 10 feet away from the end boards; (5) increasing the size of the lines to 24 inches allowing for bigger zones; and (6) eliminating ties with shootouts after overtime.[34] All of these changes are redesigning the core product of "the hockey game."

Product design is important to sport marketers because it ultimately affects consumers' perceptions of product quality. Moreover, organizations need to monitor the technological environment to keep up with the latest trends that may affect product design. Let us look at this relationship in Figure 8.5.

As you would imagine, the technological environment has a tremendous impact on product design decisions. In almost every sporting good category (e.g., exercise

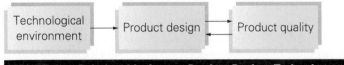

FIGURE 8.5 Relationship Among Product Design, Technology, and Product Quality

equipment, golfing equipment, and hunting equipment), sports marketers communicate how their brands are technologically superior to the competition.

The golf equipment industry thrives on the latest technological advances in ball and club design. Bicycle manufacturers stress the technological edge that comes with the latest and greatest construction materials. Tennis racquets are continually moving into the next generation of frame design and racquet length. NordicTrac exercise equipment positions itself as technologically superior to other competing brands. Nike is continually developing new lines of high-tech sports gear in its state-of-the-art Sports Research Lab. Most recently, Nike has introduced the Nike Pro Compression top and Sphere Pro undergarments that are praised for moisture control, durability, and comfort.[35] All these examples illustrate the power of technology on product design.

The product design of sporting goods, in turn, influences consumer perceptions of product quality. By definition, **product design** includes the aesthetics, style, and function of the product. Two of the eight dimensions of the quality of goods are incorporated in this definition, providing one measure of the interdependency of these two concepts.

The way a good performs, the way it feels, and the beauty of the good are all important aspects of product design. Again, think of the numerous sporting goods that are purchased largely on the basis of these benefits. Consumers purchase golf clubs because of the way they look and feel. Tennis shoes are chosen because of the special functions they perform (cross-trainers, hiking, and basketball) and the way they look (colors and style).

Color has historically been an important factor in the design of almost all licensed merchandise. Recent trends show that in hats, jerseys, and jackets, anything black is "gold." The Oakland Raiders silver and black are always near the top in NFL merchandise sales regardless of the team's record on the field. The Toronto Blue Jays have even adopted a new logo that incorporates black and moves away from the reds and blues of the past. Although fans associate certain colors with their favorite teams (e.g., Dodger Blue or the Cincinnati Reds), MLB has started to experiment with licensed products that deviate from the traditional colors. Baby blues, electric oranges, and lime greens are replacing the traditional team colors and fans seem to be responding. For example, Cleveland (red and navy uniform colors) fans are purchasing jerseys in bright orange, the color of their arch-rival Baltimore Orioles.[36] Examples like these illustrate that color alone may be a motivating factor in the purchase of many sports products. Sports marketers, therefore, must consider color to be critical in product design.

Figure 8.5 also shows that product quality may influence product design to some extent. Sports organizations are continually seeking to improve the levels of product quality. In fact, having high-quality goods and services may be the primary objective of many firms. As such, products will be designed in the highest quality manner with little concern about the costs that will be ultimately passed on to the consumers. Some major league sports organizations (e.g., New York Yankees and Detroit Red Wings) will design their teams to achieve the highest quality levels without cost consideration.

As new technologies continue to emerge, product design will become increasingly important. Organizations with a marketing orientation will incorporate consumer preferences to ensure their needs are being met with respect to product design for new and existing products. What will the future bring with respect to product design, technology, and the need to satisfy consumers? One hint comes to us via the athletic shoe industry. With advances in technology, customized shoes are now being produced for professional athletes. Gone are the days when recreational athletes could wear the same shoes as their professional counterparts. Today's professional athletes are demanding custom fit, high-tech shoes, and weekend athletes will soon require the same. Companies such as Nike are now customizing certain features of their shoes to the mass market under the Nike ID (individualized design) name.

Another perspective on the future of product design is that the design of products will stem from demand and changes in the marketing environment. One such change is the emergence of a viable market for women's sports products. For instance, ski and snowboard companies are now turning their attention to women's products based on a growing number of women hitting the slopes (some 39 percent of all skiers and snowboarders in 2002). Historically, the only difference in men's and women's ski products was the color, but today there are product design changes that truly address women's needs. Skis for women are softer and lighter. Boots are more cushioned and designed to fit the foot and calf muscles of the female skier. All of these product changes try to capitalize on the marketing environment and satisfy the needs of a growing target market.[37]

Summary

Sport products are defined as goods, services, or any combination of the two that are designed to provide benefits to a sports spectator, participant, or sponsor. Within the field of sports marketing, products are sometimes thought of as bundles of benefits desired by consumers. As discussed in Chapter 1, sports products might include sporting events and their participants, sporting goods, and sports information. The definition of sports products also makes an important distinction between goods and services.

Goods are defined as tangible, physical products that offer benefits to consumers. Conversely, services are intangible, nonphysical products. Most sports products possess the characteristics of both goods and services. For example, a sporting event sells goods (e.g., concessions) and services (e.g., the competition itself). The classification of a sports product as either a good or a service is dependent on four product dimensions: tangibility, standardization and consistency, perishability, and separability. Tangibility refers to the ability to see, feel, and touch the product. In other words, tangibility is the physical dimension of the sports product. Standardization refers to the consistency of the product or the ability of the producer to manufacture a product with little variation over time. One of the unique and complex issues for sports marketers is dealing with the inconsistency of the sports product (i.e., the inability to control the performance of the team or athlete). Perishability is the ability to store or inventory product. Pure services are totally perishable (i.e., you cannot sell a seat after the game has been played), whereas goods are not perishable and can be stored or ware-

housed. Separability, the final product dimension, refers to the ability to separate the good from the person providing the service. In the case of an athletic event, there is little separation between the provider and the consumer. That is, the event is being produced and consumed simultaneously.

Along with classifying sports products by the four product dimensions, sports products are also categorized based on groupings within the sports organization. Product lines are groups of products that are closely related because they satisfy a class of needs. These products are used together, sold to the same customer groups, distributed through the same types of outlets, or fall within a given price range. The total assortment of product lines is called the product mix. The mix represents all the firm's products. Strategic decisions within the sports organization consider both the product lines and the entire product mix. For instance, an organization may want to add product lines, eliminate product lines, or develop new product lines that are unrelated to existing lines.

Products can also be described on the basis of three interrelated dimensions or characteristics: branding, quality, and design. Branding refers to the product's name, design, symbol, or any combination used by an organization to differentiate products from the competition. Brand names, or elements of the brand that can be spoken, are important considerations for sports products. When choosing a brand name, sports marketers should consider the following: the name should be positive and generate positive feelings, be translatable into an exciting logo, imply the benefits that the sports product delivers, be consistent with the image of the sports product, and be legally and ethically permissible.

The broad purpose of branding is to differentiate your product from the competition. Ultimately, the consumer will (hopefully) establish a pattern of repeat purchases for your brand (i.e., be loyal to your sports product). Before this can happen, sports marketers must guide consumers through a series of steps known as the branding process. The branding process begins by building brand awareness, in which consumers recognize and remember the brand name. Next, the brand image, or the consumers' set of beliefs about a brand, must be established. After the proper brand image is developed, the objective of the branding process is to develop brand equity. Brand equity is the value that the brand contributes to a product in the marketplace. Finally, once the brand exhibits high levels of equity, consumers are prone to become brand loyal, or purchase only your brand. Certainly, sports marketers are interested in establishing high levels of awareness, enhancing brand image, building equity, and developing loyal fans or customers.

One of the important sports product strategies that is contingent upon building a strong brand is licensing. Licensing is defined as a contractual agreement whereby a company may use another company's trademark in exchange for a royalty or fee. The licensing of sports products is experiencing tremendous growth around the world with the latest estimate (2003) reporting over $12 billion in the sale of licensed sports products. Advantages to the licensee (the organization purchasing the license or use of the name or trademark) include positive association with the sports entity, enhancing brand awareness, building brand equity, improving distribution and retail relationships, and having the ability to charge higher prices. Disadvantages to the licensee are the possibility of the sports entity experiencing problems (e.g., athlete arrested or team performing poorly or moving). However, the licensor (the sports entity granting the permission) benefits by expanding into new markets, which creates heightened awareness. However, the licensor may not have tight controls on the quality of the products being licensed under the name.

Quality is another of the important brand characteristics. The two different types of quality that affect brand image, brand equity, and, ultimately, loyalty, are the quality of services and the quality of goods. The quality of services, or service quality, is generally described on the basis of its dimensions. Parasuraman, Berry, and Zeithaml describe service quality as having five distinct dimensions: reliability, assurance, empathy, responsiveness, and tangibles. Reliability refers to the ability to perform a promised service dependably and accurately. Assurance is the knowledge and courtesy of employees and their ability to convey trust and confidence. Empathy is defined as the caring, individualized attention the firm provides its customers. Responsiveness refers to the willingness to help customers and provide prompt service. Tangibles are the physical facilities, equipment, and appearance of the service personnel. Using this framework, sports researchers have designed an instrument called TEAMQUAL to assess the service quality within sporting events.

The quality of goods is based on whether the good conforms to specifications determined during the manufacturing process and the degree to which the good meets or exceeds the consumer's needs. Garvin has conceptualized the quality of goods from the consumer's perspective. He found seven separate dimensions of goods quality, including performance, features, conformity to specifications, reliability, durability, serviceability, and aesthetic design.

Product design is the final characteristic of the "total product." Product design is defined as the aesthetics, style, and function of the product. It is important to sports marketers in that it ultimately affects consumers' perceptions of product quality. For a sporting event, the product design might be thought of as the composition of the team. For sporting goods, product design has largely focused on the development of technologically superior products. In fact, the technological environment is believed to directly influence product design. Product design, in turn, enjoys a reciprocal relationship with product quality. In other words, product design affects perceptions of product quality and may influence product design.

Key Terms

- assurance
- brand awareness
- brand equity
- brand image
- brand loyalty
- brand mark
- brand name
- branding
- branding process
- dimensions of service quality
- empathy
- goods

- idle product capacity
- licensing
- logo
- logotype
- perishability
- product design
- product characteristics
- product line
- product mix
- product quality
- product warranties
- quality dimensions of goods

- reliability
- responsiveness
- separability
- service quality
- services
- sports product
- standardization
- tangibility
- tangibles
- TEAMQUAL
- trademark

Review Questions

1. Define sports products. Why are sports products sometimes called "bundles of benefits?"
2. Contrast pure goods with pure services, using each of the dimensions of products.
3. Describe the nature of product mix, product lines, and product items. Illustrate these concepts for the following: Converse, Baltimore Orioles, and your local country club.
4. What are the characteristics of the "total product?"
5. Describe branding. What are the guidelines for developing an effective brand name? Why is brand loyalty such an important concept for sports marketers to understand?
6. Define licensing. What are the advantages and disadvantages to the licensee and licensor?
7. Describe service quality and discuss the five dimensions of service quality. Which dimension is most important to you as a spectator of a sporting event? Does this vary by the type of sporting event?
8. Describe product quality and discuss the seven dimensions of product quality. Which dimension is most important to you as a consumer of sporting goods? Does this vary by the type of sporting good?
9. How are product design, product quality, and technology interrelated?

Exercises

1. Think of some sports products to which consumers demonstrate high degrees of brand loyalty. What are these products, and why do you think loyalty is so high? Give your suggestions for measuring brand loyalty.
2. Interview the individual(s) responsible for licensing and licensing decisions on your campus. Ask them to describe the licensing process and what they believe the advantages are to your school.
3. Construct a survey to measure consumers' perceptions of service quality at a sporting event on campus. Administer the survey to 10 people and summarize the findings. What recommendations might you make to the sports marketing department based on your findings?
4. Go to a sporting goods store and locate three sports products that you believe exhibit high levels of product quality. What are the commonalities among these three products? How do these products rate on the dimensions of product quality described in the chapter?

Internet Exercises

1. Search the Internet for a sports product that stresses product design issues on its Web site. Then locate the Web site of a competitor's sports product. How are these two products positioned relative to each other on their Web sites?
2. Search the Internet for three team nicknames (either college or professional) of which you were previously unaware. Do these team names seem to follow the suggested guidelines for effective brand names?

Endnotes

1. "Sports: Walk, Don't Schuss." www.businessweek.com/1997/49/b3556153.htm.
2. Shaquille O'Neal, http://cbs.sportsline.com/u/fans/celebrity/shaq; "Athletic Shoes by Shaquille O'Neal Now Available Only at Payless ShoeSource, PR Newswire, *Financial News* (January 14, 2004).
3. Christopher Lovelock, *Services Marketing* (Englewood Cliffs, NJ: Prentice Hall, 1984).
4. Boaz Herzog, "Rising with a Swoosh," *The Sunday Oregonian* (September 21, 2003), D1.
5. Boaz Herzog, "Nike Leaves Critics in the Dust," *Times Picayune* (September 28, 2003), 1.
6. Tom Osborn, "MLS, Potential Backers Meet," *San Antonio Express-News* (January 23, 2004).
7. See, for example, Courtland Bovee and John Thill, *Marketing* (New York: McGraw-Hill, 1992), 252.
8. Marcus Nelson, "Want a New Look? There's a Price," *The Palm Beach Post* (October 24, 2003).
9. *The Columbus Crew*, www.thecrew.com.
10. "Schools to Rule on American Indian Logos," *Associated Press Online* (August 13, 2003).
11. Marcus Nelson, "Want a New Look? There's a Price," *The Palm Beach Post* (October 24, 2003).

12. J. Gladden, G. Milne, and W. Sutton. "A Conceptual Framework for Assessing Brand Equity in Division I College Athletics." *Journal of Sports Management*, vol. 12, no. 1 (1998), 1–19.

13. G. Milne and M. McDonald, *Sports Marketing: Managing the Exchange Process* (Sudbury, MA: Jones and Bartlett Publishers, 1999).

14. Ray Melick, "Realignment Game Turns Ugly," *Scripps Howard News Service* (January 15, 2004).

15. Louis E. Boone, C. M. Kochunny, and Dianne Wilkins, "Applying the Brand Equity Concept to Major League Baseball," *Sport Marketing Quarterly*, vol. 4, no. 3 (1995), 33–42.

16. Ibid.

17. John Lombardo, "MLB makes it 5 Firsts in a Row in Brand Keys Fan Loyalty Survey," *Street and Smith's Sports Business Journal*, Vol. 8, No. 10, (August 25–31, 2003), 28.

18. "Major League Baseball Finishes First in Customer Loyalty Survey," *Business Wire* (July 11, 2000).

19. Sarah Lorge, "The Fan Plan," *Sales and Marketing Management,* vol. 151, no. 5 (May 1999), 11–13; Charles Waltner, "CRM: The New Game in Town for Professional Sports," *Information Week* (August 28, 2000).

20. S. Sleight, *Sponsorship: What Is It and How to Use It?* (London: McGraw-Hill, 1989).

21. "Sales of Sports Licensed Products Surge in 2003; Momentum Expected to Continue in 2004," Sports Licensing White Paper 2004, http://www.sgma.com/reports/2004/.

22. Ibid.

23. Eric Fischer, "License to go out of Bounds; Sports Leagues put their Names on a Variety of Off-the Wall Products," *The Washington Times* (November 23, 2001), A1.

24. Eddie Baghdikian, "Building the Sports Organization's Merchandise Licensing Program: The Appropriateness, Significance, and Considerations," *Sport Marketing Quarterly*, vol. 5, no. 1 (1996), 35–41.

25. Elliot Harris, "Spitting Image: Ink with DNA Could Put Counterfeiters on Spot at Olympics," *Chicago Sun Times* (June 8, 2000), 133.

26. Robert Thurow, "Busting Bogus Merchandise Peddlers with Logo Cops," *The Wall Street Journal* (October 24, 1997), B1, B14.

27. Rick Burton, "A Case Study on Sports Property Servicing Excellence: National Football League Properties," *Sport Marketing Quarterly*, vol. 5, no. 3 (1996), 23.

28. J. R. Lehtinen and U. Lehtinen, *Service Quality: A Study of Quality Dimensions* (Helsinki: Service Management Institute, 1982).

29. Christian Groonos, "A Service Quality Model and Its Marketing Implications," *European Journal of Marketing*, vol. 18 (1982), 36–44.

30. A. Parasuraman, Valarie Zeithaml, and Len Berry, "A Conceptual Model of Service Quality and Its Implications for Future Research," *Journal of Marketing*, vol. 49 (1985), 41–50.

31. Mark A. McDonald, William A, Sutton, and George R. Milne, "TEAMQUAL: Measuring Service Quality in Professional Team Sports," *Sport Marketing Quarterly*, vol. 4, no. 2 (1995), 9–15.

32. Sam Farmer, "Clarett Wins Another Decision Against NFL," *Los Angeles Times* (Feb 12, 2004), D.7.

33. Jack McCallum, "Going, Going, Gone," *Sports Illustrated*, vol. 84, no. 20 (May 20, 1996), 52.

34. Derrick Goold, "No Offense, But . . . Not All of the Proposed Rules Changes Deserve to be Supported," *St. Louis Post Dispatch* (February 15, 2004), D8.

35. Dave Stubbs, "Just Doing It High Tech:" *The Gazette* (September 25, 2003), C1.

36. Wendy Bounds and Stefan Fatsis, "Right Here! Get Yer Baseball Cap! Lime Green, Lavender, Baby Blue!" *The Wall Street Journal* (October 13, 1997).

37. Ski Industry Focusing on Women, sportsbusinessnews.com (January 30, 2004).

CHAPTER 9

MANAGING SPORTS PRODUCTS

After completing this chapter, you should be able to:

- Describe the characteristics of new products from an organizational and consumer perspective.
- Explain the various stages of the new product development process.
- Discuss the phases of the product life cycle and explain how the product life cycle influences marketing strategy.
- Determine the factors that will lead to new product success.
- Discuss the diffusion of innovations and the various types of adopters.

The article on SlamBall provides an interesting illustration of a new sports product that may be on the verge of taking off in the North American market. The popularity of Xtreme sports and basketball suggest the time could be right for this new product. There is obviously nothing new about basketball, jumping on a trampoline, and contact sports, but when combined they create an exciting new sport. The founders of SlamBall will have to keep this in mind when developing a marketing strategy for this emerging sports product.

NEW SPORTS PRODUCTS

Although it might seem new products are easy to describe and think about, "new" is a relative term. Think about purchasing season tickets to your favorite college basketball team for the first time. You might consider this a new product even though the tickets have been available for many years. However, consider our SlamBall example. This sports product is new to all consumers and to Spike TV, which is responsible for televising the action.

Regardless of how you define "new products," they are critical to the health of any sports organization for two reasons. First, new products are necessary to keep up with changing consumer trends, lifestyles, and tastes. Second, as unsuccessful sports products are dropped from the product mix, new products must be introduced continually to maintain business and long-term growth.

One of the key considerations for any sports organization is to continually improve the products it offers to consumers. New products seek to satisfy the needs of

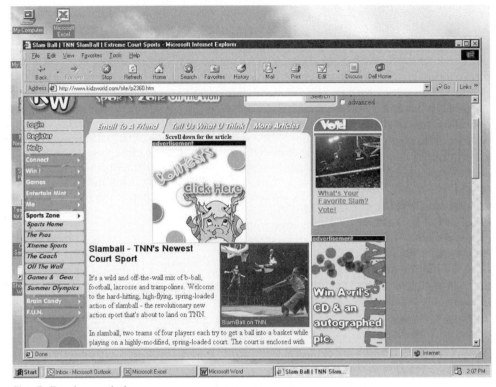

SlamBall makes a splash.

Source: Used by permission Kidzworld.com.

SlamBall: Introducing a New Sports Product

Full-contact hoops; as the crowd roars its approval, two bodies collide in mid-air, then crash violently to the floor. No harm, No Foul, no worries. This is *SlamBall.*

SlamBall is a unique combination of gymnastics, basketball, hockey, and mayhem. Trampolines add to the height, the loose interpretations of the few rules the sport has adds to the excitement.

"I know the rules aren't really set in stone," said former co-owner of the Philadelphia 76ers and currently a co-owner of the SlamBall product, Pat Croce, over a roaring crowd at UniversalCityWalk. "But as we grow, the play will get better and the rules will be better defined.

"Really, the only thing illegal in SlamBall is hitting a guy from behind. Outside of that, it's almost anything goes and as you can tell, people love it."

Players can stuff each other against a plastic wall, similar to hockey, without being called for a foul. In fact, SlamBall encourages contact. It's the mantra of the sport, hit or be hit.

"It's a very physical game," said the creator of SlamBall Mason Gordon. Gordon, 28, is not only the creator of SlamBall, but also participates. He plays for the Diablos, one of eight teams in the league. "Keeping the games to only 24 minutes, we can usually keep the players fresh and the action fast. I know people watch it on TV and, like in the old Batman TV show, they expect to see a huge graphic 'POW' flash across the screen. It's even more impressive live."

The X-man—no not Wolverine, former NBA star Xavier McDaniel is also involved in SlamBall. "It's like playing flying hockey," said McDaniel. The former NBA player has joined up as a coach for the Rapids. "My NBA experience (12 years) has helped me as a coach, but it's (SlamBall) nothing like the NBA. You plan games differently because you can actually hit guys to keep them away from the ball."

"For people who think that SlamBall is nothing more than a made-for-TV show, they should come see it live," said executive in charge of production for Spike TV, Scott Fishman.

Source: John Gonzales, *Press Enterprise* (Riverside, CA), May 15, 2003.

SPORTS MARKETING HALL OF FAME

Bill Rasmussen

Bill Rasmussen is hardly a household name, but all you have to do is mention four letters—ESPN—and his place in sports marketing history is secured. ESPN's founder developed the 24-hour sports programming channel in the fall of 1979. At that time, Rasmussen was simply looking for a way to broadcast the University of Connecticut basketball games when he happened upon satellite technology.

Today, ESPN reaches more than 87 million homes and covers 81.5 percent of all TV homes with its 4,900

hours of sports programming. A second channel, ESPN2, also reaches 85 million viewers and is growing rapidly. Product lines continue to expand with ESPN Classic, ESPNews, ESPN+Plus, ESPN radio, ESPN magazine, and others. All these networks and new products can thank Bill Rasmussen's desire to bring U Conn basketball to the people of Connecticut.

Source: Richard Hoffer, "Bill Rasmussen," *Sports Illustrated* (September 19, 1994), 121.

a new market, enhance the quality of an existing product, or extend the number of product choices for current consumers. Before discussing the process for developing new products, let us look at the different types of **new sports products.**

TYPES OF NEW PRODUCTS

As noted previously, there is no universally accepted definition of new products. Instead, new products are sometimes described from the viewpoint of the sports organization versus the consumer's perspective. The organization's definition of a new product is based on whether it has ever produced or marketed this particular product in the past. This can be important for organizations trying to understand how the new sports product "fits" with their existing products.

However, newness from the consumer's perspective is described as any innovation the consumer perceives as meaningful. In other words, the new product could be a minor alteration of an existing product or a product that has never been sold or marketed by any organization. Looking at new products from the consumer's viewpoint helps sports organizations understand the most effective way to market the product. Let us examine the types of new products from the organizational and consumer perspectives in greater detail.

NEWNESS FROM THE ORGANIZATION'S PERSPECTIVE

New-to-the-World Products   Brand new sports innovations, such as the first in-line skates, the first sailboard, or the advent of arena football, all represent new-to-the-world products. These products are new to the organization selling the product as well as to the consumers purchasing or using the product.[1]

Another interesting, **new-to-the-world sports product** is the wireless ballpark. Raley Field, home of the AAA Sacramento River Cats baseball team has become one of professional sports' most technologically advanced venues. Recently, the River Cats implemented wireless Internet access to customers in suites and the exclusive "Solon Club." By next season, the plan is to have the stadium wired for all fans. Each fan will be able to operate laptop computers, PDAs, and other wireless devices from their seats for access to up-to-the-minute stats and replays. Additionally, fans will be able to order food or tickets for future games right from their seat.[2]

New Product Category Entries Sports products that are new to the organization, but not to the world, are referred to as **new product category entries.** For example, New Balance, known only for its footwear, acquired Warrior Lacrosse, a leading manufacturer of lacrosse equipment. "Lacrosse is one of the country's fastest growing sports with young athletes that fit New Balance's high-performance, technical consumer demographic," says Jim Davis, New Balance Chairman and CEO.[3] In another example, The Hockey Company Holdings Inc., known for its CCM, JOFA, and KOHO brands acquired Roger Edwards Sport, a leading vintage sports apparel brand. The company has successfully launched lifestyle fashion lines of Vintage NHL, Hockey Night In Canada, and Team Canada Classics apparel.[4] These products are not new to the fans, but they are new acquisitions for the organizations.

Product Line Extensions Product line extensions refer to new products being added to an existing product line. For instance, the addition of expansion teams in Major League Baseball, or Daiwa's new Millionaire CV-Z casting reels, precision engineered for ultimate casting are product line extensions. The Arena Football League 2 is also a product line extension of the original Arena Football League. The league is currently fielding 25 teams and filling arenas to 70 percent capacity. Finally, another product line extension example comes from Nike Golf, which will introduce its first complete lineup of equipment designed for women.

Product Improvements Current products that have been modified and improved, such as the new shoe addition to the Jordan Brand called the Jordan XVIII (retailing at $180) are called product improvements. Another example of a product improvement is the Wilson Hyper Hammer 6.2 tennis racquet. This improved version of the ever popular (original) Hammer 6.2 includes the addition of HyperCarbon, new Step Frame

Huffy is extending their pool sports product line.
Source: Copyright © 2004 Huffy® Sports. All rights reserved.

SPOTLIGHT ON SPORTS MARKETING ETHICS

Technology Makes Golf a Brand New Ball Game

Hootie Johnson walked out to Amen Corner during the 2001 Masters in time to see Phil Mickelson play his second shot into the 455-yard 11th hole, one of the toughest at Augusta National. Mickelson had 94 yards to the green—a flip wedge. That was all Johnson needed to realize it was right to lengthen the golf course by 300 yards, the biggest overhaul in club history.

Two years later, some players question whether Augusta went far enough. "I told Hootie, 'You guys were ahead of the curve when you did this golf course last year,'" six-time Masters winner Jack Nicklaus said. "Now, they're behind the curve." The Masters isn't alone.

Torrey Pines revamped its South Course to measure 7,600 yards for the 2008 U.S. Open. Last year's U.S. Open at Bethpage Black had the two longest par 4s in its history—No. 12 (499 yards) and No. 10 (492 yards).

Why go to such lengths? To protect against the most rapid advances ever in golf technology.

It has reached a point where golf's top executives are debating whether to introduce separate equipment standards for elite and recreational players. "I really would not like to see that, but it may be inevitable," Arnold Palmer said.

Whether that would change anything is unclear. But it's not as simple as blaming the golf ball and oversized titanium drivers. Look inside the fitness trailer on tour, or in weight rooms at Kapalua and La Costa, and it's obvious that golf is starting to resemble a real sport. Players are bigger, stronger, more cut. They lift, they run, they watch what they eat. Some are trained by renowned teachers before they graduate from elementary school. By the time they mature, players can generate enormous power by swinging the club at speeds approaching 120 mph upon impact. "I've got a 9-year-old and he plays with all the kids at home, and they're all teeing it as high as a tee will allow and swinging as hard as they can," Davis Love III said. "There was only one person doing that on the range when I was growing up, and that was me."

Equipment companies are responding with drivers made of space-age metals that weigh less and have a large hitting area, allowing more room for error. They make balls that combine distance and feel, with aerodynamics that optimize lift and reduce drag. Some balls are customized for launch conditions of various players. Golf is no longer just a game. It's a science.

Nick Price learned to play when it was an art. Like most players 30 and older, he grew up using wooden drivers with a sweet spot the size of a pea. "Now the sweet spot is the size of a peach," Price laments.

Swinging for the fences often meant the ball went into the trees. Price figured out he could swing at 85 percent of his total strength before he lost control of his tee shots. Nicklaus was said to have an extra 20 yards when he needed it.

Now, it seems as though every player gives it all they have on every drive.

"As soon as you give a person a lighter, more forgiving club, guys are going to learn to swing harder," Price said. "Guys are pushing the envelope, and that's increased their ability to swing by 8 to 10 percent. That's where they pick up clubhead speed." He doesn't think rolling back the golf ball by 10 percent would solve anything.

"The game is about the ability to swing a 44-inch object 25 feet, to return it back and hit it on a sweet spot," he said. "The smaller the sweet spot, the more you test that skill."

Price, however, is in the minority. Most attribute distance gains to the variable that moves—the golf ball. Nicklaus has been lobbying against golf ball improvements for 25 years, and what happened to him last month at Doral only proved his point. When he won the 1972 U.S. Open at Pebble Beach, the defining shot was his 1-iron from 219 yards into a stiff breeze that knocked down the flag at No. 17.

Nicklaus had 219 yards into a stiff breeze to the par-5 eighth hole at Doral. At age 63, he hit 2-iron into 15 feet. "What else could it be?" Nicklaus said.

He proposes a tournament ball that would restore shotmaking and reward talent. He also fears the power game is making championship courses obsolete, and the only way to test elite players is to pinch fairways, grow rough, and make the greens as firm as concrete. Just as Ernie Els uses better equipment than Nicklaus had in his prime, Nicklaus used better equipment than Ben Hogan, who had better equipment than Bobby Jones.

"Every generation says the game changes, and the game has changed," Nicklaus said. "The only thing that hasn't had to change is the golf course—until now. How much more can people afford to keep buying land and changing the golf course because of the ego of a ball manufacturer?" Meantime, anecdotal evidence keeps piling up:

- Els hit a drive that went nearly 400 yards to the bottom of the hill on the 15th hole at Kapalua. A week later at Waialae Country Club, he reached the 501-yard ninth hole with a driver and a wedge.
- Mickelson nearly drove the green on the 403-yard 10th hole at the Phoenix Open.
- Charles Howell III hit a sand wedge for his second shot on the 451-yard 18th at Riviera, the same hole where a plaque in the fairway pays tribute to Dave Stockton for his 3-wood that helped him win the 1974 Los Angeles Open.

Still, length isn't everything. Tiger Woods is the world's best player, and he relies more on his short game and course management than hitting the ball as far as he can.

"I don't take advantage of technology fully," Woods said. "I play with a short driver (43 inches) and a steel shaft and a shallow face, so I've limited myself to what I can do. But I'd much rather control the ball and get the ball in play."

Is distance ruining golf? The fear is that technology will turn even the toughest golf course into a pitch-and-putt. Johnson didn't order changes to Augusta National because the scores were too low, he simply got tired of seeing players hit wedge shots into almost all of the par 4s. Some worry that golf will become tennis at the highest level—no longer a game of exquisite shotmaking, but sheer power.

Peter Dawson, secretary of the Royal & Ancient Golf Club, opposes two sets of rules. Still, he is not oblivious to a rapidly changing game. "What's happening now is the gap between the elite player and the average club player has widened," Dawson said. "I don't think there's any issue at the club level with technology. But because these guys get so good out here, maybe there is an issue for them."

Source: Doug Ferguson, *The Associated Press* (April 6, 2003).

design, and Iso-Zorb grommet technology. If this new racquet offers benefits that consumers are seeking (more feel and power) and is believed to be improved, then it should be successful. A final example of a product improvement comes for the Metrodome in Minnesota. Recent improvements include an upgraded food service and new concession stands in the upper deck of the stadium. In addition, the Metrodome is being resurfaced with the best artificial playing surface available. The new turf will be installed in March 2004 and will be ready when the Twins open the season.

In another example of a product improvement, any sports team or individual that improves during the off-season can be considered a product improvement. Sometimes this improvement takes place because of trades or purchasing new players, and other times an enhanced product is the result of a new coach or players who are maturing and finally performing to their potential. In either case, product improvements represent an opportunity for sports marketers to promote the improvements (either real or perceived) in product quality.

Repositionings As defined in Chapter 7, repositioning is changing the image or perception of the sports entity in the minds of consumers in the target market. Sports products such as bowling and billiards are trying to reposition themselves as "yuppie sports activities" by creating trendy and up-scale environments in sports facilities that are stereotypically grungy and old-fashioned.[5] Another repositioning example comes from the sport of cricket, which is trying to establish itself on the American sporting scene. An estimated 1.5 million people in America follow cricket on a regular basis. Amazingly, there are now at least 100 cricket teams in New York alone, with over 5,000 players.[6] Marketers of the sport must wrestle with the decision of whether to position it as a sport steeped in tradition and target mainly American immigrants, or to position it as a new cosmopolitan sport of the world.[7]

The most common examples of new products are repositioning and product improvements because of the limited risk involved from the organization's perspective. The rearrangement of existing sports products also has its advantages. For example, this type of new product can be developed more quickly than new-to-the-world or new product category entrants, and it already has an established track record with consumers.

However, new-to-the-world products must undergo more careful research and development because they are new to the organization and to consumers. Moreover, more money must be invested because heavy levels of promotion are necessary to make potential consumers aware of the product. In addition, consumers must learn about the benefits of the new product and how it can help satisfy their needs.

NEWNESS FROM THE CONSUMER'S PERSPECTIVE

Another way to describe new products is from the perspective of consumers. New products are categorized as discontinuous innovations, dynamically continuous innovations, or continuous innovations.[8] The new products are categorized on the basis of the degree of behavioral change required by consumers. Behavioral changes refer to differences in the way we use a new product, think about a new product, or the degree of learning required to use a new product. For instance, a new extra-long tennis racquet does not require us to change the way we play tennis or to relearn the sport. However, extensive learning took place for many Americans exposed to soccer for the first time in the 1994 World Cup. Similarly, learning will have to occur for the many Americans who will watch cricket or lacrosse for the first time. Let us look at the three categories of new products from the consumer's perspective in greater detail.

Discontinuous innovations are somewhat similar to new-to-the-world products in that they represent the most innovative products. In fact, discontinuous innovations are so new and original that they require major learning from the consumer's viewpoint and new consumption and usage patterns. Some of the "extreme sports," such as sky surfing, bungee jumping, and ice climbing, represented discontinuous innovations, but are now becoming more mainstream. New "extremes" such as base jumping, extreme trampolining, and kite-surfing are also becoming popular.

Many Southerners who have had limited access to ice hockey may view this sport as a discontinuous innovation. Interestingly, a study found that spectator knowledge of hockey was found to be a significant predictor of game attendance and intention to attend hockey games in the future. An equally important finding in the study was that knowledge of hockey may vary based on sociodemographic variables. In other words, the fan's age, gender, educational level, income, and marital status influence the degree of hockey knowledge.[9]

Dynamically continuous innovations are new products that represent changes and improvements but do not strikingly change buying and usage patterns. For instance, the titanium head and bubble shaft on a golf club or the liquid metal technology aluminum bat are innovations that do not change our swing, but do represent significant improvements in equipment (and hopefully our game). When the shot-clock and three-point field goal were added to basketball, changes took place in how the game was played. Coaches, players, and fans were forced to understand and adopt new strategies for basketball. Most basketball enthusiasts believe these dynamically continuous innovations improved the sport.

Another example of a dynamically continuous innovation is VTV: Varsity Television, the world's first and only 24-hour network exclusively dedicated to teenagers. For the first time ever on national television, viewers can experience the best high school sports in the country. More specifically, VTV will give viewers the opportunity to experience the first high school football super conference, where the best of the best unite on television to compete for national domination.[10]

A final example of a dynamically continuous innovation comes from the world of trading cards and technology. Topps, the historic market leader in sports trading cards has developed a new online division called etopps. "Etopps" is a unique model that works like the stock market with consumers buying and selling sports cards of specific players online for a one-week period. Typically, between 1,500 and 2,500 individual cards are printed and offered online for $6.50 each. When the sale ends, the trading begins and card owners can offer their cards for auction. Etopps prints only the ordered cards and stores them in climate controlled vaults in sealed hard plastic sleeves, to be shipped to the final owner upon request. "Only about 10 percent of our customers ever have their cards delivered to them," said etopps spokesperson Clay Luraschi.[11] Certainly, this change represents a new buying behavior for a product (trading cards) that has been on the market for decades.

Continuous innovations represent an ongoing, commonplace change such as the minor alteration of a product or the introduction of an imitation product. A continuous innovation has the least disruptive influence on patterns of usage and consumer behavior. In other words, consumers use the product in the same manner they have always used the product. Examples of continuous innovations include the addition of expansion teams for leagues such as MLB, the WNBA, or MLS. Another example of a continuous innovation comes to us from the world of sports video game technology. NHL Hitz Pro 2003 has new and improved features such as 5-on-5 gameplay (including goalies); league penalties and violations; and for the first time ever, live online gameplay.

We could debate which new product category best represents a team that has built a new arena and changed its venue or any new sports product, but few new products fall neatly into the three categories. Rather, there is a continuum ranging from minor

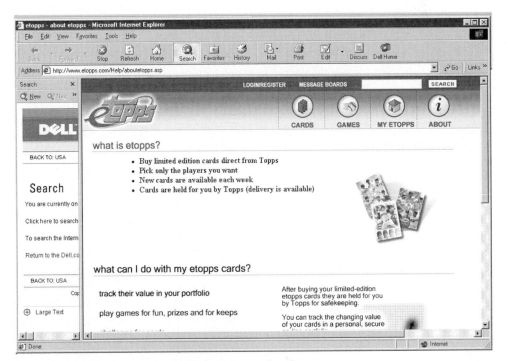

Dynamically continuous innovation in the Topps product line.
Source: Copyright © 2003. The Topps Company, Inc. All rights reserved.

Continuous innovation in baseball equipment.
Source: Copyright © 2004 Champs Sports.

innovation to major innovation, based on how consumers perceive the new product. Knowing how consumers think and feel about a new product is critical information in developing the most effective marketing strategy. Before we talk more about the factors that make new products successful and spread through the marketplace, let us look at how new products are conceived.

THE NEW PRODUCT DEVELOPMENT PROCESS

Increased competition for sports and entertainment dollars, emergence of new technologies, and ever-changing consumer preferences are just a few of the reasons sports marketers are constantly developing new sports products. As Higgins and Martin point out in their research on managing sport innovations, "Clearly, the list of innovations in sports is extensive and appears to be increasing at a rapid rate. This would suggest that spectators are seeking new and better entertainment and participants are seeking new and better challenges."[12]

Many **new sports products** are conceived without much planning, or happen as a result of chance. For instance, the sport of polo was created by British Cavalry officers in India who wanted to show off their horsemanship in a more creative way than to the parade ground allowed. Although polo represents a sport that was developed by chance, this is more the exception than the rule. More often than not, sports organizations develop new products by using a systematic approach called the **new product development process.** The phases in the new product development process include idea generation, idea screening, analysis of the concept, developing the sports product, test marketing, and commercialization. Let us briefly explore each phase in the new product development process.

IDEA GENERATION

The first phase of the new product development process is **idea generation.** At this initial phase, any and all ideas for new products are considered. Ideas for new products are generated from many different sources. Employees who work in product development teams, salespeople close to the consumers, consumers of sport, and competitive organizations are just a few of the potential sources of ideas for new sports products.

Naturally, a marketing-oriented sports organization will attempt to communicate with their consumers as much as possible to determine emerging needs. As we discussed in Chapter 4, marketing research plays a valuable role in anticipating the needs of consumers. Moreover, environmental scanning helps sports organizations keep in touch with changes in the marketing environment that might present opportunities for new product development. For instance, in our opening scenario, the entrepreneurs who established slamball understood that the environmental conditions are conducive to success.

IDEA SCREENING

Once the ideas are generated, the next step of the product development process, **idea screening,** begins. During the idea screening phase, all the new product ideas are evaluated and the poor ones are weeded out. An important consideration in the ideas screening process is to examine the "fit" of the product with the organization's goals and consumer demand. The concept of new product fit is consistent with the contingency framework, which states that product decisions should consider the external contingencies, the internal contingencies, and the strategic sports marketing process. One formal idea screening tool for analyzing the "fit" of potential products is the new product screening checklist (see Table 9.1).

Sports marketers using some variant of this new product screening checklist would rate potential new product ideas on each item. As Table 9.1 indicates, a score of less than 30 would eliminate the new product from further consideration, whereas a score of 70 or more would be further developed. Obviously, each sports organization must design its own new product screening checklist to meet the demands of its unique marketing environment and organization.

ANALYSIS OF THE SPORTS PRODUCT CONCEPT OR POTENTIAL

By the third phase of the new product development process, poor ideas have been eliminated. Now, the process continues as the firm begins to analyze potential new products in terms of how they fit with existing products and how consumers respond to these new products. As new product ideas begin to take shape, marketing research is necessary to understand consumers' perceptions of the new product concepts. One type of marketing research that is commonly conducted during the new product development process is referred to as concept testing.

During concept testing, consumers representative of the target market, evaluate written, verbal, and pictorial descriptions of potential products. The objectives of concept testing are to understand the target market's reaction to the proposed product, determine how interested the target market is in the product, and explore the strengths and weaknesses of the proposed product. In some cases, consumers are

TABLE 9.1 New Product Screening Checklist

Rate the new-product concept using a 10-point scale. Score a "1" if the concept fails the question and a "10" if it meets the criterion perfectly.

Relative Advantage

Does the new product offer a cost advantage compared with substitutes?

Does the new product have a value-added feature?

Is your innovation directed at neglected segments of the marketplace?

Compatibility

Is the product compatible with corporate practices, culture, and value systems (i.e., the internal contingencies)?

Is the new product compatible with the market's environment (i.e., the external contingencies)?

Is the new product compatible with current products and services being offered (i.e., product mix)?

Perceived Risk

Note on the following questions absence of risk should receive a higher score.

Does the consumer perceive an economic risk if they try the new product?

Does the consumer perceive a physical risk in adopting the new product?

Does the consumer fear the new technology will not perform properly?

Does the product offer a social risk to consumers?

A bottom line score of 100 (10 points for each question) suggests a new product winner. For most companies, a score of 70 or better signals a "go" decision on the new product concept. A risk-oriented company would probably consider anything that scores 50 or higher. A score of 30 or less signifies a concept that faces many consumer obstacles.

Concept testing is used to understand consumer reactions to sports such as white water rafting.

TABLE 9.2   Concept Test for the Beach Soccer World Wide Tour

The sport of beach soccer is played on a 30-by-40-yard soft sand surface with five players on each team, including the goalie. There are three periods of 12 minutes each with unlimited player substitutions (as in hockey). In the event of a tie, the game goes into a 3-minute overtime period, followed by sudden-death penalty kicks. Beach Soccer World Wide would feature nation against nation (e.g., United States vs. Italy).

What is your general reaction to beach soccer?

How likely would you be to attend an event if the tour stopped in your city?
Would definitely attend
Probably would attend
Might or might not attend
Probably would not attend
Would definitely not attend

What do you like most about this concept of BSWW?
What could be done to improve the concept of BSWW?

asked to evaluate slightly different versions of the product so that sports organizations can design the product to meet the needs of consumers.

The most important reason for conducting a concept test is to estimate the sales potential of the new product. Often, this is done by measuring "intent to buy" responses from tested consumers. Using the results of concept testing, along with secondary data such as demographic trends, sports marketers can decide whether to proceed to the next step of the new product development process, drop the idea, or revise the product concept and reevaluate. Table 9.2 shows a hypothetical concept test for the Beach Soccer World Wide tour, a new sports product that has been growing around the globe.

DEVELOPING THE SPORTS PRODUCT

Based on the results of the concept test, design of the product begins in order to conduct further testing. Ideally, if the sports organization is employing a marketing orientation, then the product design and development stem from the consumer's perspective. For instance, Nike began its product design efforts for a new baseball glove by asking 200 college and minor league baseball players what they disliked about their current gloves. Eighteen months and $500,000 later, researchers designed a prototype glove that is lightweight, held together with plastic clips and wire straps, and resembles a white foam rubber clamshell. Nike was hoping this space-age design would not be perceived by baseball purists to be too far afield from traditional models.[13] However, consumers didn't respond favorably and Nike was forced to discontinue the glove line.

In the case of a sporting good, a prototype usually is developed so consumers can get an even better idea of how the product will function and look. Today's superior engineering technology allows manufacturers to develop more realistic prototypes in a shorter period of time. It is common for prototypes to then be sent to select individuals for further testing and refinement. For instance, new golf, tennis, and ski products are routinely sent to club professionals for testing.

Another consideration in **developing the sports product** is making preliminary decisions with respect to the planning phase of the strategic sports marketing process. Potential market selection decisions (segmentation, target markets, and positioning) are considered. Furthermore, packaging, pricing, and distribution decisions are also deliberated. These basic marketing decisions are necessary to begin the next phase of new product development—test marketing.

TEST MARKETING

In the concept stage of new product development, consumers indicate they would be likely to purchase the new product or service. Now that the product has been designed and developed, it can be offered to consumers on a limited basis to determine actual sales. Test marketing is the final gauge of the new product's success or failure.

Test marketing allows the sports organization to determine consumer response to the product and also provides information that may direct the entire marketing strategy. For instance, test markets can provide valuable information on the most effective packaging, pricing, and other forms of promotion.

The three types of test markets that may be conducted include standardized test markets, controlled test markets, and simulated test markets.[14] In standardized test markets, the product is sold through normal channels of distribution. A controlled test market, also known as a forced-distribution test market, uses an outside agency to secure distribution. As such, the manufacturer of a new product does not have to worry about the acceptance and level of market support from retailers or those carrying the product because the outside agency pays the retailer for the test. A simulated test market uses a tightly controlled simulated retailing environment or purchasing laboratory to determine consumer preferences for new sports products. This type of test market may be especially important in the future as more and more sporting goods and services are being marketed through the Internet.

Whatever type of test market is chosen, it is important to keep several things in mind. First, test marketing delays the introduction of a new sports product and may allow time for the competition to produce a "me-too" or imitation, product thereby negating the test marketer's investment in research and development. Second, costs of test marketing must be considered. It is common for the cost of test marketing to range from $30,000 to $300,000. Third, the results of test marketing may be misleading. Consumers may be anxious to try new sports products and competition may try to influence the sales figures of the tested product by offering heavy discounting and promotion of their own product. Finally, test marketing presents a special challenge for sports marketers because of the intangible nature of many sports services.

COMMERCIALIZATION

The final stage of new product development is **commercialization,** or introduction. The decision has been made at this point to launch full-scale production (for goods) and distribution. If care has been taken at the previous stages of new product development, the new product will successfully meet its objectives. However, even if a systematic approach to new product development is followed, more often than not sports products fail. Just what is it that makes a small portion of new sports products successful while the large majority fail? Let us look at some of the factors that increase the chances of new product success.

NEW PRODUCTS SUCCESS FACTORS

The success of any new sports product, such as the NASCAR SpeedParks, depends on a variety of **new product success factors.** First and foremost, successful products must be high quality, create and maintain a positive and distinct brand image, and be designed to

TABLE 9.3   Critical Success Factors for New Products

Product Considerations
- **Trialability**—Can consumers try the product before they make a purchase to reduce the risk?
- **Observability**—Can consumers see the benefits of the product or watch others use the product prior to the purchase?
- **Perceived Complexity**—Does the new product appear to be difficult to understand or use?
- **Relative Advantage**—Does the new product seem better than existing alternatives?
- **Compatibility**—Is the new product consistent with consumers' values and beliefs?

Other Marketing Mix Considerations
- **Pricing**—Do consumers perceive the price to be consistent with the quality of the new product?
- **Promotion**—Are consumers in the target market aware of the product and do they understand the benefits of the product?
- **Distribution**—Is the product being sold in the "right" places and in enough places?

Marketing Environment Considerations
- **Competition**—Are there a large number of competitors in the market?
- **Consumer Tastes**—Does the new product reflect a trend in society?
- **Demographics**—Is the new product being marketed to a segment of the population that is growing?

Source: Courtland L. Bovée and John Thill, *Marketing* (New York: McGraw-Hill, 1992), 307–309.

consumer specifications. In addition to the characteristics of the product itself, the other marketing mix elements (pricing, distribution, and promotion) play a major role in the success of a new product. Finally, the marketing environment also contributes to the success of a new product. A brief description of these critical success factors is presented in Table 9.3. Let us evaluate how well the new NASCAR SpeedParks performs on each of the critical success factors.

Based on these critical success factors, would you predict that the NASCAR SpeedParks will be profitable? The NASCAR SpeedParks would seem to perform well on each of the product characteristics. Families can observe others enjoying the SpeedParks and try the sports product once with limited perceived risk. The NASCAR Go-Karts are safe and built for kids, so product complexity is low. With the NASCAR branding, the sophisticated engineering, and the authenticity, the perceived advantage of these replica cars should be far greater than "just another Go-Kart." Finally, the SpeedParks are consistent with core values, such as safe and fun entertainment for the entire family.

In addition to the product considerations, other marketing mix considerations have also been well thought out for the NASCAR SpeedParks. Initially, the SpeedParks will be placed in parts of the country known for entertainment (e.g., Myrtle Beach) and the love of NASCAR racing (e.g., Tennessee). Given the signing of Dale Jarrett, Tony Stewart, and Elliot Sadler, promotion of the SpeedParks should be solid.

The marketing environment also appears to be ready for the growth of the NASCAR SpeedParks. NASCAR is one of the fastest-growing spectator sports in the country and has a huge and loyal fan base. Moreover, there are other Go-Kart tracks, but none with the backing of NASCAR, so competition is limited. In summary, the NASCAR SpeedParks seem to perform well on all the critical success factors, but only time will tell whether this new sports product will run the victory lap.

PRODUCT LIFE CYCLE

From the time a sports product begins the new product development process to the time it is taken off the market, it passes through a series of stages known as the **product life cycle** (PLC). The four distinct stages of the PLC are called introduction, growth, maturity, and decline. As shown in Figure 9.1, the traditional PLC was originally developed by marketers to illustrate how the sales and profits of goods vary over time. However, other sports products, such as athletes, teams, leagues, and events, pass through four distinct phases over time. Regardless of the nature of the sports product, the PLC is a useful tool for developing marketing strategy and then revising this strategy as a product moves through its own unique life cycle. In a recent article, Rick Burton and Dennis Howard of the University of Oregon used the product life cycle as a tool to assess the current state of big league sports. Their conclusion was that all four big league sports (baseball, hockey, basketball, and football) have reached either late maturity or decline. The authors speculate part of the reason for this decline is that professional sports leagues have experienced "players strikes (MLB, August 1994; NHL, September 1995), player lockout (NBA, July 1998), player free agency and salary demands (all leagues, all the time), various player arrests (from the manslaughter trial of New Jersey Nets star Jayson Williams to the impending sexual assault case against Los Angeles Lakers superstar Kobe Bryant), rising ticket prices (an annual custom), stadium referendums, franchise movement, and constant legal wrangling." The authors also point out that each league should examine its current position in the marketplace and be prepared to adjust its marketing strategy based on the phase of the product life cycle. As expressed in the article, "despite all the hype and rhetoric, a case can be made that professional sports leagues are marketable brands that require sophisticated marketing plans and an understanding of how the product is perceived, received, and purchased. If a brand is in late maturity or the earliest phases of decline, then new uses, new product features, or new markets must be developed."[15]

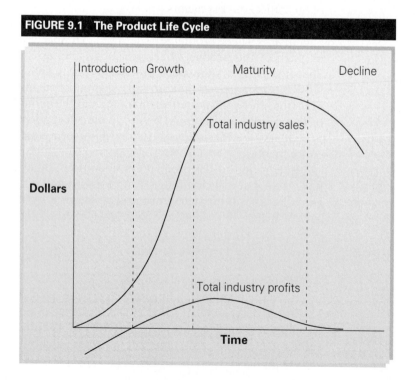

FIGURE 9.1 The Product Life Cycle

Extending the product life cycle of the waterbike.

The waterbike is an excellent example of a sports product whose life cycle mirrors the shape of the conventional PLC. The waterbike, or personal watercraft, had tremendous growth in the early 1990s. Sales of waterbikes reached their peak in 1995 with 200,000 units sold. However, unit sales have been decreasing since that year. In 2001, U.S. dealers sold 83,000 of the water machines. Sales fell further in 2002 and even James Bond couldn't help the sagging industry as he proudly rode a Sea-Doo in the movie "Die Another Day,"[16] Industry insiders want to believe the waterbike is in the maturity phase of the PLC and sales have merely reached their plateau. Others, however, contend the industry has developed an image problem because of the safety and pollution issues associated with the activity. In this case, waterbike brands such as JetSki and SeaDoo may need to find ways to extend the life of their products.

Before we explore the four phases of the PLC, keep several important factors in mind. First, the PLC originally was developed to describe product categories, such as waterbikes or baseball gloves, rather than specific brands, such as SeaDoo or Mizuno. Second, the product life cycle was designed to monitor the industry sales and profitability of goods rather than services. Third, the traditional shape and length of the product life cycle is generalized. In other words, it is assumed to look the same for all products. In reality, the length of the PLC varies for each sports product. Some products die quickly, some seem to last forever, and others die and are then reborn. Summarizing, sports marketers must carefully consider the unique PLC of each of their products on the market. Let us now explore how the PLC can be used for decision making in the strategic sports marketing process.

INTRODUCTION

When a new sports product first enters the marketplace, the introduction phase of the PLC is initiated. New leagues such as the National Pro Fastpitch and the National Women's Football Association are excellent examples of sports products being introduced. The broad marketing goal of the first phase of the PLC is to generate awareness and stimulate trial among those consumers who are willing to try new products. Typically, profits are low because of the high start-up costs associated with getting the product ready to market.

During the introduction phase, pricing of the sports product is determined largely by the type of image that has been determined in the positioning strategy. Generally, one of two broad pricing alternatives is usually chosen during the **introduction** of the product. If the product strategy is to gain widespread consumer trial and market share, a lower price is set. This low pricing strategy is termed penetration pricing. However, a higher priced skimming strategy is sometimes preferred. The advantages of skimming include recouping the early marketing investment and production costs, as well as reinforcing the superior quality usually associated with higher prices.

Distribution of the new product is also highly dependent on the nature of the product. Usually, however, distribution is limited to fewer outlets. That is, there are a small number of places to purchase the product. Incentives are necessary to push the product from the manufacturer to the consumer. Promotion activity is high during the product's introduction to encourage consumers to try the new product. In addition, promotion is designed to provide the consumers with information about the new product and to provide a purchase incentive.

GROWTH

Sales are usually slow as the new product is introduced. With the onset of the **growth** stage, sales of the product increase. In fact, a rapid increase in sales is the primary characteristic of the growth stage of the PLC. Because industry sales are growing, the broad marketing goal is to build consumer preference for your product and continue to extend the product line. Although competition is usually nonexistent or very weak at introduction, more competitors emerge during the growth phase. Promotion must stress the benefits of your brand over competitive brands.

For example, collegiate women's hockey is in the growth stage. Several decades ago there were maybe seven or eight teams on the East Coast. Today there are 61 colleges that offer Division I hockey for women and 42 were launched after the USA Women won the gold in the 1998 Olympic Games. These programs are being fueled by a growth in the sport at the high school level.[17]

During the growth stage, product differentiation occurs by making minor changes or modifications in the product or service. A premium is placed on gaining more widespread distribution of the product. Manufacturers must secure outlets and distributors at this early phase of the PLC so the product is readily available. Finally, the prices during the growth phase are sometimes reduced in response to a growing number of competitors or held artificially high to enhance perceived quality. Let us look at some of the strategic decisions discussed thus far in the context of the growth of the fantasy sports industry.

MATURITY

Eventually, industry sales begin to stabilize as fewer numbers of new consumers enter the saturated market. As such, the level of competition increases as a greater number of organizations compete for a limited or stable number of consumers. The primary marketing objective at **maturity** is to maintain whatever advantages were captured in growth and offer a greater number of promotions to encourage repeat purchases. Brand strategy shifts from "try me" to "buy one more than you used to." Unfortunately, profitability is also lessened because of the need to reduce prices and offer incentives.

If attempts to maintain sales and market share are unsuccessful in the maturity stage, an organization may try several alternative strategies to extend the PLC before the product begins to decline and eventually die. Let us look at how the powerful and popular sport of Hot Rod Racing has extended its PLC.

Fantasy Sports Industry Now Over 15 Million

More than 15 million American adults have played fantasy sports during the last year, with more than 12 million adults expected to play fantasy football this fall, according to a survey conducted for the Fantasy Sports Trade Association (FSTA), based here in St. Louis. A recent omnibus survey conducted by the Ipsos Public Affairs showed that more people are playing fantasy sports than ever before and they are playing in more leagues and spending more work time at this growing hobby.

The omnibus survey showed that in the past year, 7.2 percent of all adult Americans played fantasy sports, with 78 percent of those participants playing fantasy football. A previous FSTA survey showed that the average person plays in 2.4 fantasy football leagues per year and spends an average of $154 on fantasy football, ranging from entry fees, commissioner services, fantasy news sites, and draft publications. Today's average fantasy football participant has been playing for six years, checks his teams online at work regularly, spends almost three hours a week managing his teams, and is more likely to become even more involved in this hobby in the future.

"This survey clearly defines the size of our growing industry and shows that millions of dedicated sports fans are getting more involved in their favorite professional sports by participating in fantasy sports," said Greg Ambrosius, president of the Fantasy Sports Trade Association. "The Internet has allowed more people to get involved in fantasy sports and it is easier than ever to become a part of it. Fantasy sports is now big business and all of the major sports web sites are making it easy to transition from sports fan to fantasy sports fan."

CBS SportsLine.com, for instance, generated more than $11 million in revenue on fantasy games and services last year and its baseball revenue in 2003 jumped over 50 percent from 2002. Most fantasy businesses are expecting a record-breaking football season in 2003 as interest in fantasy football is at an all-time high. That interest is especially high in males, as 11 percent of all males surveyed play fantasy sports, with 16.6 percent of all males ages 18 to 39 playing fantasy sports, with football being the most popular.

Interestingly, 50 percent of all fantasy football players say they attended at least one professional event last year, making an average visit of 3.5 NFL games per year per person. The demographics of all fantasy players paint an upscale profile: Average age is 37, average household size is 2.7, average annual household income is $76,689, and over 90 percent of players are male. The University of Mississippi, which conducted the FSTA demographic survey in 2002, projects an 11.5 percent growth rate for football this year, meaning that hundreds of millions of dollars will be generated in 2003 through this growing industry.

Not surprisingly, 62 percent of current fantasy players say they check their fantasy football teams online during work. A whopping 73 percent of fantasy football players also use e-mail in their day-to-day mangement, likely proposing trades to other league owners. The average fantasy football player spends 2.8 hours per week managing his team.

"The average fantasy football player spends almost three hours per week visiting their fantasy teams, so it is only a matter of time before mainstream advertisers embrace our booming industry," Ambrosius added. "With that kind of frequency, advertisers will be sure their message is heard by this highly desirable demographic. While fantasy football is the current leader in our industry, interest in other sports is increasing at the same huge rate of growth, offering additional connections by advertisers to consumers. The future of fantasy sports is promising for both fantasy players and sponsors alike."

Source: Business Wire Inc. www.businesswire.com, August 14, 2003. Copyright © 2003 Business Wire, Inc.

The National Hot Rod Association is an excellent illustration of a sports organization that realized it was rapidly moving toward extinction, decided to take corrective action, and developed and implemented new marketing strategies. Table 9.4 provides additional suggestions for sports marketers who want to extend the PLC.

In another example, the NBL (National Basketball League) of Australia could be rejuvenated with live telecasts into Asia on ESPN Star Sports, which is the No. 1 pay TV sports channel in the region. A potential audience of tens of millions (Star boasts about 40 million cable subscribers) could watch the game in prime time, making it the highest-rating NBL game in the history of the sport.[18]

NHRA Lifted from the Pits to Fast Track

The National Hot Rod Association (NHRA) stood at a precarious fork in the road when its new president took over 3 1/2 years ago. R. J. Reynolds was in the process of ending its 27-year series sponsorship, a result of the tobacco companies settlement; the sanctioning body didn't have a firm television deal; and the nation's economy was at the cusp of a serious downturn.

"We were at a crossroads, on television and with Winston going away, and not having a series sponsor to replace them," said Top Fuel Dragster driver Kenny Bernstein, a six-time NHRA season champion who has been racing in the series since 1973. "Everything that you could imagine was bad about it. It was tough."

Welcome to the frying pan, Tom Compton. Compton, though, never blinked. The 45-year-old native of northern California, whose background was in business administration and marketing, formulated a plan and quickly put it in place. First, he and his officers instituted sweeping rules changes in the Top Fuel divisions, dragster and Funny Car, which picked up the pace of the competition, making it more fan-friendly while also making it safer. "They made a lot of changes in NHRA that a lot of people didn't like," 12-time Funny Car champ John Force said. "But the proof's in the pudding."

Compton next worked out a multiyear deal with ESPN, which, beginning in 2001, gained exclusive rights to the NHRA. All national events now are televised, mostly on ESPN2, with the cable network devoting more than 110 hours of original programming per season to the NHRA.

"We think it's a quality product, and it has an unbelievably loyal following," said Kelly Leferriere, ESPN's vice president of programming and acquisition. "Now, the audience knows where to find NHRA programming, and we've been consistently pleased with the ratings. It's among the highest-rating programming we have on ESPN2. We're optimistic about the future."

Next came the most crucial challenge: Finding a company willing to plunk down millions to succeed Winston as the series sponsor. Compton and his crew struck gold with Atlanta-based Coca-Cola, which wanted to promote its sports drink and agreed to fund the Powerade Drag Racing Series, beginning in 2002. "When Winston pulled out, a lot of people—maybe even myself—thought that,

'Hey, where are we going to get another sponsor in these tough times?'" said Don Prudhomme, a four-time NHRA Funny Car champ who now runs a multicar team. "And then lo and behold, Tom Compton got hold of Coca-Cola and they decided to take Powerade into our series. Man, it was a real coup."

Ben Reiling, senior manager of sports marketing for Coke, said: "We weren't searching for this opportunity. When it was presented to us, we evaluated it on a lot of different fronts. . . . We found that the plan that Tom put together and the plan we had to promote Powerade were inextricably linked. And we have partnership with ESPN, which is a tremendous benefit as well." A distinct advantage Powerade has over Winston, Compton pointed out, is its wide-open capacity to market its product while also marketing the NHRA. Winston's advertising ability was severely restricted because of the tobacco settlement.

"We're now going to be out there" in the public eye, Compton said. "They're running national television ads, they're doing in-store promotions, and you will see our champions in stores around the country. . . . We've never had the benefit of that before. Winston was a great partner, and we enjoyed working with them. But what Coca-Cola brings to the party with the Powerade brand is unprecedented."

Said Bernstein: "When you put those two pieces of the puzzle in place, these last two years we've seen (the NHRA) stabilize and get better and go forward. . . . It's stronger now than it was."

So, while other motor sports circuits—most notably, the American open-wheel circuits—struggle during difficult times, the NHRA is perking right along. Its TV ratings are solid, attendance has remained fairly steady, and its individual teams, while stretched financially, generally are making ends meet.

"We're doing surprisingly well," Compton said. "We're the No. 2 motor sport (behind NASCAR) by any measure that you can come up with. We've been that way for a number of years. We're not No. 2 perception-wise; we're probably No. 4. . . . We now have a great television package with ESPN, and we have a great series sponsor with Powerade and Coca-Cola. I think that's a powerful combination. We're pretty well positioned. I think when the economy turns around, you're going to see some of our best years."

Source: Bill Coats, "Retooling Lifts NHRA from Pits to Fast Track; New Boss, Rules, Sponsors Rejuvenate Hot-Rod Circuit," *St. Louis Post-Dispatch*, June 27, 2003 D1. Copyright © 2004. Reprinted with permission.

TABLE 9.4 Extending the Product Life Cycle

- Develop new uses for products.
- Develop new product features and refinements (line extensions).
- Increase the existing market.
- Develop new markets.
- Change marketing mix (e.g., new or more promotion, new or more distribution, and increase or decrease price).
- Link product to a trend.

Source: Joel Evans and Barry Berman, *Marketing,* 6th ed. (New York: Macmillan, 1992), 439.

DECLINE

The marketing goals for the **decline** stage of the PLC are difficult to pinpoint because decisions must be made regarding what to do with a failing product. These decisions are based largely on the competition and how the sports organization chooses to react to the competition.

The distinctive characteristic of the decline phase of the PLC is that sales are steadily diminishing. Several alternative strategies might be considered during the decline phase. One alternative is referred to as deletion. As the name implies, the product is dropped from the organization's product mix. A second alternative, harvesting (or milking) is when the organization retains the sports product but offers little or no marketing support. A final alternative is simply maintaining the product at its current level of marketing support in hope that competitors will withdraw from the market that is already in decline.

OTHER LIFE CYCLE CONSIDERATIONS

The PLC, although an excellent tool for strategic decision making, is not without limitations. These limitations include generalizing the length of the PLC, applying the PLC to broad product categories only, and using the PLC to analyze "pure" sporting goods only. Each of these potential weaknesses of the PLC model is discussed next.

LENGTH AND SHAPE OF THE PLC

Figure 9.1 depicted the traditional length and shape of the PLC. However, each product life cycle has its own unique shape and unique length, depending on the product under consideration and the nature of the marketing environment. Several variants of the typical PLC length including the fad PLC, the classic PLC, and the seasonal PLC are shown in Figures 9.2a to 9.2c.

Fad The **fad** PLC (Figure 9.2a) is characterized by accelerated sales and accelerated acceptance of the product followed by decline stages. Often, sports marketers realize their products will be novelty items that get into the market, make a profit, and then quickly exit. These one-time, short-term offerings would follow the volatile fad cycle. The ABA red, white, and blue basketball followed the fad cycle, as do many products in the golf equipment industry. Other examples of a fad cycle include the bobblehead doll as a sports promotion and retro look jerseys and sports apparel. Fitness and fads seem to go hand in hand. While some exercise routines and machines have endured the test of time to become classics, others come and go in a flash.

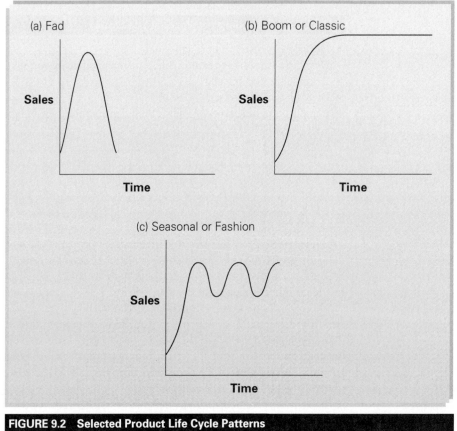

FIGURE 9.2　Selected Product Life Cycle Patterns

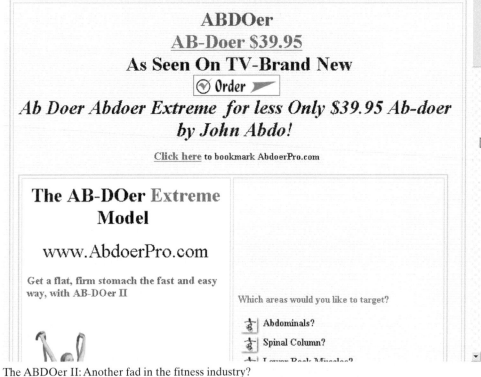

The ABDOer II: Another fad in the fitness industry?

Source: Used by permission of Ab Doer. www.surftilyoudrop.com/abdoer.

High impact aerobics might have been the first of the more modern fitness fads in the 1970s, followed by the cardio-fitness movement of the 1980s. Then came the incorporation of strength training into workouts and more recent fads include the indoor cycling program called "spinning" and cardio-kickboxing. The latest and greatest exercise fad links the mind and body in routines such as yoga and tai chi.[19] Who knows what the next fad might bring.

Classic Another variation of the PLC is characterized by a continuous stage of maturity (Figure 9.2b). Season tickets for the Green Bay Packers, Frisbees, baseball gloves and bats, tennis balls, and hockey sticks all represent other examples of the PLC know as the **classic.**

Seasonal The **seasonal** life cycle is found in most sports where the sales of sports products rise and fall with the opening and closing day of the season. To combat the seasonal life cycle, some sports have adopted year-round scheduling. Most auto racing series are run on an 8- to 10-month schedule, giving sponsors almost year-round coverage. Professional tennis has also adopted a continual schedule, but as the following paragraph indicates, this may not be the best thing for the sport.

When asked what he would do to cure the ills of tennis, former star and current TV analyst, John McEnroe did not hesitate before responding; "I would cut the amount of events. Now, there are too many tournaments, so people don't have any idea about what's really important. I would make a schedule that would be like the baseball or basketball season, so we wouldn't go 12 months a year."[20] Somewhat surprisingly, the NBA used the "less-is-more" strategy more than 20 years ago, when the league was plummeting in popularity. David Stern, then a rookie commissioner, significantly cut the number of televised games to increase long-term interest in the sport.

The fad, classic, and seasonal life cycles are three common variants of the traditional PLC. Other products, however, seem to defy all life cycle shapes and lengths. Consider skateboarding. Since its inception in the 1950s skateboarding has been a fad in nearly every decade. Now, skateboarding seems to be here to stay according to the National Sporting Good Association (NSGA). Skateboarding posted the second highest growth rate in participation for youth ages seven to 17 from 1997 to 2002. Of seven sports that saw growth in that period, skateboarding showed a 55 percent increase with the nearly 8 million in participants in 2003.[21]

THE LEVEL OF PRODUCT

Another consideration for developing marketing strategy based on the PLC is the level of the product. Historically, the PLC was based on total industry sales for an entire product category, such as basketball shoes, bowling balls, mountain bikes, or golf clubs. Although examining the PLC by category is useful, it is also necessary to understand the PLC by product form and product brand.

Product form refers to product variations within the category. For example, titanium woods, metal woods, and "wood" woods represent three variations in product form in the golf club product category. The potential marketing strategies for each of these product forms differ by the stage of the PLC. The titanium woods are in the growth stage, metal woods are in maturity, and traditional woods are near extinction.

In addition to looking at the product category and form, it is also beneficial to examine various brands. Within the titanium wood form, there are a variety of individual brands, such as Titleist Titanium 983K, Callaway Big Bertha Titanium, and Nike

450cc Titanium. Each of these brands may be in different stages of the PLC. Therefore, sports marketing managers must give full consideration to variations in the PLC, based on the level of the product (category, form, and brand).

TYPE OF PRODUCT

The PLC originally was designed to guide strategies for goods. However, the notion of the PLC should be extended to other types of sports products. For instance, individual athletes can be thought of as sports products that move through a life cycle just as products do.

The phenomenal rise and success of Tiger Woods in the professional golf ranks has skyrocketed him out of introduction and into the growth phase of his PLC. The number of products that Woods endorses is rapidly increasing and more people are becoming aware of his "star" qualities. The Cleveland Cavaliers' star, LeBron James, has emerged and continues in his introductory stage. "King" James signed a $90-million shoe contract with Nike and is being touted as the next Michael Jordan for his skills both on and off the court. Philadelphia Flyers center Jeremy Roenick, suffering the ninth concussion of his career in 2004, may be heading for retirement and decline in his individual PLC.

Interestingly, some individual athletes have a unique shape to their PLC. Think about the many professional athletes who have come out of retirement to reintroduce themselves. Mark Spitz attempted to come back to Olympic swimming 20 years after seven gold medals in Munich and was no longer able to compete. Jim Palmer, Bjorn Borg, Sugar Ray Leonard, Magic Johnson, and Muhammad Ali all tried to come back after years away from their respective sports and failed miserably. Arnold Palmer, with his incredible staying power, will undoubtedly stay in the maturity phase of his PLC and remain a classic even after playing in his last competitive golf tournament. Many aging golfers, such as Jim Colbert, who had almost no success on the regular PGA Tour are experiencing tremendous success on the senior circuit. Unfortunately, many athletes experience a life cycle that is best represented by the fad PLC. For instance, Brian Bosworth (Seattle Seahawks linebacker), Mark "The Bird" Fiydrich (Detroit Tigers pitcher), and Buster Douglas (boxing) were all athletes who had short-term success only to quickly fall into decline for a number of reasons.

Sports teams also can pass through the various phases of the PLC. For instance, the Charlotte Bobcats of the NBA began play in 2004–2005 and are in the introductory stage of their PLC. The Montreal Expos, who are owned by the other 29 teams in major league baseball, are slated to move after the 2004 season and are certainly in the decline stage. These two product examples would each require completely different marketing strategies.

Professional and collegiate sports leagues also pass through the stages of the PLC. For example, major league soccer (MLS) may be moving toward decline and is considering how to best extend its PLC. Many of the established leagues in the United States are going global and are currently in the introduction phase of their life cycles internationally. Therefore, the leagues have directed their marketing efforts toward making fans aware of and generating interest. For example, the Chinese market is attracting a lot of attention by major sports leagues in the United States as the following spotlight illustrates.

On the collegiate side, Tulsa University (TU) has gone from decline to their current (re)growth phase. After suffering through two terrible seasons that netted only two victories, the Golden Hurricane posted an eight-win season in 2003. That seven-game turnaround was the nations best and Tulsa has won its most games in a season since 1991. New coach Steve Kragthorpe has been given much of the credit for the newfound success.

SPOTLIGHT ON INTERNATIONAL SPORTS MARKETING

China Newest Frontier for U.S. Pro Sports Leagues

Most of the major pro sports leagues in the United States are making China the centerpiece of their international marketing efforts, considering it the country with the most economic potential.

A year after Yao Ming mania hit both sides of the Pacific Ocean, the NBA is airing its games regularly to more than 310 million Chinese households—nearly three times the number of American homes with a television. The league plans to stage two exhibition games this fall in Beijing and Shangai between the Yao-led Houston Rockets and Sacramento Kings.

The NFL also soon will announce exhibition games for those cities in 2005 and 2007, and it will broadcast this season's Super Bowl to about the same number of Chinese households reached by the NBA.

Major League Baseball is working with the Chinese Baseball Association on a comprehensive, grass-roots efforts designed to increase play of its game.

In each instance, the efforts are supported by extensive local marketing, native-language Web sites and game broadcasts, and youth clinics designed to foster play of basketball, football, baseball, and other sports in China.

"There are great opportunities for pro sports in China. The growth over the next several years is going to be very, very significant," said Marc Ganis, a Chicago-based sports industry consultant who is working with the Chinese government to raise the country's profile among American sports and entertainment entities.

"China is embracing a more capitalist business model and has tremendous interest in all things American. The Olympics are obviously coming in 2008 [to Beijing]. That adds up to something very powerful for all those concerned."

The 1.3 billion residents of China long have been a tempting economic carrot not only for the major sports leagues in the United States but for all of American commerce.

GROWING FORCE

Though basketball, football, and baseball are all becoming increasingly popular in China, the NBA is the most active U.S. pro sports league in marketing to Chinese fans. A numerical look at China's affinity for the NBA and basketball:

1—Other country in the world that buys more Spalding basketballs than China—the United States.

2—Exhibition games to be played this fall in China by Sacramento and Houston of the NBA, the first contests in China in league history.

25—Is the ranking of Houston center Yao Ming in the *Sporting News'* annual list of the most powerful people in sports. He is tops among active athletes.

25—Percent of total traffic to NBA.com comes from Asia. China leads the way.

17—Years since the first NBA telecast in China.

200 million—Chinese males who play basketball. The participation figure is believed to be higher than any other sport in China.

314 million—Chinese households that can access NBA games on TV through China Central Television and 14 provincial stations.

Source: Eric Fisher, *The Washington Times* (January 20, 2004). Copyright © 2004 News World Communications, Inc. Reprinted with permission of The Washington Times.

Each level of sports product must receive careful consideration by sports marketers because of the strategic implications. Sometimes the interaction of athlete, team, and league PLCs can make strategic decisions even more challenging. Take the case of Yao Ming, center for the Houston Rockets in the NBA. The Rockets and the NBA could be seen in the maturity phase of the PLC, while Yao is in introduction. What about the case of A-Rod? A-Rod is a veteran of the league, but needs to be marketed as a new product for the Yankees. As complex as this seems, sports marketers must remember not to neglect any of these products. Decisions will be made about the perceived relevance of each of these types of products.

DIFFUSION OF INNOVATIONS

New sports and sports products, or **innovations,** are continually being introduced to consumers and pass through the various stages of the product life cycle as described in the previous section. Initially, the new sport and sports product are purchased or tried by a small number of individuals (roughly 2.5 percent of the marketplace). Then, more and more people begin to try the new product. Consider the "metal wood" in golf. When this innovation was first introduced in the late 1970s, only the boldest "pioneers" of golf were willing to adopt the new technology. Now, only a very small percentage of the golfing population does not carry metal woods in their bags.[22]

The rate at which new sports products spread throughout the marketplace is referred to as the "**diffusion of innovation.**"[23] The rate of acceptance of a sport innovation is influenced by three factors, which are shown in Figure 9.3. The first factor affecting the rate of diffusion is the characteristics of the new product. These characteristics, such as trialability, observability, perceived complexity, relative advantage, and compatability, are discussed earlier in the chapter in the context of new product factors. The interaction of these factors can accelerate or slow the rate of diffusion. Perceived newness, the second factor that influences the rate of diffusion, refers to the type of new product from the consumer's perspective (continuous, dynamically continuous, and discontinuous innovations). Typically, continuous innovations have a faster rate of acceptance as they require no behavioral change and little disruption for the adopter. The third factor is the nature of the communication network. The rate and way in which information is shared about a new sports product is critical to its success, as well as the speed of acceptance. Most marketers conceptualize the communications network for innovations as a two-step flow of information. In the first step, the initial consumers try a new product or opinion leaders are influenced by mass communication such as advertising, sales promotions, and the Internet. Then, in the second step, opinion leaders use word-of-mouth communication to provide information about the new product to the rest of the target market. Martin and Higgins believe this two-step flow of information is especially important to sports innovations, because "unlike typical consumer purchase decisions, which involve only the individual, recent studies

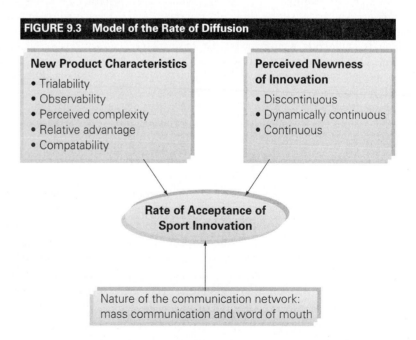

FIGURE 9.3 Model of the Rate of Diffusion

New Product Characteristics
- Trialability
- Observability
- Perceived complexity
- Relative advantage
- Compatability

Perceived Newness of Innovation
- Discontinuous
- Dynamically continuous
- Continuous

Rate of Acceptance of Sport Innovation

Nature of the communication network: mass communication and word of mouth show that of the consumers who attend sporting events, less than two percent attend by themselves."[24]

The diffusion of innovations is an important concept for sports marketers to understand because of the its strategic implications. Stated simply, the marketer must know the stage of the life cycle and the characteristics of the consumers likely to try the product at any given stage. Let us examine the characteristics of each group as a product spreads throughout the marketplace.

TYPES OF ADOPTERS

There are several **types of adopters. Innovators** represent those consumers who are the first to adopt a new sports product as it enters the marketplace. Because they are the first to adopt, these consumers carry the highest risk associated with the new product. These risks may either be social (what will others think of the product), economic (costs are high and drive up the price), and performance (will the product perform as it was intended). This younger and usually high-income group of consumers is also known for the high degree of interaction and communication they have with other innovators.

The next group of consumers to adopt a new sports product is the **early adopters.** As with the innovators, this group is also characterized by high social status. It is perhaps the most important group to sports marketers, however, because they carry high degrees of opinion leadership and word-of-mouth influence. As just discussed, these individuals are the key players in communicating the value of new sports products to the majority of consumers.

Once the new sports product has spread past the early stages of the product life cycle, the **early majority** is ready for adoption. This group is above average in social status but more deliberate in their willingness to try new products. In addition, this group is heavily influenced by information provided by the innovators and early adopters.

The late majority adopt innovations in the late stages of maturity of the product life cycle. As their name implies, over half (roughly 60 percent) the market has now purchased or tried the new product before the late majority decide to do so. These individuals are skeptical and have less exposure to mass media.

The final group of adopters is known as **laggards.** These individuals are oriented toward the past and tend to be very traditional in the sports products they choose. They begin to adopt products in the declining stage of the product life cycle. Clearly, prices must be reduced, and promotions encouraging trial and widespread distribution must all be in place for laggards to adopt new products.

Summary

Few sports products are critical to the success of any organization. Newness, however, can be thought of in any number of ways. The organizational perspective on newness depends on whether the firm has marketed the product in the past. From the organizational perspective, new products are categorized as follows: new-to-the-world products, new product category entries, product line extensions, product improvements, and repositionings.

Conversely, newness from the consumer's perspective is based on the consumer's perception of whether the product represents an innovation. From the consumer's perspective, new products are classified as discontinuous innovations, dynamically continuous innovations, or continuous innovations. Discontinuous innovations represent the most innovative new products, whereas continuous innovations are simply improvements or limitation products.

Regardless of how new products are classified, organizations are constantly searching for the next innovation that will help the firm achieve its financial objectives. Rather than leave this to chance, many organizations use a systematic approach called the new product development process. The new product development process consists of the following phases: idea generation, idea screening, analysis of the concept, developing the sports product, test marketing, and commercialization. Idea generation considers any and all ideas for new products from sources such as employees, competitors, and consumers. During the idea screening phase, these new product ideas are screened and the poorer ones are eliminated. To perform this task, organizations sometime use a new product screening checklist. In the third phase, analysis of the sports product concept, marketing research is used to assess consumer reaction to the proposed product. More specifically, concept tests are used to gauge the product's strengths and weaknesses, as well as the consumer's intent to use the new product. Next, a prototype of the new product is designed so that consumers can get an even better idea about the product. In addition, preliminary decisions regarding marketing strategy are established. In the sixth stage, the new product is test marketed. Depending on the product and the market conditions, sports marketers may use either standardized, controlled, or simulated test markets. The final stage of the new product development process is commercialization in which the new product is formally introduced in the marketplace. Whether the product succeeds is a function of a number of factors, such as the product considerations (e.g., trialability and relative advantage), other marketing mix variables (e.g., pricing), and marketing environment considerations (e.g., competition).

As a new product reaches commercialization, it moves through a series of four stages known as the product life cycle (PLC). The PLC is an important marketing concept in that the stage of the life cycle dictates marketing strategy. The four stages of the PLC include introduction, growth, maturity, and decline. At introduction, the marketing goal is to generate awareness of the new sports product. The broad goal of the growth phase is to build consumer preference for the sports product and begin to expand the product line. During maturity, the number of promotions is increased and marketers seek to maintain any competitive advantage

they have obtained during growth. Finally, the product goes through decline, where decisions must be made regarding whether to delete the product or extend the life cycle.

Although each product has a life cycle, the length of that life and the speed at which a product progresses through the four stages is unique for each product. Some sports products grow and decline at a rapid pace. These are known as fads. Other products, which seem to last in maturity forever, are called classics. The most common life cycle for sports products is known as seasonal. Other life cycle considerations are the level of product and the type of product. For example, sports marketers might analyze the life cycle of leagues, teams, and individual athletes, as well as other types of sports products.

The rate of diffusion is the speed at which new products spread throughout the marketplace. The rate of diffusion, or speed of acceptance, is based on three broad factors: new product characteristics (e.g., trialability and observability), perceived newness (e.g., discontinuous innovation), and the nature of the communications network. It is critical that sports marketers monitor the rate of diffusion and understand the characteristics of consumers that try new products as they spread throughout the marketplace.

Innovators are the first group of consumers to try a new product. They are generally younger, have higher incomes, and have a strong tolerance for risk. The next group of consumers to try a sports product are the early adopters. This is a larger group than the innovators and, as such, they are key consumers to target. After the product has passed through the initial stages of the product life cycle, the early majority adopt the product. This group is above average in income, but more deliberate in trying new things. The late majority adopt the product during the late stages of maturity and finally the laggards may try new products. Strategically, sports marketers must adopt a different marketing mix when marketing to each new product adopter group.

Key Terms

- classic
- commercialization
- continuous innovations
- decline
- developing the sports product
- diffusion of innovation
- discontinuous innovations
- dynamically continuous innovations
- early adopters
- early majority

- fad
- growth
- idea generation
- idea screening
- innovations
- innovators
- introduction
- laggards
- late majority
- maturity
- new product category entries

- new product development process
- new product success factors
- new sports products
- new-to-the-world sports product
- product form
- product life cycle
- seasonal
- test marketing
- types of adopters

Review Questions

1. What is meant by a "new sports product?" Describe a "new sports product" from the organization's perspective and from the consumer's perspective.
2. What is the difference between discontinuous, dynamically continuous, and continuous innovations? Provide examples of each to support your answer.

3. Describe, in detail, the new product development process.
4. Why is test marketing so important to sports marketers in the new product development process? What are the three types of test markets? Comment on the advantages and disadvantages of each type of test market.
5. What are the critical success factors for new sports products?
6. Describe the product life cycle concept. Why is the product life cycle so critical to sports marketers? What is it used for? How can the product life cycle be extended?
7. What are some of the variations in the shape of the traditional product life cycle?
8. Define the diffusion of innovations. What are the different types of adopters for innovations? Describe the characteristics of each type of adopter.

Exercises

1. For each of the following sports products, indicate whether you believe they are discontinuous, dynamically continuous, or continuous innovations: WNBA, titanium golf clubs, and skysurfing.
2. Contact the marketing department of three sporting goods manufacturers or sports organizations and conduct a brief interview regarding the new product development process. Does each organization follow the same procedures? Does each organization follow the new product development process discussed in the chapter?
3. In what stage of the product life cycle is Major League Baseball? Support your answer with research.
4. Find an example of a "new sports product." Develop a survey using the critical success factors for new sports products and ask 10 consumers to complete the instrument. Summarize your findings and indicate whether you think the new product will be successful based on your research.
5. Some people think boxing may be in the decline phase of the product life cycle. Develop a strategy to extend the product life cycle of boxing.

Internet Exercises

1. Search the Internet and find examples of three "new sports products" recently introduced in the marketplace.
2. Find three Internet sites of professional athletes in any sport. In what stage of the product life cycle are these athletes? Support with evidence found on the Internet.
3. Search the Internet for an example of a new sports product that could be classified as a fad. Describe the product and why you think the product is a fad.

Endnotes

1. William Zikmund and Michael d'Amico, *Marketing*, 4th ed. (St. Paul: West, 1993).
2. "Raley Field Pioneers the First Wireless Ballpark; Stadium Launches WiFi—Wireless Technology—Application Throughout Ballpark to Better Serve Fans," *Business Wire* (September 3, 2003).
3. New Balance Makes Team Move With Purchase of Warrior Lacrosse, http://www.sgdealer.com/sportinggoodsdealer/ headlines/ (February 3, 2004).
4. The Hockey Company Holdings, Inc. Announces Acquisition of Lifestyle Apparel Company—Roger Edwards Sport Ltd. *Business Wire* (August 21, 2003).
5. Mark Glover, "Taking the Cue—New Billiard Parlors Cater to Family Crowds and Aren't Shy About Giving Hustlers the Heave," *The Sacramento Bee* (January 15, 1996), El. "Billiards Growing as a Participant Sport." www.sportlink.com/individual . . . ng/96billpartstudy/96billpart.html (May 1997).
6. "Charles Laurence The Bronx is bowled over by a new ball game," *Sunday Telegraph* (November 16, 2003).
7. Rob Nixon, "As American as Cricket," *Atlantic Monthly* (July 2000), 79–81.
8. Del Hawkins, Roger Best, and Kenneth Coney, *Consumer Behavior: Building Marketing Strategy*, 7th ed. (New York: McGraw-Hill, 1998), 248–250.
9. James J. Zhang, Dennis W. Smith, Dale G. Pease, and Matthew T. Mahar, "Spectator Knowledge of Hockey as a Significant Predictor of Game Attendance," *Sport Marketing Quarterly*, vol. 5, no. 3 (1996), 41–48.
10. "VTV to Offer High School Football to a National Audience for the First Time Ever," *Business Wire* (September 11, 2003).

11. Steve Makris, "Sports cards business takes to the Internet," *The Leader-Post* (July 26, 2003).

12. Susan Higgins and James Martin, "Managing Sport Innovations: A Diffusion Theory Perspective." *Sport Marketing Quarterly*, vol. 5, no. 1 (1996), 43–50.

13. Bill Richards, "Nike Plans To Swoosh into Sports Equipment But It's a Tough Game," *The Wall Street Journal* (January 6,1998), Al.

14. Gilbert Churchill, *Basic Marketing Research*, 3rd ed. (Forth Worth: Dryden Press, 1996).

15. R. Burton and D. Howard, "Professional Sports Leagues: Marketing Mix Mayhem," *Marketing Management*, vol. 8, no. 1 (1999), 37.

16. Dan Hansen, "Personal watercraft sales take nose dive. Popularity wave crests for variety of factors, but industry promises rebound," *Spokesman Review*, (June 17, 2003).

17. Collegiate Hockey for Women a Growing Sport, www.sportsbusinessnews.com (January 6, 2004).

18. Stephen Dabkowski, "Asian Broadcasts to Chart a New Direction and Dollars for NBL," *The Age* (January 17, 2004).

19. Jason Hidalgo "Fitness fads: The mind-body approach transports itself to a gym near you," *Reno Gazette-Journal* (October 24, 2000).

20. David Hidgon, "Trim the Season to Grow the Game," *Tennis* (November 1996), 22.

21. Rhiannon Potkey "'Action' sports a growth industry," *Scripps Howard News Service* (August 13, 2003).

22. James P. Sterba, "Your Golf Shots Fall Short? You Didn't Spend Enough," *The Wall Street Journal* (February 23, 1996), B7.

23. Everett Rogers, *Diffusion of Innovations*, 3rd ed. (New York: Free Press, 1983).

24. B. J. Mullin, S. Hardy, and William Sutton, *Sports Marketing* (Champaign, IL: Human Kinetics Publishers, 1993).

CHAPTER 10

PROMOTION CONCEPTS

After completing this chapter, you should be able to:

- Identify the promotion mix tools.
- Describe the elements of the communication process.
- Understand the promotion planning model.
- Compare the advantages and disadvantages of the various promotional mix tools.
- Understand the importance of integrated marketing communication to sports marketers.

Just ask anyone the first thing that comes to mind when they think of sports marketing, and they are likely to say, "Tiger Woods' American Express advertisements" or "Michael Jordan's classic Nike ads." As we have discussed, sports marketing is much more than advertisements using star athlete endorsers. It involves developing a sound product or service, pricing it correctly, and making sure it is available to consumers when and where they ask for it. However, the necessary element that links the other marketing mix variables together is promotion.

Typically, promotion and advertising are used synonymously. **Promotion,** however, includes much more than traditional forms of advertising. It involves all forms of communication to consumers. For many organizations, sports are quickly becoming the most effective and efficient way to communicate with current and potential target markets. The combination of tools available to sports marketers to communicate with the public is known as the promotional mix and consists of the following **promotion mix elements:**

- *Advertising*—a form of one-way mass communication about a product, service, or idea, paid for by an identified sponsor.
- *Personal Selling*—an interactive form of interpersonal communication designed to build customer relationships and produce sales or sports products, services, or ideas.
- *Sales Promotion*—short-term incentives usually designed to stimulate immediate demand for sports products or services.
- *Public or Community Relations*—evaluation of public attitudes, identification of areas within the organization in which the sports population may be interested, and building of a good "image" in the community.
- *Sponsorship*—investing in a sports entity (athlete, league, team, event, and so on) to support overall organizational objectives, marketing goals, and more specific promotional objectives.

Within each of the promotion mix elements are more specialized tools to aid in reaching promotional objectives. For example, sales promotions can take the form of sweepstakes, rebates, coupons, or free samples. Advertising can take place on television, in print, or as stadium signage. Sponsors might chose to communicate through an athlete, team, or league. Each of these promotional tools is a viable alternative when considering the most effective promotion mix for a sports organization. Regardless of which tool we choose, the common thread in each element of the promotion mix is communication. Because communication is such an integral part of promotion, let us take a more detailed look at the communications process.

COMMUNICATIONS PROCESS

The communications process is an essential element for all aspects of sports marketing. **Communication** is the process of establishing a commonness of thought between the sender and the receiver. To establish this "oneness" between the sender and the receiver, the sports marketer's message must be transmitted via the complex communications process.

The interactive nature of the communications process allows messages to be transmitted from sports marketer (source) to consumer (receiver) and from consumer (source) to sports marketer (receiver). Traditionally, sports marketers' primary means of communication to consumers has been through the various promotion mix

SPORTS MARKETING HALL OF FAME

Bill Veeck

Known as the Promotion King of Baseball, Bill Veeck single-handedly changed the course of sports marketing. Veeck pioneered promotional events that today have become commonplace. For instance, Veeck initiated Ladies Night and Straight-A Night at the ballpark. One of Veeck's most memorable promotions took place on August 19, 1951, when a pinch-hitter was announced in the bottom half of the first inning in a game between the St. Louis Browns and the Detroit Tigers. Over the furious objections of the Detroit manager, Red Rolfe, the batter was declared a legitimate member of the Browns. Bill Veeck, then owner of the Browns, cautioned his pinch-hitter before he left the dugout that "I've got a man in the stands with a high-powered rifle, and if you swing he'll fire."

What was the fuss? Veeck sent in a 3 foot 7 inch midget named Eddie Gaedel to pinch-hit for the Browns. Gaedel was promptly walked on four straight pitches and removed from the game for a pinch-runner.

Gaedel was quoted as saying, "For a minute, I felt like Babe Ruth."

For all his successful promotions, Veeck is also remembered for one that turned sour in the mid-1970s. Called "Disco Demolition Night," the idea of the promotion was for fans to bring their disco albums to the ballpark to be burned in a bonfire. Unfortunately, fans stormed the field, a riot ensued, and the White Sox were forced to forfeit the second game of a doubleheader.

Veeck also instituted a promotion where fans were given signs with "yes" and "no" on them and asked to vote on strategy during a game. The "Grandstand Managers" led the Browns to a 5-3 victory. Promotions such as this led Veeck to be known as a true "fan's fan." He once stated that "every day was Mardi Gras and every fan was king," and "the most beautiful thing in the world is a ballpark filled with people." His marketing and fan orientation forged the way for later marketers of all sports.

Source: Adapted from Bill Veeck, Veeck as in Wreck: Autobiography of Bill Veeck (New York: Simon and Schuster, 1962).

elements (e.g., advertisements, sponsorships, sales promotions, and salespeople). Sports marketers also communicate with consumers via other elements of the marketing mix. For example, the high price of a NASCAR ticket communicates that it is a higher quality event than the more inexpensive Busch Series.

In addition to sports marketers communicating with consumers, consumers communicate back to sports marketers through their behavior. Most notably, consumers communicate whether they are satisfied with the sports product by their purchase behavior. In other words, they attend sporting events and purchase sporting goods.

The communications process begins with the source or the sender of the message. The source encodes the message and sends it through one of many potential communications media. Next, the message is decoded by the receiver of the message and, finally feedback, is given to the original source of the message. In the ideal world, messages are sent and interpreted exactly as intended. This, however, rarely occurs because of noise and interference.

Figure 10.1 shows a simplified diagram of the communications process. Each box in the figure represents one of the **elements in the communications process.** These elements include the sender, encoding, message, medium, decoding, receiver, feedback, and noise. To maximize communication effectiveness, it is necessary to have a better understanding of each of these elements in the communications process.

SOURCE

The sender or **source** of the message is where the communication process always originates. In sports marketing, the source of messages is usually a star athlete. For example, you might think of Mia Hamm shampooing with Pert Plus or Arnold Palmer delivering a message of behalf of Pennzoil. In a recent survey of ad agency and corporate marketing execs conducted by Burns Sports Celebrity Service, Inc., the following athletes were found to be the century's top pitchpeople.

Century's Top Product Endorsers from Sports	
1. Michael Jordan	6. Bruce Jenner
2. Tiger Woods	7. Jeff Gordon
3. Arnold Palmer	8. Jack Nicklaus
4. Muhammad Ali	9. Bo Jackson
5. Babe Ruth	10. Mia Hamm

Interestingly, Tiger and Michael topped the list of athletes to watch as spokespeople in the next century. This list also included Peyton Manning, Ken Griffey Jr., and Jeff Gordon.

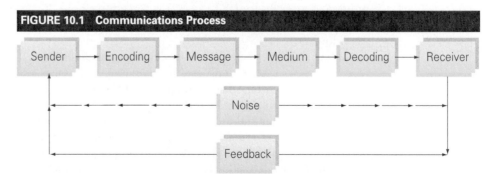

FIGURE 10.1   Communications Process

Source: Michael Solomon, *Consumer Behavior*, 3rd ed. (Upper Saddle River, NJ: Prentice Hall, 1996).

Although these sources are all individual athletes, there are many other sources of sports marketing messages. The source of a message might also be a group of athletes, a team, or even the league or sports. Additional sources of sports marketing messages are company spokespeople such as John Soldheim, the chairman of Ping golf equipment, or owners such as Mark Cuban of the Dallas Mavericks.

Sources do not always have to be well recognized and famous individuals to be effective. Sports marketers use actors playing the role of common, everyday sports participants to deliver their message from the perspective of the representative consumer of the sports product or service. Other effective sources are inanimate objects, such as the "furry Frank," the talking headcover for Tiger Woods and Nike, or the classic Little Penny featured in the Nike advertisements with Anfernee "Penny" Hardaway. In addition, sports marketers rely on sales personnel to convey the intended message to consumers. Informal sources, such as friends, family, and coworkers, are also sources of marketing information and messages. As we learned in Chapters 5 and 6, reference groups play an important role in influencing purchase behavior and transmitting the marketing message.

Whatever the source, it is agreed by researchers that to be effective, the source must be credible. **Credibility** is the source's perceived expertise and trustworthiness. A very persuasive message can be created when a combination of these two factors (expertise and trustworthiness) is present in the source. For a source to be trustworthy, that person must be objective and unbiased. Certain athlete endorsers, such as Arnold Palmer, former coach Mike Ditka, and Michael Jordan, are known for their perceived trustworthiness. We sometimes look to friends and family as information sources because of their objectivity. In fact, word-of-mouth communication is believed to be extremely persuasive because the source of the message has nothing to gain from delivering the message. Additional unbiased sources are those "man-on-the-street" testimonies given by the common consumer. For example, many of us have seen infomercials that use "regular people" to describe how they lost weight or became physically fit by using the latest and greatest fitness equipment.

Source credibility is also enhanced when the sender of the message has perceived expertise. Naturally, an athlete such as Grant Hill is believed to deliver expert messages when the product being promoted is related to athletics, or more specifically, basketball. At least this is what Fila is counting on.

In September of 1997, Hill signed an $80 million deal over seven years with Fila.[1] Hill has been picked for the NBA All-Star team every year in the league and was a member of the gold medal-winning 1996 and 2000 Olympic teams. These basketball credentials should help Fila sell the shoe that bears Grant Hill's name. In fact, Fila was hoping Hill will help build brand equity not only in the United States, but also all over the world. Unfortunately, Hill has suffered from an extensive ankle injury and after his fourth surgery was forced to sit out the entire 2003–2004 season. Injury is just one of the risks that corporations like Fila face when using athletes as endorsers.

Other examples of athletes who endorse products related to their sport include race car drivers such as Jeff Gordon promoting Chevrolet and tennis players such as Jennifer Capriati promoting Prince tennis equipment. The general rule of thumb is that the message is more effective if there is a match-up, or congruence, between the qualities of the endorser and the product being endorsed. In fact, the **match-up hypothesis** states the more congruent the image of the endorser with the image of the product being promoted, the more effective the message.[2]

If the match-up hypothesis holds true, then why do companies pay millions of dollars to star athletes to promote their nonathletic products? For example, All-Star first

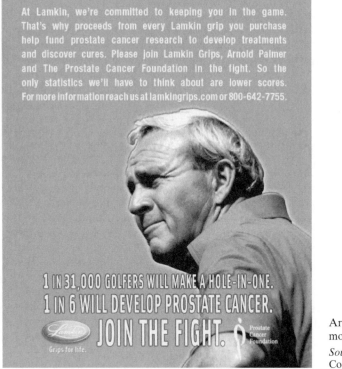

At Lamkin, we're committed to keeping you in the game. That's why proceeds from every Lamkin grip you purchase help fund prostate cancer research to develop treatments and discover cures. Please join Lamkin Grips, Arnold Palmer and The Prostate Cancer Foundation in the fight. So the only statistics we'll have to think about are lower scores. For more information reach us at lamkingrips.com or 800-642-7755.

1 IN 31,000 GOLFERS WILL MAKE A HOLE-IN-ONE.
1 IN 6 WILL DEVELOP PROSTATE CANCER.
JOIN THE FIGHT.

Arnold Palmer: One of the most credible endorsers ever.

Source: Copyright © 2004 Lamkin Corporation. All rights reserved.

baseman Rafael Palmeiro is a pitchman for Viagra, coach Dan Reeves promotes the drug Zocor, and golfer Phil Mickelson is an endorser for Ford Motor Co. First, consumers have an easier time identifying brands associated with celebrity athletes. Second, athletes are used to differentiate competing products that are similar in nature. For instance, most consumers know and associate Jeff Gordon with Pepsi. Gordon's association helps to create and then maintain the desired image of Pepsi, which in turn differentiates it from Coke.

ENCODING

After the source is chosen, encoding take place. **Encoding** is translating the sender's thoughts or ideas into a message. To ensure effective encoding, the source of the message must make difficult decisions about the message content. Will the receiver understand and comprehend the message as intended? Will the receiver identify with the message?

Consider for a moment, the slogan "We Got Next" first used to introduce the WNBA. The language of this message may be up to date and "cool," but it may also be misunderstood or misinterpreted by a large portion of the potential target audience. Likewise, even if the slogan is understood, it may be outdated quickly and seem "unhip" to the receivers of the message.[3]

Sources have a variety of tools which they use to encode messages. They can use pictures, logos, words, and other symbols. Symbols and pictures are often used in sports marketing to convey the emotional imagery that words cannot capture. The most effective encoding uses multiple media to get the message across (i.e., visually and verbally); presents information in a clear, organized fashion; and always keeps the receiver in mind.[4]

SPOTLIGHT ON SPORTS MARKETING ETHICS

Bryant Makes Case Against Idolizing Jocks

We're supposed to be shocked by Kobe Bryant's behavior, just as we were supposed to be shocked by Michael Jordan's behavior, just as we were supposed to be shocked by the behavior of (your favorite athlete here). When players' statistics include career points, rebounds, and DNA swabs, shock seems a little out of place. You say you're not shocked, just disappointed in Bryant? I have a sports survival tip for you. It's impossible to be disappointed when you have no expectations of good behavior in the first place.

When Bryant, the former Mr. Clean, sits at a news conference and says he is guilty of adultery, but not sexual assault, it should tell us something once and for all: Never trust another happy word about athletes' happy marriages. Kobe was different, we were told. Mature beyond his years. Married to the love of his life. Didn't run with the pack. A homebody. But then he wanted a few things not found on the room-service menu, had relations with a 19-year-old hotel worker who visited him while he was staying near Vail, CO, and now finds himself in trouble.

If you looked at Bryant before the recent scandal and sighed, "The perfect guy with the perfect life," you need to get yourself to a reeducation camp as soon as possible. And if you look at Jordan and still want to be like Mike, then you desperately need to bundle up in a coat of cynicism. To begin with, if people are looking to Bryant for direction in their lives, there's something very wrong with them. And if they're allowing their children to learn about life through Bryant, they have dumped their parental responsibilities on somebody's doorstep and taken off, wheels squealing. Of course, these are the same people who will give Bryant a standing ovation in his first game back with the Lakers.

There is one line of thinking that says the NBA is in big trouble if Bryant is convicted of sexual assault. But that thinking assumes we looked at Bryant any differently than we did any other pro athlete. I'd like to believe most of us, hardened by years of bad behavior by our athletes, have learned to watch the games and be skeptical of the lives of the people who play them. It's sort of like watching Sean Penn in a movie.

My interest in the NBA had nothing to do with the personalities involved, so I won't watch any more or less now that Bryant has fallen. I don't see Tim Duncan throw in a jump hook over a defender and think, "What a wonderful human being. You know, I really need to pattern my life after his." And I tell my kids to look at the players straight on and not with adoration. Drop your jaw at Allen Iverson's crossover dribble and roll your eyes at his fondness for handguns. Don't rely on anything more from Bryant than his dunks.

It's interesting, and hardly surprising, that one part of the Bryant saga is the effect of the criminal charges on his marketability. Put aside, for a second, how demeaning that topic is to all involved: to the alleged victim, to Bryant's wife, to Bryant's family, even to Bryant. But it does get at the essence of what Bryant is: a commodity, a package, a highly stylized product. And what his handlers have been trying to sell us since he came into the NBA is class, the same currency others have used to sell Jordan. Bryant was the anti-Iverson. In other words, he was supposed to feel safer to white people.

And in one of the more sick twists to a sick story, there are those who believe Bryant's legal troubles will give him more credibility among young African Americans with dollars to spend on basketball shoes and jerseys. What an insult to blacks.

Several years back I wrote a profile of a pro football player, quoting his wife as saying he had found Jesus. Apparently Jesus can be found in a strip club because a few days after the story ran, a friend of mine saw the player stuffing money into G-strings. If you allow yourself to believe in these people, there's a decent chance you're eventually going to feel like a sucker. If you marry one, there's a decent chance you're going to end up a rich sucker. Is it worth the betrayal?

Source: Rick Morrissey, Bryant Makes Case Against Idolizing Jocks, *Chicago Tribune* (July 19, 2003). Copyright © 2004. Used by permission. All rights reserved.

MESSAGE

The next element in the communications process is to develop the **message,** which refers to the exact content of the words and symbols to be transmitted to the receiver. Decisions regarding the characteristics of this message depend on the objective of the promotion, but sports marketers have a wide array of choices. These choices include one- versus two-sided messages, emotional versus rational messages, and comparative versus noncomparative messages.

The **sidedness** of a message is based on the nature of the information presented to the target audience. The messages can be constructed as either one- or two-sided. In a one-sided message, only the positive features of the sports product are described, whereas a two-sided message includes both the benefits and weaknesses of the product.

Another decision regarding the message in the promotion is whether to have an **emotional versus rational appeal.** A rational appeal provides the consumer with information about the sports product so they may arrive at a careful, analytical decision, and an emotional appeal attempts to make the consumer "feel" a certain way about the sports product. Emotional appeals might include fear, sex, humor, or feelings related to the hard work and competitive nature of sport.

A final message characteristic that may be considered by sports marketers is **comparative messages.** Comparative messages refer to either directly or indirectly comparing your sports product with one or more competitive products in a promotional message. For example, golf ball manufacturers often compare the advantages of their product with competitors' products.

Regardless of the **message characteristics,** the broad objective of promotion is to effectively communicate with consumers. What are some ways to make your sports marketing message more memorable and persuasive? Table 10.1 summarizes a few simple techniques to consider.

MEDIUM

After the message has been formulated, it must be transmitted to receivers through a channel, or communications **medium.** A voice in personal selling, television, radio, stadium signage, billboards, blimps, newspapers, magazines, athletes' uniforms, and even athlete's bodies all serve as media for sports marketing communication. In addition to these more traditional media, new communications channels such as the Internet and the multitude of sports-specific cable programming (e.g., the Golf Channel) are emerging and growing in popularity.

TABLE 10.1 Creating a More Effective Message

- Get the audience aroused.
- Give the audience a reason for listening.
- Use questions to generate involvement.
- Cast the message in terms familiar to your audience and build on points of interest.
- Use thematic organization—tie material together by a theme and present in a logical, irreversible sequence.
- Use subordinate category words—that is, more concrete, specific terms.
- Repeat key points.
- Use rhythm and rhyme.
- Use concrete rather than abstract terms.
- Leave the audience with an incomplete message—something to ponder so they have to make an effort at closure.
- Ask your audience for a conclusion.
- Tell the audience the implications of their conclusion.

Source: James MacLachlan, "Making a Message Memorable and Persuasive," *Journal of Advertising Research*, vol. 23 (December 1983–January 1984), 51–59.

TABLE 10.2 Making Media Decisions

- Cost to reach target audience
- Flexibility of media
- Ability to reach highly specialized, defined audience
- Lifespan of the media
- Nature of the sports product being promoted (e.g., complexity of product)
- Characteristics of the intended target market

Decisions on which medium or media to choose depend largely on the overall promotional objectives. Also, the media decisions must consider the costs to reach the desired target audience, its flexibility, its ability to reach a highly defined audience, its lifespan, the sports product or service complexity, and the characteristics of the intended target market. These media considerations are summarized in Table 10.2. For example, sports marketers attempting to reach the mature market may choose television as a communications medium because the elderly watch 60 percent more television than average households. In addition, the mature market watches more baseball, golf, and bowling than the average household.[5]

DECODING

The medium carries the message to the receiver, which is where decoding takes place. **Decoding,** performed by the receiver, is the interpretation of the message sent by the source through the channel. Once again, the goal of communication is to establish a common link between sender and receiver. This can only happen if the message is received and interpreted correctly. Even if the message is received by the desired target audience, it may be interpreted differently because of the receiver's personal characteristics and past experience. In addition, the more complex the original message, the less likely it is to be successfully interpreted or decoded. As the following article "I Got Game" illustrates, decoding a message is not always an easy task.

RECEIVER

The **receiver,** or the audience, is the object of the source's message. Usually, the receiver is the sports marketer's well-defined, target audience. However, and as previously mentioned, the receiver's personal characteristics play an important role in whether the message is correctly decoded. For example, the consumer's demographic profile (e.g., age, marital status, and gender), psychographic profile (e.g., personality, lifestyle, and values), and even where they live (geographic region) may all affect the interpretation and comprehension of the sports marketing message.

FEEDBACK

To determine whether the message has been received and comprehended, feedback is necessary. **Feedback** is defined as the response a target audience makes to a message. The importance of feedback as an element of the communication process cannot be overlooked. Without feedback, communication would be a one-way street, and the sender of the message would have no means of determining whether the original message should remain unchanged, be modified, or abandoned altogether.

I Got Game

"I have a fantasy," I say. "I live in Three-Pointland. I live out beyond the arc. I launch from Three-Pointland. From Downtown, Way Downtown. From another area code. From another zip code. Nothing but net."

"Uh-oh," she says.

"I shoot the trey," I say. "I handle the rock. Protect it with my life, of course. I dish. I think of myself mostly as a number 1, but I could play the 2 in a pinch. The big thing is the trey. The trifecta. I lock and load, square to the basket. I get a good look. I launch!"

"College basketball, right?" she says. "I should have known. The leaves are gone. The days are getting colder. You're going into that hibernation thing again. You and the television. College basketball."

"It's not that I'm afraid to take the rock to the rack," I say. "I'll do that. I'll go into the paint, down the lane, set up on the blocks, clean the glass, rattle the tin, grab the orange, but my strength really isn't putbacks and slams. I'm a Three-Pointland sort of guy."

"I can never get it straight," she says. "Are those all separate games you watch from now until the end of March, or is it just one long, four-month production?"

"On defense, I'm in my man's face, in his shirt," I say, "I take the charge. I give the foul. I trap. I jump switch. I help out."

"I think it is just one long game," she says. "The uniforms change, and sometimes the lighting is different from different arenas and gyms, but the horn is always sounding—honk—and the same referees are blowing their whistles, and, for sure, the same two annoying voices are describing the action in their hyped-up, cliché-filled way. Is it a rule that college basketball broadcasters can never read a book about anything except college basketball, that they can have no knowledge except about college basketball? Or am I being a little harsh?"

"I know there will be potholes and strange twists and turns on the road to the Final Four, but I am ready for that," I say. "I'm not afraid to take control. I'll throw up the tough shot, the buzzer-beater, and it'll be good if it goes. Do you know what I mean? I will work the clock and hope to get the call. If need be, I'll launch a prayer."

"The thing that bothers me most about this college basketball is the overemphasis," she says. "Do any of these kids ever go to school? One night they're playing in Hawaii, and the next night they're in Alaska. Doesn't that make it a little hard to go to the library? Some of these teams are on television more than Oprah and Ricki Lake and Alex Trebek combined. I think Georgetown played Villanova a hundred times last year. At least it seemed that way. Bobby Knight and that red sweater could be part of the wallpaper. Is that the only sweater he owns?"

"I'm not afraid to go to the floor," I say. "I'm not afraid to set a pick. Give and go. Double-down. Shake and bake. Work without the ball. Run the break. Jumpstart the offense. I'll get free with my drop step down low, my crossover dribble up high. I'll always be aware of the principle of verticality and will never put my hand in the cylinder except when I'm slamming the rock home to deliver a message."

"Is there one kid in all of college basketball who is pre-med?" she asks. "Is there one electrical engineer in the making? One English professor? I suppose there must be a couple, somewhere. The whole thing seems perverted to me. Kids from the West Coast go all the way to the East Coast to go to college. State universities fall all over each other to get tall kids from Nigeria and Serbia and Finland to go to their schools. Where's the sense in all this?"

"I'll box out. I'll put a body on people! I won't give up the baseline, but I'll hit the front end of the one-and-one, and I'll look for the cutters and the mismatches. I'll feed the hot hand, and I'll ice the shooter. I'll take off from the foul line. I'll alley and I'll oop."

"It just seems a little silly to me," she says. "The recruiting, the scandals, the money. All of this commotion . . ."

"Three-Pointland!" I say.

"It seems like so much . . ."

"Beyond the arc!"

". . . gibberish."

(Pause for a program note: ESPN will televise 194 college basketball games this season. ESPN2 will televise 87. Sports Channel will televise 58. CBS will televise 50. ABC will televise 31. NBC will televise six. ESPN and ESPN2 will televise 22 women's games. These numbers do not count the telecasts of either the men's or the women's NCAA tournaments.)

"All I know is that it's a new season," I say, "and I'm taking my game to the next level."

"Just make sure you close the door behind you," she says.

There are several ways for the consumer or target audience to deliver feedback to the source of the message. The target market might provide feedback in the form of a purchase. In other words, if consumers are buying tickets, sporting goods, or other sports products, then the sports marketers message must be effective. Likewise, if consumers are not willing to purchase the sports product, then feedback is also being provided to the source. Unfortunately, the feedback in this case is that the message is either not being received or being incorrectly interpreted.

When using personal communication media, such as personal selling, feedback is received instantly by verbal and nonverbal means. Consumers will respond favorably by nodding their head in approval, acting interested, or asking intelligent questions. In the case of disinterest or inattention, the source of the message should make adjustments and change the message as it is being delivered to address any perceived problems.

Another common form of feedback comes through changes in attitude about the object of the message. In other words, the consumer's attitude shifts toward a more favorable belief or feeling about the sports product, athlete, team, or sport itself. Generally, the more positive the attitude toward the message, the more positive the consumer's attitude toward the sports product. This should, in turn, lead to increases in future purchases. One of the many uses of marketing research is to gather feedback from consumers and use this feedback to create or redesign the strategic sports marketing process. The control phase of the strategic marketing process is dedicated to evaluating feedback from consumers and making adjustment to achieve marketing objectives.

Thus far, we have only examined feedback in one direction—from consumer of the product to producer of the product. However, feedback is an interactive process. That is, consumers also receive feedback from the sports organization. Organizations let consumers know they are listening to the "voice of the consumer" by reintroducing new and improved versions of sports products, changing the composition of teams and their coaches, adjusting prices, and even varying their promotional messages. For instance, the The Portland Pirates of the American Hockey League reduced ticket prices on nearly 4,000 seats from $11 to $6. The new plan is derived from results of a month-long marketing study that identified ticket pricing as the most critical factor affecting a fan's decision to attend a game.[6]

NOISE

The final element in the communication process is noise. Unfortunately, there is no such thing as perfect communication because of **noise,** or interference, in the communications process. This interference may occur at any point along the channel of communication. For example, the source may be ineffective, the message may be sent through the wrong medium, or there may be too many competing messages, each "fighting" for the limited information-processing capacity of consumers.

When communicating through stadium signage, the obvious source of noise is the game itself. Noise can even be present in the form of ambush marketing techniques, where organizations attempt to confuse consumers and make them believe they are officially affiliated with a sporting event when they are not. An excellent example of how noise can affect the communication process is found in ambush marketing, which will be explored in Chapter 12.

Sports marketers must realize that noise will always be present in the communications process. By gaining a better understanding of the communications process, factors contributing to noise can be examined and eliminated to a large extent.

PROMOTION PLANNING

Armed with a working knowledge of the communications process, the sports marketer is now ready to design an effective promotion plan. Not unlike the strategic marketing process, promotional plans come in all shapes and sizes but all share several common elements. Our **promotional planning** document consists of four basic steps: (1) target market consideration, (2) setting promotional objectives, (3) determining the promotional budget, and (4) developing the promotional mix.

TARGET MARKET CONSIDERATIONS

Promotional planning is not done in isolation. Instead, plans must rely heavily on the objectives formulated in the strategic sports marketing process. The first step to promotional planning is identifying **target market considerations.** During the planning phase, target markets have been identified, and promotion planning should reflect these previous decisions. Promotional planning depends largely on who is identified as the primary target audience. One promotional strategy is based on reaching the ultimate consumer of the sports product and is known as a pull strategy. The other strategy identifies channel members as the most important target audience. This strategic direction is termed a push strategy. These two basic strategies are dependent on the chosen target of the promotional efforts and guide subsequent planning. Let us explore the push and pull strategies in greater detail.

PUSH STRATEGY

A **push strategy** is so named because of the emphasis on having channel intermediaries "push" the sports product through the channel of distribution to the final consumer. If a push strategy is used, intermediaries such as a *manufacturer* might direct initial promotional efforts at a *wholesaler* who then promotes the sports product to the retailer. In turn, the *retailers* promote the sports product to the final user. When using a push strategy, you are literally loading goods into the distribution pipeline. The objective is to get as much product as possible into the warehouse or store. Push strategies generally ignore the consumer. A variety of promotion mix elements are still used with a push strategy, although personal selling is more prevalent when promoting to channel members closer to the manufacturer (i.e., wholesalers) than the end users.

PULL STRATEGY

The target audience for a **pull strategy** is not channel intermediaries but the ultimate consumer. The broad objective of this type of promotional strategy is to stimulate demand for the sports product. So much demand, in fact, that the channel members, such as retailers, are forced to stock their shelves with the sports product. Because the end user, or ultimate consumer, is the desired target for a pull strategy, the promotion mix tends to emphasize advertising rather than personal selling. It is important to note that because sports marketing is based largely on promoting services rather than goods, pull strategies targeting the end user are more prevalent. In pull strategies, your objective is to get consumers to pull the merchandise off the shelf and out the door.

Although pull strategies are more common in sports marketing, the most effective promotion planning integrates both push and pull components. For example, marketing giant Procter and Gamble's (P&G) objective was to stimulate consumer demand for its Sunny Delight and Hawaiian Punch brands. To do so, P&G designed a promotion featuring UCLA basketball coach John Wooden and one of his star players, Bill Walton. The pull strategy offered consumers a Wooden and Walton autographed picture and coin set for $19.95 and proof-of-purchase. The push promotional strategy was directed at Sunny Delight and Hawaiian Punch distributors and retailers who carried the P&G brands. If the "trade" reached their performance goals during the promotion, they earned a framed picture of Walton and Wooden that was autographed and personalized for the distributor.

PROMOTIONAL OBJECTIVES

After target markets have been identified, the next step in the promotion planning process is to define the **promotional objectives.** Broadly, the three goals of promotion are to inform, persuade, and remind target audiences. Consumers must first be made aware of the product and how it might satisfy their needs. The goal of providing information to consumers is usually desired when products are in the introductory phase of the product life cycle (PLC). Once consumers are aware of the sports product, promotional goals then turn to persuasion and convincing the consumer to purchase the product. After initial purchase and satisfaction with a given product, the broad promotional goal is then to remind the consumer of the sports product's availability and perceived benefits.

Informing, persuading, and reminding consumers are the broad objectives of promotion, but the ultimate promotional objective is to induce action. These consumer actions might include volunteering to help with a local 10K race, donating money to the U.S. Olympic Team, purchasing a new pair of in-line skates, or just attending a sporting event they have never seen. Marketers believe promotions guide consumers through a series of steps to reach this ultimate objective—action. This series of steps is known as the hierarchy of effects (also sometimes called the hierarchy of communication effect).

THE HIERARCHY OF EFFECTS

The **hierarchy of effects** is a seven-step process by which consumers are ultimately led to action.[7] The seven steps include unawareness, awareness, knowledge, liking, preference, conviction, and action. As shown in Figure 10.2, consumers pass through each of these steps before taking action.

- *Unawareness*—During the first step, consumers are not even aware the sports product exists. Obviously, the promotional objective at this stage is to move consumers toward awareness.
- *Awareness*—The promotional objective at this early stage of the hierarchy is to make consumers in the desired target market aware of the new sports product. To reach this objective, a variety of promotional tools are used.

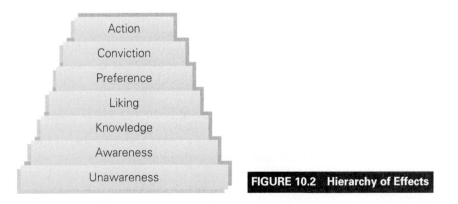

FIGURE 10.2 Hierarchy of Effects

- *Knowledge*—Once consumers are aware of the sports product, they need to gather information about its tangible and intangible benefits. The primary promotional objective at this stage is to provide consumers with the necessary product information. For instance, the NHL.com Web site has a link called "Learn to Play," which is designed to give youth players tips on how to play the game. Another example of creating and enhancing knowledge is the proliferation of classes called Football 101 targeted toward women and novice fans. Football 101 primers have been held at the Super Bowl XXXVIII Fan Experience, The Ohio State University's homecoming week, and even been offered in Spanish to Oakland Raider fans. Teams and organizers hope that once the fans become more knowledgeable, they will then move to the next level of the hierarchy—liking.
- *Liking*—Having knowledge and information about a sports product does not necessarily mean the consumer will like it. Generating positive feelings and interest regarding the sports product is the next promotional objective on the hierarchy. The promotion itself cannot cause the consumer to like the product, but research has shown the linkage between attitude toward the promotion (e.g., advertisement) and attitude toward the product.[8] The objective is to create a feeling of goodwill toward the product via the promotion.
- *Preference*—After consumers begin to like the sports product, the objective is to develop preferences. As such, the sports marketer must differentiate their product from the competition through promotion. The sports product's differential advantage may be found in an enhanced image and tangible product features.
- *Conviction*—Moving up the hierarchy of effects, consumers must develop a conviction or intention to take action. Behavioral intention, however, does not guarantee action. Factors such as the consumer's economic condition (i.e., financial situation), changing needs, or availability of new alternatives may inhibit the action from ever taking place. The objective of the conviction step of the hierarchy of effects is to create a desire to act in the mind of the target audience.
- *Action*—The final stage of the hierarchy, and the ultimate objective of any promotion, is to have consumers act. As stated previously, actions may come in a variety of forms, but usually include purchase or attendance.

Theoretically, the hierarchy of effects model states that consumers must pass through each stage in the hierarchy before a decision is made regarding purchase (or other behaviors). Some marketers have argued this is not always the case. Consider, for instance, purchasing season tickets to a professional sport for business purposes. The purchaser does not have to like the sport or team to take action and buy the tickets. Regardless of what the hierarchy of effects proposes to do or not do, the fact remains that it is an excellent tool to use when developing promotional objectives. Knowing where the target audience is on the hierarchy is critical to formulating the proper objectives.

ESTABLISHING PROMOTIONAL BUDGETS

Total advertising spending in the United States was expected to climb to $266.4 billion, up 6.9 percent from the 2003 estimate.[9] In part, this growth has been attributed to a surge in spending for the 2004 summer Olympic games. In fact, NBC estimates that it will generate 1 billion dollars in revenue for Olympic advertisement spots. In fact, over the past several years TV ad expenditures have increased for most sports with tennis and NASCAR experiencing the greatest percentage increases in spending. The NFL is still king, however, with over 2 billion dollars being spent by companies in 2002 according to Nielsen Media Research. As you might have guessed, the companies that lead the way in ad spend for sports are beer and cars with Anheuser Busch, Chevrolet, and Ford at the top.[10]

Having greater knowledge of sports such as hockey, moves consumers through the hierarchy of effects.

In addition to companies spending huge dollars on sports advertising, teams and leagues are constantly promoting the sport. For instance, the NHL released the somewhat controversial "Get It" campaign, MLB is trying to capture fans with the "I Live For This" campaign, and the NBA is still using the classic "I Love This Game" promotion. In the case of the NHL, increases in advertising were needed to make potential fans more knowledgeable about and able to appreciate hockey. Major League Baseball wanted to stress the passion that their players have for the game and generate the same passion in their fans. In all cases, teams and leagues are advertising to keep up with the tremendous competitive threat of other entertainment choices for the fans.

In theory, the promotional budget of the NHL or the NBA would be determined based on the many objectives set forth by the leagues marketing strategy. In practice, **promotional budgeting** is an interactive and unscientific process by which the sports marketer determines the amount spent based on maximizing the monies available. Some of the ways promotional budgets may be established include arbitrary allocation, competitive parity, percentage of sales, and the objective and task method.

ARBITRARY ALLOCATION

The simplest, yet most unsystematic, approach to determining promotional budgets is called **arbitrary allocation.** Using this method, sports marketers set the budget in isolation of other critical factors. For example, the sports marketer disregards last year's promotional budget and its effectiveness, what competitors are doing, the economy, and current strategic objectives and budgets using some subjective method. The budget is usually determined by allocating all the money the organization can afford. In other words, promotional budgets are established after the organizations' other costs are considered. A sports organization that chooses this approach does not place much emphasis on promotional planning.

COMPETITIVE PARITY

Setting promotional budgets based on what competitors are spending (**competitive parity**) is often used for certain product categories in sports marketing. For example, the athletic shoe industry closely monitors what the competition is doing in the way of advertising efforts. adidas (annual budget of roughly $50 million), Reebok ($44 million), and K-Swiss ($15 million) must keep pace with Nike's (annual budget of roughly $150 million) promotional spending if they intend to increase market share.

One athletic shoe company that does not follow its competitors huge promotional spending is New Balance. The New Balance ad budget was $10 million in 2002, following a year that saw sales nearly double. In fact, New Balance's sales have grown from $221 million in 1992 to $1.3 billion in 2002, representing an average annual growth rate of over 25 percent during the past decade. Instead of using famous athletes, New Balance has paved its success by understanding its primary consumer, the 35- to 59-year-old baby boomer. Rather than paying celebrities to endorse its products, they prefer to invest in research, design, and domestic manufacturing. This unique positioning is illustrated on the New Balance Web page which states "N is for mileage, not for image" and ads that explain "N is for Fit."[11]

PERCENTAGE OF SALES

The **percentage of sales** method of promotional budget allocation is based on determining some standard percentage of promotional spending and applying this proportion to either past or forecasted sales to arrive at the amount to be spent. It is common for the percentage to be used on promotional spending to be derived from some industry standard. For example, the athletic shoe industry typically allocates 5 percent of sales to promotional spending. Therefore, if a new athletic shoe company enters the market and projects sales of $1 million, then they would allocate $50,000 to the promotional budget. Likewise, if Converse totaled $7 million in sales in the previous year, then it might budget $350,000 to next year's promotional budget.

Although the percentage of sales method of budgeting is simple to use, it has a number of shortcomings. First, if percentage of forecast sales is used to arrive at a promotional budget figure, then the sales projections must be made with a certain degree of precision and confidence. If historical sales figures (e.g., last year's) are used, then promotional spending may be either too high or too low. For example, if Converse has a poor year in sales, then the absolute promotional spending would be decreased. This, in turn, could cause sales to slide even further. With sales declining, it may be more appropriate to increase (rather than decrease) promotional spending. A second major shortcoming of using this method is the notion that budget is very loosely, if at all, tied to the promotional objectives.

OBJECTIVE AND TASK METHOD

If arbitrary allocation is the most illogical of the budgeting methods, then objective and task methods could be characterized as the most logical and systematic. The **objective and task method** identifies the promotional objectives, defines the communications tools and tasks needed to meet those objectives, and then adds up the costs of the planned activities.

Although the objective and task method seems the most reasonable, it also assumes the objectives have been determined correctly and the proper promotional mix has been formulated to reach those objectives. For instance, suppose the Vanderbilt University women's basketball team wanted to achieve an attendance increase of 15 percent from the previous season. To this end, the Director of Marketing for Athletics must develop a promotional mix that includes local advertising, related sales promotions, and public relations in an effort to reach all target audiences. Even if the attendance goal is achieved, it is difficult to determine whether the money required to achieve this objective was spent in the most efficient and effective fashion.

CHOOSING AN INTEGRATED PROMOTIONAL MIX

The final step in building an overall promotional plan is to determine the appropriate promotional mix. As stated earlier, the traditional promotional mix consists of advertising, personal selling, public relations, and sales promotions. The sports marketing manager must determine which aspects of the promotional mix will be best suited to achieve the promotional objectives at the given budget.

In choosing from among the traditional elements, the sports marketer may want to broadly explore the advantages and disadvantages of each promotional tool. For example, personal selling may be the most effective way to promote the sale of personal seat licenses, but it is limited in reaching large audiences. Table 10.3 outlines some of the considerations when deciding on the correct mix of promotional tools.

Although the factors listed in Table 10.3 are important determinants of which promotional tools to use to achieve the desired objectives, there are other considerations. The stage of the life cycle for the sport product, the type of sports product, the characteristics of the target audience, and the current market environment must also be carefully studied. Whatever the promotion mix decision, it is critical that the various elements be integrated carefully.

Promotional planning for sports is becoming increasingly more complex. With the rapid changes in technology, new promotional tools are being used to convey the sports marketer's message. In addition, it is becoming harder and harder to capture the attention of target audiences and move them along the hierarchy of effects. Because of the growing difficulty in reaching diverse target audiences, the clarity and coordination of integrating all marketing communications into a single theme is more important than ever.

The concept under which a sports organization carefully integrates and coordinates its many promotional mix elements to deliver a unified message about the organization and its products is known as **integrated marketing communications.** Think for a moment about the promotional efforts of the WNBA. The promotional goals are to increase awareness and develop excitement about the league. To accomplish this, the WNBA will combine national advertisements, sponsorships, cable and network broadcast schedules, and tie-ins with the NBA. All of these communications media must deliver a consistent message that produces

TABLE 10.3 Evaluating the Promotional Mix Elements

	Promotional Tools			
	Advertising	*Personal Selling*	*Sales Promotion*	*Public Relations*
Sender's control over the communication	Low	High	Moderate to low	Moderate to low
Amount of feedback	Little	Much	Little to moderate	Little
Speed of feedback	Delayed	Immediate	Varies	Delayed
Direction of message flow	One way	Two way	One way	One way
Speed in reaching large audiences	Fast	Slow	Fast	Typically fast
Message flexibility	None	Customized	None	Some
Mode of communication	Indirect and impersonal	Direct and face to face	Usually indirect and impersonal	Usually indirect and impersonal

a uniform image for the league to be successful. Not only must the WNBA deliver an integrated promotional mix, but the league's sponsors and the 14 teams must also transmit a unified message.

The primary advantage of integrating the promotional plan includes more effective and efficient marketing communications. Unfortunately, determining the return on investment (ROI) for an integrated promotion plan is still difficult, if not impossible. Professor Don Schultz has identified four types of information that must be available to begin to measure ROI for integrated communications.[12] These factors include the following:

- *Identification of Specific Customers*—identification of specific households, including information on the composition of those households to make inferences.
- *Customer Valuation*—placing a value on each household based on either annual purchases or lifetime purchases. Without this information on the purchase behavior of the household or individual, the calculation of ROI is of limited value to the marketer.
- *Track Message Delivery*—understanding what media consumers or households use to make their purchase decisions, and how a household receives information and messages over time. In addition, this involves measuring "brand contacts" or when and where consumers come into contact with the brand.
- *Consumer Response*—to establish the best ROI, behavioral responses are captured. In other words, consumer responses such as attitudes, feelings, and memory are deemed unimportant and purchases, inquiries, and related behaviors (e.g., coupon redemption) are evaluated.

Summary

Promotional planning is one of the most important elements of the sports marketing mix. Promotion involves communicating to all types of sports consumers via one or more of the promotion mix elements. The promotion mix elements include advertising, personal selling, sales promotions, public relations, and sponsorship. Within each of these promotion mix elements are more specialized tools to communicate with consumers of sport. For example, advertising may be developed for print media (e.g., newspapers and magazines) or broadcasts (e.g., radio and television). However, regardless of the promotion mix element that is used by sports marketers, the fundamental process at work is communication.

Communication is an interactive process established between the sender and the receiver of the marketing message via some medium. The process of communication begins with the source or sender of the message. In sports marketing, the source of the message might be an athlete endorser, team members, a sports organization, or even a coach. Sometimes the source of a marketing message can be friends or family. The effectiveness of the source in influencing consumers is based largely on the concept of source credibility. Credibility is typically defined as the expertise and trustworthiness of the source. Other characteristics of the source, such as gender, attractiveness, familiarity, and likeability may also play important roles in determining the source's effectiveness.

After the source of the message is chosen, message encoding occurs. Encoding is defined as translating the sender's thoughts or ideas into a message. The most effective encoding uses multiple ways of getting the message across and always keeps the receiver of the message in mind. Once encoding takes place, the message is more completely developed. Although there are any number of ways of constructing a message, sports marketers commonly choose between emotion (e.g., humor, sex, or fear) and rational (information-based) appeals.

The message, once constructed, must be transmitted to the target audience through any number of media. The traditional media include television, radio, newspapers, magazines, outdoor billboards, and stadium signage. Nontraditional media, such as the Internet, are also emerging as powerful tools for sports marketers. When making decisions about what medium to use, marketers must consider the promotional objectives, cost, ability to reach the targeted audience, and the nature of the message being communicated.

The medium relays the message to the target audience, which is where decoding occurs. Decoding is the interpretation of the message sent by the source through the medium. It is important to understand the characteristics of the target audience to ensure successful translation of the message will occur. Rarely, if ever, will perfect decoding take place because of the presence of noise.

The final elements in the communications model are the receiver and feedback. The message is directed to the receiver, or target audience. Again, depending on the purpose of the communication, the target audience may be spectators, participants, or corporate sponsors. Regardless of the nature of the audience, the sports marketer must understand as much as possible about the characteristics of the group to ensure an effective message is produced. Sports marketers determine the effectiveness of the message through feedback from the target audience.

Understanding the communications process provides us with the basis for developing a sound promotional plan. The promotional planning process includes target market considerations, setting promotional objectives, determining the promotional budget, and developing the promotional mix.

The first step in the promotional planning process is to consider the target market identified in the previous planning phase of the strategic sports marketing process. The two broad target market considerations are the final consumers of the sports product (either spectator or participants) or intermediaries, such as sponsors or distributors of sports products. When communicating to final consumers, a pull strategy is used. Conversely, push strategies are used to promote through intermediaries. After target markets are considered, promotional objectives are defined. Broadly, objectives may include informing, persuading, or reminding the target market.

One model that provides a basis for establishing promotional objectives is known as the hierarchy of effects, which states that consumers must pass through a series of stages before ultimately taking action (usually defined as making a purchase decision). The steps of the hierarchy of effects include unawareness, awareness, knowledge, liking, preference, conviction, and action. Once objectives have been formulated, budgets are considered. In the ideal scenario, budgets are linked with the objectives that have been set in the previous phase of the promotion planning process. However, other common approaches to promotional budgeting include arbitrary allocation, competitive parity, and percentage of sales. Most sports organizations use some combination of these methods to arrive at budgets. The final phase in the promotion planning process is to arrive at the optimal promotion mix. The promotion mix includes advertising, personal selling, public relations, sales promotion, and sponsorship. Decisions about the most effective promotion mix must carefully consider the current marketing environment, the sports product being promoted, and the characteristics of the target audience. Ideally, the sports marketer designs an integrated promotion mix that delivers a consistent message about the organization and its products.

Key Terms

- arbitrary allocation
- communication
- comparative messages
- competitive parity
- credibility
- decoding
- elements in the communications process
- emotional versus rational appeal
- encoding
- feedback

- hierarchy of effects
- integrated marketing communications
- match-up hypothesis
- medium
- message
- message characteristics
- noise
- objective and task method
- percentage of sales
- promotion

- promotion mix elements
- promotional budgeting
- promotional objectives
- promotional planning
- pull strategy
- push strategy
- receiver
- sidedness
- source
- target market considerations

Review Questions

1. Define promotion and then discuss each of the promotion mix elements.
2. Describe the elements of the communication process. Why is communication so important for sports marketers? What is the relationship between communication and promotion?
3. Define the source of a sports marketing message and provide some examples of effective sources. What is source credibility? What are the two components of source credibility?
4. What is meant by encoding? Who is responsible for encoding sports marketing messages?
5. Discuss the various message characteristics. What are the simple techniques used to create more effective messages?
6. Why is television considered to be the most powerful medium for sports marketing messages?
7. Define feedback. How is feedback delivered to the source of the message?
8. Outline the basic steps in promotion planning.
9. What is the fundamental difference between a push and a pull strategy?
10. Describe the three broad objectives of any type of promotion. What is the hierarchy of effect, and how is this concept related to promotional objectives?

11. What are the various ways of setting promotional budgets? Comment on the strengths and weaknesses of each.
12. Comment on how you would choose among the various promotion mix tools. Define integrated marketing communication.

Exercises

1. Evaluate the promotional mix used for the marketing of any intercollegiate women's sport at your university. Do you believe the proper blend of promotional tools are being used? What could be done to make the promotional plan more effective for this sport?
2. Find any advertisement for a sports product. Then describe and explain each of the elements in the communications process for that ad. Do the same (i.e., explain the communications process) for the following scenario: A salesperson is trying to sell stadium signage to the marketing director of a local hospital.
3. Conduct an interview with the Marketing Department of a local sports organization and discuss the role of each of the promotional tools in the organization's promotion mix. In addition, ask about their promotional budgeting process.
4. Describe three television advertisements for sports products that are designed to inform, persuade, and remind consumers. Do you believe the advertisements are effective in reaching their promotional objectives?
5. Locate advertisements for three different sports products. Comment on which response on the hierarchy of effects you believe each advertisement is trying to elicit from its target audience.
6. Find an example of a comparative advertisement. What do you believe are the advantages and disadvantages to this type of message?

Internet Exercises

1. Using the Internet, find an example of an advertisement for a sports product and a sports-related sales promotion. For each, discuss the targeted audience, the promotional objectives, and the message characteristics.
2. How do organizations get feedback regarding their promotions via the Internet? Find several examples of ways of providing sports marketers with feedback about their promotions.
3. Consider any sports product and find evidence of advertising and sales promotion *not* on the Internet. Then locate the product's promotion on the Internet. Comment on whether or not this organization practices integrated marketing communications.

Endnotes

1. Joseph Pereira, "Fila Scores on an Assist From Grant Hill," *The Wall Street Journal* (November 5, 1996); Stefan Fatsis, "Grant Hill Signs New Fila Deal for $80 Million," *The Wall Street Journal* (September 23, 1997).
2. Michael Kamins, "An Investigation into the Match-Up Hypothesis in Celebrity Advertising: When Beauty May Be Only Skin Deep," *Journal of Advertising,* vol. 19, no. 1 (1990), 4–13.
3. Martha Irvin, "If Not on Point, Slang Can Make A Tight Campaign Sound Wack," *The Commercial Appeal* (November 29, 2002), C1.
4. Charles Lamb, Joseph Hair, and Carl McDaniel, *Principles of Marketing,* 2nd ed. (Cincinnati: South-Western Publishing, 1994), 487.
5. Michael Solomon, *Consumer Behavior,* 3rd ed. (Upper Saddle River, NJ: Prentice Hall, 1996).
6. Jenn Menendez, Pirates slash price on most seats; Nearly 4,000 seats fall from $11 to $6 as the team rolls out an aggressive new marketing campaign. Portland Press Herald (Maine) (March 5, 2004), 3D.
7. Robert Lavidge and Gary Steiner, "A Model for Predictive Measurements of Advertising Effectiveness," *Journal of Marketing,* vol. 24 (1961), 59–62.
8. Rajeev Batra and Michael Ray, "Affective Responses Mediating Acceptance of Advertising," *Journal of Consumer Research,* vol. 13 (September 1986), 236–239; Leon Shiffman and Leslie Kanuk, *Consumer Behavior,* 4th ed. (Upper Saddle River, NJ: Prentice Hall, 1996), 237–239.
9. US 2004 advertising spend seen healthy, Europe to lag—industry forecasters AFX.COM December 9, 2003.
10. Nielsen Media: Sports Advertising Spending Rises in '02, www.sportsbusinessdaily.com; Top Sports Advertisers, www.sportsbusinessjournal.com.

11. Sean Gallagher and Larry Barrett, "Case 093 Shoe Fits," *Baseline* (November 1, 2003), 44.; www.newbalance.com.

12. Don Schultz, Stanley Tannenbaum, and Robert Lauterborn, *Integrated Marketing Communications: Putting It Together and Making It Work* (Lincolnwood, IL: NTC Publishing Group, 1992); Don Schultz, "Rethinking Marketing and Communications' ROI," *Marketing News* (December 2, 1996), 10; Don Schultz and Paul Wang, "Real World Results," *Marketing Tools* (April–May 1994).

CHAPTER 11

PROMOTION MIX ELEMENTS

After completing this chapter, you should be able to:

- Describe each element of the promotion mix, in detail.
- Understand the basic process for designing a successful advertising campaign.
- Discuss emerging forms of promotion.
- Outline the strategic selling process and explain why sports marketing should use this process.
- Identify the various forms of promotion.
- Specify the importance of public or community relations to sports marketers.

The CoActive Marketing Group, one of America's leading marketing agencies, designed a unique sales promotion for Hiram Walker to increase short-term sales of Canadian Club Classic (a 12-year-old whiskey). In this case, the promotion (called a premium) was a baseball card signed by one of four Hall of Fame players, including Willie Stargell, Billy Williams, Ernie Banks, and Brooks Robinson. With each purchase of a 750-ml bottle of Canadian Club Classic, consumers were able to collect one card from the series of cards.

In addition to the end users, Hiram Walker distributors were also involved in the sales promotion. Distributors could win a customized shelf unit to display the set of baseball cards and autographed baseballs. They could win these items for participating in the promotion and selling the idea to their retailers. The prizes motivated distributors to push cases into their retail accounts. By all accounts, the promotion was a huge success. In fact, it was so well received that a second series of cards were issued. To make the sales promotion work, personal selling was needed to secure the baseball legends. Other forms of communication were also necessary to inform the Hiram Walker distributors and consumers about the promotion.

As demonstrated in the Hiram Walker promotion, sports marketers must carefully integrate the promotion mix elements to establish successful promotions to consumers and trade. In Chapter 10, we explored the importance of communication and the basic concepts of promotional planning. This chapter examines each of the **promotional mix elements** in greater detail. By doing so, sports marketers will be in a better position to choose the most effective promotional elements for the construction of the promotional plan. Let us begin by looking at one of the most widely used forms of promotion—advertising.

Stadium signage was one of the earliest forms of promotion.

ADVERTISING

Advertising remains one of the most visible and important marketing tools available to sports marketers. Although significant changes are taking place in the way sports products and services are advertised, the reasons for advertising remain the same. Advertising creates and maintains brand awareness and brand loyalty. In addition, advertising builds brand image and creates a distinct identity for sports products and services. Most important, advertising directly affects consumer behavior. In other words, it causes us to attend sporting events, buy that new pair of running shoes, or watch the NCAA Women's Basketball tournament on television.

Most of us associate the development of an advertisement with the creative process. As you might imagine, advertising is more than a catchy jingle. To develop an effective advertisement, a systematic process is employed. Some of the steps in this process are very similar to the promotional planning process discussed in Chapter 10. This is not unexpected, as advertising is just another form of communication, or promotional tool, used by sports marketers.

The advertising process is commonly referred to as designing an advertising campaign. An advertising campaign is a series of related advertisements that communicate a common message to the target audience (see Figure 11.1). The advertising campaign (similar to the promotional planning process) is initiated with decisions about the objectives and budget. Next, creative decisions, such as the ad appeal and execution, are developed. Following this, the media strategy is planned and, finally, the advertising campaign is evaluated. Let us explore each of the steps in designing an advertising campaign in greater detail.

ADVERTISING OBJECTIVES

The first step in any advertising campaign is to examine the broader promotional objectives and marketing goals. The overall objectives of the advertising campaign

FIGURE 11.1 Designing an Advertising Campaign

Ad objectives → Ad budget → Creative decisions → Media strategy → Ad evaluation should, of course, be consistent with the strategic direction of the sports organization. The specific objectives and budgeting techniques for advertising are much the same as those discussed in Chapter 10. Namely, advertising is designed to inform, persuade, remind, and cause consumers in the target market to take action.[1] In addition to these broad objectives, **advertising objectives** are sometimes categorized as either direct or indirect.

The purpose of **direct objectives** in advertising is to elicit a behavioral response from the target audience. In sports marketing, this behavioral response may be in the form of purchasing tickets to a game, buying sporting goods that were advertised on the Internet, or even volunteering at a local event. Sometimes, an advertisement asks consumers to make multiple behavioral responses—for instance, go to snickers.com to vote for the "hungriest player," watch ABC Monday Night Football and grab a Snickers bar, are all directives in an advertisement for Snickers candy bars.

Direct advertising objectives can be further categorized into two distinct types: advertising to end users and sales promotion advertising. Both direct response objectives, however, are designed to induce action.

Advertising by Sports Organizations to End Users In this case, the objectives of advertising are not to enhance the perceived image of the event, the team, or the league, but rather to generate immediate response. With this type of objective, the sports

Vanderbilt advertisement using direct objective.
Source: Copyright © 2001, Follett Corporation.

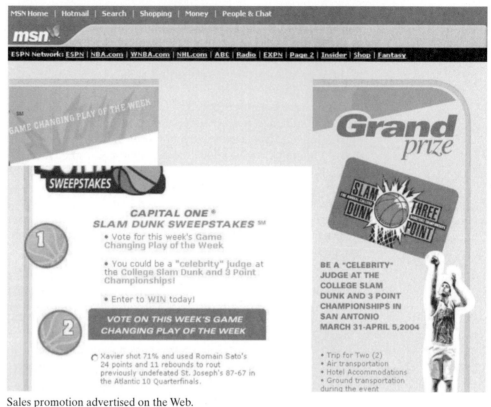

Sales promotion advertised on the Web.
Source: Reprinted courtesy of ESPN.com.

marketer is attempting to build immediate sales. As such, the specific objective of advertising to end users is usually stated in terms of increasing sales volume.

Sales Promotion Advertising It is common for contests, sweepstakes, coupons, and other forms of sales promotions to be advertised via any number of media. As such, the objectives of direct response advertisements are to have consumers participate in the contests and sweepstakes or redeem coupons. Objectives, therefore, are measured in terms of the level of participation in the sales promotion.

Indirect objectives are based on establishing prebehavioral (i.e., prior to action) responses to advertising. That is, accomplishing goals, such as increasing awareness, enhancing image, improving attitudes, or educating consumers. These indirect objectives should, in turn, lead to more direct behavioral responses. Consider the ad for American Express featuring coach Phil Jackson, who led the Bulls and Lakers to multiple NBA Championships. The ad simply is a picture of Jackson with the caption "The Official Card of Ringleaders." . . . The objective of this advertisement is solely to enhance the image of the brand. Ultimately, the advertisements sponsor hopes these indirect objectives will lead to the behavior response of securing new cardholders and reminding existing customers to purchase more products and services using the American Express card.

Indirect objectives, such as image enhancement, are always present to some extent in advertising. Sports leagues, such as the NBA, use indirect advertising ("I Love This Game") to generate awareness and interest in the league, whereas individual teams are more concerned with direct, behavioral objectives (such as the Pittsburg Pirates "Come See Us Play").

ADVERTISING BUDGETING

As with advertising objectives, budgeting methods for an ad campaign are largely the same as those for other forms of promotion. For example, techniques such as competitive parity, objective and task, and percentage of sales are again relevant to advertising. Whatever the methods used, it is important to remember that **advertising budgeting** should ideally stem from the objectives the advertising is attempting to achieve. However, other factors, such as monies available, competitive activity, and how the sports organization views the effectiveness of advertising, should be kept in mind.

CREATIVE DECISIONS

After the objectives and the budget have been established, the creative process becomes the focus of the advertising campaign or **creative decisions.** The **creative process** has been defined as generating the ideas and the concept of the advertisement. Advertising and sports marketing agencies hire individuals who possess a great deal of creativity, but even the most innovative people use a systematic process to harness their creativity.

To begin the creative process, most advertising agencies prepare a creative brief. The purpose of any creative brief is to understand clients' communication objectives so the creative process will be maximized. The **creative brief** is a tool used to guide the creative process toward a solution that will serve the interests of the client and their customers. When used properly, the creative brief can be thought of as a marketing-oriented approach to the design of an advertising campaign. Table 11.1 shows a sample of the creative brief used by CoActive Marketing Group (mentioned at the beginning of the chapter).

The three outcomes of the creative process are (1) identifying benefits of the sports product, (2) designing the advertising appeal—what to say, and (3) developing the advertising execution—how to say it. Each of these three elements in the creative decision process is discussed.

IDENTIFYING BENEFITS

Designing a distinctive advertising campaign involves identifying the key benefits of the sports product. We have briefly discussed the importance of understanding benefits in the context of segmenting consumer markets. As defined in Chapter 7, benefits describe why consumers purchase a product or service or what problem the product solves for the consumer. For advertising purposes, describing the benefits or reasons why consumers should buy the sports product is a must. Marketing research is used to understand the benefits desired or perceived by consumers who might use or purchase the sports product.

ADVERTISING APPEALS

Understanding benefits and developing **advertising appeals** go hand in hand. Once the desired benefits are uncovered, the advertising appeal is developed around these benefits. In short, the advertising appeal recounts *why* the consumer wants to purchase the sports product. The major advertising appeals used in sports marketing include health, emotion, fear, sex, and pleasure.

Health appeals are becoming prevalent in advertising, as the value placed on health continues to increase in the United States. Obviously, advertisements for the fitness industry and fitness centers capitalize on this growing concern of Americans. One important consideration when using health appeals in advertisements is the demographic profile of the target audience. According to the International Health, Racquet and Sportsclub Association, the strongest growth in health club membership is in the 55 + age range. There were 6.9 million members over the age of 55 in 2002, which represents a 350 percent increase from 1987.[2] The demographics of the audience and the health benefits desired from fitness centers should be carefully studied in the advertising process.

TABLE 11.1 The Creative Brief

"Thinking about the situation is much better than hoping."
Strategic thinking leads to insight, which leads to high-quality execution.
Question: Why do a creative brief?
Answer: Our objective is to help our clients build their business. To do that, we must learn as much as we can so we can best deploy our creative resources to help the client meet their business objectives.

Creative brief elements
1. Project description
2. Target audience description (demographics, psychological data, etc.)
3. Long-term strategy
4. Competitive distinctiveness
5. Desired customer response (1–2 "desires" maximum; e.g., trial, change perception)
6. Mandatory executional elements (1–2 maximum)
7. Known key customer insights

What does the creative brief do?
1. Raises key issues about the business
2. Organizes learning already known about the consumer or business
3. Suggests areas for needed additional learning
4. Can help uncover new insights important to helping the customer
5. Contributes to the creative process

Questions to ask when developing a creative brief
1. Are there proven insights from other products or categories that we could use?
2. Is there a negative perception in category or product that our client's product could refute? Is there a tradeoff or compromise that the client's product could eliminate?
3. Are there specific usage habits that could be leveraged into strong executions? How can we breathe creative life into research reports?
4. Is there a potential consumer negative in your principal competitor's strength?
5. Is there a perceived standard of excellence in your category? How does your brand compare with it? Can you create a standard of excellence for your brand?
6. What are the realities of how the client's brand fits their customer's needs? How does this affect the consumer's mindset when considering the alternatives available in the product category?
7. Is there a positive piece of consumer psychology your product can latch onto? Is there an emotional side to the client's brand? How does it interrelate with the practical side?
8. How does the client's consumer perceive their "brand"—not the product—"the brand"?

Source: © 1996 Optimum Group.

A number of **emotional appeals,** such as fear, humor, sex, pleasure, and the drama associated with athletic competition, are also used in sports marketing promotions. One of the unique aspects of sports marketing is the emotional attachment that consumers develop for the sports product. As discussed in Chapter 6, many fans have high levels of involvement and identification with their favorite athletes and teams.[3] Some fans may even view themselves as part of the team. Recognizing this strong emotional component, many advertisers of sports use emotional appeals. The infamous "Thrill of victory and agony of defeat" message used for decades for ABC's *Wide World of Sports* opening captures the essence of an emotional appeal. Emotional appeals that allow fans to relive the team's greatest moments and performances of past years are often used to encourage future attendance.

One specific type of an emotional appeal is a fear appeal. **Fear appeals** are messages designed to communicate what negative consequences may occur if the sports product or service is not used or is used improperly. Scare tactics are usually inappropriate for sports products and services, but in some product categories moderate amounts of fear in a message can be effective. Consider, for example, messages concerning exercise equipment or health club membership. Many promotional campaigns are built around consumers' fears of being physically unfit and aging. Even athletic promoters use moderate fear appeals by telling consumers that tickets will be sold out quickly and that they should not wait to purchase their seats. Effective sports marketers identify their sports products as solutions to the common "fears" of consumers. For example, manufacturers of bike and skateboard helmets are quick to cite the plethora of head injuries that result without the use of proper headgear.

Another emotional appeal is sex. **Sex appeals** rely on the old adage that "sex sells." Typically, marketers who use sex appeals in their messages are selling products that are sexually related, such as perfumes and clothing. This is true also in sports marketing, as demonstrated by Polo Sport fragrance by Ralph Lauren or the Michael Jordan cologne, which made $60 million in sales during its first six months on the market.

In sports marketing, sex appeals are sometimes used, but this is always a delicate subject. ProBeach Volleyball has been criticized for relying too much on the sex appeal of its players (both male and female) to attract fans. Notably, top player Gabrielle Reece has been used as a model in *Sports Illustrated*'s swimsuit edition and in other advertisements. Incidentally, the annual sales of the *Sports Illustrated* swimsuit edition generates nearly three times the number of readers as the typical, male clad edition, pointing again to the old adage that "sex sells."

FIFA president Sepp Blatter was recently under fire for his comments that women soccer players should wear "more feminine uniforms such as tighter shorts to raise fan interest and attract new sponsors." This certainly was the case for the Australian Women's Soccer Team, also known as "The Matildas," that created a stir with the release of a 2000 calendar where team members posed nude. Interestingly, the calendar was sponsored by the Australian Women's Soccer Association in hopes of boosting the image of the team prior to the 2000 Summer Games in Sydney.[4] An additional proponent of sex appeals is female golfer Jan Stephenson, who originally caused a stir in 1986 by posing nude in a bath of golf balls. Stephenson, now 51 years old, plans to play on the Champions Tour with the men and insists the women's tour has to "sell sex" to attract fans and sponsors to the game in the face of competition from the PGA Tour, Seniors Tour, and other sports.[5] Of course, a discussion of sex and sports marketing would be remiss without any discussion of tennis star Anna Kournakova, who has been openly criticized for her mediocre play and better than average exposure.

Pleasure or fun appeals are designed for those target audiences that participate in sports or watch sports for fun, social interaction, or enjoyment. These advertising appeals should stress the positive relationships that can be developed among family members, friends, or business associates by attending games or participating in sports. A recent advertisement by a major credit card company captured the pleasure of a father taking his son to a baseball game. The essence of the appeal was that, although you might not be able to afford it at the time, you will never be able to replace the priceless moment of taking your child to his or her first ball game. Another classic example of fun appeals is the Budweiser "Whassup" ads. The campaign, featuring four buddies shouting to each other over the phone, specifically targeted young sports fans.

ADVERTISING EXECUTION

The **advertising execution** should answer the appeal that the advertiser is trying to target. In other words, it is not what to say, but how to say it. Let us look at some of the more common executional formats, such as message sidedness, comparative advertisements, slice of life, scientific, and testimonials.

SPOTLIGHT ON SPORTS MARKETING ETHICS

LPGA Looks to Put Some Gloss on Image

The LPGA, trying to increase its fan base, is looking for some glitter, glitz and maybe a little sex appeal. The tour is hoping to light up with personality beginning Thursday at the year's first major, the Kraft Nabisco Championship at Rancho Mirage, Calif. "Right or wrong, society has decided that it's important to be attractive," Commissioner Ty Votaw says. "If we're just about being pro golfers, then our players will not reach their potential."

Votaw, whose tour dropped six events from its schedule this year, in part because of a lack of corporate sponsorships, will be watching TV ratings and attendance this week. His goal, as part of a five-year plan, is to increase viewers by 10 percent and attendance by 15 percent each year. Votaw announced those goals, and the players were coached on how they can help reach them during a summit two weeks ago. The players were told that becoming a more fan-friendly, personality-driven tour can turn female pro golfers into celebrities. "There are five points of celebrity," he says. "The first is performance. If you don't perform, the others won't matter." Votaw says the players must play with joy and passion and have a good appearance.

He does not emphasize sex appeal because he says as a marketing plan, "It has a short shelf life. If you perform well and relate to the public, then you will be attractive to everyone." The summit, which focused on the importance of marketing, was designed to teach players how the tour works as a business.

"I don't think the LPGA is doing anything different from the PGA Tour," says Donna Lopiano of the Women's Sports Foundation. "Both have dress regulations. You don't come to work looking like you just tumbled out of bed." Laura Diaz, a young pro who won last Sunday's event in Tucson, says attractiveness has many elements, including a neat appearance and a pleasing personality. She adds, "The better we appear, the better the LPGA will be."

The plan, coming under the slogan "Fans first," starts in a year in which Nancy Lopez, the most popular player in the LPGA's 52-year history, is phasing out of competitive golf. "Society expects women to dress neatly, look pretty, and be feminine," Lopez says. "That's just part of life."

Source: Jerry Potter. "LPGA Looks to Put Some Gloss on Image." *USA Today* (March 27, 2002). Used by permission.

One executional format is whether to construct the message as **one-sided versus two-sided.** A one-sided message conveys only the positive benefits of a sports product or service. Most sports organizations do not want to communicate the negative features of their products or services, but this can have its advantages. Describing the negatives along with the positive can enhance the credibility of the source by making it more trustworthy. In addition, discussing the negative aspects of the sports product can ultimately lower consumers' expectations and lead to more satisfaction. For instance, you rarely hear a coach at any level talk about how unbeatable a team or player is. Rather, the focus is on the weaknesses of the team, which reduces fan (and owner) expectations.

Comparative advertisements, another executional format, contrast one sports product with another. When doing comparative advertisements, sports advertisers stress the advantages of their sports product relative to the competition. For new sports products that possess a significant differential advantage, comparative advertisements can be especially effective. The risk involved with comparative advertisements is that consumers are exposed to your product as well as the competitor's product.

Because of the unique nature of sport, many advertisements are inherently comparative. For example, boxing advertisements touted the "Fight of the Century" between Muhammad Ali and Joe Frazier. In fact, there have been many "Fight of the Century" advertisements that are strikingly similar, comparing two boxers' strengths and weaknesses. Other sporting events, such as the made-for-television Skin's Game, use a similar comparative format for promoting the events. Many home teams skillfully

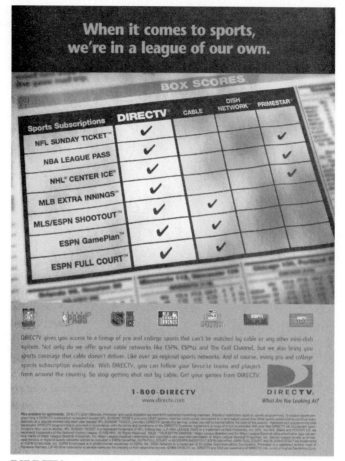

DIRECTV uses comparative advertising.
Source: Used by permission of DIRECTV.

use comparative advertisements to attract moderately involved fans interested in the success of the local team. These fans are attracted by the allure of the visiting team or one of its star athletes. For instance, many basketball advertisements promote the big-name athletes of the opposing team, rather than highlight their own stars.

Slice-of-life advertisements show a "common" athlete or consumer in a common, everyday situation where the consumer might be using the advertised sports or non-sports product. For example, Campbell's Chunky Soups, features football stars Donovan McNabb and Michael Strahan eating soup prepared by their moms. A slight variation of this style is the **lifestyle advertisements,** wherein the advertisement is intended to portray the lifestyle of the desired target audience. For example, the classic "Just Do It" campaign uses a slice-of-life format that appeals to the participant in each of us. In another slice-of-life example, Zest soap ran a very effective campaign for their product using football star Ironhead Hayward as their "showering" spokesperson.

Another executional style that is also readily used in sports advertising is called **scientific advertisements.** Advertisers using this style feature the technological superiority of their sports product or use research or scientific studies to support their claims. For instance, many golf ball manufacturers use scientific claims to sell their product. The Srixon UR-X is touted as having the "largest core," which means longer distance. Callaway markets the HX Tour as having "revolutionary hexagonal aerodynamics," and the Titleist Professional ball, which has a core of corn syrup, water, and salts, surrounded

TABLE 11.2 Most Effective Retired Athlete Endorsers

National Basketball Association: Michael Jordan
National Football League: Terry Bradshaw
Golf: Arnold Palmer
Major League Baseball: Cal Ripken
National Hockey League: Wayne Gretzky
Boxing: George Foreman
Tennis: John McEnroe
NASCAR: Richard Petty

Source: Total Sports and Entertainment, http://www.tsesports.com/press/index.php. Used by permission.

by a rubber and plasticlike covering. As Bill Morgan, Titleist's vice president of golf ball research admits, "A lot of times, chemical words or technical words are talked about in marketing and nobody really knows what they are talking about. But it sounds high tech. There is a little deception there, really."

One of the most prevalent executional styles for sports advertising is the use of **testimonials.** Testimonials are statements about the sports product given by endorsers. These endorsers may be the "common" athlete, professional athletes, teams, coaches and managers, owners, or even inanimate objects, such as mascots. For example, in advertising designed to increase tennis participation among children, kids are seen playing with cartoon characters. Michael Jordan and his "Space Jam" friends represented a great example of inanimate objects used as endorsers. Even retired athletes are making a comeback as popular endorsers as shown in Table 11.2.

Why are athlete testimonials so popular among sports advertisers? The answer to this question is the ability of sports celebrities to persuade the target audience and move them toward purchase. Athletes' persuasive power stems from their credibility and, in some cases, attractiveness. **Credibility** refers to the expertise and the trustworthiness of the source of the message. **Expertise** is the knowledge, skill, or special experience possessed by the source about the sports product. Of course, successful athletes who promote products needed to participate in their sport have demonstrable expertise. Examples of the athlete–athletic product match-up include Steve Francis and Cheryl Swoopes—basketball shoe contracts; Tiger Woods, Greg Norman, and Jack Nicklaus—golf equipment; Jeff Gordon and Dale Jarrett—automotive industry; Ken Griffey Jr. and Mike Piazza—baseball gloves; Martina Navratilova and Juan Carlos—tennis racquets; and Eric Lindros and Curtis Joseph—hockey equipment.

The other dimension of source credibility is **trustworthiness.** This refers to the honesty and believability of the athlete(s) endorser(s). Trustworthiness is an intangible characteristic that is becoming harder and harder for professional athletes to establish. Today's consumers realize athletes with already large salaries are being paid huge sums of money for endorsements. Because of this, the athlete's believability is often suspect. Nevertheless, even some of the highest paid athlete endorsers, such as George Foreman, Arnold Palmer, and Tiger Woods, seem to have established themselves as trustworthy sources of information.

In addition to credibility, another factor that makes athletes successful endorsers is **attractiveness.** Although attractiveness is usually associated with physical beauty, it appears to have another, nonphysical dimension based on personality, lifestyle, and intellect. Attractiveness operates using the process of identification, which means that the target audience identifies with the source (athlete) in some fashion. Gatorade's classic "I wanna be like Mike" campaign, featuring Michael Jordan, is a good example of the identification process. Perhaps, an even better example is Nike's "I am Tiger

MEN'S AND WOMEN'S COLLECTION   2004

Fred Couples creates a powerful image for the Ashworth Collection.
Source: Courtesy of Ashworth, Inc. www.ashworthinc.com

Woods" campaign, where kids of all races and ages were found putting themselves in the shoes of Tiger.

Who will be the most successful and appealing athlete endorsers of the new century? In 2003, a study was conducted by Burns Sports Celebrity Service, Inc. to answer this question.[6] The survey asked over 2,000 creative directors at national advertising agencies and corporate marketing executives, who hire athletes, to rate the most appealing athlete endorsers. Not surprisingly, the results indicated that the appeal of Tiger Woods continues to grow at an extremely rapid pace. Woods has firmly established himself as one of the top sports celebrity endorsers today, and Burns Sports' President, Bob Williams, believes, "If Tiger Woods takes an aggressive approach accepting endorsements, he could become the first athlete to earn a billion dollars in endorsements. Woods' golf career could last 30 years or more, unlike athletes from other sports whose average career is in the single digits. Hence, the real opportunity to earn a billion dollars from endorsements is within reason for a megastar like Tiger Woods."

Although athlete endorsers can be extremely effective, there are risks involved. Athletes are costly, may have career threatening injuries, or just do foolish things. Here are just a few classic examples of the many athlete endorsers gone bad.

In an unprecedented move, the Golden State Warriors terminated Latrell Sprewell's four-year, $32 million contract after he threatened to kill his coach, P. J. Carlesimo, during a scrimmage. After exchanging words, Sprewell grabbed Carlesimo and choked him for 10 to 15 seconds before the other players could stop him. The NBA suspended him for one year without pay, and Converse terminated Sprewell's endorsement deal, which was estimated to pay between $300,000 and $600,000 annually. Kobe Bryant, one of the most well-liked players in the NBA, was accused of sexually assaulting a 19-year-old woman in 2003. His endorsement deals with McDonald's, Nike, Sprite, Upper Deck, and Spalding, totaling some 20 million dollars, are all on hold as Bryant awaits trial.[7]

Dennis Rodman, a notorious bad boy, was fined $50,000 for making derogatory comments about Mormons during the 1997 NBA Championship Series against the Utah Jazz. The fine was Rodman's third of the season. His previous two incidents involved kicking a courtside photographer ($25,000) and striking Joe Wolf of the Bucks ($7,500). In response to Rodman's insensitive comments, his television advertisements for Carl's Jr. (fast food restaurant) were yanked permanently. Robert W. Wisely, senior vice president of marketing for Carl Karcher Enterprises, commented that "Derogatory comments made about any religious or racial group are inexcusable."

O. J. Simpson was enjoying a successful run with Hertz when he was charged with the murder of his former wife, Nicole Brown Simpson. Magic Johnson's public announcement that he was HIV positive caused a stir with his sponsors. John Daly (problems with alcohol, wife abuse) and Fuzzy Zoeller (racist remarks after the 1997 Masters) represent two examples of problematic endorsers in golf. And the list goes on and on.

For these reasons, many sports advertisers are shying away from signing megastar, individual athletes to huge contracts and are instead using teams or events as their advertising platform. For instance, Reebok reduced its football endorsement stable from 250 to 150. Baseball endorsers were reduced from 350 to 100 and basketball endorsers were reduced from 100 to 25. Gatorade Vice President of Sports Marketing, Tom Fox, said it best: "The paradigm in the athlete marketplace has changed. . . . Like a lot of companies, we question the ability of any single athlete to reinforce brand equity to such a huge extent that it would move product off the shelf."[6] Nonetheless, many companies are still using athletes, and as you might suspect Nike is leading the way. Over the past year, Nike has signed the following stable of athletes to multiyear contracts: NBA stars LeBron James ($90 million), Carmelo Anthony ($15 million), and Kobe Bryant ($45 million); tennis superstar Serena Williams ($40 million); 14-year-old U.S. soccer star Freddy Adu ($1 million); and Canadian world champion hurdler Perdita Felicien ($1 million).[7] Nike estimated its total endorsement commitments for 2004 will be $338.6 million, which represents more than a 50 percent increase from last year.[8] Table 11.3 presents some general guidelines for using sports celebrities in advertising campaigns.

TABLE 11.3 Guidelines for Using Sports Celebrities as Endorsers

- Sports celebrities are more effective for endorsing sports-related products. Match-up hypothesis again holds true—does not matter if consumers recognize the athlete if they cannot remember the product that is being endorsed
- Long-term relationships or associations between the product and the endorser are key— cannot be short-term or one-shot deals to be effective. Examples include Arnold Palmer with Pennzoil and Michael Jordon with Nike
- Advertisements using athlete endorsers who appear during contests or events in which the athlete is participating are less effective
- Athletes who are overexposed may lose their credibility and power to influence consumers. Tiger Woods's manager Hughes Norton of IMG says that he is planning to limit the golfing phenom to an association with just five global brands to avoid overexposure

Source: Adapted from Amy Dyson and Douglas Turco, "The State of Celebrity Endorsement in Sport," *Cyber-Journal of Sport Marketing.* www.cad.gu.edu.au//cjsm/dyson.htm.

One promising alternative that reduces the risk of potential problems is to use athletes who are no longer alive. Nike ran a series of 10 commercials using former Green Bay Packer coach Vince Lombardi. Other corporations which have featured departed stars in their ad campaigns, included Citibank (Babe Ruth), Microsoft (Lou Gehrig and Jesse Owens), McDonald's, Coca-Cola, Apple Computer, General Mills (Jackie Robinson), and Miller Brewing (Satchel Paige). Dead athletes are more cost effective, scandalproof, and are icons in the world of sports. Ruth was chosen to represent Citibank in an ad campaign—49 years after his death and 62 since his last homer—for similar reasons. "Babe's an American sports icon, instantly recognizable," says Ken Gordon, a Citibank vice president, explaining why Ruth got the nod over contemporary ballplayers.[9]

MEDIA STRATEGY

As presented in Chapter 10, a medium or channel is the element in the communications process by which the message is transmitted. Traditional mass media, such as newspapers, television, radio, or magazines, are usually thought of as effective ways of carrying advertising messages to the target audience. However, new technologies are creating alternative media. The Internet, for example, represents an emerging medium that must be considered by sports advertisers. Deciding what medium or media to use is just one aspect in developing a comprehensive media strategy. **Media strategy** addresses two basic questions about the channel of communication. First, what medium or media mix (combination of media) will be most effective in reaching the desired target audience? Second, how should this media be scheduled to meet advertising objectives?

MEDIA DECISIONS OR MEDIA SELECTION

The far-ranging (and growing) number of media choices make selecting the right media a difficult task. Choosing the proper media requires the sports advertiser to be mindful of the creative decisions made earlier in the advertising process. For instance, an emotional appeal—best suited to television—would be difficult to convey using print media. It is also critical that the media planner keep the target market in mind. Understanding the profile of the target market and their media habits is essential to developing an effective advertising campaign.

Every type of media has strengths and weaknesses that must be considered when making advertising placement decisions. As the previous article illustrates, print may be the most cost-effective medium for sports marketers. Table 11.4 demonstrates selected advantages and disadvantages when choosing advertising media.

ALTERNATIVE FORMS OF ADVERTISING

Because of the advertising clutter present in traditional advertising media, sports marketers are continually evaluating new ways of delivering their message to consumers. Alternative forms of advertising range from the more conventional stadium signage to the most creative media. Consider the following innovative illustrations of alternative forms of advertising: The International Cricket Council has allowed players to sell the top 23 centimeters of their bats for advertising; and in Connecticut 35 public golf courses have signed up for a program that will put advertisements in the bottom of their holes.

STADIUM SIGNAGE

Stadium signage, or on-site advertising, is back.[10] For some time, nary a sign was found on the outfield wall of a MLB team or on the boards at an NHL game. Now, stadium signage prevails on every inch of available space. Not unlike other forms of advertising, stadium signage is designed to increase brand or corporate awareness,

TABLE 11.4 Profiles of Major Media Types

Medium	Advantages	Limitations
Internet	Allows messages to be customized, reaches specific market interactive capabilities	Clutter, audience characteristics, hard-to-measure effectiveness
Newspapers	Flexibility; timeliness; good local market coverage; broad acceptability; high believability	Short life; poor reproduction quality; small pass-along audience
Television	Good mass market coverage; low cost per exposure; combines sight, sound, and motion; appealing to the senses	High absolute costs; high clutter; fleeting exposure; less audience selectivity
Direct mail	High audience selectivity; flexibility; no ad competition within the same medium; allows personalization	Relatively high cost per exposure; "junk mail" image
Radio	Good local acceptance; high geographic and demographic selectivity; low cost	Audio only, fleeting exposure; low attention ("the half-heard" medium); fragmented audiences
Magazines	High geographic and demographic selectivity; credibility and prestige; high-quality reproduction; long life and good pass-along readership	Long advertisement purchase lead time; high cost; no guarantee of position
Outdoor	Flexibility; high repeat exposure; low cost; low message competition; good positional selectivity	Little audience selectivity; creative limitations

Source: Adapted from Philip Kotler and Gary Armstrong, *Marketing: An Introduction,* 4th ed. (Upper Saddle River, NJ: Prentice Hall), 471.

create a favorable image through associations with the team and sport, change attitudes or maintain favorable attitudes, and ultimately increase the sale of product.

One current estimate is that $15 billion is spent each year on stadium signage, but this is expected to increase, given the advent of new technologies allowing stadium billboards to be changed and customized for local markets.[11] As the following article illustrates, there is sometimes more to a stadium sign than meets the eye.

Although stadium signage can be an effective means of advertising, it can also be costly. For instance, the rotating scorer's and press table stadium signage can cost between $50,000 and $100,000 for NBA games, given the current demand for the space. How is expensive stadium signage sold and justified by sports marketers? First, research has shown that locations considered to be part of the game (e.g., scorer's table or on the ice) are more effective than those locations removed from the action (e.g., scoreboards). One researcher found that spectators had improved recognition of and attitudes toward eight courtside advertisers for an NCAA Division I men's basketball team. This finding is, of course, extremely important to sponsors considering the cost and effectiveness of this type of stadium signage.[12]

OTHER OUTDOOR

A new form of outdoor advertising is also becoming popular at national sporting events. This type of outdoor promotion uses live product demonstrations or characters to attract fans' attention. For example, the U.S. Army staged a live combat reenactment prior to the start of the Charlotte 500 NASCAR race. In another example, Juan Valdez, the very recognizable brand character for Columbian Coffee, showed up in the stands of

Coca-Cola creates a positive association with baseball by using stadium signage.

Source: Courtesy of the Coca-Cola Company.

the U.S. Open tennis tournament. Similarly, Ronald McDonald attended the Kentucky Derby and a Chicago Bulls game to promote new products from McDonald's.

In a related fashion, sports marketers sometimes use variations of product placement techniques. Product placement occurs when manufacturers pay to have their products used in television shows, movies, and other entertainment media such as music videos. For instance, "The Best Damn Sports Show Period" on Fox SportsNet, incorporates product placement into each show. Each day a dinner from Outback Steakhouse is eaten by the hosts as they discuss the sports news of the day. Gordon and Smith surfboards were prominently featured in the movie *Blue Crush*, written about female surfers; and perhaps the earliest sports product placement was when James Bond, 007, used Slazenger golf balls on the links in the classic *Goldfinger*. In the ultimate product tie-in, the Anaheim Mighty Ducks of the NHL were named after the series of movies created by their then parent company, Disney.

Are these product placements effective? Top-rated TV shows aren't necessarily the best places for product placement. That's the conclusion of a new study of television product placement effectiveness conducted by New York-based Intermedia Advertising Group (IAG), a four-year-old research company whose roots are in measuring the effectiveness and performance of network television commercials.[13] "We both poll viewers and measure the exposure ourselves," IAG co-CEO Alan Gould said. "We code the exposure type, we measure the duration and note factors such as whether the product is embedded into the story line, used as intended, and in the foreground or background."[14] Even though this study seemed to find little support for the

Virtual Advertising: Wave of the Future

First used by a minor league baseball team in 1995, the latest technological advancement in sports stadium signage is called the "virtual advertisement" or "virtual sign." Virtual advertisements or signs are ads that are not really there. The ads can appear on the field, ice, tennis court, or just about anywhere, but can only be seen by the television viewing audience rather than those in attendance.

The technology, called L-VIS, was developed by Princeton Video Image (PVI) of Princeton, New Jersey. The system can distribute different video images simultaneously to different audiences around the globe, and as such is geared primarily for large global advertisers. As PVI vice president Sam McCleary points out, "The L-VIS system allows advertisers to modify the message to fit the market. Customized signage by market is an increasingly more valuable component to marketing."[a] Princeton Video Imaging currently does the 1st Down Line for CBS and virtual advertising with Major League Baseball and Major League Soccer.

Benefits of virtual signs include state-of-the-art graphics, a way to hold viewers attention, and cost effectiveness. For instance, a half inning of virtual advertising costs $20,000, roughly the same as a 30-second conventional commercial. In addition, virtual signage will help keep the stadium and playing surfaces free of unwanted signage. This may even help the players, as signage on the ice or right behind home plate or a tennis end line may be disturbing.[b] McCleary says that viewers "don't seem to make the distinction" between real signage and virtual signage.[c] Most important, virtual signage will give teams the opportunity to be flexible and creative with potential sponsors. For instance, BMW of North America will launch a five-month ad campaign on Fox Sports en Espanol to pitch the brand to upscale Hispanic consumers. Central to the package, which gives BMW exposure across network soccer broadcasts and daily news reports, is a "virtual" advertising format that "brands" the playing field with BMW's signature logo and sends virtual vehicles across the field.

[a]Chad Rubel, "What You See on TV Is Not What You Get at Stadium," *Marketing News* (May 6, 1996) 2.
[b]Brian Fenton, "Truth in Advertising," *Popular Mechanics* (January 1997) 34.
[c]Karl Greenberg, Targeting: BMW's Goal—Score with Virtual Soccer Pitch, *Brandweek* (May 12, 2003).
Source: Rich Thomaselli. Targeting new revenue: Sports tech firms seek ad sponsors; Princeton Video, Sportsvision in talks to offer on-screen deals. *Advertising Age* (May 13, 2002).

effectiveness of product placement, anecdotal evidence shows that product demonstrations seem to work. RAM Sports, Inc., in Denver, with $10 million in sales and 50 employees, spends up to 20 percent of its $250,000 marketing budget to place Classic brand sport balls, which compete with Wilson and Spalding. Its products have appeared in *Flubber*, *He Got Game*, and other films. RAM coowner and CFO Randy Jones says, "When we have an exposure, our phone rings off the hook."[15] The advantages that have been cited for these alternative forms of advertising include[16]:

- **Exposure**—A large number of people go to the movies, rent movies, or could be exposed to a live-product demonstration if they are attending a sporting event or watching television.
- **Attention**—Moviegoers are generally an attentive audience. Sports spectators are also a captive audience when they are waiting for the action to begin.
- **Recall**—Research has shown that audiences have higher levels of next-day recall for products that are placed in movies than for traditional forms of promotion.
- **Source Association**—For product placements, the audience may see familiar and likable stars using the sports product. As such, the product's image may be enhanced through association with the celebrity.

Another alternative form of advertising is using the athlete as a "human billboard."[17] The history of athletes wearing an advertisement can be traced back to the 1960s, when organizations began establishing relationships with stock car drivers. Soon, the practice of drivers wearing patches on their clothing spread to other sports, such as tennis and golf. The use of athletes as advertisers is much more common in individual sports because these individuals have the ability to negotiate and wear whatever they want, as opposed to the tight controls imposed on athletes in team sports by their respective leagues.

Today, the use of athletes as human billboards is part of the integrated marketing communications plan rather than a stand-alone promotion. Steve Elkington, Tiger Woods, Chip Beck, David Berganio Jr., and Ben Crenshaw of the PGA Tour wear Buick visors, sweaters, and shirts, in addition to the other advertisements and promotions they perform for Buick. The major appeal of this form of advertising is the natural association (classical conditioning) formed in consumers' minds between the athlete and the organization or product.

How much does it cost sponsors to rent advertising space on an athlete's body? An IndyCar driver's helmet might cost between $50,000 and $250,000, depending on the driver. The precious space on a professional golfer's visor would cost between $250,000 and $500,000. Although these prices may seem outrageous, organizations are willing to pay the price for the exposure and enhanced brand equity.

In addition to these more conventional examples, basketball player Rasheed Wallace was asked by a candy company to tattoo his body for the NBA season. This offer was ultimately rejected as it was thought to potentially violate the NBA Uniform Player contract. Additionally, boxers have started to use their bodies as billboards by tattoing corporate logos on their chest and back. The Nevada State Athletic Commission tried to ban body billboards, but ultimately lost to the state court's ruling protecting boxers' right to free speech.

INTERNET

Another major player in the world of advertising media is the Internet. As discussed in Chapter 3, the Internet has already become a valuable source of sports information for participants and fans. In addition, the Internet is fast becoming the favorite promotional medium for sports marketers. A total user base of over 150 million people exists in the United States alone, which is just one advantage to promotion via the Internet. In addition, the Online Publishing Association recently estimated that U.S. consumers spent $30 million on paid online sports content.[18] Let us take a look at some of the other advantages to promotion via the Internet.

These runners all exemplify the human billboard.

Perhaps, the most substantial advantage to using the Internet as a promotional tool is the good fit between the profile of the sports fan and the Internet user. The typical Internet user is described as an entertainment-minded, educated male between 18- and 34-years-old. For instance, the demographic profile of espn.com users is 94 percent male, 47 percent single, with 66 percent between the ages of 18 and 34.[19] Sound familiar? These characteristics closely match the traditional sports fan.

A study of online users showed that nearly a third of all Internet users (roughly 50 million people) visited some sort of sport site, with espn.com being the leader. In addition, over 50 percent of all male Internet users between the ages of 25–34 visited a sports site. Slightly older males (35–44) spend the most time surfing sport sites, with an average of 107 minutes spent per visit. Finally, the Internet is the ideal medium to target college sports fans due to greater access and usage rates among students. Generally, the Internet allows the sports advertiser to reach an extremely focused targeted market.[20]

Another distinct advantage of promotion via the Internet is the interactive nature of the medium. Promotions attract the attention of the target audience and then create involvement by having consumers point and click on the information they find of interest. For instance, the major league soccer site (www.mlsnet.com) has an interactive advertisement for MardiGras paper towels and napkins. A point and click of the mouse will take fans to the the Georgia Pacific soccer link, which features the ability to download player screen savers and wallpapers, enter a shootout online contest, and, of course get more information on MardiGras products.

Other advantages of the Internet versus more traditional media include the Internet's ability to be flexible. Web promotions can be updated, and changes can be made almost instantly. This flexibility is a tremendous advantage for sports marketers, who are constantly responding to a changing environment. In fact, the Internet seems to be the perfect tool for sports marketers using the contingency framework for strategic planning.

The Internet has become a popular advertising medium.
Source: Copyright © 2003–2004 PGA/Turner Sports Interactive. All rights reserved.

A final benefit of promotion via the Internet is its cost effectiveness. The Internet provides organizations with a means of promoting sports to consumers around the world at a low cost. The ability to reach a geographically diverse audience at a low cost is one of the primary advantages of Internet promotion.

Although there are many advantages, promotion via the Internet can also pose potential problems. As with other forms of advertising, it is difficult to measure the effectiveness of sports promotion over the Internet. Often, marketers use the "number of hits" as a proxy for effectiveness, but this cannot be used to determine the interest level of the consumer or purchase intent.

Promotional clutter is another difficulty with Internet promotions. As the Internet becomes a more popular advertising medium, more organizations will compete for the audience and its attention. To break through the clutter, sports marketers must design new Internet promotions. Differentiating among Web promotions will become increasingly important in gaining the attention of consumers and developing a unique position for organizations.

A final disadvantage of promotion on the Internet is its inability to reach certain groups of consumers. Although the Internet is a great medium to reach younger, college-educated, computer-literate consumers, it may be extremely inefficient in trying to promote to the mature market or, perhaps, consumers of lower socioeconomic standing.[21]

Although we have looked at some of the pros and cons of promotion via the Internet, the fact remains that the Internet is here to stay. The low costs, ability to target sports fans and participants, and high flexibility far outweigh the disadvantages of this medium. Certainly, sports marketers have accepted the Internet as another important tool in their integrated communications efforts.

CHOOSING A SPECIFIC MEDIUM

Once the medium or media mix is chosen by the sports organization along with the advertising agency, the specific medium must be addressed. In other words, if the advertisement will appear in a magazine, then the choice of magazine will be most effective. Do we want our advertisement to promote the 2002 World Champion U.S. Women's Softball Team to appear in *Sports Illustrated, Sporting News Magazine, The Softball Magazine*, or some combination of these specific media? To answer this question, we must consider our reach and frequency objectives.

Reach refers to the number of people exposed to an advertisement in a given medium. For the advertiser who wants to generate awareness and reach the largest number of people in the target audience, perhaps *Sports Illustrated,* with a circulation of 3.3 million, would be the most effective medium.[22] However, if the target audience is women, then *Sports Illustrated* might be reaching people who are not potential users.

The reach of an advertisement is determined by a number of factors. First, the nature of the media mix influences reach. The general rule is that the greater the number of media used, the greater the reach. For example, if the advertising campaign for U.S. Women's Softball were broadcast on television, printed in magazines, and also appeared on the Internet, reach would be increased. Second, if only one medium is to be used, increasing the number and diversity within this medium will increase the reach. For instance, if cable television was chosen as the sole medium for the U.S. Women's Softball campaign, reach would be increased if the commercial were aired on ESPN, Lifetime, and Fox Sports versus ESPN alone. Finally, reach can be enhanced by airing the advertisements during different times of the day or day parts. The advertisement might be shown at night after 9:00 P.M. and also in the morning to reach a greater percentage of the target audience.

Along with reach, another consideration in making specific media decisions is frequency. **Frequency** refers to the number of times the individual or household is exposed to the media vehicle. An important point is that frequency is measured by the number of exposures to the media vehicle rather than the advertisement itself. Just because an advertisement is shown on television during the Super Bowl does not mean that the target audience has seen it. Consumers might change channels, leave the room, or simply become involved in conversation. A study examined this issue using Super Bowl viewers in a bar setting.[23] It found that visual attention levels for the game are similar to attention levels for the advertisements, attention to commercials varies by their location in the cluster of advertisements and time of game, and that Super Bowl commercials may receive more attention than commercials on other programs.

MEDIA SCHEDULING

Four basic **media scheduling** alternatives are considered once the medium (e.g., magazines) and specific publications (e.g., *Sports Illustrated*) are chosen. These schedules are called continuous, flighting, pulsing, and seasonal. A **continuous schedule** recognizes that there are no breaks in the demand for the sports product. This is also called steady, or "drip," scheduling. During the advertising period, advertisements are continually run. Most sporting goods and events are seasonal and, therefore, do not require a continuous schedule. Some sporting goods, such as running shoes, have roughly equivalent demand and advertising spending throughout the year.

A **flighting schedule** is another alternative, where advertising expenditures are varied in some months and zero is spent in other months. Consider the case of the Houston Astros. Heavy advertising expenditures are spent in March, April, and May leading up to the season. Reminder-oriented advertising is placed over the course of the rest of the season, and no advertising dollars are spent in the winter months. This type of scheduling is most prevalent in sports marketing due to the seasonal nature of most sports.

A **pulsing schedule** is a variant of the flighting schedule. Ad expenditures may vary greatly, but some level of advertising is always taking place. Although it sounds similar to a flighting schedule, remember that a flighting schedule has some months where zero is spent on advertising.

PERSONAL SELLING

Now that we have looked at the advertising process in detail, let us turn to another important element in the promotion mix—personal selling. Personal selling is used in a variety of ways in sports marketing, such as securing corporate sponsorships, selling luxury suites or boxes in stadiums, and hawking corporate and group ticket sales. In the marketing of sporting goods, the primary applications of personal selling are to get retailers to carry products (push strategy) and consumers to purchase products (pull strategy).

Personal selling represents a unique element in the promotion mix because it involves personal interaction with the target audience rather than mass communication to thousands or millions of consumers. The definition of personal selling reflects this important distinction between personal selling and the other promotion tools. **Personal selling** is a form of person-to-person communication in which a salesperson works with prospective buyers and attempts to influence their purchase needs in the direction of their company's products or services.

All the advantages of personal selling described in Table 11.5 make it an attractive promotional tool, so the ability to use personal selling to develop long term relationships with consumers is becoming increasingly important to sports marketers. In fact, building long term relationships with consumers has become one of the critical issues for marketers.[24] More formally, **relationship marketing** is the process of creating,

TABLE 11.5 Benefits of Personal Selling

- Personal selling allows the salesperson to immediately adapt the message they are presenting based on feedback received from the target audience.
- Personal selling allows the salesperson to communicate more information to the target audience than other forms of promotion. Moreover, complex information can be explained by the salesperson.
- Personal selling greatly increases the likelihood of the target audience paying attention to the message. It is difficult for the target audience to escape the message because communication is person to person.
- Personal selling greatly increases the chances of developing a long-term relationship with consumers, due to the frequent person-to-person communication.

maintaining, and enhancing strong, value-laden relationships with customers and other stakeholders.[25]

As Kotler and Armstrong point out, the key premise of relationship marketing is that building strong economic and social ties with valued customers, distributors, dealers, and suppliers leads to long-term profitable transactions. Many sports organizations are realizing it is cheaper to foster and maintain strong relationships with existing customers rather than find new customers or fight the competition for a stagnant consumer base.

Two examples of building relationships with consumers of sport were described in an article entitled, "Pursuing Relationships in Professional Sport."[26] In the first example, a promotion was developed by the Pittsburgh Pirates and Giant Eagle Supermarkets. The basic premise of the promotion was that fans could earn discounts and special offers at Pirates' games by participating in the Giant Eagle preferred shoppers program. For example, fans with an Advantage Card (given to program participants) were offered discounted ballpark meals for a month, half-price tickets to five games throughout the season, and discounts on Pirates' merchandise. The relationship-building program was deemed successful by the Pirates, Giant Eagle, and the fans.

Another relationship-building effort was designed for the fans of the San Diego Padres. The program, initiated in the 1996 season and called the Compadres Club, rewards fans for attending predetermined numbers of games. In addition, the fans receive frequency points based on player performance. Ultimately, fans can redeem their frequency points for Padres' merchandise, posters, and dinners. For example, the top earners receive an authentic baseball bat autographed by a Padres' player and presented on the field at a special pregame ceremony. More than 50,000 fans enrolled in the program's initial year (now up to 150,000 members), and the Padres have gathered a wealth of information on their fans.

Although both the Pirates and the Padres have developed marketing programs to build relationships with fans, the importance of personal selling should not be over looked. Personal selling was necessary for the Pirates to communicate the benefits of the partnership to Giant Eagle. As a result of selling a successful program to Giant Eagle, the company increased its Pirates-related marketing budget by roughly 25 percent. The Padres, armed with a database of the demographic and buying habits of its most loyal fans, will use personal selling to secure additional sponsorship and advertising dollars.

THE STRATEGIC SELLING PROCESS

Now that we have defined personal selling and discussed some of its major advantages, let us examine how the selling process operates in sports marketing. As previously discussed, sports marketers are generally concerned with selling an intangible service versus a tangible good. Most salespeople view the selling of services as a much more difficult process, because the benefits of the sports product are not readily observable or easily communicated to the target audience. It is much easier to sell the new and improved R360 XD driver from TaylorMade when the consumer can see the design, feel the weight of the club, and swing the club. In essence, the product sells itself. Contrast this with the sale of a luxury box to a corporation in a stadium that is yet to be built. Selling this sports product is dependent on communicating both the tangible and intangible benefits of the box to the prospective buyer. In addition to the problems associated with selling a service versus a good, the sale of many sports products requires several people to give their approval before the sale is complete. This factor also makes the selling process more complex.

In the ever-changing world of sports marketing, the "good ol' boy" approach to selling is no longer valid. To be more effective and efficient in today's competitive environment, a number of personal selling strategies have been developed. One process, developed by Robert Miller and Stephen Heiman, is called **strategic selling.**[27]

Miller and Heiman suggest the first step in any strategic selling process is performing an analysis of your current position. In this instance, position is described as understanding your personal strengths and weaknesses as well as the opportunities and threats that are present in the selling situation. In essence, the salesperson is constructing a mini-SWOT analysis. Questions regarding how prospective clients feel about you as a salesperson, how they feel about your products and services, who the competition is, and how they are positioned must all be addressed at the initial stages of the strategic selling process.

Good salespeople realize that they must adapt their current position for every account before they can be successful. To change this position, six elements in the strategic selling process must be considered in a systematic and interactive fashion. These elements, which must be understood for successful sales, include buying influences, red flags, response modes, win-results, the sales funnel, and the ideal customer profile. Let us take a brief look at how these elements work together in the strategic selling process.

BUYING INFLUENCES

A complex sale was earlier defined as one where multiple individuals are involved in the buying process. This is true of large organizations considering a sponsorship proposal or families considering the purchase of exercise equipment for a new workout facility in their home. One of the first steps in the strategic sales process is to identify all the individuals involved in the sale and to determine their buying roles.

Roles are patterns of behavior expected by people in a given position. Miller and Heiman believe there are generally four critical buying roles that must be understood in a complex sale (no matter how many people play these roles). The **economic buying role** is a position that governs final approval to buy and that can say yes to a sale when everyone else says no, and vice versa. The **user buying role** makes judgments about the potential impact of your product or service on their job performance. These individuals will also supervise or use the product, so they want to know "what the product or service will do for them." The **technical buying role** screens out possible suppliers on the basis of meeting a variety of technical specifications that have been determined in advance by the organization. The technical buyers also serve as gatekeepers, who screen out potential suppliers on the basis of failing to meet the stated specifications. Finally, the **coach's role** is to act as a guide for the salesperson making the sale. The coach is a valuable source of information about the organization and can lead you to the other **buying influences.** As Miller and Heiman point out, identifying the individuals playing the various roles is the foundation of the strategic selling process.

RED FLAGS

Once the individuals have been identified, the next step in the strategic selling process is to look for red flags, or things that can threaten a complex sale. Red flags symbolize those strategic areas that can require further attention to avoid mistakes in positioning. In addition, red flags can be used to capitalize on an area of strength. Some of the red flags that can threaten a complex sale include either missing or uncertain information, uncontacted buying influences, or reorganization. For example, any uncontacted buying influences are considered a threat to the sale. These uncontacted buying influences are analogous to uncovered bases in baseball. Teams cannot be fielded or successful when there is no shortstop or catcher. Likewise, a sale cannot be successful until all the relevant players have been contacted.

RESPONSE MODES

After the buyer(s) have been targeted and you have correctly positioned your products or services by identifying red flags, the next step in the strategic selling process is to determine the buyer's reaction to the given sales situation. These varying reactions are categorized in four **response modes.** These modes include the growth mode, trouble mode, even keel mode, and overconfident mode.

The **growth mode** is characterized by organizations who perceive a discrepancy between their current state and their ideal state in terms of some goal (e.g., sales or profits). In other words, the organization needs to produce a higher quality sports product or put more people in the seats in order to grow. In this situation, the probability of a sale is high.

The second response mode is known as the **trouble mode.** When an organization is falling short of expectations, it is in the trouble mode. Here again, there is a discrepancy between the current and ideal states. In the growth mode the organization is going to improve upon an already good situation. However, the trouble mode indicates that the buyer is experiencing difficulties. In either case, the potential for a sale is high.

The **even keel mode** presents a more difficult case for the salesperson. As the name implies, there is no discrepancy between the ideal and current results and, therefore, the likelihood of a sale is low. The probability of a sale can be enhanced if the salesperson can demonstrate that a discrepancy actually exists, the buyer sees growth or trouble coming, or there is pressure from another buying influence.

The final response mode is the **overconfident mode.** Overconfidence is generally the toughest mode to overcome from the salesperson's perspective in that the buyers believe things are too good to be true. Just think about individual athletes or teams who are overconfident. Invariably they lose because of their false sense of superiority. Organizations that are overconfident are resistant to change because they are exceeding their goals (or at least they think so), so sales are difficult. NASCAR is one the fastest growing sports in the world, but organizers don't want to alienate long-time loyal fans. As such, NASCAR aired a series of TV ads at the start of the 2004 season that attempted to please the old knowledgeable NASCAR fan and address the new, novice fan of the sport. "We are always going to be very careful, while continuing to grow the sport, about alienating the avid fan," said Roger VanDerSnick, NASCAR's managing director of brand and consumer marketing. "We are very cognizant of the balancing act."[28] In this stage of the strategic sales process, the response mode of the organization should be analyzed. In addition, each of the buying influences should be examined to determine their perception of the current situation. By analyzing the buying influences and their perceptions, the salesperson is in a position to successfully adapt his or her approach to meet the needs of each buying influence and each customer.

WIN-RESULTS

Much of sports marketing today is based on the premise of strategic partnerships. The same is true for the strategic sales process. In strategic partnerships, the sales process produces satisfied customers, long-term relationships, repeat business, and good referrals. To achieve these outcomes, the salesperson must look at clients as partners rather than competition that must be beaten.

Miller and Heiman define the **win-results** concept in the strategic selling process as an objective result that gives one or more of the buying influences a personal win. The key to this definition is understanding the importance of both wins and results. A result is the impact of the salesperson's product or service on one or more of the client's business objectives. Results are usually tangible, quantifiable, and affect the entire organization. Wins, however, are the fulfillment of a promise made to oneself. Examples of personal wins for the potential client include gaining recognition within the organization, increasing responsibility and authority, and enhancing self-esteem. It is important to realize that wins are subjective, intangible, and do not benefit all the people in the organization the same way.

THE SALES FUNNEL

The sales funnel is another key element in the strategic sales process. This is a tool used to organize all potential clients, as opposed to developing a means for understanding an individual client. Basically, the **sales funnel** is a model that is used to organize clients so salespeople might organize their efforts in the most efficient and effective manner. After all, allocating time and setting priorities are two of the most challenging tasks in personal selling.

The sales funnel divides clients into three basic levels—above the funnel, in the funnel, and the best few. Potential clients exist above the funnel if data (e.g., a call from the prospective client wanting information or acquiring information from personal sources) suggest there may be a possible fit between the salesperson's products or services and the needs of the potential client. The salesperson's emphasis at this level is to gather information and then develop and qualify prospects.

Potential clients are then filtered to the next level of the sales funnel. If clients are placed in the funnel (rather than above it), then the possibility of a sale has been verified. Verification occurs once a buying influence has been contacted and indicates that the organization is in either a growth or trouble response mode. Remember that these two response modes represent ideal conditions for a sale to occur.

When all the buying influences have been identified, red flags have been eliminated, and win-results have been addressed, sales prospects can be moved from in the funnel to the "best few." At this final level of the sales funnel, the sale is expected to happen roughly 90 percent of the time.

IDEAL CUSTOMERS

The ideal customer concept in strategic selling extends the notion of the sales funnel. In this case, all potential customers outside the funnel are evaluated against the hypothetical "ideal customer." The strategic sales process is based on the belief that every sale is not a good sale. The **ideal customer** profile is constructed to cut down on the unrealistic prospects that should not be in the sales funnel in the first place.

When constructing the ideal customer profile, the salesperson must judge each prospect with respect to organizational demographics, psychographics, and corporate culture. Current prospects can then be evaluated against the ideal customer profile to determine whether additional time and energy should be invested.

SALES PROMOTIONS

Another promotion infix element that communicates to large audiences is sales promotions. **Sales promotions** are a variety of short-term, promotional activities that are designed to stimulate immediate product demand. A recent Krispy Kreme doughnut sales promotion illustrates how a simple game promotion can affect short-term sales.

The promotion allows each Kansas City Royal fan to redeem his or her ticket stub for a dozen free doughnuts whenever the Royals have 12 or more hits. In the season preceding the promotion, the Royals reached the 12-hit plateau while playing at home just 21 times. By June, the Royals had already reached 10 games with 12 or more hits and fans had turned in about 25,000 stubs for the equivalent of more than 2.1 million doughnuts, and a retail value of nearly $1 million. "*We never expected this in a million years,*" said Kelly Lehman, Krispy Kreme's director of marketing for Missouri and Kansas.[29]

The sales promotions used in sports marketing come in all shapes and sizes. Think about some of the sales promotions with which you may be familiar. Examples might include the Bud Bowl; Straight-A Night at the ballpark; a lifesize, cutout figure of Shaquille O'Neal placed inside Taco Bell restaurants; coupons for reduced green fees at public golf courses; a sweepstakes to win a free trip to the SuperBowl; a click of the mouse for a special free collector's edition of *Sports Illustrated* from Campbell's Soup; Miller Lite's "make the call for Miller Lite" baseball promotion, which includes banners, display cards, posters, and merchandise; and many other examples.

Minor League Baseball has always been known for its creative sales promotions and the Pacific Coast League's Portland Beavers provide a number of great examples. Every Thursday the Beavers offer two dollar beers on Thirsty Thursday, and Wednesdays are Dollar Dog nights, where fans can get a hot dog for a buck. The Beavers have also gained the attention of fans with their "Bark in the Park" promotion where fans can bring their dogs to the ballpark and "Two Dead Fat Guys" night in honor of Elvis and Babe Ruth.

As stated in the definition, all forms of sales promotions are designed to increase short-term sales. Additional objectives may include increasing brand awareness, broadening distribution channels, reminding consumers about the offering, or inducing a trial to win new customers. To accomplish these objectives, sports marketers use a variety of sales promotion tools.

PREMIUMS

Premiums are probably the sales promotion technique most associated with traditional sports marketing. **Premiums** are items given away with the sponsors product as part of the sales promotion. Baseball cards, NASCAR model car replicas, water bottles, hats, refrigerator magnets, posters, and almost anything else imaginable have been given away at sporting events. Although premiums are often given away to spectators at events, they can also be associated with other sporting promotions. For example, *Sports Illustrated* magazines gives away hats, T-shirts, and videos to induce potential consumers to subscribe. In another example, many credit card companies are giving away hats with the logo of the fan's favorite team for applying for a line of credit.

Perhaps the most effective and exciting premium over the past several years has been the Bobblehead. Recently, LeBron James' Bobbleheads were promoted by the Cleveland Cavaliers and fans lined up for more than three hours prior to the tipoff to get their hands on one the 10,000 being given away. While the Bobblehead remains popular, the latest and greatest premium is the Russian nesting doll, also known as a matroyska. The San Diego Padres honored Tony Gywnn with his own nesting doll and the giveaway prompted the third largest crowd of the year. Who knows what the next premium craze might be in sports?

Although premiums can bring people to games who would not otherwise attend, they can also have negative consequences and must be carefully planned. In the now defunct World Hockey Association (WHA), the Philadelphia Blazers handed out souvenir pucks at the first home game. Unfortunately, the game had to be postponed because the ice was deemed unfit for skating. When the Blazer's Derek Sanderson announced the game cancellation to the crowd at center ice, he was pelted with the pucks.[30] In a similar scenario, the LA Dodgers had to forfeit a game because fans began throwing baseballs (that they had been given) onto the field, endangering players and other fans. The

Giveaways are a popular promotional technique.

Dodgers can also be used to illustrate the height of premium marketing. In 1984, the Los Angeles Olympic Games created a regionwide craze for pin collecting. Sensing the "legs" of this mania, the Dodgers created six pin-give-away nights at their stadium, Chavez Ravine. They picked games that would typically have low attendance. The result was that all six of these games sold out on the strength of a $.60 per unit collector's pin!

CONTESTS AND SWEEPSTAKES

Sweepstakes and contests are another sales promotional tool used by sports marketers to generate awareness and interest among consumers. Contests are competitions that award prizes on the basis of contestants' skills and ability, whereas sweepstakes are games of chance or luck. As with any sales promotion, the sports marketing manager must attempt to integrate the contest or sweepstakes with the other promotion mix elements and keep the target market in mind.

One of the classic contests sponsored by the NFL was the punt, pass, and kick competition. In this competition, young athletes competed for a chance to appear on the finals of nationally televised NFL games, making the NFL the winner for promoting youth sports. Other contests have capitalized on the growing popularity of rotisserie sports. Dugout Derby, Pigskin Playoff, and Fairway Golf are all examples of "rotisserie" contests conducted via toll-free numbers where fans could earn prizes for choosing the best fantasy team or athletes. In return, marketers capture a rich database of potential consumers.[31] As sweepstakes become more and more popular, companies are constantly looking for new ways to break through the clutter. Consider this tremendous opportunity for race fans offered by RadioShack and Samsung. They have designed the "Call Your Driver" sweepstakes where fans can enter by purchasing any Samsung wireless phone at RadioShack or by requesting an official entry code. Participants "call their driver" by selecting the driver they think will win the Samsung/RadioShack 500 in Fort Worth, Texas. The winning bounty includes the following: flying the winning fan and three guests to the Samsung/RadioShack 500 where they will spend five nights in a state-of-art RV on the infield of the race, receive passes to tour the pits, and tickets to watch the race from the grandstands.

In addition, the grand prizewinner will receive a RadioShack scanner, race intercom system, and headset, allowing them to listen as pit crews and drivers discuss racing strategies. Afterward, the grand prize winner will visit Victory Lane for an experience

Visa and NASCAR team up for an on-line contest.
Source: Courtesy of NASCAR and Visa.

of a lifetime as the winning driver is presented with the coveted Texas Motor Speedway "boot" trophy. To top it off, if the driver in Victory Lane is the same one the grand prize winner selected on his or her Call Your Driver sweepstakes entry form, they'll be presented with a 2004 car in the same make and model. Now that's a sweepstakes![32]

Other sweepstakes are taking advantage of the Internet and its growing audience. For example, Pontiac sponsored a contest in 2004 in which sports fans had a chance to win $10,000 by picking the most winners in the NCAA basketball tournament. The sweepstakes was promoted through the ESPN Web site, and the only information required to win this prize was a name, phone number, and e-mail address. Again, the marketers for Pontiac are collecting a database of potential consumers for their product by running this sales promotion. The typical by-product of this database would be an invitation to visit a dealership, test drive a car, or have information mailed to participants.

SAMPLING

One of the most effective ways of inducing customers to try new products that are being introduced is **sampling.** Unfortunately, it is very difficult to give away a small portion of a sporting event. However, sports have been known to put on exhibitions to give consumers a "taste" for the game. Squash demonstration matches have been held in the middle of New York's Grand Central Station, attracting thousands of fans who would have never otherwise been exposed to the sport. The Olympics, of course, have used demonstration sports since 1904, in sports such as roller hockey and Bandy (soccer on ice), to provide a "sample" of the action to spectators. If fan interest is high enough (i.e., attendance), the sport can then become a medal sport in the next Olympiad. In yet another example, one million samples of Nivea for Men will be distributed in conjunction with NCAA March Madness. Employees outfitted as referees, cheerleaders, and basketball players will distribute the products both on college campuses and in the streets to prospective consumers.

POINT-OF-PURCHASE DISPLAYS

Point-of-Purchase or **P-O-P displays** have long been used by marketers to attract consumers' attention to a particular product or retail display area. These displays or materials, such as brochures, cut-outs, and banners, are most commonly used to communicate price reductions or other special offers to consumers. For instance, tennis racquet manufacturers, such as Prince, design huge tennis racquets, which are then displayed in the storefronts of many tennis retail shops to catch the attention of consumers.

COUPONS

Another common sales promotion tool is the coupon. **Coupons** are certificates that generally offer reductions in price for sports products. Coupons may appear in print advertisements, as part of the product's package, inserted within the product packaging, or be mailed to consumers. Although coupons have been found to induce short-term sales, there are disadvantages. For instance, some marketers believe continual coupon use can detract from the image of the product in the mind of consumers. In addition, most coupon redemption is done by consumers who already use the product, therefore limiting the use of coupons to attract new customers.

PUBLIC RELATIONS

The final element in the promotional mix that we discuss is public relations. Quite often, public relations gets confused with other promotional mix elements. Public relations is often mistaken for publicity. This is an easy mistake to make because the goals of public relations and publicity are to provide communication that will enhance the image of the sports entity (athlete, team, or league). Before we make a distinction between public relations and publicity, let us define public relations. **Public relations** is the element of the promotional mix that identifies, establishes, and maintains mutually beneficial relationships between the sports organizations and the various publics on which its success or failure depends.

Within the definition of public relations, reference is made to the "various publics" with which the sports organization interacts. Brooks divides these publics into the external publics, which are outside the immediate control of sports marketers, and the internal publics, which are more directly controlled by sports marketers. The external publics include the community (e.g., city and state officials, community members, corporations), sanctioning bodies (e.g., NCAA), intermediary publics (e.g., sports marketing agencies), and competition (e.g., other sports or entertainment choices). The internal publics, such as volunteers, employees, suppliers, athletes, and spectators are associated with manufacturing, distributing, and consuming the sport itself.[33]

Sports marketers have a variety of public relations tools they can use to communicate with the internal and external publics. The choice of tools depends on the public relations objective, the targeted audience, and how public relations is being integrated into the overall promotional plan. These tools and techniques include generating publicity (news releases or press conferences), participating in community events, producing written materials (annual report or press guides), and even lobbying (personal selling necessary for stadium location decisions).[34]

One of the most important and widely used public relations tools is publicity. Publicity is the generation of news in the broadcast or print media about a sports product. The news about a sports product is most commonly disseminated to the various sports publics through news releases and press conferences. Although public relations efforts are managed by the sports organization, publicity can sometimes come from external sources. As such, publicity might not always enhance the image of the sports product. Because publicity is often outside the control of the sports organization, it is seen as a highly credible source of communication. Information that is coming from "unbiased" sources, such as magazines, newspaper articles, or the televised news, is perceived to be more trustworthy.

In addition to publicity, another powerful public relations tool used to enhance the sports organization's image is **community involvement.** A study was conducted to determine what, if anything, professional sports organizations are doing in the area of community relations. The survey specifically examined the NBA, NHL, NFL, and MLB to determine how they are involved in community relations and how important community relations is to their overall marketing program. All the responding teams indicated they were involved in some sort of community programs, with the most common form of community involvement being (1) sponsoring public programs (e.g., food and toy drives, medical programs and services, auctions, and other fundraisers); (2) requiring time commitment from all of the sports organizations' employees); (3) partially funding programs; and (4) providing personnel at no charge. Interestingly, the study found no differences among the importance of community relations by type of league. In other words, the NBA, NHL, NFL, and MLB are all equally involved in community relations.[35]

There are a variety of public relations techniques that can help achieve public relations and promotion objectives. When developing an integrated marketing communications strategy, sports marketers need to know how to coordinate public relations efforts with the other promotional mix tools. In addition, sports marketers must understand how to best synthesize each public relations tool. The following example illustrates how Benson and Hedges planned, implemented, and evaluated an integrated public relations and sponsorship plan. As you read, pay special attention to how the public relations tools were carefully blended to achieve Bensen and Hedges objective of establishing a mutually beneficial relationship with the international sport of snooker.

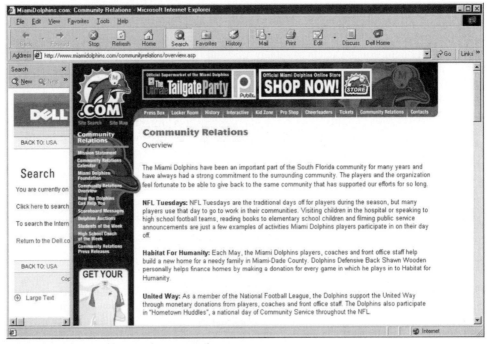

Miami Dolphins reach out to the community.

Source: Used by permission of Miami Dolphins.

Benson & Hedges Masters

BACKGROUND

Benson and Hedges has sponsored this leading snooker tournament since 1975. KES manage the full sponsorship—including all PR. All PR activities must be within the restrictions of tobacco regulations.

OBJECTIVES

- Create awareness of the Benson & Hedges Masters Tournament.
- Drive ticket sales.
- Work alongside governing body to help snooker reposition itself to a younger age group and more appealing demographic.

STRATEGY

- Create original angles for preview features away from the table that focus on the player's personalities to build appeal of the tournament.
- Create hype around big head-to-head matches mid-tournament.

ACTION

Player Feature Campaign

- KES set up a number of different opportunities for TV, print, and radio with players taking part in the tournament. These included:
- A Silverstone Driving day, which appeared on BBC National News, Sky News, and in *The Sun*.
- A day "At the Races" with Jimmy White. This was featured on London Tonight and in *The Daily Mail* and *The Mirror*.
- A press conference at Stirling Castle, which resulted in features on Grampian TV, BBC TV Scotland, in six Scottish national newspapers, and on two radio stations.
- A day with Ronnie O'Sullivan "Keeping in Shape" at a health club featured on BBC London News and in *The Times*.

- A Paul Hunter Fashion Makeover at Harrods was featured in the *Express Magazine*.

Radio Prepromotion

- Live links and syndicated interviews were aired on over 134 stations including BBC Radio 2, TalkSport, Five Live, and Team Talk.
- A number of on-air phone-ins were arranged with wild card Steve Davis, "Snooker Steve."
- Eighty-two radio ticket competitions ran.
- There were 12 hours 15 minutes of B&H snooker coverage aired.

Regional Press

- Ninety percent of SE-based press titles ran promotions to win tickets and carried tournament previews.
- Syndicated player interviews ran across all these titles.

Tournament Activity

- Preview of "head-to-heads."
- Celebrity attendance from Ronnie Wood. Featured in four national dailies.
- BBC London News aired a live interview with Jimmy White broadcast from the B&H Masters.

RESULTS

- BBC total audience figures were up by 4.6 million over the week.
- The B&H Masters final audience was the highest for eight years.
- Ticket sales increased by 28 percent over 2001.
- Radio values were up by 23 percent over 2001.
- Press values were up by 43 percent over 2001.
- Total media value: £2,696,500.
- Pretournament activity value: £948,000.
- PR Budget: £15,000.

Source: Benson & Hedges Masters. Copyright © Karen Earl Sponsorship 2001. www.karen-earl.co.uk. All rights reserved.

Summary

Chapter 11 focuses on gaining a better understanding of the various promotional mix elements. Advertising is one of the most visible and critical promotional mix elements. Although most of us associate advertising with developing creative slogans and jingles, there is a systematic process for designing effective advertisements. Developing an advertising campaign consists of a series of five interrelated steps, which include formulating objectives, designing an ad budget, making creative decisions, choosing a media strategy, and evaluating the advertisement.

Advertising objectives and budgeting techniques are similar to those discussed in Chapter 10 for the broader promotion planning process. Advertising objectives are sometimes categorized as either direct or indirect. Direct advertising objectives, such as advertising by sports organizations to end user and sales promotion advertising, are designed to stimulate action among consumers of sport. Alternatively, the goal of indirect objectives is to make consumers aware, enhance the image of the sport, or provide information to consumers. After objectives have been determined, budgets for the advertising campaign are considered. Budget techniques, such as competitive parity, objective and task, arbitrary allocation, and percentage of sales, are commonly used by advertisers.

Once the objectives and budget have been established, the creative process is considered. The creative process identifies the ideas and the concept of the advertisement. To develop the concept for the advertisement, benefits of the sports product must be identified; ad appeals (e.g., health, emotional, fear, sex, and pleasure) are designed; and advertising execution decisions (e. g., comparative advertisements, slice of life, and scientific) are made. After creative decisions are crafted, the next phase of the advertising campaign is to design media strategy. Media strategy includes decisions about the what medium (e.g., radio, television, and Internet) will be most effective and how to best schedule the chosen media.

Another communications tool that is part of the promotional mix is personal selling. Personal selling is unique in that person-to-person communication is required rather than mass communication. In other words, a salesperson must deliver the message face to face to the intended target audience rather than through some nonpersonal medium (e.g., a magazine). Although there are many advantages to personal selling, perhaps none is greater than the ability to use personal selling to develop long-term relationships with customers.

In today's competitive sports marketing environment, a number of strategies have been developed to maximize personal selling effectiveness. One process, designed by Miller and Heiman, is called the strategic selling process and consists of six elements. The elements, which must be considered for successful selling, include buying influences, red flags, response modes, win-results, the sales funnel, and the ideal customer profile.

Sales promotions are another element in the promotional mix that are designed primarily to stimulate consumer demand for products. One of the most widely used forms of sales promotion in sports marketing includes premiums, or items that are given away with the core product being purchased. In addition, contests and sweepstakes, free samples, point-of-purchase displays, and coupons are forms of sales promotion that often are integrated into the broader promotional mix.

A final promotional mix element considered in Chapter 11 is public, or community, relations. Public relations is the element of the promotional mix that identifies, establishes, and maintains mutually beneficial relationships between the sports organization and the various publics on which its success or failure depends. These publics include the community, sanctioning bodies, intermediary publics, and competition. Other publics include employees, suppliers, participants, and spectators. The tools with which messages are communicated to the various publics include generating publicity, participating in community events, producing written materials such as annual reports and press releases, and lobbying.

Key Terms

- advertising
- advertising appeals
- advertising budgeting
- advertising execution
- advertising objectives
- attractiveness
- buying influences
- coach's role
- community involvement
- comparative advertisements
- continuous schedule
- coupons
- creative brief
- creative decisions
- creative process
- credibility
- direct objectives
- economic buying role
- emotional appeals
- even keel mode

- expertise
- fear appeals
- flighting schedule
- frequency
- growth mode
- health appeals
- ideal customer
- indirect objectives
- lifestyle advertisements
- media scheduling
- media strategy
- one-sided versus two-sided
- overconfident mode
- personal selling
- pleasure or fun appeals
- P-O-P displays
- premiums
- profit appeals
- promotional mix elements
- public relations

- pulsing schedule
- reach
- relationship marketing
- response modes
- roles
- sales funnel
- sales promotions
- sampling
- scientific advertisements
- sex appeals
- slice-of-life advertisements
- stadium signage
- strategic selling
- sweepstakes and contests
- technical buying role
- testimonials
- trouble mode
- trustworthiness
- user buying role
- win-results

Review Questions

1. What are the major steps in developing an advertising campaign?
2. Explain direct advertising objectives versus indirect advertising objectives.
3. Describe the creative decision process. What are the three outcomes of the creative process?
4. Discuss, in detail, the major advertising appeals used by sports marketers. Provide at least one example of each type of advertising appeal.
5. What are the executional formats commonly used in sports marketing advertising?
6. Comment on the advantages and disadvantages of using athlete endorsers in advertising.
7. What two decisions do advertisers make in developing a media strategy? What are the four basic media scheduling alternatives? Provide an example of each type of media scheduling.
8. Discuss the strengths and weaknesses of the alternative forms of advertising available to sports marketers.
9. When is personal selling used by sports marketers? Describe, in detail, the steps in the strategic selling process.
10. Describe the various forms of sales promotion available to sports marketers.

Exercises

1. Design a creative advertising strategy to increase participation in Little League Baseball.
2. Design a survey instrument to assess the source credibility of 10 professional athletes (of your choice) and administer the survey to 10 individuals. Which athletes have the highest levels of credibility, and why?
3. Attend a professional or collegiate sporting event and describe all the forms of advertising you observe. Which forms of advertising do you feel are particularly effective, and why?
4. Visit a sporting goods retailer and describe all the sales promotion tools that you observe. Which forms of sales promotion do you believe are particularly effective, and why?
5. Interview the director or manager of ticket sales for a professional organization or collegiate sports program to determine their sales process. How closely does their sales process follow the strategic selling process outlined in this chapter?
6. Interview the marketing department (or director of community/public relations) from a professional organization or collegiate sports program to determine the extent of their community or public relations efforts. How do sports organizations decide in which community events or activities to participate?

Internet Exercises

1. Using the Internet, find two examples of advertisements for sports products that use indirect objectives and two examples of advertisements that use direct objectives.
2. Find 10 advertisements on the Internet for sports products and describe the executional format for each advertisement. Which type of execution format is most commonly used for Internet advertising?

Endnotes

1. See, for example, Joel Evans and Barry Berman, *Marketing*, 6th ed. (New York: Macmillan, 1994), 610.
2. IHRSA Notes: "Nesting" Americans Predicted to Flock to Fitness Centers in Record Numbers in 2004; IHRSA Offers Seven Tips Every Prospective Club Member Should Know, "*Business Wire*" (December 3, 2003).
3. William A. Sutton, Mark A. McDonald, George R. Milne, and John Cimperman, "Creating and Fostering Fan Identification in Professional Sports," *Sport Marketing Quarterly*, vol. 6, no. 1 (1997), 15–22.
4. Rachel Lehmann-Haupt, Does Sex Still Sell? *Folio* (March 1, 2004) 3; Women's Soccer News. www.hankerin.com/jan00/soccer/matildas.html.
5. "Stephenson in "Sex" Appeal," *Irish Independent* (October 15, 2003).
6. Terry Lelton, "The Post-Mike Millennium"—Gatorade Advertising, *Post*-Michael Jordan, Brandweek, (January 3, 2000).
7. "Kobe Bryant's Endorsement Deals." http://advertising.about.com/library/weekly/aa072903a.htm
8. Rich Thomaselli "$192 million: Nike bets big on range of endorsers." *Advertising Age* (January 5, 2004) 8.

9. Mark Hyman, "Dead Men Don't Screw Up Ad Campaigns," *Business Week* (March 10, 1997), 115.

10. Douglas M. Turco, "The Effects of Courtside Advertising on Product Recognition and Attitude Change," *Sport Marketing Quarterly*, vol. 5, no. 4 (1996), 11–15.

11. Jay Gladden, "The Ever Expanding Impact of Technology on Sport Marketing, Part II," *Sport Marketing Quarterly*, vol. 5, no. 4 (1996), 9–10.

12. Douglas M. Turco, "The Effects of Courtside Advertising on Product Recognition and Attitude Change," *Sports Marketing Quarterly*, vol. 5, no. 4 (1996), 11–15.

13. Wayne Friedman, "Intermedia Measures Product Placements; Study Shows No Correlation Between Ratings, Effectivenes, *Television Week* (December 15, 2003), 4.

14. Marla Matzer Rose, "Firms gauge product placements," *The Hollywood Reporter* (January 20, 2004).

15. Dale Buss, "You Ought to Be in Pictures." www.businessweek.com/smallbiz/news/columns/98–25/e3583060.htm.

16. George Belch and Michael Belch, *Advertising and Promotion: An Integrated Marketing Communications Perspective*, 4th ed. (New York: Irwin, McGraw-Hill, 1998), 431–434.

17. Joe Layden, "Human Billboards," *Mark McCormack's Guide to Sports Marketing*, International Sports Marketing Group (1996), 129–136.

18. Media Metrix Announces Top 50 U.S. Internet Property Rankings for September 2003; U.S. Internet Population Breaks the 150 Million Mark. *PR Newswire* (October 21, 2003).

19. //http://espn.go.com/mediakit/research/demographics.html

20. Masha Geller, "Reaching Young Sports Fans Online," http://www.mediapost.com/dtls_dsp_news.cfm?news ID = 198732 (March 13, 2003).

21. Rachel Johns, "Sports Promotion & The Internet," *Cyber-Journal of Sport Marketing*. www.cad.gu.edu.au/market/cv. . . urnal_of_sport_ marketing/htm.

22. "Top Magazines by Paid Circulation: Six Month Averages Ended June 30, 1997." www.adage.com/ns-search/datapla. . . 3/aaaa004Chf33977&NS-doc-offset50&.

23. Fred Beasley, Matthew Shank, and Rebecca Ball, "Do Super Bowl Viewers Watch the Commercials," *Sport Marketing Quarterly*, vol. 7, no. 3 (1998), 33–40.

24. Philip Kotler and Gary Armstrong, *Marketing: An Introduction*, 4th ed. (Upper Saddle River, NJ: Prentice Hall, 1997).

25. Ibid.

26. Sean Brenner, "Pursuing Relationships in Professional Sport," *Sport Marketing Quarterly*, vol. 6, no. 2 (1997), 33–34.

27. Robert Miller and Stephen Heiman, *Strategic Selling* (New York: Warner Books, 1985).

28. Stephanie Stoughton, "NASCAR concerned about racing's image," *The Associated Press* (February 5, 2004) 2B.

29. Royals' fans taking advantage of Krispy Kreme promotion (June 23, 2003). sportsbusinessnews.com.

30. Ed Willes, "A Legacy of Slapstick and Slap Shots," *New York Times* (November 30, 1997), 33.

31. Howard Schlossberg, *Sport Marketing* (Cambridge, MA: Blackwell, 1996).

32. "Samsung and RadioShack Encourage Racing Fans to 'Call Your Driver' in National Sweepstakes." *PR Newswire* (February 12, 2004).

33. Christine Brooks, *Sports Marketing: Competitive Business Strategies for Sports* (Upper Saddle River, NJ: Prentice Hall, 1994).

34. William Zikmund and Michael d'Amico, *Marketing*, 4th ed. (St. Paul, MN: West, 1993).

35. Denise O'Connell, "Community Relations in Professional Sports Organizations," Unpublished Master's Thesis, The Ohio State University, Columbus, Ohio.

CHAPTER 12

SPONSORSHIP PROGRAMS

After completing this chapter, you should be able to:

- Comment on the growing importance of sports sponsorships as a promotion mix element.
- Design a sponsorship program.
- Understand the major sponsorship objectives.
- Provide examples of the various costs of sponsorship.
- Identify the levels of the sports event pyramid.
- Evaluate the effectiveness of sponsorship programs.

GROWTH OF SPONSORSHIP

The opening scenario is just one example of a company using sponsorship to help achieve its marketing objectives. A wide variety of organizations are realizing that sports sponsorships are a valuable way to reach new markets and retain an existing customer base. Sponsorships can increase sales, change attitudes, heighten awareness, and build and maintain relationships with consumers. It is no wonder that sponsorships became the promotional tool of choice for marketers in the 1990s and continues to grow in importance. Before we turn to the growth of sponsorship as a promotional tool, let us define sponsorship.

In Chapter 10, sponsorships were described as one of the elements in the promotional mix. More specifically, **sponsorship** was defined as investing in a sports entity (athlete, league, team, or event) to support overall organizational objectives, marketing goals, and promotional strategies. The sponsorship investment may come in the form of monetary support and trade. For example, Under Armour has signed a five year deal to be The University of Maryland's exclusive uniform provider beginning with the 2004 season. The contract includes two one-year renewal options and is valued at $520,000 annually, which includes $200,000 in sponsorship payments, $195,000 in apparel and footwear allowances, and an average of $125,000 in marketing support for Maryland football. Under Armour will do this to support their marketing objective of increasing awareness of their brand and to associate with a winning NCAA program. Understanding how sponsorship can help achieve marketing goals and organizational objectives is discussed when we look at the construction of a sponsorship plan or program. For now, let us turn our attention to the dramatic growth of sponsorship as a promotional tool.

Brewer Will Be the "Official Beer Sponsor" of the U.S. Olympic Team

Anheuser-Busch announced the company has signed a multiyear agreement with the United States Olympic Committee (USOC) extending its Budweiser and Bud Light beer brands as the "official beer sponsors" of the U.S. Olympic Team through 2008.

The sponsorship will give Budweiser, Bud Light, and Michelob ULTRA use of the U.S. Olympic five-ring logo in all marketing and advertising activities to support Team USA's efforts at the XX Olympic Winter Games in Torino, Italy, in 2006; the XXIX Olympic Games in Beijing, China, in 2008; and the 2005 and 2007 Pan-American Games. The company's previous agreement as the "official beer sponsor" runs through the 2004 Olympic Games in Athens, Greece.

In addition, Anheuser-Busch will be the exclusive malt-beverage advertiser on all Olympic Games telecasts on NBC and its family of networks through 2008. "Anheuser-Busch has been a proud supporter of the USOC since 1984, and we're thrilled to continue supporting America's best athletes in their pursuit of winning a gold medal," said Tony Ponturo, vice president of Global Media and Sports Marketing, Anheuser-Busch, Inc. "Throughout history, the Olympic Games have captured some of the most remarkable and memorable moments in sports, and Budweiser and Bud Light are honored to be a part of these events as an official sponsor."

"The tremendous partnership our athletes have enjoyed with Anheuser-Busch has been instrumental in our efforts to field the best athletes in the world, while inspiring Americans in their everyday lives," said Jim Scherr, chief executive, United States Olympic Committee. "We are very fortunate and grateful to have a committed partner like Anheuser-Busch, a company that embodies the Olympic spirit of quality, excellence, and determination."

Budweiser has been an Olympic supporter since 1984 when the brand was the "official beer sponsor" of the Olympic Games in Los Angeles. Also, Budweiser and Bud Light were the "official beer sponsors" of the 1996 Olympic Games in Atlanta and the 2002 Olympic Winter Games in Salt Lake City.

In addition to the USOC sponsorship, Anheuser-Busch has signed a separate agreement making Budweiser the "official beer sponsor" of the XX Olympic Winter Games in Torino, Italy. This deal marks Anheuser-Busch's first sponsorship of Olympic Games held outside the United States. The sponsorship will give Budweiser official use of the 2006 Olympic Winter Games marks in Italy and a significant number of other countries.

In addition to the Olympic Games, Anheuser-Busch is the "official beer sponsor" of the National Basketball Association (NBA); Major League Baseball (MLB); 27 of the 32 National Football League (NFL) teams; the National Hockey League (NHL); NASCAR and NASCAR driver Dale Earnhardt Jr.; Major League Soccer (MLS) and each of its 12 teams; and the PGA TOUR, LPGA Tour and Champions Tour. Budweiser also sponsors a variety of international sports properties including the FIFA World Cup$^{(TM)}$, the BMW WilliamsF1 Team, the English Premier League, and Manchester United.

Source: Used by permission of Anheuser-Busch Inc.

In our brief discussion of sponsorship, we have alluded to the "dramatic growth" of sponsorship, but just how quickly is sponsorship growing? Review the following facts and figures regarding sponsorship activities:

- International Events Group (IEG) estimates that $10.25 billion were spent in North America by companies sponsoring special events in 2003 and this number is expected to rise to $11.14 billion in 2004. Of this $10.25 billion, $7.08 billion (or roughly 69 percent) were spent to sponsor sporting events.[1]
- IEG estimates that global spending on sponsorship will rise to $28 billion in 2004.[2]
- In 2003 soccer sponsorships totaled 1.9 billion making this sport first in sponsorship dollars spent. Golf and motorsports were the second and third highest sport for sponsorship spending respectively.[3]
- Sponsorship growth has exceeded traditional forms of promotion. For example, in 2003, advertising expenditures grew 5.2 percent while sponsorship sales grew 6.2 percent.[4]
- In 2002, companies spent $751 million sponsoring the Winter Olympic Games in Salt Lake City.[5]

- In 2003 the top valued sponsorship deals included: Nextel (with NASCAR) at $311 million; Nike (with Arsenal FC soccer) at $210 million; and General Electric (with the Olympics) at $200 million.[6]
- By 2010 estimates suggest that the sponsorship spending will reach $50 billion according to Sponsorship Research International.[7]

Not unlike other forms of promotion, sponsorship marketing is also reaching its saturation point in the marketplace. Consumers are paying less attention to sports sponsorships as they become more the rule than the exception. Sponsorship clutter is causing businesses, such as Anheuser-Busch, to design more systematic sponsorship programs that stand out in the sea of sponsorships. In addition, businesses are fighting the clutter of sponsoring mainstream sports by exploring new sponsorship opportunities (e.g., X-Games, women's sports, and Paralympics) and by becoming more creative with existing sponsorship opportunities.

One example of a creative sponsorship approach in a traditional sports medium comes from the world of pharmaceuticals and the race to capture the male impotence market. In an attempt to battle the market leader Viagra, GlaxoSmithKline and Bayer recently introduced a competing drug called Levitra. Viagra has gained widespread awareness, in part, because of the Mark Martin NASCAR sponsorship; and Levitra has countered with a NFL-sponsorship deal. Glaxo and Bayer signed a three-year deal with the NFL for a reported $6 million a year and will also spend an additional $10 to $15 million per year in advertising. To this end, the companies hired Mike Ditka to be their spokesperson. As is the case with most sponsorship deals, the agreement simply allows the drug makers to use the NFL logo and identify themselves as NFL sponsors. However, Glaxo and Bayer are willing to pay the price to break through the clutter and reach the desired target market. Glaxo spokesperson, Michael Fleming stated that 'it will give us access to the NFL's loyal, enthusiastic fan base and an opportunity to reach over 120 million football fans a week who watch the games."[8]

The Levitra example illustrates the nature of sponsorship. In essence, a sports sponsorship program is just another promotion mix element to be considered along with advertising, personal selling, sales promotions, and public relations. One difference, however, between sponsorship and the other promotion mix elements is that sports marketing relies heavily on developing successful sponsorship programs. In fact, sponsorship programs are so prevalent in sports marketing that the field is sometimes defined in these terms. The rest of this chapter is devoted to understanding how to develop the most effective sponsorship program.

DESIGNING A SPORTS SPONSORSHIP PROGRAM

Sports sponsorship programs come in all shapes and sizes. Following are just a few examples:

- George Mason High School has signed a five year, $50,000 deal to name its new football stadium Moore Cadillac Stadium.
- Skateboarder Mitchie Brusco has signed deals with Termite Skateboards, Lego, and Jones Soda to receive free merchandise in exchange for endorsements. He is only six years old!
- Manchester United announced a 13-year strategic alliance with Nike beginning August 2002. The 302.9 million pounds will hand Nike worldwide rights to all United merchandise and global operations.

- The NBA announced a new multiyear partnership with America's Dairy Farmers and Milk Processors to make milk the official promotion partner of the NBA.
- The Athens 2004 Olympic Committee has secured more than $50 million from a Greek telephone company (OTE) in what it says is the largest national sponsorship in the games' history.

What do each of these sponsorship examples have in common? First, they were developed as part of an integrated marketing communications approach in which sponsorship is but one element of the promotion mix. In addition, each of the sponsors has carefully chosen the best sponsorship opportunity (with individual athletes, teams, and leagues) to meet their organizational objectives and marketing goals.

To carefully plan sponsorship programs, a systematic process is being used by an increasing number of organizations. The process for designing a sports sponsorship program is presented in Figure 12.1. Before explaining the process, it is important to remember that sponsorship involves a marketing exchange. The sponsor benefits by receiving the right to associate with the sports entity (e.g., team or event), and the sports entity benefits from either monetary support or product being supplied by the sponsor. Because the marketing exchange involves two parties, the sponsorship process can be explored from the perspective of the sponsor (e.g., Nokia) or the sports entity (e.g., Sugar Bowl). We look at the process from the viewpoint of the sponsor rather than the entity sponsored.

As shown in the model, decisions regarding the sponsorship program are not made in isolation. Rather, the **sponsorship program** is just one element of the broader promotional strategy. It was suggested earlier that all the elements in the promotional mix must be integrated to have the greatest and most effective promotional impact. However, sponsorship decisions influence much more than just promotion. Sponsorship decisions can affect the entire marketing mix. For example, Nike signed a 10-year, $200-million contract to sponsor Brazil's World Championship soccer club. This will certainly present an opportunity for Nike to design and market a number of product tie-ins (shoes and apparel) to the sponsorship.[9] There are two important things to consider before signing a sponsorship agreement: (1) all your organization is getting is the right to be called a sponsor, not a completed sponsorship plan; and (2) you should spend two to three times your sponsorship fee to leverage your relationship as a sponsor—if you do not have the funds to promote, do not buy the sponsorship.

When designing the sponsorship program, the initial decisions are based on sponsorship objectives and budgets. These two elements go hand in hand. Without the money, the most meaningful objectives will never be reached. Alternatively,

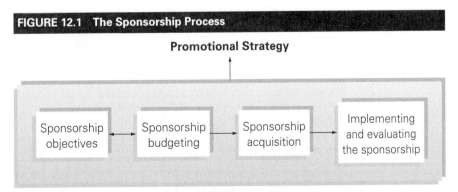

FIGURE 12.1 The Sponsorship Process

Promotional Strategy

Sponsorship objectives → Sponsorship budgeting → Sponsorship acquisition → Implementing and evaluating the sponsorship

Source: Hawkins et al., *Consumer Behavior*, 6th ed. (New York: McGraw-Hill, 1995). Reproduced with permission of the McGraw-Hill Companies.

Nike—a major sponsor of Brazilian football.

Source: Used by permission Brasil Futebol Shop. www.brasilfutebolshop.com.br/scripts/default.asp.

appropriate objectives must be considered without total regard to cost. If the objectives are sound, senior-level managers will find a way to allocate the necessary monies to sponsorship.

After the objectives and budget have been agreed upon, the specific sports sponsorship opportunity is chosen from the hundreds available. For example, Pepsi receives approximately 500 sponsorship proposals each year, and Pennzoil reports that they receive 200 proposals annually. Others estimate that several corporations receive over 100 sponsorship proposals each week (for an example of proposal guidelines, see Table 12.1). Regardless of the exact number, there are a wealth of sponsorship opportunities available to potential sponsors. Table 12.2 illustrates how U.S. Men's and Women's Under-19 World Lacrosse teams are presenting information to potential sponsors.[10]

When choosing from among many sponsorship opportunities, three decisions must be addressed. The first decision is whether to sponsor a local, regional, national, or global event. Second, the organization must choose an athletic platform. For instance, will the organization sponsor an individual athlete, team, league, or stadium. Third, once the broad athletic platform is chosen, the organization must decide on a specific sports entity. For example, if a league is selected as the athletic platform, will the organization sponsor the WNBA, the MLS, or the NFL?

The final stage of the sports sponsorship process involves implementation and evaluation. Typically, the organization wants to determine whether their desired sponsorship objectives have been achieved. Measuring the impact of sponsorship on awareness levels within a targeted audience is a relatively easy marketing research task. However, as the costs of sponsorships continue to increase, there is a heightened sense of accountability. In other words, organizations want to assess the impact of sponsorship on the bottom line—sales. The shift from philanthropy to evaluating sponsorship return on investment

TABLE 12.1 Castrol North America—Sponsorship Criteria Requirements

As you might imagine, we receive a number of requests for a variety of sponsorships from across North America. In order for us to most effectively evaluate each proposal we receive, we have established criteria that will provide us with the pertinent information we need. Including all of the data requested below will improve your chances of a prompt response.

Timeframe:

1. **Submitting a proposal to Castrol North America:** To allow us enough lead-time to line up appropriate resources, your proposal must be submitted at least 6 months prior to the start date of the event/project. We will not consider proposals submitted outside of this timeframe.
2. **Castrol North America Response:** You should expect a reply within 3 months.

What to send and where to send it:

1. **Brief detailed description of sponsorship**
2. **Contract Information**
3. **Fees and Payment Terms/Schedule:** All costs Castrol is expected to pay, including sponsorship fee, Value In Kind, promotional fees, signage, literature, printing costs, creative/production costs, equipment, merchandising, etc.
4. **Direct On-site Sales Opportunities:** Include a three-year history of Castrol or non-Castrol motor oil product sales as well as projected motor oil product sales over the next three years. If this is a new venue with no previous motor oil related sales, please explain why this is an ideal Do-it-Yourself (DIY) automotive demographic.
5. **Castrol Benefits:** Include items such as TV, radio, and newspaper exposure, Website visits, complimentary tickets, hospitality, and access to special events at the property and quantity as appropriate.
6. **Product/Category Exclusivity**
7. **Marketing Opportunities:** On-site and off-site, such as co-sponsor promotional activities, Consumer and Trade promotions available to Castrol, etc.
8. **List of Other Sponsors:** Indicate whether they are potential or committed. Also please indicate historical sponsors and length of association.
9. **Term:** (Annual, two-year, three-year, etc.)
10. **Number of Events per annum**
11. **Attendance:** Annual ticket sales, paid and unpaid, trend history for the last three years, future projections for three years
12. **Demographics:** Include where applicable (i.e., if noticeably different), the following demographics for both attendees *and* the media audience.

    a. age;
    b. gender;
    c. % do it yourself (i.e., change their own oil);
    d. ethnic origin;
    e. income profile; and
    f. any other applicable information

13. **Any Other Pertinent Information**

Please include as much of this information as possible when sending your proposal to Castrol. Once your proposal is complete, please forward by mail to the address below:

Sponsorship Department
Castrol Consumer North America
1500 Valley Road
Wayne, NJ, 07470
USA

We appreciate your interest in Castrol North America as a potential sponsor and look forward to receiving your sponsorship proposal.

Source: www.refresh.castrolusa.com/sponsors/.

TABLE 12.2 Sponsorship Opportunity for U.S. Men's and Women's Under-19 World Lacrosse Teams

Flagship Sponsor* ($10,000 or more)

- Logo identification as Flagship Sponsor in all team promotional materials
- Corporate patch on all game jerseys (max. 2 patches per team)
- One framed commemorative event poster, signed by the U.S. team
- One framed U.S. team commemorative team jersey, signed by the U.S. team
- Two framed team photos signed by the U.S. team
- Five World Championship programs
- Ten commemorative pins.
- View Flagship Sponsors: *Men Women*

Premium Sponsor* ($5,000–$9,999)

- Logo identification as Premium Sponsor in all team promotional materials
- One framed commemorative event poster, signed by the U.S. team
- One U.S. team commemorative team jersey, signed by the U.S. team
- One framed team photo signed by the U.S. team
- Two World Championship programs
- Five commemorative pins
- View Premium Sponsors: *Men Women*

Supporting Sponsor* ($2,500–$4,999)

- Listing as a Supporting Sponsor in all promotional materials
- One framed commemorative event poster, signed by the U.S. team
- One framed team photo signed by the U.S. team
- One World Championship program
- Five commemorative pins
- View Supporting Sponsors: *Men Women*

Contributing Sponsor ($1,000–$2,499)

- Listing as a Contributing Sponsor in all promotional materials
- One commemorative event poster, signed by the U.S. team
- One team photo signed by the U.S. team
- Two commemorative pins
- View Contributing Sponsors: *Men Women*

Booster ($500–$999)

- One team photo
- One event poster
- Two commemorative pins
- View Boosters: *Men Women*

Friend ($100–$499)

- One team photo
- One commemorative pin
- View Friends: *Men Women*

*Sponsorship packages may include additional items.
Source: U.S. Lacrosse. Used by permission of the U.S. Lacrosse-News. All rights reserved.

(ROI) is also documented in the academic sport sponsorship literature and new models are emerging to understand the complexities of sponsorship evaluation (see, for example, Stotlar[11]). As Glenn Wilson, professor at Griffith University, points out, "The task of assessing the financial benefit [of sponsorship] remains a difficult one."[12]

Now that we have a rough idea of how the sponsorship process works, let us explore each stage of the sports sponsorship model in greater detail.

SPONSORSHIP OBJECTIVES

The first stage in designing a sponsorship program is to carefully consider the sponsorship objectives. Because sponsorship is just one form of promotion, the **sponsorship objectives** should be linked to the broader promotional planning process and its objectives. The promotional objectives will, in turn, help achieve the marketing goals, which should stem from the objectives of the organization. These important linkages were stated in our definition of sponsorship.

Not unlike advertising objectives, sponsorship objectives can be categorized as either direct or indirect. **Direct sponsorship objectives** have a short-term impact on consumption behavior and focus on increasing sales. **Indirect sponsorship objectives** are those that ultimately lead to the desired goal of enhancing sales. In other words, the sponsor has to generate awareness and create the desired image of the product before consumers purchase the product. The indirect sponsorship objectives include generating awareness, meeting and beating competition, reaching new target markets, building relationships, and improving image.[13]

One of the reasons that sponsoring sporting events has risen in popularity is that sponsorship provides so many benefits to those involved in the partnership. In other words, both the sponsor and the sports entity (event, athlete, or league) gain from this win–win partnership. Let us look at some of the primary objectives of sponsorship, from the sponsor's perspective.

AWARENESS

One of the most basic objectives of any sponsor is to generate **awareness** or raise levels of awareness of its products and services, product lines, or corporate name. Sponsors must understand which level to target (i.e., individual product versus company name) based on the broader promotional or marketing strategy. For a new company or product, sponsorship is an important way to generate widespread awareness in a short period of time.

From the event or sports entity's perspective, having a large corporate sponsor will certainly heighten the awareness of the event. The corporate sponsor will design a promotional program around the event to make consumers aware of the sponsor's relationship with the event. The corporate sponsor will also want to ensure their promotional mix elements are integrated. In other words, advertising, sponsorship of the event, and sales promotion will all work in concert to achieve the desired promotional objectives. However, a study conducted by Hoek, Gendall, Jeffcoat, and Orsman[14] found that sponsorship generated higher levels of awareness than did advertising. In addition, sponsorship led to the association of a wider range of attributes with the brand being promoted than did advertising.

COMPETITION

Another primary objective of sponsorship is to stamp out or meet any competitive threats or **competition.** Many corporate sponsors claim they are not that interested in sponsorship opportunities, but they cannot afford not to do so. In other words, if they do not make the sponsorship investment, their competitors will. Sponsorship is thought of as a preemptive tactic that will reduce competitive threat. For instance, Texaco sponsors virtually every national governing body of U.S. Olympic sports. They promote only a handful of these sports, but their sponsorship of the others effectively keeps other competitors out of any chance of ambushing their Olympic efforts. Another example of competitive threat comes from the the America's Cup and the fierce rivalry between Louis Vuitton and Rolex. For nearly two decades, Louis Vuitton has been the principal partner of the event and because of the growing popularity of the competition, the close association with the America's Cup has proved effective in enhancing the company's image and reputation. However, the French company recently had to fend off a challenge from Rolex, one of Switzerland's leading watch makers and luxury brands, Rolex clearly saw a chance to preempt Vuitton.

Securing the sponsorship would have given Rolex an opportunity to snub its French rival, which decided to take on Rolex on its own turf last year by developing and launching its own high quality Swiss watch manufacturing business. "Rolex were clearly not too happy we entered the market, just as we would not be too happy if they decided to make luxury bags and suitcases," said Yves Carcelle, Louis Vuitton's chief executive. Despite the Vuitton's long association with the competition, the sponsorship deal is negotiated each year before the event. Vuitton renewed the sponsorship for a "high" price and was pleased not only to have fought off the Rolex challenge but also to have expanded the partnership.[15]

Unfortunately, the sponsoring company, such as Vuitton, can still be harmed by competitors who use ambush marketing tactics. **Ambush marketing** is a planned effort (campaign by an organization) to associate themselves indirectly with an event to gain at least some of the recognition and benefits that are associated with being an official sponsor.[16] One of the earliest examples of ambush marketing at its finest was Nike's 1984 "I Love LA" marketing campaign. Although not an official Olympic sponsor, this campaign inextricably tied Nike to the city and event. Most sports marketers consider this ambush campaign the catalyst for the steady rise in ambush marketing practices.[17]

Today, many examples of ambush marketing exist. However, the Olympic Games seems to be the "sporting event of choice" for ambush marketers. Consider this 2000 Olympic ambush moment:[18]

- Quantas, an Australian airline, commissioned an extensive and high-priced advertising campaign before the start of the summer games. The ads featured Australian Olympians Cathy Freeman and Ian Thorpe. Because of its reputation as the Australian airline, consumers believed Quantas was an official sponsor of the games. Ansett, the actual sponsor, started a legal battle with Quantas, which the two airlines eventually settled out of court.
- adidas was not an Olympic sponsor, but research showed that consumers believed the company to be the seventh most recognized sponsor of the games. This was due largely to the publicity surrounding the new adidas body suits worn by the Australian swim team. The adidas logo was visible on the suits throughout the broadcast coverage of the swimming events.
- The National Australia Bank (NAB) was not an Olympic sponsor, but it had been promoting basketball legend Andrew Gaze and its Team National for five years up to the start of the summer games. The NAB branch banks were filled with sporting images for months prior to the start of the games, causing an association between the bank and Olympic sponsorship.

Do ambush marketing tactics work for organizations that do not want to pay the cost for official Olympic sponsorship? The answer to this question seems to be an overwhelming yes. Studies have shown that most consumers cannot correctly identify the true Olympic sponsors. Research from the Chartered Institute of Marketing (CIM) revealed that brands that adopted ambush marketing strategies enjoyed more public recognition than the official Olympic sponsors.[19] The study, which questioned 1,000 adults regarding brands associated with the Olympics in an official or nonofficial capacity, found that 33 percent of consumers linked either adidas or Reebok with the Sydney Games despite the fact that neither were official Olympic partners.

On the positive side, Coca Cola, an official partner of the games, achieved the most recognition with 22 percent of respondents associating the soft drinks brand with the Olympics. However, other sponsors fared less well, with Visa International, Samsung, Panasonic, and IBM all scoring less than 5 percent in terms of public recognition. In the case of Visa, this lack of awareness was put into even more perspective by the fact the its main rival, American Express, scored higher recognition despite not being an official sponsor.

Because ambush marketing tactics are effective and consumers do not really care (only 20 percent of consumers said that they were angered by corporations engaging in ambush marketing), it appears that there is no end in sight for this highly competitive tactic. However, some preventative measures are taking place to protect the investments of the actual sponsors of the Olympic Games.

The Atlanta Committee for the Olympic Games (ACOG) contracted with an advertising intelligence firm to monitor all television and radio advertisements for ambush attempts. In addition, ACOG sent 900 letters to corporate executives informing them of their intent to identify and remove ambush attempts. If a company was found to have engaged in ambush attempts, ACOG threatened to take out full-page advertisements in national newspapers to embarrass the offending organization.[20]

New legislation is continuing to emerge to prevent ambush marketing. In Australia, new antiambush legislation was announced by the Federal Minister for Sport, Territories, and Local Government to protect sponsors and organizers of the 2000 Summer Games in Sydney. Moreover, the Sydney Olympic Games Organizing Committee (SOGOC) launched a $2 million dollar advertising campaign against ambushers. The advertisements featured six Olympians and highlighted the contributions made to the games by the official sponsors.[21]

The South African parliament passed the Merchandise Marks Amendment Act in 2002 that gives protection to sponsors involved in selected major events staged in South Africa. This legislation was enacted specifically to prevent ambush marketing at the Cricket World Cup. In essence, any spectator carrying a product made by a competitor of one of the main sponsors is liable to have it confiscated. Water bottles are permitted, but the labels must be removed and T-shirts, hats, and flags bearing competitors' logos are not welcome. With Pepsi among the tournament's four primary sponsors, the most visible sign of the rules has been the sight of ushers removing bottles of Coke from fans' cooler bags to protect Pepsi's investment. One fan, approaching the rows of metal detectors that are a familiar sight at World Cup venues, summed up the mood of spectators. "Here we go," he said. "It's not a bomb check, it's the Coke police."

So stringent are the rules that offenders could find the real police getting involved. The legislation allows for prison terms against serious offenders. A Johannesburg businessman, watching South Africa's match against New Zealand with his family last Sunday, found himself evicted for drinking a can of Coke.[22]

REACHING TARGET MARKETS

Reaching new target markets is another primary objective of sponsorship programs. One of the unique features and benefits of sponsorship as a promotional medium is its ability to reach people who are attracted to sports entities because they share a common interest. Therefore, sporting events represent a natural forum for psychographic segmentation of consumers. That is, reaching consumers with similar activities, interests, and opinions (AIOs). Sue Tougas, assistant vice president of corporate communications at Mass Mutual sums up their worldwide sponorship of the U.S. Open

Ambush Marketing

Unofficially, it does work. Ambush marketing, stunts, and tactics used to promote brands at events sponsored by a rival, is growing in sophistication. And now the Rugby World Cup is looming...

Tensions are rising among marketers Down Under as preparations for next month's Rugby World Cup get under way. The Cup organizers are preparing to prevent "ambush marketing"—ploys and stunts employed by brands and companies looking to jump on the marketing bandwagon and steal the official sponsors' thunder.

The World Cup's organizers are promising official backers a "clean stadium," free of brands and advertisers that are not sponsors.

For consumer goods and services companies, international sporting events are an excellent way of building awareness and increasing sales and marketing share. And sponsorship has become such an important part of international sport that organizers are desperate to keep ambush marketing—otherwise known as hijack or parasite marketing—at bay.

The problem is that ambush marketing has become so sophisticated, with many campaigns having more impact than the millions spent by official sponsors. For example, during the 2002 Winter Olympics in Salt Lake City, Anheuser-Busch of Budweiser fame paid 50 million dollars for the rights to use the word "Olympic" and the five-ring logo—enabling a small microbrewery to paint its trucks with the words "Wasatch Beers. The Unofficial Beer. 2002 Winter Games."

Then there was Nike's decision to run five-a-side football games, complete with ad campaign, during last year's football World Cup. As a result, although the event was sponsored by adidas, many consumers assumed that Nike was an official sponsor.

And it's not just sporting events where ambush marketers are successful. Take ad agency WCRS' promotional tactics with the new BMW Mini Cooper during the Gay Mardi Gras in Manchester. Although the event was officially sponsored by Ford, WCRS decorated the Mini with fake leather bondage gear and the car ended up leading the parade.

Ambush marketing often occurs when one big brand is trying to dilute the presence of a rival which is sponsoring an event, thus diminishing the return on the official sponsor's investment. As Raman Mangalorkar, at consultants AT Kearney, explains: "If you don't do it, they will gain all the benefit."

Another popular ambush scenario is the minnow, with a small marketing budget, challenging the established blue-chip brand. "Challenger brands can afford to be risky and daring," says Adrian Stannard at agency Cunning Stunts, which specializes in guerrilla and ambush marketing.

However, the risks are high, as clumsily done, ambush marketing can be detrimental to the brand. "You do have to amuse people, because if you're ambushed by something boring, it's just irritating," says Julian Hough, business development director at WCRS. "It has to be the right tone and the right style or you end up looking cheap and dirty," agrees Steve Martin, who runs the sports sponsorship business for PR firm Ketchum.

However, done well, it can be a powerful marketing tool. While official sponsors are limited in what they can or can't do, brands opting for ambush marketing are less constrained about injecting humor.

Ambush marketing also works because of its subversive nature. While admittedly the hijacker is also marketing itself, it seems to appeal to consumers' deep-rooted aversion to large companies taking over an event to sell its products. "It's a little less corporate and a little less straight down the line," says Sundeep Gohil, a planner at ad agency BBH. "Ambush media is terribly potent."

For a company sponsoring an event, countering ambush marketing is imperative. However, again, the right approach is crucial.

South Africa and Pepsi showed us how not to do it during the World Cup cricket earlier this year. The South African government amended its trademark and marketing laws to try to stamp out attempts at ambush marketing. With Pepsi as a sponsor, spectators drinking Coca-Cola were ejected from the grounds.

Pepsi tried to distance itself from the event, but overt and heavy-handed regulation has a negative effect among consumers. "Rather than build affinity with consumers and show that you care about the sport, you confirm that you are the nasty large corporation just looking to sell things," says Gohil at BBH.

The case of Coke handing out branded cups for people to drink beverages out of at last year's World Cup football is an example of a more subtle approach.

There will always be ambush marketing at large international events, and organizers and sponsors need to do more research into light-touch enforcement. Otherwise costs will go up for the organizers, who will be forced to spend more money on enforcement and demands from sponsors for discounts on rights fees, says AT Kearney's Mangalorkar. "People need to dedicate resources to research consumers' perception about enforcement. It has to move in that direction."

Source: Emiko Terazono, *Financial Times* (September 2, 2003), 6.

Tennis event by saying, "Viewership and audience attendance for the U.S. Open continues to be among the largest in professional sports, and the demographics of tennis fit precisely with our target consumer audience."[23]

Consider the following examples of how sponsors have attempted to reach new and sometimes difficult-to-capture audiences: The X-Games represent a perfect opportunity to reach Generation Xers, a target market that is "difficult to reach through traditional media." Another target market that has been neglected includes the millions of disabled Americans. With the growth of the Paralympic Games and programs such as Sporting Chance, which provide opportunities for people with disabilities to participate in sports, marketers are now addressing this market. Begun in 1960 as an event "parallel" to the Olympics, the Paralympics have blossomed into a major competition of their own. The Paralympic Games are a multisport, multidisability competition of elite, world-class athletes held approximately two weeks after the regular Olympics in the same host city.[24]

Just consider some of the impressive numbers from the 2000 Summer Games. More than one million tickets were sold to the Sydney Paralympic Games, including the opening and closing ceremonies. In 2004, more than 4,000 athletes from 140 countries will be competing and 1,500 media representatives are expected to cover the event. Additionally, more than 15,000 volunteers will help organize and run the event. In fact, the Paralympic Games will be the second largest sporting event in the world after the Olympic Games.[25]

Furthermore, women represent a growing target market for many marketers interested in sports sponsorship opportunities as discussed in the following article.

Disabled athletes compete in paralympics games.

Source: U.S. Paralympics is a division of U.S. Olympic Committee. Copyright © U.S. Paralympics. All rights reserved.

Factors Affecting Corporate Sponsorship of Women's Sport

There is little doubt that women's sport and the consumers that follow it are becoming the greatest growth sector for sports marketers in the new millennium. The growth of women's sports is taking place at all levels. More and more women are participating in sports and watching sports, which has created opportunities for equipment and apparel manufacturers as well as for broadcast media. In addition, marketing to women through the athletic medium has become an interesting and valuable tool for corporate America. In short, women are becoming the target market of choice for sports marketers.

Although women are growing in importance to sports marketers, relatively little is known about the sponsorship decisions relative to women's sport. A study by Nancy Lough of Kent State University was designed to better understand corporate sponsorship of women's sport. Summarized results of the research follow:

What are the benefits realized by corporations that have sponsored women's sports?

Benefits	Rank (1 is the greatest perceived benefit)
Extended audience profile	1
Demographic fit	
Size	
Extended media coverage	2
Local	
National	
Public relations factors	3
Customer presence	
Hospitality provided	
Community leader presence	

What factors are influential in the development of corporate involvement in sponsorship?

Category	Rank (1 is the greatest perceived benefit)
Budget considerations	1
Cost effectiveness	
Affordability	
Access to potential buyers	
Targeting of market	2
Demographic fit	
Access to users of product	
Immediate audience	
Size	
Proposal considerations	3
Competent staff running event	
Evaluation procedures described or employed	

What factors are utilized by corporations in sponsorship selection decisions?

Category	Rank (1 is the greatest perceived benefit)
Meeting sponsorship goals	1
Achievement of objectives	
Cooperation of organizers with sponsors	
Value/ROI	

Category	Rank (1 is the greatest perceived benefit)
Performance of event organizers	
Corporate direction and strategy	
Positioning/Image	2
Product–Sport image fit	
Image–Target market fit	
Targeting Women	3
Visible connection of sponsor and women's event	
Women as potential consumers of company's products	
Ability to promote sales to women	
Unique opportunity vs. other options	
Research supporting involvement with women's sport	

In addition to these findings of women's sport sponsorship, Lough offers the following observations:

- Gender-appropriate sports are still the most attractive to sponsors of women's sport.
- Sponsors are interested in creating ties to the sport or event image via media coverage and/or advertising.
- Corporate interest in sponsoring women's sports will continue to grow.
- Establishing the Women's Sport Cable Channel will give sponsors the perfect vehicle to reach this emerging market.
- As competition for ownership of women's events increases, so too will the value of sponsorships.
- Women's sports sponsorship appears to represent a better value than a comparably priced sports package.

Source: Nancy L. Lough, "Factors Affecting Corporate Sponsorship of Women's Sport," *Sport Marketing Quarterly,* vol. 5, no. 2 (1996), 11–19. Reprinted with permission of Fitness Information Technology, Inc. Publishers.

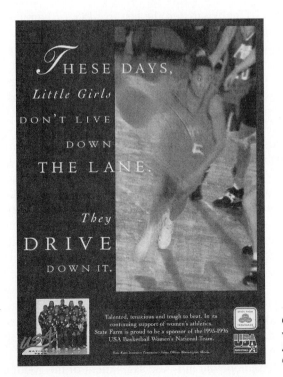

Corporate sponsorship targeting women's sport.
Source: State Farm Insurance Companies.

RELATIONSHIP MARKETING

As discussed in Chapter 11, **relationship marketing,** building long-term relationships with customers, is one of the most important issues for sports marketers in today's competitive marketing environment. Building relationships with clients or putting the principles of relationship marketing to work is another sponsorship objective. Corporate hospitality managers see to it that sponsors are given ample space to "wine and dine" current or perspective clients. The prevalence of luxury boxes at stadiums or arenas is just one small piece of evidence that corporate sponsors will go to great lengths and spend great amounts of money to build and maintain working relationships with their clients and employees.

For example, 37 companies paid the PGA of America $165,000 each to rent a tent at the 2000 PGA Tournament held at Valhalla in Louisville, Kentucky. Included in that price are enough furnishings, food, and beverages to make you forget you are in the middle of a field. There are tables with floral arrangements, three television sets, and a computer with access to tournament scoring and statistics. The bar is stocked, and the meals are catered. It is all air-conditioned, with wooden doors and glass windows to keep out the almost 90-degree heat and high humidity. Bill Sutton, a sports marketing professor at the University of Massachusetts, explains the reaction companies are hoping to get from their guests: "If they (UPS) can deliver on The Masters, I know they're going to get my packages there on time."

But for some, that standard package is not enough. At past tournaments, companies have done their tents up as a Scottish pub, the Taj Mahal, or the New York Stock Exchange. At Valhalla, the Anheuser-Busch tent has faux marble columns and the company's eagle logo carved into a wood-paneled bar. Another tent features bar stools that appear to be made from the shaft heads and grips of golf clubs. Two other tents have high-speed Internet connections.[26]

For a price that can soar to $300,000 past the standard tent fee, Barton G. Weiss can handle almost any request. Weiss, who goes by the trade name "Barton G.," heads a company that has put together corporate hospitality villages at several sports events, including the Super Bowl, Final Four, and the last five PGA Championships. His company designed, built, and stocked all the corporate hospitality tents at this week's tournament, including any special touches for which companies wanted to pay.

Companies began throwing more lavish sports-related parties at the Super Bowl during the mid-1980s. David M. Carter of The Sports Business Group, a Los Angeles-based sports consulting firm, says the demand for corporate sports hospitality has grown "exponentially" since then. "As sports' fan base has shifted from the everyday fan to the corporate fan, these events have increasingly catered to fans who are there to conduct business-to-business marketing," Carter says. These companies are trying to generate new business and keep current clients as well. In another golfing example, companies shelled out $6,000 to $50,000 for private tables, skyboxes, and corporate tents during The International in Castle Rock, Colorado. "Qwest Communications International, the tournament's lead sponsor, locked up a $15-million-a-year contract with a big East Coast bank, and that was just on the first day," said Stephen M. Jacobsen, a senior executive at Denver-based Qwest. "That's what this is all about," Jacobsen said, estimating that 700 customers would attend. "We're working deals everywhere."

Very few studies have explored company attitudes towards corporate hospitality or the effectiveness of this activity, but recently Bennett looked at this growing sports marketing function. He found that two-thirds of the companies believed that "highly formal" procedures were applied to the management of corporate hospitality and that one-third of the expenses were incorporated into marketing budgets. Additionally, two-thirds of the companies responding to the survey said that the decision on choice of events for corporate hospitality was based on "the in-house assessment of the goodness of the match between corporate hospitality activities and specific clients." Two-thirds of the companies felt that corporate hospitality was a vital element of the marketing mix and even if faced with a recession would not cut their budget in this area. Finally, companies stated that the greatest benefit of corporate hospitality activities was retaining profitable customers.[27]

The community is another public with which sponsors want to build relationships. Many corporate sponsors believe returning something to the community is an important part of sponsoring a sporting event. Buick has recently signed on as the title sponsor for the Greater Hartford Open and strongly believes in the charitable and community benefits the tournament offers the community. It is estimated that the tournament has raised over $24 million for Greater Hartford Jaycee-supported community projects, charitable grants, and scholarships. In addition, the tournament is thought to contribute over $20 million annually to the local economy and generates over $200,000 annually in state income taxes. The final benefit is promoting the Greater Hartford region to over 140 countries worldwide through the international telecast of the tournament.

IMAGE BUILDING

Perhaps the most important reason for sponsorship of a sports entity at any level is to maintain or build an image. **Image building** is a two-way street for both the sponsoring organization and the sports entity. The sponsoring organization associates itself and/or its brands with the positive images generated by the unique personality of the sporting event. Ferrand and Pages describe the process of finding a congruence between event and sponsor as "looking for the perfect wedding."[28] The researchers also point out that "any action toward sponsoring an event should begin with an analysis of the common and unique attributes of the event and the brand or product."

Consider an event like the Summer Extreme Games (X-Games), which possess a well-defined image that includes characteristics such as aggressiveness, hip, cool, no fear, and no rules. The image of extreme sports such as skysurfing, street luge, or the adventure race will certainly "rub off" or become associated with the sponsoring organization. Taco Bell, Nike, and Mountain Dew will take on the characteristics of the extreme sports, and the image of their products will be maintained or enhanced.

In Chapter 10, the **match-up hypothesis** was described as the more congruent the image of the endorser with the image of the product being promoted, the more effective the message. This simple principle also holds true for sponsorship. However, the image of the sports entity (remember this may be an event, individual athlete, group of athletes, or team) should be congruent with the actual or desired image of the sponsor's organization or the product being sponsored. In Figure 12.2, we can see how the image of Taco Bell has shifted toward the X-Games and how the image of the X-Games also shifts toward the sponsor.

Sometimes the "match up" between sponsor and sports entity is not seen as appropriate. For example, Anheuser-Busch's $50 million sponsorship of the 2002 Winter Olympics in Salt Lake City, Utah, may be scrutinized because of the religious beliefs of Mormons. Anheuser-Busch may be forced to call their products malt beverages. In another alcohol-related example, increasing pressure has been put on the NCAA by The Center for Science in the Public Interest (CSPI) to prohibit alcohol advertising and sponsorship. The CSPI said alcohol producers spent nearly $600 million on sports programming in 2002. Of that, nearly $60 million was spent on college sports programs, funding more than 6,200 ads. The NCAA basketball tournament in 2002 had 939 beer ads, more than the Super Bowl, World Series, college football bowl games, and NFL Monday Night Football combined.[29]

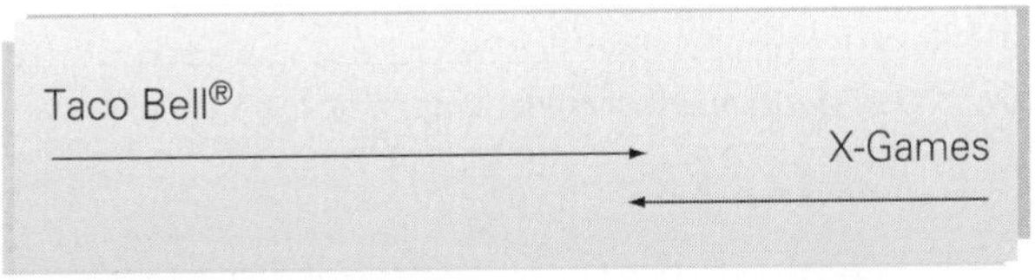

Taco Bell®

X-Games

FIGURE 12.2 Sponsorship Match-Up

SALES INCREASES

The eventual objective for nearly all organizations involved in sponsorship programs is **sales increases.** Although sometimes there is an indirect route to sales (i.e., the hierarchy of effects model of promotional objectives, which states that awareness must come before action or sales), the major objective of sponsorship is to increase the bottom line. Organizations certainly would not spend millions of dollars to lend their names to stadiums or events if they did not feel comfortable about the return on investment. Likewise, the events are developed, in some cases (e.g., the Skins Game, and the Showdown at Sherwood featuring Tiger Woods and David Duval), for the sole purpose of making a profit. Without sponsorship, the event would lose the ability to do so.

It is clear that when organizations are considering a sponsorship program, the first step is to determine the organizational objectives and marketing goals that might be achieved most effectively through sponsorship. However, the primary motivation for organizations participating in sports sponsorships is still unclear. Historically, organizations entered into sponsorships to create awareness and enhance the image of their brands, product lines, or corporations. Three studies examining the primary reasons for engaging in sponsorship found increasing awareness and enhancing company image to be the most important objectives. More recently, studies have shown that increasing sales and market share are the primary motives of sponsorship (see Table 12.3).

Regardless of the relative importance of the various sponsorship objectives, organizations must carefully evaluate how the sponsorship will help them achieve their own unique marketing objectives. Along with examining the sponsorship objectives, the organization must find a sponsorship opportunity that fits within the existing promotion budget. Let us look briefly at the basic budgeting considerations, the next step in the sponsorship model.

SPONSORSHIP BUDGETING

As with the promotional budget, determining the **sponsorship budgeting methods** include competitive parity, arbitrary allocation, percentage of sales, and the objective and task method. Because the fundamentals of these budgeting methods have already been discussed, let us examine the sponsorship budgeting process at several organizations.

TABLE 12.3 Importance of Sponsorship Objectives

Objectives	Mean Importance Rating
Increase sales and market share	6.14
Increase target market awareness	6.07
Enhance general public awareness	5.88
Enhance general company image	5.47
Enhance trade relations	4.60
Enhance trade goodwill	4.55
Involve community	4.48
Alter public perception	4.15
Enhance employee relations	3.84
Block competition	3.68
Develop social responsibility	3.13
Develop corporate philanthropy	3.12

Source: Doug Morris and Richard L. Irwin, "The Data-Driven Approach to Sponsorship Acquisition," *Sport Marketing Quarterly*, vol. 5, no. 2 (1996), 9. Reprinted with permission of Fitness Information Technology, Inc. Publishers.

SPOTLIGHT ON INTERNATIONAL SPORTS MARKETING

The Cost of Sponsorship

Sport is a costly business, but lucrative sponsorship deals are becoming hard to find.

Corporate Australia will be asked to cough up about $500 million in the next three years as sports seek to renew sponsorship and television rights deals. The amount is significant: the business sector pumps about $1.1 billion into sport each year through sponsorship, broadcast, and naming rights agreements.

Competition is intense for the corporate dollar from a long list of big-ticket sports. On the agenda before 2006 are television broadcasting rights deals for the four main football codes, cricket, and tennis. Golf and horse racing are also chasing sponsorship and broadcast deals. And the 2006 Melbourne Common-wealth Games is scouring the market for about $130 million in corporate sponsorship.

Meanwhile, the free-to-air networks could be facing more competition from Foxtel if the federal government changes its controversial antisiphoning list, which limits pay-television's access to live broadcasts of most of the popular sports.

Craig Dodson, group account director of the consulting firm Sponsorship Solutions, says the elite sports should be able to maintain their levels of sponsorship, although second-tier sports such as basketball and athletics could struggle. "Take rugby union. After a successful world cup [last year] the prices for that sport will definitely go up," Dodson says. "But the lower level of sponsorships will suffer because everyone wants to be involved only at the top end now."

Some new agreements have already been signed. The Australian Football League (AFL) and Toyota have agreed on a five-year naming rights deal that could be worth up to $11 million a year.

Tennis Australia has renewed its agreement with the Seven Network and Foxtel to broadcast the Australian Open and Davis Cup for $25 million over the next five years. And the Australian Rugby Union (ARU) has signed an estimated $3 million, three-year deal with brewer Lion Nathan for naming rights to the Super 12 provincial championship for its Tooheys New brand.

Yet after the boom of the past decade, there are doubts about what the television companies will pay for broadcast rights. Several networks have made substantial losses from televising sport in the past five years, in Australia and worldwide.

The AFL's five-year, $500-million broadcast deal with Nine Network, Network Ten, Foxtel, and Telstra was signed at the height of the television sports rights boom in 2001. Already many AFL executives have admitted that the sport will struggle to sign a similar deal again because Nine and Foxtel have made losses on their investments.

Rugby union is the next big broadcasting deal up for grabs. The ARU, and its New Zealand and South African counterparts, signed a 10-year, $US500-million ($634-million Australian) deal with News Limited in 1995. The outgoing ARU chief executive, John O'Neill, has conceded that rugby may have to sign for less, or the same amount, next time.

The National Rugby League's deal with Nine Network and Foxtel, worth a combined $80 million a year, expires in 2007. Channel Seven will reportedly enter the bidding against Nine Network.

Ahead of the Game: What it will cost to back the winners

Estimated Annual Event	Value ($ m)	Due
Commonwealth Games	130	2006
Australian Football League broadcast deal	100	2006
National Rugby League broadcast deal	80	2007
Rugby Union broadcast deal	63	2005
Horse racing broadcast deal	30	2004*
National Rugby League naming rights	7	2006
Rugby Union naming rights	7	2004
Australian Open tennis European broadcast rights	5	2004
Australian Open tennis associate sponsor	4	2004
Australian Open golf naming rights	2–3	2004

*Rolling deal with different expiration dates for Sydney and Melbourne races.

Source: BRW.

(Continued)

(Continued)

Other TV sport sponsorship deals on the horizon include a European TV deal for the Australian Open tennis. Starting next year, the men's final will be broadcast in a more favorable timeslot for Europe.

The Open is also searching for an associate sponsor, worth about $4 million a year, to replace brewer Heineken. Other sports without naming rights deals include soccer (which will launch a revamped national league later this year), basketball, and golf.

The Australian Open golf tournament naming rights are worth $2–$3 million a year. Jonathan Field, the director of golf at sports management company IMG, which jointly runs the Open with the Australian Golf Union, is confident of finding a sponsor.

The ARU is yet to find a naming rights sponsor (it would cost about $7 million a year) for the national team, the Wallabies. An ARU spokesman says it is confident of agreeing to a deal soon.

Source: John Stensholt, "Playing For Keeps," *Business Review Weekly (Australia)* (February 26, 2004), 22.

The only generality to be made about the budgeting process is that decision making varies widely based on the size of the company and its history and commitment to the practice of sponsorship.[30] Larger organizations that have used sponsorship as a form of communication for many years tend to have highly complex structures and those new to sponsorship tend to keep it simpler.

Consider, for example, the budgeting process at Anheuser-Busch. Anheuser-Busch's budgeting process begins with determining the corporate-wide marketing budget. This is usually anywhere from three to five percent of the previous year's sales (percentage of sales method discussed in Chapter 11). The total budget is then divided among the company's 32 brands, with Budweiser, the flagship brand, receiving the largest share of the budget. The final decision on budget allocation is made by two high-level management teams, who receive and review potential sponsorships. The first team looks at how the managers plan on supporting their sponsorships with additional promotional mix elements such as point-of-sale merchandising. The second team hears the brand managers present their case and defend their budget.

Although Anheuser-Busch's budgeting process represents a more complex and structured approach, Marriott uses a simpler technique. Marriott, a relative newcomer to sports sponsorship, leaves the whole business to its corporation's hotel and time-share properties. The same practice holds true for Philip Morris, where managers of individual brands like Virginia Slims decide which sponsorship opportunities to pursue and how much money to allocate. The brand managers of Yukon Jack and Jose Cuervo, two alcoholic beverage brands of IDV/Hublein, also make their budgeting decisions independently. Yukon Jack and Jose Cuervo spend 60 and 30 percent, respectively, of their marketing budget on sponsorship.[31]

Once specific budgets are allocated, the organization must look for sponsorship opportunities that will meet objectives and still be affordable. To accommodate budgetary constraints, most sports entities offer different levels of sponsorship over a range of sponsorship fees. One example of the cost of sponsorship and the tangible benefits received by the sponsor is the Giant Eagle LPGA Classic (see Table 12.4).[32] The professional golf tournament in Warren, Ohio, attracts an almost equal number of men (48 percent) and women (52 percent), who have attended or graduated college and have an average household income of $65,000. Sponsorship packages are presented in the following areas: skyboxes, souvenir program or pairings guide, course promotions, and corporate hospitality. The preceding example demonstrates the potential costs of sponsoring a sporting event. Table 12.5. shows several other miscellaneous sponsorship fees. It is important to note that the sponsorship fee is not the only expense that should be considered by organizations. As Brant Wansley of

TABLE 12.4 Sponsorship Opportunities: Giant Eagle LPGA Classic

Community Club

Entertain your guests among tournament sponsors and enjoy complimentary food and beverage service in the exclusive Community Club pavilion.

- Individual Community Club pass: $550
- 6 Community Club passes: $3,150
- 10 Community Club passes: $5,000
- 15 Community Club passes: $7,125

Packages of six or more include 2 VIP Parking passes and identification on the sponsor board and Web site.

Corporate Hospitality Tents

Separate yourself from the competition by entertaining your guests in the exclusivity and privacy of a Corporate Hospitality Tent. Each package includes:

- 25 weekly Corporate badges
- Four VIP Parking passes
- $2' \times 2'$ sign featuring your company logo
- Private rest room facilities
- 20 percent discount off Souvenir Program advertising
- Right to purchase additional tickets, up to 20% of your daily allotment, at a discounted rate
- Identification on the tournament sponsor board and Web site

Package A: $8,500

- $16' \times 16'$ tent with $16' \times 16'$ fenced patio
- 300 tickets, 60 each day Wednesday–Sunday

Package B: $11,750

- $20' \times 20'$ tent with $20' \times 20'$ fenced patio
- 625 tickets, 125 each day Wednesday–Sunday

Package C: $15,400

- $20' \times 20'$ tent with $30' \times 16'$ fenced patio
- 1,000 tickets, 200 each day Wednesday–Sunday

Package D: $21,300

- $30' \times 30'$ tent with $30' \times 16'$ fenced patio
- 1,600 tickets, 320 each day Wednesday–Sunday

Skybox

Skyboxes combine the benefits of premium seating and corporate hospitality to create a distinctive entertainment venue.

Executive Skybox: $4,500

- 20 reserved seats in your private section
- 100 tickets, 20 each day Wednesday–Sunday
- 100 transferable Executive Skybox passes, 20 each day Wednesday–Sunday
- Cash bar access and wait staff service
- 2 VIP Parking passes

18th Green VIP Skybox: $250

- One reserved seat in the 18th Green VIP Skybox
- Five tickets, one each day Wednesday–Sunday

(Continued)

(Continued)

- Five transferable VIP Skybox passes, one each day Wednesday–Sunday
- Cash bar access and wait staff service
- Identification on the sponsor board and Web site (four-seat minimum)

9th Green VIP Skybox: $200

- One reserved seat in the 9th Green VIP Skybox
- Five tickets, one each day Wednesday–Sunday
- Five transferable VIP Skybox passes, one each day Wednesday–Sunday
- Cash bar access and wait staff service
- Identification on the sponsor board and Web site (four-seat minimum)

Souvenir Program

An annual collector's item, the Giant Eagle LPGA Classic Souvenir Program is complimentary to all tournament spectators.

Type	Tickets	Price
Back Outside Cover, Four-Color	Two Season Clubhouse badges, Four Good-Any-One-Day passes	$3,500
Full-page, Four-Color	Two Season Clubhouse badges, Two Good-Any-One-Day passes	$2,000
Full-Page, Black and White	Two Season Clubhouse badges, Two Good-Any-One-Day passes	$1,500
Half-Page, Black and White	Eight Good-Any-One-Day passes	$1,000
Quarter-Page, Black and White	Four Good-Any-One-Day passes	$ 550

Pairing Guide

A daily guide to all the tournament action from Wednesday–Sunday, your advertisement appears adjacent to each day's pairings.

- Inside Panel—Sunday only: $3,450
- Outside Panel: $4,750
- Inside Panel: $5,250
- Inside Panel under Course Map: $6,000

Each panel includes one full-page, four-color ad in the Souvenir Program and one Classic Ticket Package.

- Promotional Tents: $3,100
- Daily interaction with tournament spectators awaits organizations that use a Promotional Tent.
- $10' \times 10'$ Promotional Tent
- Two 8' tables and four chairs
- One Classic Ticket Package

Staff tickets

Tee Sponsorship: $3,500

Uniting prominent signage on the tee and a two-page spread in the Souvenir Program provides Tee Sponsors with integrated exposure to tournament spectators.

- Logo identification on the hole, par, yardage sign
- One full-page, four-color ad in the Souvenir Program facing the hole layout

Putting Green Sponsor: $3,500

- Two signs at the putting green with color company logo
- Identification on course map legend
- Listing on sponsor board, sponsor prize, program, and on Web site.

Leaderboard Advertising: $2,950

Source: Courtesy of Giant Eagle LPGA Classic.

TABLE 12.5 The Cost of Sponsorship

Match Sponsor for Welsh All Blacks Rugby Union	$1,500
The Premium Sponsorship Box is a superb setting to entertain 20 clients and guests and includes drinks reception, hot buffet for 20 guests, afternoon tea, matchday program for each guest company, branding in matchday program, and front cover advertising on Stadium Tannoy.	
Specialty Signage for Midland Rock Hounds (Minor League Baseball)	
Tarp Cover	$3,200
Dugout Tops	$4,500 each
Concourse Signs	$3,900
Turnstile	$3,200 each
Super Bowl Package Includes one commercial in the game, four ads before the game, and an exclusive sponsorship of a 30-minute pregame program.	$3–4 million
Title Sponsor of the Durango Pro Rodeo	$10,000
Primary sponsor of NASCAR team	$15 million/year

BrandMarketing Services, Ltd., points out, "Buying the rights [to the sponsorship] is one thing, capitalizing on them to get a good return on investment is another. . . . Purchasing a sponsorship is like buying an expensive sports car. In addition to the initial cost, you must invest in the maintenance of the car to ensure its performance."[33] Sponsorship must be integrated with other forms of promotion to maximize its effectiveness. Rod Taylor, senior vice president of the CoActive Marketing Group, adds, "The only thing that you get as a sponsor is a piece of paper saying you've paid to belong. It is up to you as the marketer to convince consumers that you do, in fact, belong!" Bill Chipps, of the TEG Sponsorship Report, says that "the rule of thumb is that for every dollar a company spends on a rights fee, to maximize the sponsorship, they spend another $2 to $3 on leverage." This figure is substantiated in a study conducted by IEG Sponsorship that found the average ratio of activation spending to rights fees is 2.4 to 1.[34]

An excellent example of an organization leveraging its Olympic sponsorship is Anheuser-Busch. In addition to print and broadcast advertisements, Anheuser-Busch produced commemorative Olympic cans and accompanying P-O-P displays to stimulate sales at the retail level. Bob Lachky, group vice president of Budweiser brands at Anheuser Busch, says, "When you can drill [sponsorship] all the way through every element of the marketing mix—from advertising all the way through point-of-sale . . . and if you can get something that looks seamless from top bottom, you're going to have a successful promotion."[35]

CHOOSING THE SPONSORSHIP OPPORTUNITY

Once sponsorship objectives have been carefully studied and financial resources have been allocated, organizations must make decisions regarding the appropriate sponsorship opportunity. Whatever the choices, thoughtful consideration must be given regarding the potential opportunities.

Choosing the most effective sponsorship opportunity for your organization necessitates a detailed decision-making process. Several researchers have examined the organizational decision-making process in attempts to understand the evaluation and selection of sponsorship opportunities. A conceptual model of the corporate decision-making process of **sport sponsorship acquisition** developed by Arthur, Scott, and Woods is shown in Figure 12.3.

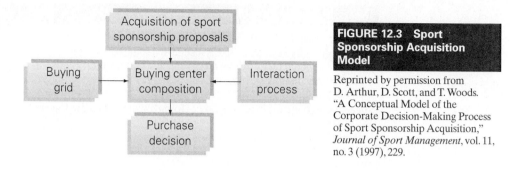

FIGURE 12.3 Sport Sponsorship Acquisition Model

Reprinted by permission from D. Arthur, D. Scott, and T. Woods. "A Conceptual Model of the Corporate Decision-Making Process of Sport Sponsorship Acquisition," *Journal of Sport Management*, vol. 11, no. 3 (1997), 229.

The process begins with the acquisition of sponsorship proposals. Generally, this is a reactive process in which organizations receive the multitude of sponsorship possibilities from sports entities wanting to secure sponsors. Within the sponsorship proposal, potential sponsors commonly look for the following information to assist in decision making:

- fan attendance and demographic profile of fans at the event,
- cost or cost per number of people reached,
- length of contract,
- media coverage,
- value-added promotions, and
- sponsorship benefits.

After the proposals have been acquired, the next step is to form the buying center. The buying center is the group of individuals within the organization responsible for **sponsorship evaluation** and choice. The buying center usually consists of four to five individuals who each play a unique role in the purchase. Typically, these roles are described as gatekeepers, influencers, decision makers, and purchasers. These roles were previously discussed in the context of personal selling. You will recall that one of the sales activities was to identify the individuals within the organization who performed these roles. Similarly, the sponsorship requester must learn who these individuals are before submitting the proposal. Hopefully, the proposal can then be tailored to meet the unique needs of the individuals who comprise the buying center.

Gatekeepers control the flow of information to the other members of the buying center. They are able to pass on the relevant proposals to other group members and act as an initial filtering device. The **influencers** are individuals who can impact the decision-making process. These individuals often have information regarding the sports entity that is requesting the sponsorship. The influencers have acquired this information through contacts they have in the community or industry. The **decision maker** is the individual within the buying center that has the ultimate responsibility to accept or reject proposals. In our earlier examples, describing the budgeting process for Jose Cuervo and Yukon Jack, the brand managers were the ultimate decision makers in the sponsorship acquisition process. Finally, the **purchasers** are responsible for negotiating contracts and formally carrying out the terms of the sponsorship.

The composition of the buying center, in terms of the number of individuals and the interaction between these individuals, is a function of the type of sponsorship decision. The buying grid refers to the organization's previous experience and involvement in sponsorship purchases. If this is the first time the organization has engaged in sport sponsorship, then more information will be needed from the sponsorship requester. In addition, the buying center will have additional members with greater interaction. However, if the sponsorship is simply being renewed (also known as a straight sponsorship rebuy), the buying center will play a less significant role in the decision-making process.

The next step in the sponsorship acquisition model is to make the purchase decision. Typically, it takes an organization three to six weeks to make a final sponsorship decision. While this may seem slow, purchasing a sponsorship is a complex decision that requires the coordination and interaction of all the members in the buying center.

The purchase decision consists of three interrelated steps. In the first step, the organization must consider the desired scope of the sponsorship (e.g., international versus local). To do this, a simple scheme for categorizing sponsorship opportunities has been developed, called the Sport Event Pyramid. The second interrelated step requires the organization to select the appropriate athletic platform for the sponsorship. Does the organization want to sponsor an event, a team, a league, or an individual athlete? Finally, after the organization has chosen the scope of sponsorship and the athletic platform, it specifies the particular sports entity. After the final decision is made, a quick audit can be conducted to determine whether the organization has made the appropriate choice of sponsorship. Let us examine the three steps in the purchase decision-making process in greater detail.

DETERMINING THE SCOPE OF THE SPONSORSHIP

The first step in the purchase decision phase of sponsorship acquisition is to determine the desired scope of the sponsorship. David Shani and Dennis Sandler have developed a way to categorize various sponsorship opportunities called the **Sports Event Pyramid.**[36] The Sports Event Pyramid is an excellent first step in reducing the number of sponsorship proposals to a smaller subset.

The Sports Event Pyramid consists of five levels: global events, international events, national events, regional events, and local events. Each level of the Sports Event Pyramid classifies events on the basis of the width and depth of interest in the event. Shani and Sandler describe the width as the geographic reach of the event via the various communications media, and the depth of the event refers to the level of interest among consumers.

Global events are at the apex of the pyramid. As the name implies, global events have the broadest coverage and are covered extensively around the world. In addition to their wide coverage, global events generate a great deal of interest among consumers. Shani and Sandler suggest that the World Cup and the Olympic Games are the only examples of truly global events. Corporations that want to position themselves in the global market should be prepared to pay top dollar for sponsorship of these events due to the tremendous reach and interest in the events.

International events are the next level in the hierarchy. For any event to be considered international in scope, it might (1) have a high level of interest in a broad, but not global, geographic region, or (2) be truly global in scope but have a lower level of interest in some of the countries reached. Examples of international events include Wimbledon, European Cup Soccer, America's Cup (yachting), the Rugby Union World Cup, and the Pan-American Games. Sponsoring these types of events is useful for corporations that have more narrowly targeted global markets.

Extremely high interest levels among consumers in a single country or two countries is categorized in the Sports Event Pyramid as a **national event.** National events, such as the World Series, the NCAA Final Four, and the Super Bowl, attract huge audiences in the United States.

Regional events have a narrow geographic focus and are also characterized by high interest levels within the region. The Big East conference tournament in basketball and the Boston Marathon are considered good examples of regional events.

In the lowest level of the pyramid are **local events.** Local events have the narrowest geographic focus, such as a city or community, and attract a small segment of consumers

Little League World Series—an international event.
Source: Copyright © 2003 Little League. All rights reserved.

that have a high level of interest in the event. High school sports, local races, and golf scrambles are examples of local events.

The primary purpose of the pyramid is to have marketers first develop an understanding of what level of sponsorship is consistent with corporate sponsorship objectives and budgets. Next, the corporation can decide upon which specific sporting events at the correct level present the best match. The organization may start small and choose to sponsor local events at the beginning. The larger the organization gets, the more likely it will be involved in sponsorship at each of the five levels of the pyramid. For example, Coca Cola is deeply involved in sponsorships at all five levels.

Although the Sports Event Pyramid is a great tool for marketers developing a sponsorship program, it does have some potential flaws. First, the local events are shown at the base of the pyramid. To some, this may imply the broadest geographic focus whereas, in fact, the local events have the most narrow focus. Second, it may be extremely difficult to categorize certain events. For example, the Super Bowl is cited as a national event that, by definition, has a one- or two-country focus with a high level of interest. The Super Bowl, of course, is broadcast in hundreds of countries, but may have limited interest levels in most. Therefore, it is uncertain as to whether the event should be categorized as a national event, an international event, or both.

DETERMINING THE ATHLETIC PLATFORM

After the general level of sponsorship reach is considered via the sponsorship pyramid, a more specific sponsorship issue must be considered. Namely, choosing the appropriate athletic platform. University of Michigan Professor Christine Brooks defines the **athletic platform** for sponsorship as being either the team, the sport, the event, or the athlete.[37] In addition, choice of athletic platform could be further subdivided on the basis of level of competition. For instance, common levels of competition include professional, collegiate, high school, and recreational.

The choice of athletic platform (or, in some instances, platforms) is based on sponsorship objectives, budget, and geographic scope. More specifically, when selecting the athletic platform, several factors should be considered.

- What is the sponsorship budget? What type of athletic platform is feasible given the budget?
- What is the desired geographic scope? How does the athletic platform complement the choice made in the sports sponsorship pyramid?
- How does the athletic platform complement the sponsorship objectives?

Let us take a closer look at each of the broad choices of athletic platform for sponsorship. These include athletes, teams, sports/leagues, and events.

Athletes We have previously examined the opportunities and risks of athletes as endorsers in Chapters 10 and 11. To summarize, athletes can have tremendous credibility with the target audience and can create an immediate association with a product in the consumer's mind. For example, NASCAR fans talk about Ward Burton driving the "NetZero HighSpeed " car or Tony Stewart driving the "Home Depot" car. Interestingly, when it comes to athletes as sponsors, golfers have always been at the head of the pack.[38] In fact, most believe the entire sports marketing industry was built on the backs of professional golfers, such as Arnold Palmer, Jack Nicholas, and Gary Player. Of course, Tiger Woods is now carrying the flag with appearance fees and endorsement deals worth an estimated $70 million in 2003, making him the world's best paid golfer (see Hall of Fame that follows). The problem, however, is that athletes can perform poorly or be seen as trouble-makers.

One athlete that is always surrounded by controversy and seems to exemplify the bad boy image is Allen Iverson. Allen's latest problems are based on assault charges. The police charged Iverson with threatening to kill two men after a domestic dispute with his wife. Iverson could have ben sentenced to 65 years in prison, but eventually all the charges were dismissed. In his latest controversy, Iverson was questioned about a shooting involving one of his friends outside a Philadelphia nightclub. Who knows what will happen next and what risk it will impose on Iverson's sponsors and the NBA.

Teams Teams at any level of competition (little league, high school, college, and professional) can serve as the athletic platform. Although sponsorship is typically associated with professional teams, college athletic departments also rely heavily on sponsorship partnerships.

The marketing of collegiate sports has skyrocketed in recent years. Anywhere from 10 percent to 20 percent of college basketball tournaments have title sponsors. One estimate states that corporations spend nearly $70 million annually on college sports sponsorships. The Collegiate Licensing Company, which handles licensing for about 180 schools, estimates the college market to be roughly $2 billion per year. Add to that the multimillion-dollar television contract and deals that most university coaches have with Nike, Reebok, and adidas, and college athletics is a huge business[39] (see Table 12.6).

Becoming the official outfitter for a university's athletic teams has become especially lucrative for colleges and has given sponsors great exposure. For instance, The University of North Carolina recently extended an eight year 28.3 million dollar contract with Nike to fuel the growth of the university's athletic program. Nike will provide North Carolina's athletic department with the following: (1) $18 million in footwear, apparel, and equipment; (2) $200,000 annually, of which half will go to the North Carolina general fund and half will go to an academic and athletic excellence fund; (3) $100,000 annually to the Chancellor's Academic

SPORTS MARKETING HALL OF FAME

Tiger Woods

Although sports marketing takes on many different meanings to different people, its essence is captured in the multimillion dollar phenom named Eldrick "Tiger" Woods. Tiger seems to have it all. He's handsome, charming, young, multiethnic, and, most important, is oozing talent. *In fact, in 2003 Tiger earned the PGA Tour player of the year award for the fifth consecutive time.* The world's best golfer made $70 million last year from appearance fees and endorsements and Tiger's sponsors certainly think that he is worth the money. For example, in 2004 Buick re-signed Woods for another five years, in a deal reportedly worth $40 million. Buick is happy with its investment, pointing out that more than 130,000 Rendezvous vehicles were sold in 2002 and 2003, which exceeded all forecasts and was attributed to Tiger's endorsement.

Nike, Titleist, Buick, American Express, Rolex, and the All-Star Cafe have all purchased a piece of Tiger for a total of tens of millions of dollars in sponsorship fees. Woods' latest multiyear agreement is his first business-to-business endorsement, with Accenture, the management consulting and technology services firm. Nike, of course is the most prominent sponsor of Tiger and has long reaped the benefits of its $105-million contract. The company's golf revenues continue to increase and Tiger is expected to help the entire golf equipment industry grow at a significant pace. Thomas Crow, Cobra golf founder and vice chairman, states that "All the manufacturers have an opportunity to feed off Tiger."

PGA Tour Commissioner Tim Finchem has stated that "It's conceivable that in terms of overall impact on the sport—when you figure in media, dollars on the table for him, his ability to be a role model—that if he succeeds he might be the most important player ever. He has the potential to have a profound impact on our sport as an entertainment sport. He could have a real impact on the overall growth of the game, which would be a much more lasting impact than the week-to-week sort of Tigermania which has been referred to."

The sport of golf has already seen short-term benefits of the new Tiger era. Interest in the sport has rocketed, by 67 percent since 1995, according to an ESPN poll, including a 21 percent increase in the past 12 months. Participation among African Americans from 1996 to 1999 has increased 30 percent from 676,000 to 882,000. In addition, Woods' participation in a tournament increases attendance by about one third.

Source: Lisa DiCarlo, "Six Degrees Of Tiger Woods," forbes.com (March 18, 2004); Andy Dworkin, "Woods Drives Nike Marketing Effort," *The Times Picayune* (July 30, 2000); Gerard Wright, "Tiger Inc Puts Golf in the Big Picture," *The Independent* (December 10, 2000),

Enhancement Fund; (4) up to $175,000 funding for each of five foreign exhibition trips for men's and women's basketball teams and the women's soccer team.[40]

Sport or League In addition to sponsoring teams, some companies choose to sponsor sports or leagues. One example of this is Procter & Gamble (P&G) and the WNBA. P&G, hoping to attract female audiences, has agreed to a multiyear deal with the league that will

TABLE 12.6 University Merchandise Sales Leaders

1. Michigan
2. North Carolina
3. Notre Dame
4. Texas
5. Georgia
6. Tennessee
7. Oklahoma
8. Florida
9. Penn State
10. Alabama

Sponsorship of teams can occur at any level of competition.

include the marketing of brands such as Secret, Head and Shoulders, Herbal Essences, Cascade, Swiffer, Cheer, and Joy. The agreement also allows P&G to leverage their sponsorship through advertising, cross-promotion activities, and team sponsorships.[41] One advantage to sponsoring women's sports and the WNBA is that there is less sponsorship clutter. Fewer companies are sponsoring women's sports or leagues and those that do are creating a unique position and differentiating themselves.[42]

MCI is a corporation that has chosen an integrated approach in sponsoring a number of sports or leagues. MCI's athletic platform at the sport or league level includes being the official communications company of Major League Baseball, Historic Sportscar Racing, CART; and it is also the official telecommunications company of NASCAR.

The "Ben Hogan Tour" was established in 1990 as a breeding ground for golf professionals who have not cracked the PGA. In 1993, Nike sponsored the tour, followed by Buy.com, which ended its sponsorship in 2002. . . . Currently, the tour is sponored by Nationwide, which signed a five-year agreement beginning in 2003. Although the Nationwide Tour was initially thought of as the "minor league" of professional golf, it has become a viable tour in and of itself. Since 1990, purses have increased from $3 million to $12.8 million, with the average purse increasing 68 percent from $255,000 to $427,500 over the past year. Also, the top 15 players on the Nationwide Tour money list automatically become eligible for the PGA Tour.

Nike has thrown itself into the sponsorship of soccer. By agreeing to pay the U.S. Soccer Federation $120 million over eight years, Nike has boosted U.S. soccer into the big leagues. Nike aspires to dominate the world's most popular sport and capture the largest share of the billions being spent on soccer shoes and apparel. In addition to their deal with the U.S. Soccer Federation, Nike currently spends about $3 million sponsoring MLS, the premier professional league in the United States.

Lately, leagues have been trying to organize themselves to become more attractive to sponsors. MLS is structured as a single entity, which means that each team owner has a financial stake in the league. This is different from the other professional sports leagues, which consist of individual franchise owners (i.e., every person for themself). This structure decreases the opportunity for ambush marketing and offers organizations an integrated sponsorship and licensing program.[43]

The MLS was not the first league to think about how best to serve the interests of sponsors. NFL Properties was designed in 1963 primarily to meet and beat the

The A10 corporate partner program.

Source: Copyright © 2002–2003, The Atlantic 10 Conference. All rights reserved.

competition posed by Major League Baseball. The league, in attempting to offer a competitive advantage to sponsors, built a system whereby potential sponsors receive collective and individual team rights. That is, sponsors can create opportunities or promotions that feature all NFL teams and local teams in a local market.[44]

Sponsors choose to use the power of the league and its recognizable league logo and, therefore, support all the teams. From the sponsors' perspective, this represents easy and less expensive one-stop shopping. As Burton points out, "If an NFL corporate partner had to design individual local contracts to secure key markets, the collective local team fees would quickly surpass the single sponsorship fee." By allowing sponsors the opportunity to receive collective team rights, the league gains enhanced exposure. An example of this national exposure through marketing collective team rights include Coke's "Monsters of the Gridiron."

Events An athletic platform that is most commonly associated with sports marketing is the event. Examples of sporting events sponsorship are plentiful, as are the opportunities to sponsor sporting events. In fact, sometimes the number of events far outweighs the number of potential corporate sponsors. For example, the city of Winnipeg staged two national and international sporting events over the space of 16 months. In a city that ranks as the eighth largest in Canada and has a population of only 680,000, the challenge was to find enough corporate sponsors. In response to this challenge, event organizers were forced to be more creative in designing sponsorship packages that appeal to organizations of all sizes.[45]

The advantages to using an event as an athletic platform are similar to those benefits gained by using other athletic platforms. For instance, the event will hopefully increase awareness and enhance the image of the sponsor. In addition, the event often allows the consumer a forum to use and purchase the sponsor's products. For example, Motorola recently sponsored its DraftMeMoto challenge at the 2004 Super Bowl. The promotion allows fans to participate in a series of activities based on NFL draft-like tests to see how they compare with the pros in kicking field goals and passing. They could even try their hand at announcing some of the great moments in NFL history. Upon completion of events at DraftMeMoto, participants were able to try out Motorola cell phones free of charge. As with the other athletic platforms, one of the primary disadvantages of using events as the athletic platform is sponsorship clutter. In other words, sponsors are competing with other sponsors for the attention of the target audience. One popular way to combat this clutter is to become the title sponsor of an event. Every college football bowl game now has a title sponsor, with the exception of the Rose Bowl—and this too has changed. In 1999 the Rose Bowl added a sponsor's tag line. More formally, this is called a presenting sponsor (i.e., the Rose Bowl presented by Sony Playstation).

CHOOSING THE SPECIFIC ATHLETIC PLATFORM

The choice of a particular athletic platform follows the selection of the general platform. At this stage of the sponsorship process, the organization makes a decision regarding the exact athlete(s), team, event, or sports entity. For instance, if the organization decides to sponsor a professional women's tennis player, who will be chosen—Venus Williams, Monica Seles, or Anna Kournikova? As with the previous decisions regarding sponsorship, the choice of a specific sponsor is based largely on finding the right "fit" for the organization and its products.

A recent trend is for sports marketers to ensure and control the fit by manufacturing their own sporting events. For example, Nike has created a new division to create and acquire global sporting events. By creating their own events, Nike will be able to control every aspect of how each event is marketed. Moreover, Nike will be able to develop events that are the perfect fit for their multiple target markets.[46] Other organizations, such as Honda, are pursuing a similar strategy. They have put pressure on their advertising agency to develop sporting events that will be the ideal match for the Honda target market.

Once the decision regarding the general level of sponsorship and the specific athletic platform have been addressed, it may be useful to review carefully the choice(s) of sponsorship before taking the final step. To do so, Brant Wansley of BrandMarketing Service, Ltd. Offers the following suggestions for choosing a sponsorship[47]:

- Does the sponsorship offer the right positioning?
- Does the sponsorship provide a link to brand image?
- Is the sponsorship hard for competitors to copy?
- Does the sponsorship target the right audience?
- Does the sponsorship appeal to the target audiences' lifestyle, personality, and values?
- How does the sponsorship dovetail into current corporate goals and strategies?
- Can the sponsorship be used for hospitality to court important potential and current customers?
- Is there a way to involve employees in the sponsorship?
- How will you measure the impact of the sponsorship?
- Can you afford the sponsorship?
- How easy will it be to plan the sponsorship year after year?
- Does the sponsorship complement your current promotion mix?

SPONSORSHIP IMPLEMENTATION AND EVALUATION

Once the sponsorship decisions are finalized, plans are put into action and then evaluated to determine their effectiveness. Do sponsorships really work? The findings to this million-dollar question are somewhat mixed. In Chapter 16, we discuss the techniques organizations use to determine whether the sponsorship has met their objectives. For now, let us look at the results of several studies that were conducted to determine consumer response to sponsorship. In a poll conducted by Performance Research, more than half of the respondents indicated they would be "not very likely" or "not at all likely" to purchase a company's products because it was an Olympic sponsor.[48] Surveys by Performance Research have found that if given the choice between two similar products, 72 percent of NASCAR fans would purchase the product of a NASCAR sponsor. That so-called "loyalty rate" compares with about 35 percent for the NFL and baseball, and 40 percent for the NBA. The only groups that have loyalty rates close to NASCAR's are nonprofits and the performing arts, both in the 60 percent range, according to the firm's data.

TABLE 12.7 Why Sponsorships Fail?

No Budget for Activation—Be prepared to spend several times your rights fees to leverage the property.

Not Long-Term—One year commitments generally don't work. It takes time to build the association.

No Measurable Objectives—Must have internal agreement on sponsorship goals.

Too Brand-Centric—Sponsorship should be based on the needs of consumers not brands.

Overlook Ambush and Due Dilligence—Know what you are not getting is as important is as what you are getting.

Too Much Competition for Trade Participation—When products sold through the same distribution channel sponsor the same property, the impact is diluted.

Failure to Excite the Sales Chain—A sponsorship program will not work unless the concept is sold throughout the entire distribution channel.

Insufficient Staffing—Additional staffing is needed to meet the time demands of sponsoring an event.

Buying at the Wrong Level—Higher sponsorship levels equate to more benefits. Make sure you are reaping all the benefits or buy at a lower level.

No Local Extensions—National brands must create localized execution overlays for a sponsorship to truly reach their audiences.

No Communication of Added Value—For maximum impact, sponsors must be viewed as bringing something to the event. The activity should be "provided by" the brand rather than "sponsored by" it.

Most studies report that sponsorship is having a positive impact on their organizations. For example, Visa reported that since its affiliation with the Olympic Games its market share in the United States increased by one-third, but the number of consumers who considered it the best overall card doubled to 61 percent.[49] Delta Air Lines also increased awareness levels from 38 percent to 70 percent due to its Olympic sponsorship. A recent study by the International Olympic Committee found that 22 percent of respondents would be more likely to buy a product if it were an Olympic sponsor's product.[50] In another study, roughly 60 percent of consumers indicated that they "try to buy a company's product if they support the Olympic Games."[51] In addition, 57 percent of consumers around the world agreed that "they look favorably towards a company if it is associated with the Olympics."

However, some researchers found that the majority of consumers say sponsorship makes no difference to them and their purchase behavior. For example, Quester and Lardinoit conducted a study and found that Olympic sponsors could not expect to find higher levels of brand recognition or loyalty.[52] Additionally, a study by Pitts and Slattery found that over 60 percent of respondents said they would not be more likely to purchase a product just because they knew it was a sponsor's product. One potential reason for these less than encouraging findings is the amount of sponsorship clutter. Other reasons that sponsorships fail are highlighted in Table 12.7.

Summary

The element of the promotional mix that is linked with sports marketing to the highest degree is sponsorship. A sponsorship is an investment in a sports entity (athlete, league, team, or event) to support overall organizational goals, marketing objectives, and/or promotional objectives. Sports sponsorships are growing in popularity as a promotional tool for sports and nonsports products (and organizations). For example, an estimated $4.56 billion was spent on

sports sponsorships in 1998. Because so much emphasis is placed on sponsorship, an organization must understand how to develop the most effective sponsorship program.

The systematic process for designing a sponsorship program consists of four sequential steps, which include setting sponsorship objectives, determining the sponsorship budget, acquiring a sponsorship, and implementing and evaluating the sponsorship. Because sponsorship is one of the promotional mix elements, it is important to remember the relationship it has with the broader promotional strategy. As suggested in Chapters 10 and 11, all the elements of the promotional mix must be integrated to achieve maximum effectiveness.

The sponsorship process begins by setting objectives. These objectives, not unlike advertising objectives, can be categorized as either direct or indirect. Direct sponsorship objectives focus on stimulating consumer demand for the sponsoring organization and its products. The sponsoring company benefits by attaching their product to the sports entity. The sports entity also benefits by increased exposure given by the sponsor. As such, both parties in the sponsorship agreement benefit through the association. Indirect objectives may also be set for the sponsorship program. These objectives include generating awareness, meeting and beating the competition, reaching new target markets (e.g., disabled) or specialized target markets (e.g., mature market), building relationships with customers, and enhancing the company's image.

After objectives have been formulated, the sponsorship budget is considered. The techniques for setting sponsorship budgets are also in accord with the promotional budgeting methods discussed in the previous chapter. Generally, sponsorship of sporting events is not an inexpensive proposition—especially given the threat of ambush marketing. Ambush marketing is the planned effort by an organization to associate themselves indirectly with an event to gain at least some of the recognition and benefits that are associated with being an official sponsor. In past years, the Olympics have been a playground for ambush marketing techniques. For example, Nike, not an official sponsor of the 1996 Summer Olympics, constructed a building overlooking the Olympic Park to associate themselves with the festivities of the Olympic Games. Today, more stringent policing and regulation of ambush marketing is occurring by the sporting event organizers to protect the heavy financial outlay of official sponsors.

The third step of the sponsorship process is to choose the sponsorship opportunity, or acquire the sponsorship. This means making decisions about the scope of the sponsorship, choosing the general athletic platform, and then choosing the specific athletic platform. The scope of the sponsorship refers to the geographic reach of the sports entity, as well as the interest in the entity. Shani and Sandler describe the scope of athletic events using a tool called the Sports Event Pyramid. The Sports Event Pyramid is a hierarchy of events based on geographic scope and level of interest among spectators. The five-tiered hierarchy ranges from international events, such as the Olympic Games, to local events, such as a Little League tournament in your community. Once the scope of the sponsorship has been chosen, the athletic platform must be determined. The athletic platform for a sponsorship is generally a team, sport, event, or athlete. In addition, the athletic platform could be further categorized on the basis of level of competition (i.e., professional, collegiate, high school, or recreational). Decisions regarding the choice of athletic platform should be linked to the objectives set in the previous stages of sponsorship planning. After choosing the general athletic platform, the potential sponsor must select the specific platform. For example, if a collegiate sporting event is to be the general platform, then the specific athletic platform may be the Rose Bowl, the Championship Game of the Final Four, or a regular season baseball game against an in-state rival.

The final phase of the sponsorship process is to implement and evaluate the sponsorship plans. Organizing a sponsorship and integrating a sponsorship program with the other promotional mix elements requires careful coordination. Once the sponsorship plan is put into action, the most critical question for decision makers is "Did the program deliver or have we met our sponsorship objectives?" The implementation and evaluation of the strategic sports marketing process and, more specifically, sponsorships are considered in Chapter 16.

Key Terms

- ambush marketing
- athletic platform
- awareness
- competition
- decision maker
- direct sponsorship objectives
- gatekeepers
- global events
- image building

- indirect sponsorship objectives
- influences
- international events
- local events
- national event
- match-up hypothesis
- purchasers
- reaching new target markets
- regional events

- relationship marketing
- sales increases
- sponsorship
- sponsorship budgeting methods
- sponsorship evaluation
- sponsorship objectives
- sponsorship program
- sport sponsorship acquisition
- sports event pyramid

Review Questions

1. Define sponsorship and discuss how sponsorship is used as a promotional mix tool by sports marketers? Provide evidence to support the growth of sports sponsorships worldwide.
2. Outline the steps for designing a sports sponsorship program.

3. Discuss, in detail, the major objectives of sports sponsorship from the perspective of the sponsoring organization.
4. What is ambush marketing, and why is it such a threat to legitimate sponsors? What defense would you take against ambush marketing tactics as a sports marketer?
5. In your opinion, why are sports sponsorships so successful in reaching a specific target market?
6. How are sponsorship budgets established within an organization?
7. Describe the various levels of the sponsorship pyramid. What is the Sports Event Pyramid used for, and what are some potential problems with the pyramid?
8. Define an athletic platform. In determining what athletic platform to use for a sponsorship, what factors should be considered?
9. What questions or issues might an organization raise when choosing among sponsorship opportunities?
10. Describe the different ways that sports sponsorships might be evaluated. Which evaluation tool is the most effective?

Exercises

1. Design a proposed sponsorship plan for a local youth athletic association.
2. Provide five examples of extremely good or effective match-ups between sporting events and their sponsors. In addition, suggest five examples of extremely poor or ineffective match-ups between sporting events and their sponsors.
3. Find at least one example of sponsorship for each of the following athletic platforms: individual athlete, team, and league.
4. Contact an organization that sponsors any sport or sporting event and discuss how sponsorship decisions are made and by whom. Also, ask about how the organization evaluates sponsorship.
5. Design a survey to determine the influence of NASCAR sponsorships on consumers' purchase behaviors. Ask 10 consumers to complete the survey and summarize the findings. Suggest how NASCAR might use these findings.

Internet Exercises

1. Search the Internet and find an example of a sponsorship opportunity at each level of the Sports Event Pyramid.
2. Locate at least three sports marketing companies on the Internet that specialize in the marketing of sponsorship opportunities. What products or services are these organizations offering potential clients?

Endnotes

1. IEG Sponsorship Report, 2004.
2. Ibid.
3. Ibid.
4. Ibid.
5. Matt Ball and Andrew Miller, "Go for the Greed," *Newsweek* (January 25, 1999).
6. IEG Sponsorship Report, 2004.
7. Ibid.
8. Linda Loyd. "Glaxo and Bayer announce 3-year sponsorship deal with NFL," *Philadelphia Inquirer* (July 17, 2003).
9. Linda Himelstein, "The Game's the Thing at Nike Now," *Business Week* (January 27, 1997), 88; Oscar Waters, "Nike Hopes for Big Kicks from Brazilian Soccer," *St. Louis Post-Dispatch* (December 16, 1996), B19.
10. Lacrosse Junior.

11. David Stotlar, "Sponsorship Evaulation: Moving from Theory to Practice," *Sport Marketing Quarterly*, vol. 13, no. 1 (2004), 61–64.
12. Glenn Wilson, "Does Sport Sponsorship Have a Direct Effect on Product Sales?" *Cyber-Journal of Sports Marketing*, www.ausport.gov.au/fulltext/1997/cjsm/v1n4/wilson.htm.
13. See, for example, Nigel Pope. "Overview Of Current Sponsorship Thought," www.cad.gu.edu.au/cjsm/pope21.htm; R. Abratt, B. Clayton, and L. Pitt, "Corporate Objectives in Sports Sponsorship," *International Journal of Advertising*, vol. 6 (1987), 299–311; Christine Brooks, *Sports Marketing: Competitive Business Strategies for Sports* (Englewood Cliffs, NJ: Prentice Hall, 1994).
14. Janet Hoek, Philip Gendall, Michelle Jeffcoat, and David Orsman, "Sponsorship and Advertising:

A Comparison of Their Effects," *Journal of Marketing Communications* (1997), 21–32.

15. Paul Betts, "America's Cup luxuriates in fierce battle between sponsors," Yachting: *Financial Times* (London, England) December 3, 2003.

16. D. M. Sandler and D. Shani, "Ambush Marketing: Who Gets the Gold?" *Journal of Advertising Research*, vol. 29 (1989), 9–14.

17. *Atlanta Constitution Journal* (December 29, 1995). www.atlantagames.com/WEB/oly/getcoke2.html.

18. Matthew Garrahan, "Stringent Measures Taken to Prevent Ambush Marketing," *Financial Times* (September 16, 2000), 8; Simon Lloyd, "Airlines, the Unfriendly Skies." vol. 22, no. 41, www.brw.com.au.

19. "Sports Marketing Brands Set Sponsor Ambush," (November 2000), 2.

20. Peter J. Graham, "Ambush Marketing," *Sport Marketing Quarterly*, vol. 4, no. 1 (1997), 10–12.

21. Chris Pritchard, "Aussie Olympic Committee Takes on Ambush Marketing." www.marketingmag.ca/Content/32.97/int1.html.

22. Paul Kelso, "Logos are no-go for World Cup crowds: New law means a fan can be thrown out for drinking a can of Coke," *The Guardian (London)* (February 20, 2003), 8.

23. "MassMutual Signs New Five-Year Deal for US Open Sponsorship; Expanded Relationship Includes New US Open Series," (March 1, 2004) prnewswire.com.

24. Mike Tierney, "2000 Paralympic Games: Big Wheels Training in Warm Springs," *The Atlanta Journal and Constitution* (June 24, 2000).

25. International Paralympic Committee and Visa sign partnership agreement, *PR Newswire European*, (September 17, 2003).

26. Chris Jenkins, "A Look under the Big Top," *USA Today*. www.usatoday.com/sports/golf/pga00/fs30.html; Andrew Backover; "Courting Clients: The Game in Tournament's Tent City," *The Denver Post* (August 4, 2000), E-01.

27. Roger Bennett, "Corporate Hospitality: Executive Indulgence or Vital Corporate Communications Weapon," *Corporate Communications: An International Journal*, vol. 8, no. 4 (2003), 229–240.

28. Alain Ferrand and Monique Pagés, "Image Sponsoring: A Methodology to Match Event and Sponsor," *Journal of Sport Management*, vol. 10, no. 3 (July 1996), 278–291.

29. Jennifer C. Kerr, "Consumer group wants college sports to nix the beer ads," *The Associated Press*, (November 12, 2003).

30. Roger Williams, "Making the Decision and Paying for It," *Mark McCormack's Guide to Sports Marketing*, International Sports Marketing Group (1996), 166–168.

31. Roger Williams, "Making the Decision and Paying for It," *Mark McCormack's Guide to Sports Marketing*, International Sports Marketing Group (1996), 166–168; Paula Hendrickson, "Sports Marketing: Gaining the Competitive Advantage," *Sales and Marketing: Strategies & News*, vol. 7, no. 4 (May–June 1997).

32. "Giant Eagle LPGA Classic," www.tpgaclassic.com/spon_opps.htm.

33. Brant Wamsley, "Best Practices Will Help Sponsorships Succeed," *Marketing News* (September 1, 1997), 8.

34. "IEG/Performance Research Survey Reveals What Matters Most to Sponsors," *IEG Sponsorship Report* (March 11, 2002).

35. "Scoring with Sports Fans," *Beverage Industry* (November 1996), 46, 48, 49.

36. David Shani and Dennis Sandler, "Climbing the Sports Event Pyramid," *Marketing News* (August 26, 1996), 6.

37. Brooks (1994).

38. Damon Cline, "Endorsements Lucrative for Progolfers," *The Augusta Chronicle* (April 11, 2000), www.augustachronicle.com/stories/640900/bus_124_1859.shtml.

39. Dianna P. Gray, "Sponsorship on Campus," *Sport Marketing Quarterly*, vol. v, no. 2 (1996), 29–34; Sporting Goods Manufacturers Association, "Sports Licensed Products Report," www.sportlink.com/research/. . . h/industry/98_licensed_report.html.

40. "Nike Swoosh Expands in $28.3 Million Contract," *North Carolina General Alumni Association On-Line* (October 16, 2001).

41. "P&G Teams with WNBA," *Cincinnati Business Courier*, www.bizjournals.com/cincinnati (May 27, 2003).

42. Margaret Littman, "Sponsors Take to the Court with the New Women's NBA," *Marketing News* (March 3, 1997), 1, 6.

43. "A Look Back at the First Two Years of MLS," www.mlsnet.com/aboum/#The Structure.

44. Rick Burton, "A Case Study on Sports Property Servicing Excellence: National Football League Properties," *Sport Marketing Quarterly*, vol. 5, no. 3 (1996), 23–30.

45. Nancy Boomer, "Winnipeg's Next Flood," www.marketingmag.ca/Content/1.98/special.html.

46. Jeff Jenson, "Nike Creates New Division to Stage Global Events," *Advertising Age* (September 30, 1996), 2.

47. Brant Wamsley, "Best Practices Will Help Sponsorships Succeed," *Marketing News* (September 1, 1997), 8.

48. Howard Schlossberg, *Sports Marketing* (Cambridge, MA: Blackwell Publishers, 1996).

49. Carol Emert, "Olympic Seal of Approval," *The San Francisco Chronicle* (September 2, 2000), D1.

50. Pascale Quester and Thierry Lardinoit, Sponsors impact on attitude and purchase intentions: Longitudinal Study of the 2000 Olympic Games—December 2001, http://130.195.95.71:8081/WWW/ANZMAC2001/home.htm

51. Stuart Elliott, "After $5 Billion Is Bet, Marketers Are Racing to Be Noticed Amid the Clutter of the Summer Games," *The New York Times* (July 16, 1996), D6.

52. Brenda Pitts and Jennifer Slattery, "An Examination of the Effects of Time on Sponsorship Awareness Levels," *Sport Marketing Quarterly*, vol. 13, no. 1 (2004), 43–54.

CHAPTER 13

DISTRIBUTION CONCEPTS

After completing this chapter, you should be able to:

- Describe the core distribution concepts in sports marketing.
- Discuss the various types of channels of distribution.
- Explain the nature of sports retailing and discuss the current state of the sports retailing industry.
- Explore the major issues in facilities and stadium management and marketing.
- Understand the role of sports media in the distribution process.

Historically, distribution has been one of the most important marketing functions. The ability of consumers to purchase or gain access to sports products in a timely fashion at a convenient location is the essence of the distribution function. Without distribution, every consumer interested in purchasing a new pair of Nike running shoes would need to travel to one of their manufacturing facilities around the world. Without the sports media, another form of distribution, we would have to travel with our favorite major league team to away games to watch the action. As illustrated in the opening scenario, without distribution, baseball fans from around the world would have to come to the United States to see Major League Baseball.

Fortunately, we are able to purchase our Nike shoes from department stores, sporting goods outlets, catalogs, shoe stores, and a variety of other convenient sources. We can tune in and watch every one of our team's games because of specialized, cable television programming, such as DIRECTV.

To just what length will sports marketers go to bring their products to consumers? Consider the following examples:

- The Buffalo Bills chartered an Amtrak train that ran 290 miles from Albany to Buffalo, bringing fans to games. With minimal publicity, 980 people purchased tickets to the first tailgate party on rail. Another 1,500 people put their name on the waiting list. The response has local and state officials debating whether to spend millions on rail improvements that would bring the fans practically to the stadium's front gate. A few other NFL teams offer commuter rail packages to their stadiums, but none has brought in fans from so far. Bill Munson, the Bills' assistant general manager, says, "We feel this train is an important part of what we want to try to do to become as regional as we can."[1]
- V1 golf is now offering golf lessons via the Internet. The product is promoted on the web by telling golfers that "you can work on your game knowing you have

SPOTLIGHT ON INTERNATIONAL SPORTS MARKETING

Major League Baseball International

With the 100th anniversary World Series under way, the first word in its title has actually started to mean something. These days, about 28 percent of all major leaguers, including the Florida Marlins' Miguel Cabrera (Venezuela) and the New York Yankees' Hideki Matsui (Japan), come from parts of the planet outside the 50 states. The figure is an astounding 46 percent in the minors.

And in the last few years, the people who run baseball have made renewed efforts to bolster the international fan base. "Our efforts in that regard are absolutely critical," commissioner Bud Selig said. "The potential to grow the game is great here, but the potential elsewhere is tremendous." Why do the people at Major League Baseball care so much about globalizing the game?

They're not thinking about establishing franchises outside North America; logistics make that impractical, at least for now. Mostly, they are thinking about getting added revenue from three sources:

- The sale of overseas broadcast rights.
- Sponsorship arrangements, primarily with U.S. companies that do business in Asia and Latin America.
- The marketing of team-logo merchandise, which, in some countries, has considerable sales appeal as Americana.

To grow that part of the business, Major League Baseball International is going to considerable lengths. During the World Series, it is producing its own video feed, separate from that of Fox Sports, which is being broadcast to well over 200 countries. Announcers Gary Thorne and Rick Sutcliffe are explaining the game to foreign viewers and highlighting foreign players.

Earlier this year, Major League Baseball opened a new office in Tokyo to go along with existing outposts in London and in Sydney, Australia. For the 2005 season, serious consideration is being given to playing a regular-season series somewhere in Europe, most likely in Italy, perhaps just before the All-Star Break. Last fall, about the time the New York Mets' Mike Piazza was posing outside the Coliseum in Rome, a baseball official was looking at Rome's Olympic Stadium as a possible venue.

Also in the talking stages is a baseball World Cup that might be held in this country during spring training. The competition would involve national teams made up largely of major-leaguers, teams representing Japan, South Korea, the Dominican Republic, Puerto Rico, Venezuela, Mexico, Cuba, and the United States, among other countries.

"The NBA's international business exploded after the Dream Team played in the 1992 Olympics," said Paul Archey, baseball's senior vice president for international business operations. "We think a World Cup could do the same for us. And we wouldn't have just one Dream Team. We'd have eight or nine, with no guarantee the United States would win."

While baseball won't reveal how much money it's making overseas, Archey says that the amount has grown substantially over the last few years and that 70 percent of the total comes from broadcast rights. In Japan, the most lucrative overseas market, the 2003 All-Star Game got better television ratings than it did in the United States.

To try to spur interest in other countries—the kind of interest that results in higher rights' fees, more sponsorship deals, and more sales of Yankees caps and Red Sox jerseys—baseball is moving on several fronts. The most noticeable is the staging of overseas events. There's the semiannual All-Star tour of Japan, with similar trips being contemplated for Australia, South Korea, and Taiwan. And this season, as part of baseball's broader outreach, the Montreal Expos played 22 "home" games in San Juan, Puerto Rico.

But the prospective European excursion has particular appeal to baseball executives because of what Europe has going for it—a lot of money, a lot of new cable and satellite television stations in need of programming, and, to put the best face on it, a lot of room for growth.

"Europe has been a tough market for us because it's so soccer crazy," said Russell Gabay, baseball's executive producer of television operations. "You've got to get people to see baseball and touch it. The philosophy under which Major League Baseball International operates is that it can't make money someplace long-term unless people there are playing the game. Only then, the theory goes, will they watch games on television or buy licensed products.

With that in mind, baseball has poured about $25 million into a number of development programs. One introduces the game to youngsters in grade-school gym classes. Another sends U.S. college coaches overseas. A third provides equipment to national baseball federations. A fourth offers a "road show" featuring a batting cage and pitching tunnel. A fifth sends American stars abroad as ambassadors. Piazza, for instance, went to Berlin and Rome last November.

Baseball's goal is to help countries develop national teams and ultimately send a few players to the major leagues. "Establishing heroes in each country is critical to the development of our sport," said James Pearce, baseball's director of market development. "The nationalistic nature of sports is so powerful."

It's no accident that Major League Baseball's revenue in Japan soared with the arrival of Ichiro Suzuki in Seattle and Matsui in the Bronx. Or that the interest level is high among Venezuelans and Dominicans, who have plenty of their own players to watch. More foreign stars means higher foreign broadcast fees and more merchandise sales. What Bud Selig wouldn't give for a superstar from Italy.

Source: Larry Eichel, "America's pastime going truly global" *Philadelphia Inquirer.* (October 21, 2003).

ready access to professional guidance at any time." In essence, your video golf swing is uploaded to the Internet via specialized software and then downloaded by your V1 golf coach, bringing golf lessons to your home when you don't have time to get to the course.

- The 2004 NCAA basketball tournament will be webcast and feature all 56 games of the first and second rounds and the regional semifinals. The video webcasts are being promoted as "NCAA March Madness on Demand" and will appear on ncaasports.com.[2]

DIRECTV distributes customized sports programming to consumers.
Source: DIRECTV, Inc.

Distribution planning, as shown in the foregoing examples, is a complex process to understand because of the many shapes it takes in sports marketing. For sporting goods, **distribution** involves moving the product from producer to end users. This task is accomplished through a **channel of distribution,** or a coordinated group of individuals or organizations that route the sports product to the final consumer. Those individuals or organizations that take part in the distribution process are referred to as **channel members.** Channel members are responsible for facilitating the exchange between manufacturers or service providers and consumers.

For sporting events, there is a direct channel of distribution. The fans attending the event are consuming it as quickly as the sports product (entertainment) is being produced. Consumers not attending a sporting event may also want access to the event. In this case, the sports marketer must seek alternative ways to deliver the sporting event to a widespread audience. Television, radio, or the Internet can be considered a distribution medium for fans who want to consume the game via one of the many broadcast media.

Distribution is also important to sports marketers who are seeking new markets in which to sell existing sports products. Sports marketers are developing new **sports delivery systems** to bring their sports to new markets. In addition to televising games worldwide, the NFL may play several regular season games in Mexico to promote the sport of football south of the border. NASCAR also distributed its product internationally, holding several events in Japan in the late 1990s.[3] Likewise, in October 1997, the NHL broke the ice in Japan by holding its first-ever official league game outside of North America.[4] As discussed in the following article, Major League Baseball will not be left behind in the race to gain international distribution and increase the fan base as the 2004 regular season officially begins when the New York Yankees meet the Tampa Bay Devil Rays in Tokyo.

Distribution of NFL products over the Web.

Source: Copyright © 2004, NFL Enterprises. All rights reserved.

Big-League Baseball Booms in Japan

Japanese children swinging in the batting cages pretend they're him, the news photographers at the ball park act is if there's no one else here besides him, and when the newspaper headlines scream his nickname, Godzilla, the exclamation marks are taken for granted.

That's the public story of New York Yankee, Hideki Matsui's, triumphant homecoming, Japan's most beloved baseball slugger returning to a unified display of adulation from a proud nation. He came back for Major League Baseball's regular-season opener here tonight (7 p.m., same-day tape, RSE), and for an exhibition Sunday against his old team, Tokyo's Yomiuri Giants.

But Japanese society, perhaps more than any other, is one of public stories shared and private feelings masked—a social peculiarity characterized by the Japanese terms *tatemae* and *honne*. The happy tale of Godzilla's return is certainly an authentic one, more than just a facade of *tatemae*, but it also has a complicated inner *honne*, a concealed anxiety about the surging popularity of America's major-league baseball and the declining state of the Japanese pastime he left behind.

Matsui ensured the public homecoming story would be a good one. He hit a home run Sunday in his first at-bat to earn a standing ovation from a sellout crowd of 55,000 at the Tokyo Dome. The fans chanted "Home run, home run, Matsui!" every time he went to the plate, and booed in disappointment when he was walked. Even when he was just standing in the outfield, television cameras regularly made sure the viewers at home saw him waiting for the next batted ball. His fans seemed satisfied enough, as he helped his Yankees beat the hometown Giants 6–2, but some might also reflect on how Japan defines success.

"In the world of baseball and other American sports, players must go to America to become the world's best. This is an imperialistic act, promoting the American way of sports to the world," Masayuki Tamaki, a sports writer and author of the book *What Is Sports?*, said in an interview. "This American colonization can be seen behind Major League Baseball's strategy for the Japanese market."

This is the flip side of a phenomenon viewed favorably by many fans here, the "Japanification" of the major leagues in the past decade. Three of Japan's best players are successful stars in the United States—Hideo Nomo of the Los Angeles Dodgers, Ichiro Suzuki of the Seattle Mariners, and now Matsui—creating a huge following among fans here. They get up early in the morning to watch their heroes' games on television or buy travel packages to see them in person. And this year, hopes are high for another star, New York Mets shortstop Kazuo Matsui, or Little Matsui, who is unrelated to Hideki.

Last year, the league's 272 games on broadcast television here drew an average audience of 1.5 million, according to league officials; and one of every six households watched Game 1 of last year's World Series, featuring Matsui's Yankees and the Florida Marlins. Even players who struggle in the United States can produce a spike in viewers here, as long as they are in the lineup or on the pitching mound.

"Japanification" has begun to accomplish what Major League Baseball wants, increasing fan recognition here of teams with Japanese players, especially the Yankees, and building a "brand" for their television broadcasts, sponsorships, and Americana merchandising. The league earned $60 million in revenues from Japan last year, more than from all other foreign countries combined. Three hundred games will be broadcast on free network television this year, the first of a six-year, $275-million (U.S.) television deal. The league opened an office in Tokyo last year and is planning a baseball World Cup event, possibly as soon as next year, to extend its reach here and elsewhere.

But it is unclear whether all this will help develop or undermine Japan's proud baseball tradition, which dates back to at least 1872, when an American teacher in Tokyo, Horace Wilson, introduced the game to his students at what would later become Tokyo University. Since then, Japanese baseball has produced the world's home-run king, Sadaharu Oh, who hit 868 home runs; one of history's best left-handed pitchers, Masaichi Kaneda, who won 400 games and struck out 4,490 batters; and early pitching legend Eiji Sawamura, who struck out Babe Ruth, Jimmie Foxx, and Lou Gehrig in succession in a 1–0 loss to a visiting All-Star team in 1934.

That might help explain why Matsui's signing with the Yankees last year carried so much cultural weight, for good and for bad. Unlike the Japanese stars who left before him, Matsui played for the powerhouse Yomiuri Giants. The Yomiuri Giants are owned by a media conglomerate, The Yomiuri Shimbun Holdings, whose flagship newspaper, *The Yomiuri Shimbun*, is the world's largest daily, with a morning circulation of 10 million and an evening circulation of 4 million.

For decades the Giants have had most of the best players, won by far the most pennants, and have had all or most of their games broadcast on network television. Oh, Kaneda, and Sawamura all played for the Giants, as did Japan's arguably most popular player ever, Oh's teammate Shigeo Nagashima. Nicknamed Mr. Baseball, Nagashima, who was also manager of the Giants and a mentor to Matsui, recently suffered a stroke, making his

(Continued)

(Continued)

medical condition as important front-page news as Godzilla's return.

So when, after 10 years as a star for the Giants, Matsui was presented with the opportunity to leave for America's most famous team, it was a choice laden with cultural significance. He made that much clear after he had decided. "When he started his press conference last spring, he said: 'I hope people don't think I'm a traitor,'" said Robert Whiting, author of *The Meaning of Ichiro*. "On the other hand, if he didn't go, people would say he was a wimp."

He went, and instead of becoming a wimp, he became, like Ichiro before him, a made-in-Japan version of Michael Jordan. The reaction has been mostly favorable, especially from younger fans less devoted to the domestic game. "We all have dreams for Matsui right now," said Taku Harada, 22, who just graduated from college. "The guys around me, we don't watch Japanese baseball much anymore. They have more interest in major-league baseball."

That is what concerns the fans of Harada's parents' generation. Surveys show baseball is still the favorite sport of more than half of Japanese. But the domestic game has been losing fan support to soccer, video games, and new choices on TV, including, notably, major-league baseball.

With Matsui gone, the television ratings for Giants' games dropped to an all-time low last year, to slightly more than half the audience of 20 years ago. This year's major-league games at the Tokyo Dome also are drawing attention away from the beginning of the Japanese season.

MLB commissioner Bud Selig said here Sunday that the American game's impact here is good for the Japanese game: "The more popular baseball gets, whatever the reasons, the better it is for everybody here, and that includes Japanese baseball."

Source: Gady A. Epstein, "Big-league ball booms in Japan: Japanese players' success in the U.S. has boosted popularity of Major League Baseball in the Land of the Rising Sun, but it also mirrors a growing decline in the country's domestic game," *The Baltimore Sun*, (March 30, 2004), C1.

In this chapter, distribution is examined from three distinct perspectives. First, we explore basic distribution concepts for the delivery of sports products. Second, the distribution function is investigated from the sporting-event standpoint. Ticket distribution and the stadium as "place" are examined as a portion of this distribution function. Finally, distribution is discussed from the viewpoint of sports media, or those organizations interested in bringing sporting events to widespread audiences.

BASIC DISTRIBUTION CONCEPTS

As stated earlier, distribution involves getting sports products to consumers. This is accomplished through a channel of distribution that is defined as organizations or individuals who direct the flow of sports products from producer to consumer. The organizations or individuals who make up the channel of distribution are commonly referred to as channel members. Channel members include producers, intermediaries, and consumers. Producers of sports products may range from two teams, competing products, at a manufacturer of sporting goods, such as Head. As we discussed in earlier chapters, the ultimate consumers of the sports products are either spectators or sports participants.

Channel intermediaries are organizations or individuals that are in the middle (thus, the term *middlemen*) of producers and consumers. The two most common types of intermediaries for sporting goods are wholesalers and retailers. Wholesalers sell to other intermediaries, such as retailers and other wholesalers. Retailers, such as The Sports Authority or Dick's, sell to ultimate consumers, or end users. Although these are traditional intermediaries for sporting goods, intermediaries are also present in the channel of distribution for attending sporting events or watching sports. For instance, the ticket distribution agency (or the scalper) can be considered an intermediary in getting you to the sports product. In addition, the televised sporting event is distributed to you via a cable or a national network. In this case, the media can be thought of as an intermediary.

Iznad golf illustrates direct marketing in action.

Source: Copyright © Iznad Golf, Inc. Used by permission. All rights reserved.

One job of the sports marketer is to ensure products flow smoothly through this "pipeline" of intermediaries to you, the ultimate consumer. Through the proper management of channels of distribution, products arrive to consumers in the most timely and cost-effective manner. Intermediaries, in fact, make this possible. In the next section, we look at why intermediaries advance the distribution process.

INTERMEDIARY FUNCTIONS

Intermediaries perform a number of broad functions in the distribution process. Each broad function is essential to the distribution process. The structure of the distribution channel and the type of sports product dictate the functions of the intermediary. It is important to realize that, in most cases, the functions are necessary and cannot be eliminated, although responsibilities can be shifted among channel members.

The first channel function is referred to as the **information function.** Because intermediaries such as sporting goods retailers are closer to the end users of the product, they are in a position to provide insight into consumer needs and the benefits desired by consumers. Aside from marketing research, channel intermediaries may also help producers monitor the marketing environment. For example, a retailer monitors trends in consumer demand for products and informs the manufacturer of the sporting good. The information can also flow in the other direction. That is, retailers provide consumers with information to assist in purchase decisions. Intermediaries such as the sports media also need to provide information to consumers regarding the nature of the broadcast.

Another of the core **intermediary functions** of channel members is the **marketing communications function.** As we learned in Chapters 10 and 11, the communications function involves a number of activities, such as advertising and promotion, personal selling, and public relations. Typically, many of the marketing communications functions are performed by retailers to stimulate demand by end users. For example, Lady Foot Locker promotes Reebok shoes using a collegiate woman athlete. The objective of this promotion is to increase demand for Reebok and for Lady Foot Locker.

The **physical distribution function** is perhaps most synonymous with distribution activities. Without physical distribution, products would not be moved from producer to consumer. Imagine having to drive to Louisville every time you wanted to purchase a baseball bat or to Indonesia, to buy Nike shoes. One of the critical distribution issues is making deliveries in a timely fashion. New technologies are emerging, such as a computerized order processing system that reduces the time between placing an order and receiving goods.

Inventory management is yet another of the important functions performed by channel intermediaries. Inventory management tasks include ordering the correct assortment of merchandise (i.e., popular product lines and items), maintaining appropriate levels of merchandise, and storing the merchandise that has been ordered. Today, just-in-time (JIT) management systems are being used to minimize the amount of inventory that needs to be stored. In essence, goods arrive when needed to reduce inventory costs.

Although each of these functions is necessary, the channel member who performs each is largely dictated by the type of channel. In other words, various routes can be navigated from producer to consumer. In the next section, we examine several of the more common marketing channels for sports products.

TYPES OF CHANNELS

Channels of distribution can vary in length, depending on the total number of channel members. Broadly speaking, channels can be described as either direct or indirect. **Direct channels** are the shortest in length because producer and end user are the only two channel members (see Fig. 13.1).

With the increasing number of direct mail catalogs for sports and the use of the Internet for shopping, direct distribution is becoming a popular channel for sports marketers. Virtually all types of sporting goods can be purchased using direct mail. For example, discounted golf equipment can be purchased from GolfSmith or GolfWorks catalogs, running shoes and gear can be purchased from Soark or Roadrunner catalogs; volleyball equipment is sold in the magazine *Volleyball*; and tennis equipment is sold in the magazine *Tennis*.

The other type of channel structure is called an **indirect channel** because intermediaries are present. Two common indirect channels of distribution look like the following:

Producer $\longrightarrow$ Wholesaler $\longrightarrow$ Retailer $\longrightarrow$ Consumer

Producer $\longrightarrow$ Retailer $\longrightarrow$ Consumer

As you can see, wholesalers and retailers are all added to the distribution process when indirect channels are being used. In addition, agents or brokers, who have the legal authority to act on behalf of the producer, can become important members of an

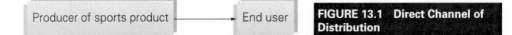

Producer of sports product $\longrightarrow$ End user

FIGURE 13.1 Direct Channel of Distribution

indirect channel. Sports agents, in fact, are intermediaries who act on the behalf of athletes, who are being hired by the consumer (in this case, the sports organization).

SINGLE VERSUS MULTIPLE CHANNELS

The previous section provided a brief discussion of traditional channel structure. Another decision that must be made by sporting goods manufacturers is whether to use a single-channel versus a multiple-channel strategy. A **single-channel strategy** is described as using only one channel of distribution to reach potential consumers. For example, Sea Ray boats are sold through authorized Sea Ray dealerships around the world. This channel structure allows the manufacturer greater control over the entire distribution process.

The other, more common, alternative for channel design is to distribute sports products via the **multiple-channel strategy.** In this case, more than one channel structure is used. For example, Calloway golf clubs can be purchased in golf specialty stores, through direct mail-order catalogs, and at pro shops. Professional and college athletic programs also offer multiple channels of distribution. Games and events can be attended, watched on television, listened to on the radio, or even broadcast via the Internet. For many sports organizations, multiple channels are considered advantageous because they allow multiple opportunities or places to purchase the sports product, and they reach different market segments.

DEGREES OF MARKET COVERAGE

One item related to the idea of single versus multiple retailing channels is determining the desired level of market coverage. **Market coverage** refers to the number of outlets used in the distribution of the sports product. The extent of market coverage is defined in terms of exclusive, selective, or intensive distribution.

Exclusive distribution occurs when only one outlet is used to market products per geographic market. For instance, the phrase "exclusive coverage" of sporting events illustrates the concept of exclusive distribution. NBC has paid some $3.5 billion to secure the exclusive rights to televise the **Winter** and Summer Games from 2006 to 2012.[5] Other examples of exclusive distribution include the long-standing coverage of the Masters and the NCAA Men's Basketball Tournament by CBS.

Selective distribution, as the name implies, refers to making products available in several, but selectively chosen, outlets. For instance, the NFL selectively distributes its regular season contests on Fox, CBS, ESPN, and ABC. **Intensive distribution** involves selling sports products in a large number of available outlets. Nike athletic shoes, for example, are sold in NikeTown retail stores. Nike factory outlet shops, a number of retail athletic shoe stores (e.g., Foot Locker and Footaction), department stores, discount stores, and catalogs. As such, Nike has chosen an intensive distribution strategy. However, specific models of Nike shoes are selectively or exclusively distributed.

SPORTS RETAILING

A critical member of most channels of distribution for sporting goods is the sports retailer. Sports retailers, such as The Sports Authority, Foot Locker, and Dick's Sporting Goods, are linked with sports marketing in that they provide products to the final consumer so that they may participate in sports. By definition, **sports retailers** are channel members who are involved in all the activities of selling products and services to end users, or final consumers.

In this definition of sports retailing, a few important points must be considered. First, retailers are channel members who differentiate themselves from other channel members in that they sell to end users, or consumers, who use the products or service. If more than 50 percent of an organization's sales are to end users, they may be called retailers. However, if less than 50 percent are sold to final consumers, the organization is considered a wholesaler. By contrast, a wholesaler purchases products that are sold to other businesses for resale.

Second, retailers are involved in a variety of activities, such as promotion, creating a desirable store image in which to shop, and providing wide assortments of sporting goods to consumers. Each of these retailing activities are explored in the next section of this chapter.

Third, the definition of sports retailing points to the notion of selling not only goods, but also providing needed services. Most sports retailers provide both goods and services to consumers. For example, a tennis retailer will sell equipment and apparel and also provide racquet repair and stringing services. Some tennis retailers may also offer lessons. Other sports retailers may provide ticket distribution services for sporting events.

Some sports retailers, such as health and fitness clubs, are known as service retailers because they primarily offer services rather than goods to end users. Other examples of service sports retailers would be golf club repair shops and tourist attractions, such as the Baseball Hall of Fame and the Louisville Slugger Museum. In addition, sports medicine clinics, which not only rehabilitate you when you are injured but also help to make you a better athlete, are sports retailers.

THE NUMBER AND TYPES OF SPORTS RETAILERS

The continued reduction in the total number of sporting goods outlets and the consolidation of key players continues to be the trend in the retail sporting goods industry as we look past 2004. The Sporting Goods Manufacturers Association expects the nearly $50 billion industry to grow slightly by roughly 1.3 percent.

The large retailers continue to transform the marketplace. Woolworth's has put together an empire of brands, including Foot Locker, Lady Foot Locker, Kid's Foot Locker, and Champs. In the biggest merger yet, Gart Sports has combined forces with the Sports Authority creating the closest thing to a national retail chain in the sporting goods industry. Additionally, sports retailers are increasing the number of private label products in their stores in both the equipment and apparel categories.[6]

Another huge development that has influenced sports retailing is the sports e-tailing trend. Forrester Research predicts that the market for online sporting goods sales will grow from $1.7 billion in 2003 to over $6 billion in 2008, for an amazing growth rate of 350 percent. Interestingly, about one-third of this grow will be based on the sale of used sporting goods.[7] Online licensed market retailer Fanbuzz.com, which had just $3 million in overall sales in 1999, grew to more than $20 million in sales in 2002. Since its launch in 1996, the company has seen its sales figures grow each year and FanBuzz was recently acquired by ValueVision. Another example of the potential growth of online sales is the entry of Amazon into the sporting goods sector. Amazon will not stock or ship any products, but is paid an undisclosed commission by manufacturers who want to display their items on the well-known site. Dan Head, the vice president for e-commerce at sportline.com explains the attraction of the sporting goods industry for Amazon and other online companies. "It's impossible to put a good bricks and mortar sporting goods store together. There are at least 500,000 products in the sporting goods industry—probably double that. Imagine trying to put all that stuff into one building so you can satisfy the consumer. But you can do it online."[8]

SPORTS RETAILING MIX

Like all marketers and retailers, sports retailers must also design an effective marketing mix for their retail environment. With the nature of sports retailing constantly changing, sports retailers must be able to quickly adapt their marketing mix to meet the changing needs of consumers.

Profiling the Sports E-tailing Consumer

Ever wonder how sports e-tailers acquire new customers and drive business toward profitability. Gomez marketing research surveyed approximately 3,000 Internet-enabled sporting goods buyers who currently shop online, off-line, or both online and off-line. The purpose of the study was to understand the online and off-line buying habits, behaviors, and intentions of these consumers. Although the study uncovered a wealth of compelling information, this focuses on only a fraction of the study's insights—understanding customers who do not yet purchase sporting goods online.

To better understand customer intentions, the study segmented buyers who are not currently purchasing sporting goods online into three waves: Wave 1, which is more likely to purchase sporting goods online in the future; Wave 2, which is less likely to purchase sporting goods online in the future; and Wave 3, which are resisters and unlikely to buy sporting goods online. Both Wave 1 and Wave 2 are comprised of respondents who watch and participate in at least one or more sports activities and who have purchased items other than sporting goods online within the past six months.

The methodology behind the wave segmentation incorporates existing Gomez market research and predicates purchasing intentions based on previous behavior. Research showed that sporting goods are typically not the first item that consumers buy online. Most consumers' first transactions online are commodity goods, such as music, computers, and books. A second group of products that consumers are likely to purchase prior to purchasing sporting goods consists of apparel, electronics, and toys. We also learned that sporting goods purchasers' median Web tenure is four years or more. This information tells us that sporting goods consumers, as a group, are generally seasoned online veterans and tend to expect a higher level of service from the stores with which they interact.

Here are measures retailers can take to acquire customers on the precipice of making a sporting goods purchase online.

- Grab the Low-Hanging Fruit—Focus on Wave 1 versus Wave 2 as they are more likely to purchase online. Wave 1 respondents have stated their intentions to purchase online within the next six months, and this upcoming holiday may be the time to capture this market segment and retain those customers. Market aggressively to this group through whatever means possible. Highly effective, low-cost marketing campaigns such as newsletters or e-mail alerts announcing

sales, promotions, and newsworthy information can be successful in driving new customers to your site.

- Target the Demographic—Now that you can identify the customer's sweet spot, market to their preferences and lifestyle. For example, retailers should know that women represent 56 percent of the next generation of sporting goods buyers and, thus, focus marketing efforts to capture these shoppers. Our research also indicates that women are most likely to shop at a discount store within the next six months, followed by a brick-and-mortar store and Internet-only store. Leverage this knowledge by providing equal or higher-quality services and resources to that of discount stores and make consumers aware of the benefits of shopping online.

- Make It As Easy As Possible To Transact Online—Both waves of buyers stated convenience, selection, and price, in that order, are the top three motivators to shopping online. Sites should make it extremely convenient for consumers to become online shoppers by employing standardized navigation that is clearly defined and empowering the consumer with useful decision support tools while shopping. E-tailers should offer a deep and wide selection of products and allow consumers the ability to make comparisons by developing at-a-glance methods that allow browsing shoppers to make product and pricing comparisons.

- Offer Incentives for Purchasing Online—As illustrated previously, future buyers overwhelmingly prefer to shop at conventional off-line sales channels. Sites should incentivize these consumers to shop online by developing programs such as frequent flyer miles, promotional dollars on every purchase, and discounts for first-time online sports shoppers. In addition, stores with physical locations should entice off-line customers to use their online channel by providing in-store coupons that are redeemable online and existing customer discounts as well as Internet kiosks in the physical stores. Stores that offer a variety of purchase choices are providing a better experience for consumers.

Retailers can learn a great deal from the consumers who are both buying and not buying from their sites. Gomez identifies these consumers and offers some advice on how to capture the portion of the market that has yet to purchase sporting goods online, but is ready to take the plunge off the virtual diving board.

Source: John Lovett, "The Wave of the Future: The Next Online Sporting Goods Customer." www.esportsreport.com/directory/web_zine/market_ research/wave.htm.

The first step in designing an effective retail marketing mix is to understand just who your customers are or who you want them to be. Sports retailers segment and target groups of consumer in a number of ways. Some sports retailers, such as Lady Foot Locker, use demographic segmentation and target women. Other retailers, such as the many tennis and ski shops, segment on the basis of psychographics and lifestyle, knowing that a large proportion of consumers who ski also participate in tennis.

Just as in the broader strategic sports marketing process, after target markets have been chosen the next step in retailing is to develop a unique position in the marketplace. If you recall, positioning was defined in Chapter 7 as fixing the sports product in the mind of consumers. In retailing, positioning is fixing the retail outlet in the minds of consumers. This is accomplished by developing a marketing mix that will be the most appealing to the chosen target market and create the desired image. Let us examine retailing mix decisions and retail image in greater detail.

SPORTS RETAILING PRODUCTS

One of the biggest challenges facing sports retailers is choosing the right product mix to satisfy their target market(s). Remember, the product mix describes all the different product lines that are carried by the organization, as well as the depth and breadth of that assortment. In sports retailing, this translates into decisions about what sports products to carry and what variety and depth of product lines to carry in each sport. For example, some sporting goods retailers may not choose to sell hunting and fishing equipment, whereas others may specialize in only these two sporting activities. Obviously, these two sports retailers would be positioned very differently from each other.

An excellent example of a sports retailer that has chosen to differentiate itself based on the type of merchandise carried is Play It Again Sports. These retailers specialize in selling preowned (used) sporting goods at a fraction of the cost of new products. Consumers bring in their old merchandise and may either sell it or trade it for other merchandise. By selling used sporting goods, Play It Again Sports targets price-sensitive consumers who, for whatever reason, do not want to pay a lot for their sporting goods.

Planning the assortment of goods and services to offer consumers is often referred to as merchandising. In fact, merchandising is at the heart of sports retailing. If sports retailers did not provide some assortment of products, stores would have to be highly specialized. For example, you would have to go to a soccer store for shin guards, a baseball store for a glove, a hockey store for a stick, and so on.

Merchandisers are also concerned with the issue of presenting the products in the retail environment. The type of merchandise sold by a sports retailer and the way that it is presented to consumers have a tremendous impact on the image of the retailer. Store layout and the way the products are stocked are critical to the atmosphere of the retail outlet. NikeTown outlets could sell their actual products on a fraction of the retail space they actually use. If they reduced their space, however, they would not convey the sports experience message that they are trying to transmit to consumers.

A recent trend in sports merchandising is to carry products in the retail environment that are not necessarily focused on sports. This practice of selling "unrelated merchandise" is referred to as scrambled merchandising. Sports retailers are beginning to scramble merchandise by offering consumers a much wider variety of active wear and clothing than they have ever done in the past. In addition, some stores are beginning to offer consumers a wide array of sports services, such as batting cages, a bowling center, basketball courts, and workout facilities. The NBA Store in Manhattan is one prime example of a retailer offering much more than products alone. The NBA Store serves as a museum, gym, event center, and merchant with a unique design. The store averages roughly 4,000 visitors a day and has some 35,000 square feet of selling space. It also features a half-court shooting area, an arena-sized Jumbotron, and a Center Court that has the capacity to hold 1,100 people for events ranging from concerts to birthday parties.[9]

SPORTS RETAILING PRICING

Pricing decisions also allow sports retailers to differentiate themselves from competitors. Many independent and smaller sporting goods retailers charge higher than normal prices and position themselves as excellent customer service providers. Sports retailers, such as the nearly 450 "team stores" across the United States that specialize in college and professional licensed merchandise, may also charge higher prices for their deep but narrow product lines. In contrast, sports discounters, such as Hibbett Sporting Goods, offer lower prices and a wider assortment of products.

Again, the decision of what price strategy to follow at the retail level is based on the target market that has been chosen, the desired positioning, and the competition. It is important to understand that not all consumers are necessarily looking for the lowest price. The various categories of price orientation among consumers are presented in Table 13.1.

Again, the sports retailer must identify the price orientation of its target market and plan the rest of the retail mix accordingly. For instance, the independent sports retailer may charge more but offer higher levels of customer service, convenience, and, hopefully, establish "store-loyal" consumers. However, sports superstores may offer limited service but the lowest prices in town.

SPORTS RETAILING DISTRIBUTION

The most critical retail distribution decision is the location of the store. As the old saying goes, the three most important factors in the success of a retail outlet are location, location, location. Although this is generally true, certain types of shoppers, as we have learned, are more price sensitive than others and will be willing to travel to more remote locations to get the best deals. Alternatively, the prestige shoppers may have to go out of their way to purchase that one-of-a-kind product.

Because location is so critical, how do retailers choose the ideal location? As with all retail mix decisions, store location is largely a function of the target market and positioning. Table 13.2 presents general guidelines for choosing a store location.

SPORTS RETAIL PROMOTIONS

Retail promotions refer to decisions sports retailers make with respect to the proper mix of personal selling, advertising, sales promotions, and public relations.

TABLE 13.1   Price Orientation Among Consumers

- **Brand-Loyal Customers**—Consumers who believe their chosen brand is superior to other brands and are willing to pay a fair price for the sports product, even if it is slightly higher than competitors.
- **Status-Seeking Customers**—Consumers who will only purchase the highest-quality, most prestigious, name brand sports products and will pay higher prices. In fact, higher prices are welcomed by these consumers because of the prestige and status associated with the price tag.
- **Service-Seeking Customers**—Consumers who are also willing to pay slightly higher prices if compensated by higher levels of service. This is especially important for consumers who require higher levels of information from store personnel.
- **Convenience Customers**—Consumers who value the location of the store and the ease of purchasing products that this offers. They are less likely to "shop around" and thus more likely to pay above-average prices.
- **Price-Shopping Customers**—Consumers who will "shop around" for the best deal at the lowest possible price.

Source: Joel Evans and Barry Berman, *Marketing*, 6th ed. (New York: Macmillan, 1994), 680.

TABLE 13.2 General Guidelines for Choosing Store Location

- Consider the types of retail outlets that will surround yours. An upscale tennis and ski shop would not want to be placed next to a heavy price discounter such as a "Big Lots" or a "Dollar Store." Are other retailers located near you compatible with your product offerings?
- Consider retail saturation or how the demand for goods and services is being served by existing retailers. Stated simply, consider the number and quality of competitors in the area.
- Consider the characteristics of the consumers in the area. Does the demographic profile (age, income, or education) and psychographic profile (lifestyle) match the desired target market.
- Consider the accessibility of the potential location. Is the location easy to get to? What are the traffic flow and congestion in the area? In addition, the retailer must consider the parking considerations.
- Consider the cost of the potential location. What are the basic rent payments, taxes, maintenance costs, or length of the lease?

Source: Patrick Dunne, Robert Lusch, Myron Gable, and Randall Gebhardt, *Retailing* (Cincinnati: South-Western, 1992).

Promotional decisions also play a key role in retail positioning, or establishing the store in the mind of the target market.

Typically, advertising at the local retail level has short-term, direct objectives for stimulating sales. Retail sports advertising tends to emphasize price discounts and is usually run in conjunction with other sales promotions. Ultimately, retailers' advertising wants to draw consumers to a specific store with the hope that once they arrive, they will make multiple purchases.

At the national level, retail advertising tends to be more institutional, stressing the image of a chain of stores. These national advertisements promote the atmosphere of the store, product selection, or brand names carried, and often feature a well-known athlete endorser. For example, a Finish Line advertisement uses NBA stars Yao Ming, Vlade Divac, and Jamal Mashburn, and also features the Reebok brand logo. Finish Line hopes to enhance its image through association with a name brand shoe and the high-profile NBA stars.

Personal selling at sports retailers is also an essential part of the retail promotional mix. The amount of personal selling is often a key positioning factor for sports retailers. Sales personnel are an important part of a consumer's perception of a retailer. The level of knowledge and the customer service the sales personnel possess can shape the image of the retailer. In essence, sales personnel are a retailer's foot soldier in the constant war for consumers' discretionary income.

RETAIL IMAGE

As previously stated, the retailer's positioning strategy is thoughtfully carried out by choosing the appropriate marketing mix and by creating the desired store image. In fact, nothing may be as important to a sports retailer than the image of the store. Most retailers realize they need to create an image that consumers find entertaining and fun. Simply putting quality products on the shelves is no longer acceptable. As such, sporting goods retailers are undergoing a "Disneylike" transformation. One emerging leader in merchandising and image is the Bass Pro Shop Outdoor World, which positions itself as bring the outdoors inside. The Web site promotes the "gorgeous waterfalls, giant aquariums, incredible wildlife mounts, delicious food, and more that make Bass Pro Shops stores a must-see attraction for sporting families around the world."[10]

Just what makes up store image? This concept is as difficult to describe as someone's personality. In fact, a good way to conceptualize store image is to think of it as "store personality" made up of many tangible and intangible traits. Retail store image

TABLE 13.3   Dimensions of Retail Store Image

- Atmospherics
- Location
- Sales personnel
- Clientele
- Type of merchandise carried
- Type of promotional activities

is made up of a number of interrelated factors that together produce the overall store experience (see Table 13.3). These factors include atmospherics, location, store sales personnel, clientele, types of merchandise carried, and types of promotional activities. As we discuss the dimensions of retail store image in greater detail, pay special attention to the relationship between each factor and the marketing mix.

ATMOSPHERICS

The term that best encompasses the many facets of in-store image is atmospherics. **Atmospherics** are a retail store's visual, auditory, and olfactory environments, designed to attract and keep consumers in the store. Of all the factors that comprise retail store image, atmospherics are perhaps the most important in creating and reinforcing the store image. In addition, store atmosphere plays a role in encouraging people to visit a store, stay in a store for longer periods of time, and make more impulse purchases. In fact, some research

Retailers such as Kmart appeal to price-sensitive customers.
Source: Kmart Corporation.

suggests that atmosphere becomes even more important as the number of competing stores increases and as these stores begin to carry similar products at similar prices.

As seen in this definition, the three dimensions of atmospherics are the visual, auditory, and olfactory. Each of these dimensions relates to the consumer's senses and has an impact on the overall "feel" of the sports retail outlet. The visual dimension refers to those things that we can see in the store environment, such as the way the merchandise is displayed, the store layout, the color of the walls and carpeting, the in-store promotional displays, lighting, and even the appearance of employees. The auditory dimension of atmosphere refers to the sounds that are present in the retail environment. Most notably, music is an integral part of any sports retailing environment. The sports marketer must carefully choose the music or sounds that are consistent with the desired store image and target market. For example, you might want to play up-tempo, high-energy music in a store selling aerobics and exercise equipment and soft, relaxing music in a store specializing in golf equipment.

NikeTown is well-known for its visual and auditory effects within the store. For example, just look at this description of NikeTown in San Francisco:

Customers ascend from the ground floor to the third floor of this 49,840 square-foot sports showcase store on an escalator flanked by the multimedia collage wall featuring graphics video and archival displays. The three-story Town Square central space contains a full height concept pavilion, surrounded by product pavilions. The Town Square area features four banks of video monitors with inspirational videos designed by Nike Film and Video. On the screens customers will see footage of Nike athletes on the field, on the course, on the court, and on the lanes. Above, shoppers circulate through the upper floor on translucent glass bridges (etched with the Nike Waffle outsole pattern).[11]

The olfactory dimension is based on the sense of smell. Studies have shown that smell influences the amount of time consumers spend in a retail setting, purchase intentions, and spending behavior. Although smell has the greatest-impact on our emotions, memory, and purchase behavior, it is seldom considered by retailers. In the future, sports retailers might manipulate the olfactory environment of their stores by producing scents that replicate the "smell of the ballpark" that consumers remember from their childhood.

LOCATION

Location of the store was previously discussed in the context of the retail mix. First, the location of the store in relation to the community is a determinant of image. For instance, is the store in a downtown metropolitan area, in a suburban neighborhood, or in a rural community? Second, important to the store's image is the location of the store with respect to the store cluster. In other words, is the store located in a shopping center, in a strip mall, or perhaps in an outlet mall? Finally, the location of the store relative to surrounding stores is an important element in establishing and maintaining the retail image.

All these location factors interact to create part of the image. A golf specialty store located in an upscale part of the community surrounded by other high-end retailers creates an extremely positive image for that store. In fact, this is an especially important part of image because even those consumers who never enter the store will still form an image of the store because of the location factors.

SALES PERSONNEL

Store sales personnel are also an important ingredient in the image of the retail outlet for a number of reasons. First, the physical appearance of the sales staff may enhance or detract from the store image. For example, the sales personnel at The Finish Line are required to wear striped referee shirts to create a "sports authority image."

Second, the level of customer service provided by the sales personnel adds to the "service image" of the store.

Customer service refers to the activities that take place before, during, and after the transaction. It is the knowledge and caring that sales personnel provide customers. Studies that examine the traits of successful sales personnel have shown the importance of the role of empathy, or the ability to feel as the customer does and put oneself in the other's position to appreciate his or her situation. Most researchers have found that empathy is a highly desirable characteristic in personal selling. However, a study found that sales performance and empathy are not related in a linear fashion. In other words, the sales performance does not directly increase as empathy increases.[12]

In addition, and of special importance to those sports retailers that target consumers with a service orientation, customer service means the extent to which extra services are provided to consumers. For example, golf pro shops will often let you play a few rounds with a set of clubs before making a purchase decision or bicycle shops will offer test rides and maintenance discounts for consumers.

CLIENTELE

Other consumers who shop at the same retailer comprise the clientele. The demographic and psychographic characteristics of the target market can influence the overall image of the store. For example, if trendy, high-income consumers are seen shopping at a tennis and ski shop, then the store will take on some of the characteristics of the consumers. In turn, consumers who desire to be seen as more trendy may visit this store to enhance their self-image. This is another demonstration of the "matchup" hypothesis, or image congruence hypothesis, discussed in Chapter 11. Rather than the matchup between celebrity endorser and product being featured in the ad or the matchup between sponsor and event, we have the congruence between consumer and retail outlet.

MERCHANDISE ASSORTMENT

Another essential, if not the most important, determinant of store image is the type of merchandise carried. If the merchandise is considered to be high quality and high priced, the image of the store will follow. In the Kentucky Store, all the merchandise carried is licensed by the University of Kentucky and the NCAA. The image of the store is directly related to the image of the University of Kentucky and its prominent and successful basketball program.

PROMOTIONAL ACTIVITIES

The nature and number of promotional activities a sports retailer implements are another factor that may affect store image. It is important to remember that promotional activities do not just include the advertising done by the sports retailer. They also include the personal selling that affects customer service, sales promotions, sponsorships, and public relations.

The greater the number of promotional activities, the greater the communication the sports retailer has with its target audience. As such, the retailer increases their chances to develop or maintain its image with every promotional opportunity. However, this is not to say that all promotional activities are viewed positively. For example, some consumers may equate continual price discounting of merchandise with a lower quality of product.[13] This practice could have a detrimental effect on overall store image.

As you have seen, store image is a function of many different factors. Perhaps one way to think about these factors is that each one is somehow related to the retailing mix. The critical principle to be gathered from the previous discussion of retailing image is that image is a powerful tool sports retailers use to differentiate themselves from their competition.

NONSTORE RETAILING

Another form of retailing that is growing in popularity is nonstore retailing. As the name implies, nonstore retailing includes purchases made outside the traditional retail outlet and usually in the home. Interactive shopping via the Internet, television home shopping networks, and mail-order retailing are all types of nonstore retailing. It is predicted that as many as 40 percent of all shoppers will try some form of home shopping within the next several years. Generally, consumers are shopping at home for convenience, time savings, potentially lower prices, and no pressure from salespeople.[14]

Somewhat surprisingly, consumer safety may also be a reason that consumers are shopping at home.[15] One study reports that consumers no longer feel safe in heavily crowded malls or downtown shopping areas. This finding has tremendous implications for sporting goods retailers and for professional sports franchises. Strategies need to be developed and implemented to promote a safe environment for shopping or attending events. This also has implications for the location of new sports facilities. A number of new stadiums are being built in impoverished areas to spur economic development. If this finding can be generalized, then sports organizations may need to rethink where they are "relocating" and rebuilding.

INTERNET SHOPPING

One of the fastest-growing home shopping media is the Internet. Forrester Research believes that total online sales will reach $123 billion in 2004 and continue to grow over the next few years as more people use the Internet and have faster connections.[16] As mentioned previously, the sale of online sporting goods and sports products is expected to reach $6 billion by 2008. However, the percentage of online shoppers is predicted to grow with further advances in technology and consumer acceptance. Other factors that will help to increase the amount of Internet shopping include addressing concerns with security of payment and being assured companies on the Web are reputable.

One of the primary advantages of Web shopping is the ability of sports marketers to reach a highly uniform target market. In other words, the target market on the Internet is highly homogeneous and has very similar interests and behaviors. This target marketing approach, driven by the rapid growth in computer technology, has facilitated the use of database marketing techniques.

Database marketing measures customers' buying behavior so the sports marketer is able to distinguish loyal fans from first-time purchasers. Once these loyal customers are captured on the Internet, they can be reached when they go online next time or via more traditional direct marketing approaches, such as being mailed postcards inviting them to attend a pregame team function or social event for fans after the game. Sports marketers have recently started to successfully use these traditional database marketing techniques.

One example of an organization that assists both college and professional teams with database marketing is SmartDM. Recently, Comcast-Spectacor combined the customer databases of the Philadelphia Flyers, 76ers, and other sport properties that they own using the SmartDM, customer relationship management (CRM) software. Comcast realized that it had over 5,000 sources of data on their customers, but none of it was integrated in any way. The SmartDM system allowed Comcast-Spectacor enter all their data into a universal data warehouse; the information can then be retrieved to best meet the needs of the organization. Having all their data in one place and easily accessible will provide Comcast-Spectacor with the opportunity to easily cross-promote among a number of their events. Comcast President Peter Luukko sings the

Fogdog sports—leading online sports retailer.

Source: GSI Commerce Solutions, Inc. All rights reserved.

praises of database marketing and states, "With the change in the business of selling tickets, we are attempting to be innovative in our sales and marketing techniques. We have found one of the best methods of reaching our customers is through direct mail, e-mail, and customer relationship management telemarketing."[17]

STADIUM AS "PLACE"

As we discussed earlier in the chapter, the distribution channel for services, such as attending a sporting event, varies dramatically from the distribution of a sporting good. The primary distinction is that the game is produced and consumed simultaneously at the "place" of distribution. As such, the service "factory," or place where the service is consumed, becomes an integral part of the service experience for consumers. "The Death of the Stadium" article provides an elegant description of the stadium experience and its importance to sport.

THE EMERGENCE OF NEW VENUES

Over the last 10 years, almost every city and their professional sports franchise have talked about building a new facility or renovating an existing facility. This is certainly the greatest building boom in the history of sports. In some areas, such as Greater Cincinnati, three new stadia have been built—Paul Brown Stadium for the Bengals (football), the Great American Ballpark for the Reds (baseball), and the Kentucky Speedway for auto racing. Moreover, an estimated $16 billion were spent on new stadia in the United States and Canada as more than 160 new or renovated stadiums were completed in the last decade. In addition, almost two-thirds of the professional teams in the four major leagues were playing in new facilities in 2003.[18]

The Death of the Stadium

Walt Disney said at the opening of Disneyland in 1955, "It will be a place for people to find happiness and knowledge." In an ideal world, the same aspirations should be expressed at the opening ceremony of a modern stadium—unfortunately, this is not the case.

These special places—these cathedrals of sport we call stadia—have not lived up to their potential since they evolved out of the codification of sport last century. That is unfortunate, because stadia are very special buildings: They are designed to bring communities together, to react with each other, and as one with the event. We gather inside them to celebrate a unique experience—whether it is a sporting event or music event. But these buildings, which have taken on the responsibility of providing us with this special experience, are often dull and uninteresting places. Sometimes they lack the most basic amenities and are bleak and unfriendly; their owners are obsessed with head counts at the turnstiles rather than the heartbeats of experience.

The good news is that these inhospitable concrete bowls are dying.

A New Generation

Great performances are difficult to achieve in a hostile environment, any more than spectator commitment can be expected from people who have to queue, are jostled and uncomfortable, have restricted views, and are herded out at the end of the event.

A new generation of stadia are in the making and will live up to their potential of being very special places. But mediocrity in design, management, catering, safety, or comfort has no place in the new sporting cathedrals. At long last we have woken up to the fact that the long-term health of any stadium is directly dependent on two things: the quality of the event and the quality of the spectator experience. The people creating these buildings are learning to protect those qualities, creating venues that can command the respect and admiration of the athletes and the spectators.

There is no doubt that the average living room provides a higher level of comfort than do most stadia; and television coverage generally provides a better view of the game, with the added benefit of close-ups, replays, commentary, and interviews. But the critical ingredient that sets the live experience apart from its televised replica is this—the crowd: this gathering of people focusing on a show of human endeavor.

The Experience

This physical and emotional experience is the product the stadium sells, and it is unique in modern life. The opportunity to be part of the crowd, to cheer and applaud at the same time as 100,000 other people just like us, to join in the wave, the national songs, or the club chant, provides a deep bonding reassurance that we are part of a whole.

The spirit, the camaraderie, the emotion, and the atmosphere of a great sporting occasion are improved by a great stadium. The venue is not a passive backdrop but is a set that can enhance the experience through its design and its management. It is this experience that is the core business of the stadium, and it must be nurtured and encouraged if it is to survive and prosper.

Source: "The Death of the Stadium." Sport Business International. www.sportbusiness.com. Courtesy of Sport Business, Ltd.

Rather than build a new facility, some sports complexes are choosing less costly renovations. The Jacksonville City Council has approved some $40 million in upgrades intended to get Alltel Stadium ready for the 2005 Super Bowl XXXIX. The project will include new luxury suites, club seats, a sports bar, escalators, and a new south end zone deck. Who will be asked to pay for these major stadium renovations or sparkling new arenas? Although the logical answer to this question would be the millionaire owners or huge corporations who own the teams, 80 percent of all monies come from the taxpayers. Since 1990, 10.4 billion dollars have been spent on new or renovated stadiums with the NFL and MLB leading the way.[19] Ironically, the average citizen may not be able to afford the price of admission to the new stadium or arena that he or she just helped fund. The stadium that the taxpayers just funded may be obsolete in less than 10 years. For example, the Miami Heat of the NBA built a brand new facility for the expansion team in 1988, but it has already been replaced by the new and improved $200 million American Airlines Arena. As business consultant Marc Ganis pointed out, "It was obsolete before the concrete dried."[20]

The primary reason the stadium was quickly outdated was the absence of luxury seating and other amenities that are standard in today's new arenas. Modern sports

SPOTLIGHT ON SPORTS MARKETING ETHICS

Publicly Funded Stadiums

Public subsidies for sports facilities don't pay off in economic benefits, a professor of urban and regional planning said. "With most of these public-private partnerships, the public sector creates the opportunities and the private sector reaps all the rewards," said Tim Chapin of Florida State University.

In his doctoral research, Chapin asked whether sports stadiums generate downtown redevelopment. "I found that the Camden Yards ballpark has done remarkably little for the city in terms of urban redevelopment," he said. "Most of the glitter in downtown Baltimore has been there long before the ballpark. . . . It was touted as the anchor for revitalizing the west side of downtown Baltimore. But in nearby rundown neighborhoods, about the only economic benefit is that residents charge fans $20 to park on game days."

"Every reputable, empirical study has concluded that these are not good financial investments," said Chapin, who prepared his study for the Lincoln Institute of Land Policy. Why, then, have sports tycoons been able to get away with socializing the cost of doing business? "It's a good sell." Chapin replied. "If you're the mayor of a town like Baltimore or Cleveland, and they say, 'Let's build a new ballpark,' you say, 'Sounds good to me.' "

Sports stadiums have been built with public money in the United States for almost half a century.

Chapin said he probably was the first to look specifically at urban redevelopment, but many studies—beginning in the early 1970s—have shown that cities generally do not make money from these projects.

So why have we heard so few arguments against them?

"I actually think there's more of that than we think there is," Chapin answered. "But that side of the story is often very poorly funded. Opponents are often characterized as malcontents and misanthropes who don't want to spend money on anything."

"The sports teams spend a lot of money and hire very big, powerful consulting firms to generate these glossy studies to suggest that there's tremendous impact. But these studies inflate the benefits and understate the costs," he said. "They make tremendous assumptions that invariably don't hold true." Chapin said a consultant in Cleveland predicted that the Gateway Complex would generate some 28,000 jobs. "But it turned out that it was well less than 2,000 jobs," the professor said. And those that are created are usually low-paying seasonal service-sector jobs that cannot serve as the basis for a robust local economy.

How do people keep getting away with making these unfounded claims? "There's wonderful sociological theory that talks about the idea of a growth machine," Chapin replied. "The idea of a growth machine is that powerful people who own land in downtowns are very good friends with mayors and city councils, the people who run newspapers, the bankers, and the construction industry. And they all want this to happen, because it's good for them for whatever reason. They do a real good job of selling something that, if you look at the details, doesn't make sense."

In a statement prepared with FSU's Jill Elish, Chapin added more detail. "Publicly financed stadiums are a growing trend," he said. "In the 1990s alone, more than 40 major league facilities were built, at a cost of more than $9 billion. About 55 percent of that was public money. I'm a firm believer that the public should be involved to some degree," Chapin said, "but the local governments should be able to get some of the money back to at least help them pay off the debt."

Debt service is only one cost that tends to be underestimated. Others are the cost of land, construction, operation and maintenance, the relocation of other businesses, police and ambulance services for public events, new highway interchanges, water and sewer lines, and lost tax revenue.

Chapin replied that he wanted to learn if stadiums and arenas catalyze redevelopment. "In the case of Cleveland, the answer is yes, and in the case of Baltimore, the answer is no. So what I concluded was that they offer opportunities for redevelopment. Now, that's a different question from, 'Is it worth it?' Economically, if you trace dollar flows and ask, 'Did the public sector get back what it put into the project?' the answer's still no. Cleveland is still paying for that stadium. It cost more than they thought it would."

"There are a lot of economic . . . costs and benefits that are attached to these facilities," Chapin said. For example, the Gateway Complex has brought in thousands of suburbanites who used to be "deathly afraid" of coming to downtown Cleveland. "That's a tremendous benefit," he said. But at the same time, the land is "forever tied up in that," lost to tax revenue or "whatever other uses might have popped up."

"There's also tremendous opportunity cost. If you spend $200 million on a stadium, that's $200 million you can't spend on other stuff."

Source: Lou Marano, "Publicly funded stadiums don't pay off." *United Press International* (May 16, 2003).

TABLE 13.4 What a New Stadium Is Worth (ranked by potential new revenues)

Team	New Stadium	Debut	Cost ($ mil)	New Revenue ($ mil)*
Seattle Mariners	Safeco Field	1999	$517	$44.78
Cincinnati Reds	The Great American Ballpark	2003	297	44.01
Montreal Expos	Labatt Park	2002	250	43.51
Detroit Tigers	Comerica Park	2000	260	43.35
Milwaukee Brewers	Miller Park	2001	367	43.17
Pittsburgh Pirates	PNC Park	2001	228	42.61
Boston Red Sox	Under proposal	n/a	545	41.52
Minnesota Twins	Under proposal	n/a	439	40.84
N.Y. Yankees	Under proposal	n/a	600	39.58
San Francisco Giants	Pac Bell Park	2000	306	37.88
Houston Astros	Minute Maid Park	2000	265	28.41
San Diego Padres	Petco Park	2002	268	25.64
		Totals	$4,342	$475.31

*Difference between 1998 stadium revenue and estimated stadium revenue during initial season at new facility.
Source: "$4.3 Bil. In New Ballparks to Usher in Grand Slam Gate, According to New Kagan Sports Business Study." www.kagan.com/kmarket/press.htm.

complexes with luxury boxes, restaurants, and other entertainment facilities seem to guarantee revenues for owners. For instance, the Staples Center in Los Angeles generates an estimated $68 million per year in suite sales. Andrew Zimbalist, an economist at Smith College, agrees. He believes a new stadium or arena can add between $10 million and $40 million to a team's annual income. Table 13.4 illustrates the cost and additional revenues that new stadiums can generate. The Kagan analysis reveals that teams playing in stadiums no more than 10 years old pulled in an average of $47 million at the gate in 1998. The remaining MLB teams averaged $28 million in gate revenue while playing in stadiums mostly built in the 1960s and 1970s. The difference in stadium revenue is reflected in payroll, where teams playing in new stadiums spent $10 million more on payroll than teams playing in old stadiums—and still managed a profit.

What are new stadiums doing to enhance the entertainment value of attending games? Most new facilities have created their own unique "neighborhoods" within the ballpark or arena with different themes and environments. For instance, Petco Park in San Diego has a large grassy picnic area beyond the outfield dubbed the "Park at the Park" for picnics and gatherings. In the Great American Ballpark in Cincinnati, fans can enjoy the game from the "Party Deck," which offers great views of right field, or they can take a seat in the Party Deck's padded ballpark seating for up-close views of the game. The primary goal of these modern theme parks is to create value for the price of admission and attract more families to the games. The reality is that the majority of fans want these new sports venues—even if the funding comes out of their own pockets.[21]

New technologies are also adding to the "entertainment" value of new stadiums. For example, a company called Istadium is now marketing interactive videogames played on existing arena Jumbotrons. The Istadium system measures how loudly fans yell when teams on the video board need to hit a ball or slap a puck. Their enthusiasm—or lack of it—determines which video team gets on base or scores a goal. Another example of new stadium technology is ChoiceSeat's seat-side computers, which allow fans at a number of stadiums, including Tropicana Field in St. Petersburg, to order hot dogs and beer or pull up a player's stats.[22]

Although the latest technology is present and expected as a feature in all new stadiums, the look and feel is anything but new. The architectural style in almost all new stadium construction is "retro." Having a "retro" park is based not only on the stadium's appearance, but also on the feeling of how the ballpark fits in with the surrounding neighborhood. For instance, Camden Yards in Baltimore is highlighted by a warehouse that sits outside the stadium and provides part of the old feel that is attractive to fans. This old feel at Camden Yards is maintained down to the most minute details, such as the typeface and lettering used on signage.

An attractive stadium atmosphere, good location, and providing a variety of entertainment options for fans would seem to be the right formula for increasing attendance and attracting new fans, but is it working? There certainly appears to be a novelty effect and new stadiums are attracting more fans in the first few years, but this newness seems to wear off quickly.

The Milwaukee Brewers, for example, were forced to cut their player payroll in 2004 for an already poorly performing team because their costs at the 3-year-old Miller Park were too burdensome on top of escalating player salaries. Brewers' attendance has dropped about 40 percent from their first year in their new stadium.

The turnout at games of the Detroit Tigers (17,080) and the Pittsburgh Pirates (20,984), whose stadiums are 4 and 3 years old, respectively, has also declined sharply. The Tigers' attendance dropped about 44 percent from their first year in the new stadium; the Pirates' fell 32 percent. The sellout crowds at the Cleveland Indians' Jacobs Field have also become a thing of the past. Regarded as one of the best new "retro" stadiums even though it's 10 years old, Indians' attendance dropped about 40 percent from their stadium's first year.[23]

TICKET DISTRIBUTION

Revenues generated through media continue to rise in the revenue mix of professional sports teams. Even with this trend in broadcast revenues, ticket revenues remain critical to the financial health of sports organizations. As such, ticket distribution practices are one of the most important considerations of sports marketing managers.

A common misperception is that ticket distributors simply provide fans with tickets at a convenient location. However, ticket distributors, not unlike the channel members for other sports products, provide a variety of necessary functions. Modern ticket distribution tasks include marketing the game, advertising, sales force management, sales force operations, technical support, and customer service. As such, these tasks have an impact on the fan's overall satisfaction with the sporting experience. In addition, if these functions are performed effectively and efficiently, fans may also benefit from lower prices.

As Miller and Fielding point out in their study of 113 professional sports franchises, ticket distribution practices of professional sports franchises have evolved over the years.[24] In 1968, Ticketron became the first organization to offer computerized distribution services. Today, 67 percent of the responding professional sports franchises use outside ticket distribution services. However, 81 percent stated that the ticket agencies sell less than 33 percent of their tickets. This is because of the large percentage of season ticket sales for professional sports. In fact, some of the franchises that do not employ ticket agencies sell all their tickets on a seasonal basis.

Although ticket distribution agencies generally provide a much-needed service for fans and professional sports franchises, they have also received a great deal of criticism from consumers. The primary complaint is that ticket distribution agencies add an "excessive" service fee to the face value of the ticket. The agencies believe the service fee is reasonable to cover the costs of providing the basic distribution tasks (e.g., handling

TABLE 13.5 Advice for Sports Marketing Managers Involved with Ticket Distribution Agencies

- No one agency operates as a monopoly, so negotiate for the best deal.
- Require that the ticket agency's staff has proper training in customer service.
- Require that the ticket agency's staff know your facility inside and out.
- Inquire about the bonus provisions paid to you in exchange for long-term agreements.
- Consider limiting the number of service fees that the ticket agency charges fans.
- Negotiate the hours the box office is open for consumers.
- Retain the right to audit the ticket distribution agency.
- Carefully consider the location and number of ticket distribution sites with the agency.
- Decide on who will incur costs, such as ticket production on information systems.
- Determine the agency's position on refunds or cancellations.
- Agree on the appropriate number of phone lines to be used.
- Require the ticket agency to communicate all service fees prior to the transaction.
- Specify the amount of liquidation damages in case a breach of contract occurs.
- Determine whether controls are in place to safeguard against employees involved in the scalping market.
- Require that the ticket agency, use print technology to guard against counterfeiting.
- Understand the state laws regarding ticket distribution practices.
- Determine whether your contract with the ticket agency conflicts with existing contracts.
- Clarify whether the ticket distribution agency can subcontract to other distributors.
- Agree that your franchise may provide ticket distribution for charitable events.
- Agree that your franchise may provide ticket distribution for season tickets and other promotional packages.

Source: Lori K. Miller and Lawrence W. Fielding, "Ticket Distribution Agencies and Professional Sport Franchises: The Successful Partnership," *Sport Marketing Quarterly*, vol. 6, no. 1 (1997), 47–55. Copyright © 1997 by Fitness Information Technology. Used by permission.

charge and mailing charge), but fans feel like they are being "ripped off." Not only does this cause problems for the distribution agent, but the negative feelings also spill over onto the professional sports franchise. Of those professional sports franchises responding to the survey, 27 percent indicated they receive more than 50 complaints each year from dissatisfied consumers regarding service fees. Table 13.5, provides sports marketers with suggestions for dealing with ticket distribution agencies.

Of course, the trend in ticket distribution for all sporting events is online sales. The growth of online ticketing continues and nearly half of all tickets sold through Ticketmaster were purchased online. More than 60 percent of NHL fans buy their single game tickets online and Major League Baseball hopes to sell around 15 million tickets online each year within the next five years. In addition to the driving ticket sales, online purchasing also provides an additional benefit to teams and fans. It creates a venue for fans to forward unused tickets to friends or resell tickets on line, alleviating the problem of no-shows, which ultimately reduce revenues.[25]

SPORTS MEDIA AS DISTRIBUTION

Another form of distribution that is continuing to grow in importance to sports is the sports media. Network and cable television, radio, and the Internet can all be considered channel intermediaries that deliver the sports product to the final consumer. Sports media, most notably television, has been considered the driving force of sports marketing in the past decade and continues to be implemented. Let us look at what Dick Ebersol, president of NBC Sports and voted the most powerful person in sports in 1996, had to say about the significant role of the media in sports:

SPORTS MARKETING HALL OF FAME

Roone Arledge

If television has done more for sports and sports marketing than anything, then Roone Arledge is the man who has done the most to guide the course of sports television. He is responsible for, among other things, creating Wide World of Sports, The American Sportsman, and Monday Night Football. In addition, modern television coverage of the Winter and Summer Olympics was defined by Arledge's production of the 1964 Mexico City games.

Arledge, later to become the president of ABC News, pioneered sports broadcasts by using instant replay, handheld cameras, isolation cameras, graphics, and field microphones. All these things have brought the fans closer to the game. Mr. Arledge passed away in December 2002 after a long and memorable career in sports broadcasting.

Sources: Bill Carter. "Roone Arledge, 71, a Force in TV Sports and News, Dies", *The New York Times* (December 6, 2002) A1; Steve Rushin, "Roone Arledge," *Sports Illustrated* (September 19, 1994), 55.

Look at the impact of television on the growth of sports. Because advertiser interest is so strong, the broadcast and cable networks are in a position to pay much more money for rights than anyone would have imagined 15 to 20 years ago. That means more money has gone to the leagues and teams. The results? Expansion, newer stadiums, and the ability of many of these teams to attract free agents.

As long as sports—particularly on television—is a worthwhile business enterprise, the people at the top of The Sporting News' *list [of the most powerful people in sports] will keep the tent poles firmly in place. If interest falls, the poles will crack and the tent will come down. And the interest is from the fan. Your living room is the voting booth, and your remote control is the voting device. Though you did not elect us, your "votes" send us a clear message about what you want to see.*[26]

Another way to examine the growing importance of the media as a distribution tool is to look at the trend in revenues among sports franchises. Twenty-five years ago, the majority of revenues generated by professional sports franchises were based on gate receipts. For example, in 1974, 55 percent of the operating income of NFL franchises was generated from ticket sales and 34.5 percent from media revenues.

There has been a tremendous shift in all the sports, with the exception of hockey, toward a reliance on media revenues (see Table 13.6). In fact, the NFL media revenues more than double the gate receipts. Media revenues will only increase with the recent television rights agreements reached between the NFL and the major networks for $17.6 billion.

The NFL's pact with ABC, ESPN, CBS, and Fox shows once again just how much the television networks, their ratings battered by cable, video, satellite television, and the Internet, simply must have national sports to stay relevant in a splintering media market. "We anticipated we would get a big boost, but nothing like this," said Rich McKay, general manager of the Tampa Bay Buccaneers. "This is unbelievable." Why are networks willing to pay these astronomical prices to televise football? Is this a reasonable price for networks to pay? Consider the benefits[27]:

- Professional football and other professional sports are the last bastion of a guaranteed mass audience. In particular, big-time sports programming delivers the young, male target market that advertisers want to reach.

TABLE 13.6 Broadcast Rights to Major Sports Properties

Rights holder(s)	Property	Length	Total value	Final season of contract
Fox				
	NFL	8 years	$4.4 billion*	2005
	MLB	6 years	$2.5 billion	2006
	NASCAR	8 years	$2.4 billion**	2008
ABC				
	NFL	8 years	$4.4 billion*	2005
	NBA	6 years	$4.6 billion	2007–08
	NHL	5 years	$600 million	2003–04
	MLS	5 years	(a)	2006
	PGA	4 years	$850 million	2006
	IRL	5 years	$60 million–$65 million	2004
	NCAA Bowl Championship Series	4 years	$400 million	2005–06
	U.S. Figure Skating Championships	8 years	$96 million	2006
CBS				
	NFL	8 years	$4 billion*	2005
	PGA	4 years	$850 million	2006
	NCAA Men's Basketball Tournament	11 years	$6 billion	2012–13
	CART	4 years	(b)	2004
	USTA US Open	4 years	$38 million/year	2004
	The Masters	1 year	(c)	Year-to-year
NBC				
	Olympics	Winter and Summer Games	(d)	2012
	PGA	4 years	$850 million	2006
	NASCAR	6 years	$2.4 billion**	2008
	Arena Football League	NA	(e)	NA
	Triple Crown	5 years	$51.5 million	2005
	Wimbledon	4 years	$52 million	2006
	Notre Dame football	5 years	$45 million	2004

Source: Sports Business Journal, www.sportsbusinessjournal.com.

- Television ratings for football are declining, but at a slower rate than the ratings for other network programming. For instance, *Monday Night Football's* (which incidentally gets $360,000 per 30-second advertising spot) ratings have dropped about 9 percent in 2000. Even so, the ratings still have MNF as the fifth-ranked prime time network program.
- On cable television, professional football remains the most watched programming.
- The networks use the NFL telecasts to create and enhance their image. In addition, they are saving money they would have had to spend on developing other programming. Compared with the 10 percent success rate for new programs, broadcasters know sports leagues (usually) finish their seasons.

The Future of Sports and TV

It is March 2020. The San Francisco Giants are prohibitive favorites to extend the Steroid League's nine-year reign of World Series dominance over the Still Natural League. Thirty-five-year-old LeBron James, having signed for short money to win a championship ring with the Lakers, is grumbling about his minutes. UCLA and USC are back in the NCAA basketball tournament, testament to a recommitment to defense, discipline, and the newly expanded 128-team tournament field.

And how will we be consuming all this exciting sports action? Would you believe hand-held wireless pay-per-view high-definition video-on-demand, with an interactive proposition-bet gambling component and real-time second-by-second updates on how your fantasy-league players are performing?

No? Wanna bet? That's the spirit of 2020, as envisioned by a group of sports media executives toying with a crystal ball during the World Congress of Sports conference in Newport Beach last week. Before looking ahead to 2020, sportsline.com founder Mike Levy advised looking back 20 years.

"Twenty years ago, nobody knew what the Internet was," he said. "Twenty years ago, PCs were just starting out. Modems weren't built into those PCs. . . . And there were no online services to go on except for text-based services. So 20 years from now, who knows?

"I can tell you one thing that was true 20 years ago and will be true 20 years from now—and that is that people are going to be gambling a lot of money on sports . . . and gamblers are looking for more interactive ways to do it. The Internet made it possible for these guys to open offshore accounts. And fantasy leagues have come on strong. "I think you're going to see a lot more interactivity in fantasy leagues. Every office in America is starting to put one together. If you're not in the league, you want to be in one next year, because everybody's having fun with it."

Levy imagines telecasts of sporting events catering more to betting interests, with television viewers toggling their remote controls to place down-by-down proposition bets during NFL games. (Brace yourself for the accompanying ESPN studio show, "Oddsmakers.") He also foresees interactive poker tournaments, open to the public, beginning with 1,000 tables of 10 players each and a television program showing highlights as tournament play progresses.

Steve Bornstein, president and chief executive of the NFL Network, said "it's pretty clear" the future of sports consumption will be on demand. "I don't think it will be 100 percent on demand," he said. "Television will still be primarily a passive experience. But ultimately, when you look out into the future, the majority of the consumption will be on demand."

It is happening now. TiVo represents the tip of the video-on-demand iceberg, with networks already worried about becoming TV Titanics. DIRECTV founder Eddy Hartenstein said TiVo was viewed "by some segments of our world as an anti-Christ. It is the ultimate form of empowerment to the consumer we are after. It's an on-demand type of world that we're coming to, and as we're able to have the economics to produce every single game that's out there, once it's out there, how do you put it into a format by which consumers can literally watch what they want to watch when they want it?

"Imagine for a moment, instead of the 1 million people that have TiVo today, if you get very quickly to 10 million and then 50 million, it's not too wild [to envision that in] about five, six years from now, TiVo penetration in the 100 million television households that [will be similar] to what DVD penetration is. And then what happens to the very economics, the advertising-over-the air television model?"

Because TiVo enables viewers to record programs and fast-forward through the commercials, traditional television advertising could be rendered obsolete. How will advertisers compensate? If you watched last year's World Series on Fox, glutted with virtual billboards behind the batter and Joe Buck fooling around with mid-game mobile phone calls to plug the manufacturer of that mobile phone, you have glimpsed the future.

"Product placement is going to become more and more popular," Fox Sports President Ed Goren predicted. So will pay-per-view, in Goren's estimation, as networks try to cope with escalating sports rights fees. "Long-term, if these rights keep going up, we're going to stop writing the checks and the free ride 20 years from now will be over," Goren said. "One way or another, the consumer is going to pay. Either in higher cable fees, higher satellite fees, or 'Let's take the Super Bowl and make it pay-per-view, $49.95, just like a heavyweight championship fight.' "

What sports will we be watching in 2020? Twenty years ago, the idea of stock car racing drawing better TV ratings than the NBA was as unthinkable as life on Mars. A decade ago, hockey in this country was considered a boom sport. There's no accounting for tastes 16 years down the line, but *Sports Illustrated* Managing Editor Terry McDonell sees popular new sports developing from the surf and hip-hop cultures. "There is so much coming out of those cultures," he said. "They are churning down there. The clothing business, music, whatever. The potential of those sports in China, for example, is staggering to me, and I can't believe that won't be part of our niche 20 years down the road."

The panel agreed that the NFL would remain prosperous in 2020. "The NFL is the 2,000-pound gorilla," Goren said. "They're in great shape. They don't need to change. Everybody else is chasing."

Source: The Future of Sports and TV, www.sportbusinessnews.com (March 13, 2004).

- Despite inroads by the NBA, professional football remains the United States' favorite spectator sport, says the Chilton/ESPN Sports poll, with about one-fourth of all Americans picking it as their favorite.

Aside from the traditional media, other distribution systems that allow the fans to customize their own sports products are becoming popular. Direct broadcast satellite services that use a DSS system allow fans to subscribe to all the major league sports, collegiate sports, and the more than 25 specialty sports networks (e.g., the Golf Channel or Speed Vision). For instance, DIRECTV's NBA League Pass allows fans to watch more than 40 games per week outside of their local area. Even more important, the fans are able to choose which games they want to watch. As more distributors compete for subscribers, the number of games to choose from should increase.

Along with television, radio and Internet broadcasts are other sports media for distributing games. The power of the radio is usually underestimated, as some fans live and die by their ability to listen to their favorite team from other states. For example, fans as far away as Tulsa, Oklahoma, or Cincinnati, Ohio, are able to receive all the St. Louis Cardinals' baseball broadcasts transmitted from KMOX-AM, aptly dubbed the "Sports Voice of St. Louis." The broadcast of games via the Internet even takes this one step further. Fans from all over the world are able to listen to and watch sports on their computers.. Although the technology is not quite ready, consumers will soon be able to enjoy their favorite teams from anywhere on the planet.[28] The previous article looks at what else the future of sports and TV will bring to fans.

Summary

The focus of Chapter 13 is the distribution element of the sports marketing mix. Distribution refers to the ability of consumers to receive sports products in a timely fashion at a convenient location. The complex process of distribution has many meanings in sports marketing. In this chapter, we explored distribution from three distinct perspectives: distribution concepts for the delivery of sporting goods; distribution to consumers who attend sporting events; and distribution to consumers who experience the event via one of several sports broadcast media.

One of the most important concepts in the distribution of sporting goods is the channel of distribution. A channel of distribution is an organization or individual who directs the flow of sports products from producer to consumer. The individuals or organizations who comprise the channel include producers or manufacturers, intermediaries, and consumers. As discussed in Chapter 1, all these channel members play an important role in the sports industry.

Producers are those sports entities that manufacture the sports product. This may be two competing athletes or the manufacturer of sporting goods needed to participate in sports events. Intermediaries are organizations that are in the middle of the channel of distribution, and thus they perform a number of functions (e.g., providing information, promotion, physical distribution, and inventory management) that help sports products flow smoothly from producer to consumer. Two common intermediaries for sporting goods are wholesalers and retailers.

The strategies used to select channels of distribution depend on a number of factors, such as the type of product, the phase of the product life cycle, the characteristics of the target market, and the organizational objectives and marketing goals of the producer. These factors are all considered when deciding which type of channel structure to pursue and the distribution intensity. The types of channels that may be used range from direct channels of distribution with no intermediaries to more complex and lengthy structures. The distribution intensity, or degree of market coverage, refers to the number of outlets being used to sell the sports products. The extent of market coverage ranges from intensive distribution, which seeks to sell the sports product in as many places as possible, to exclusive distribution, in which the sports product is available only at one location.

Sports retailers are an important member of most channels of distribution. By definition, retailers are involved in all the activities of selling products and services to end users or final consumers. Critical to the success of sports retailers is the designing of an effective and coordinated retail mix. Similar to the marketing mix, the retailing mix consists of sports products, pricing, place, and promotion. To support the retailing mix, sports retailers seek to create a unique image for their retail outlets. The store image of the retailer is influenced by factors such as atmospherics, location, sales personnel, clientele, types of merchandise carried, and types of promotional activities. Finally, nonstore retailing is growing in importance to sports marketers, as more and more products are being sold via home shopping media such as the Internet, television, and direct mail.

The second broad sports distribution issue discussed in this chapter is distributing the sport product to spectators who are attending events. Two primary issues in distribution to spectators at the event are the stadium as retailer and ticket distribution. New stadiums are being constructed at an alarming pace, as owners of professional sports franchises realize the potential for increased revenues through personal seat licenses and luxury boxes. Interestingly, the taxpayers are choosing to subsidize the cost of these "entertainment" venues as the owners threaten to move the team if new facilities are not built. Ticket distribution is another important component of the complex distribution process in sports marketing. Ticket distribution tasks involve more than just handling transactions at the ticket booth. Other functions, such as

marketing the game, advertising, sales force management and operations, technical support, and customer service, are also ticket distribution responsibilities. The nature of the tasks performed by the ticketing agency has an impact on fans' overall satisfaction with the sporting experience.

The third issue in the distribution of sports products is to provide the game experience to spectators not at the event, but through a mediated source such as television or the Internet. One example of the importance of media to the sports industry is to consider the astronomical $17.6 billion television rights agreement between the NFL and the four major networks. In professional sports such as football, the media revenues more than double the teams' take at the box office. In addition to the traditional broadcast media, companies such as DIRECTV are offering satellite services that allow consumers more sports programming than ever before.

Key Terms

- atmospherics
- channel intermediaries
- channel members
- channel of distribution
- customer service
- database marketing
- direct channels
- distribution

- exclusive distribution
- indirect channel
- information function
- intensive distribution
- intermediary functions
- inventory management
- market coverage
- marketing communications function

- multiple-channel strategy
- physical distribution function
- selective distribution
- single-channel strategy
- sports delivery systems
- sports retailers

Review Questions

1. Define distribution planning for sports marketers. What is meant by the terms *channel of distribution* and *channel members*?
2. What are some of the emerging ways of delivering sports products to widespread audiences?
3. Describe, in detail, the significant functions of channel intermediaries.
4. What are the major types of channels of distribution? Provide an example of each type of channel of distribution. What are the pros and cons of purchasing sports products through direct channels of distribution?
5. Differentiate between single versus multiple channels of distribution. Do professional sports franchises use single or multiple channels of distribution for ticket sales? For merchandise?
6. What is meant by degree of market coverage? Compare exclusive distribution, selective distribution, and intensive distribution. How would you determine which degree of market coverage to use for any given sports product?
7. Discuss the current state of sports retailing? What are the dimensions of the retail store image?
8. Describe what is meant by nonstore retailing. What is the quickest-growing form of nonstore retailing?
9. Why are sports media considered a form of distribution?

Exercises

1. Choose any sports product and describe the channel of distribution(s) used for that product.
2. Decide on the appropriate market coverage—intensive, selective, or exclusive—for the following sports products: New York Rangers hockey, Reebok golf shoes; and Speedo swimwear.

3. Comment on some of the consequences (positive and negative) of "selling out" any professional sporting event.
4. Conduct a brief environmental analysis (opportunities and threats portion of the SWOT analysis) to determine what type of sports retail outlet you believe will be successful in the coming years.
5. Discuss the trends in sports retailing with the store manager of a local sporting goods outlet. What products are performing well and which ones are phasing out? How does the store manager develop his or her strategic plan?
6. Design a survey to assess the impact of using celebrity athletes to endorse sporting goods retailers (e.g., Terry Bradshaw for Dicks Sporting Goods chain). Have 10 consumers complete your survey and report the findings. What are the implications of your results to strategic market planning?
7. Visit a local sporting goods retailer and comment on how the outlet targets its marketing efforts toward women. Is the emphasis placed on women more or less than you expected? Discuss the retailer's store image.
8. Perform a search for information regarding the television rights for the NBA, NHL, and PGA. How do these compare with the NFL? Comment on why these other sports organizations cannot demand the fees paid to the NFL.

Internet Exercises

1. Find a virtual sporting goods retailer via the Internet. Comment on the advantages and disadvantages of Internet shopping.
2. Find an Internet site for a stadium that was built recently. Comment on the atmospherics of the stadium as described on the Web site.
3. Perform a search for three sites that provides sports news. Which do you believe is the best site and why?

Endnotes

1. The Associated Press, "Bills Begin Running Football Fans in on a Rail," *Cincinnati Enquirer* (November 23, 1996), 5.
2. NCAA Division I Men's Basketball Championship Games to be Streamed Live on NCAAsports.com, (March 17, 2004), prnewswire.com.
3. Corinne Economaki, "Out of the Box," *Brandweek* (November 17, 1997), 23–25.
4. Peter Lardner, "NHL Stars Break the Ice in Tokyo," *Reuters Ltd.* (October 1, 1997).
5. Meredith Amdur, "Going for the Gold," *Daily Variety* (January 14, 2004), 6.
6. Today's Sporting Goods Industry: The 2004 Report, www.sgma.com.
7. 25 Million New Households to Shop Online Over Next 5 Years, Forrester Says, *Internet Retailer* (August 12, 2003), www.internetretailer.com
8. Bob Tedeschi, "As Amazon Moves Into Sporting Goods, Online Retailers Wonder Whether to See it As a Competitor or a Partner," *The New York Times* (September 29, 2003), C8.
9. Thomas Ryan, "Driving to the Register," *Sporting Goods Business* (January, 2004), www.sbrnet.com.
10. www.basspro-shops.com.
11. "NikeTown San Francisco, Retail San Francisco Info." www.info.nike.com/retail/info_sanfran.html

12. "New Survey Indicates How to Increase Consumer Confidence in Shopping Online." www.biz.yahoo.com/prnews/980127/va_better_1.html.
13. Ibid.
14. "Why We Might Shop at Home." www.duke.edu/, bjones/lit/iiiwhy.html.
15. Ibid.
16. Dan Fost, "Shoppers Clicking, Buying: Online Retail Sales Soar to $17.2 Billion in Fourth Quarter," *The San Francisco Chronicle* (February 24, 2004), B1.
17. "Philly teams build data warehouse, learn how to find what they need." www.sportsbusinessjournal.com (September 8, 2003).
18. "Recent Facility Spending," By the Numbers," *Sports Business Journal*. www.sportsbusinessjournal.com.
19. Ibid.
20. "The Death of the Stadium," *Sport Business International*. www.sportbusiness.com.
21. Cliff Peale, "Adding Spice to the Ballpark," *Cincinnati Post* (October 2, 1996), 5B.
22. Chana Schoenberger, "Striking Out," *Forbes Magazine* (November 27, 2000).
23. Aron Kahn, "New arena carries no guarantee of fans," *Pioneer Press*, Twincities.com. (March 30, 2004).
24. Lori K. Miller and Lawrence W. Fielding, "Ticket Distribution Agencies and Professional Sport Franchises: The Successful Partnership,"

Sport Marketing Quarterly, vol. 6, no. 1 (1997), 47–55.

25. Bob Tedeschi, "Sports Teams Have Discovered That They Can Put More Spectators in the Seats Through Online Ticket Sales," *The New York Times* (November 10, 2003), C11.

26. Dick Ebersol. "The Box and I." *The Sporting News*. www.sportingnews.com/features/powerful/ebersol.html.

27. Stephan Fatsis and Kyle Pope, "Why TV Networks Splurge on NFL Deals," *The Wall Street Journal* (December 12, 1997), B1, B8.

28. Mark Hyman, "Do You Love the Orioles and Live in L.A.?" *Business Week* (May 12, 1997), 108.

CHAPTER 14

PRICING CONCEPTS

After completing this chapter, you should be able to:

- Explain the relationship among price, value, and benefits.
- Understand the relationship between price and the other marketing mix elements.
- Describe how costs and organizational objectives affect pricing decisions.
- Explain how the competitive environment influences pricing decisions.

If you were an executive of a sports franchise, what price would you charge your fans? What factors would you consider when making your pricing decision in a continually changing marketing environment? How would you estimate the demand for tickets? Will the financial benefit of increasing prices offset the negative fan relations?

In this chapter, we explore the subjective nature of pricing sports products. More specifically, we consider how factors such as consumer demand, organizational objectives, competition, and technology impact pricing. Also, we examine how pricing interacts with the other elements of the marketing mix. Let us begin by developing a basic understanding of pricing.

WHAT IS PRICE?

Price is a statement of value for a sports product.[1] For example, the money we pay for being entertained by the Boston Celtics is price. The money that we pay for shorts featuring the Notre Dame logo is price. The money we pay for a personal seat license, which gives us the right to purchase a season ticket, is price. The money we pay on tuition to the Dave Pelz Golf Academy is price. In all these examples, the price paid is a function of the value placed on the sports product by consumers.

The essence of pricing is the exchanging process discussed in Chapter 1. Price is simply a way to quantify the value of the objects being exchanged. Typically, money is exchanged for the sports product. We pay $26 in exchange for admission to the sporting event. However, the object of value that is being exchanged does not always have to be money. For instance, Play It Again Sports, a new and used sporting goods retailer, allows consumers to trade their previously owned sports equipment for the store's used or new equipment. This form of pricing is more commonly referred to as barter or trade. It is common for kids who exchange baseball cards to use this form of trade. Many golf courses hire retirees and pay them very low wages in exchange for free rounds of golf.

Racing Pays Price for High Prices

This town has been deserted all week. The restaurants are empty. The hotels are vacant. Tickets are available.

All that may change today when Dale Earnhardt Jr. flexes his muscle in NASCAR's twin 125s. Certainly Daytona International Speedway officials hope the last four days of SpeedWeeks go better than the previous, though it remains to be seen if President Bush's decision to drop in on Sunday's Daytona 500 will help fill these 168,000 seats.

What's the problem? Well, put simply, it's the economy, and a sport that has become overpriced in too many ways. A lot of these NASCAR Dads may be having a hard time subsidizing this sport with its $200 a night hotel rooms right now. It's not just fans.

Alan Kulwicki won the NASCAR championship on a budget of $1.9 million in 1992. This season he would be facing an engine bill of $3 million alone and then a tire bill of $1 million, even before the meat and potatoes. No wonder stock-car team owners are wearing long faces. The dollars don't make sense, even for some of the richest, much less racing stalwarts such as car owners Travis Carter, Bill Baumgardner, and Jim Smith, endangered species in this world. When Dale Earnhardt Inc. and Jack Roush can't find sponsors to back their teams, NASCAR has a major problem.

Part of the problem, to hear some drivers, crew chiefs, and car owners, is NASCAR: Not only is the sanctioning body unable or unwilling to cut costs, or disinterested, it is actually allowing costs to escalate drastically, adding more test dates this season, and throwing yet more rules changes at teams within the past few days. Crew chiefs in particular are bitter about NASCAR's latest round of rules changes in the past three weeks, which they criticize as expensive, useless, busy work.

NASCAR executives, Jimmy Spencer said, are spending too much time trying to find new ways to milk the sport and exploit sponsors and not enough time trying to help the fans and the teams that helped get the sport to where it is today. NASCAR, Spencer said, has forgotten its roots. NASCAR, Spencer said, may be getting richer than ever, but NASCAR is losing its way, and he decries what he sees as its arrogance.

"The problem is NASCAR keeps looking at how they can make more money and answer to the stockbrokers . . . but screw the stockbrokers—they didn't make this sport," Spencer said. "These punks coming out of college and just reading numbers are not what made this sport. The men who made this sport are the guys who worked their tails off from 8 to 5, who religiously followed Richard Petty and David Pearson and Bobby Allison and Dale Earnhardt.

"He comes to the races now and says 'I might not like this Ryan Newman but I like this Kurt Busch.' Or 'I might not like this Kurt Busch but I like that Jimmie Johnson. But I still like Bobby Allison and Rusty Wallace.' But NASCAR isn't looking at it that way. It's 'These guys are over 40 and ancient history, they can't do this any more.' Hey, wait a minute, I grew up watching Bobby and David and Richard. These (NASCAR) guys now aren't doing anything to keep the base of their sport."

Only 4,000 or so showed up on Sunday for Daytona 500 qualifying, which is a shocker. "Ticket prices," Spencer said with a shake of his head. "Something is really wrong with our sport. We only had 43 cars for the Daytona, only 43 cars. It's incredible. There are a lot of little things that are wrong that are starting to get big. They need to restructure the purse."

To fill some fields, NASCAR officials have even brought in ARCA drivers with cars that, according to some, didn't come anywhere close to fitting Cup templates and one that even had an illegal rollercam engine. The price tag for a top NASCAR sponsorship is $16-plus million, so companies being pitched for $10 million deals realize they don't have a chance of competing. On top of that, there is the widespread perception among sponsors and potential sponsors that NASCAR's television partners don't spread the coverage around enough, that teams buying TV ads get preferential TV treatment.

"We've lost sight of what television should be doing—scanning through the field and talking about each car," Spencer said. "Some sponsors aren't getting any mentions. We're too focused on two or three teams, because those teams buy commercial time. That goes back to NASCAR—they can go back to Fox and NBC producers, especially NBC, and say, 'You guys have got to quit what you're doing and give us some help here and here and here.' They say, 'It'll work itself out.' But that's not true. That stuff doesn't work itself out.

"Still, for a sponsor this sport, at $10 million is still the best deal going. If all the pieces of the puzzle fall together, NASCAR is doing good, they'll help you, work with you. But NASCAR needs to go one step further and work the media more and work this TV package better. There are a lot of things NASCAR needs to do to ensure a full field of 43 cars. Of course NASCAR's solution would be a 38-car field, if it could."

Source: Mike Mulhern, "Racing Pays Price for High Prices." *Winston-Salem Journal* (February 12, 2004), C1.

To some, golf lessons may be priceless.

Regardless of how pricing is defined, value is the central tenet of pricing. The value placed on a ticket to a sporting event is based on the relationship of the perceived benefits to the price paid.[2] Stated simply,

$$Value = \frac{perceived\ benefits\ of\ sports\ product}{price\ of\ sports\ product}$$

The perceived benefits of the sports product, or what the product does for the user, are based on its tangible and intangible features. The tangible benefits are important in determining price because these are the features of the product that a consumer can actually see, touch, or feel. For example, the comfort of the seats, the quality of the concessions, and the appearance of the stadium are all tangible aspects of a sporting event. The intangible benefits of going to a sporting event may include spending time with friends and family, feelings of association with the team when they win (e.g., BIRGing), or "being seen" at the game.[3]

The perceived benefit of attending a St. Louis Cardinals' game is a subjective experience based on each individual's perception of the event, the sport, and the team. One consumer may pay a huge amount to see the game because of the perceived benefits of the product (mostly intangible), whereas another consumer may attend the game only if given a ticket. In either case, the perceived benefits either meet or exceed the price, resulting in "perceived value."

For the high-involvement sports fan the Cardinals' ticket represents a chance to be able to tell his grandchildren that he saw 2001 Rookie of the Year, Albert Pujols. To the no- or low-involvement individual, the same game may appear to be a complete waste of time. Again, it is important to recognize that the value placed on attending the sporting event is unique to each individual, even though they are consuming the same product (in this case, the Cardinals' game). As researcher Valerie Zeithaml points out, "What constitutes value—even in a single product category—appears to be highly personal and idiosyncratic."[4]

Using a different example, a Reggie Jackson rookie baseball card in mint condition may be priced at $600. A collector or baseball enthusiast may see this as a value because the perceived benefits outweigh the price. However, the noncollector (or the mom or dad who threw our cards away) may perceive the card as having barely more value than the cost of the paper on which it is printed.

The Value of a Seat

Personal Seat Licenses, or PSLs, have become one of the new sports marketing "buzzwords" of the last decade. This increasingly common phenomenon is a sports stadium financing strategy in which fans pay thousands of dollars for rights to future tickets. With stadium costs soaring to $200 million-plus in a time of scarce public resources, PSLs—like million-dollar salaries for .220 hitting infielders and $50 pay-per-view fights that last 90 seconds—have become a permanent fixture in the economics of professional sports. In fact, PSLs are also familiar at the collegiate level, with many seat locations being tied into required annual donations to the booster clubs.

"Basically you were giving people legacy rights for their tickets," says Max Muhleman, sports marketing executive, who developed the idea of the PSL for the then expansion Charlotte Hornets in 1987.

With the Hornets leading the league in attendance during three of their first four years, however, tickets became a scarce—and valuable—commodity in Charlotte. Against that backdrop, Muhleman came across a classified ad in a Charlotte newspaper asking for $5,000 for the rights to two seats.

"I called early in the morning and asked the guy, 'Is this a joke?'" Muhleman recalled. "And he said, 'No, I sold them to the first caller and you're about the tenth caller. I should have asked $10,000.'" For Muhleman, the realization that fans were willing to spend thousands of dollars simply for the right to buy future tickets caused the

proverbial light to go on over his head. Today, licenses for prime midcourt seats cost as much as $25,000.

The Pros

To those who support—however grudgingly—the seat license concept, the idea is a way of minimizing the public money needed to build major facilities. In return, the fan also receives something of value: the right to control the destiny of his seats, even after he stops buying them. Until now, in most professional sports, when a season ticket holder stopped renewing his order, his seats usually reverted back to the team for sale—though in a limited number of cases immediate family members could sometimes acquire them. Under the new plan, charter season ticket holders could pass on their seats to friends or even sell them, although no one saw much value in that possibility.

The Cons

Detractors feel that PSLs are simply a slick marketing gimmick that dramatically escalates major ticket costs, shifting more fan dollars to wealthy team owners and players. One man, in a Charlotte newspaper, stated that "Football is a working person's game" and that PSL prices had made Ericsson Stadium (home of the Carolina Panthers) the preserve of "wine and cheesers." "I thought I could send a kid to college, house him, feed him, and buy him a car for what these seats cost," said Charlotte real estate broker Walker Wells, who three years ago paid $42,000 for 14 seat licenses.

Source: Adapted from Barry Horstman, "Seat Licenses Hated, But They Work," *Cincinnati Enquirer* (September 23, 1996), 1A, 3A.

In yet another example, professional sports franchises are assigned monetary values based on tangibles such as gate receipts, media revenues, venue revenues (e.g., concessions, stadium advertising, and naming), players costs, and operating expenses. Further consideration in the value of a professional sports franchise is brand equity, a highly intangible characteristic. In 2003–2004, NFL franchises increased the most in value (an average of 19 percent), followed by the NBA (7 percent), MLB (3 percent), and the NHL with a 3 percent decrease.[5] Table 14.1 provides a list of the franchises having the highest values in each sport and the respective percentage change from the previous year.

Two important points emerge from the previous examples of value. First, value varies greatly from consumer to consumer because the perceived benefits of any sports product will depend on personal experience. Second, pricing is based on perceived value and perceived benefits. As such, consumers' subjective perceptions of the sports product's benefits and image are fundamental to setting the right price. In this case, image really is everything.

All too often, price is equated incorrectly with the objective costs of producing the sports product. Because many sports products are intangible services, setting prices based on the costs of producing the product alone becomes problematic. For instance, how do you quantify the cost of spending time with your friends at a sporting event or having the television rights to broadcast NFL games?

How do sports organizations provide a quality experience for fans so they feel they are getting their money's worth? Many event promoters believe the solution is to add

TABLE 14.1 2003–2004 Top Franchise Values

Major League Baseball	Current in millions	1-Year Change
Yankees	$832	−2%
Red Sox	$533	+9%
Mets	$442	−11%
National Football League	**Current in millions**	**1-Year Change**
Redskins	$952	+13%
Cowboys	$851	+9%
Texans	$791	NA
National Basketball Assoc	**Current in millions**	**1-Year Change**
Lakers	$447	+5%
Knicks	$401	+1%
Bulls	$356	+10%
National Hockey League	**Current in millions**	**1-Year Change**
Rangers	$272	+4%
Stars	$270	+7%
Maple Leafs	$263	+9%

more value via interactive experiences for the fan. For example, the Indy Racing League (IRL) has added a Fan Experience allowing racing fans to compete on the simulated Indy Racing Challenge, change tires at the Indy Racing League Pit Stop Challenge, purchase merchandise at the Racing Gear tent or visit the kid-friendly Indy Racing Kids area. The Experience has reached some 1.6 million fans. Bill Long, vice president of marketing for the IRL believes "this is the largest traveling fan exhibit of any sports property in terms of numbers of locations and event days, as we made over 600 appearances this year."[6] In a similar vein, the NCAA has created Hoops City for the men's and the women's Final Four in 2004. The interactive experience gives basketball fans a chance to participate in a number of hoop skills contests, get autographs, and share the excitement of the national championship.[7]

The stadium experience has also been jazzed up to enhance value. One of the best examples of in-arena experiences was at the Miami Sol, where kids under 12 formed a human "Sol train" and paraded around the court during intermissions to a bongo beat. They were able to set foot on the court and provide audience entertainment. Kids who attended the game were selected from the audience during the pregame and instructed on their involvement in the action. Small, in-seat video screens are also becoming popular at stadiums and arenas that want to offer the ultimate balance between watching the action live and on TV. Each seat is equipped with a video monitor that can offer game replays, other cable TV networks, stock market updates, and online service.

The ultimate question is whether these "extras" create value and add benefits for the fans. SMRI research has found that nine out of 10 fans attend sporting events out of a love for the game or team. So are these extras creating real fans or trying to buy the way into fans hearts? Do stadiums and arenas pay more for the interactive fan elements and end up receiving much less in the end—a fan that attends for the extras, not for the love of sports, the competitive element, the rivalry, the action, in other words—the game?[8]

THE DETERMINANTS OF PRICING

Now that we have discussed the core concept of price, let us look at some of the factors that affect the pricing decisions of sporting marketers. Pricing decisions can be influenced by internal and external factors, much in the same way that the contingency

SPORTS MARKETING HALL OF FAME

Pete Rozelle

Pete Rozelle led the National Football League for nearly three decades, helping it survive bidding wars with three rival leagues and three players strikes, before retiring unexpectedly in 1989.

Rozelle's pioneering sports marketing accomplishments include Monday Night Football and the Super Bowl, which blossomed into America's most-watched sporting event. The "Father of the Super Bowl" put the NFL on television just about everywhere and transformed the way Americans spend Sunday afternoons.

Rozelle arrived at about the same time as the rival American Football League, a development that created competition for players and television ratings. In 1962, Rozelle negotiated a $9.3 million television contract with CBS, a deal that earned him reelection as commissioner and a $10,000 bonus that pushed his salary to $60,000. By 1966, the two warring leagues, weary of the battle for player talent, merged, creating a single professional football league, with Rozelle as commissioner. The merger also produced a world championship game, which would eventually come to be known as the Super Bowl.

It was Rozelle who brought sports into 10 figures when he negotiated a landmark five-year, $2.1 billion

contract with television's three major networks in 1982. Then he expanded to cable, selling a Sunday night series to ESPN in 1986. The current television contract, for which Rozelle set the groundwork, gets $1.58 billion for four years from Fox alone, more than 2,000 times what Rozelle got in his first contract with CBS in 1962.

Along with these accomplishments, Rozelle's biggest contribution may have been introducing revenue sharing in pro football 30 years before it created havoc in other sports. Doing so allowed teams in minor markets like Green Bay to equally share TV revenues—the biggest part of the NFL pie—with teams in New York, Chicago, and Los Angeles.

Rozelle is also credited, along with Roone Arledge, for creating Monday Night Football, now the nation's longest-running sports series. Because the NFL had an agreement not to televise on Friday night or Saturday in competition with high school and college football, he decided Monday night would be the obvious time to showcase a single game nationally. Overall, Rozelle's impact was as much social as it was financial. He changed the nation's leisure habits and lifestyle by making Sunday afternoons and Monday nights sacred during football seasons.

Source: "Innovator Rozelle Dies at 70," *Cincinnati Enquirer* (December 7, 1996), C1, C5.

framework for sports marketing contains both internal and external considerations. **Internal factors,** which are controlled by the organization, include the other marketing mix elements, costs, and organizational objectives. **External (or environmental) factors** that influence pricing are beyond the control of the organization. These include consumer demand, competition, legal issues, the economy, and technology. Figure 14.1 illustrates the influence of the internal and external forces on pricing decisions. Let us look at each of these forces in greater detail.

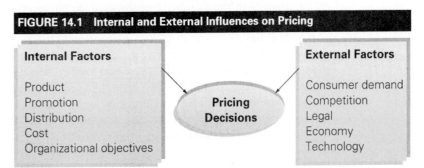

FIGURE 14.1 Internal and External Influences on Pricing

Internal Factors

Product
Promotion
Distribution
Cost
Organizational objectives

Pricing Decisions

External Factors

Consumer demand
Competition
Legal
Economy
Technology

Source: Gary Armstrong and Philip Kotler, *Marketing: An Introduction,* 7th ed. © 2005. (Reprinted by permission of Pearson Education, Inc. Upper Saddle River, NJ.)

INTERNAL FACTORS

OTHER MARKETING MIX VARIABLES

Price is the element of the marketing mix that has been called a "pressure point" for consumers. That is, price can make or break a consumer's decision to purchase a sports product. Although price is critical, the other **marketing mix variables** must be carefully considered when determining the price of a sports product. Pricing must be consistent with product, distribution, and promotional planning. For marketing goals to be reached, all the marketing mix elements must work in concert with one another.

How is price connected to other marketing mix variables? Let us begin by examining the relationship between price and promotional planning. Each of the promotional mix elements discussed in Chapter 10 (advertising, public relations, personal selling, sales promotions, and sponsorships) is related to price. Broadly, the promotion function communicates the price of the sports product to consumers. For example, advertisements often inform consumers about the price of a sports product. In comparative advertisements, the price of a sports product versus its competition may be the central focus of the message.

Many forms of sales promotion are directly related to price. For example, price reductions are price discounts designed to encourage immediate purchase of the sports product. Coupons and rebates are simply another way for consumers to get money back from the original purchase price. Moreover, premiums are sometimes offered for reduced prices (or for free) to build long-term relationships with consumers. For instance, kids aged 16 and under can join the St. Louis Blues' Junior Blue Note Club for $24.95 and receive two free tickets for a Blues' game, a chance to attend a skating party, a subscription to the Junior Blue News, and a membership kit consisting of merchandise such as a Blues' school bag, umbrella, binoculars, and a lunch bag.

The relationship between pricing and promotion also extends to personal selling. Depending on the sports product, sales personnel sometimes negotiate prices. Although not the case for most sports products, some prices are negotiable. The sale of boats, golf clubs, squash lessons, scalped tickets, and luxury boxes each represents an example of a sports product that has the potential for flexible pricing.

The public relations component of the promotional mix is also related to pricing in several ways. First, publicity and public relations personnel often stress the value of their ticket prices to potential consumers. For example, the Montreal Expos' public relations department includes information about how little a family of four will have to spend to attend a game. In addition, the Twins may emphasize that they have the lowest average prices in baseball at $10.82 per ticket, compared with other major league sports and teams.[9]

Second, public relations are important in the launch of a new sports product. Media releases that alert the public to the features of the new product, as well as the pricing, are an important aspect of creating awareness. In addition, sources not only inside but also outside of the sports organization play roles in providing information about changes to the product. For instance, when a professional sports team raises its ticket price, you can bet that the story will generate "negative public relations."

A final link between price and promotion is the cost of the promotion itself. The price of running a promotion may influence potential consumers. The price of a Super Bowl advertisement (a record $2.3 million for a 30-second spot in 2004),[10] upon becoming public knowledge, may shape consumers' expectations and perceptions of not only the advertisement, but also the product and the company. Consumers' expectations for advertisements featured during the Super Bowl are generally higher because of the hype and the advertisement's high price tag. At the same time, the high levels of free publicity generated by Super Bowl advertisements, both prior to and after the event itself, can offset the exorbitant expense and render the advertisements cost effective.

The distribution element of the marketing mix is also related to pricing. The price of a sports product is certainly dictated (in part) by the choice of distribution channel(s).

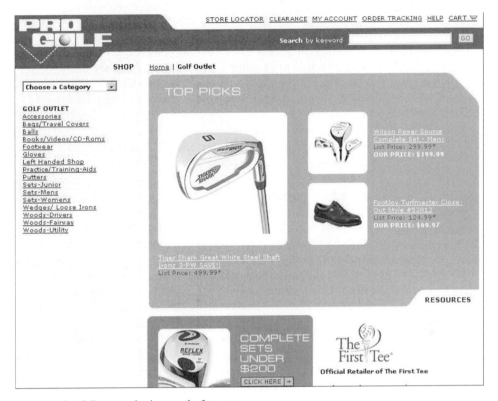

An example of discounted prices on the Internet.

Source: www.progolf.com.

In a traditional channel (manufacturer of the sporting good to wholesaler to retailer to consumer), the costs of covering the various functions of the channel members are reflected in the ultimate price charged to consumers. In a more nontraditional channel, such as purchasing a product over the Internet, prices are generally reduced. For example, the Callaway ERC Fusion driver may cost $500 in a golf specialty store but is sold for hundreds of dollars less via the Internet.

The retailer is also a common member of the distribution channel that shapes pricing decisions. More specifically, the type of retailer selling the sporting good or facility where the sporting event takes place will affect price perceptions. For instance, consumers expect to pay more for golf equipment in a country club pro shop than they do at a local golf discount outlet. Likewise, consumers who attend a baseball game at Citizen's Bank Field in Philadelphia expect to pay higher ticket prices for the state-of-the-art facility than do consumers at an aging facility like Montreal's Olympic Stadium. A concern facing professional sports is that the new sports palaces being built around the country may drive the common fan out of professional sports markets.[11]

A final element of the marketing mix related to price is the sports product itself. The price of attending a sporting event is related to expectations of service quality. The higher the ticket price being purchased, the higher fan expectations of customer service. Likewise, the higher the price of the sporting good, the higher the consumer expectations of product quality. In this way, price is used to signal quality to consumers, especially to those who have little or no previous experience using the sports product.[12]

Pricing is also used to differentiate product lines within the sports organization. An organization will offer product lines with different price ranges to attract different target markets. For example, Converse still offers a canvas basketball shoe at a low price for traditionalists who prefer canvas over the more popular—and more expensive—leather style.

The product life cycle also suggests the strength of the price–product relationship. As illustrated in Chapter 9, pricing strategies vary throughout the stages of the product life cycle. For example, during the introductory phase, products are typically priced either low to gain widespread acceptance or high to appeal to a specific target market and signal quality. Product prices are slashed during the decline phase of the life cycle to eliminate inventory and related overhead costs.

The design of sports products is the final factor that demonstrates the close relationship between product and price. Product design and pricing are interdependent. Sometimes, product design is altered during the manufacturing process to achieve a target price. For instance, Jerry Colangelo's dismantling of the Arizona Diamondbacks following their 2001 World Series triumph was a dramatic move to reduce the payroll. In this case, the product design refers to the quality of the team; the manufacturing process is the team's performance on the field. Unfortunately, the team and its fans may suffer from this move to achieve target price. Other times, prices must be adjusted (usually upward) to achieve the desired product design. New York Yankee owner George Steinbrenner has historically spent large sums of money to build a winning team (with a record high payroll of $184 million in 2004), with success as the team has appeared in the World Series Championships six times between 1996 and 2003.[13]

Clearly, price is closely associated with the rest of the marketing mix. Usually, there are two ways of coordinating the element of price with the rest of the marketing mix variables: nonprice and price competition. Let us look at these two distinctly different pricing strategies in greater detail.

NONPRICE VERSUS PRICE COMPETITION

Nonprice competition is defined as creating a unique sports product through the packaging, product design, promotion, distribution, or any marketing variable other than price.[14] This approach permits a firm to charge higher prices than its competitors because its product has achieved a competitive advantage. In turn, consumers are often willing to pay more for these products because the perceived benefits derived from the product are believed to be greater. Nevertheless, an element of risk is attached to using this nonprice competition approach.

Consider a commodity like a golf ball. Bridgestone may adopt a nonprice competition strategy for its brand of golf balls (Precept) by featuring the packaging, the product design, or something other than price. This can be a risky strategy for Bridgestone. What if consumers fail to recognize the superiority of the Precept golf ball? They may instead purchase a competitor's lower-priced golf ball that offers the same benefits.

When adopting the distinctly different **price competition** strategy, sellers primarily stimulate consumer demand by offering consumers lower prices. For example, minor league franchises successfully use price competition to attract dissatisfied fans unable or unwilling to spend large sums of money to attend major league sporting events. In response to a price competition strategy, and to offset its own higher ticket costs, a major league franchise is likely to stress the greater intangible benefits associated with attending its more prestigious events. These benefits include the higher quality of competition, the more exciting atmosphere, and the greater athletic abilities of the stars.

COSTS

Costs are those factors associated with producing, promoting, and distributing the sports product. Consider the cost of owning a minor league hockey franchise. To produce the competition or event, players are necessary. These players require salaries and equipment in order to perform. In addition, these players require support personnel such as coaches, trainers, equipment managers, and so on. Also, these players need a place to play, which includes the costs of rent, utilities, cleaning, and maintenance. These represent some of the basic costs for producing a hockey game. However, they do not tell the entire story.

In addition to these core costs, other costs can include advertising, game promotions, and the salaries of front-office personnel (secretaries, general managers, and scouts). Team transportation is another cost. All these costs, or the **total cost** of owning a minor league hockey franchise, can be expressed as the sum of the variable and fixed costs, as shown:

$$TC = FC + VC$$

where TC = total cost
FC = fixed cost
VC = variable costs

Fixed costs are the sum of the producer's expenses that are stable and do not change with the quantity of the product consumed. Almost all costs associated with the minor league hockey team in the preceding example would be considered fixed. For example, rent on the arena, salaries, and transportation are all fixed costs. They do not vary at all with the amount of the product consumed (or in this case the team's attendance). The bulk of the game promotions are determined prior to the season and, as a result, are also considered fixed costs.

Variable costs are the sum of the producer's expenses that vary and change as a result of the quantity of the product being consumed. Advertising may represent a variable cost for the minor league hockey franchise. If advertising expenditures increase from one month to the next because the team is doing poorly at the box office, then the dollar amount spent varies. Similarly, advertising could represent a variable cost if additional advertising or promotions are used because attendance is higher than expected.

Although an athletic team experiences very few variable costs in the total cost equation, a manufacturer of pure sporting goods would encounter a significantly greater number of variable costs. Usually, variable costs for manufacturing a sporting good range between 60 and 90 percent of the total costs. For example, the cost of the packaging and materials for producing the good varies by the number of units sold.

Costs are considered an internal factor that influences the pricing decision because they are largely under the control of the sports organization. The minor league hockey team management makes decisions on player salaries, how much money to spend on advertising and promoting the team, and how the team travels. These costs loom large in the sport franchise because they affect the prices charged to the fans.

In addition to the more traditional male athletes, women are also starting to enjoy big paydays. Women sports stars are also reaping the benefits of endorsement deals, sponsorship fees, and all the money coming into sports through television rights. The Williams sisters are certainly cashing in on this trend. Venus Williams signed a five-year endorsement deal with Reebok worth $40 million; and in late 2003, Serena was added to the stable of Nike women endorsers, signing a five-year deal worth at least $4 million a year.[15] However, these earnings pale in comparison to their male counterparts like LeBron James who earned over $100 million pitching products in his rookie year.

The increasing cost of player salaries has been passed on, in part, to the fans. Table 14.2 shows an example of the Fan Cost Index (FCI) for the NBA. The FCI represents the total dollar amount that a family of four would have to pay to attend a home game. This total cost includes the price of four tickets, two small beers, four sodas, four hot dogs, parking, two game programs, and two twill caps. The other costs indicate the pricing of one unit. In other words, the cost of one beer at the Knicks game is $6.00.

There are many recent examples of professional teams that attempt to control their costs. They may decide to reduce payrolls by trading players with top salaries and not actively pursue players in the high-priced free-agent market. Teams may elect not to travel

SPOTLIGHT ON SPORTS MARKETING ETHICS

Astronomical Athlete Salaries: Are They Worth It?

It is a great day to take in a ball game, do not you think? With our hustling, bustling jaunt through the economy, we probably deserve a relaxing afternoon of hot dogs and peanuts with my favorite baseball team—the Shady Valley Primadonnas. Of course, the hot dogs and peanuts are overpriced, and you might need a second mortgage on your house to buy the ticket, but the expense is worth watching the finest athletes in the world display their world-class athletic abilities. We might even coax an autograph from the Primadonnas' all-star centerfielder—Harold "Hair Doo" Dueterman.

Are These Guys Worth It?
Although we thoroughly enjoy the game—the Primadonnas come from behind to win in the bottom of the ninth—our favorite player, Hair Doo, strikes out four times and commits an error in centerfield. This raises a really, really important question in the grand scheme of the universe: Is Hair Doo worth his $10 gadzillion salary? Should Hair Doo get 100 times the salary of an average, overworked, underappreciated member of the third estate?

Hair Doo's salary really raises another more general question: Why does anyone get paid what they get paid? Any questions we ask about Hair Doo Dueterman's salary could also be asked about the wage of any average, overworked underappreciated member of the third estate—Hair Doo's numbers just happen to be bigger. Because wages and salaries are nothing more than prices, the best place to look for answers is the market.

The Market Says Yes!
Let us first ponder the supply side of the market. Hair Doo performs his athletic prowess before thousands of adoring fans—supplies his labor—because he is willing and able to take on his designated duties for a mere $10 gadzillion. If Hair Doo was not willing and able to play baseball for $10 gadzillion, then he would do something else.

Hair Doo's willingness and ability to play our nation's pastime depends on his opportunity cost of other activities, such as deep sea diving, coal mining, ballet dancing, or game show hosting. By selecting baseball, Hair Doo has given up a paycheck plus any other job-related satisfaction that could have been had from those pursuits. He has decided that his $10 gadzillion salary and the nonmonetary enjoyment of playing baseball outweigh his next best alternative. We should have little problem with this decision by Hair Doo, because we all make a similar choice. We pursue a job or career that gives us the most benefits.

But . . . (this is a good place for a dramatic pause) . . . someone also must be willing to pay Hair Doo Dueterman $10 gadzillion to do what he does so well. This is the demand side of the process, which we affectionately call the market. It deserves a little more thought.

The someone who's willing to pay Hair Doo's enormous salary, the guy who signs Hair Doo's paycheck, is the owner of Shady Valley Primadonnas—D. J. Goodluck. You might remember D. J.'s grandfather from Fact 3, "Our Unfair Lives," a wheat farmer on the Kansas plains who had the good fortune of homesteading 160 acres with a BIG pool of crude oil beneath. (The Goodlucks still visit the toilet each morning in a new Cadillac. They did, however, sell their ownership in Houston, Texas, and bought South Carolina.)

Why on earth would D. J. and his Shady Valley Primadonnas baseball organization pay Hair Doo this astronomical $10 gadzillion salary? D. J. must have a pretty good reason. Let us consider D. J.'s position.

Hair Doo's statistics are pretty impressive. In the past five years, he has led the league in umpire arguments, souvenir foul balls for adoring fans, product endorsements for nonbaseball-related items, and instigation of bench-clearing fights. All these have made Hair Doo an all-star, number-one fan attraction.

While Hair Doo may or may not help the Shady Valley Primadonnas win the championship, he does pack fans into the stands. And he has packed fans into the stands for the past five years.

Fans in the stands translates into tickets for the Shady Valley Primadonnas, national television broadcasts, and revenue for D. J. Goodluck. D. J. is willing to pay Hair Doo $10 gadzillion to perform his derring-do, because Hair Doo generates at least $10 gadzillion in revenue for the team. If Hair Doo failed to generate revenue equal to or greater than his $10 gadzillion salary, then D. J. would trade him to the Oak Town Sludge Puppies (the perennial last-place cellar-dwellers in the league), send him to the minor leagues, or just release him from the team.

The bottom line on Hair Doo's salary is the same for any average, overworked, underappreciated member of the third estate—an employer is willing and able to pay a wage up to the employee's contribution to production. If your job is making $20 worth of Hot Mamma Fudge Bananarama Sundae's each day, then your boss—Hot Mamma Fudge—would be willing to pay you $20 per day.

Many Are Worth Even More

As entertainers, athletes are paid for fan satisfaction. The more fans who want to see an athlete perform, the more an athlete is paid. In fact, most athletes—even those who make gadzillions of dollars for each flubbed fly ball, dropped pass, and missed free throw—probably deserve even higher salaries. The reason is competition. The degree of competition on each side of the market can make the price too high or too low. If suppliers have little or no competition, then the price tends to be too high. If buyers have little or no competition, then the price tends to be too low.

In the market for athletes, competition is usually less on the demand side than on the supply side. The supply of athletes tends to be pretty darn competitive. Of course, Hair Doo is an all-star player, but he faces competition from hundreds of others who can argue with umpires and hit foul balls into the stands.

The demand side, however, is less competitive. In most cases, a particular team, like the Shady Valley Primadonnas, has exclusive rights to a player. They can trade those rights to another team, like the Oak Town Sludge Puppies, but the two teams usually do not compete with each other for a player's services. There are a few circumstances—one example is "free agency"—where two or more teams try to hire the same player, but that is the exception rather than the rule.

With little competition among buyers, the price tends to be on the low side. This means that Hair Doo Dueterman's $10 gadzillion salary could be even higher. It means that the Shady Valley Primadonnas probably get more, much more, than $10 gadzillion from ticket sales and television revenue. It means that D. J. Goodluck would probably be willing and able to pay more, much more, than $10 gadzillion for Hair Doo Dueterman's athletic services. The only way to find out how much Hair Doo is worth to the Shady Valley Primadonnas is to force them to compete for Hair Doo's services with other teams.

This is a good place to insert a little note on the three estates. Most owners of professional sports teams, almost by definition if not by heritage, tend to be full-fledged members of the second estate. The players, in contrast, usually spring from the ranks of the third. The idea that one team owns the "rights" of a player stems from the perverse, although changing notion, that the third estate exists for little reason other than to provide second-class servants for the first two estates.

Colleges Are Worse

If professional athletes who get gadzillions of dollars to play are underpaid, how do college athletes, who get almost nothing, compare? It depends on the sport.

Big-time college sports, especially football and basketball, are highly profitable entertainment industries. Millions of spectators spend tons of money each year for entertainment provided by their favorite college teams. Star college athletes can pack the fans into the stands as well as star professional athletes. With packed stands come overflowing bank accounts for the colleges.

What do the athletes get out of this? What are their "salaries?" Being amateurs, college athletes are not paid an "official" salary. They are, however, compensated for their efforts with a college education, including tuition, books, living accommodations, and a small monthly stipend. Although a college education is not small potatoes—$100,000-plus at many places—this compensation tends to fall far short of the revenue generated for the school. The bottom line is that big-time college athletes, like the pros, are usually underpaid.

The reason is very similar to that of the professional athletes. College athletics have limited competition among the "employers" but a great deal of competition among the "employees." Many more high-school athletes hope to play big-time college ball than ever realize that dream. While different colleges may try to hire—oops, I mean recruit—the same athlete, the collegiate governing bodies, most notably the National Collegiate Athletic Association, limit the degree of competition and fix the "wage" athletes can receive. You often hear about the NCAA penalizing a college because it went "too far" in its recruiting efforts. This translates into the charge that college paid an athlete "too much" to play, such as new cars, bogus summer jobs with high wages, and cash payments from alumni.

Underpayment is most often a problem for big-time football and basketball revenue-generating sports. Athletes in sports with less spectator interest, such as tennis, gymnastics, or lacrosse, actually may be overpaid based on their contribution to their colleges' entertainment revenue.

Here's a tip to keep in mind in the high-priced world of athletics: Athletes are paid based on their contribution to fan satisfaction. If you think athletes are paid too much, then do not contribute to their salaries by attending games or watching them on television. If, however, you enjoy their performance and are willing to pay the price of admission, then worry not about their pay.

Source: Orley Amos, "Those Astronomical Athlete Salaries," *A Pedestrian Guide.* www.amos.bus.okstate.edu/guide/ISO2.html. Courtesy of Orley M. Amos Jr.

TABLE 14.2 Fan Cost Index: National Basketball Association: 2003–2004

Team	Avg. Ticket	% Change	Prem. Avg. Ticket	Ticket Rank	Beer	(oz.)	Soda	(oz.)	Hot Dog	Parking	Program	Cap	FCI	% Change
LA LAKERS	$75.40	6.1	$176.12	1	$7.75	16	$2.75	16	$3.75	$10.00	$5.00	$12.00	$387.10	4.1
NEW YORK	$64.10	0.0	$272.57	2	$6.00	20	$3.25	24	$4.25	$20.00	$10.00	$12.00	$362.39	1.3
HOUSTON[3]	$59.05	6.6	$423.62	4	$5.00	12	$3.00	22	$2.50	$10.00	$10.00	$16.00	$330.19	15.6
SACRAMENTO[1]	$63.20	7.4	$164.23	3	$5.75	18	$2.50	16	$3.00	$8.00	$0.00	$16.00	$324.30	5.2
BOSTON	$57.02	18.4	$307.87	5	$4.00	14	$2.50	14	$3.00	$20.00	$10.00	$10.00	$318.09	13.3
NEW JERSEY	$54.36	0.0	$208.28	6	$5.00	14	$2.75	20	$3.00	$8.00	$10.00	$15.00	$308.45	0.0
DALLAS	$53.07	5.4	$136.41	7	$4.00	12	$2.75	12	$3.75	$9.00	$6.00	$15.99	$299.25	3.8
CHICAGO	$50.67	0.0	$85.87	7	$5.00	16	$3.00	16	$3.25	$13.00	$5.00	$16.00	$292.69	1.4
MIAMI[1]	$46.25	−10.0	$188.50	10	$5.50	21	$3.00	24	$3.50	$25.00	$0.00	$15.99	$278.98	−6.8
WASHINGTON	$46.83	0.0	$135.07	9	$4.50	16	$2.50	16	$2.50	$13.00	$5.00	$15.00	$269.32	−1.8
PORTLAND[2]	$44.12	−2.1	$110.00	11	$4.50	16	$2.50	16	$2.50	$13.00	$4.00	$18.00	$262.50	−1.5
LEAGUE AVERAGE	$44.68	1.6	$152.93		$5.10	16	$2.78	17	$3.13	$10.99	$4.63	$14.23	$261.26	1.8
LA CLIPPERS	$43.40	8.0	$105.24	13	$7.25	16	$3.50	16	$3.75	$10.00	$5.00	$12.00	$261.10	5.2
SAN ANTONIO	$41.23	−1.6	$162.61	15	$5.75	21	$3.50	24	$3.75	$8.00	$5.00	$16.00	$255.43	2.3
PHILADELPHIA	$42.09	0.0	$149.48	15	$4.25	16	$3.50	24	$3.50	$10.00	$4.00	$13.99	$250.84	0.0
INDIANA	$42.33	0.0	$106.06	14	$5.00	16	$3.25	16	$2.50	$8.00	$5.00	$15.00	$250.33	2.9
ATLANTA	$37.50	0.0	$74.83	22	$5.75	20	$2.00	14	$3.75	$10.00	$8.00	$15.99	$242.47	0.0
PHOENIX[1]	$44.08	4.2	$123.21	12	$5.00	16	$2.50	16	$3.00	$8.00	$0.00	$12.00	$240.34	1.4
MEMPHIS[1]	$38.22	6.5	$148.13	21	$6.25	16	$3.00	16	$3.50	$10.00	$5.00	$18.00	$237.38	9.6
NEW ORLEANS	$33.35	−12.1	$128.38	27	$5.00	12	$4.00	12	$4.00	$10.00	$5.00	$20.00	$235.39	−7.3
TORONTO[4]	$40.82	0.0	$126.58	17	$4.60	14	$2.08	20	$2.40	$12.80	$3.20	$12.79	$235.19	−5.1
MILWAUKEE	$39.13	0.0	$110.00	20	$5.00	16	$3.00	16	$3.00	$10.00	$4.00	$12.99	$234.49	0.0
CLEVELAND[1]	$40.15	4.2	$115.78	20	$5.00	16	$2.50	16	$3.00	$10.00	$0.00	$13.99	$230.60	2.9
UTAH	$39.77	2.2	$199.17	19	$5.25	20	$2.75	22	$2.75	$8.00	$5.00	$10.00	$229.57	0.6
MINNESOTA	$37.01	1.0	$160.49	23	$4.25	16	$2.75	16	$3.00	$6.00	$5.00	$12.00	$219.54	0.7
ORLANDO	$35.90	−13.6	$95.02	24	$3.00	12	$2.50	16	$3.00	$5.00	$5.00	$15.00	$216.59	−5.5
SEATTLE	$34.01	0.0	$141.86	25	$4.75	16	$2.50	16	$2.75	$15.00	$2.00	$10.99	$207.52	0.0
DETROIT	$33.60	9.8	$82.88	26	$5.00	12	$2.00	12	$3.00	$7.00	$5.00	$13.00	$207.40	6.1
DENVER	$32.77	0.0	$91.48	28	$5.25	16	$3.25	12	$2.00	$10.00	$5.00	$11.00	$204.58	0.0
GOLDEN STATE	$26.38	0.0	$105.24	29	$4.50	14	$2.00	14	$3.00	$12.00	$3.00	$16.00	$184.52	0.0

[1]Denotes teams that do not produce a game program or provide it to fans at no cost.
[2]Portland's Guaranteed Pricing Plan is a multiyear season ticket agreement that offers savings by signing a 3-, 5-, or 7- year agreement.
[3]Houston is playing at the new Toyota Center this season. The percent of change reflects a comparison with the Compaq Center, where the team was a resident last season.
[4]Prices for Canadian teams are converted to U.S. dollars and comparison prices were converted using the current exchange rate.
Source: TMR's Fan Cost Index. Used by permission of TMR. *www.teammarketing.com.*

first class. Former Cincinnati Reds owner Marge Schott wanted to eliminate the organ player so she would not have to pay him. These types of cost-cutting or controlling decisions may affect employee satisfaction, fan support, and, consequently, long-term profits.

Although cost is usually considered to be an internal, controllable factor for organizations, it can have an uncontrollable component. For instance, the league imposes a minimum salary level for a player that is beyond the control of the individual team or owner. The costs of raw materials for producing sporting goods may rise, representing a cost increase that is beyond the control of the manufacturer. Players' unions for professional teams may set minimum standards for travel that are not under the individual team's control. All these examples describe the uncontrollable side of costs that must be continually monitored by the sports marketer.

ORGANIZATIONAL OBJECTIVES

The costs associated with producing a good or service are just one factor in determining the final price. Cost considerations may determine the "price floor" for the sport product. In other words, what will be the minimum price that an organization might charge to cover the cost of producing the sports product? Covering costs, however, may be insufficient from the organization's perspective. This depends largely on the organization's objectives. As we have stressed throughout this text, marketing mix decisions—including pricing—must consider the broader marketing goals. Effective marketing goals should be consistent with the organizational objectives.

There are four categories of **organizational objectives** that influence pricing decisions. These include income, sales, competition, and social concerns. **Income objectives** include achieving maximum profits or simply organizational survival. In the long term, all professional sports organizations are concerned with maximizing their profits and having good returns on investment. Alternatively, amateur athletic events and associations are in sports not necessarily to maximize profits but to "stay afloat." Their organizational objectives center around providing athletes with a place to compete and covering costs.

Sales objectives are concerned with maintaining or enhancing market share and encouraging sales growth. If increasing sales is the basic organizational objective, then a sporting goods manufacturer or team may want to set lower prices to encourage more purchases by existing consumers. In addition, setting lower prices or offering price discounts may encourage new groups of consumers to try the sports product. By doing so, the team may increase fan identification and, ultimately, fan loyalty. This will, in turn, lead to repeat purchases.

Another broad organizational objective may be to compete in a given sports market. An organization may want to meet competition, avoid competition, or even undercut competitive pricing. These **competitive objectives** are directly linked to final pricing decisions. Traditionally, professional sports franchises are the "only game in town," so competitive threats are less likely to dictate pricing as they would in other industries.

A final organizational objective that influences pricing is referred to as a **social concern.** Many sports organizations, particularly amateur athletic associations, determine the pricing of their sporting events based on social concerns. For example, consider a local road race through downtown St. Louis on St. Patrick's Day. The organizational objective of this race is to encourage as many people as possible to participate in the community and festivities of the day. As such, the cost to enter the race is minimal and designed only to offset the expense of having the event.

Regardless of which organizational objective is established, each has a large role in setting prices for sports products. In practice, more than one objective is typically set by the sports organization. However, prices can be determined more efficiently and effectively if the organization clearly understands its objectives. Let us look at an example of how the MLS mission statement provides a direction for pricing.

Major League Soccer's mission statement is

To create a profitable Division I professional outdoor soccer league with players and teams that are competitive on an international level, and to provide affordable family entertainment. MLS brings the spirit and intensity of the world's most popular sport to the United States. Featuring competitive ticket prices and family oriented promotions such as "Soccer Celebration" at the stadium, MLS appeals to the children who play and the families who support soccer. MLS players are also involved with a variety of community events.

As indicated in the mission statement, MLS is concerned with profitability for its league and teams. Moreover, the pricing of MLS games should be affordable so families who support soccer will be financially able to purchase tickets, reflecting a social concern. Finally, the mission statement reflects the competitive nature of pricing. The interaction of the organizational objectives of the MLS should exert a great influence on the price that fans pay to see U.S. professional soccer.

EXTERNAL FACTORS

Thus far, we have described the internal, or controllable, determinants of pricing and factors believed to be under the control of the sports marketer. The uncontrollable or **external factors** also play an important role in pricing decisions. The uncontrollable factors that influence pricing include consumer demand, competition, legal issues, the economy, and technology. Let us turn our discussion to each of these major, external factors.

CONSUMER DEMAND

One of the most critical factors in determining the price of a sports product is **consumer demand.** Demand is the quantity of a sports product that consumers are willing to purchase at a given price. Generally, consumers are more likely to purchase products at a lower price than a higher price. More formally, economists refer to this principle as the **law of demand.**[16] To better understand the nature of the law of demand and its impact on any given sports product, let us examine the price elasticity of demand.

Price elasticity explains consumer reactions to changes in price. **Price elasticity** or **price inelasticity** measures the extent to which consumer purchasing patterns are sensitive to fluctuations in price. For example, if the St. Louis Cardinals raise their general admission prices from $7.50 to $9.00, will the demand for general admission seats decline? Similarly, if the ticket prices are reduced by a given amount, will the demand increase?

Mathematically, price elasticity is stated as

$$e = \frac{DQ/Q}{DP/P}$$

where e = price elasticity
DQ/Q = percentage change in the quantity demanded
DP/P = percentage change in the price

Consumer price elasticity may be described in one of three ways: elastic demand, inelastic demand, or unitary demand. **Inelastic demand** states that changes in price have little or no impact on sales. In the previous example, demand would have probably been inelastic, because even relatively large increases in the ticket prices would have had little impact on the number of fans attending each game. If demand is inelastic, then e is less than or equal to 1 (see Figure 14.2a). Because of the great demand for tickets, the Green Bay Packers, who have been sold out on season tickets since 1960, could probably raise their minimum ticket price to $300 and still sell out all their games.

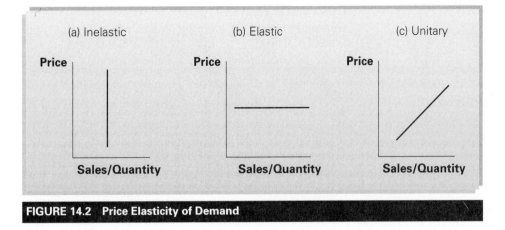

(a) Inelastic

(b) Elastic

(c) Unitary

Price — Sales/Quantity

Price — Sales/Quantity

Price — Sales/Quantity

FIGURE 14.2   Price Elasticity of Demand

Elastic demand refers to small changes in price producing large changes in quantity demanded. For example, if the average price of a ticket to an Orlando Magic game is reduced from $45.00 to $35.00, and if the number of units sold increases dramatically, then demand is considered elastic, because e is greater than 1 (see Figure 14.2b).

Finally, **unitary demand** is defined as a situation where price changes are offset exactly by changes in demand. In other words, price and demand are perfectly related. A small change in price produces an equally small change in the number of units sold. Similarly, a large change in price causes an equally large change in the number of units sold. In a situation where demand is unitary, e is equal to 1 (see Fig. 14.2c).

ESTIMATING DEMAND

The basic notion of demand allows sports marketers to explore the relationship between price and the amount of sports product that is sold. In practice, a sports marketer cannot continually change the price of a product and then determine the impact of this price change. Rather, the sports marketer must develop estimates of demand. The three basic factors that are used in **estimating demand** are consumer trends and tastes, availability of substitute sports products, and the consumer's income. Let us briefly explore the three demand factors.

Soccer is one of the fastest growing participant sports in the United States.

CONSUMER TASTES

Consumer tastes play an influential role in estimating demand. Consumer demand for football is at an all-time high,[17] which influences ticket prices (and the price of rights to televise football). Similarly, paintball games, water skiing, and weight lifting are the hottest participant sports (measured by percentage change in participation rates) according to the National Sporting Goods Association (see Table 14.3). The increased demand for these "popular" sports will also affect pricing of equipment to consumers.

With sophisticated statistical techniques, sports marketers can understand what, when, and how factors are influencing consumer tastes and the likelihood of purchasing products. For example, demand for a new design of in-line skates in any given market may be expressed as a function of a number of factors other than price. These factors can include the number of consumers currently participating in this recreational activity, the desire of recreational skaters to have more technologically advanced skates, the amount that the new skates have been advertised or promoted, or the availability of the skates.

Marketing research (as discussed in Chapter 4) allows us to estimate demand for new and existing sports products. Firms conduct research to determine consumers' past purchase behavior and the likelihood of their buying a new product. In addition, businesses rely on environmental scanning to monitor changes in the demographic profile of a market, changes in technology, shifts in popular culture, and other issues that may affect the size or tastes of the consumer market.

Environmental scanning and marketing research assist sports marketers in understanding what consumers expect and are willing to pay for sports products. Let us look at how consumers evaluate price (see Fig. 14.3).

In the **consumer pricing evaluation process,** acceptable price ranges are determined by consumers' expectations. These expectations are influenced by communicating with other consumers (i.e., word of mouth), promotions or advertising, and, to some extent, past experience in purchasing the products. If the gap between expectations and the actual price is too large, a problem arises for the sports organization. If prices are much higher than expected, the consumer will be much less likely to purchase. However, if prices are much lower, then the quality of the sports product may be called into question.

The sport of professional boxing provides an excellent example of the role past experience plays in determining an acceptable price range for consumers. Fan

TABLE 14.3 2002 Participation—Ranked by Percent Change

Sport	Total	Percent Change*
Paintball Games	6.9	24.4
Water Skiing	6.9	18.4
Weight Lifting	28.1	17.4
Hiking	30.5	17.0
Exercising with Equipment	50.2	14.4
Camping (vacation/overnite)	55.4	13.8
Mountain Biking (off road)	7.8	12.6
Canoeing	7.6	11.5
Boating, Motor/Power	26.6	11.4
Muzzleloading	3.6	11.0

*Participated more than once (in millions); seven (7) years of age and older; ranked by percent change.
Source: National Sporting Goods Association, 2002 Participation.

satisfaction with professional boxing has reached an all-time low because of the short length of heavyweight fights and the heavyweight prices paid by pay-per-view (PPV) customers to watch these fights. To combat this problem of short telecasts, Cablevision introduced a controversial pricing strategy. Consumers who wanted to view the 1996 title fight between Evander Holyfield and Mike Tyson, fight paid a $10-a-round price with a $50 cap.[18]

This innovative strategy apparently sparked a 200 percent jump in sales in Cablevision's 1.9 million PPV homes (a PPV record). Equally important, the product quality was not called into question. Cablevision paid a flat fee (roughly $4 million) for the rights to the fight, and the boxers did not receive any additional money based on the fight's length.

Along with a consumer's previous experience with pricing, expectations of future pricing also influence the acceptable range of prices a consumer is willing to pay. For example, when an innovative sports product, such as the Quik Change Dumbell System, is in the introductory phase of the product life cycle, little competition exists and start-up costs are high. Most consumers would expect the price of this product to drop over time, and some may be willing to wait for this to occur. However, sports fans may expect prices to continually rise in the future and purchase the new product immediately rather than waiting for the inevitable higher prices.

Along with expectations of current and future prices, a number of other individual consumer judgments will also play a role in determining the acceptable price range for any given sports product. As shown in Figure 14.3, these variables include consumer income, situational factors, price of substitutes, cost of information search, and perceptions of value.

Consumer income, one of the three demand factors, refers to the consumer's ability to pay the price. Generally, the higher the consumer's income, the wider the range of acceptable prices. For example, a sports fan who has an annual income of $100,000 might perceive a $7 increase in ticket prices as still within his or her price range. However, the same $7 increase in price may be unaffordable to the fan earning $30,000 per year. Significantly, both fans may find the increase in ticket prices unacceptable, but only the latter finds it unaffordable.

The **situational factors** that may affect a consumer's acceptable range of prices include the presence or absence of time, the usage situation, and social factors. Consider the following situations and how each might affect the price you would be willing to pay. First, you are getting ready for a much anticipated round of golf when you discover you only have one ball left in your bag. Typically, you purchase golf balls at your local discount store for roughly $6 a sleeve (package of three) Given the situation (absence of time), you are forced to "cough up" $12 at the pro shop for the three

---

FIGURE 14.3 Consumer Pricing Evaluation Process

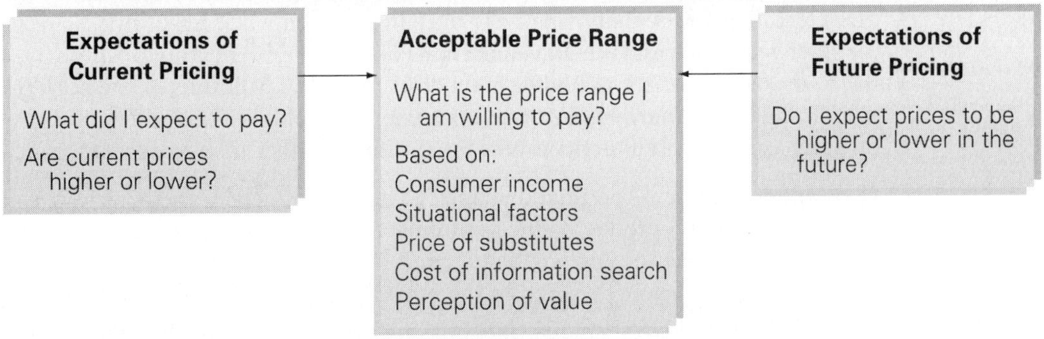

Expectations of Current Pricing	**Acceptable Price Range**	**Expectations of Future Pricing**
What did I expect to pay? Are current prices higher or lower?	What is the price range I am willing to pay? Based on: Consumer income Situational factors Price of substitutes Cost of information search Perception of value	Do I expect prices to be higher or lower in the future?

balls needed to get you through the round. This absence of time to shop for less expensive golf balls caused the acceptable price range to double in this situation.

The next scenario illustrates how your usage situation influences the range of acceptable prices. Imagine you are purchasing a new set of golf clubs that will be used only once or twice a month at the local public course. In this situation, the acceptable price range for this set of clubs might be from $200 to $300. It is likely that you may even purchase less expensive, previously owned clubs. However, if you are planning to use the clubs once or twice a week and are more concerned about their quality and your image, the acceptable range of prices would increase.

The final situation places you in the position of purchasing tickets for the Sharpie 500 NASCAR race. The cost of purchasing one ticket is approximately $100. You are not a huge NASCAR fan and the thought of spending $100 for a ticket seems disagreeable. However, a group of your best friends are attending the event and encourage you to "go along for the ride." You agree and purchase the ticket because of the social situational influence.

Another interesting social situational influence is referred to as the "mob effect." The **mob effect** (or the crowd effect) describes a situation in which consumers believe it is socially desirable to attend "special" sporting events, such as the NBA Finals, bowl games, or the World Series. Because these events constitute unique situations that can never be duplicated, consumers are willing to pay more than usual for the "right" to be a part of the mob (or crowd).

An additional consumer determinant of acceptable prices is the **expected price range of substitute products.** The prices of competitive products will have a major influence on what you deem acceptable. If a sports organization's pricing becomes out-of-line (higher) versus competition, then consumers will no longer pay the price.

The **cost of information search** also determines what a consumer considers acceptable. A consumer wanting to purchase a series of tennis lessons has a relatively low cost of information search because information is easily obtained from friends or by calling various tennis professionals. In this case, the cost of the search is less than the benefit of finding the best value. Interestingly, in purchasing a sports product, the cost of information search may be negligible because fans may find the search itself to be intriguing.

Finally, as discussed previously, **perception of value** will dictate acceptable price ranges for sports products. Remember, perceptions of value will vary from individual to individual and are based on the perceived benefits. The greater the perceived benefits of the sports product, the higher the range of acceptable prices. Most people would consider $400 an outrageous price to attend a single pro football game. However, that cost might look like the bargain of a lifetime if that single game were the Super Bowl.

Availability of Substitute Products   Another demand factor, other than price alone, that may affect demand is the **availability of substitute products.** Generally, as the number of substitute products for any given sports product increases, demand for the product will decrease. Consider the case of almost any professional sports franchise and substitute products. Typically, there is no substitute product for the professional sports team. Therefore, demand remains relatively unchanged, even when ticket prices are increased (in other words, demand is highly inelastic). For example, there is no substitute product for the St. Louis Cardinals, although baseball is played in St. Louis at the collegiate, high school, and amateur levels. However, consumers may choose to spend their sports dollars on purchasing televised broadcasts of the Cardinals, rather than pay the price increase.

Consumer's Income   The final demand factor that influences the consumer's ability to purchase the sports product is the **consumer's income.** Simply stated, the more income a consumer realizes, the higher the demand for various sports products. This "income-related" demand factor is related to the cost of the sports product under consideration. That is, the higher the cost of the sports product, the more "consumer income" matters.

The potential consumer's personal income and ability to purchase products is also highly related to the state of the economy, in general. The economy is one of the "other external factors" that influences pricing, which is discussed in the next section.

ECONOMY

The current economic cycle, or **economy,** also influences pricing decisions. A recessionary period, for instance, is characterized by reduced economic activity. During these times, there is a reduced demand for goods and services. In addition, unemployment rates are typically higher. Although this sounds grim for consumers and sports fans, imaginative sports marketers might be able to take advantage of these slowdowns in the economy by holding or slightly reducing prices, while stressing the continued value of the sports product.

Periods of inflation also require a pricing review. During inflationary periods, the cost of inputs (e.g., supplies or raw materials) necessary to produce the sports product will rise and ultimately increase prices to consumers. Rather than increase prices, sports marketers may adopt a cost reduction strategy during inflation. Such a strategy necessitates reducing or stabilizing costs of producing the product so consumer prices need not be increased.

Whatever the phase of the economic cycle, it is important to understand the direct relationship between pricing and the economy. In the preceding discussion, prices were adjusted due to changes in the economy. The prices set by manufacturers and sports organizations equally have a tremendous impact on the demand for these products and services and, in turn, affect the economy.

COMPETITION

As stated earlier, **competition** is one of the most critical factors in determining prices. Every sports organization must closely monitor the pricing structure of competing firms to successfully implement prices for its own products. One key to understanding the relationship between price and competition is exploring the sports organization's competitive environment. These four competitive environments include pure monopolies, oligopoly, monopolistic competition, and pure competition.

Most professional sports organizations operate in a pure monopoly, which means they are the only seller who sets the price for a unique product. With the exception of New York, Chicago, and California, there are few areas large enough to support two professional sports franchises in the same sport (e.g., the Cubs and White Sox). As such, most professional sports are free to manipulate prices as they want. The same would hold true for many college athletic programs, where college sports may be "the only show in town."

An oligopoly is where a small number of firms control a market. Conditions for an oligopoly exist when no one seller controls the market, but each of the few sellers has an impact on the market. In the sports industry, an example of an oligopoly is the sports news networks where ESPN and Fox have dominant control over the market.

In the case of many sporting goods, monopolistic competition is the norm. There are dozens of brands with identical products to sell. This competitive environment requires both price competition and nonprice competition. For example, all tennis balls are designed the same, but the many different brands compete based on lower prices and/or other marketing mix elements (promotions, product image, and sponsorships). The same holds true for golf balls, basketballs, and so on.

Pure competition is a market structure that has so many competitors that none can singularly influence the market price. The market conditions that must exist for pure competition include homogeneous products and ease of entry into the market. Although pure competition exists in industries selling uniform commodities such as agricultural products, it does not exist in the sports industry.

TABLE 14.4 Laws Influencing the Pricing of Sports Products

- **Sherman Act, 1890**—Establishes legality of restraint/price of trade and fixing. It also restricts the practice of predatory pricing to drive competition from the marketplace through pricing.
- **Clayton Act, 1914**—Restricts price discrimination.
- **Robinson-Patman Act, 1936**—Limits the ability of firms to sell the same product at different prices to different customers.
- **Wheeler-Lea Act, 1938**—Ensures pricing practices are not deceiving to consumers.
- **Consumer Goods Pricing Act, 1975**—Eliminates some control over retail pricing by wholesalers and manufacturers. It allows retailers to establish final retail prices in most instances.

LEGAL ISSUES

In addition to the other external factors, sports marketers must consider **legal issues,** such as constraints imposed on pricing. Several key laws that affect sports marketers were presented in Chapter 3. Table 14.4 presents U.S. legislation that specifically affects the pricing of sports products.

TECHNOLOGY

Without a doubt, all sports products are becoming more and more technologically advanced. The trend toward **technology** can have an indirect or direct influence on pricing decisions. Experience tells us that greater technology costs money. The high cost of research and development, as well as the higher costs for production and materials, drive up the price of the sports product. For example, if our stadiums are equipped with miniscreen monitors at every seat, the consumer would be expected to

Technology allows easy access to price information and discounting.

Source: Copyright © 2004. MLSnet.com. All rights reserved.

pay the price for this technology in the form of higher ticket prices. In this case, an advance in technology has a direct impact on the pricing.

Although technology and higher prices are typically believed to go hand in hand, technology does not always have to increase pricing. For example, a consumer may be able to buy a King Cobra titanium driver for $299 using electronic commerce (in other words, purchasing it through the Internet). The same driver may cost $125 more if purchased in a traditional retail outlet. In this case, technology is having an indirect influence on pricing, happily reducing the price of goods to consumers.

Summary

The pricing of sports products is becoming an increasingly important element of the sports marketing mix. Price is a statement of value for a sports product, and understanding consumers' perceptions of value is a critical determinant of pricing. Value is defined as the sum of the perceived benefits of the sports product minus the sum of the perceived costs. The perceived benefits of the sports product, or what the product does for the user, are based on its tangible and intangible features. Each consumer's perception of value is based on his or her own unique set of experiences with the sports product.

A variety of factors influences the pricing decisions for any sports product. Similar to the internal and external contingencies that affect the strategic sports marketing process, pricing influences can be categorized as internal or external factors. Internal factors are those under the control of the sports organization, such as the other marketing mix elements, cost, and organizational objectives. External factors are those factors beyond the control of the sports organization that influence pricing. These include consumer demand, competition, legal issues, the economy, and technology.

Marketing mix elements other than price must be carefully considered when determining the price of the sports product. Promotional mix elements (e.g., advertising and sales promotions) often communicate the price (or price reductions) of the sports product to consumers. The channel of distribution that is selected influences the price of sports products. For instance, consumers expect to pay higher prices (and are charged higher prices) when purchasing tennis equipment from a pro shop versus directly from the manufacturer. Product decisions are also highly related to pricing. Simply, price is used to signal product quality. Generally, the higher the price that is charged, the greater the perceived quality of the product.

Two distinct pricing strategies that emerge based on the emphasis of marketing mix elements are price and nonprice competition. As the name suggests, nonprice competition tries to establish demand for the sports product using the marketing mix elements other than price. Price competition, however, attempts to stimulate demand by offering lower prices.

In addition to other marketing mix variables, costs play a major role in pricing decisions. Costs are those factors that are associated with producing, promoting, and distributing the sports product. The total cost of producing and marketing a sports product is equal to the sum of the total fixed costs and the total variable costs. The fixed costs, such as players' salaries, do not change with the quantity of the product consumed, whereas variable costs change as a result of the quantity of the product being consumed. Today, the costs of running a professional sports franchise are skyrocketing because of players' salaries.

A final internal factor that influences pricing is organizational objectives. The four types of pricing objectives include income, sales, competitive, and social objectives. Typically, a combination of these four objectives is used to guide pricing decisions.

External factors, which are beyond the control of the organization, include consumer demand, competition, legal issues, the economy, and technology. Demand is the quantity of a sports product that consumers are willing to purchase at a given price. Price elasticity measures the extent to which consumer purchasing patterns are sensitive to fluctuations in price. For some sports products, such as a ticket to the Super Bowl, demand is relatively inelastic, which means that changes in price have little impact on game attendance. However, when demand is elastic, small changes in price may produce large changes in quantity demanded. Sports marketers try to estimate the demand for products by examining consumer trends and tastes, determining the number of substitute products, and looking at the income of the target market.

One of the most critical factors in determining pricing for sports products is to examine the prices charged for similar products by competing firms. Most professional sports franchises operate in a monopolistic environment in which no direct competitors exist. Because of this market condition, the price of attending professional sporting events is continually increasing. In fact, many "average" fans believe they are being priced out of the market and can no longer afford the cost of admission. In addition to competition, laws influence the pricing structure for sports products. For example, the Sherman Act was designed to protect freedom of competition, thereby freeing prices to fluctuation subject to market forces. The phase of the economic cycle is another important consideration in pricing. During periods of inflation, prices may rise to cover the higher costs, and during periods of recession, prices may be lowered. Finally, advances in technology are related to pricing decisions. Typically, consumers are willing to, and expect to, pay more for "high-tech" sports products. However, this is not always the case, as sometimes technological change can reduce pricing by facilitating marketing of the sports product.

Key Terms

- availability of substitute products
- competition
- competitive objectives
- consumer demand
- consumer income
- consumer pricing evaluation process
- consumer tastes
- cost of information search
- costs
- economy
- elastic demand
- estimating demand
- expected price range of substitute products

- external (or environmental) factors
- fixed costs
- income objectives
- inelastic demand
- internal factors
- law of demand
- legal issues
- marketing mix variables
- mob effect
- nonprice competition
- organizational objectives
- perception of value
- personal seat licenses
- price

- price competition
- price elasticity
- price inelasticity
- sales objectives
- situational factors
- social concern
- technology
- total cost
- unitary demand
- variable costs

Review Questions

1. Define price, perceived value, and perceived benefits. What is the relationship among price, value, and benefits?
2. Discuss the advantages and disadvantages of personal seat licenses from the consumer's perspective and the sports organization's perspective.
3. Outline the internal and external factors that affect pricing decisions. What is the primary difference between the internal and external factors?
4. Provide examples of how the marketing mix variables (other than price) influence pricing decisions.
5. Define fixed costs and variable costs and then provide several examples of each type of cost in operating a sports franchise. Do you believe costs should be considered controllable or uncontrollable factors with respect to pricing?
6. What are the four organizational objectives, and how does each influence pricing? Which organizational objective has the greatest impact on pricing?
7. What is meant by the law of consumer demand? Explain the difference between elastic and inelastic demand.
8. Describe, in detail, how sports marketers estimate the demand for new and existing sports products. What are the three demand factors, and which do you believe is the most critical in estimating demand?
9. What laws have a direct impact on pricing? Briefly describe each law.
10. How do advances in technology influence pricing? How does the economy influence pricing decisions?
11. Describe the different types of competitive environments. Why is competition considered one of the most critical factors influencing pricing?

Exercises

1. Interview five consumers and ask them, "If a new athletic complex was built for your college or university basketball team, would you be willing to pay higher seat prices?" Summarize your results and discuss the findings in terms of perceived value and perceived benefits.
2. Interview five consumers and ask them to describe a sports product they consider to be of extremely high value and one they consider to be of extremely poor value. Why do they feel this way?

3. Find two examples of sports products you consider to compete solely on the basis of price. Provide support for your answer.
4. For any professional sports franchise, provide examples of how the rest of its marketing mix is consistent with its pricing.
5. Provide two examples of sports organizations that have (either in whole or in part) a social concern pricing objective.
6. Interview five people to determine whether demand could be characterized as elastic or inelastic for the following sports products: season tickets to your favorite basketball team's games, golf lessons from Greg Norman, and Nike Air Jordans.
7. Provide examples of how technology has increased the ticket prices of professional sporting events. Support your examples from a cost perspective.

Internet Exercises

1. Using the Internet, find three examples of promotions for sport products that provide consumers with pricing information.
2. Find an example of a sports product that is being sold via the Internet for a lower price than offered via other outlets. How much cheaper is the sports product? What does the consumer have to give up to purchase the product at a lower price over the Internet?

Endnotes

1. See, for example, William Zikmund and Michael d'Amico, *Marketing,* 4th ed. (St. Paul, MN: West, 1993).
2. Christopher Lovelock, *Services Marketing,* 3rd ed. (Upper Saddle River NJ: Prentice Hall, 1996).
3. See, for example, R. B. Cialdini, R. J. Borden, A. Thorne, M. R. Walker, S. Freeman, and L. R. Sloan, "Basking in Reflected Glory: Three (Football) Field Studies," *Journal of Personality and Social Psychology,* no. 34 (1976), 366–375.
4. Valerie Zeithaml, "Consumer Perceptions of Price, Quality, and Value: A Means-End Chain Model and Synthesis of Evidence," *Journal of Marketing,* vol. 52 (July 1988), 2–21.
5. 2004 Team valuations, http://www.forbes.com.
6. Tom Savage, "IRL Fan Experience Reaches Fans Nationwide," indyracing.com; http://irl.autoracing sport.com/ 2003_novnews/irl_1113_fan_ experience.html.
7. 2004 NCAA® Hoop City® and March Madness™ Heading to San Antonio and New Orleans http://www.hostcommunications.com/ 0,6032,1_1410_0_52107,00.html.
8. Kathleen Davis, "Val-pac: Assessing the Value in Attending Sporting Events," (August 10, 2000). FoxSportsBiz.com.
9. Team Marketing Report, Fan Cost Index, Major League Baseball 2004, http://www.teammarketing.com/ fci.cfm.
10. Michael McCarthy, "To Ad Buyers Super Bowl = Young Men," *USA Today* (January 14, 2004), 1B.
11. Rick Morrissey, "Sold Out While Owners Chase Higher Revenues, Average Fan Pays the Price," *Rocky Mountain News* (February 18, 1996), 16B.
12. See, for example, A. R. Rao and K. B. Monroe, "The Effect of Price, Brand Name, and Store Name on Buyers' Perceptions of Product Quality," *Journal of Marketing Research* (August 1989), 351–357; J. Gotlieb and D. Sarel, "The Influence of Type of Advertisement, Price, and Source Credibility on Perceived Quality," *Journal of the Academy of Marketing Science* (Summer 1992), 253–260.
13. Hal Bodley, "Yanks payroll soars as MLB average falls," *USA Today* (April 9, 2004), 1C.
14. See, for example, William Zikmund and Michael d'Amico, *Marketing,* 4th ed. (St. Paul, MN: West, 1993).
15. Boaz Herzog, "Nike Adds Star Serena Williams as Endorser," *The Oregonian* (December 12, 2003), B1.
16. See, for example, Joel Evans and Barry Berman, *Marketing,* 6th ed. (New York: Macmillan, 1994), 677.
17. Richard Turner, "Send in the Refs," *Newsweek* (November 25, 1996), 91–93; Stephan Fatsis and Kyle Pope, "Why Networks Will Splurge on NFL Deals," *The Wall Street Journal* (December 12, 1997), B1, B8.
18. Rudy Martzke, "SET Expects Pay-Per-View Recordbreaker," *USA Today* (November 8, 1996), 2C.

CHAPTER 15

PRICING STRATEGIES

After completing this chapter, you should be able to:

- Understand the components for designing a successful pricing strategy.
- Explain and apply the differsent ways to arrive at an approximate price level (differential pricing, new sports product pricing, psychological pricing, product mix pricing, and cost-based pricing).
- Describe how and when price adjustments should be made in the final stage of pricing.

In Chapter 14, we discussed the internal (controllable) and external (uncontrollable) influences on pricing decisions made by a sports organization. This chapter describes a strategic process for determining price within the context of these internal and external factors. Setting approximate prices to achieve the sports organization's objectives is largely based on choosing from among several pricing strategies. The various **pricing strategy models** that we discuss include differential pricing, new sports product pricing, psychological pricing, product mix pricing, and cost-based pricing.

DIFFERENTIAL PRICING STRATEGY

One of the most common pricing strategies for sports marketers is known as differential pricing. **Differential pricing** is selling the same product or service to different buyers at different prices. Because the market is heterogeneous and unique target markets exist, differential pricing strategies are common practice.

Theoretically, differential pricing may constitute the illegal practice of price discrimination—the practice of charging different prices to different buyers for goods of like grade and quality. However, differential pricing in sports marketing is considered legal if the product in question is a service rather than a good and if the price discrimination does not substantially lessen competition.[1]

Second-market discounting is the most common differential pricing strategy used for pricing sporting events. **Second-market discounting** occurs when different prices are charged to different segments of consumers. For example, students are given a $4 discount off the regular price of admission to the Cincinnati Mighty Ducks hockey games. Similarly, faculty and student discounts are common when attending collegiate sporting events.

Second-market discounting is also prevalent in sports participation. Golf courses commonly offer different pricing for weekend versus weekday tee times. In fact, courses also offer discounts for greens fees during nonpeak times, such as after 6:00 P.M. Similarly, ice rinks offer reduced pricing in the summer to stimulate demand.

Ticket prices for the Nashville Predators.

Source: Used by permission of the Nashville Predators. All rights reserved.

NEW SPORTS PRODUCT PRICING STRATEGY

As the name implies, **new sports product pricing** strategies are used when the sports organization sets approximate price levels for products being introduced in the marketplace for the first time. Regardless of which of these pricing strategies is used, competition is a major consideration in setting prices at the introductory stage of the product life cycle.

The two pricing strategies that are commonly employed for new products include penetration pricing and price skimming. **Penetration pricing** occurs when the new sports product is being introduced at a low initial price relative to the competition. This low price will encourage consumers to try the product or service, especially when consumers are price sensitive. In addition, penetration pricing is useful when demand is relatively price elastic, that is, when small decreases in price produce high levels of increased demand for the product. Generally, penetration pricing is useful for gaining a large market share and generating high sales volume as a sport product is being introduced.

One example of penetration pricing strategy being used to stimulate demand for a relatively new product is the WNBA. Most of the teams in the league offer tickets for as low as $6 and as high as $50. The Cleveland Rockers offer tickets for $8, $15, $18, $25, and $30. This, of course, is a far cry from the NBA and its average ticket price of nearly $45. The WNBA's decision to use penetration pricing is an attempt to expose as many fans as possible to women's games, so they can see the high quality and entertaining brand of basketball being played by women. Another example of penetration pricing comes from the The Calgary Roughnecks of the National Lacrosse League. Rather than raising ticket prices in 2004 after their first season, the club announced a new pricing structure that promotes the best available seats, which actually have been dramatically reduced in price. "Following our first season we made a promise to our fans to greatly improve the club, we did, and the fans responded. Now with this new ticket pricing structure we are taking a calculated gamble that rather than increasing revenue by raising ticket prices, we will increase revenue by reducing ticket prices, increasing our fan base, and filling the Pengrowth Saddledome," said Roughnecks' president, Brad Banister.[2] Another example of penetration pricing would be when the San Diego Clippers moved their NBA franchise to Los Angeles. This move brought them head-to-head with the more successful LA Lakers franchise. The "new" LA Clippers discounted their tickets in an effort to build fan attendance during their first few seasons.

Price skimming is an entirely different pricing strategy, in which a sports organization initially sets high prices or charges prices higher than do the competition. Price skimming refers to the practice of skimming the "cream of the top" of the market. In other words, skimming targets those consumers who are price insensitive. The price must not be too high, but high enough to induce certain target markets to adopt the new product. To successfully adopt a price-skimming strategy, the sports organization must be certain that the rest of the marketing mix is consistent with the pricing. In other words, if the price is high, perception of product quality and image must be high, distribution must be more selective, and the promotional strategy must be image enhancing.

The risk of using a price skimming approach is that competitors of "knockoff or imitation" products may quickly enter the market and attempt to grab sales and market share by offering a comparable product at a substantially lower price. An added danger of price skimming is that fewer consumers are likely to pay the higher prices for the products. Given this, it is important for the sports organization to monitor sales and charge a high enough price to be profitable. Golf and tennis tournaments use price skimming techniques effectively to sell their best seats to a select few customers.

Other issues that may lead to decisions of penetration versus skimming pricing include[3]:

- *Production Capacity*—Limited production capacity tends to favor a skimming strategy because the marketer may be more assured that you can sell all you can produce. A good example of this is limited stadium seating, where the sports organization can only accommodate a relatively small number of fans and, therefore, charges higher prices because it is relatively assured of sellouts. This happens for many teams in the United States and abroad, as the following article suggests.
- *Rate of Technological Change*—In the sporting goods industry, where there are rapid changes in product design based on technology (e.g., skiing, tennis, and golf), skimming strategies may be more appropriate.
- *Barriers to Entry*—If there is some barrier (e.g., patent or high start-up costs) that will reduce the threat of competition, a skimming pricing strategy may be more appropriate.
- *Economic Conditions*—In periods of high inflation, a price skimming strategy is recommended. The sports organization would want to charge "all that the market could bear" because the additional revenues will be worth much less in the future.

SPOTLIGHT ON INTERNATIONAL SPORTS MARKETING

Brazil's Poor Priced Out of Matches

When Pele was still known as Dico, he used to wear a flour sack and trawl the streets of Sao Paulo looking for used cigarette butts from which he would extract tobacco to sell. A member of a barefoot side known as The Shoeless Ones, he once broke into a peanut warehouse and stashed the haul in a cave, and although he progressed to better things and got a job sewing welts on boots, he is precisely the sort of person Brazil's football clubs are now hoping to price out of the beautiful game.

The country's 24 first-division clubs have agreed to set minimum ticket prices for next season's championship in the unashamed hope of attracting a more elite public. "Poor people cannot afford to take the bus, pay for food or clothes, they live in misery," Mario Cesar Petraglia, the president of Atletico Paranaense, said. "We have to work with people who can afford to go to the stadiums."

To borrow from John Lennon, Petraglia wants football fans to lose their working-class roots and rattle their jewelery rather than clap their appreciation. But the move has been criticized by Agnelo Queiroz, the Brazilian Minister of Sport, who argued that football remained a passion for the country's 170 million people. "Brazilian football would completely lose its meaning without the presence of the masses," he said.

Nevertheless, any club that develops a social conscience and charges less than the agreed figure will be fined the minimum ticket price multiplied by the match attendance. The prices will start at £1.50 (in British pounds) to stand in the "Geral" area, where fans have a poor view and are liable to be pelted with objects from the upper tiers, with the next cheapest area, the "Arquibancada," costing £3.

The prices may sound affordable, given that one can pay £40 to watch a domestic match in England, but Brazil is a country blighted by poverty and social inequality.

"This is all very unfortunate," Queiroz said. "A lot of this sport's success is owed to children from poor families."

Is football now a middle-class game?

Source: Rick Broadbent, "Brazil's poor priced out of matches," *The Times (London),* (December 17, 2003), 39. Used by permission.

- *Desired Image*—If the desired position of the sports product is higher quality and prestige, then a price skimming strategy would be consistent. However, price penetration may be useful for a sports organization stressing good value for the price. Realistically, the NFL could charge $500 per seat for a Super Bowl ticket and still sell every seat due to the tremendous interest in this event (and its halftime shows).

PSYCHOLOGICAL PRICING STRATEGIES

Why would anyone purchase a pair of Air Jordan XIX for $165, a Taylor Made® R510 TP driver for $700, or a courtside ticket to the New York Knicks basketball game for $1,000? One possible answer is that price says something about the quality of the product or service. Perhaps, even more important, the price that consumers are willing to pay says something about the person and their self-concept. This notion of pricing being based on the consumer's emotion and image, rather than economics alone, is known as **psychological pricing.**

Several different types of psychological pricing are commonplace in sports marketing. In the examples just listed, prestige pricing is being used for setting approximate price levels for sports products. **Prestige pricing** is setting an artificially high price to provide a distinct image in the marketplace. Examples of prestige pricing include professional basketball teams charging extremely high ticket prices for courtside seats. For example, the Boston Celtics raised the ticket prices of courtside seats to $700 per seat for an individual game or $30,100 for one season ticket.

Another example of prestige pricing comes from the world of professional golf. As part of a special spectator package called GolfWatch, 1,000 fans are provided access to the action from inside the traditional gallery ropes. The fans will be provided with this exclusive viewing area, an on-course concierge, hospitality oases, and other extras not given to the average paying customer. However, the price tag for the prestigious spectator accommodations will be roughly $1,500 per head.[4]

Sports marketers also use a psychological pricing strategy known as reference pricing. In **reference pricing** consumers carry a frame of reference in which they evaluate products. Typically, these referenced prices are either based on past experience with the product or service or obtained by gathering high levels of information when evaluating alternative products. Knowing this, sports marketers might provide consumers with comparative information on various brands so consumers "feel" like they are getting a deal. Often, lesser-known brands might be featured next to name brands in sporting goods retailers to reflect the value.

A variant of reference pricing is known as the **"lure of the middle pricing."** A new product is introduced into the product line at a price higher than the current highest priced product. In essence, consumers are now attracted to the midpriced product (formerly the highest priced product). Its selling price has not been altered, but its reference price has changed.

Odd–even pricing is another form of psychological pricing that may be used in conjunction with other strategies. Consumer perceptions are altered by using an odd-number price ($9.95) versus an even-number price ($10). Interestingly, consumers might perceive the odd-number pricing as a greater value than the $10 even with a meaningless $.05-cent difference in price. Likewise, consumers associate even pricing with higher quality products or services. Ticket pricing for most sporting events follows an even-pricing strategy, whereas many sporting goods are sold using odd-pricing.

A final psychological pricing strategy is called **customary or traditional pricing.** Consumers' expectations of price and beliefs about what prices are historically charged for sports products form the basis of traditional pricing. For instance, many Major League Baseball franchises try to keep bleacher seating at or below $7, to uphold the tradition of the "cheap seat." Any attempt to dramatically increase these customary prices usually elicits a highly negative reaction among consumers. Unfortunately, other related products (e.g., concessions and merchandise) may be increased to offset the inexpensive ticket prices for bleachers or general admission seating.

PRODUCT MIX PRICING STRATEGIES

One of the pricing objectives discussed in Chapter 14 was profit oriented. This pricing objective suggests that firms can set prices to achieve maximum profitability. In this case, pricing strategy may be guided by exploring the profitability of an entire product mix or product line, rather than setting prices for individual products independently. As such, pricing decisions made around the entire mix of products become more complex due to the various factors that influence demand for each product. Let us take a look at the more commonly used **product mix pricing strategies.**

In Chapter 8, we learned that a product line is a group of products that are closely related because they satisfy a class of needs, are used together, are sold to the same customer groups, are distributed through the same type of outlets, or fall within a given price range. **Product line pricing** establishes a range of selling prices and price points within that range.[5] Some of the items are priced lower and designed to appeal to a more price-sensitive group of consumers; other items within the product line are higher priced and targeted to a more affluent or price-insensitive group of consumers.

Product line pricing strategies are used for selling tickets to most sporting events. For example, the Washington Capitals offer tickets to all regular season home games at the MCI Center for $10, $25, $39, $55, $80, $85, $90, $99, $150, and $230.

Sports card manufacturers also use product line pricing strategies when they offer special, limited edition card sets at grossly inflated prices. The only thing "limited" in these sets is often the value to the consumer.

When using product line pricing strategies, sports marketers must be careful in choosing the approximate prices to set for the various products within the line. The image of the higher-priced products might suffer if consumers apply the limited quality and features of the lower-priced items to the upper-end items. However, the higher-priced items within the line may enhance the image of the lower-priced sports products.

Frequently, marketers are exposed to the perceptual law that states "the whole is greater than the sum of its parts." This is the basic premise of bundle pricing. A **bundle pricing strategy** refers to the grouping of individual sports products and services into a "single package" price. Golf and tennis balls are each sold using bundle pricing, with multiple balls being lumped together in one sleeve or canister and sold at a single price. Another example of a bundling strategy is when sweatpants and jacket are sold together as a single unit for a single price.

Often, we hear of golf vacation packages that incorporate greens fees, breakfast, lodging, and sometimes travel costs into one low price. This is usually more attractive to the potential consumer, because prices are generally lower for the package than they would be for the individual items and greater convenience is offered. Another example of bundle pricing in sports marketing is the bundling of individual game tickets into a "mini" season ticket package. For example, the Minnesota Twins offer a 20-game season ticket package called "Extra Innings." This ticket bundling package offers fans the opportunity to purchase seats for discounted prices and also offers the benefits of post-season ticket priority, free Twins publications, pro shop discounts, Twinfest tickets, and to top it off, a free Twins bobblehead. In yet another example, the Goodwill Games in New York offer discounts of 20 percent on tickets for groups of 20 or more.

Finally, price bundling occurs when selling season tickets for nearly all sports. For instance, the New England Revolution of Major League Soccer offer a season ticket package called the Revolution Center Circle for as low as $240, where members receive "special access" credentials and amenities not offered as part of other season ticket packages. The price, which is more than just a ticket includes: Complimentary *autographed* copy of 2004 Revolution Yearbook (per account); early access into special Center Circle Stadium Gates; Option to purchase discounted Reserved Parking Passes; Center Circle Member Game Notes e-mailed to you prior to gameday; Access to special Center Circle Member Web Site; Revolution Rewards Program points for season ticket referrals; and $10 Gillette Stadium voucher.[6]

The converse of bundle pricing strategy is **captive product pricing** where multiple sports products are separated and sold at a single price. In captive product pricing, sports manufacturers or organizations sell products and services used in conjunction with or in addition to the primary product. Typically, the primary product is sold at a low price and profits are made on the purchase of additional product(s). For businesses providing services, this type of pricing strategy is referred to as **two-part pricing,** where the service charge has a fixed fee and a variable component based on usage.

Consider purchasing a ticket to a sporting event. The ticket price represents a fixed fee, and the additional products and services consumed while watching the event vary based on the individual consumer. Most people at the event will have something to eat or drink and possibly purchase other souvenir items. Using a captive pricing strategy involves charging a moderate price for the ticket to enter the event and then setting higher markups on the related items. Anyone who has attended a major sporting event

Price bundling in sports travel and tourism.

Source: Used by permission EscortedGroupTours.com. www.escortedgrouptours.com/sports.htm.

and has paid $3.50 for a soft drink and $5 for a hot dog has experienced captive pricing techniques at work (although fans often sneak in their own food and drink).

Another familiar example of a two-part pricing strategy is country club membership. Typically, fixed fees are charged for membership and monthly dues, and additional fees are assessed for using other facilities, such as the golf course, tennis courts, or dining. In fact, many golf courses (to the dismay of people who enjoy walking) require golfers to use carts to speed up play and increase course throughput, or the number of golfers that participate each day.

Racquet club membership often uses two-part pricing strategies.

COST-BASED PRICING STRATEGIES

Perhaps the most straightforward of all pricing strategies are **cost-based pricing strategies.** As the term implies, the sports organization examines all the costs associated with producing the sporting good or event before determining the price. Traditionally, organizations that use cost-based methods will set costs to achieve the desired levels of profitability. The lowest possible selling price a firm can charge and still attain its profit objectives is known as the price floor. A sports organization will be reluctant to price its products below the price floor because doing so will result in the organization eventually running itself into the ground. To avoid this problem, sports marketers put a great deal of emphasis on understanding the costs associated with producing any given product.

Cost-plus pricing represents the simplest type of cost-based pricing strategy. In this strategy, the price is derived by computing the total cost (fixed + variable costs) of producing the individual product and then adding an additional cost to achieve the desired profitability. This extra charge, which is added to the cost of the product, is referred to as a standard markup. Let us look at an example of cost-plus pricing for a souvenir baseball autographed by Cal Ripken Jr. of the Baltimore Orioles and trace how a $6.50 baseball is sold for $79.95. The initial cost of the baseball is $6.50, but Cal Ripken is paid $20.00 for signing each ball (incidentally, Ripken will sign roughly 10,000 balls each year). The next cost to add is a licensing fee of $2.50, paid to Major League Baseball for each ball and $2.00 for a nameplate, holder, and certificate of authenticity. The marketing company, Score Board, Inc., adds a $14.00 markup, selling each ball for about $45.00 wholesale. Finally, retailers like Hammacher Schlemmer mark up each ball $34.95 to cover their costs and make a profit. The cost to you, the collector, is $79.95.[7]

How do sports marketers determine the size of the markup on products and services? As stated previously, profit objectives and consumer demand typically drive the percentage markup. In addition, the markup is based on the effort required to sell products and services (the more effort and time, the greater the markup), the quantity of products and services sold (the greater quantity sold, the less the markup), and also industry standards (use markup similar to that of the competition).

Target profit pricing is another variation of the cost-based methods. Here, sports marketers set approximate prices based on the target profit they determined when setting objectives. To decide on price levels, a break-even analysis is typically conducted.

The basic premise of this **break-even pricing strategy** is for the firm to determine the number of units it will have to sell at a given price to break even (or recoup costs). Simply stated, if it costs Miami University of Ohio approximately $727,000 in expenses to run their women's basketball program each year and they generate $727,000 in total revenues each year, then the program has "broken even."

To look at the number of units needed to break even at any given price, the following formula is applied:

$$\text{Break-Even Point} = \frac{\text{Fixed Cost}}{\text{Price} - \text{Variable Costs per Unit}}$$

To illustrate, suppose we wanted to calculate the break-even point for a new fiberglass hockey stick. If the fixed costs for the stick are estimated to be $1.5 million, the variable costs per unit are $5, and the suggested selling price is $25, then the company would need to sell 75,000 hockey sticks to break even.

$$\text{Break-Even Point} = \frac{\$1.5 \text{ million}}{\$25 - \$5.00/\text{unit}}$$

$$\text{Break-Even Point} = 75,000 \text{ sticks}$$

SPOTLIGHT ON SPORTS MARKETING ETHICS

Athletic Spending Grows as Academic Funds Dry Up

As colleges at all levels of the NCAA's top competitive division struggle through lean times for their overall campus budgets, many of their athletic departments are not feeling a similar squeeze. Average athletic budgets rose at a pace more than double the increases in average university spending at Division I schools between 1995 and 2001, according to an analysis by *USA TODAY* and *The Des Moines Register* of the most recently available NCAA and U.S. Department of Education data.

Spending on Division I intercollegiate athletics has increased on average about 25 percent, while university spending has increased on average 10 percent, after inflation. Increases in basic costs such as scholarships and travel have had an impact. But the escalating costs of college sports also are fueled by universities' desires to reap the benefits of a winning season, which can boost attendance and TV ratings, maintain alumni support, and lift student, and even regional, morale.

Small and midsize schools are particularly squeezed, unable to generate big-time funds like major schools but still facing student, alumni, and community pressure to win. Athletics-generated revenues aren't keeping pace with costs. Only about 40 schools claim their athletic departments are self-sufficient. To compensate for deficits, most athletic departments are increasingly relying on money from their schools—money that otherwise could be used for academics or other enterprises. Student bodies also are helping pay the tab, sometimes without knowing it. About 60 percent of all Division I schools rely on student fees to help the athletic department. These fees generally range from $50 to $1,000 a year for full-time students. In return, students get free admission to games.

These developments have deepened the tension between athletics and academics on many campuses. Most states have had several consecutive years of double-digit cuts in higher education funding, which have forced schools to cut jobs, increase class sizes, and raise tuition. For example, at the College of William & Mary in Williamsburg, VA, some faculty members felt that the 1 percent cut in the athletic department's budget last year seemed small compared with the campuswide cuts imposed to absorb a 30 percent drop in state funding.

"If a university is under duress financially, I think everyone ought to share in the pain, and as far as I can tell, that's not the case," says Terry Meyers, a William & Mary English professor. "Essentially, the athletic people are getting a free ride." School officials there and else-where counter that athletic programs have done their share of cost-cutting and that athletics benefit everyone on campus. Athletics directors are left with conflicting demands: integrate their programs into their schools' educational missions but independently generate the revenue that will enable them to have competitive teams.

While the most recent publicly available data *USA TODAY* analyzed are nearly three years old, NCAA financial consultant Daniel Fulks says the trend of rising athletic spending has not changed. Also, the numbers don't include expenditures on capital improvements—athletic or nonathletic—or compensation paid to coaches beyond their base salaries. Billions have been spent nationally in the last decade on new or enhanced stadiums, arenas, and practice facilities. And million-dollar coaching deals have become so common it takes a $2 million-a-year package to make headlines, though there are at least six of those in football and men's basketball.

Schools weigh costs, benefits. For most schools, the decision to maintain—or even grow — athletic programs is unquestioned because of the perceived benefits to the campus as a whole. "Education and athletics are linked in this country. That's the way our society is organized," says David Larimore, an education professor and former athletics director at Tennessee Tech. "It projects an image, and people come to expect that if a school has a major sports franchise, they also have a major institution attached. So if you want to become invisible, downgrade (athletics) or get out of it."

Among the Division I-A schools, those playing big-time football, a primary interest is establishing, or enhancing, chances of reaching a Bowl Championship Series game or advancing far in the NCAA men's basketball tournament. That, for example, can mean trying to hire or retain a brand-name coach at millions a year. In Division I-A, the average head football coach's base salary—now at $388,600—increased 83 percent after inflation, between 1998 and 2002. These figures don't include money tied to shoe, apparel, or TV deals—money often guaranteed by athletic departments.

The University of Louisville hired Rick Pitino in 2001 with a six-year, $12.4 million contract, hoping he would restore the men's basketball team to its former glory. Meanwhile, the athletic department also had to pay about $2.5 million in the subsequent three years to Pitino's predecessor, Denny Crum. For nearly 20 years,

Louisville had been paying for its athletic programs entirely with sports revenue and contributions. But about the time of Pitino's hiring, the school also built a football venue with a corporate name, Papa John's Stadium; added several women's sports to improve gender equity; and paid rising insurance, travel, and scholarship costs.

Suddenly, the athletic program was in debt. A series of cost-cutting measures, ticket price increases, and new corporate sponsorships wouldn't be enough to keep the program at a competitive level. "If you want to grow, you're going to have to find ways to do it," athletics director Tom Jurich says. "My vision when I started six years ago was to grow this program to be something special . . . one of the biggest I-A programs in the country—and not just in basketball."

The university agreed to begin supporting the athletic department. A gradual tuition increase that started this year, plus other university funds, will supply about $3 million annually to the $31.9 million athletic budget. Jurich: "We all need to be under one umbrella. Because when we take the field, our uniforms say University of Louisville. They don't say Louisville Incorporated."

Louisville's competitive aspirations are far from unique. Since the 1994–1995 school year, 12 schools that had been playing Division I-AA football moved to the more expensive I-A, where bowl games and national TV attention beckon.

During the same period, the number of schools in Division I—which has the popular and lucrative men's basketball tournament but requires more spending on athletics—has increased by 24.

Texas A&M-Corpus Christi relaunched an athletic program in 1998 that had been defunct for more than 25 years and gained Division I standing in July 2002. It gradually has grown to 14 teams but does not have football. The bulk of the funding came from student fees, and the remainder of the $3.4 million annual athletic budget came from ticket sales, money raised through the bookstore and vending machines, and state money from tuition revenue bonds, money typically used for academic facilities. Upset faculty members and student government leaders were appeased somewhat last year when the athletic department stopped using money that would otherwise be spent on academics.

Faculty members are among the most vocal critics of using university funds or student fees to pay for athletics. Several national groups, composed primarily of faculty, have met in recent months to consider recommendations for reforming aspects of intercollegiate athletics—including finances. B. David Ridpath, an executive board member of the Drake Group, an asso-

ciation of current and former athletics officials and academics, says the problem of rising athletic costs in the midst of a university budget crisis has reached a point "that some kind of reform is going to happen." "The message we are sending is that we accept a watered-down educational institution at the expense of having an essentially professionalized college sports," says Ridpath, director of judicial programs at Marshall University.

Students Pony Up

A widely used alternative or supplement to funding from university coffers or commercial sources is a student athletic fee. At Division I schools, about 20 percent of athletic funding on average comes from students. About 60 percent of Division I schools in 2001 reported using some money from fees for athletics. That is down from 70 percent in 1995, according to NCAA data, but Fulks says that percentage may have increased again in the last two years as dozens of schools have added the fee.

The highest student athletic fees tend to be at smaller schools, such as William & Mary, where the athletic program can't generate big-time money. William & Mary fields 23 teams (the Division I average is about 15), with a philosophy that athletics are an extension of a student's educational experience. "If we were competing (with big programs), we'd have revenues that come with big-time athletics, but because we don't we're put in a much more difficult fiscal position," says Bill Walker, associate vice president for public affairs.

The school pays 52 percent of its athletic costs with an annual $916 student fee. The rest comes from donations, ticket sales, and a small amount of NCAA revenue. Virginia prohibits the use of state appropriations for athletics. The state's higher education authority has asked the school to reduce its dependence on student fees to 50 percent, down from 60 percent four years ago. The student fee has generated controversy on campus this year. Meyers, the English professor, launched a campaign to convince the school to make the athletic fee more apparent. The fee is not itemized on bills or in the course catalog but is on the school's Web site.

Sam Jones, the university's vice president of finance, says the school does not want to itemize the expense on bills because it would have to list 18 other fees. "I think if parents and students knew they were paying $916 per year to essentially support football and men's and women's basketball, they would be startled," Meyers says. "There's something insidious in this because athletic folks can depend on a steady, secret source of funding."

Source: MaryJo Sylwester and Tom Witosky, "Athletic spending grows as academic funds dry up." *USA TODAY* (February 18, 2004) 1A.

If the price of the hockey stick is decreased by $5 to a selling price of $20, then the new break-even point would be 100,000 hockey sticks. The problem, however, is that the marketing manager cannot necessarily predict the impact the price change will have on the demand for the product. Dropping the price may not lead to an increase in demand large enough to still break even.

It is important to remember that when using a target profit pricing objective, the firm is not content to merely break even but seeks to earn a profit. That is, revenues must be greater than costs. Clearly, price plays a critical role in assuring profit objectives are met.

PRICE ADJUSTMENTS

As with most things in sports marketing, prices are dynamic. Initial prices are determined by a variety of internal and external issues that are continually changing with new market conditions. For instance, more or less competition may provide the impetus for price changes. Also, **price adjustments** may be made to stimulate demand for sporting products when sales expectations are not currently being met. Finally, prices might be adjusted to help meet the objectives that have been developed. The next section explores some of the ways in which price adjustments are implemented by sports marketers.

PRICE REDUCTIONS AND INCREASES

For the second consecutive season, the Denver Broncos will raise ticket prices by roughly 5 or 6 dollars for the lucky fans who sit in the upper-levels of Invesco field. This strategy followed an increase in the 2003 season which increased prices for the lower-level tickets. The price increases were justified as a "necessary step to ensure that we put the best team of the field." This logic was hard to follow for most fans, as the Broncos haven't won a playoff game since 1999.[8] The Baltimore Orioles also increased prices for the "rich" while attempting to hold ticket prices in check for the average fan. Upper deck seat prices will remain unchanged for the 2004 season, but lower-level seats will experience a price increase of 28 percent. The Orioles said that the price increase was a matter of supply and demand, raising prices of the seats that sell out year after year.[9]

Similarly, universities are joining most of their professional counterparts and raising ticket prices to meet the higher cost of operations. For instance, the University of Nebraska announced a $3 per ticket increase in 2004, bringing the average cost of a ticket to $45. The increased revenues are expected to be in the million dollar range, but will do little to cover the loss of $2.5 million expected from playing six home games versus seven.[10] Another big name football program, Penn State, also announced raising ticket prices $2 despite a drop in attendance in the 2003 season when the Nittany Lions posted a 3-9 record.[11]

Not all teams are increasing prices. In fact, many teams in the NHL are planning price reductions given the potential lockout and problems with labor expected in the 2004–2005 season. The Dallas Stars are reducing prices of more than 2,000 season tickets and lowering the prices of other seats. In a very proactive move, Stars' President Jim Lites announced that the decreased prices were to "fulfill our pledge to fans to reduce the burden escalating payrolls have put on ticket prices."[12] The New Orleans Hornets of the NBA are also cutting prices in an effort to generate more season ticket sales and keep current fans happy.[13]

Although teams commonly reduce or increase prices after the season, sports organizations rarely reduce or increase the price charged to consumers during the course of the season to stimulate demand. It is much more common, however, for marketers of sporting goods to reduce and increase prices. Typically, **price reductions** are efforts to enhance sales and achieve greater market share by directly lowering the original price. In addition to the direct reductions in price, rebates or bundling products are other types of price breaks commonly employed. Simply said, the Los Angeles Dodgers will never have an end-of-the-season sale of tickets. You will, however, be able to find any number of sales of baseball equipment at the end of the summer.

Whatever the form of price reductions, they are frequently risky for sports manufacturers for a number of reasons. First, consumers may associate multiple price reductions with inferior product quality. Second, consumers may associate price reductions with price gouging (always selling products at a discount so the initial price must be unreasonably high). Third, price reductions may wake a sleeping dog and cause competition to counter with its own price decreases. Finally, frequent price changes make it more difficult for the consumer to establish a frame of reference for the true price of sports products. If tennis balls regularly sell for $4.99 for a package of three, and I conduct three sales over the season that offer the balls for $2.99, then what is the perceived "real" price?

Price increases represent another important adjustment made to established prices. In recent years, many sports organizations have had to increase prices for a variety of reasons, even though consumers, retailers, and employees discourage such actions. One of the primary reasons for increasing prices is to keep up with cost inflation. In other words, as the cost of materials or running a sports organization increases, prices must be increased to achieve the same profit objectives. Another reason for implementing a price increase is because there is excess demand for the sports product. For example, if the Boston Celtics have season tickets sold out for the next 10 years, then slight increases to these ticket prices may be acceptable.

Because of the negative consequences of raising prices, sports organizations may consider potential alternatives to straight price increases. These alternatives include eliminating any planned price reductions, lessening the number of product features, or unbundling items formerly "bundled" into a low price.

If there are no viable alternatives to increasing prices, it is important to communicate these changes to fans and consumers in a straightforward fashion to avoid potential negative consequences. Remember, much of pricing is based on consumer psychology. If fans or consumers of sporting goods are told why prices are being increased, they may believe price increases are justified.

An important concept when making price adjustments (either up or down) is known as the **just noticeable difference (JND).**[14] The just noticeable difference is the point at which consumers detect a difference between two stimuli. In pricing, the two stimuli are the original price and the adjusted price. In other words, do consumers perceive (notice) a difference when prices are increased or decreased from their previous price? The following examples illustrate the importance of the just noticeable difference.

Dick's Sporting Goods may sell Wilson softball gloves at a regular price of $49.99 (note the psychological price strategy of odd pricing being used). With softball season right around the corner, Dick's decides to reduce prices and sell the gloves for $44.99. Does this $5 reduction surpass the difference threshold? In other words, does the consumer believe there is a noticeable difference between the regular price and sale price? If not, then the price reduction will not be successful at stimulating demand.

Increasing Ticket Prices—In Praise of Ticket Scalping

Suppose you and your buddy had two tickets to the Super Bowl. Because you were at the front of the ticket line, you had good seats. Unexpectedly, your boss, in spite of your apoplectic protests, sends you both on an emergency business trip.

So what do you do with the tickets? Give them away? Not likely. You paid full freight for them. Let them go unused and eat the $250 per ticket? You have got to be kidding. Sell them to your neighbor for what you paid for them? Maybe, but the odds on the game have narrowed, and the tickets seem worth a lot more.

What about scalping them for maybe $1,500 each, the market price on the street? What is wrong with that? Whose tickets are they, anyway?

Any normal NFL fan (and any market economist) would say nothing at all because that is the market price. And besides, they are your tickets, right?

Well, no, say the owners of the teams. By scalping the tickets, you are making a profit that belongs to us. Or in the words of Jerry Colangelo, president of the Phoenix Suns, in an exchange with Arizona State University students, scalpers "made money off of him without his permission and that was not right." Further, he noted that he paid taxes on the money he earned on the original sale, and the scalpers paid no taxes on the resale. Peter Luukko, CEO of the Core States Center in Philadelphia, puts it differently: "By selling your tickets on the scalping market, you are stealing from the teams."

Of course, scalping is against the law in about half the states and in most of the cities where major sporting and concert events are held. There are several reasons for the laws. First, most of them were passed when markets were not in favor and government regulation was. Second, there is a fairness issue: All the tickets to a popular event should not go to the wealthiest people; some should be rationed to lower income buyers and "true fans" on a first-come, first-served basis.

Third, the owners of the teams and the promoters of the events want a sellout, both for public relations purposes and to maximize revenues from parking, popcorn, and pizza sales at the game. They dread a bust, a lousy game at which the parking lot ticket price before the game falls, signaling empty seats, less revenue, and general embarrassment.

Finally, owners, officials, and fans alike are rightly concerned with two aspects of scalping: the hassling of fans at the stadium and the possibility of sales of counterfeit or misrepresented tickets.

Fallout from scalping can be good and bad. Dennis McGlynn, the president and CEO of Dover Downs (Delaware) Entertainment, where NASCAR auto racing draws thousands of fans, notes that his track can be the fall guy. "When a scalper sells tickets for $290, promising they are on the straightaway right near the finish, when in fact they are bleacher seats on the far turn that any fan could have bought for $32, Dover Downs gets the flak for misrepresentation." And the scalper has moved to the next event.

These pressures have resulted in all sorts of anti-scalping statutes. Sometimes, to be sure, the law of unintended consequences strikes. A few years back, the city of Cleveland began enforcing a 50-year-old statute that prohibits the reselling of two or more tickets "at a price varying from the regularly advertised box-office price."

In 1995, more than two dozen fans were busted by the Cleveland police for trying to sell something like $24 worth of Indians tickets for $20 just to get rid of them. Even the mayor recognized the folly of such a policy and stopped enforcing the law. So some teams have established "Scalp-Free Zones" at the stadium where fans can sell tickets at face value or lower—but not at more than face value.

But there is a better idea. Stephen K. Happell and Marianne Jennings, professors at Arizona State University, proposed letting the market work. Scalping, they note, is inevitable and a fact of life at every stadium at every event. So why not set aside an area at the stadium where scalpers have the right to operate and trade tickets at will? Scalpers would buy a license, bringing some revenue to the owners, and the designated areas would keep scalpers from harassing uninterested fans. Tickets would be available to fans who want them—and without the fear of being nabbed as a criminal if they buy them.

Happell and Jennings persuaded the city of Phoenix to adopt such a plan in 1995, and it has been working well. They correctly predicted that if all the scalpers were segregated in one place, the market would clear and the price of scalped tickets would fall. Tickets to Phoenix Suns' games dropped to face value, and even at the 1996 Super Bowl in Phoenix, fans could buy tickets at face value, almost unheard of at America's premier sporting event.

In other words, let the market work and everyone wins—the owners reinforce their ticket-pricing structure, fans get tickets, crime is reduced, and nobody is hassled. Only you and your buddy are at risk, for your $1,250-per-ticket profit may evaporate. But, hey, you win some and lose some, right?

Source: Pete du Pont, "In Praise of Ticket Scalping" (December 4, 1997). www.intellectualcapital.com/issues/97/1204/iced, asp. With permission of IntellectualCapital.com (www.intellectualcapital.com).

Let us continue the example of the Wilson softball glove. Suppose, now, that because of the increasing cost of raw materials needed to produce the gloves, the price has to be increased from $49.99 to $54.99. Again, the sports marketer has to determine whether consumers will notice this increase in price. If not, then the price increase may not have negative consequences for the sale of Wilson softball gloves.

PRICE DISCOUNTS

Combined with straight price decreases, **price discounts** are other incentives offered to buyers to stimulate demand or reward behaviors that are favorable to the seller. The two major types of price discounts that are common in sports marketing are quantity discounts and seasonal discounts.

Quantity discounts reward buyers for purchasing large quantities of a sports product. This type of discounting may occur at all different levels of the channel of distribution. Using the previous softball glove example, Wilson may offer a quantity discount to Dick's Sporting Goods for sending in a large purchase order. Consumers hope that Dick's Sporting Goods will pass the savings on to them in the form of price reductions. The purchase of group ticket sales is another common example of quantity discounts in sports marketing.

Seasonal discounts are also prevalent in sports marketing because of the nature of sports. Most sports have defined seasons observed by both participants and spectators. Seasonal discounts are intended to stimulate demand in off-peak periods. For example, ski equipment may be discounted in the summer months to encourage consumer demand and increase traffic in skiing specialty stores. Ski resorts also frequently offer seasonal deals. For instance, the Hunter Mountain Ski Resort in New York is offering ValuePASS from March 1 through next season. For $229 you get unlimited skiing seven days a week at five different resorts for the rest of the season starting Sunday.[15]

In addition to sporting goods, seasonal discounts are often offered for ticket prices to sporting events. The Kroger Senior Classic (golf) event provides discounts for customers purchasing tickets in advance during the winter months for this summer event. The Holiday Badge promotion allows consumers to purchase an all-week ground badge for $55 and get the second one free.

Ski resorts may use seasonal discounting.

Summary

This chapter discusses several pricing strategies that are used to determine the price of sports products. The pricing strategies examined in Chapter 15 include differential pricing, new sports product pricing, psychological pricing, product mix pricing, and cost-based pricing.

Differential pricing is selling the same sports product to different buyers at different prices. When using differential pricing, care must be taken not to discriminate against consumers. As you will recall from Chapter 14, the Robinson–Patman Act of 1936 limits the ability of firms to sell the same product at different prices to different customers. The most common form of differential pricing is second-market discounting, where different prices are charged to different segments of consumers.

New sports product pricing strategies are used to determine the selling price for sports products about to be introduced to the marketplace. The two new sports product pricing strategies that are commonly employed are penetration pricing and price skimming. Penetration pricing strategies attempt to stimulate demand and product trial by offering the new sports product at a low price. Alternatively, price-skimming strategies set prices at or above the competition to enhance perceived product quality.

Psychological pricing strategies are based on the image that the organization wants to project for its sports product. Prestige pricing, reference pricing, odd–even pricing, and traditional pricing are all different types of psychological pricing. Prestige pricing uses high prices to convey a distinct and exclusive image for the sports product. Reference pricing uses the consumers' frame of reference that is established through either previous purchasing experience or high levels of information search. Odd–even pricing is setting prices at odd numbers (e.g., $9.95) to denote a lower price or a "good deal" or setting prices at even numbers (e.g., $10.00) to imply higher quality. Finally, traditional pricing uses historical or long-standing prices for a sports product to determine the pricing.

Product mix strategies consider all the organization's products at set prices to maximize the profitability of each individual product. Product line pricing, a type of product mix strategy, sets price steps (also known as price points) between products in the line to appeal to different groups of consumers. Another product mix strategy, called price bundling, clusters two or more sports products into a single packaged price. Conversely, captive product pricing unbundles two or more sports products and sells each at a separate price. This type of product mix strategy is also referred to as two-part pricing.

Cost-based pricing strategies calculate all the costs associated with producing and marketing a sports product and then determine the price based on the total cost. The simplest type of cost-based strategy is known as cost-plus pricing, where total costs are determined and an additional cost is added to achieve the desired profitability. Another cost-based method is target profit pricing, which sets approximate prices based on the target profit that the organization determined when setting objectives. To decide on price levels using any of the cost-based methods, a break-even analysis is typically conducted.

Once the price of the sports product has been determined, adjustments are constantly necessary as market conditions, such as consumer demand change. Price reductions or increases are used to reach pricing objectives that have been determined. Generally, price reductions are used to help achieve sales and market share objectives, whereas increases are used to keep up with rising costs. Regardless of whether adjustments are made to raise prices or lower prices, an important consideration in pricing is the concept known as the JND, or just noticeable difference. The JND is the point at which consumers can detect a "noticeable" difference between two stimuli—the initial price and the adjusted price. Depending on the rationale for price adjustments, sports marketers sometimes want the change to be above the difference threshold (i.e., consumers will notice the difference) and sometimes it will be below the difference threshold (i.e., consumers will not notice the difference).

Key Terms

- break-even pricing strategy
- bundle pricing strategy
- captive product pricing
- cost-based pricing strategies
- cost-plus pricing
- customary or traditional pricing
- differential pricing
- just noticeable difference (JND)
- lure of the middle pricing
- new sports product pricing strategies
- odd–even pricing
- penetration pricing
- prestige pricing
- price adjustments
- price discounts
- price increases
- price reductions
- price skimming
- pricing strategy model
- product line pricing
- product mix pricing strategies
- psychological pricing
- quantity discounts
- reference pricing
- seasonal discounts
- second-market discounting
- target profit pricing
- two-part pricing

Review Questions

1. Outline the steps for developing a pricing strategy. How do the internal and external factors affect this process?
2. Discuss differential pricing strategies. What is second-market discounting?
3. Describe the major differences between penetration pricing and price skimming. What conditions lead sports marketers to use penetration pricing versus price-skimming strategies?
4. What is psychological pricing? Provide several examples of reference pricing for sports products. Do you believe odd–even pricing is an effective psychological pricing strategy? Why?
5. Discuss the various product mix pricing strategies. Keeping the overall strategic marketing process in mind, why are product mix strategies so important?
6. Define cost-based pricing. Why are cost-based pricing strategies considered to be the simplest way of establishing prices? Explain the logic of break-even analysis.
7. What are the risks associated with reducing the price of sports products? Describe two common types of price discounting.

Exercises

1. Design a study that will establish a consumer's just noticeable difference for two sports products: (1) a season ticket package initially priced at $250, and (2) a soccer ball initially priced at $23.95. What are your findings? Does the initial price (the starting point) matter?
2. Calculate the break-even point for a manufacturer of golf balls, given the following: the fixed costs for the balls are estimated to be $1.3 million, the variable costs per unit are $2, and the suggested selling price is $10.
3. Name two sports products that use price-skimming strategies and two sports products that use a penetration pricing strategy. Comment on how the rest of the marketing mix follows the pricing strategy. Do you agree with the sports marketer's pricing decision?
4. Conduct a simple study of odd–even pricing by producing a rough (mock-up) advertisement for a sports product. Produce two versions of the advertisement—one using odd pricing for the sports product and an identical version using even pricing for the sports product. Then measure demand for the product (potential sales) by assessing purchase intent and consumer perceptions of quality. Which product will sell the best (odd or even priced)? Which product is perceived to be of higher quality (odd or even priced)?
5. Interview the organizer of a local or neighborhood road race (e.g., 5K or 10K) and determine the costs of staging such an event. Categorize the costs as either fixed or variable. Assess the role of cost in the price of the entry fee for participants.

Internet Exercises

1. Using the Internet, find an example of price bundling sports products.
2. Using the Internet, find an example of product line pricing for the pricing of a sponsorship package (i.e., sponsorship levels at different prices).
3. Searching the Internet, find an example of a sports product that uses prestige pricing. Comment on the construction of the Web site itself. Is it consistent with the prestige pricing?

Endnotes

1. See, for example, William Zikmund and Michael d'Amico, *Marketing,* 4th ed. (St. Paul, MN: West, 1993).
2. NLL.com, Roughnecks Lower Ticket Prices for 2004 (July 3, 2003), 14:13.
3. Eric Berkowitz, Roger Kerin, Steven Hartley, and William Reidelius, *Marketing,* 3rd ed. (Homewood, IL: Irwin, 1992), 339–340.
4. "Diamond Vision," *Sports Illustrated* (July 29, 1996), G22.
5. Joel Evans and Barry Berman, *Marketing,* 6th ed. (New York: Macmillan, 1994), 720.
6. http://www.revolutionsoccer.net/
7. Sabra Chartrand, "When the Pen Is Truly Mighty," *The New York Times* (July 14, 1995), D1.
8. Adam Schefter, "Broncos announce 'necessary' ticket increase," *The Denver Post* (January 30, 2004), D1.
9. Ed Waldman, "Prices rising for Orioles' best tickets," *The Baltimore Sun* (January 29, 2004), 1C.

10. Rich Kaipust, "Pederson: Hike not tied to facilities: The average cost of a Nebraska football ticket will be $45, up $3 from 2003 and $1.25 from 2002, *Omaha World Herald* (April 2, 2004), 1C.

11. "Nittany Lions raise football ticket prices," *The Associated Press*, (March 11, 2004).

12. "Stars lower some tickets in anticipation of NHL changes," *The Associated Press* (January 14, 2004).

13. Jimmy Smith, "Hornets to cut some ticket prices; Plan will go into effect next season," *Times-Picayune* (New Orleans, LA), (February 28, 2004), 1.

14. See, for example, John Mowen and Michael Minor, *Consumer Behavior,* 5th ed. (Upper Saddle River, NJ: Prentice Hall, 1998),

15. "Hit Slopes on the Cheap," *The New York Post* (February 26, 2004), 61.

MK Timer

Jim Kauffman gazed out the window of his office and thought again about his dilemma. Jim was the dean of students at a small Southeastern college. He knew he should be concerning himself with the matters of student life at the college but his mind kept coming back to the product he and a partner had developed. They had reached a critical point in regard to the development and sale of that product and he was thoroughly confused as to what he should do.

The product that he and Rocky Ferron, his partner, had developed was a timing device that could be used as a teaching aid in baseball. The product, which they had named the MK Timer, was not a new concept, but rather an improvement on an already existing product. Another company had developed a timing device under the trade name "Jugg Gun." It measured the speed at which a baseball pitcher threw a ball. The MK Timer did that, but it could also be used to measure the time required by a catcher to throw a ball to second base to catch a base runner attempting to steal a base or the time it took a pitcher to throw to first base to hold a base runner at that base. The product could do all this, and Jim thought it could be sold for less than the existing products in the market.

Jim's invention, as so many inventions often do, came about by accident. Shortly after assuming his role as dean of students at the college, the baseball coach had resigned. The chancellor of the school, aware that Jim had played some baseball in college, asked him to take over the position until a new coach could be hired. Jim accepted the role with some hesitation but found once he started coaching that he really enjoyed it. He became totally absorbed in the job and searched for ways to improve his players' performances. There is an old adage in baseball that states that 80 percent of the game is pitching. Jim believed strongly in that adage and he searched desperately for ways to improve the performance of his pitchers. In an effort to help his pitchers become more effective at changing the speed of their pitches, he developed the MK Timer.

Successful pitchers are able to throw with speed and control and vary the speed of their pitches. The key to hitting a baseball is the timing of the batter. If a pitcher can disrupt a hitter's timing by varying the speed of his pitches, he can be very successful. Jim was aware of this and he searched for a method he could use to train his pitchers to change the speed of the pitches they threw. He videotaped his pitchers to improve their throwing motions and in the process of reviewing the tapes he discovered the importance of the release point of the throwing motion. He decided that timing a pitch from this point until the pitch reached the catcher's glove could be a more

effective way to teach how to change a pitches' speed than the Jugg Gun.

Through experimentation, Jim developed the idea of a timing device that had three major elements. The first was a small pad that was placed on the pitcher's rubber. The pitcher placed one foot on the pad and an electronic signal was sent when the pitcher released the ball from his hand. From observation, Jim had discovered that a pitcher's foot came off the rubber at the same instant that the ball left his hand. The two motions were simultaneous. Therefore, if a timing device was attached to the rubber that could detect when all pressure was removed from it, an accurate measurement could be made.

The second element was a digital meter. It gave a reading of the speed at which the ball was thrown. The third element was a type of watch worn on the catcher's wrist. It was a timing device that sent a signal to the digital meter. It recorded the time required for a pitch to travel from the pitcher's hand to the catcher's glove. The impact of the ball entering the catcher's glove sent an impulse to the timing meter, which displayed the speed of the pitch. This three part system was quite simple and Jim believed just as effective as the existing technology being used to measure the speed of pitches.

When Jim and Rocky, an assistant coach, first developed the idea for the MK Timer, they knew they had to have help in building it. Neither of them had any experience in electronics. The solution was to hire an engineering firm to construct a prototype for them. Jim and Rocky made an initial trip to an engineering office in Alabama to explain what they wanted and in a few months they returned to examine what had been developed. They tested the timer on the college's baseball field, and after their pitchers got used to the pressure pad on the pitching rubber, there were no problems. Jim was elated. He had developed a device that could help his players. His pitchers could now see immediately how fast they were throwing their fastballs, curves, and most important, their off-speed pitches. Jim knew that varying the speed of two consecutive pitches by as little as five to seven miles per hour would make his pitchers much more difficult to hit.

An additional application for the timer was to record the time required for a catcher to throw to second or third base to keep an opposing base runner from stealing a base. An accurate measure of the time required for the catcher to rise out of his crouch behind home plate and throw to a base would make it possible to compare times and see if the catcher could improve his speed. The device also had a third application. This was to record the time required for a pitcher to throw to first base to keep a base runner from stealing. Once timed properly, the pitcher could work on different aspects of this motion to improve his quickness and to make it more difficult for the base runner to determine if the pitcher was throwing to first base or to home plate.

As Jim continued to work with the device he began to realize that he might have a marketable product. If the device worked for his team, why not for other college baseball teams and also for women's softball teams? There might even be a market for the product among high school teams and American Legion or other amateur teams. The technology was applicable to different types of baseball and softball teams and significantly less expensive than the existing product in the marketplace.

Competitive Products

The most popular product presently in the market was the Jugg Gun—a hand-held electronic device used to measure the speed of a thrown pitch. All major league baseball teams own at least one, and often several, of these devices. The minor league teams affiliated with the major league clubs typically have at least one Jugg Gun each, also. There were 30 major league teams and approximately four minor league teams associated with each major league team. This represented a total professional market of 150 teams. Jim did not expect to be able to sell his device to this market segment. He believed the primary market for the MK Timer was the college market and a portion of the high school market. There were two other competitors in the marketplace besides the Jugg Gun, but they had experienced very limited success.

The strategy that Jim and Rocky developed for their product was to sell it for less than the existing products and to appeal primarily to colleges and high schools. Based on their discussions with the engineers who built the prototype, the MK Timer could be mass produced for a cost of less than $200. Jim and Rocky thought they could sell the device for $500. This would cover the initial marketing and distribution costs. This price was quite attractive when compared to price of $1,500, which was be charged by the manufacturers of the Jugg Gun.

Jim decided that before he went any further with the development and marketing of this product he needed to do two things. First he needed to determine if he could patent the device so that he would have exclusive rights to its sales. Second, he needed to develop at least a rough estimate of the number of potential customers for the timer. He estimated that it could be sold to at least half of all colleges in the United States that had baseball or softball teams. He had no idea, however, how many schools actually had teams. Many of the smaller schools with limited budgets might not be able to afford his product, but certainly the Division I schools and many of the Division II schools could afford the timer. Also, if the men's and women's teams shared the device as a teaching tool this would make it more affordable for the school.

Jim contacted a patent lawyer in the area. The attorney told him it would cost a minimum of $2,500 to secure a patent for the timer. Jim was a bit shocked at this cost and settled for a limited search, which cost approximately $750. After some analysis, the attorney determined that Jim had a good chance of receiving a patent on the timer if he were willing to incur the expense.

At this point Jim was starting to realize the extent of the commitment he would have to make if he were going to try to market this device himself. He and his partner had already invested over $2,500 in this product and he estimated it would require an additional $5,000 to $7,000 to introduce the product into the marketplace. He had no real training in business. His academic background was in student affairs and not in management or marketing. His partner owned a small business, but he had no experience in manufacturing or distribution. Also, Rocky was less committed to the timer than Jim. He now realized there was more to making this product a success then he had first thought and that he needed some additional guidance.

Endorsement

Jim and his partner discussed what their next step should be. They decided that attending the college baseball coaches' national meeting would allow them to determine if there was actually interest in the device among the coaches. Also, Jim hoped to enlist the aid of his college coach in endorsing the product.

Jim's coach at Florida State University had been a major league outfielder for the St. Louis Cardinals and the Philadelphia Phillies. After retirement from major league baseball he became a college coach and had become quite successful at the Florida school. He was well known among college coaches and if he were to endorse this product it could be a real boost to sales. If the coach liked the product then Jim planned to use his name in the sales efforts for the timer. He left for the conference with the MK Timer and high hopes.

This was the first time that Jim had ever attended the national coaching conference and he felt a bit out of place. He was a baseball coach, but only an interim one, at a very small school. He knew the coaches of the large schools by reputation only or as a result of watching the College World Series on television. Upon his arrival at the conference hotel he contacted his old coach and asked if he might meet with him to discuss the timer. Coach Litwhiler was hesitant at first but, when Jim explained to him how much time and effort he had invested in the product, he agreed to a demonstration.

Jim was a bit nervous as he rode the elevator up to the twelfth floor to Coach Litwhiler's room. He knew this product had helped the players on his team, but the trick was to convince his old coach in one evening that this was a viable product and one with which he should want to be associated.

After spending several minutes discussing the old college days with the coach and his new coaching position, Jim brought the conversation around to the timer. Coach Litwhiler wanted to know what made this product better than the existing timing devices in the market. Jim explained the multiple uses of the timer and that it could be sold for much less than the Jugg Gun. Litwhiler listened intently but did not say much. Finally, Jim asked if he would like to see a demonstration. The coach agreed but said he did not have time to go outside to see it demonstrated. Jim was a bit surprised by this but realized this was his one chance to demonstrate the product to Litwhiler, so he agreed.

He suggested they move out into the hall where there would be enough space to throw pitches. The pressure pad and electronic clock were set up and Jim had a friend serve as a catcher as he threw several pitches. To Jim's amazement the clock would not register the speed of the pitches. He tried repeated throws and adjustments of all three elements of the system, but nothing he did produced a proper reading. Jim was flabbergasted and could not understand why the timer did not work. Litwhiler said he was sorry but he could not possibly endorse a product that did not perform any better than this had. Jim took the timer back to his room and checked it for any loose parts or connections. He found none and was still baffled by the lack of performance. The next day he took it outside to test it and it worked properly.

It was not until two weeks later that Jim discovered why the timer had not worked in the hotel. He contacted the engineers who had built the prototype. After some tests they explained to him that the electronic impulse sent from the pressure pad was affected by the steel girders used to construct the multistory hotel. When it was used outside, as the product was designed to be used, there was no problem. Unfortunately, Coach Litwhiler had only seen the feeble attempts inside the hotel.

Jim returned home deeply disappointed. He had failed to secure Litwhiler's endorsement. Without it or some other well-known coach or player's endorsement, he knew it would be difficult to sell the timer. If he were to go forward with the device he would have to invest money to do a complete patent search. Also, he had to draw up a contract with a manufacturer to produce the product, and he needed to determine where and to whom he would sell it. He knew he and his partner would have to invest an additional $5,000 to $7,000 to bring the product to market with no guarantee of success. Jim believed strongly in the product and he had even contemplated the possibility of taking a leave of absence from his job to devote all his time to the manufacture and sale of the MK Timer. This option involved the greatest risk. Jim still viewed himself as a college administrator and not an entrepreneur. There must be some way for him and his partner to introduce the timer into the market without changing careers.

DISCUSSION QUESTIONS

1. Does Jim have a product that can be sold successfully to colleges and universities or has he simply gotten carried away with this idea?
2. What can Jim do to determine the potential sales for this product?
3. How important is it for Jim to have a well-known coach or player endorse this product?
4. Should Jim try to manufacture this product himself or contract for a separate firm to perform this task?
5. Is it worth Jim quitting his job to produce and sell this product on a fulltime basis?
6. What other options are available to Jim if he does not want to pursue manufacturing or marketing the timer?

IMPLEMENTING AND CONTROLLING THE STRATEGIC SPORTS MARKETING PROCESS

CHAPTER 16

IMPLEMENTING AND CONTROLLING THE STRATEGIC SPORTS MARKETING PROCESS

After completing this chapter, you should be able to

- Describe how the implementation phase of the strategic sports marketing process "fits" with the planning phase.
- Explain the organizational design elements that affect the implementation phase.
- Identify the general competencies and the most important skills that effective sports marketing managers possess.
- Describe the basic characteristics of total quality marketing (TQM) programs and how TQM might be implemented in sports organizations.
- Identify some of the guidelines for designing reward systems.
- Define strategic control and how the control phase of the strategic sports marketing process "fits" with the implementation phase.
- Explain the differences among planning assumption control, process control, and contingency control.

The opening scenario presents an excellent example of how sports organizations operate in uncertain and changing conditions. Moreover, sports organizations must consider the internal and external environments and formulate a plan that achieves a "fit" with these environments. The strategic sports marketing process is ultimately directed toward the achievement of the organization's mission, goals, and objectives. The contingency theory of sports marketing suggests that there are a variety of marketing plans that can achieve these goals. However, not all these plans are equally effective. Likewise, organizations have a variety of ways to implement and control the strategic sports marketing plan they have developed, all of which are not equally useful for putting the plan into action. Thus, sports marketers should allocate the time and effort necessary to develop a program that will lead to the desired outcomes and most effectively implement and control the planning process.

PART IV

IMPLEMENTING AND CONTROLLING THE STRATEGIC SPORTS MARKETING PROCESS

SPOTLIGHT ON INTERNATIONAL SPORTS MARKETING

All Set to Muscle In On Moscow

Dressed in baggy khakis and a rumpled blazer, 25-year-old James "Jake" Weinstock might be mistaken for a struggling actor. When he stabs at his unruly locks and gushes about hitchhiking in Zimbabwe, he projects the boyish charm of Tom Hanks in *Big*. In the Wild East, however, where the high-octane capitalism of the post-Soviet era has turned convention on its head, appearances can be deceiving.

Though he looks like a slacker, the history major from the University of Pennsylvania could teach a Harvard MBA a thing or two. Straight out of college and with little experience in business, Weinstock and two other partners raised $2.5 million to realize a dream of starting a business in Russia, a country Weinstock fell in love with while roaming the world during a year's leave of absence from Penn. In the year and a half of teeth-grinding frustration since the enterprise was conceived in a Moscow bar, he has hopped across continents in search of start-up capital, boned up on accounting and contract law, and staved off the Russian mafia.

RATTLED RIVALS

The result: a soccer-field-size, state-of-the-art Gold's Gym in Moscow's center—the name licensed from California's renowned Gold's Gym, which has 500 franchises around the world. The facility has shaken up the city's sluggish health club industry and rattled its once complacent Russian rivals. With Astroturfed tennis courts, a Nike-built basketball court, high-tech Cybex workout machines, tanning salons, a Western-style emphasis on service, a day care center, and in-house medical staff, Gold's has fired up the city's fitness-starved business community. In the run-up to February's grand opening, the gym has been taking members at reduced rates, which include hefty corporate discounts. Weinstock has fielded hundreds of calls from affluent Muscovites and expatriate residents, signing up more than 400.

"I'm biting my nails. We're just this close to the end," says Weinstock in the gym's bare-bones office, his words almost drowned out by the rattle of jackhammers and the roar of blowtorches as workers race around the clock to meet the opening deadline.

DREAMS

Weinstock was merely upholding his family's independent streak when, after only six months of employment, he chucked his comfortable marketing job at Moscow's

Ernst & Young for "plain pasta dinners" and heady dreams. Both Weinstock's parents are also boss-dodgers: His mother, a freelance editor, worked for *The New Yorker*, while his father runs his own small consulting firm. Weinstock's brothers are writers. "I wanted to do my own thing," he says. "And the fact that it's so difficult here makes success that much more rewarding."

An avid sports fan, who claims he would join a pickup basketball game anywhere, Weinstock got the idea for a gym venture on his second day in Moscow. An expatriate fraternity brother introduced him to 31-year-old Paul Kuebler, at that time financial director at Andersen Consulting. "The project was a perfect fit for both of us: making money while having fun," says Weinstock. Kuebler had been at Andersen for almost eight years and was itching for something more adventurous. In May 1995 he brought on board a Russian friend of two years, Vladimir Grumlik. Then things really began to roll.

Weinstock is not unique in the New Russia. Other brash, adrenaline-charged Generation Xers, both Russians and Westerners, have braved the chaos and rampant criminality of post-Soviet Russia to follow their stars—opening diners, movie theaters, casinos, and even banks, and transforming the city's landscape in the process.

Weinstock and his partners are among the few entrepreneurs, however, who braved quitting their jobs without the security of prior backing, simply hoping venture capital might emerge in time to save them.

Their gamble paid off. But raising capital was much tougher than just passing the hat. Despite a licensing agreement with Gold's and an upbeat business plan that promised a 60–70 percent return, few investors in either Russia or the United States took the bait. "Our proposal was a bit offbeat: too small for the big funds and too big for the small ones," says Kuebler, who admits that he naively expected things to fall into place within three months of leaving Andersen last October.

The venture seemed doomed when the Communists swept to victory in December's parliamentary elections, just when Weinstock was in New York seeking investors. Potential financiers, already wary of both Russia and Weinstock's youth, lost interest when the specter of communism reappeared.

CHARACTER

The partners did not despair, however. Smashing open their combined nest eggs of about $150,000—Weinstock

(Continued)

(Continued)

claims that even his high school ball-boy savings went into the project—and with a little help from friends and relatives, they persisted. When a Boston real estate developer, Commonwealth Property Investors (CPI), decided to pump in a cool million last June after a presentation by the two Americans, things began to click. "Jake and Paul's character was crucial in our decision. They're mature, levelheaded, dedicated, and complement each other well. I was impressed that they staked their nest eggs on this project," says CPI's Moscow rep, Greg Getshow. He added that although Gold's was not in CPI's line of business, it was excited by the idea.

With CPI's $1 million paving the way, 10 other private investors jumped on board, a Russian among them. The savvy partners say they made sure, however, to keep a controlling interest in the business, which is registered as an offshore company in Cyprus with a local Russian subsidiary.

Keen to upstage Reebok International, Ltd., and increase its visibility in Moscow, Nike, Inc., while wary of sponsoring an exclusive gym, agreed to build a basketball court, on the condition that it be made available on demand for company-sponsored sports clinics for the young. It is also providing staff outfits.

Investors agree that the Americans' fluency in Russian helped. More important, their extensive contacts with Moscow officialdom through a trustworthy local partner helped seal their backing. Vladimir Grumlik, an intense, no-nonsense former athlete who once sold Nikes in Russia's caviar capital, Astrakhan, got to know Moscow officials through his earlier business ventures. He has been crucial.

Grumlik scoured Moscow for potential gym sites, helping to find a crumbling but spacious soccer arena belonging to the Stadium of Young Pioneers, a now privatized wing of the Soviet-era youth organization. They got the building under a 25-year renewable lease. "I love working with Paul and Jake. They're more responsible and farsighted than the Russians I've dealt with," says Grumlik. With his sports mentor, Alexei Spirin, a World Cup Russian soccer referee, he helped them strike the kind of deal that in Moscow keeps the mafia at arm's length. A power broker back in Soviet times, Spirin is cozy with Moscow's elite and knows well how to make things happen in Russia.

"On Spirin's recommendation, we hired a security firm tied to the former KGB," says Kuebler. "We pay them above-market rates plus a 'consulting' fee, and they make sure no one messes with us." The cost is no more than 5 percent of revenue.

NO POOL

Although the security issue may be resolved for now, the partners still have plenty to worry about. Competitors have their knives out for the brash American upstarts. "They're just a bunch of kids with no experience," sniffs Olga Antonova, manager of their biggest rival, World Class Fitness, which has more than 3,000 members. Spurred by Gold's debut, World Class has spruced up service, extended hours, and is rushing to open a new gym.

While Gold's equipment might be a notch above its competitors', Gold's lacks the clincher—a swimming pool. Then there is the cost: A year's membership, while $500 cheaper than many rival gyms, still runs $2,500. Says Greek businessman Konstantinos Tsakonas: "[Membership in] the Gold's franchise in Cyprus costs $600. Why are they charging me four times more?" Many of the city's wealthy, including expats, prefer working out in cheaper Soviet-style sports clubs. And although the partners are chummy now, Russians have been known to fall out, often violently.

Some outsiders, however, are cautiously optimistic. "This city could absorb scores more world-class gyms. If Gold's doesn't alienate Russians by being too American, it could take off," says Andrei Kulikov, a correspondent for the Russian sports daily, Sport Ekspress.

Even before liftoff, Weinstock is amazed by what has happened. "I never imagined we'd come this far," he says, "When I can have a café latte and watch people enjoying themselves, then I'll finally be able to relax."

Maybe. But if members sign up in droves and if branches appear in St. Petersburg and Ukraine as planned, Weinstock should not count on relaxing for long.

Source: Vajai Maheshwari, "All Set to Muscle in on Moscow," *Business Week* (December 16, 1996). Reprinted from *Business Week* by special permission. Copyright © 1996 by the McGraw-Hill Companies, Inc.

The remainder of this chapter looks at the last two phases of the strategic marketing process—implementation and control. We begin by examining a model of the implementation process and the organizational design elements that facilitate or impede the execution of the marketing plan. Then, we shift our focus to the control phase and look at some of the common forms of strategic control.

IMPLEMENTATION

Implementation can be described as putting strategy into action or executing the plan. As illustrated in the opening scenario, Jake Weinstock's dream of opening the first Gold's Gym in Moscow was realized after overcoming considerable obstacles. Although most sports marketers need not worry about the Russian mafia, they do need to continually monitor the implementation process to make sure plans are being carried out in the correct manner.

To successfully manage the implementation process, the sports marketer must consider a number of organizational design elements. These organizational design elements include communication, staffing, skills, coordination, rewards, information, creativity, and budgeting. Implementation must begin with **communication.** Effective communication requires a leadership style that allows and encourages an understanding of the marketing plan by all members of the sports marketing team. A second critical element involves **staffing** and developing the **skills** in those people who are responsible for carrying out the plan. These people must also be placed within the organization so they can work together to implement the plan, thus a third critical design element is **coordination. Rewards** that are congruent to the plan can provide the motivation and incentives necessary for people to work effectively toward the achievement of the goals and objectives outlined within the plan. **Information** must be available to those people who will carry out the plans so effective decisions can be made throughout the implementation phase. Effective work environments also allow for and encourage **creativity** from individuals who are expected to find ways to carry out the strategic marketing plan. Finally, a supportive **budgeting** system is critical to the successful achievement of strategic goals and objectives. These seven organizational design elements of implementation and their relationship to the strategic sports marketing process are outlined in Figure 16.1.

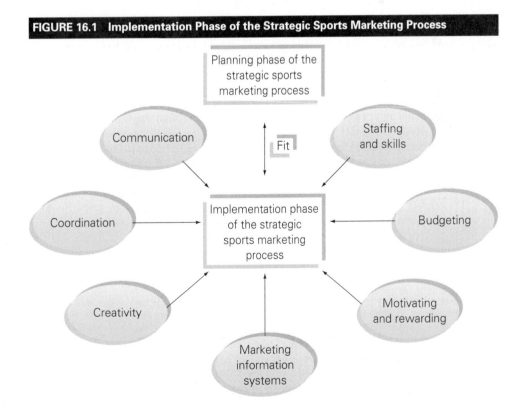

FIGURE 16.1   Implementation Phase of the Strategic Sports Marketing Process

XFL: What Went Wrong?

After plunging into the sports arena with unparalleled fanfare and first-day success, the XFL closed its initial season with a whimper. If this were a wrestling match, it would have been stopped. XFL President Basil Devito acknowledged as much before the title game. "The biggest mistake was starting too quickly," he said. "In Week 1, we were not prepared either from a football or television production side. Following the season, we will be moving forward with what the new shape of the XFL will be. We have to improve it."

Attendance averaged 23,410 a game in the regular season, 17 percent above initial projections. But this is a made-for-TV league, and the TV audience dwindled. The XFL produced some interesting images, using cameramen on the field, cameras over the field, and shooting from other unconventional angles. But while cinematography can enhance the viewers' enjoyment of the game, it means little if there are no viewers. The season average for the XFL was 3.3. Only 2.5 percent of the homes with television sets in the nation's 49 largest markets tuned in, according to Nielsen Media Research. That was the story of the made-for-television league from Week 2 onward.

In February, when the league started, the World Wrestling Foundation's Vince McMahon had ventured that his latest promotion would dazzle the public with "real football" and teach the "pantywaist" NFL a thing or two along the way. "We know how to listen and we know what the people want," McMahon had said. "This league isn't just going to survive. It's going to thrive. . . . We'd have to be blithering idiots for this not to succeed."

Midway through the first, and perhaps last XFL season, New York/New Jersey Hitmen Coach Rusty Tillman was asked to assess the quality of play in his league compared with what he saw in more than 30 years of playing and coaching in the NFL. "We've got some great kids out here really busting their butts," Tillman said. "But here's the biggest problem. The quarterbacks pretty much stink, and the receivers pretty much stink. Basically, it's still football, and it's getting better every week. These kids try real hard, but it is what it is."

"The quality of play is decent," said Mike Keller, director of football operations for the new league. "We knew it wouldn't be the NFL. We were always looking for the best players who were not in the NFL. Sure we're struggling at quarterback, like everyone does. But our games have been fairly compelling and many of them are very close."

Where did the league go wrong? Tony Ponturo is vice president of media and sports marketing at Anheuser-Busch and was ranked by *The Sporting News* among the top 10 most powerful people in sports last year because of the vast amount of advertising money he and his associates spend on sporting events. He blames much of the league's demise on McMahon.

"He personally may have been his own worst enemy," Ponturo said from his St. Louis office, pointing out that McMahon already had a sullied reputation in the media because he used many distasteful tactics in his wrestling shows. "If he was John Doe starting with lower expectations (and less negative press), things might have been different."

The league started with a roar as curiosity seekers were lured by what XFL officials said was the biggest promotional effort ever directed at a start-up league. Many weeks of commercials aired during WWF and NBC programming, and the campaign seemed to work. According to Nielsen, the first telecast was seen in 9.5 percent of the nation's homes with a TV, far above projections.

Only 2.4 percent of the homes with TVs tuned in for the rest of NBC's regular-season telecasts. Advertisers had been guaranteed a 4.5 rating, which was reached only once in the final nine weeks, so the network gave away free commercials to offset the shortfall.

Another problem with the league may have been a lack of marketing planning. The XFL elected to use mostly no-name players instead of stocking up with high-priced National Football League-caliber talent. It played games that were nothing like the offense-dominated contests that made the AFL the only successful start-up pro football league in the past 50 years.

Ponturo also said the XFL erred by rushing into things. It failed to do enough test marketing and enough training sessions for players, who went to camp only about a month before the first game and played no formal exhibition contests. He compared it to Anheuser-Busch rolling out a new brand but failing to introduce it in test markets—a small geographical proving ground to get feedback—before going national. "It's one thing to fail in a rollout market," he said. "But when you go full bore without testing, you pay the consequences."

Sources: Kevin Modesti, "First XFL Season Is History; TV Viewers Ignored It, but League Had Its Fans." *Star Tribune* (April 23, 2001), 12C; Leonard Shapiro, "The XFL: 'It's Not Very Good Football'; Started with a Bang, Ending with . . . " *The Washington Post* (April 18, 2001), D10; Dan Caesar, "XFL Seems Destined to Exit NBC, as Sex Didn't Sell; A-B Marketing Exec Says League Misread Audience and Was Poorly Planned." *St. Louis Post-Dispatch* (April 25, 2001), D1.

Each of these seven elements must be carefully considered within the strategic marketing process by the sports marketing manager. The implementation design must be appropriate for the plan. In other words, a "fit" between the planning phase and the implementation phase is required. Thus, a change in the strategic marketing plan of a sports organization could lead to the need to make changes in one or more of these design elements. As you read the previous article on the demise of the XFL, think about what design elements could have been changed to save the league.

COMMUNICATION

Effective communication is critical to the successful implementation of the strategic sports marketing plan. Before we discuss the issues involved in effective communication, it is important to understand the importance of having a leader who is committed to the strategic sports marketing plan. Without such commitment, the best communication efforts will be ineffective. The values of the marketing leader not only affect the strategic sports marketing process, but also the way the plan will be implemented. Strategy leadership requires a "champion," someone who believes so strongly in the strategic marketing plan that they can share the "what," "why," and "how" with those who will be responsible for its implementation.

The commitment of the leader to the plan usually dictates the level of commitment among those who will carry it out. In addition, different strategies require different skills, even among leaders. Therefore, when strategy changes, a change in leadership often follows. That relationship may also be reversed. A change in leadership will often lead to a change, or at least an adjustment, to the strategy. In fact, because of the close relationship between strategy and leadership, it is sometimes necessary to bring in outside sports marketers to implement a changed or new strategy. Organizations will also often bring in someone new when they believe a new marketing strategy is needed to enhance performance.

For example, Ty Votaw, commissioner of the Ladies Professional Golf Association (LPGA) was hired to broaden the scope of the league and increase exposure.[1] Votaw brings a wealth of experience in his new role, having worked for the LPGA since 1991. He was responsible for handling business transactions, including tournament sponsorships and television rights negotiations, as vice president of business affairs. Votaw stated that "Our focus will be on getting more of our tournaments on television, increasing the size of purses and expanding internationally, with more lucrative television packages from foreign nations such as Korea, Australia, and Sweden." Although this will be challenging, Votaw has the support of the players, sponsors, and golf industry executives. In addition, Votaw has the popularity of women's golf on his side.

Organizational leadership sets the tone for communication within the sports organization. Communication may be formal or informal and may use a number of different channels. For example, some organizations may require all communications be written and meetings be scheduled and documented. Other organizational leaders may have an informal, open-door policy and allow for more "spur of the moment" meetings and "hallway" discussions. Either policy can be effective when it comes to implementing strategy within the sports organization, as long as the necessary information is clearly and accurately communicated.

Strategy was once considered a "top-down" only process where those who had a "big-picture" view of the organization were considered the best candidates for formulating strategy. This often led to huge communication requirements as organizational leaders attempted to inform those who had to carry out the strategy about not only the strategy, but also the rationale for strategic choices made by the top management. Experience has shown that the communication process is easier when those who are expected to

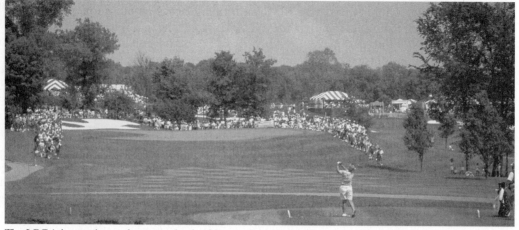

The LPGA is growing under strong leadership.

implement the plan are involved throughout the process. Thus, involving the entire sports marketing team throughout the strategic sports marketing process can usually be more effective than attempting to communicate the plan after it has been developed.

Even when everyone responsible for implementing the plan is involved in its development, strategic sports marketing plans should be communicated often. Due to the contingent nature of the strategic sports marketing process, plans and circumstances can change, and people can forget the original plan and the basic premise on which the plan was formulated. Employees can learn about or be reminded about the content and purpose of the plans in a variety of ways. This information can be communicated in regularly scheduled meetings or at gatherings where the strategic plan is the primary agenda item. Printed material can also be useful. Some sports organizations may give employees desk items, such as calendars or paperweights, with keywords that remind them of the strategy. They may even program screen savers on computers with words that will remind employees of the strategic thrust of the marketing plan. Promotional literature that can be displayed around the office or sent to employees through e-mail is also useful. In essence, sports marketing organizations that can provide daily reminders of the strategy are more likely to keep everyone involved on the same strategic path. Many forms of internal promotion can be used to achieve this goal.

Communication with groups and individuals outside the marketing department is also important. Many such individuals and groups, both within the organization and outside the organization, have a stake in the marketing strategy and can have an impact on the implementation of the plan. For example, it is important to inform other departments within the sports organization who affect or are affected by the strategy or the strategic marketing direction. For example, many teams and leagues are in the process of trying to develop long-term relationships with their fans. One of the ways to build these relationships is to allow fans more access and contact with the players. At the collegiate level, Xavier Women's Basketball Team has implemented a Kid's Club where young Musketeer fans are sent a handwritten note by a member of the team inviting them to a pregame pizza party. This creative plan can only be executed by communicating its importance to coaches and members of the XU team.

On the professional front, many teams hold an annual fan appreciation day to enhance fan relations. The Orlando Magic, for example, feature a pregame party outside the T.D. Waterhouse Center with a Magic yearbook giveaway to the first 8,000 fans. During halftime, the Magic Dancers and Stuff (the mascot) will sign autographs and select food discounts will be offered during the game. Additionally, over 400 t-shirts are

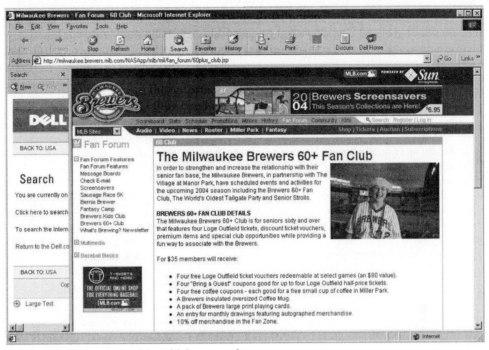

Building long term relationships with long term fans.

Source: Used by permission of MLB. All rights reserved.

launched into the crowd during a single time-out break. After the game, each player will give away his home jersey to a 15-year season ticket holder, and his away jersey to a community recipient. All of these activities contribute to strengthening the team–fan relationship, but as shown in Table 16.1, the Magic aren't even among the top fifteen in professional sports.

As with internal promotion, external promotion and communication of the strategic sports marketing plan can take many forms. Some channels for these communications include Web sites, annual reports, mailers, marketing specialties such as calendars, or meetings. Again, the key to effectively communicating to outside or inside groups is committed and competent leadership. It is with this leadership and effective communication efforts that the foundation for successful implementation of the strategic sports marketing plan is provided.

TABLE 16.1 Professional Sport Teams—2004 Fan Relations* Rankings

1. San Antonio Spurs	9. Tennessee Titans
2. Dallas Mavericks	10. Colorado Avalanche
3. Green Bay Packers	11. Anaheim Angels
4. Kansas City Chiefs	12. Vancouver Canucks
5. Detroit Red Wings	13. Columbus Blue Jackets
6. Minnesota Wild	14. Sacramento Kings
7. Detroit Pistons	15. St. Louis Cardinals
8. Houston Texans	

* FRL (Fan Relations): Ease of access to players, coaches, and management.
Source: SportsNation. The Ultimate Standings ESPN The Magazine's Fan Satisfaction Rankings: Where fans rate every team, from 1 to 121. Reprinted courtesy of ESPN.com.

SPORTS MARKETING HALL OF FAME

Gary Davidson

Gary Davidson was once called the man who has had the greatest impact on professional sports in America. A former lawyer, Davidson founded and served as president of the American Basketball Association (ABA), the World Hockey Association (WHL), and the World Football League (WFL) in the late 1960s and early 1970s.

These leagues, of course, offered alternatives for professional athletes that would have never existed otherwise. By breaking the virtual monopoly held on talent by the existing NBA, NHL, and NFL franchises, Davidson attracted stars such as Wayne Gretzky, Bobby Hull, "Dr. J." Julius Erving, and Rick Barry to play in his rebel leagues. Davidson and his leagues are also credited with some major rule changes that subsequently were adopted by the existing professional leagues. For instance, the three-point shot was created to add excitement to the ABA and has changed the entire course of modern basketball.

In addition to his ambush marketing tactics, Gary Davidson broadened the scope of professional sports. He placed professional franchises in cities that were previously considered too small to support major league sports. For example, San Antonio and Indianapolis were two of his original ABA teams that are now successful NBA franchises. Davidson's leagues have benefited the fans, the players, and major league sports.

Source: Steve Rushin, "Gary Davidson," *Sports Illustrated* (September 19, 1994), 145.

STAFFING AND SKILLS

As we just discussed, it is critical to the success of the strategic sports marketing plan to have a leader who can "champion" and communicate the strategy. As important as the leader is to effective implementation, it is equally important to have a staff who cares about and is capable of implementing the strategy. A group of individuals must be assembled who have the appropriate mix of backgrounds, experiences, know-how, beliefs, values, work and managerial styles, and personalities.

It is important to consider strategy prior to hiring and training new employees and in retraining those who are already with the marketing team. This is especially vital in managerial or other key positions. However, staffing for the implementation of strategic sports marketing plans must go much deeper into the organizational ranks. In fact, putting together an effective marketing team is one of the cornerstones of the implementation process.

A few studies have examined the relationship between types of strategy and staff characteristics. One study of corporate executives and their perceptions regarding the relationship between managerial characteristics and strategy offered two interesting findings.[2] First, experience and exposure to a particular type of strategy has been viewed by corporate executives as being essential for managers. Previous experience and exposure to a strategy can provide an opportunity for these experienced individuals to provide important input into the implementation of the plan. However, the second finding suggests that a "perfect match" between managerial characteristics and strategy is likely to result in an overcommitment to a particular strategy. In other words, managers may not be able to change strategic direction when contingencies change if they are perfectly matched in education, training, experience, and personality to one particular strategy. These findings may be particularly relevant for sports organizations. Because sports organizations operate in changing, uncertain, and unpredictable environments where the internal and external contingencies can change frequently, staffing must consider the capacity for change among employees.

Sports careers on the Web.

Source: Copyright © 2004. Work in Sports L.L.C. All rights reserved.

To develop a staff capable of implementing the strategy, three categories of characteristics must be considered: education, training, and ability; experience and previous track record; and personality and temperament. With any team-building activity, it is important to consider the compatibility of the individuals who will work together to implement the strategic sports plan.

Just what skills are necessary to land and keep your dream job in sports marketing? The answer to this question is best addressed in two parts. First, what knowledge is required for an individual to be successful in all sports management positions? In other words, what are the foundation skills for a successful career. Second, what are the marketing-specific core competencies of the sports marketing manager?

In addressing the first question, the general competencies necessary for all sports marketing management careers include being able to[3]:

- direct the work effort of people or groups of people,
- interrelate with the community,
- negotiate to arrive at a solution to a problem,
- function within a specified budget,
- use supervision techniques,
- evaluate the results of your decisions in light of work objectives,
- self-evaluate employee's job performance,
- use problem-solving techniques,
- interpret basic statistical data,
- speak before large audiences,

TABLE 16.2 Most Important Skills for Sport Marketing Managers

Presented in Rank Order Where 1 Is the Most Important Skill and 20 Is the Least Important Skill

1. Establish a positive image for your sporting organization.
2. Achieve sponsors' promotional goals.
3. Stimulate ticket sales.
4. Maximize media exposure for events, athletes, and sponsors.
5. Acquire sponsors through personal contacts.
6. Maintain good relations with community, authorities, and partners.
7. Acquire sponsors by formal presentations.
8. Develop special promotions.
9. Improve budget construction.
10. Negotiate promotion contracts.
11. Evaluate sports marketing opportunities and performance.
12. Design and coordinate content of events.
13. Coordinate press coverage of events.
14. Create contracts.
15. Provide corporate hospitality of events.
16. Build public image and awareness of athletes.
17. Schedule events and facilities.
18. Establish event safety factors.
19. Build rapport with editors, reporters, and other media reps.
20. Buy and resell media rights.

Source: Peter Smolianov and David Shilbury, "An Investigation of Sport Marketing Competencies," *Sport Marketing Quarterly*, vol. 5, no. 4 (1996), 27–36. Reprinted with permission of Fitness Information Technology, Inc. Publishers.

- apply the knowledge of the history and evolution of sport into the structure of today's society, and
- appreciate the psychological factors that pertain to an athlete's performance and attitude on the playing field.

These general skills are required of all sports marketing managers to some extent, but what about more specific marketing skills? This question was posed to sports marketing professionals employed in sports marketing firms, amateur sports organizations, professional sports organization, and college athletics. The results of this study are presented in Table 16.2.

Remember, changes in strategy may lead to modification of the staff and skill base. Thus, employee training and retraining is often an important part of the implementation process. As strategy is developed and the implementation plan formulated, sports marketers must consider not only new staffing needs, but also new skill needs. Training and retraining programs should be designed and included in the implementation plans so the staff is prepared to implement the new or modified strategy. Until all the staff and skills are in place, it is unlikely that the sports organization can proceed with the successful implementation of the marketing plan.

COORDINATION

Successful implementation of the marketing plan depends not only on capable and committed leadership who can effectively communicate internally and externally and a staff with the necessary skills, but also on the effective organization of those people and their tasks. Structure helps to define the key activities and the manner in which they will be coordinated to achieve the strategy. A fit between strategy and structure has been shown to be critical to the successful achievement of strategy and the performance of organizations. According to one important study of organizations, when a new strategy was chosen, a decline in performance was observed and administrative problems occurred until a new method of organizing people and activities was put into place. Once the new method was implemented, organizational performance began to improve, and the strategy was more likely to be achieved.[4] Thus, the strategic marketing plan must dictate how people and tasks are organized.

One way of coordinating people and tasks in a sports organization is by practicing **Total Quality Management (TQM).** Quality improvement programs have become an important and powerful tool for organizations of the 1990s, including sports organizations.[5] Nearly all major corporations and industries in the United States have adopted some type of quality initiative to meet competitive challenges. Traditionally, TQM programs have been focused on manufacturing quality. To manufacturers of sporting goods, quality is likely to mean an excellent consistency of goods and deliveries made by their suppliers. In a manufacturing environment, TQM has been primarily concerned with both the counting and reduction of defects and reducing the cycle time taken to complete any given process.

Even though TQM philosophies originally were used in manufacturing companies, a large number (69 percent) of service organizations are also using the principles of TQM. Although the nature of services is vastly different from those of manufactured products (see Chapter 8), Roberts and Sergesketter argue that the fundamental quality issues are similar.[6] A service organization, as with a manufacturing organization, must concentrate on the reduction of defects and cycle times for important processes. As such, the philosophies of TQM are just as applicable for sports services as they are for manufacturing.

Although TQM represents a quality philosophy, there is little agreement as to what TQM (or quality) actually is and how best to manage the TQM process in an organization.[7] Evans and Lindsay define TQM as an integrative management concept for continuously improving the quality of goods and services delivered through the participation of all levels and functions of the organization.[8] In addition, TQM is described as incorporating design, control, and quality improvement, with the customer as the driving force behind the process.

Although the definitions of TQM may vary on the basis of wording and relative emphasis, all quality improvement programs share a common set of features or characteristics.[9] These characteristics, include, but are not limited to, the following:

1. **Customer-Driven Quality**—Quality is defined by customers, and all TQM practices are implemented to please the customer.
2. **Visible Leadership**—Top management is responsible for leading the quality charge and places quality above all else.
3. **Data-Driven Processes**—All TQM processes are driven by data collection, use of measurement, and the scientific method.
4. **Continuous Improvement Philosophy**—It is always possible to do a better job, and continual, small changes in improvement are just as critical as an occasional major breakthrough.

REWARDS

As we discussed previously, the execution of strategy ultimately depends on individual members of the organization. Effective communication, staffing, skill development and enhancement, and coordination are vital to implementation efforts and should be planned for and considered throughout the strategic sports marketing process. Another critical component in the design of an implementation plan is to provide for motivating and rewarding behavior that is strategy supportive. Thus, a reward system is a key ingredient in effective strategy implementation.

There is no one "correct" reward system. From a strategic perspective, rewards must be aligned with the strategy; therefore, the best reward system is "contingent" upon the strategic circumstances. These rewards and incentives represent another choice for management. Thus, reward systems will reflect the beliefs and values of the individuals who design them. However, to successfully motivate desired behavior, reward systems must consider the needs, values, and beliefs of those who will be "motivated" by and receiving the rewards.

Management can choose from several types of motivators, which can be classified on the basis of three types of criteria. Motivators can be positive or negative, monetary or nonmonetary, and long run or short run. Some examples include compensation (salary or commission), bonuses, raises, stock options, benefits, promotions, demotions, recognition, praise, criticism, more (or less) responsibility, performance appraisals, and fear or tension.

Experience has shown that positive rewards tend to motivate best in most circumstances; however, negative motivators are also frequently used by organizations. Many organizations assume that only financial motivators will lead to desired behaviors. However, many organizations have obtained great success with nonfinancial rewards. Typically, a combination of both provides optimal results. Timing is also an important consideration in motivating performance with reward systems. Rewards systems should be based on both short and long term achievements so that employees can receive both immediate feedback and yet be motivated to strive for the longer term strategic goals.

Although reward systems are contingent upon the internal and external contingencies and the specific circumstances around which a sports marketing group must operate, there are some important general guidelines for developing effective reward systems (see Table 16.3).

In summary, reward systems are critical to the successful achievement of the strategic sports marketing plan. To be effective, these systems must motivate behavior that "fits" with and ensures adequate attention to the strategic plan.

INFORMATION

Accurate information is an essential guide for decision making and action, and necessary for all phases of the strategic sports marketing process. Execution of the sports marketing plan depends on effective information systems. These systems should provide

TABLE 16.3 Guidelines for Designing Reward Systems

1. Rewards must be tightly linked to the strategic plan.
2. Use variable incentives and make them part of the compensation plan for everyone involved in strategy execution.
3. Rewards should be linked to outcomes that the individual can personally effect.
4. Performance and relationship to the success of the strategy should be rewarded rather than the position held by the individual.
5. Be sensitive to the discrepancies between top and bottom of the organization.
6. Give everyone the opportunity to be rewarded.
7. Being fair and open can lead to more effective reward systems.
8. Reward success generously—make the reward enough to matter and motivate.
9. Do not underestimate the value of nonfinancial rewards.
10. Be willing and open to adapting the reward system to people and situation changes.

Source: John Pearce and Richard Robinson, *Formulation, Implementation, and Control of Competitive Strategy*, 5th ed. (Boston: Irwin, 1994).

the necessary information but should not offer more than is needed to give a reliable picture of issues critical to the implementation of the strategy.

Reports of information must be timely. The flow of information should be simple, including all the critical data being reported only to the people who need it. In other words, reports do not necessarily need "wide distribution."

To aid strategy implementation, information reports should be designed to make it easy to flag variances from the strategic plan. In designing these reports, the critical questions to ask are as follows:

1. Who is going to need this information?
2. For what purpose will they need it?
3. When do they need it?

The NHL provides an example of a sports organization who enhanced their ability to implement marketing strategy through an information system.[10] One of the organizational objectives of the NHL was to make better use of emerging technologies. Led by the vision at the top, NHL Commision Gary Bettman believes "everything is connected to everything else" and that the league needs to be a leader in the use of technology to achieve its goals. Toward this end, the NHL has implemented a program called NHL-ICE (Interactive Cyber Enterprises), which has developed information systems for the media, fans, coaches, and players. The NHL-ICE programs also includes the design and content of the NHL Web site, implementing a real-time scoring system that captures statistics for every hockey game, and integrating network computing solutions into the marketing of the league's products and services.

The NBA's Detriot Pistons also present another fine example of information driving strategies. The Pistons have implemented ePrize's Intelligent Promotion Platform (IPP), a proprietary interactive marketing technology used via the Internet. The primary feature of the IPP includes customizing content so that fans can enjoy special offers, coupons, and game experiences based on their registration information and past consumption behaviors In addition, the IPP allows the Pistons to learn more and more about their fans by creating a fan profile through an interactive survey. The system seems to be paying of as the Pistons have increased ticket sales by more than $500,000 in the past two years.[11]

CREATIVITY

The design of the strategic sports marketing plan's implementation phase is concerned with putting in place an effective system for executing marketing programs that will lead to the achievement of goals and objectives developed by the organization. The premise of this book is that the changing and uncertain environments in which sports organizations operate often require the need to adjust or change plans based on changing internal and external contingencies. Innovative plans and processes are vital to finding a fit with those contingencies. Thus, innovation, in the context of the strategic sports marketing process, is concerned with converting ideas and opportunities into a more effective or efficient system.

The **creative process** is the source of those ideas and, therefore, becomes an important component in the successful formulation and implementation of strategic sports marketing plans. Without creative endeavors, innovation is unlikely, if not impossible. An increase in creative efforts should likewise lead to an increase in innovative plans and processes.

When we talk about creativity, it is important to consider both the creative process and the people who engage in that process. The creative process can be learned and used by virtually anyone. However, some people have more experience with and confidence in their ability to be creative than others.

Many organizations can encourage creativity within their employees. This process of creating and innovating within an organization has been referred to as intrapreneurship, or corporate entrepreneurship. Intrapreneurial efforts have become popular as organizations have acknowledged the value of innovation in changing and uncertain environments. The watchword of today's businesses, sports organizations included, is change. As we discussed, innovation is vital to an organization's ability to change and adapt to internal and external contingencies. There are two general steps that can lead to an increase in the number of creative efforts and the resulting innovations: education and training regarding the creative process and establishing an organizational culture and internal environment that encourages creativity.

THE CREATIVE PROCESS

Although creativity is usually associated with promotion, it is important for all elements of the marketing mix. To be competitive, sports organizations must be creative in their pricing, in developing new products and services, and in getting new sports products to the consumer. The first step in increasing creative efforts within a sports organization is educating employees about the creative process. Creativity is a capability that can be learned and practiced. It is a distinctive way of looking at the world and involves seeking relationships between things that others have not seen.

Although they are referred to by different names, there are four commonly agreed-upon steps in the creative process. They are knowledge accumulation, incubation, idea generation, and evaluation and implementation.

The *knowledge accumulation phase* is an often overlooked, but absolutely vital, stage in the process of creating. Extensive exploration and investigation must precede successful creations. Because creations are simply putting together two existing ideas or tangibles in a new way, it is necessary to have an understanding of a variety of related and unrelated topics. This information gathering provides the creator with many different perspectives on the subject under consideration. Information can be gathered through reading, communication with other people, travel, and journal keeping. Simply devoting time to natural curiosities can be useful in this stage. The key is that the more the creator can learn about a broad range of topics, the more they will have to choose from as the new creation is being developed.

In phase two, *the incubation period*, the creative individual allows his or her subconscious to mull over the information gathered in the previous stage by engaging in other activities. The creative effort is dropped for other pursuits. Routine activities, play, rest, and relaxation can often induce the incubation process. "Getting away" from the creative endeavor allows the subconscious mind to consider all the information gathered.

Often, when the creator least expects it, solutions will come. The next stage, *idea generation*, is the stage that is often portrayed as the "lightbulb" coming on in one's mind. The opportunity for this has been set, however, in the first two phases. As the body rests from the research and exploration, the subconscious mind sees the creative opportunity or the "light."

The last stage, *evaluation and implementation*, is often the most difficult. It requires a great deal of self-discipline and perseverance to evaluate the idea and determine whether it will lead to a useful innovation. Following through with that implementation is often even more challenging. This is especially true because those individuals who are able to generate creative ideas are often not the ones who can turn those ideas into innovations. Often creators will fail numerous times as they attempt to implement creative efforts. And as the following article illustrates, sometimes the innovative ideas that do reach the marketplace aren't always the most welcomed.

Worst Sports Innovations

This is a list of the worst innovations in sports and their ranking, voted on by the fans, officials, and the players.

1. **Performance-enhancing drugs**—Steroids, human growth hormone, greenies, and God-knows-what else. Have sports gotten more exciting since these products flooded the market? No. Everyone gets better at pretty much the same rate (just wait— soon the pitchers will catch up to the hitters, and the old 20 strikeout mark will be obliterated). In the meantime, records become meaningless, and athletes get all kinds of gruesome side effects. Lyle Alzado was a harbinger. More, inevitably, will die young.

2. **Artificial turf**—Dick Allen said in 1970, "If a horse can't eat it, I don't want to play on it." Norman Mailer said, "The injuries are brutal and the fields stink; at the end of the game they smell of vomit and spit and blood because it doesn't go into the earth. All the odors just cook there on this plastic turf." There you have it: Players hate it, fans hate it. Now that test tube strains of green blades can flourish in all kinds of climates, and real grass fields can be cultivated outdoors and slid indoors when it's time to play, it's time for the plastic stuff to go.

3. **BCS**—Bowl Championship Series? No. Bad College System. Bowls make big bucks, but the BCS is just a lousy idea that's eventually going to give way to college football playoffs. As the Atlanta Journal Constitution's Tim Tucker wrote last December, "By putting Nebraska—last seen giving up 62 points and losing by 26 to Colorado— in the national championship game, the BCS surrendered all credibility and exposed itself as even worse than we thought, which was plenty bad enough."

4. **Aluminum bats**—Politicians often do the wrong things, and sometimes say the right things. So we'll just quote from a speech given by Illinois representative Richard H. Durbin in 1989: "Designated hitters, plastic grass, uniforms that look like pajamas, chicken clowns dancing on the baselines, and of course the most heinous sacrilege, lights in Wrigley Field. Are we willing to hear the crack of a bat replaced by the dinky ping? Are we ready to see the Louisville slugger replaced by the aluminum ping dinger? Is nothing sacred?"

5. **Enormous tennis rackets, grooved golf club heads, liquid-centered golf balls, and titanium**—Equipment on steroids. Big, titanium rackets result in 150 mph serves, which lead to lots of aces. Yippee. Big titanium clubs result in 350-yard drives, which lead, inevitably, to longer golf courses. What fun. Altogether, this new equipment has changed the whole balance of power in these sports, it has also changed the meaning of records and history.

6. **Contraction**—Bud Selig does the math and figures that MLB lost $232 million. Forbes magazine does the math and finds that MLB racked up $75 million in profits. As Twins' outfielder Denny Hocking put it, "Gee, should I believe a magazine that spends 365 days a year researching finances? Or a guy who has zero credibility?" Can one former used-car dealer from Milwaukee ruin the national pastime? Twenty-nine other owners are hoping to find out. Proof that making a bundle of money doesn't make you an economic genius.

7. **Indoor football (NFL domes)**—Another strategy masher, for a sport that needs to encourage more innovation, not more sameness. Last year's great Patriots-Raiders playoff game in the snow was a tantalizing glimpse of all we've lost to climate control.

8. **Naming rights**—We have no beef with Campbell Soup Field, the home of the Camden (N.J.) Riversharks. But think about it. Enron. PSInet. TWA. Fruit of the Loom. What do these companies have in common? They all went bankrupt. What else? They all bought stadium naming rights. Fans don't benefit, and what ballclub benefits by association with the losers of the business world?

9. **Off-Track Betting (OTB)**—OTB seemed like a spiffy idea when it was launched in New York City on April 8, 1971—state-sanctioned gambling for days when a player couldn't get out to the track. But over the years, it's proved a losing proposition. OTB has ruined racing in New York and in lots of other places all over the country—the tracks have become wastelands, with attendance falling precipitously almost everywhere. Major stakes races have disappeared, purses have dropped, fields have gotten smaller, racing has gotten worse, as the state drains much-needed money away from a dying sport without giving much back. The sport of kings is becoming largely a studio sport, with little to differentiate it from state lottery gimmicks, except it's a lot slower.

(Continued)

(Continued)

10. **Olympic hockey shootout**—Although numerous pundits clamored for the NHL to adopt many of the international rules showcased in Salt Lake City, there's no disputing the NHL's sudden-death, let-'em-play-until-somebody-scores overtime method is the best way to determine a winner. Penalty shots are a nice skills showcase, but it's like having a free throw or slam dunk contest to decide a winning team in basketball.

Also receiving votes:

- The save statistic in baseball
- NHL's glowing puck
- Penalty kicks to decide a winner in soccer
- Publicly funded ballparks
- Body armor for hitters
- Zone defenses in the NBA
- 3-pointers
- Personal seat licenses

Source: ESPN.com, "Worst Sports Innovations," ESPN staff report, 2003. Reprinted courtesy of ESPN.com.

ENCOURAGING INTRAPRENEURSHIP

Creative efforts and the innovations within organizations are a function of both individual and organizational factors. Entrepreneurial employees add value to the organization and enhance implementation by finding creative ways to achieve the strategic plan. However, these efforts can flourish only if organizational features foster creativity. To encourage an intrapreneurial environment, staff members must be rewarded for entrepreneurial thinking and must be allowed and even encouraged to take risks. Failure and mistakes must be allowed and even valued as a means to creative and innovative expression.

The key to successfully creating a climate that encourages creativity and innovation is to understand the components of such an atmosphere. Those components include management support, worker autonomy, rewards, time availability, and flexible organizational boundaries. To understand these components, consider the following guidelines used at 3M Company[12]:

- *Do Not Kill a Project*—If an idea does not seem to find a home in one of 3M's divisions at first, 3M staff member can devote 15 percent of their time to prove it is workable. In addition, grant money is often provided for these pursuits.
- *Tolerate Failure and Encourage Risk*—Divisions at 3M have goals of 25–30 percent of sales from products introduced within the last five years.
- *Keep Divisions Small*—This will encourage teamwork and close relationships.
- *Motivate Champions*—Financial and nonfinancial rewards are tied to creative output.
- *Stay Close to the Customer*—Frequent contact with the customer can offer opportunities to brainstorm new ideas with them.
- *Share the Wealth*—Innovations, when developed, belong to everyone.

The NHL is just one league that is constantly thinking about creative and innovative approaches to make the game more exciting for its fans. Currently, offensive firepower in the league is sagging and the average number of goals per game is shrinking, One creative solution under consideration to generate more offense is making the rink larger. More specifically, the width of the rink would be expanded from 85 feet to roughly 100 feet. While innovative approaches are typically thought of in terms of adding elements of technology, sometimes change takes place by removing technological advances to sport. For instance, John McEnroe and other retired tennis stars have said that modern tennis technology is killing the game. McEnroe and colleagues have urged the International Tennis Federation to reduce the width of the racquet head from 12.5 inches to 9 inches, which would reduce the amount of baseline play and cause more volleying.

Sports television programmers are continually looking for innovation and creativity to attract viewers. Not long ago, there were no virtual first-down markers, no net cams, and no microphones clipped to managers or coaches. One innovation in sports programming that has received positive feedback is the camera analysis of a baseball bat in motion. ESPN presents information on bat speed and the length of time that the bat is level through the strike zone. This innovation allows viewers to see that the classic advice of "swing level" holds true.[13]

BUDGETING

Budgets are often used as a means of controlling organizational plans. However, the budgeting process can be an important part of the implementation plan if budget development is closely linked to the sports marketing strategy. In fact, the allocation of financial resources can either promote or impede the strategic implementation process.

Marketers within the sports organization must typically deal with two types of budgetary tasks. First, they must obtain the resources necessary for the marketing group to achieve the marketing plan goals. Second, they must make allocation decisions among the marketing activities and functions. These two types of activities require working with individuals and groups internal and external to the sports marketing function.

To develop strategy-supportive budgets, those individuals responsible should have a clear understanding of how to use the financial resources of the organization most effectively to encourage the implementation of the sports marketing strategy. In general, strategy-supportive activities should receive priority budgeting. Depriving strategy-supportive areas of the funds necessary to operate effectively can undermine the implementation process. However, overallocation of funds wastes resources and decreases organizational performance.

In addition, just like the rest of the strategic sports marketing process, the budgeting process is subject to changing and often unpredictable contingencies that may necessitate changes in the marketing budget. A change in strategy nearly always calls for budget reallocation. Thus, those individuals who are responsible for developing budgets must be willing to shift resources when strategy changes.

CONTROL

In the uncertain and changing environments in which sports organizations operate, it is critical to consider four questions throughout the strategic sports marketing process.

1. Are the assumptions on which the strategic marketing plan was developed still true?
2. Are there any unexpected changes in the internal or external environment that will affect our plan?
3. Is the marketing strategy being implemented as planned?
4. Are the results produced by the strategy the ones that were intended?

These questions are considered the basis of strategic control and the fundamental issues to be considered in the **control** phase of the strategic sports planning process model. **Strategic control** is defined as the critical evaluation of plans, activities, and results—thereby providing information for future action. As illustrated in Figure 16.2, the control phase of the model is the third step to be considered. However, it is important to note that the arrows allow for "feedforward." In other words, even though we

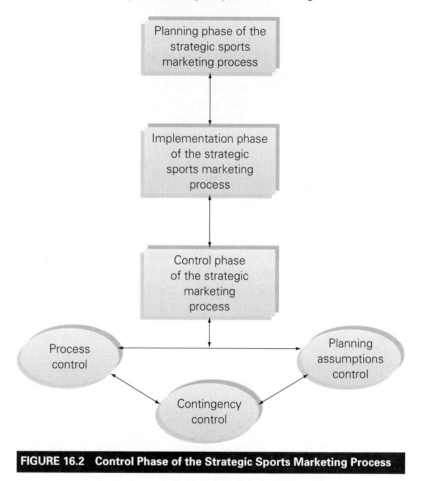

FIGURE 16.2 Control Phase of the Strategic Sports Marketing Process

consider control as the third phase of the model, it is considered as earlier phases of the process are developed. Once the initial plan is developed, the assumptions on which the plan was developed and the internal and external contingencies must be examined and monitored. As the implementation process is set in place and as the plan is executed, strategic control reviews the process as well as the outcomes. Variances from the original assumptions, plans, and processes are noted and changes are made as needed.

The three types of strategic control that sports marketers must consider are planning assumptions control, process control, and contingency control. The following sections outline each of these three types of control.

PLANNING ASSUMPTIONS CONTROL

As we have discussed throughout this text, it is vital to understand internal and external contingencies and formulate strategic sports marketing plans that establish a fit with those contingencies. During the planning phase, it is often necessary to make assumptions concerning future events or contingencies about which we do not have complete information. In addition, individual planners may perceive and interpret data differently. In other words, the strategic sports marketing plan is based on a number of situation-specific premises and assumptions. This level of control attempts to monitor the continuing validity of these assumptions. Thus, in **planning assumptions control,** the sports marketer asks the question: "Are the premises or assumptions used to develop the marketing plan still valid?" To fully evaluate the responses to this question, the assumptions used during the development of the marketing plan must be listed. This step is vital to the success of this control mechanism so those individuals who are responsible can monitor them throughout the process.

A good example of planning assumptions control at work was the merger of Depaul University, Marquette University, University of Louisville, University of South Florida, and the University of Cincinnati into the Big East Conference. The move from Conference USA to the Big East is set to take place in July 2005 and commissioner Mike Tranghese couldn't be happier. The schools' assumption is that they are moving to a stronger conference in terms of both athletic and academic success (enhancing their product), while the Big East is capturing even more media exposure with some major markets in the United States (enhancing their chance to spromote the league and capture more revenues).[14] Another example of a planning control assumption no longer being valid was the marketing of the All-American image of Kobe Bryant. The corporations that market through Bryant had to seriously rethink their plans when Bryant was accused of rape in 2003.

Because of the complexity of the decision-making process, it may be impossible to monitor all the assumptions or premises used to formulate the strategic sports marketing plan. Therefore, it is often practical not only to list the premises, but also to prioritize them based on those that may most likely effect a change in the marketing plan.

Although all assumptions should be considered in this form of control, there are two categories of premises that are most likely to be of concern to the sports marketer: external environmental factors and sports industry factors. As we discussed earlier, strategic sports marketing plans are usually based on key premises about many of these variables. Some examples of external environmental factors include technology, inflation, interest rates, regulation, and demographic and social changes. The relevant sports industry in which a sports organization operates is also usually a key premise aspect in designing a marketing plan. Competitors, suppliers, league regulations, and leadership are among the industry-specific issues that need to be considered when identifying the critical assumptions used to develop the strategic plan.

Although monitoring the premises or assumptions used to develop the strategic sports marketing plan is vital to the control phase of the strategic sports marketing process, it is not sufficient. In other words, this form of control does not measure how well the actual plan is progressing or is it able to take into account the aspects of the internal and external environment that could not be detected during the planning phase when the premises were developed. Thus, effective control must consider two additional forms of evaluation: process control and contingency control.

PROCESS CONTROL

Process control monitors the process to determine whether it is unfolding as expected and as desired. This type of control measures and evaluates the effects of actions that have already been taken in an effort to execute the plan.

Because of changes in premises and contingencies, the realized strategic marketing plan is often not the intended strategic marketing plan. Changes and modifications to the plan usually occur as a result of the process control activities carried out by marketers. In other words, during this stage of control, sports marketers attempt to review the plan and the implementation process to determine whether both remain appropriate to the contingencies. Either the marketing plan or the implementation process put in place to execute the plan may not proceed as intended. These variances may lead to a need to change the plan or the process or both. Thus, the key question asked by this form of control is: "Should either the strategic plan or the implementation process be changed in light of events and actions that have occurred during the implementation of the plan?" It is important to note that to change or modify the marketing plan or implementation process is not necessarily a decision to avoid. The benefit of this form of control is that sports marketers can minimize the allocation of resources into a strategic plan or implementation process that is not leading to achievement of the objectives and goals deemed important by the sports organization.

To answer the preceding question, two measures are typically used: *monitoring strategic thrusts* and *reviewing milestones*. As we discussed earlier, the strategic sports marketing plan is a means of achieving strategic and financial organizational goals and marketing objectives. An important part of evaluating the plan and process is to review the achievement of these objectives and goals during the execution of the plan. Because objectives are not time specific or time bound (as discussed in Chapter 3), strategic thrusts can be examined to evaluate progress in the direction of strategic and financial objectives. On the other hand, reviewing milestones typically examines achievement of marketing objectives. Let us look at each of these two forms of process control more closely.

MONITORING STRATEGIC THRUSTS

Monitoring strategic thrusts attempts to evaluate or monitor the strategic direction of the plan. As a part of the overall strategic plan, smaller projects are usually planned that will lead to the achievement of the planned strategy. Successful pursuit of these smaller projects can provide evidence that the strategic thrust is the intended one. However, if these projects are getting lost to other "nonstrategic" projects, it could mean that the overall strategy is not progressing as planned.

One strategic thrust of special interest to sports organizations and organizations marketing their products through sports is, of course, sponsorship. Determining the effectiveness of a sponsorship program is becoming increasingly more important as the costs of sponsorship continue to rise. Just how, then, do we measure or determine whether we are seeing a return on our marketing investment. Lesa Ukman, president of IEG Chicago, which publishes the IEG sponsorship report, believes sponsorship return can be measured. Ukman stresses the following regarding sponsorship measures[15]:

Sponsorship return can be measured. The key lies in defining objectives, establishing a presponsorship benchmark against which to measure, and maintaining consistent levels of advertising and promotion so that it is possible to isolate the effect of sponsorship.

The lack of a universal yardstick for measuring sponsorship is a problem, but it is also an opportunity. The problem is that sponsorships often are dropped, not

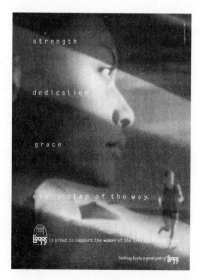

Sponsorship represents a strategic thrust that must be monitored.

Source: Used by permission of Sarah Lee Corporation.

because they don't have measurement value, but because no one has actually measured the value.

The lack of a single, standardized measurement is also an opportunity because it means sponsors can tailor their measurement systems to gauge their specific objectives.

Although there are no universal measures, here are a few of the more popular ways of measuring sponsorship effectiveness against the objectives of awareness and exposure, sales, attitude change, and enhancing channel-of-distribution relationships:

- Number of stories and mentions in popular media, such as newspapers, televised shows, and magazines, serve as a measure of exposure. For example, John Hancock Financial Services measures the impact of its football bowl sponsorship using this method. In one year, approximately 21 binders of newspaper clippings were collected at an estimated advertising equivalency of $1 million.[16]

Awareness is also assessed through "media equivalencies." That is, determining how much "free" time the sponsor has accumulated through television coverage. For example, Julius Joyce and Associates has estimated that Budweiser was the biggest exposure winner among the sponsors of the 2003 Daytona 500 as the brand collected more than 27 minutes of on-camera time and 20 mentions, bringing about a comparable value of $16.1 million. While the measurement of brand exposure has historically used human observation, new companies like Margaux Matrix are testing electronic tools to perform the same operation more accurately.[17] Not all researchers are sold on the notion of media equivalences. In fact, public relations firm Jeffries-Fox's most recent study conclusions led to the official Institute for Public Relations (IPR) position that "The IPR Commission does not endorse Ad Value Equivalencies as a measurement tool."[18]

Sponsorship ROI evaluation.

Source: Used by permission of Joyce Julius & Associates, www.joycejulius.com. All rights reserved.

• Sales figures for products and services can be examined both prior to (pre) and after (post) the event to estimate the potential impact of the sponsorship. Other methods of tracking sales include looking at sales for the sponsorship period versus the same time period in prior years or measuring sales in the immediate area versus national sales. In addition, sales might be tied directly to the sponsored event. For example, discounts for products might be offered with proof of attending the event (show ticket stub); therefore, the number of redemptions might be tracked. Of course, many other factors, such as competitive reaction and additional sales promotions, will influence the sales figures.

One final variation of measuring the impact of sales is to involve the sales force in tracking the value of leads and contacts generated through sponsorship.

• To assess consumer attitudes toward various products and services, as well as the sponsored event, research is conducted in the form of surveys or in-depth interviews. This primary market research is used to gauge the image of the event and its sponsors, attitudes that consumers have toward the event and its sponsors, and awareness of events and sponsors' products and services. Let us look at the following example taken from the Western Open golf tournament, which is featured on CBS over the Fourth of July holiday.[19]

In early 1994, Motorola decided to become a title sponsor of the Western Open golf tournament. Motorola's objectives where to enhance awareness levels and change attitudes toward Motorola's products and services among their target market. In this case, the target audience was defined as adults in the United States with annual household income levels of $25,000 or more and who indicated that they regularly or sometimes follow professional golf.

Their research approach consisted of a two-phased, before and after design that would help understand whether promotional objectives were being met. Phase one consisted of a telephone survey of a representative sample of 500 eligible adult respondents two months prior to the tournament. The purpose of this survey was to determine general awareness levels and attitudes of Motorola's products and services. Phase two was a follow-up telephone survey of a second representative sample two weeks after the tournament to assess whether awareness and attitudes had changed.

Sponsors such as Jaguar and Castrol must design controls to evaluate sponsorship effectiveness.

The research found that over one third of the golf enthusiasts interviewed had watched the Motorola Western Open on CBS. Using aided recall, one of four respondents was able to identify Motorola's title sponsorship of the tournament. Large groups of respondents reported that Motorola's title sponsorship of the tournament directly influenced their attitudes toward the company. Nearly half of the respondents agreed Motorola's image as a quality company improved because of the sponsorship. In addition, nearly 40 percent of the respondents in the follow-up study claimed they now had even higher regard for Motorola than they did before the event. Almost 33 percent stated they were now more likely to purchase Motorola's products, and 26 percent reported their awareness of the company's products and services had increased.

When determining the impact of sponsorship on channels of distribution, it is common practice to track the number of outlets carrying the given product before and after the sponsored event. In addition, sponsors may want to assess the number of retailers or dealers participating in a program versus previous promotions. Finally, companies may measure incremental display at the point of purchase in retail outlets.

For example, Kraft General Food, Inc.'s, primary objective for sponsorship of a NASCAR team for Country Time Drink Mix was to enhance distribution in the Southeast and in-store merchandising nationally. To this end, Kraft created a promotion in which consumers, who had a proof of purchase, could get to ride in a race car simulator. The simulator ride offer increased sales 66 percent in the Southeast and generated more than 40 incremental case displays at each retail stop nationwide.[20]

MILESTONE REVIEW

The second form of process control is **milestone review.** Marketing managers at sports organizations usually establish milestones that will be reached during the execution of the marketing plan. These milestones may be critical events, major allocations, achievements, or even the passage of a certain amount of time. As these milestones are reviewed on a continuous basis, an evaluation of the advisability of continuing with the plan and the process is afforded.

FINANCIAL ANALYSIS

Financial information can be used to understand and control the process of strategic marketing plan implementation; that is, to perform **financial analyses.** It is important for any sports organization to have a good accounting system. In terms of process control, the accounting system can provide the following:

- A ready comparison of present financial performance with past performance, industry standards, and budgeted goals.
- Reports and financial statements that can be used to make appropriate strategic decisions.
- A way of collecting and processing information that can be used in the strategic sports marketing process.

Two important components of a good accounting system are the *income statement* and *balance sheet*. Income statements provide a summary of operating performance. These documents summarize both money coming into and going out of the sports organization and the marketing department or division. Because income statements are a good measure of customer satisfaction and operating efficiency, they should be prepared frequently—at least every three months, if not monthly. Balance sheets provide a summary of the financial health of the sports organization at a distinct point in time. The balance sheet provides the sports marketer with a summary of what the organization is worth; what has been invested in assets, such as inventories, land, and equipment; how the assets were financed; and who has claims against the assets. Tables 16.4A and 16.4B

TABLE 16.4A   Rich Creek Rockers

Income Statement for the Year Ended December 31, 1998

Revenues:		
Single game admissions	$140,000	
Season ticket holders	275,000	
Concessions	250,000	
Advertising revenue	95,000	760,000
Expenses:		
Cost of concessions sold	100,000	
Salary expense—players	235,000	
Salary and wages—staff	130,000	
Rent	150,000	615,000
Profits before taxes		145,000
Income tax		33,000
Income after taxes		$112,000

TABLE 16.4B   Rich Creek Rockers

Balance Sheet at December 31, 1998

Assets		*Liabilities and Owner's Equity*	
Cash	$10,000	Accounts payable	$20,000
Accounts receivables	82,000	Capital stock	50,000
Equipment	40,000	Retained earnings	62,000
Total assets	$132,000	Total liabilities and owner's equity	$132,000

provide simple examples of the information typically found on income statements and balance sheets.

One of the more useful methods of financial analysis for control purposes is known as **ratio analysis.** Financial ratios are computed from income statements and balance sheets. These ratios can tell the sports marketing manager a lot about the progress and success of the strategic sports marketing plan. In other words, using financial ratios can help a sports marketing manager assess whether the marketing strategy continues to provide an appropriate fit with internal and external contingencies. There are several types of financial ratios that can be categorized as follows:

- *Profitability Ratios*—Provide an indication of how profitable the organization or division is during a period of time.
- *Liquidity Ratios*—Indicate the ability of the organization to pay off short-term obligations without selling off assets.
- *Leverage Ratios*—Measure the extent to which creditors finance the organization.
- *Activity Ratios*—Measure the sales productivity and utilization of assets.
- *Other Ratios*—Determine such things as return to owners in dividends, the percentage of profits paid out in dividends, and discretionary funds.

Table 16.5 lists some of the more commonly used ratios, how each is calculated, and what each can tell the sports marketing manager. Examples of how these ratios are applied and interpreted are shown in Table 16.6.

TABLE 16.5 Summary of Selected Key Financial Ratios

Ratio	Calculation	Question(s) Answered
Gross profit margin	$\dfrac{\text{Sales} - \text{Cost of goods sold}}{\text{Sales}}$	What is the total margin available to cover operating expenses and provide profit?
Net profit margin	$\dfrac{\text{Profits after taxes}}{\text{Sales}}$	Are profits high enough given the level of sales? Are we operating efficiently?
Return on total assets	$\dfrac{\text{Profit after taxes}}{\text{Total assets}}$	How wisely has management employed assets?
Asset turnover	$\dfrac{\text{Sales}}{\text{Average total assets}}$	How well are assets being used to generate sales revenue?
Current ratio	$\dfrac{\text{Current assets}}{\text{Current liabilities}}$	Does our organization have enough cash or other liquid assets to cover short-term obligations?
Debt-to-assets load	$\dfrac{\text{Total debt}}{\text{Total assets}}$	Is the organization's debt excessive?
Inventory turnover	$\dfrac{\text{Cost of goods sold}}{\text{Average inventory}}$	Is too much cash tied up in inventories?
Accounts receivables turnover	$\dfrac{\text{Annual credit sales}}{\text{Accounts receivables}}$	What is the average length of time it takes our firm to collect for sales made on credit?

TABLE 16.6 Examples of Financial Ratios

Net profit margin $\qquad \dfrac{112,000}{760,000} = 14.7\%$

Interpretation—Approximately 15 percent of sales is yielding profits. This percentage should be compared with industry (similar sports organizations) averages and examined over a period of several years. Declining or subpar percent could mean expenses are too high, prices are too low, or both.

Return on assets $\qquad \dfrac{112,000}{132,000} = 84.8\%$

Interpretation—This is a measure of the productivity of the assets in the sports organization. Once again, this number should be compared with similar sports organizations and examined over several years. If this number is declining, it may indicate that assets are not being used as effectively or efficiently as they were in previous years.

Inventory turnover $\qquad \dfrac{2,500,000}{100,000} = 25$ times

Interpretation—Inventory turnover is a measure of the number of times inventory is sold during a period of time. Assuming an average inventory of $100,000 (beginning inventory + ending inventory/2) the inventory (in this example—concessions) was sold 25 times. If this number is higher than the average for this type of sports organization, then ordering costs may be too high and stockouts may be occurring. If the number is lower, it may mean too much inventory is being stored, tying up money unnecessarily, and the products (in this case—food) may lack freshness.

CONTINGENCY CONTROL

The third form of control, **contingency control,** is based on the assumption that sports marketers operate in an uncertain and unpredictable environment and that the changing nature of the internal and external environments may lead to the need to reassess strategic choices. Although it is included as a part of the control phase, this form of control should be of concern throughout the strategic sports marketing process.

The goal of contingency control is to constantly scan the relevant environments for internal and external contingencies that could affect the marketing planning process. Unlike planning assumptions control, the goal here is to remain unfocused so any unanticipated events will not be missed. In other words, the "big picture" is of most concern in this phase of control. The primary question to be addressed here is: "How can we protect our marketing strategy from unexpected events or crises that could affect our ability to pursue the chosen strategic direction?" The following spotlight on sports marketing ethics presents one major event that could impact the very nature of intercollegiate athletics and the way it is marketed.

Attempts to control without a prestructured list of variables of concern may not seem to make sense at first. However, it is easier to understand this form of control if one thinks in terms of how a crisis usually occurs. The daily events leading up to an unpredicted event lead to a focus in the form of a crisis. Previously unimportant or unnoticed events become more problematic until an actual crisis requires some action. Learning to notice and interpret signals thus becomes an important way to circumvent crises. Thus, the goal of contingency control is to learn to notice these signals and to have a plan of action in place to cope with a crisis if it occurs.

Sports scandals and crises are not infrequent. Anyone who reads a newspaper sports section has observed situations that could lead to a public relations nightmare for a sports organization or individual athlete. For example, some of the bigger scandals in professional sport for 2003 included the following: Laker star Kobe Bryant being charged with sexual assault; Sammy Sosa being suspended for using an illegal corked bat; the baseball steroids issue implicating slugger Barry Bonds; Pirate first baseman Randall Simon hitting a "sausage" in a mascot race with his bat; the Hootie Johnson and Martha Burk showdown at the Masters Tournament; and these are just a few of the stories in professional sports.[21]

College athletes and athletic programs have also been frought with scandals: St. Bonaventure University forfeits six games for using an ineligible player and players refuse to take the court for the last two games—ultimately the Chair of the Board commits suicide; Iowa State assistant coach resigns after charges of child pornography; the University of Georgia fires basketball coaches Jim Harrick Jr. and Sr. for academic fraud; NCAA takes scholarships from University of Arkansas after finding a booster improperly paid players; the University of Alabama fires its football coach after learning he visited a strip club; the University of Washington fires its football coach after learning about his betting on NCAA games; Patrick Dennehy of Baylor is shot by teammate Carlton Dotson; and Ohio State suspends Maurice Clarett for filing a false report of stolen property. . . . and that's just half the number of major scandals facing colleges and universities.[22]

Although crises such as these are unpredictable, it is useful to plan so the chosen response can be not only faster, but also more effective. A **crisis plan** should include the following[23]:

- Well-defined organizational response strategies,
- Specific procedures that will lead to more efficient and effective response,

SPOTLIGHT ON SPORTS MARKETING ETHICS

Should We Pay Them for Play?

As another year of college sports will soon end, we are thankful for the athletes. Without receiving paychecks, college athletes play their hearts out for their schools. Some feel that college athletes, who spend many hours on the practice field and bring much prestige to their schools, deserve to be paid for their efforts. The payment of college athletes presents many problems to universities, however, and it should not be permitted.

Athlete salaries would cause greater financial strain for the many major colleges whose athletic programs lose money. To turn a profit, most major athletic programs require the input of money from the school itself. An NCAA survey reports that, without this institutional support, only 35 percent of Division I-A athletic programs and fewer than 10 percent of I-AA programs were profitable in 2001. According to the same NCAA survey, the average 2001 financial positions for I-A and I-AA athletic programs, minus institutional support, were losses of $600,000 and $3.4 million, respectively. Many athletic departments already spend millions on scholarships, which are appropriate remuneration for student athletes. The payment of athletes will needlessly draw more institutional funds away from appropriate areas of spending.

While the spirit of a big game can unite nonathletes with their teams, athlete salaries will cause divisions in student bodies. Colleges will become the athletes' "employers," and "fellow" students will be the customers who help pay their salaries. Nonathletes will feel alienated from the athletes, though they both share the same campus and even the same classes. If athletes are paid based on revenue their sports produce, divisions may form even among the athletes. Football, on average, generates far more revenue than any other college sport, according to the NCAA. Football players, who would be paid the most, could develop condescending attitudes toward "less-important" athletes.

Further, paid college athletes are more likely to fall into academic apathy. Why should athletes care about school when they are getting paid to shoot a basketball? Writing paychecks for athletes implies that they are at college to perform on the playing field and prepare for the pros—not to learn in the classroom. This message is a disservice to the athlete, who must be encouraged to persevere in academics despite the time demands of a sport. It is also an insult to the studious nonathlete, who may be paying a hefty tuition for an education that many athletes receive for free or at a discount.

With the demands of college athletics today, many athletes do not have time for jobs while school is in session. How can colleges support athletes financially without paying salaries? For one, the NCAA permits colleges to pay stipends for housing and some meals to athletes who live off-campus. The NCAA Special Assistance Fund is also available to cover $500 of transportation and clothing costs and some medical expenses for financially needy athletes. Athletic department personnel can also make a greater effort to help athletes find jobs during summer and breaks. The NCAA permits athletes to earn as much as they can during these vacations. Lastly, universities can commit more money to athletic scholarships. Scholarships, not salaries, indicate that an education is the real purpose for attending college, even if they are awarded based on athletic skill.

It is vital that the NCAA adamantly preserve the amateur status of college sports. Though college athletes should be praised for their talents, they do not deserve to be paid for them. As Ralph Waldo Emerson observed, "Money often costs too much." With the negative repercussions for nonathletes and athletes alike, the cost of paying college athletes is just too great.

Source: Kevin Hansen, "College athletes: Don't pay them," *South Bend Tribune* (Indiana) (May 8, 2003), A11. Used by permission. All rights reserved.

- Steps that will deal effectively with potential media impact and will enhance image, and
- Efficient ways to deal with a variety of problems that could occur.

Moreover sports organizations may benefit from an informal and a formal crisis response plan. The key is that any crisis plan should offer priorities for proactive and reactive response under a variety of circumstances. It should have the capacity to both alert and calm people during an unexpected event that could have potential for major consequences.

Summary

Implementing and controlling the strategic sports marketing process is the emphasis of Chapter 16. After the planning phase of the strategic marketing process is completed, the implementation and control phases are considered. Implementation is described as an action step where strategic marketing plans are executed. Without the proper execution, the best plans in the world would be useless. To facilitate the implementation process, seven organizational design elements must be addressed. The organizational design elements include communication, staffing and skills, coordination, rewards, information, creativity, and budgeting. To begin, the organization must effectively communicate the plan and its rationale to all the members of the sports marketing team who will play a role in executing the plan. In terms of staffing and skills, there must be enough people and they must have the necessary skills and expertise to successfully implement the strategic marketing plan. Research has shown that the skills deemed most important for sports marketing managers include establishing a positive image for your sports organization, achieving sponsors' promotional goals, stimulating ticket sales, maximizing media exposure for events, athletes, and sponsors, and acquiring sponsors through personal contacts.

Coordination is another of the organizational design elements that influences implementation. Coordination involves determining the best structure for the organization to achieve the desired strategy. Research has shown the importance of good fit between structure and successful implementation. One way of coordinating people and tasks that has received considerable attention over the last decade is through total quality management (TQM). TQM philosophies are based on aligning the organizational structure to best meet the needs of the customers.

Another important organizational design element that affects implementation is the rewards structure of the sports organization. With proper pay and incentives, employees may be motivated to carry out the strategic plan. Some guidelines for designing effective rewards systems include linking rewards to the strategic plan, using a variety of incentives: link performance with rewards, give everyone the opportunity to be rewarded, and be willing to adapt the rewards system.

Information is one of the most essential elements of effective implementation. To aid in the gathering and dissemination of information for strategic decision making, organizations must design information systems. Before gathering information, consideration must be given to who is going to need this information, for what purpose the information is needed, and when do they need it?

Fostering creativity, another organizational design element, is yet another important aspect of implementation. Creativity and innovation within the organzation is called intrapreneurship or corporate entrepreneurship and is developed through education and training. To enhance employee creativity the creative process, consisting of four steps, is used by organizations. These steps include knowledge accumulation, idea generation, evaluation, and implementation. Efforts to encourage intrapreneurship are also enhanced by creating an organizational environment that cultivates such thinking.

The final organizational design element that has a direct impact on implementation is budgeting. Without proper monies, the strategic sports marketing plan cannot be properly implemented or carried out. Budgets must be secured for all marketing efforts within the larger organization. Once these monies are obtained, they must then be allocated within marketing to achieve specific marketing goals that have been prioritized.

After plans have been implemented, the control phase of the strategic sports marketing process is considered. Strategic control is defined as the critical evaluation of plans, activities, and results, thereby providing information for future action. In other words, the control phase explores how well the plan is meeting objectives and makes suggestions for adapting the plan to achieve the desired results. Three types of strategic control considered by sports marketers include planning assumptions control, process control, and contingency control.

Planning assumptions control asks whether the premises or assumptions used to develop the marketing plan are still valid. Two categories of assumptions that should receive special consideration from sports marketers are those concerned with the external contingencies and the sports industry. Because plans are typically developed by carefully considering the external environment and the sports industry, assumptions with respect to these two issues are critical.

Process control considers whether the plan and processes used to carry out the plan are being executed as desired. The key issue addressed by process control is whether the planning or implementation processes should be altered in light of events and actions that have occurred during the implementation of the plan. To make decisions about whether plans or the implementation process should be changed, sports organizations review milestones that have been set or monitor strategic thrusts. Milestones such as financial performance are more specific objectives that can be examined, while strategic thrust evaluates whether the organization is moving toward its intended goals.

Key Terms

- activity ratios
- budgeting
- communication

- contingency control
- control
- coordination

- creative process
- creativity
- crisis plan

- financial analyses
- implementation
- information
- leverage ratios
- liquidity ratios

- milestone review
- monitoring strategic thrusts
- planning assumptions control
- process control
- profitability ratios

- ratio analysis
- rewards
- staffing and skills
- strategic control
- total quality management (TQM)

Review Questions

1. What are the organizational design elements that must be managed for effective implementation?
2. Why must there be a fit between planning and implementation phases of the strategic sports marketing process?
3. What are some of the common ways of communicating with groups both inside and outside the sports organization?
4. What are the marketing-specific core competencies of the sports marketing manager?
5. Define TQM. What are the common characteristics of any TQM program? Why is it important for sports organizations to practice a TQM philosophy?
6. What are the guidelines for designing rewards systems?
7. What is intrapreneurship? What are the four steps in the creative process? How can sports organizations encourage intrapreneurship?
8. Define strategic control. What are the three types of strategic control that sports marketers must consider?
9. What two measures are typically used during process control?
10. How can we evaluate sponsorship effectiveness?
11. Describe the different financial ratios that can be calculated to assess whether a sports organization's financial objectives are being met.
12. What are the fundamental components of a crisis plan?

Exercises

1. Describe three sports organizations that have a strong leader who communicates well outside the sports organization. What are the common characteristics of these leaders, and why do these leaders communicate effectively?
2. How does the training that you are receiving compliment the marketing-specific skills required of sports marketing managers?
3. Locate the organizational charts for the marketing department of two professional sports organizations. How will this structure facilitate or impede the implementation of their strategic marketing effort?
4. Design a rewards system to encourage intrapreneurship.
5. Discuss the last three major "crises" in sport (at any level). How did the organizations or individuals handle these crises?
6. Discuss how being the quarterback of a football team is similar to being a marketer responsible for implementing and controlling the strategic sports marketing process.
7. Interview three marketing managers who are responsible for sponsorship decisions in their organization. Determine how each evaluates the effectiveness of their sponsorship.

Internet Exercises

1. Browse the Web site of the National Sporting Goods Association (www.sgma.com) and discuss how the information found on this site might be useful for developing a strategic marketing plan for the new IBL.
2. Find two Web sites that would provide sports marketing managers with information about whether their planning assumptions regarding demographics of the U.S. population remained valid.
3. Find examples of three nonsports organizations that advertise on ESPN's Web site (www.espn.com). How might these companies evaluate the effectiveness of their Web-based advertising?

Endnotes

1. "Votaw Outlines His Plans for LPGA." www.golftoday.co.uk/news/yeartodate/news99/lpga.html.

2. A. K. Gupta and V. Govindarajan, "Build, Hold or Harvest: Converting Strategic Intentions into Reality," *Journal of Business Strategy* (Winter 1984), 41.

3. Peter Smolianov and Dr. David Shilbury, "An Investigation of Sport Marketing Competencies," *Sport Marketing Quarterly*, vol. 5, no. 4 (1996), 27–36.

4. A. D. Chandler, *Strategy and Structure* (Cambridge, MA: MIT Press, 1963).

5. L. Marlene Mawson, "Total Quality Management: Perspectives for Sport Managers," *Journal of Sport Management*, vol. 7 (1993), 101–106.

6. Harry Roberts and Bernard Sergesketter, *Quality Is Personal* (New York: Free Press, 1993).

7. George Easton and Sherry Jarrel, "The Effects of Total Quality Management on Corporate Performance: An Empirical Investigation," *Journal of Business*, vol. 71, no. 2, 253–261.

8. James Evans and William Lindsay, *The Management and Control of Quality*, 2nd ed. (St. Paul, MN: West, 1993).

9. Ibid.

10. "NHL Teams with IBM to Promote and Enhance Hockey through New Alliance, NHL-ICE." www.issc2.boulder.ibm.com/telmedia/prnhl996.htm; "NHL-ICE: A Virtual Power Play." www.domino.www.ibm.com/ebusine . . . s/ 35E438D34E58CD4A852651E00639D54.

11. "Technology driving the Pistons," http://www.sportandtechnology.com/news.php?pageId=0135#5.

12. Russell Mitchell, "Masters of Innovation," *Business Week* (April 10, 1989), 58–63.

13. Wayne Scanlon, "TV Shows the Swing is Still the Thing," *The Ottawa Citizen* (July 3, 1998), Fl.

14. Lindsey Willhite, "Joining the beast, DePaul sees nothing but upside to making the move with four others from Conference USA to the Big East," *Chicago Daily Herald* (November 5, 2003), 1.

15. Lesa Ulkman, "Evaluating ROI of a Sponsorship Program," *Marketing News* (August 26, 1996), 5.

16. "And Now a Word From Our Sponsors." *Marketing Tools* (June 1995); www.demographics.com/publications/mt/95_mt/9506_mt/mt169.htm; John Burnett, Anil Menon, and Denise Scott, "Sports Marketing: A New Ball Game with Old Rules," *Journal of Advertising Research* (September–October 1993), 21–38.

17. "Sponsorship: Keeping an eye on the ball," *Marketing Week* (October 30, 2003), 43.

18. "Institute for Public Relations Releases First-Ever Guidelines for Measuring Importance of Internet Audience," *U.S. Newswire* (February 17, 2004).

19. "Measuring Effectiveness for Motorola." www.prcentral.com.

20. Lesa Ulkman, "Evaluating ROI of a Sponsorship Program," *Marketing News* (August 26, 1996), 5.

21. Don Bowman "2003 had plenty of feel-good stories, along with a lot of scandal," *Fort Worth Star-Telegram* (December 30, 2003).

22. Welch Suggs "A Hard Year in College Sports: Academic scandals, coaching embarrassments, raids by conferences, and other problems set the tone in 2003," *Chronicle of Higher Education*, http://chronicle.com/prm/weekly/v50/i17/17a03701.htm

23. "Defining Crisis and Crisis Planning." www.sports.mediachallenge.com\crisis\index.html#feature.

Career Opportunities in Sports Marketing

Many of us have dreamed of becoming a professional athlete. Unfortunately, reality sets in rather quickly. We discover that we cannot throw a 90 mile-per-hour fastball or even touch the rim—much less slam-dunk. However, there are many other opportunities for careers in sports. In fact, there are a wide variety of sports careers in sports marketing. In this appendix, we will explore some of the career options in sports marketing and present some interview and resumé writing tips for landing that dream job. Finally, we will examine some additional sources of information on careers in sports marketing.

Before we look at some of the career alternatives in sports marketing, it is useful to think about how the concepts discussed in this text can be useful in your job search. As you know, the strategic marketing process begins by conducting a SWOT analysis. You should build a SWOT into your career planning. First, ask questions about your own strengths and weaknesses. You can be sure the organizations you interview with will be asking similar questions. Next, try to identify the opportunities that exist in the marketplace. What sports are hot? Where are the growth areas in sports marketing?

The next step of your strategic career search should be to gather information and conduct research on prospective employers. Research could be conducted by talking to people within the organization to gain a better understanding of the culture. In addition, observation might take place both before and certainly during the interview.

Next, you need to consider your target market. Do not apply for all of the sports marketing jobs in the world. Target the job opportunities based on location, type of position, and how the position or organization fits with your current and potential strengths. You also need to position yourself. Remember, careers in sports marketing are in demand and you need to find a way to market yourself and stand out from the competition.

The marketing mix variables also should be considered in your job search. The product, in this case, is you. You are the bundle of benefits that is being offered to the prospective organization. You should also enter into the strategic career search with some understanding of price. What is the value you attach to the service and expertise that you will provide? Are the salary and benefits package being offered a satisfactory exchange?

Your resumé, cover letter, interviewing skills, and ability to sell yourself are the elements of the promotion mix. These elements communicate something about you to prospective employers. Finally, the place element of the marketing mix is the location in which you are willing to work.

From this brief discussion, you can begin to understand that finding the right job for yourself in sports marketing can be done in a systematic, organized fashion. By using the basic principles of the strategic marketing process, you will be in a better position to land your dream job. Let us turn our attention to some of the job opportunities that exist in the field of sports marketing.

JOB OPPORTUNITIES IN SPORTS MARKETING

There are a wide variety of jobs in sports marketing that may be of interest to you. Here are just a few of the opportunities that exist. As you look through this section, pay attention to the sample advertisements and the qualifications that are stressed for each position. In addition, remember not to suffer from marketing myopia when you look for your first job. Have a broad perspective and think of your first job as an entrée into the sports industry.

INTERNSHIPS

Nearly 70 percent of sports marketing executives began their careers interning for a sports organization, and 90 percent of sports organizations offer some type of internship. Many sports marketing students believe they will secure high-paying, glamorous, executive-level positions upon completion of their degree. The truth is, jobs in sports marketing are so competitive that internships are usually the only route to gaining the experience needed for a permanent position. By working as an intern, you become familiar with the organization and learn about the sports industry. In turn, the organization learns about you and reduces its risk in hiring you for a permanent position.

Sample Advertisements

- **Sales and Marketing Manager**—Interns will assist the marketing department in the following areas: sponsorship fulfillment, lead qualification, sampling/couponing programs, health and fitness expo at the Los Angeles Convention Center, and race day festival. Must be hardworking, detail-oriented, friendly, energetic, computer-literate, and have good communication skills. Hours would be flexible to fit interns' schedule.
- **Marketing Intern**—We have an opening for a sports marketing intern to assist in marketing programs

designed to facilitate the growth of our products and services. Ideal person should have a sports marketing or sports management background. Computer, organization, and strong communication skills are essential. Internet experience preferred.

FACILITIES MANAGEMENT

Whatever the sport, there must be a place to play. From brand new multimillion-dollar sports complexes such as Citizens Bank Park in Philadelphia to community centers used for recreational sports, facilities management is an important function. Although facilities management positions are more managerial in nature, they do include a strong marketing emphasis. For example, facilities managers are expected to perform public and community relations' tasks, as well as having a strong promotion management background.

Sample Advertisements

- **Advertising and Public Relations Manager**— Opportunity for a creative, energetic, hands-on individual to develop and implement advertising and PR programs for an established golf course facility. Minimum of five years' experience in advertising, design, broadcast production, and media planning. Desktop experience a must. Internet experience a plus. Must be able to maximize pre-established budgets.
- **Facility Manager**—The Special Events Center is seeking candidates for the position of Facility Manager. Candidates should be sales and marketing driven with experience in event planning, marketing and promotions, and facility management. Bachelor's degree with three years' related experience required. Primary liaison between users and facility staff. Provide leadership in event planning, on-site event management, and customer service.

PROFESSIONAL SERVICES

As the sports industry grows, the need for more and more business professionals in all areas is increasing. Today, sports careers are automatically associated with being a sports agent because of the Jerry McGuire "show me the money" phenomenon. However, professional services are also needed in sports law, advertising, accounting, information systems, marketing research, finance, and sports medicine. Having the appropriate educational background before attempting to secure sport industry experience is a must. Salaries for professional services positions vary greatly depending on the job type and responsibilities.

Sample Advertisements

- **Director of Special Olympics**—Seeking persons with excellent communication, fundraising, and management skills. Special Olympics is a year-round program of sports training and competition for children and adults with mental retardation. Responsibilities include planning and organizing competitive events,

training programs, public awareness campaigns, and fund-raising activities. Candidates for position must possess excellent communication and fund-raising skills as well as administrative, organizational, and volunteer management experience. Previous Special Olympics experience not required, but helpful.
- **Global Advertising/Merchandising Manager**— Multinational manufacturer of cycling components. Responsible for leading the creation and execution of global advertising; athlete and event sponsorship; media planning and communication; global product merchandising; global cost center management. This position requires an analytical thinker with excellent leadership and execution skills. A successful candidate is an MBA who has in-depth knowledge of ad strategy, planning, and production.

HEALTH AND FITNESS SERVICES

As the sports-participant market continues to grow, so will jobs in the health and fitness segment of the sports industry. Numerous jobs are available in management and sales for health clubs. Additionally, health and fitness counseling or instruction (personal trainer or aerobics instruction) represents another viable job market in health and fitness. Careers in sports training and sports medicine are also increasing. In addition to working for sports organizations as a trainer or physical therapist, a number of sports medicine clinics (usually affiliated with hospitals) are targeting the recreational participant and creating a host of new jobs in the prevention or rehabilitation of sports injuries.

Sample Advertisements

- **Director of Campus Recreation**—Major responsibilities: provide opportunities to enhance participant fitness, personal skills, and enjoyment for a variety of student recreational activities; supervise, coordinate, and evaluate the activities of the department; prepare operating and capital expenditure budgets; develop goals, objectives, policies, and procedures; and perform personnel administration within the department. Qualifications: Master's degree and three years' experience in recreation or a similar field, two years' experience in administrative position, and current CPR and first aid certification required.
- **Fitness Club Operations Director**—Oversee all pool and tennis associates. Duties include hiring, training, supervising, and reviewing the performance of staff; administering weekly payroll; designing employees work schedules; and overseeing maintenance/ cleanliness of facilities and inventory. Bachelor's degree; minimum two years' experience in athletic club/resort and one year in club management; basic knowledge of tennis, fitness and aquatics; excellent communication skills. Sales and marketing experience, with a strong member services background and experience developing/implementing member retention programs preferred.

SPORTS ASSOCIATIONS

Nearly every sport has a governing body or association that is responsible for maintaining the integrity and furthering the efforts of the sport and its constituents. Examples of sports associations include Federation International Football Association (FIFA), National Sporting Goods Association (NSGA), United States Tennis Association (USTA), and the Thoroughbred Racing Association (TRA). Each sports association has executive directors, membership coordinators, and other jobs to help satisfy the members' needs.

Sample Advertisements

- **U.S. Tennis Association**—Assist Director of Marketing in sponsorship, donations, and ad sales. Professional tournament operations for one tournament and booth promotions at all Northern California tournaments.
- **Research Associate**—A nonprofit golf association. Duties include survey research, statistical analysis, report writing, and database management. Knowledge of SAS and related Bachelor's degree a must. Proficiency required in mapping, spreadsheet, and word processing software. Position requires demonstrated experience in technical writing and good verbal communication skills. Knowledge of the golf industry a plus. Entry-level position.

PROFESSIONAL TEAMS AND LEAGUES

Along with being a sports agent, the types of jobs most commonly associated with sports marketing are in the professional sports industry segment. Working as the director of marketing for one of the "big four" sports leagues (NBA, MLB, NHL, or NFL), or one of the major league teams, requires extensive experience with a minor league franchise or college athletic program and a Master's degree. Job responsibilities include sales, designing advertising campaigns to generate interest in the team, and supervision of game promotions and public relations.

Sample Advertisements

- **Assistant Marketing Director**—Develops season ticket campaign strategies, negotiates advertising and media tradeouts, directs promotion coordinator, sales representative. Master's degree preferred; Bachelor's degree required, preferably in marketing. Excellent communication skills a must. Should have extensive experience in working with corporate sponsors and developing a client base to support athletic sales.
- **Advertising Sales**—Major sports league seeks account executive to sell print advertising for event publications. The ideal candidate will possess two to four years' consumer or trade publication sales experience; excellent written and verbal communication skills; a proven track record of increasing sales volume; and the ability to work in a fast-paced environment and the flexibility to travel.

COLLEGE ATHLETIC PROGRAMS

If your ultimate career objective is to secure a position with a professional team or league, college athletic departments are a great place to start. Nearly all Division I and Division II athletic programs have marketing, sales, and public relations functions. In fact, most of the larger Division I programs have an entire marketing department that is larger than most minor league franchises.

Sample Advertisements

- **Coordinator of the Goal Club**—Responsibilities include identifying, cultivating, soliciting, and stewarding donors together with managing special events and direct mail programs. Candidates must possess a Bachelor's degree and two or three years of fund-raising experience.
- **Athletic Recruiting Coordinator**—Responsibilities include developing and organizing a vigorous recruiting program for eight sports within the guidelines of NCAA III, represent the athletics department at college fairs, and coordinate all recruiting activities with the admissions department.

SPORTING GOODS INDUSTRY

Sporting goods is a $50 billion industry that is growing and presents career choices in all of the more traditional marketing or retailing functions. Opportunities include working for sporting goods manufacturers' (e.g., Nike, adidas, Callaway, or Wilson) or retailers such as Dick's, Sports Authority, or Footlocker.

Sample Advertisements

- **Associate Buyer**—Lady Foot Locker is looking for a professional. To qualify you will need chain store buying experience. Sporting goods exposure a plus.
- **General Manager/Catalog Division**—An outdoor recreation equipment retailer in the burgeoning backpacking/mountaineering/climbing industry is looking for a hands-on GM with full responsibility for its fast growing catalog division. Responsibilities include bottom-line profitability, strategic planning/execution, financial planning, marketing, prospecting, circulation and database management, catalog development and production, purchasing and inventory control, and systems coordination. Qualifications include five-plus years' management in a mail-order operation.

EVENT PLANNING AND MARKETING

Rather than work for a specific team or league, some sports marketers pursue a career in events marketing. Major sporting events such as the World Series, All-Star games, or the Olympics do not happen without the careful planning of an events management organization. The largest and most well-known events management company is the International Management Group (IMG) with offices worldwide. Event marketers are responsible for promoting the event and selling and marketing sponsorships for the event.

Sample Advertisements

- **Event Management Leader**—A service management association serving the bowling industry. Candidates will have a Bachelor's degree in business or hotel management along with a proven track record of professional event production.
- **Event Planner**—National sports marketing firm organizing sports leagues and special events for young professionals, is seeking an entry-level candidate to assist with operations and promotions of sports leagues, parties, and special events. Should be sports minded, extremely outgoing, and organized for this very hands-on position.

RESEARCHING COMPANIES

The previous section gives you a good idea of the types of job opportunities in sports marketing. Having considered your options, it is now time to get serious about finding that first job that will launch an exciting career. You will soon send out cover letters and resumés tailored to each position and organization. If they are not, the prospective employer will sense you have not done your homework. Your research efforts should include the following types of information: age of the organization, services or product lines, competitors within the industry, growth patterns of the organization and of the industry, reputation and corporate culture, number of employees, and financial situation.

Today, most of the organizational information can be obtained quickly and easily via the Internet. Other popular sources of industry and company information include the following: *Team Marketing Report's Inside the Ownership of Professional Sports Teams, Million Dollar Directory* (Dun & Bradstreet), *Standard and Poor's Register,* and *Ward's Business Directory of U.S. Private and Public Companies.*

COVER LETTERS AND RESUMÉS

Once you have researched prospective employers, you are ready to communicate with the organizations that you wish to pursue. Let us look at how to construct simple, yet persuasive, cover letters and resumés. Remember, these documents are within your complete control (think of this as an internal contingency); use this to your advantage and present yourself in the best possible light. Let us begin with the fundamentals of cover letter preparation.

COVER LETTERS

The major objective of any cover letter is to pique the interest of the prospective employer. First impressions are everything and the cover letter is the employer's first glimpse of you. There are a few basic guidelines that you can follow to make your cover letters more effective.

In the first paragraph, state the letter's purpose and how you found out about the position. Follow this with an overview of your most impressive job-related attributes such as skills, knowledge, and expertise. Obviously, the attributes you choose should relate to the position in mind. The third part of the cover letter should stem from all the research previously gathered on the organization. Show off your knowledge of the company and their current needs. Finally, let the organization know how you can help solve their current needs. Stress the fit between your background and values and the organization's culture.

RESUMÉS

Now that your cover letter has been constructed, you are ready to begin work on an effective resumé. Here are seven tips for writing a resumé that are guaranteed to tell your story.

1. **Be Thorough**—A good resumé should give the employer an indication of your potential based on your previous accomplishments. Include things such as job-related skills, previous work experience, educational background, volunteer experiences, special achievements, and personal data.

   Activities that you might deem to be unimportant could provide a great deal of insight into your ability to succeed on the job. For example, how about the student that has coached a little league team throughout his or her collegiate career? Some candidates might view this as totally unrelated to the job. However, the wise candidate will see how this activity could be used to demonstrate unique aspects of their personality such as patience, leadership, and good organizational skills.

2. **Be Creative**—Most students are under the false impression that there is a right way and a wrong way to organize their resumé. In fact, most career development centers use a boilerplate format making every student's resumé standard and neglecting the job and the industry.

   All resumés should include topical areas such as job objectives, skills, knowledge, accomplishments, personal data, education, employment history, observations of superiors, and awards. Organizing and writing these sections is limited only by your imagination. The most important thing to remember is that the format should reflect both you and the job you are seeking.

3. **Use Quotations**—A powerful tool that is not widely used in resumé preparation is the use of quotations. These quotes can be found in old performance evaluations or letters of recommendation. Here is an example of a quote that was used to reinforce the strength of an application.

   "Ms. Verst has contributed in a positive manner to the success of the athletic department at WPU by organizing and implementing an effective game day promotional plan."
   Ed Vanderbeck, promotions manager, athletic department, WPU.

Quotes like this can provide further evidence of your abilities while relieving you of having to toot your own horn.

4. **Make the Resumé Visually Appealing**—Looks are everything. In one study, 60 percent of employers indicated that they formed an opinion about the candidate on the basis of their resumé's appearance. The resumé that looks good will be given more consideration than one that does not. The resumé that is badly written and produced will be tossed, regardless of the applicant's qualifications. A few things to think about when designing your resumé include length (keep it to one page), paper (high-quality stock in white or off-white), spelling, grammar, and neatness (any error is unacceptable).

5. **Include a Career Objective**—Most employers consider the career objective to be the most important part of the resumé. Why? A specific career objective indicates that you know what you want in a job. This type of goal-directed behavior is what employers want to see in a candidate.

On the other hand, some resumé preparation experts strongly disagree with this line of reasoning. They argue that by placing an objective on your resumé, you are limiting the potential position. In other words, if you leave your options open, the employer will direct your resumé to the job that best suits your qualifications.

The best advice is to have multiple resumés prepared and ready to go with multiple career objectives. Most people have multiple career interests and do not have to settle for just one job. If you are truly practicing target marketing, you should have several different resumés ready. You should try to make the career objective sound like the description of the job you are targeting. Here is a sample career objective for a student who wishes to pursue a public/community relations position at a major university or professional sports franchise:

Public Relations Assistant—Interested in copy writing, editing, writing speeches and news releases, photography, graphics, etc. Desire experience on organization's internal and external publications. Good writing and speaking skills with communications background should assist in advancement to a management position within the athletic department of a major university or professional sports organization.

6. **Honesty Is the Best Policy**—Employers are checking prospective candidates' qualifications more than ever before, due to a wave of people falsifying their credentials. Obviously, deceiving the employer about what you have done, or what you are able to do, is no way to start a positive relationship.

7. **Spread the Word**—You should seek feedback and constructive criticism about your resumé by showing it to everyone you know. Ask for comments from other students, your professors, and career development specialists at school. In addition, you should circulate it among people in the sports industry. Resumé writing is a dynamic process that requires constant changes and improvement.

INTERVIEWING

Most jobs in sports marketing require a high degree of interpersonal communication; therefore, the interview becomes a place to showcase your talents. Each person should have his or her own interview style, but here are some tips that should assist all job candidates with their interviewing skills.

1. **Be Mentally Prepared**—As with athletes, mental preparation is the name of the game for job seekers. Most job candidates do not come to the interview fully prepared. To get ready, you should have thoroughly researched the sports organization. Next, you need to learn as much as possible about the person or people who will be conducting the interview. Being mentally prepared means being able to ask intelligent questions. Naturally, the types of questions you ask will vary by the position of the interviewer. Here are just a few of the potential questions that you might ask of the personnel manager or human resource representative:

- What do employees like best about the company? What do employees like least about the company?
- How large is the department in which the opening exists? How is it organized?
- Why is this position open?
- How much travel would normally be expected?
- What type of training program does a new employee receive? What type of professional development programs are offered? Who conducts them?
- How often are performance reviews given and how are they conducted?
- How are raises and promotions determined? What is the salary range of the position?
- What are the employee benefits offered by the company?

Possible questions for your potential supervisor include:

- What are the major responsibilities of the department?
- What are the major responsibilities of the job?
- What would the new employee be expected to accomplish in the first six months or year of the job?

- What are the special projects now ongoing in the department? What are some that are coming in the future?
- How much contact with management is there? How much exposure?
- What is the path to management in this department? How long does it typically take to get there, and how long do people typically stay there?

Here are some questions that might be asked of would-be colleagues:

- What do you like most or least about working in this company? What do you like most or least about working in this department?
- Describe a typical workday.
- Do you feel free to express your ideas and concerns? Does everyone in this department?
- What are the possibilities here for professional growth and promotion?
- How much interaction is there with supervisors, colleagues, external customers? How much independent work is there?
- How long have you been with the company? How does it compare with other companies where you have worked?

2. **Be Physically Prepared**—Image is important to all organizations, and a large part of the image that you project is largely a function of your physical appearance. In other words, if you look the part, the chances of getting the job increase exponentially. The key to dressing for an interview is not only to be professionally dressed, but to convey an image that is consistent with the company and the position. An interview is not the time to redefine the meaning of professional dress. Make sure you feel comfortable in the clothes that you choose to wear to the interview. If you look good and feel good, you will undoubtedly convey these positive feelings throughout the interview.

3. **Practice Makes Perfect**—Many marketing experts have discussed the similarities between finding a job and personal selling. When you are job hunting, you are, in essence, marketing or selling yourself. If you were selling a product, you would strive to become as familiar as possible with that product. You would not only learn the positive features and benefits of the product, but understand the limitations of the product. In this case, you have to know everything the interviewer could conceivably ask about you. This should not be difficult, but you have to be prepared. The best way to prepare is through practice and repetition, so that you feel confident answering questions about yourself.

   The following is a list of questions regarding school, work, and personal experiences that are often asked during the interview. The more you have thought about these questions prior to the interview, the better your responses. Questions pertaining to school experiences might include:

- Which courses did you like most? Why?
- Which courses did you like least? Why?
- Why did you choose your particular major?
- Why did you choose to go to the school you attended? What did you like most or least about this school?
- If you could start college again, what would you do differently?

Questions pertaining to work experiences might include:

- What did you like most or least about the job?
- What did you like most or least about your immediate supervisor?
- Why did you leave the job?
- What were your major accomplishments during this job?
- Of all the jobs you have had, which did you like the most and why? Of all the supervisors you have had, which did you like the most and why?

Questions pertaining to personal experiences might include:

- Of all the things that you have done, what would you consider to be your greatest accomplishment and why?
- What do you consider to be your major strengths? What do you consider to be your major weaknesses?
- What kind of person do you have the most difficulty dealing with? Assuming that you had to work with such a person, how would you do it?
- What do you think are the most valuable skills you would bring to the position for which you are applying?
- What are your short-term goals (within the next five years), and what are your long-term goals?

4. **Maintaining a Proper Balance**—A good interviewee will know when to talk and when to listen. Your job is to present a complete picture of yourself without dominating the conversation. The best strategy for success is adapting to the interviewer and following his or her lead. When you are answering questions, do not let your mouth get ahead of your mind. Take a moment to think and construct your answers before rushing into a vague and senseless reply.

5. **The Interview Process Does Not End with the Interview**—After the interview be sure to write a letter expressing your thanks and desire for future consideration. It is a good idea to mention something in the body of the letter that will trigger the memory of the interviewers. Look for unique things that happened or were said during the interview and write about these. Too often, students neglect writing this simple letter and lose the opportunity to present their professionalism one more time.

Where to Look for Additional Information

1. Beatty, Richard. *The Perfect Cover Letter,* 2nd ed. (New York: John Wiley and Sons, 1996).
2. Carter, David. *You Can't Play the Game If You Don't Know the Rules: Career Opportunities in Sports Management.* San Luis Obispo, CA: Impact, 1994.
3. Field, Shelly. Career Opportunities in the Sports Industry. (Checkmark Books, 1998).
4. Fischer, David. *The 50 Coolest Jobs in Sports: Who Got Them, What They Do, and How Can You Get One!* (New York: Arco, 1997).
5. Grappo, Gary Joesph, and Adele Beatrice Lewis. *How to Write Better Resumés,* 5th ed. Barrons Educational Series, 1998.
6. Karlin, Leonard. *Careers in Sports.* (E. M. Guild Publishers, 1997).
7. Taylor, John. *How to Get a Job in Sports.* (New York: Macmillan, 1992).
8. Heitzmann, William Ray. *Opportunities in Sports and Fitness Careers.* (McGraw-Hill/Contemporary Books, 2003).
9. Tepper, Ron. *Power Resumés.* (New York: John Wiley and Sons, 1998).
10. Yate, Martin John. *Cover Letters That Knock 'Em Dead,* 3rd ed. Adams, 1997.
    www.onlinesports.com/pages/jobs.html
    www.sportscareers.com
    http://www.teammarketing.com/jobs.cfm
    http://www.sgma.com/jobs/index.html
    www.womenssportscareers.com
    www.sportsworkers.com www.jobsinsports.com

APPENDIX B

Sports Marketing Sites of Interest on the Internet

CATEGORY	URL	ANNOTATION
Professional sports	www.nba.com	Official site of the NBA (basketball)
	www.nhl.com	Official site of the NHL (hockey)
	www.nfl.com	Official site of the NFL (football)
	www.mlb.com	Official site of MLB (baseball)
	www.mlsnet.com	Official site of MLS (soccer)
	www.wnba.com	Official site of WNBA (women's basketball)
	www.pga.com	Official site of PGA (golf)
	www.lpga.com	Official site of LPGA (women's golf)
	www.nascar.com	Official site of NASCAR racing
	www.pba.org	Official site of PBA (bowling)
	www.atptour.com	Official site of ATP (tennis)
	www.minorleaguebaseball.com	Official site of Minor Leagues (baseball)
International sports	www.sportcal.co.uk	Database of international sporting events
	www.ausport.gov.au	Australian Sports Directory
	www.ismhome.com	Institute of Sport Management (Australia)
	www.olympic.org	International Olympic Committee
	www.nbcolympics.com	NBC Olympics information
	www.paralympic.org	Paralympic information
	www.nfleurope.com	Official site of NFL Europe
	www.cfl.ca	Official site of CFL (Canadian Football League)
Sports media	www.espn.go.com	ESPN sports
	www.cnnsi.com	CNN & *Sports Illustrated* sports
	www.sportingnews.com	The *Sporting News* sports
	www.sportsline.com	CBS sports
	www.sportsnetwork.com	Sportsnetwork sports
	www.cardmall.com/sportsmap	Sports News
Women in sports	www.womenssportsfoundation.org	Women's Sports Foundation
	www.womenssportswire.com	Women's Sports Wire
	www.lifetimetv.com/WoSport	Women's Sports
	www.sportquest.com/resources/women/	Links to women in sports
	www.gslis.utexas.edu/~lewisa/womsprt.html	Links to women in sports
	www.faculty.babson.edu/turner/fish/women.htm	Links to women in sports
	www.womenssportscareers.com	Women's sports career
Careers in sports	www.sportsjobs.com	Job openings in sports & recreation industry
	www.onlinesports.com/pages/CareerCenter.html	Job openings in sports & recreation industry

CATEGORY	URL	ANNOTATION
	www.sportscareers.com	Job openings in sports & recreation industry
	www.grinnell.edu/careerdevelopment/Library/sports.html	Job openings in sports & recreation industry
	www.jobsinsports.com	Job openings in sports & recreation industry
	www.espn.go.com/special/careers/	Job openings in sports & recreation industry
	www.sportsbusinessjobs.com	Job openings in sports & recreation industry
	www.workinsports.com	Job openings in sports & recreation industry
Sporting goods industry information	www.sgma.com	Sporting Goods Manufacturers Association
	www.americansportsdata.com	Sporting goods and fitness industry research
	www.sportinggoodsresearch.com	Sporting goods industry research
	www.nsga.org	National Sporting Goods Association
	www.esportsreport.com	E-Commerce in the sporting goods industry
College sports	www.ncaa.com	Official site of the NCAA
Sports marketing industry information and research	www.teammarketing.com	General sports marketing information
	www.sportsbusinessdaily.com	General sports marketing information
	www.cjsm.com	*Cyber-Journal of Sports Marketing*
	www.nasss.org	North American Society for Sociology of Sport
	www.sportseconomics.com	Sports economics information
	www.sportsbusinessjournal.com	*The Sports Business Journal*
	www.sportsbusinessnews.com	Sports business news
	www.users.pullman.com/rodfort	Sports business links
	www.nassm.org/	North American Society of Sport Management
	www.kagan.com/sports/sports_page.html	Kagan sports business news
	www.joycejulius.com	Joyce Julius Sponsorship evaluation
	www.sportsvueinc.com	Sports business news
	www.sbrnet.com	Sports business research network
	www.gameops.com/content/news/	Sports promotion news and information
	www.users.pullman.com/rodfort/SportsBusiness/BizFrame.htm	Sports business data sources
	www.sportslinkscentral.com/Sports_Business/Sports_Business.htm	Sports business links
	www.niles-hs.k12.il.us/kevkel/Sports_Marketing/links.html	Sports marketing links
Other sports	www.soccer-links.com	Soccer links
	www.auto.com/links_motor.htm	Motor racing links
	www.flakezine.com	Snowboarding
	www.gymn.com/links	Gymnastics
	www.churchilldowns.com	Horse racing
	www.thoroughbredtimes.com	Horse racing

CATEGORY	URL	ANNOTATION
	www.baseball-links.com	Baseball links
	www.baseballprospectus.com/	Baseball
	www.tennis.com	Tennis links
	www.golflink.com	Golf links
	www.tenpin.org/sites.html	Bowling links
	www.hockeyzoneplus.com/ salair_e.htm	Hockey business news and information
Indices	www.el.com/elinks/sports/	Index for general sports links
	www.sports.yahoo.com	Index for general sports information
	www.refdesk.com/sports.html	Index for general sports links
	www.sportslinkscentral.com	Index for general sports links of sports
	www.oldsport.com	Index of general sports & sporting goods links
Educational opportunities	www.nassm.com/universities.htm	Colleges and universities offering sports business
Stadium issues	www.stadianet.com	Stadium and venue news
	www.fortunecity.com/athena/ thatcher/2042/	Stadium information
	http://garnet.acns.fsu.edu/~tchapin/ stadia/stadia.html	Stadium information

GLOSSARY

advertising A form of one-way mass communication about a product, service, or idea paid for by an identified sponsor.

advertising appeals The reason that the consumer wishes to purchase a sports product.

agent Intermediaries whose primary responsibility is leveraging athletes' worth or determining their bargaining power.

amateur sports participants Participants who do not receive compensation for playing a sport.

ambush marketing A planned effort or campaign, by an organization to associate itself indirectly with an event in order to gain some of the recognition and benefits associated with being an official sponsor.

antecedent states The temporary physiological and mood states that a consumer brings to the participant situation.

assurance The knowledge and courtesy of employees and their ability to convey trust and confidence.

athletes Participants who engage in organized training in order to develop skills in particular sports.

athletic platform The type of sports entity (team, sport, event, or athlete) chosen to produce the best return on sports sponsorship objectives.

atmospherics A retail store's visual, auditory, and olfactory environments that are designed to attract and keep consumers in the store.

attitude Learned thoughts, feelings, and behaviors toward a given object.

behavioral segmentation The process of grouping consumers based on how much they purchase, how often they purchase, or how loyal they are to a product or service.

benefits segmentation The process of grouping consumers based on why they purchase a product or service or what problem the product solves for the consumer.

brand equity The value that a brand contributes to a product in the marketplace.

brand image The consumers' set of beliefs about a brand, which shapes their attitudes.

brand loyalty A consistent preference for, or repeat purchase of, one brand over all others in a product category.

brand mark The element of a brand that cannot be spoken (also known as the *logo* or *logotype*)

brand name The element of the brand that can be vocalized, such as the Nike Air Jordan, the Cincinnati Reds, or the University of Kentucky Wildcats.

branding Any combination of name, design, and symbol that a sports organization uses to help differentiate its products from the competition.

break-even pricing strategy Pricing strategy where the basic premise is for the firm to determine the number of units it will have to sell at a given price to break even (or recoup costs).

bundle pricing The grouping of individual sports products and services into a single-package price.

buying influences The individuals involved in the sale and their buying roles.

captive product pricing Pricing where multiple sports products are separated and sold at a single price and where sports manufacturers or organizations sell products and services used in conjunction with or in addition of the primary product.

channel of distribution A coordinated group of individuals or organizations that route a sports product to the final consumer.

cognitive dissonance Feelings of doubt or anxiety that may occur after consumers have made an important participation decision.

commercialization The introduction of a new product in the final stage of its development.

communication The process of establishing a commonness of thought between the sender and the receiver.

competition A contest among sellers trying to reach their market objectives by filling the same customer need.

consumer demand The quantity of a sports product that consumers are willing to purchase at a given price.

consumer pricing evaluation process The way in which acceptable price ranges are determined by consumers' expectations.

consumer socialization Consumer learning about the skills, knowledge, and attitudes necessary for participating in sports.

contingency control Control based on the assumption that sports marketers operate in an uncertain and unpredictable environment and that the changing nature of the internal and external environments may lead to the need to reassess strategic choices.

contingency framework for strategic sports marketing A system for understanding and managing the complexities of the sports marketing environment.

contingency strategy Being prepared for either positive or negative changes in the environment that are out of the sports marketer's control, acknowledging and managing those changes, and finally being prepared to cope with these rapid changes.

control The process of measuring results, comparing the results to the marketing objectives, communicating the results to the entire organization, and modifying plans to achieve the desired results.

convenience sampling techniques Sample elements are chosen based on being readily available to the researcher.

costs Those factors associated with producing, promoting, and distributing the sports product.

cost-based pricing The pricing schemes in which the sports organization examines all of the costs associated with producing the sports product and then determines the price.

coupons Certificates that offer reductions in price for sports products.

creative brief A tool used to guide the creative process toward a solution that will serve the interests of the client and their customers.

credibility The expertise and the trustworthiness of the source of a message.

culture The shared values, beliefs, language, symbols, and tradition that are passed on from generation to generation by members of a society.

cultural values Widely held beliefs that affirm what is desirable by members of a society.

customary or traditional pricing Pricing where consumers' expectations of price and beliefs about what prices are historically charged for sports products form the basis of traditional pricing.

data collection techniques A function used to attain information for problem definition and research design type.

decision-making process The foundation of our model of participant consumption.

demographic environment Observing and monitoring trends and shifts in the population.

demographic factors Variables, such as population, age, gender, education, occupation, and ethnic background, that are also found to be related to game attendance.

developing the sports product A prototype of the new product is designed so that consumers can get a better idea about the product; in addition, preliminary decisions regarding marketing strategy are established.

differential pricing Selling the same product or service to different buyers at different prices.

diffusion of innovation The rate at which new sports products spread throughout the marketplace and are accepted by consumers.

direct competition The competition between sellers producing similar products and services.

direct sponsorship objectives The objectives that have a short-term impact on consumption behavior and focus on increasing sales.

distribution The movement of a sports product from producers to consumers.

economic activity The flow of goods and services between producers and consumers.

economic buying role A position that governs final approval to buy and that can say yes to a sale when everyone else says no, and vice versa.

economic factors Both the controllable and uncontrollable variables that can affect game attendance.

elements in the communication process The elements to maximize communication effectiveness include the sender, encoding, message, medium, decoding, receiver, feedback, and noise.

empathy The caring, individualized attention a firm provides its customers.

environmental scanning A firm's attempt to continually acquire information on events occurring outside the organization.

eustress Positive levels of arousal that are provided to spectators of sports.

evaluative criteria Features and characteristics that potential consumers look for when choosing a sport in which to participate.

exchange A marketing transaction in which the buyer gives something of value to the seller in return for goods and services.

experimentation Research in which one or more variables are manipulated while others are held constant in order for results to be measured.

extensive problem solving (or extended problem solving) The exhaustive decision process which involves problem recognition and heavy information search (both internal and external), followed by the evaluation of many alternatives on many attributes.

external contingencies All influences outside of the organization that can impact the organization's strategic marketing process.

facility aesthetics The interior and exterior appearance of a stadium.

fad A product life cycle characterized by accelerated sales and accelerated acceptance of the product followed by a rapid decline.

family life cycle A progression of individuals through various life stages (e.g., young and single, married with children).

fan identification The personal commitment and emotional involvement customers have with a sports organization.

fan motivation factors Those variables that make spectators want to attend sporting events.

fixed costs The sum of the producer's expenses that are stable and do not change with the quantity of the product consumed.

focus group A structured discussion with 6–10 people led by a moderator.

frequency The number of times an individual, or a household, is exposed to a media vehicle.

game attractiveness A situational factor that varies from game to game and week to week whereas the perceived quality of a single game or event is based on the skill level of the individuals participating in the contest (i.e., the presence of any star athletes), team records, and league standings or if the game is a special event.

geodemographic segmentation The process of grouping consumers who live in close proximity and are also likely to share the same lifestyle and demographic composition.

goal A short-term purpose that is measurable, challenging, attainable, and time specific.

goods Tangible physical products that offer benefits to consumers.

idle product capacity "Down time" in which the service provider is available, but there is no demand for the sports product.

implementation Decisions in the strategic sports marketing process such as who will carry out the plans, when the plans will be executed, and how the plans will be executed.

indirect competition The true competition between other forms of products and services, which is more general in nature and may be the most critical of all for sports marketers.

indirect sponsorship objectives The objectives that ultimately lead to the desired goal of enhancing sales.

inelastic demand A situation in which changes in price have little or no impact on demand.

information search When a participant seeks relevant information that will help them resolve the problem.

innovations New sports products that are continually being introduced to consumers.

integrated marketing communications The concept by which a sports organization carefully integrates and coordinates its many promotional mix elements to deliver a unified message about the organization and its products.

intermediaries Organizations or individuals that are in the middle of producers and consumers; also called middlemen.

internal contingencies All influences within the organization that can impact the organization's strategic marketing process.

inventory management Ordering the correct assortment of merchandise, maintaining appropriate levels of merchandise, and storing the merchandise that has been ordered.

judgment sample Sample elements chosen subjectively and based on the judgment of the researcher that they best serve the purpose of the study.

learning Relatively permanent changes in response tendencies due to the effects of experience.

licensing A contractual agreement whereby a company may use another company's trademark in exchange for a royalty or fee.

macroeconomic elements The economic activities that examine the big picture, or the national income.

majority fallacy The false assumption that the largest group of consumers should always be selected as the target market.

management problem statement A statement from management defining a problem.

market coverage Refers to the number of outlets used in the distribution of the sports product. The extent of market coverage is defined in terms of exclusive, selective, or intensive distribution.

market niche A relatively tiny part of a market that has a very special need not currently being filled.

market segmentation Grouping consumers together based on common needs.

market selection decisions Choosing market segments, target markets, and positioning in the planning phase of the strategic sports marketing process.

marketing mix variables Variables that must be carefully considered when determining the price of a sports product, such as product, distribution, and promotional planning, which must work in concert with one another.

marketing myopia The practice of defining a business in terms of goods and services rather than in terms of the benefits sought by customers.

marketing orientation Concentration on understanding the consumer and providing a sports product that meets consumers' needs, while achieving the organization's objectives.

marketing research The systematic process of collecting, analyzing, and reporting information to enhance decision making throughout the strategic sports marketing process.

marketing sources Important information sources, such as advertisements, sales personnel, brochures, and Web sites on the Internet.

Maslow's hierarchy of needs A popular theory of human motivation based on classification of needs.

match-up hypothesis The belief that the more congruent the image of the endorser with the image of the product being promoted, the more effective the message.

media The element in the communications process by which the message is transmitted.

microeconomic elements The smaller economic activities that make up the big picture or the national income.

mob effect A situation in which consumers feel it is socially desirable to attend "special" sporting events.

motivation An internal force that directs behavior toward the fulfillment of needs.

multiple channels Using more than one channel of distribution to reach potential consumers.

new product category entries Sports products that are new to the organization, but not to consumers.

new product development process Sports organizations develop new products by using a systematic approach.

new product success factors Variables, such as high quality, creation and maintenance of a positive and distinct brand image, being designed to consumer specifications, and other marketing mix elements, play a major role in the success of a new product.

new sports product pricing strategies Strategies ussed when the sorts organization sets approximate price levels for products being introduced for the first time in the marketplace.

new-to-the-world products Brand new sports innovations such as the first in-line skates, the first sailboard, or the advent of arena football.

niche marketing The process of carving out a relatively tiny part of a market that has a very special need not currently being filled.

nonprice competition The creation of a unique sports product through the packaging, product design, promotion, distribution, or any marketing variable other than price.

nonprobability sampling Techniques used whose sample units are chosen subjectively by the researcher; as such, there is no way of ensuring whether the sample is representative of the population of interest.

odd–even pricing A form of psychological pricing where consumers might perceive the odd-number pricing ($9.95) as a greater value than even-number pricing (e.g., $10).

organizational culture The shared values and assumptions of organizational members that shape an identity and establish preferred behaviors in an organization.

organizational objectives Signposts that help an organization focus on its purpose as stated in its mission statement.

organized sporting events Sporting competitions that are sanctioned and regulated by a controlling authority such as a league, association, or sanctioning body.

out-of-market technology Out-of-market packages that use direct-to-home (DTH) technology to give subscribers a selection of sports telecasts not available on regular cable.

participant-consumption behavior Actions performed when searching for, participating in, and evaluating the sports activities that consumers feel will satisfy their needs.

perception The complex process of selecting, organizing, and interpreting sports-related stimuli.

penetration pricing Selling a new sports product at a low initial price relative to the competition in order to gain market share.

perceived risk The uncertainty associated with decision making and concern for the potential threats of making the wrong decision.

perceptual maps A tool created to examine positioning by providing marketers with three types of information.

personal seat licenses (PSLs) A sports stadium financing strategy in which fans pay for rights to purchase future tickets.

personal selling A form of person-to-person communication which a salesperson works with prospective buyers and attempts to influence their purchase needs in the direction of his or her company's products or services.

personal training Products designed to benefit participants in sports at all levels of competition (e.g., fitness centers and health services, sports camps and instruction).

personality A set of consistent responses an individual makes to the environment.

planning assumptions control Control that makes assumptions concerning future events or contingencies about which we do not have complete information.

point-of-purchase (P-O-P) displays A promotional display designed to attract consumers' attention to a particular product or retail display area.

positioning Fixing the sports product in the minds of the target market by manipulating the marketing mix.

premiums Items given away with the sponsors product as part of the sales promotion.

prestige pricing Setting an artificially high price to provide a distinct image in the marketplace.

price A statement of value for a sports product.

price competition Stimulating consumer demand primarily by offering consumers lower prices.

price discounts Incentives offered to buyers to stimulate demand or reward behaviors that are favorable to the seller.

price elasticity The extent to which consumer purchasing patterns are sensitive to fluctuations in price.

price reductions Efforts to enhance sales and achieve greater market share by directly lowering the original price.

price skimming Selling a new sports product at a high initial price relative to the competition to enhance perceived quality.

primary data Data gathered for the specific research question at hand.

probability sampling A technique used whose sample units have a known and nonzero chance of being selected for the study and are considered stronger than the nonprobability sampling because the accuracy of the sample results can be estimated with respect to the population.

problem definition Specifying what information is needed to assist in solving problems or identifying opportunities.

problem recognition Discrepancy between a consumer's desired state and an actual state large enough and important enough to activate the entire decision-making process.

process control Control that monitors the process to determine whether it is unfolding as expected and as desired and that measures and evaluates the effects of actions that have already been taken in an effort to execute the plan.

product design The aesthetics, style, and function of the sports product.

product life cycle A useful tool for developing a marketing strategy and then revising this strategy as a product moves through the stages of introduction, growth, maturity, and decline.

product line A group of products that are closely related because they satisfy a class of needs, are used together, are sold to the same customer groups, are distributed through the same type of outlets, or fall within a given price range.

product line pricing Pricing that establishes a range of selling prices and price points within a given price range.

product mix The total assortment of product lines that a sports organization sells.

product mix pricing strategy Pricing strategy that includes product line pricing, bundle pricing, captive product pricing, and two-part pricing.

product line extensions New products being added to an existing product line.

product quality The degree to which the goods meet and exceed consumers' needs.

projective techniques Any variety of methods that allow respondents to project their feelings, beliefs, or motivations onto a relatively neutral stimulus.

promotional mix elements The combination of elements—including advertising, personal selling, sponsorship, public relations, and sales promotion—designed to communicate with sports consumers.

promotional planning Armed with a working knowledge of the communications process, the sports marketer is now ready to design an effective promotion plan using four basic steps: (1) target market consideration, (2) setting promotional objectives, (3) determining the promotional budget, and (4) developing the promotional mix.

psychological or internal factors The elements such as personality, motivation, learning, and perception that are unique to each individual and guide sports participation decisions.

psychological pricing Pricing based on the consumer's emotion and image, rather than economics alone.

public relations The element of the promotion mix that identifies, establishes, and maintains a mutually beneficial relationship between the sports organizations and its publics.

quality dimensions of goods How well the product conforms to specifications that were designed in the manufacturing process and the degree to which the goods meet and exceed consumers' needs.

quantity discounts Rewarding buyers for purchasing large quantities of a sports product by lowering prices.

quota sampling Sample elements chosen on the basis of some control characteristic or characteristics of interest to the researcher.

reach The number of people exposed to an advertisement in a given medium.

reference groups Individuals who influence the information, attitudes, and behaviors of other group members.

reference pricing Pricing in which consumers carry a frame of reference in which they evaluate products, typically based on past experience with the product or service or obtained by gathering high levels of information when evaluating alternative products.

relationship marketing Marketing that builds long-term relationships with customers.

reliability The ability to perform a promised service dependably and accurately.

repositioning Changing the image or perception of the sports entity in the minds of consumers in the target market.

research design The framework or plan for a study that guides the collection and analysis of data.

research proposal A document that describes all the information necessary to conduct and control a study.

responsiveness The willingness to help customers and provide prompt service.

sales promotions A variety of short-term promotional activities designed to stimulate immediate-product demand.

sample A subset of the population from which data is gathered to estimate some characteristic of the population.

sanctioning bodies Organizations that not only market sports products, but delineate and enforce rules and regulations, determine the time and place of sporting events, and provide athletes with the structure necessary to compete.

seasonal discounts Reduction in prices to stimulate demand during off-peak periods.

secondary data Data that has been collected previously but is still relevant to the research question.

services Intangible, nonphysical products.

service quality The degree to which the service meets and exceeds consumers' needs.

simplified model of the consumer–supplier relationship A framework for describing the various products, suppliers, and consumers in the sports industry.

simulated test market Typically, respondents in a simulated test market participate in a series of activities, such as (1) receiving exposure to a new product or service concept, (2) having the opportunity to purchase the product or service in a laboratory environment, (3) assessing attitudes toward the new product or service after trial, and (4) assessing repeat purchase behavior.

single channel strategy Using only one channel of distribution to reach potential consumers.

situational factors Temporary factors within a particular time or place that influence the participation decision-making process.

spectators Consumers who derive their benefit from the observation of the event.

sponsorship The element in the promotional mix using investing in a sports entity (athlete, league, team, or event) to support overall organizational objectives, marketing goals, and promotional strategies.

sponsorship budgeting The budgeting for investing as a sponsor that includes several considerations: competitive parity, arbitrary allocation, percentage of sales, and the objective and task method.

sponsorship objectives Objectives that should be linked to the broader promotional planning process and its objectives.

sport A source of diversion, or a physical activity, engaged in for pleasure.

sporting goods Tangible products that are manufactured, distributed, and marketed within the sports industry.

sport involvement The perceived interest in and personal importance of sports to an individual attending sporting events or consuming sport through some other medium.

sportscape The physical surroundings of a stadium that impact spectators' desire to stay at and ultimately return to the stadium.

sports delivery systems The manner in which sports marketers are developing ways to bring their sports to new markets.

Sports Event Pyramid A way to categorize various sponsorship opportunities, which consists of five levels: global events, international events, national events, regional events, and local events.

sports marketing mix The coordinated set of elements that sports organizations use to meet their marketing objectives and satisfy consumers' needs.

sports marketing research The systematic process of collecting, analyzing, and reporting information to enhance decision making throughout the strategic sports marketing process.

sport sponsorship acquisition A reactive process whereby organizations receive sponsorship possibilities from sports entities wishing to secure sponsors.

sports product map The map showing the multidimensional nature of sports products using two dimensions: goods–services and body–mind.

sports camps and instruction Organized training sessions usually designed to provide instruction in a specific sport.

sports equipment manufacturers Organizations responsible for producing and sometimes marketing sports equipment used by consumers who are participating in sports at all different levels of competition.

sports information Products that provide consumers with news, statistics, schedules, and stories about sports.

sports involvement The perceived interest in and personal importance of sports to an individual sport consumer.

sports marketing The specific application of marketing principles and processes to sports products and to the marketing of nonsports products associated with sport.

sports product A good, a service, or a combination of the two that is designed to provide benefits to a sports spectator, participant, or sponsor.

sports retailers Channel members who are involved in all the activities of selling products and services to end users or final consumers.

sports sponsorship Exchanging money or product for the right to associate a name or a product with a sports entity.

social class The homogeneous division of people in a society sharing similar values, lifestyles, and behaviors that can be hierarchically categorized.

sociological factors Influences outside of the individual participant that influence the decision-making process.

stadium factors The variables such as the newness of the stadium, stadium access, aesthetics or beauty of the stadium, seat comfort, and cleanliness of the stadium.

strategic control The critical evaluation of plans, activities, and results, providing information for future strategic action.

strategic selling The process for successful sales consists of six elements: buying influences, red flags, response modes, win-results, the sales funnel, and the ideal customer profile.

strategic sports marketing process The process of planning, implementing, and controlling marketing efforts to meet organizational objectives and satisfy consumers' needs.

strategic windows A period of time during which the characteristics of a market and the distinctive competencies of a firm fit together well.

tangibles The physical facilities, equipment, and appearance of the service personnel.

target marketing Choosing the segment(s) that will allow an organization to attain its marketing goals most efficiently and effectively.

target profit pricing Pricing that is a variation of the cost-based method, where sports marketers set approximate prices based on the target profit they determined when setting objectives.

test marketing Introducing a new product or service in one or more geographic areas on a limited basis.

total quality management (TQM) A practice where quality is likely to mean an excellent consistency of

goods and deliveries made by suppliers to meet competitive challenges.

trademark An identifier that indicates a sports organization has legally registered its brand name or brand mark, thus preventing others from using it.

two-part pricing Pricing where the service charge has a fixed fee and a variable component based on usage.

types of adopters The characteristics of each group of consumers as a product spreads throughout the marketplace.

value The perceived benefits of a sports product, or what the product does for the user, based on its tangible and intangible features.

variable costs The sum of the producer's expenses that vary as a result of the quantity of the product being consumed.

vision A long-term roadmap to guide where the organization is headed.

warranties Statements indicating the liability of the manufacturer for problems with the sports product.

PHOTO CREDITS

Chapter 1
11 Ken Karp/Pearson Education-PH College; **15** Getty Images, Inc./PhotoDisc; **20** National Baseball Hall of Fame

Chapter 2
35 Harlem Globetrotters; **42** Getty Images, Inc./PhotoDisc; **49** Monica Almeida/New York Times Pictures

Chapter 3
68 Getty Images, Inc./PhotoDisc

Chapter 4
108 Getty Images, Inc./PhotoDisc; **110** Alliance Research, Inc.

Chapter 5
128 Getty Images, Inc./PhotoDisc; **130** Ed Bock/CORBIS, CORBIS-NY; **135** Matthew D. Shank/Matthew D. Shank Ph.D.; **138** Getty Images, Inc./PhotoDisc; **151** Getty Images, Inc./PhotoDisc; **152** Getty Images, Inc./PhotoDisc

Chapter 6
158 AP/Wide World Photos; **159** Getty Images, Inc./PhotoDisc

Chapter 7
185 Kevin Fleming/CORBIS, CORBIS-NY; **194** Getty Images, Inc./PhotoDisc

Chapter 8
217 Getty Images, Inc./PhotoDisc

Chapter 9
258 Getty Images, Inc./PhotoDisc; **263** Getty Images, Inc./PhotoDisc

Chapter 10
290 Getty Images, Inc./PhotoDisc

Chapter 11
298 AP/Wide World Photos; **313** AP/Wide World Photos; **322** Getty Images

Chapter 12
357 Larry Fleming/Pearson Education-PH College

Chapter 14
398 Index Stock Imagery, Inc.; **411** Getty Images Inc./PhotoDisc, Inc.

Chapter 15
426 Jim Cummins/Getty Images, Inc.-Taxip; **433** Getty Images, Inc./PhotoDisc

Chapter 16
448 Jack Stohlman/LPGA Ladies Professional Golf Association; **464** Jose Goitia/AP/Wide World Photos

INDEX